Author's Note

The characters portrayed in this book are real and the events described took place, but fictional names and descriptive detail have been used in parts where I have felt this would protect privacy.

Lucy Irvine

PART ONE

Sunny Day

Chapter One

A green field in England on a sunny day. It was early summer, the time of dog roses and fallen fledglings along country lanes. The sun, now high, would last until early evening and then give way to a sudden chill. Yet again, I would miss all but the last half hour of it. And that would be wasted hanging round the bus stop listening to talk of teachers, homework and the cost of aniseed balls.

I craned forward to catch a glimpse of the stream. Light tickled ripples hide-and-seeking in the reeds. How good to be beside the water now, or better still floating on it, dipping a hand to break the play of beams. I drew my head back. Julia Fosdyke's ponytail was in the way.

Miss Eccleston's voice crackled out, weary, automatic: 'Turn to page two hundred and forty-two, exercise five. Caroline Austin, begin, please.'

Caroline's effortful voice stumbled among the phrases full of *silvae*, *agricolae* and soldiers laying waste. Miss Eccleston's grey head wobbled as she shook it. The sunlight caught a fall of powder from her jowls.

'Next.'

Slowly up and down the rows of small, blond-wood desks, chairs scraped back and hesitant voices, some earnest, some bored, pushed on through the woods and wastes. A bee droned against the window, exhausted. Finally he knocked himself out. He would never escape. I looked at the timetable for the afternoon: R.I., Maths, Singing. Then the bus to 309, tea, homework, television, bed. School again tomorrow. And so on until I was eighteen. I looked again towards the water and the field.

Miss Eccleston's eyes fell on my raised hand.

'Yes?'

'Please may I be excused?'

'You should have gone at breaktime.'

'I know. I'm sorry I didn't.'

'Go along, then.'

I left the classroom quietly, closing the door behind me.

In the corridor I pulled off my shoes and, holding them in one hand, sprinted silently past all the classrooms until I reached the top of the stairs where, breath held, I listened for footsteps below. Not a sound. I tiptoed down and with a sudden surge of confidence took the last four steps at a bound, sliding expertly on the polished floor below. In the cloakroom I emptied all the textbooks out of my case and replaced them with gymshoes and a blank exercise book. I left my blazer but remembered to grab my beret at the last minute. It was forbidden to be seen outside in school uniform without a beret and its absence from my head might attract more attention than my absence from class if I bumped into anyone.

Clear of the pupils' exit, I stood for a second looking across the field. My feet were on the grass and I was no longer just wishing, but there. One small dream realized. Careless of eyes that might be following, I plotted a clear diagonal to a gate in the far corner and walked out into the sun.

Outside the gate I stopped to work out the next move. If I went to 309 now there would be nobody in. Good. I could get rid of the school clothes and find some useful things to put in the case. Then I would let Richard, my father, know I had left. We always told each other about important things in our lives. Absently, as I crossed the bridge over the school stream, I took off my beret and tossed it in. It spun as it floated away.

The bus was slow, packed with women lugging shopping, and when I reached 309 I had to rush to avoid meeting my mother. She would be upset and not understand. It would cause a messy delay. Upstairs I changed quickly and ripped a small blanket off my bed. On the way through the kitchen I swept four apples into the case and swiftly downed a glass of milk. I looked around for the cat to say goodbye. She was curled up on the grand bishop's chair in the hall. Lifting her warm body I kissed the surprised old face once, then plonked her back on the chair, where she began to sneeze. It was the last sound I heard before I banged the front door and set off down the road.

Richard's office was in Kensington, St Mary Abbot's Place. I expected him to be on the telephone when I arrived, or at a meeting. Instead he was sitting sideways in a leather chair, munching bread and honey and talking to a smart woman in a green trouser-suit. She had a lot of rather exciting red hair. He stopped in mid-munch when he saw me, eyebrows raised.

'Hello, no school today?'

I looked him straight in the eye.

'I've left.'

He finished his mouthful and said lightly, 'Have you? You don't think it might be a bit soon?'

I shook my head. Twelve seemed old enough to me. The smart woman went out quietly and I thought they exchanged a look over my shoulder. Richard jabbed the bread and honey gently in my direction. I took a bite and we both chewed for a minute, looking at each other. His casual reaction to my announcement did not surprise me. Richard's reactions were usually different to those of other grown-ups. That was what made him so special.

'Listen,' he said, 'I'm doing some filming at Windsor Horse Show tomorrow. Do you want to come?'

'I might.'

I knew I would not but he was being so nice I wanted to show willing. The phone rang suddenly and he picked it up. He talked for what seemed a long time and when he had finished, said he had to go out.

'We'll talk later, hmm?'

I nodded noncommittally, knowing that 'later' would be no good. But at least he knew now that I had left and I trusted him not to do anything embarrassing, like call the police.

Back on Kensington High Street I took a 73 bus and changed

in Richmond for one that went to Kingston, knowing I had to go through there to get out on to the road south. Kay, my mother, always used to say this was the worst part of the journey. That was when Richard kept his boat near Chichester and we used to go down at weekends, a family of five with a dog and a cat.

I had never hitch-hiked before but I knew how it was done. I had seen people do it on the motorway when we drove up to Scotland. Sometimes, if it was two girls, Richard would joke: 'Not pretty enough' and drive on. He frowned if it was long-haired youths.

It struck me that the middle of Kingston was not the best place to start, so I followed the main street until I was past the last shop, then stuck out my thumb. I held it out for a long time. A number of cars went by and several passers-by stared. Then two cars passed with the passengers grinning and waving. I blushed. I was not being taken seriously.

Waiting until there were no pedestrians approaching – I did not want anyone to think I was giving up – I started to walk, head down and arm well out. I swung my thumb vigorously and was concentrating so hard on technique that when the window of a parked car rolled down and a man spoke, I jumped.

'Where are you trying to get to, lass? You'll never get a car stopping here.'

He had a northern accent and a blotchy, sincere kind of face. I bent down to the window.

'I'm trying to get out on the road to Dorking. Actually I'm heading for somewhere near Chichester.'

'Well, you've got the wrong road for a start, unless you want to go via Guildford. Tell you what, hop in and I'll put you on the road you want.'

'Thank you.'

I sat in the front with the case on my lap. The driver was chatty and I realized, as I felt my way cautiously round his questions, that it might be an idea to evolve a few stock replies. It was not long before the matter of age came up.

'Bit young to be doing this, aren't you? How old are you? Fourteen, fifteen?'

Not wanting to push credibility too far, I said fourteen. He raised his eyebrows and with admonitions to 'Take care, lass' let me out on the Dorking road.

After only a few minutes a lorry stopped. The engine was noisy and I shouted above it, one foot on the step of the cab.

'Dorking?'

The driver nodded and I scrambled up. I liked the way his red, knobbly hands manipulated the controls of the big lorry and his eyes stayed businesslike on the road. I gazed out of the window, happy on this warm, swiftly moving day. Briefly, as my stomach gurgled, I thought of what they would be having for lunch at school. Friday: fish fingers. I was not missing much.

The lorry went fast and soon the driver was pulling into a lay-by and saying that my best bet was to try for a lift here without getting mixed up in the town. He handed down my case, waved, and was on his way.

The next lift came quickly but the man warned that he was only going as far as a village outside Horsham. Was that OK? So long as it was in the general direction of Chichester, that was fine with me. I was learning fast. In years to come I was to find that a dead set on the final aim but flexibility on the way was a healthy policy for most things.

This driver was annoying. He fiddled constantly with the radio, talked over it, and a jacket he had hanging in the back swung around on a squeaky hanger. I asked him 'what he did' and was irked when he hedged around. It seemed a very adult question.

'Guess, go on, what do I look like?'

I thought he looked like an office sort of person and said so. He laughed and pulled a pamphlet from the mouth of an open briefcase beside him.

'There you are, that's me – a traveller in baby powder – or if you want to be more down to earth about it, a sales rep.'

He offered me a free sample but I refused. I did not want anything unnecessary in my case.

He dropped me on a small road where there was hardly any traffic and there followed a period of walking. Two cars went by without stopping and one man made a silly face. A woman on her own shook her head and looked angry.

I took out an apple and crunched it as I walked along. The sun was still high and I felt good. The last of the apple was still in my mouth when an elderly man in a small van stopped. I went through the routine of making sure he was going the right way. He spoke stiffly.

'If you don't mind going by the small roads I can take you nearly all the way. I've got to pick something up in Petworth, but after that I'm going straight on down. I live that way.'

I climbed in. Petworth rang a bell. My sister, Marianne, had a friend whose parents had a country cottage near there. We had gone there for a weekend once and had had two midnight feasts in one night. I thought of Marianne. She would probably be in the school toilets now, dodging Games. She had done that ever since she started getting thin; ever since Richard and Kay's silent war started to get louder. The driver's voice, sounding stern, broke into my thoughts.

'I don't know what a young girl like you is doing taking lifts. You want to be careful. You don't know what might happen. I don't generally stop for anybody but I thought I'd better pick you up before somebody not quite nice came along. Lot of funny folk around these days.'

I told him I had been very lucky with lifts so far.

'Doesn't matter,' he said. 'Only has to happen once. I wouldn't have any youngster of mine taking lifts on the road.'

A lecture in exchange for the ride seemed fair enough, but I hoped it would not happen too often.

The stop in Petworth was brief. He left the engine running while he went to the back of a house and picked up a box of vegetables. When he got back into the van he put five little apples on the seat beside me.

'There you are, put them in your bag. I like to see young people eating what's good for them.'

Gratefully, I fitted the apples into my case and we drove on. He took me so near my destination I could walk the rest of the way. I knew this last part of the journey well.

*   *   *

Birdham Pool lay next to Chichester yacht basin, much smaller and less grand. Rows of boats, mostly small yachts with one or two motor launches dotted tubbily among them, sat quietly on the water, tall masts swaying gently, making occasional whirrs and pings. In the days when Richard and Kay brought me and Marianne and our brother James here, there had been swans, a whole family with cygnets, sailing elegantly round the boats hoping for crumbs. In the evenings they would retire among the reeds at a shallow end of the Pool, smooth vees in the water marking their passage as the sun went down. We always had crusts to throw and Richard used to imitate their funny sideways looks, making us all laugh. The swans were not there now.

Across the road was a big, marshy lake, and it was something in the woods on the far side of this I had come to find. Slowly I made my way round the lake, following the muddy path where I used to go with Marianne. This was where we had found a lame duck. We had adopted her for a while, called her Martha. Leaving the path, I pushed into the woods, feet sinking into layers of mashed leaves. Twigs caught in my hair and there was a dark moss stain on one trousered knee.

Suddenly that knee came up hard against something large and I grabbed a tree so as not to fall. I had stumbled on what I was looking for. Joyfully I set to work clearing away branches and long grass. It was warm and I rolled up my sleeves, bending over with legs braced, hair in my eyes. But as my treasure was revealed, enthusiasm ebbed. The little dinghy I had hoped to paddle to the farthest reaches of the lake – maybe even round the coast if the weather were fair – was nothing more than a bottomless shell. Two winters had eaten away the planking, ferns had grown under the rowing seat and where I pulled at a section of gunwale, it came apart in my hands. I tossed the broken pieces away and stood looking out through the trees at the calm water. I very much wanted to be out on it, floating, to complete the realization of the morning's classroom dream.

On Birdham Pool I had noticed a small tender lying in the mud not far from where the swans used to glide when the sun went down. Determinedly, I stomped back along the muddy path. On the other side of the road I checked to see there was no one about, then took off my socks and shoes and rolled up my trousers. I left the case behind a tree and made straight for the white tender. I had to rock it a few times to break the suction of the mud but after that it slid easily. One good push and she was afloat.

For an hour, perhaps two, I drifted around in that little boat. I could not go far – there was not far to go – but that did not matter. There was a spidery tangle of overhanging branches along the bank. For a while, as the boat rocked gently in the reeds, I lay and looked up through a mesh of twigs at the sky. It was very big, making me and my world look very small. There was something about that I liked. The words and tensions that cluttered life at 309, and made it hard to concentrate at school, slid away to nothing in that big sky.

When the sun went in and there were sounds of cars and children, I sat up. Friday-evening families had begun to arrive, unloading cars piled high with provisions for a boating weekend. Just as we used to in the old days. It made me feel strange to watch them and soon I put the boat away.

Back on the road, like an old hand, I began to hitch. It was time I found somewhere to stay the night.

Chichester always seemed a grand place to me. This was where the family had come for major shopping, when more was needed than could be found at Birdham Pool store. I must have been to the town centre dozens of times but I was thoroughly lost now and it did not seem so grand. I stopped in front of a café and put down my case. I wished I could see in to tell what kind of place it was but the front was all smoked-yellow panes covered with whorls and dimples and luncheon voucher signs. I tweaked my plaits to straighten them before walking in.

A loud jangle announced my entrance but the woman behind the steaming cylinders of the coffee machine did not look up. Voices and the tinkle of cutlery floated up from below. I wondered if I could get past the service counter without having to buy anything. With her pink powdered face and frizzy yellow hair, the woman looked like a sleazy version of my old Geography mistress. I would not have been able to get past her. But I made it safely to the top of the stairs and there was a momentary lull in the voices as I walked down.

In a corner behind a post there was one empty table. I moved towards it but knew that if I sat down I would be stuck. I would have to order something and pretend that this was what I did every day. Standing where I was, I fixed my eyes on an advertisement pinned to the post. It read: JOLLY JACK TAR SEA-BOOTS: THE BEST BY FAR. I gripped the handle of my case more tightly. The eating faces were a blur beyond the seaboots.

'Excuse me' – my voice would have won top marks for clarity in an elocution class – 'does anyone know where the nearest, cheapest dosshouse is?'

As soon as the words were out I knew I had made a mistake. There was dead silence in the café. Still staring at the seaboots I felt my cheeks flame. I fled up the stairs and into the street, shutting the jangling door on the frizzy-haired woman's face, her mouth wriggling soundlessly in surprise.

Charging along furiously, smarting inside and out, I zoomed past shops and lamp-posts and across roads without any idea where I was going. My legs, in my newest, most grown-up trousers, took enormous strides.

It was some time before I realized I was being followed. A man, trotting to keep up, was trying to attract my attention from behind. I did not stop but slowed down enough for him to come alongside. He was young, with dark hair, wearing a flecked fisherman's sweater. His face had an anxious-to-be-friendly expression on it.

'You were in the café just now, weren't you?' he said.

I said nothing, and kept on walking.

'I didn't want to say anything in there, but look, if you're looking for somewhere to stay . . .'

My pace slackened again subtly.

'. . . Me and some friends, we've got this place in Littlehampton. You'd have to sleep on the floor.'

'That'dbeallright.'

I shot the words out as though they were one and followed quickly with a question.

'Is it far?'

'Not far, no, but we'd have to take the train. I was on the way to the station myself.'

He slowed down and stopped. I stopped with him.

'It's the other way,' he said lamely and we turned round and set off again.

'How much will the train be?' I asked. I had a pound note and twelve and six in change.

'Oh well,' he said, 'I usually dodge the guard.'

I flashed him a sharp look.

'It's all right,' he said, 'it's easy. Just do what I do.'

I said doubtfully that if we got caught I would probably be able to pay.

'Naah,' he said disparagingly, 'you don't want to waste your money.'

The guard-dodging went smoothly, although I suffered in suspense as a white-haired guard, punching tickets rhythmically, moved up the carriage towards where we were.

'What are we going to do?' I hissed. The young man put a finger to his lips and said to follow him. While the guard's back was turned we casually walked past him and up to the end of the carriage which had already been checked. I was amazed that he did not pursue us. My companion shrugged.

'Can't be bothered,' he said. But I did not relax until we were off the train.

That hurdle safely over, I became curious about what sort of place we were going to, what the friends he had mentioned were like. Here on the streets of Littlehampton, his home territory, our positions were reversed. Now I was the one trotting alongside asking questions.

'Oh,' he said vaguely, 'you know, it's just a place where we doss. Sometimes there's two of us, sometimes seven or eight. I think there's about three now, so should be room for you. Got a doss-bag?'

I told him about the blanket.

'Doss-bag's better. I'll lend you mine – we could share it if you like.'

He said this last as a joke and I put on the man-freezing expression which made Richard laugh.

'Only kidding,' he said, 'you're safe with us.' Then he added, as if it explained everything, 'We like bikes.'

It seemed a long walk from the station. In the sun, earlier, I had been too hot in my jersey, but now the day was drawing in and I was glad of its warmth. Littlehampton looked all grey. Wind, smelling faintly of sea, rushed around corners on to wide grey streets, blowing up newspapers and chasing grey dust swirls along gutters. We stopped at a small shop.

'Hope you like beans,' my companion said.

'Baked beans?'

'What else?'

I didn't, but kept quiet. He also bought a loaf of white sliced bread – the sort Richard would call cottonwool – and a bottle of Tizer.

'I've got some apples,' I offered, wanting to contribute.

'Never eat apples,' he said as we swung back into stride.

We turned into a long road at the end of which was the sea. It was distant, grey as the town, but I loved the sharp tang on the air and the faraway whisper of breaking waves.

'That's us. One or two of the boys around, I see.'

He gestured ahead to a small two-storeyed house. What distinguished it from similar houses on either side was the jumble of machinery in the front garden. There were four motorbikes drawn up in neat formation in the road outside.

'What's your name?' he asked as we went in. 'Mine's Bill. You don't have to tell me your real one.'

'Susan,' I said promptly. Unwittingly, Bill had laid the foundations of a habit that was to stay with me for years: when among strangers I always gave the first name that came into my head, rarely my own.

Bill's companions greeted me with casual nods. I nodded back, doing as in Rome. One of them I found impressive. He was tall, with rather long fair hair and a mauve scarf knotted at his throat. It contrasted pleasingly with the rest of his outfit which was heavy and black. I noticed that they all wore black, except for Bill with his fisherman's sweater. They sat around and chatted, using expressions I did not always understand, until someone said it was time for eats. Bill pulled out a camping Gaz ring from under a bed – we were sitting upstairs – and started to open a can of beans.

'Here, Susie, butter some of this, will you?' He tossed me the loaf and I buttered carefully, stacking the slices in face-together piles on a square of paper. There seemed to be a shortage of plates.

'Run away from school then, did you?' said the tall one conversationally as the bean pot went round.

'Yes.'

'First time?'

'Yes.'

'Cops aren't after you, I hope?'

I finished my mouthful before replying. The beans tasted all right here.

'No cops, no. I told my father I had left.'

'Did he give you a row?'

'No.'

There was a pause and a hint of surprise before he dismissed the subject.

'Well, lucky, aren't you? Do you like bikes?' Motorbikes were not something I had ever really thought about but I said yes.

'All right, we'll give you a ride tomorrow if you're good.'

He seemed to be the boss. Later, when he was leaving, I heard him say to the others: 'Keep your old ladies downstairs while that kid's around.'

'He's nice, isn't he?' I said to Bill.

Bill reflected for a moment, then agreed.

'Yeah – got the best bike in the gang.'

I spent the night on the floor, comfortable enough in Bill's sleeping-bag, but I did not like being so close to the grubby carpet or the smell of smoke that clung to my hair. In the morning I was sent out to buy more beans. That was to be my job while I was with the boys. They called me Susie the Bean.

22

The others were there again when I got back and as the morning went on the row of motorbikes outside the front door grew. It was another sunny day and I sat contentedly in the machine-strewn garden, sleeves and trousers rolled up, watching all the new arrivals. Then somebody brought a radio and there was loud, angry-sounding music. A girl with greasy hair and torn jeans turned up with one of the boys. She smoked all the time with her head hanging down and I wondered why her hair did not catch fire. I hoped the fair-haired leader had not forgotten about my ride. I hung around while he did things to his bike and when he looked hot, went indoors and poured him a glass of Tizer. I was fascinated by a tanned section of belly that appeared as he moved around under the bike and his shirt wriggled out of his jeans. I could not tell whether it was hair or dirt that made his belly button so brown.

At last they were ready. A dozen leather and denim legs were thrown over saddles and starters were kicked. Nobody talked any more. They all knew what they were doing. The level of noise mounted as one after another the engines erupted into life. The boys were putting on headgear. A few wore crash helmets but most had blue or black peaked caps. One had a German army helmet and goggles. The leader, to my surprise, had a red beret not unlike the one I had recently thrown into the school stream.

As some of the bikes began to circle in the road, angry faces appeared at the windows of neighbouring houses. A door was banged meaningfully. Nobody paid any attention. Just as I thought they were about to go without me the leader said, 'Jump on then, we'll give you a spin.'

I jumped on and as the big machine vroomed into the road my casually dangling arms leapt around the jacketed waist and my knees gripped the seat hard.

The ride began slowly. In three lines of four we cruised down the road towards the sea, a loud black and silver phalanx. When we reached the esplanade there was a pause and the lines broke. The bikes wove slowly between each other, tracing figures of eight. A few day-trippers further along stopped to watch; a woman hustled her little boy away. Then, one by one, the bikes

23

left the group and rolled down a steep slope on to the beach. Some of the riders used their booted feet to steady their machines through the dry sand, others took the slope at a graunching zig-zag, swirling up yellow clouds. The bike I was on was last to go and I screwed up my eyes and clung tight as we crunched and slid among the clumps of marram grass and spraying sand. Once on the level again I sat up straight.

Out on the water there were a few boats. A man in a dinghy with red sails flapping stared curiously as singly and in pairs, the bikes milled, revs gathering. Then, rearing in unison, the first two shot away. The leader held back, watching the others go, one foot on the sand, the machine under us moving backwards in small curves as though it were alive.

Suddenly, launched in one dynamic motion, we were off, cutting like a chainsaw through the stillness of the day. The noise and the speed, ever rising, seemed to take us into another dimension where all the wind and sound in the world was our own. Passing the others now, tyres gliding on the hard-packed sand near the water, the machine achieved its final level of speed. Eyes in visor slits against the wind, I saw the sea flash by as a silver frieze, the line of foam at the edge a wild, white whiplash.

The end came with no cessation of noise. First at the finish, where a jetty blocked the way, the leader revved and wheeled while one by one the others swept in and swerved into triangular formation. Dazed, I dismounted, the flesh still fluttering on my thighs where I had gripped the seat so hard. The leader held the bike still beside me for a moment and playfully tugged one of my plaits.

'Like it?' he mouthed, inaudible above the engine roar.

I nodded. I had more than liked it. It had been something new: fear and elation fiercely combined.

'OK, stay here.'

I moved back and flopped down against one of the jetty legs, bottom squirming into the sand, elbows on knees, as I watched them go. They were doing tricks now, performing hard-practised stunts, rigorous in their attention to detail. Over and over they spun and jumped, using a thin plank and a drum as a ramp, and then each other's bodies as obstacles. High into the air they flew and then wove between an evenly spaced line of men. They hardly spoke, going through the routines like soldiers carrying out a familiar drill. When the black and silver missiles flew straight at them they did not flinch and their faces were empty of all expression. Finally they lined up to race, engine noise rising to a blurred howl as the invisible flag went down. Then all I could see was the wavering mirage of their exhausts and the wrecked sand after they had gone.

Left suddenly in silence I got up and stood with my feet in the sea. The line of foam was back to normal now, bubbles breaking and spilling over my toes. I climbed on to the jetty and walked to the end. After the thrill of the ride my mind felt pleasantly numb. The sea winked, becoming one with the sky on a hazed horizon.

The sun was low by the time they came to fetch me, just three of them, gliding at top speed in single file. Quickly I took my place and once again felt wonder surge as we passed the mad brink of that other dimension, seeming, in our hurtling flight, to slice the pinkening sky in two.

Back in the house, the evening followed the pattern of the day before: baked beans, smoking and the same strange, jargoned talk. They had their music going, music that snarled and jerked and made it impossible to think. It was exciting and disturbing at the same time. I did not sleep well that night, wishing there was a bath, that the music would stop and the smell of smoke go away.

On Sunday they took the bikes out again but this time I was not invited. There were jokes, something about things I should not see. The leader said he would take me for another ride on Monday. He was wearing a different hat today, with DAY-TRIPPER inked in jokey writing on the brim. I nodded and said OK. Upstairs I looked at the room with the sticky Gaz ring, the rumpled bed and Bill's doss-bag on the floor and knew I did not want to stay there any more. My world and theirs only overlapped outside, on the bikes. There was nothing to pack in my case; it held the same as when I arrived – minus a few apples.

The day was not so warm, the sun an intermittent yellow splurge, the sea a weakened blue. I found a pebbled bay where

I was alone and there, forcing myself to crouch in knickers and teen-bra under the cold waves, I bathed. I had no towel and the blanket I used instead was gritty. I spread it out on the rocks to dry but it was still damp at the end of the day when I put it back in the case. I had opened the blank exercise book once during the afternoon and closed it again a little later, still blank. It was chastening to find I had nothing to say.

When it was too cold to sit any longer I walked back towards the town. I had noticed a row of tiny cottages behind the railway. One of them had a Bed and Breakfast sign.

The woman who answered the door was old and very small. She stared at me through misty bi-focals and shot words in quick succession out of a mouth like a knitted buttonhole.

'How many nights? Cooked breakfast or Continental? Twelve-an'-six all in.'

The buttonhole closed and the misty glasses raked me for a reply. Behind her in a cramped hallway a terrier was mauling a rubber rat.

'Yes, please, one,' I said vaguely and to cover up the inadequacy of the answer smiled briskly in a way that Kay did at shopkeepers and men who served her in the garage. I was shown up to a bare room with a bible on the windowsill and a chamber-pot under the bed.

'Lavvy's outside. Breakfast at half past seven. Payment in advance.'

I counted out the money and thanked the old woman politely. Her tiny mauve-veined hand stuffed the coins into an apron pocket and she backed on orthopaedic shoes to the door. Just before she closed it she gave a startlingly pretty smile.

'Shall I bring a drop of hot water up in the morning so's you can have a warm wash? I don't bother for the gentlemen.'

I said that would be very kind. Later, snuggled in the big bed, I reflected. I had never been to an outside toilet or stayed in a house without a proper bathroom. But then I had never walked out of school before or left home. With those two doors closed behind me a whole new set had opened and there were different lives going on behind each one. I pulled the covers higher, revelling in the warmth but knowing that tomorrow I would have to come up with a plan. Beyond the borrowed doss-bags and the Bed and Breakfasts of Littlehampton was a big, mysterious world I had chosen to confront alone.

Chapter Two

But that confrontation was postponed, for the next day curiosity and a desire to experience once more the crazy, other-dimensional thrill of a bike ride landed me firmly back in the lap of adult care.

I lay stunned in a white cocoon of quiet while again and again, the same short scene repeated itself in my mind: high, twisted iron arches, spiralling verticals, elegant fleurs-de-lis; my arms stretching up to fly; a woman in a brown skirt with a gaping mouth; a sharp pain in the jaw, then blank.

At first, I thought I was at the dentist's. There was that same circular drilling motion ending each time with a savage yank. But it was somewhere on the outside that it hurt, not a tooth. Something was pulling at my chin. My hand explored cautiously and found a big square of plaster. As I traced the edges my fingers were taken and held. I opened my eyes and the first thing I saw was the back of my exercise book in somebody's hands. It was open, being read.

Indignation cut across confusion. I did not know where I was, did not know who these people were, but I did know they had no business to be reading my diary.

'Hey!' I cried, and the plaster on my chin stretched painfully.

'Stay quiet, dear. You don't want to break your stitches.'

I looked up at the speaker, a stocky woman in a black uniform. It was she who was holding my hand.

'Nurse,' she called, 'young lady here is with us again.'

The man reading my diary closed it. There was another man

standing back a little, a cap in his hands. Police. A nurse came bustling over.

'How are we feeling? Got a nasty little cut on your chin, you did, but otherwise you are a very lucky girl. How's your head?'

I moved my head on the pillow. It seemed all right.

'All right.'

The man with my diary stepped forward.

'Now young lady, since you seem to be none the worse for wear, I'd like a few words with you. Perhaps you'd like to tell me just what you think you've been up to.'

'As you've read my diary,' I said clearly, 'you know.'

I was furious. It had been a long entry made just that morning while I was waiting for the old lady to appear with my hot water.

'I'll tell you straight away,' said the man, who had outsize ears and yellowish bags under his eyes, 'there's no point taking that attitude. You've caused a lot of worry all round.'

Had he been in touch with Richard and Kay? How did he know where to find them?

'Whose motorbike was that you were on?'

'I don't know.'

It was true. I did not know the leader's name.

'Well, whose ever it was isn't going to be very pleased. It's a mess.'

The black-gate scene flashed through my mind again, but this time I remembered more of it.

I had met some of the bike boys shortly after leaving the Bed and Breakfast place and jumped at the offer of a ride straight away. I did not notice until I was on the back of the leader's bike that they were all in a strange mood, laughing a lot, with goggling, bloodshot eyes. I heard one of them say he had not stopped tripping since last night. I wondered where he had been. We did not go to the beach this time but cruised around the backstreets of the town. It was not the same and I began to fidget. I muttered that one day I would like to drive a bike myself. The leader said he would give me a go.

We came to a quiet place where there was a path with an expanse of grass on one side, houses on the other. First he put me on the seat in front of him and drove along slowly with my hands on the controls under his own. He showed me how to use the accelerator. Then we stopped by the others and he got off. They all seemed very tired, lolling on the ground and grinning. I sat on the bike with the engine running. One of them said, 'Go on, take her round on the grass.'

Nervous, because I knew the bike was too heavy for me to steady with my feet, I clutched the rubber handgrips tightly. The bike lurched crazily and the leader jumped to his feet, shouting. Looking to see where the brakes might be, both my wrists went down. There was a terrible noise and the bike flew forward jerking, then shot in a straight line along the path. Sound and speed were chaotic, a mad cacophony, but my understanding of what was going to happen was perfectly clear. The path was not long. There were big wrought-iron gates at the end. I was going to hit them.

I tried to do things with the handgrips to make the machine and the madness stop but it only went faster, thundering, screaming. I stared at the top of the wrought-iron gates rushing closer, noted the curves of the high, twisted arches, the spiralling verticals, elegant fleurs-de-lis. My arms stretched up to fly and I saw the gaping mouth of a woman in a brown skirt. Pain in the jaw then blank. And here I was with a plaster on my chin and that man holding my diary.

The memory produced an inner slump. I was just a silly little girl. My defiance collapsed and I answered the man's questions flatly, letting things take their course. When a woman took his place I answered her questions too. They had already telephoned 309, the address was on the inside of my school case. I could imagine the expression on Richard's face when he heard. He would not be angry, but puzzled. What had I been up to? What was the idea behind this escapade? And looking back over the events of the last few days, I had no good answer. It all seemed silly now.

They put me on a train back to 309. A social work woman came with me. She kept saying how Mummy and Daddy would be pleased to see me back safe and sound. I turned away and stared out of the window at the drearily whizzing countryside. I was so bitterly ashamed of the mess I had made of things I did not even want to see the cat.

When I walked out across the school field that sunny day I failed to appreciate both the glamour and the iniquity of my crime. Ideally, when shunted back, tail between legs, I would have liked to retire to some quiet corner, nurse my injured pride and brew up a better plan for next time – something which covered such contingencies as scarcity of funds and non-guaranteeable sunshine. This was not to be. From the moment I walked into 309 and saw the delighted, conspiratorial gleam in Marianne's eyes, I realized that my status had undergone a major change. Things would never be the same again.

'Mummy's been livid,' she said as soon as we were alone.

'You've got to see Stew.'

Stew was what we called the headmistress of the school I had left, Miss Margery Stewart-Grange.

'Why's Kay been livid?' I asked.

'Because you went and told Daddy before her.'

'Ah.'

Marianne, who was fifteen months older than I, followed other people's relationships closely.

'Does James know?'

James, our little brother, was five years my junior.

'Sort of – he doesn't really understand. What are you going to say to Stew?'

The prospect of my audience with the head intrigued her.

'I don't know. I'll see at the time.'

'You'll have to wear your uniform to see her.'

'Why?'

'It's a school rule. Have to wear full uniform on the premises.'

'I don't go to that school any more.'

I had to stand in the corridor until Miss Stewart-Grange was ready to receive me. The timing was unfortunate. Thirty seconds after the break bell rang, the corridor was aswirl with girls, many of them from my year. Those who dared hissed things as they passed.

30

'Latin was fantastic after you'd gone. You should have seen Eccleston. She thought you'd fainted in the loo.'

'You'll never be allowed to be form captain again, even if we vote you, I heard them say ...'

But the most repeated remark was: 'Golly, you're not in uniform!'

I was glad when they had gone. The girl I had been closest to had not said anything. Now that I was not one of them any more, I found I had nothing to say to her either.

At last I was told I could go in. Miss Stewart-Grange stood erect behind her desk, dignity drawn smoothly round her like a robe. The lecture she delivered had two parts, the first based on the words 'surprised' and 'disappointed'. ('We are surprised and disappointed by your behaviour.') The second was more complicated, dealing with the charity of forgiveness. It sounded like a speech we had been reading in English recently – 'the quality of mercy' – and ended on a magnanimous flourish.

'It has been decided that owing to your promising reports up to this time, and the fact that we understand there have been difficulties at home, you are to be allowed to return to school immediately.'

My eyes left her face and travelled down to the tip of one polished shoe. The mention of 'difficulties at home' disturbed me. Its inclusion as a reason for my being forgiven somehow sounded deprecating to my family, making them into a mitigating circumstance. I remained silent.

Miss Stewart-Grange's last words were: 'Don't ever let me see you out of school uniform on these premises again.'

'No, Miss Stewart-Grange.'

I did not mention that she was never going to see me in it again, either.

Although it was accepted that I would not go back to that school, it was required by law that efforts were made to continue my education somehow. Richard, seeing what was expected of him, spoke dutifully of the occasional need for 'compromise' in one's attitude. I think the word sounded as strange to him as it did to me. When people talked about him they used words like 'single-minded' and 'determined'. Sometimes they said 'ruthless', too, which I thought sounded rather thrilling. Kay, more conventional and anxious to steer me back on to the rails, equipped herself with a thick blue book listing hundreds of different schools. It was felt that a boarding establishment might be best and for a while my bedtime reading consisted of long academic records and parochial triumphs of the field in brochures bright with crested photographs of formidable–looking buildings in attractive settings. The dining-rooms always looked spartan and the dormitories huge. There were invariably long lists of uniform.

As efforts were continued and I remained polite but unyielding, patience began to fray. There was an undercurrent of tension in the house which sometimes simmered to the surface and burst in snappy bubbles off Kay's tongue. Although I knew I was only partly the cause, I felt I must do something soon.

Often I was tempted to fill my case with books and apples and take to the road again. Having once tasted the ease of mobility, it was hard to discard as a way out, however temporary. But the lessons learned on that first walk into the sun had gone deep. The indignity of having my diary read and the misery of the train ride with the social worker were still vivid. I realized that stabs at an independence for which I was not yet equipped were not only damaging to self-esteem, they were dangerous. To maintain what little freedom I had gained I must remain as uninvolved with the authorities as possible which, in effect, meant cooperating to some degree. In a moment of frustration the words 'approved school' had been flung at me. Although my quiet, non-delinquent behaviour did not qualify me for such measures, I took heed of the warning. The last thing I wanted was to have my options restricted by law.

One day a brochure arrived which was different from the others. It showed an artist's impression of a place neither grand nor stately, but rather a cluster of houses set in grounds which looked encouragingly unkempt. There were boys as well as girls in the photographs and none of them wore uniform. It came under the heading 'progressive school'. I had to do something. I would give St S—'s a try.

There were few possessions to which I was greatly attached but one thing I did not leave behind when packing for St S—'s was my music. From the age of six, when I began to learn, I had had an ambivalent relationship with the piano. Publicly, I disliked practising and shrank from the rigours of scales and theory, but privately, I was very drawn to certain pieces. There was satisfaction in making the music say things I felt but could not describe in words. I also had a lot of respect for my music teacher, a dedicated, highly principled woman who disapproved of me strongly but saw potential behind my capricious moods. Under her guidance, I took and passed the practical and theory examinations up to grade seven. Then suddenly, I baulked. That was around the time Kay and Richard started to be more open in their hostilities to one another. Without any explanation to anyone, I stopped playing altogether. Nevertheless, into the bottom of my St S—'s case went Heller, Paderewski and Beethoven, graffiti'd indelibly with my teacher's annotations in green ink. Those tattered sheets of music were the first objects of conscious nostalgia in my life, representing a brief era of discipline, security and achievement gone forever.

St S—'s, I soon discovered, was not the place to be reintroduced to the benefits or otherwise of discipline hailing from the adult world. Although, paradoxically, one of the main ideas behind the school was to nurture the talents of the individual, there was a slant towards the communal way of living which isolated me from the start. Only ever at ease in groups when way out in front or so far behind as to be off the map, I was an unhappy misfit in a system where everything was 'fair'. Democratic was a word frequently used.

And, with the special 'free' structure of the school, there was a whole new set of rules to learn. These were not rules made by the staff, they were the unwritten decrees as to what constituted good and bad set up by the children in the absence of any other code. 'Freedom' as a catchword was held aloft and waved like a militant banner. To the pupils of St S—'s, freedom meant extremism. It was their way of coping with a concept too daunting to handle. Using the conventional mores of the establishment as a wall to kick against, they formed a solid anti-culture which bristled with as rigid a set of values as those they claimed to despise.

I was welcomed as a shining example of anti-establishment when it was learned that I had run away from my last school. But as it became clear that, far from having a tearaway attitude, I was quiet and spent a great deal of time reading, respect dwindled and I was labelled dismissively as a goody-goody. Not even getting into trouble for the sin of eating sardines under the bedclothes helped: freedom for animals meant we all had to be vegetarian.

'How *could* you?' I was asked.

'I like sardines.'

A well-meaning girl, who was nearly fourteen, tried to make me understand.

'Don't you see how wrong it is to eat those poor little fish? What right have you to take their lives?'

'I'm a bigger fish.'

'That's a really fascist remark!'

She turned to the rest of the dorm and there were nods. Now I was a goody-goody *and* a fascist. It all seemed very complicated. I went on quietly eating sardines.

One afternoon Richard came to see me. We made the arrangement on the spur of the moment by telephone and, to avoid wasting any time, fixed to meet outside the school grounds. Richard was as bored at the thought of going through the usual formalities as I was. After lunch recess, instead of getting changed for Netball, I slipped unnoticed through an opening in the hedge and walked along the road to our rendezvous. He had a Bristol at the time, a big, sleek bomb of a car, and I felt proud as he turned up right on time with a rich slur of tyres on the verge.

We went for a drive in the country and talked. Or rather he talked. I was only dimly aware that this was for him as well as me a period of major changes. He was not specific, but hinted that things would be different from now on. There was talk of sailing a new boat up to Scotland, selling this car. I knew without

34

asking that he would not be sailing with Kay and it crossed my mind that it might be the lady with red hair from his office who was to be the crew. I nodded as I listened to him, catching the thread of his enthusiasm and spinning visions of my own. It had been too long since he had said those exciting words: 'I've got a plan!'

He smiled in a special way that was just for me and him and told me 'not to breathe a word'. Then, as if just checking, he said, 'You like Scotland, don't you? Remember those holidays we had? The cottage? The sea?'

I remembered, and knew then that I was not being cut out of his plan.

When we stopped for tea at a deathly silent hotel, where Richard made me giggle by imitating the sour-faced waitress behind her back, he broached the subject of how I was getting on at St S—'s. 'I'm not,' I said flatly, only ever afraid to hide the truth from him. For a moment he looked irritated, then sighed, searching for something positive to pull from this confession which would no doubt cause problems for us both.

'Well, I suppose it means I won't have those exorbitant fees to pay any more.'

He looked down at the tea tray with its fussy white doily. There was one biscuit left on the plate.

'Do you want that biscuit?'

I shook my head and he popped it whole into his mouth. I loved the way he ate so neatly and with such relish, dabbing up the last of the crumbs with a finger.

As he drove me back to school I reflected that I had never once heard him speak of a plan without it being put into action sooner or later. He was a *doer*, and I wanted to be a doer too. I could not imagine that anyone could ever take his place in my heart.

Richard's failure to go through the proper channels before visiting gave rise to a disturbing confrontation. Shortly after I got back to St S—'s I was summoned to the houseparents' quarters.

Housemother was a square woman: square shoulders, square bust, square frown. Her husband was taller but similarly angled, a rectangle. They both faced me, standing, in the kitchen of their apartment. Housemother began.

'How can we be expected to do anything for you youngsters when parents set an example like this? How were we supposed to know where you were? For all we knew you could have been kidnapped.'

She leaned her square buttocks against a dresser and folded her arms. Housefather chipped in.

'What is he? In films or something? Same old story. Half the messed-up kids here come from theatrical families.'

The disparaging way he spoke startled me. He had got it all wrong. I began to explain that Richard made commercials and fishing documentaries but was cut short.

'Whatever he does, he has behaved irresponsibly and encouraged you to do the same. There are plenty like that. Coming here in their big cars and filling their kids' heads with all sorts of fancy ideas, then going off and leaving them flat for God knows how long. Happens all the time and we're in the middle of it, supposed to be doing a job.'

I did not care about this man's job and Richard was not going to go off and leave me flat for God knows how long. 'Leaving me flat' was an expression I had heard Kay use, and it scared me. Angry that I could not bring myself to glare into their faces, addressing instead a stain on the wall behind, I blurted, 'If it weren't for *people like my father*, *people like you* would not even have a job. He pays for you.'

My taunt could not have been more unfortunate. Housefather was quick to bite back.

'Oh no, girlie, that's just where you're wrong.' He rocked a chair at the kitchen table with his long arms and his blockish face loomed close. 'What we do we do because we believe in it. Getting paid has precious little to do with it.' There was a grunt of agreement from his other half. 'And besides, if I am not mistaken, your dad has had more than one reminder about fees due before the beginning of term . . .'

Housemother put out a restraining hand. This was perhaps going too far. I took in nothing of what was said during the rest of the interview, conscious only that the voices were placatory and an arm around my deliberately stiffened shoulders was meant to be sympathetic. I shook it off.

Back in the dormitory, relieved to find myself alone, I flung on my anorak and felt in the pocket for the two half-crowns Richard had given me. One had vanished and as I descended to the ground via the fire ladder, I cursed the thief with a word once torn from Kay's lips in a moment of fury. I knew who the culprit was. It was that girl with the tapeworm who dyed her hair and kept dope in a Tampax tube. I muttered the word again and when a fat boy called out to ask if I wanted to 'go to Winkley' – the standard St S—'s formula for a fumble – I turned my venom on him.

He grinned appreciatively and bounced it back.

'Bugger off!'
'Bugger off!'
'Bugger off!'
'Bugger off!'

It went like a chant with the rhythm of my stride and the blotting ugliness of it cancelled all other thought and made me feel strong.

In the High Street of the local town the shops were beginning to close. I slipped into Woolworth's just as a man with a swab bucket was about to lock the doors, and for seven pence halfpenny equipped myself with a lump of pink and white slab cake the size of a brick. St S—'s could keep their nut rissole supper. Moments later I regretted the indulgence when I learned that a half-fare bus ticket to anywhere within ten miles of 309 cost two and sixpence. If I had wanted to go badly enough I could have hitched, but I did not. I did not know what I wanted. Richard probably would not even be there.

Aimlessly, I wandered back into the High Street and started to munch on the slab cake. Only when a woman wheeling a pram-load of groceries stared did I realize that tears were running down my cheeks, making salty trifle of the crumbs.

That Easter it was suggested that I spend the holidays with my godmother in France. I leapt at the chance, not caring where I

went so long as it was away. I knew I would not be going back to
St S—'s.

Chapter Three

I came back from France armed with a sort of mental carapace
– it was a word I had recently learned – which shielded me from
the worst chunks now beginning to crack off my parents' marriage. I had enjoyed the foreign-ness of the holiday. A limited
understanding of the language made me see people from a distance and observe their behaviour dispassionately, as if I were a
fly on the wall. I took refuge in this point of view now, turning
it on my family and myself. As a defence system it was only
partially successful.

This term my name was on the register of a local grammar
school and I was also, perhaps belatedly, putting in appearances
at a Child Guidance clinic where a gracious lady in maroon gave
me coffee and ink-blot tests. She asked me to tell her what games
I liked and I told her about being a fly on the wall, and Chatter.

Chatter was a game Marianne and I used to play when we
shared the Big Room at 309 – a room at the top of the stairs
which Richard could cross with one magnificent leap when he
came to say good-night in an exuberant mood. The rules of the
game were flexible and developed in pace with our own minds
and bodies. We called it Chatter in honour of frequent yells from
below to 'Stop that chatter!' It went on for years.

Immediately after Lights Out one or other of us would whisper,
'Up to?'

This was the signal to begin. Our principal character was stolen
from a TV serial about a horse. The horse's owner, Joey, was our
hero. In fact we discovered that on close examination Joey was

38

not up to much as a hero, so we made improvements of our own, giving him more height, changing his American accent to King's English and toning down the loud check of his lumberjack shirts. We also dealt fairly summarily with the horse, putting it out to grass after it had served its purpose in the initial episode and allowing it to age gracefully while Joey got on with his adventures. For Chatter was an endless saga of how Joey got himself into and out of a wide variety of challenging situations.

The other characters we chose to bring into Chatter were selected from books, films, history and our own social circle. At first we surrounded Joey with animal friends, allowing him to steal Long John Silver's parrot and somehow having Guy the gorilla and King Kong produce an endearing miniature called Little Ho, after Horatio Nelson. A small, ugly dog by the name of Benji went everywhere with Joey and was a constant source of embarrassment. He turned up in a suitcase when Joey, in a reckless fling with Peter Pan's Wendy, eloped to Penang. (I had just started reading Somerset Maugham.) The dog's squeaking, puddling presence ruined the romance of the occasion and sent Wendy rushing back to Never-Never Land, while Joey sat on the balcony sipping a manly stengah with David Copperfield, who was having similar trouble with Dora. They both decided they were better off without girls and Copperfield was shortly replaced by Dick West, the Lone Ranger's sidekick, who was tanned and dashing and always had sandwiches in his saddlebag.

Gradually, as our early adolescent curiosities became defined, we placed Joey in situations where, through him, the questions in our own minds could be aired. What did it feel like to be a grown-up woman? Briskly we thrust upon Joey a pair of breasts, a tight skirt and high heels, making him, for the sake of continuity, the temporary victim of a surgical slip. The result was disappointing, lasting only one episode. After he had dressed up and done his hair differently a few times, been shopping and had a giggly candlelit dinner with Dick, we could not think what else to give him to do – beside the washing up, and Joey certainly wasn't going to do that.

Being a baby lasted longer. Both Marianne and I found the

concept of infant helplessness fascinating. Imagine knowing what you wanted but not having any way of expressing it except by crying. The thought was appalling. Time after time we forced babyhood upon Joey, surrounding him with adults who sometimes listened but never fully understood his needs. We could imagine no worse hell than being entirely at the mercy of grown-ups. Eventually even this palled and Joey reverted to his original, enviable form: a young man in charge of his own life who did not have to depend on anyone for anything. For that, before puberty stepped in, was how we wanted to be.

The game recalled a time when Marianne and I took the closeness of each other for granted and when our parents and the future were solid, unquestionable things. I told the lady in maroon about Chatter but not about what happened when that, and so many other things in my life, suddenly came to an end. I did not tell her how Marianne changed, overnight it seemed, into someone who was always ill; how I ran away, was brought back, left again; how the cat was run over and Marianne's Dobermann puppy, gone wild because she was no longer strong enough to take it for walks, ate my pet hen and savaged the last of our rabbits. I said nothing of the evening Kay appeared with a black eye saying she had fallen against a door knob or of how, when I tip-toed down to Marianne's room, I found Richard with her, white-faced, rocking her thin body against him. They were both crying.

After that Richard often came home from work too late to say good-night. And sometimes he did not come at all.

If I missed Marianne sharing the Big Room or Richard's long good-nights, I did not admit it. I cried many times, secretly, when Perdita the cat died, but when Kay sat on the end of my bed and told me unhappily that things were going on between her and Richard which I could not be expected to understand, I felt curiously little interest. Knowing that some kind of sympathetic response was being solicited, I would nod with appropriate gravity and offer non-committal comments from inside my carapace. As soon as she had gone I would dive back into the book I was reading, taking advantage of the fact that in her present state of mind she was more lenient about Lights Out time.

It was different for Marianne. When Kay went to talk to her she listened with her whole being, her eyes, ever-widening as her face grew thinner, alive to every nuance, every hint as to what was going on. And when Richard sat with her she gave him the same breathless attention. She also gave him a small ocean of childish loyalty and everything she knew of love.

I had accepted from an early age that Marianne was not only brighter than me – described as 'the academic one' – but also more attractive. Dark and fine-boned with pale, clear skin and glossy brown hair, she was like a pretty Arab pony, beside whom I remained for years a scruffy Shetland – what bones I had lost beneath cheeks stubbornly rosy and round. The change that came over Marianne when the family began to divide was profound, and she used every ounce of her considerable intelligence to conceal it from the rest of the world.

It began when she announced that from now on she would make her own breakfast. She went down ahead of the rest of the family, fed Annie, the little mongrel who outlived and outsmarted all our more exotic pets, and made herself a piece of toast. The first morning I found the toast, still warm and unbitten, under a scrumple of paper in the dustbin, I was mildly surprised, but after a while it became automatic to check it was there. Sometimes I ate it. Marianne's plate, knife laid across a strategic scattering of crumbs, was left by the sink with a mug in which milk had been swirled. Tacitly loyal, I said nothing about this regular waste either to Marianne or the grown-ups. But I wondered at it all the same.

Avoiding lunch was not difficult for her. She simply tipped the contents of her lunchbox down the school lavatory. And at tea, as soon as Kay's back was turned, she shovelled everything she did not want into our brother James's eager mouth. It was Richard, with his casual habit of offering a bite of whatever was especially good on his plate, who presented the only real problem, and in dealing with this Marianne employed her most subtle tactic: she accepted. Richard did not know for a long time that

41

the odd nibbles she took from his hand were often the only nourishment she had. When he did not come home to supper, she starved.

Weeks, perhaps months, went by while her crusade continued undetected. It was only when she started to avoid Games at school, hiding in the cloakrooms because she knew she was too weak to run, that people began to wake up to what was going on. By then it was almost too late to arrest the downward trend. And inside her shrinking body other insidious things were happening.

Words had always interested me. Now there were several new ones around. *Anorexia* was repeated often enough to become ordinary sounding after a while. Then there was *duodenal colic* with a question mark, followed by *psychosomatic* and then *peritonitis*, no question mark, and finally *peritoneal abcess*. Somewhere here the non-medical term *adultery* slipped in and somewhere here, too, Kay, under pressure miles beyond my ken, gave vent to a revelation for which, with childish brutality, I punished her for years.

It was after the grown-ups' supper and James was in bed. Marianne was in her room, ill, and Richard had left the house after a row I had not heard. I went into the dining-room, where Kay was slowly clearing the table. Her movements were wooden and her face frighteningly sad. The paisley apron she wore for washing up hung over the back of a chair. She put it on now, carelessly flattening her hair. I hesitated by the door, wanting to go through to the kitchen for a glass of water but not wanting to get involved with Kay. I guessed there had been a row and knew there was very little safe to say.

'Can I just get some water?'

I hovered with my glass, poised to bolt through. Kay pulled a plate towards her, rucking the table-cloth.

'What?' she said, the word a small, bitter explosion, 'are you talking to me? Of course you can get some water. Do what you like. You all do what you like in this house.'

I started to walk past the huge painting on the wall, Madonna and Child with fruit. The baby in it looked vacant and old and the mother had a sixth finger half erased. Kay held out a pile of plates.

'Take these with you as you go.'

Her voice sounded brittle, as though it would break if she allowed it to soften. The dishes she was collecting slithered together and a fork fell to the carpet, strewing an arc of cold gravy. She asked me to bring a cloth.

In the kitchen I found the cloth screwed up in a ball beside the sink. A few days before I had seen her kill a spider with it, a spider I had pointed out because I liked the way it walked. She used it now on the bread board with slow, crumb-crushing swipes. Her eyes, cold with misery, stared ahead unseeingly.

All at once I no longer wanted to escape but to smash this mood I had seen so often. I knew she was in pain but I did not care. I ploughed in pitilessly with a line guaranteed to make her explode.

'Where's Richard? What did you say to make him go away?'

Her hands gripped the bread board, holding the knife slotted down one side.

'What did I say? What did *I* say? Why don't you take a look at your wonderful father for a change? What do you think he is doing right now – thinking about you, thinking about Marianne up there half dead because of him? No, I'll tell you . . .'

I hated the writhing shape of her lips.

'Shut up, shut up!'

One of Kay's hands flew out from the bread board. The knife was in it.

'Don't you dare tell me to shut up! Who the hell do you think you are? If it wasn't for a hole in a condom you wouldn't even be here – I never planned to have you so soon after Marianne. Don't you think I had enough on my plate?'

'Well, I *am* here!' I shouted, grabbing the bread board and leaving her waving the knife. 'I *am* here! And if I was an accident' – I looked at the spilled gravy, the rumpled cloth – 'I bet it was your fault. I bet you used an old *thing*!'

'Get out of my sight, you little bitch!'

I went.

As usual, I felt ashamed for having deliberately baited Kay, but from the detached, fly-on-the-wall point of view I was intrigued. The bit about the condom was new. Her words conjured up a film-strip image of myself in miniature, boxing my way through a hole in the void to burst upon the universe with fists raised.

'I am here!' I thought again excitedly, as I stood on my head before going to bed that night. And the knowledge that I had entered the world uninvited made me feel fierce and special.

'I am here!' I thought again and again. 'I am alive!'

For a long time Marianne was in hospital. When she came out, her bags were taken into a downstairs room, Richard's old studio. I was called to come and say hello. Pleased that she was back I bounded down the stairs, bursting with things to say. Just inside the door I stopped short, every word eclipsed.

A set of clothes had been made for her while she was away, a skirt, waistcoat and jacket in green tweedy material. Marianne had just finished putting it on when I came in. And that was the only reason I believed it was her. From beneath a short pudding-basin of thin, mouse-coloured hair, one side of her mouth twitched upwards. Lines like pencilled algebraic symbols broke out where a dimple used to be.

'Hello, duck.'

It was our private greeting. At least her voice was her own. Very slowly, as if her body were a jumble of glass coat-hangers, she stooped to pull up her tights. Thick nylon mesh was bunched in wrinkles over each transparent ankle. Her calves were bowed out and flattened like stripped wishbones. There were heavy suede shoes on her feet. I sat down on the edge of a big lounge chair watching as her white fingers tugged at the laces.

' 'lo, duck. Why are you wearing those old-lady shoes?'

'Mummy bought them specially. They're "sensible".'

'Sensible' to us meant boring and unattractive. Teachers were sensible. There was a knock on the already open door and Kay came in smiling, her brightness painfully strained. She had a friend with her in the lounge and had made coffee. There was a mug for each of us and a plate of ginger biscuits. In a moment

44

she bustled out and we heard the tail end of a sentence – 'leave the girls to get on with it' – as she went in to join her friend. I wriggled under the formality, feeling like a visitor.

'Shall I get Annie?' I said, thinking the presence of the dog might help.

'Not allowed,' said Marianne, indicating a Kay decree with a familiar movement of her head.

'Do you want her?'

There was a nod and a tiny hint of the old conspiratorial gleam. I opened one of the windows on to the garden. It was easy just to step out. Annie was very excited to see Marianne and her cries of welcome had to be stifled with a cushion. When she was calmer we sat her on a chair and threw ginger biscuits for her to catch.

'Was it horrible?' I asked, meaning the hospital and everything.

'Yes,' said Marianne, and then rather proudly, 'I've got lesions.'

There was a pause as I wondered how best to respond to this.

'Foreign lesions?'

We giggled. Suddenly I found myself telling her how I had been kissed for the first time on my last day in France. It was in a lift and the man had put a lot of spit in my mouth and I did not know what to do with it.

'So what did you do?'

Marianne's great eyes were right there with me in the lift.

'Pretended to bury my face in his chest and dribbled it down his jumper. It was awful, left a great wet stain.'

Marianne laughed, a lovely, tinkly sound. I wished I did not think of glass coat-hangers every time her bones moved.

'Tell me more,' she said, 'more, more, more.'

And telling true stories of things that happened to me became the role I played with Marianne: the more details of faces, dialogues and scenes I remembered, the more raptly she listened. It was like a living version of Chatter: I had stepped into Joey's shoes.

The day came for me to meet 'the other woman'. We had all known there was one for some time. I furrowed my brow at Richard when he made the suggestion.

'What on earth will we talk about?'

He looked wicked for a moment, screwing up his eyes in imitation of Annie at her most prima donna'ish, wagging an imaginary tail and saying, 'Me!'

Then he sat up properly and thought for a moment.

'Horses. You're both mad about horses. She used to teach riding.'

Oh no, I thought. I was not mad about horses, I was terrified of them; had only endured the years of Saturday-morning hacks in Bushy Park to keep up with Marianne.

'And she's done quite a lot of acting,' he went on. 'She was in a feature film when she was twelve.'

Worse and worse. When I was younger, keen on dancing and reciting poetry, I had announced that I wanted to be an actress. This had made Kay bite her lip and lit Richard's face with a smile which said: 'I've been waiting for this,' but that ambition was out of date now. I wondered if I ought to wash my hair before visiting Edwina.

In the end I went as I was, in an old brown duffel coat with a book in each pocket; the *Odyssey* and a James Bond. Arriving early, I sat against some railings near her flat, reading until it was time to go in. I was still mentally lashed to the mast as Odysseus' ship passed the island of the Sirens when Edwina opened the door, and I gave a jump when I recognized her.

If I had been expecting a familiar face at all it was that of the woman in the green trouser-suit. But this was another, a girl glimpsed fleetingly on an occasion when I played a part in one of Richard's commercials. The impression then had been of a tall, wind-ruffled figure always in a hurry. She looked different now, much more sophisticated. The flat she lived in was very tidy. The only thing that matched the former dashing image was a huge colourful bedspread woven of subtly matched silks. I fingered its rich texture while she was out of the room. From the kitchen she called to ask if I would like to hang up my coat. I did, noticing that she had a duffel coat too, then I wandered through to watch her arranging tea things on a tray. Her hands were businesslike. The teapot had been properly warmed.

We sat at a low table in the main room. The minutes while the tea brewed seemed very long. Edwina brought in some shortbread still warm from the oven.

'That smells good,' I said, and sought for the right descriptive word, '... homely.' An unfortunate choice.

Edwina poured, holding the lid on the teapot. The weewee gurgle of the sound brought a hysterical lump into my chest. I was enormously relieved when it stopped. It was not a good moment to giggle.

'Do you like cooking?' asked Edwina pleasantly.

'Quite. I can make fudge.'

She offered me a piece of shortbread. The inside of it was exactly the same colour as the jerkin she wore, which complemented her dark hair well but looked as though it were made out of a blanket.

'Richard says you're a good cook,' I said, keen not to let the conversation die, 'and very economical.'

Edwina gave a loud neigh of laughter, long eyebrows moving up and down merrily. She was not wearing any make-up and her face had little natural colour. It was the dark eyes and wide, laughing mouth that made her attractive. I wanted to know how often she washed her hair, which shook like a mane. That reminded me of the horses. We both started speaking at the same time.

'I gather that...'

'Richard says that...'

There was a silly moment of confusion while we both apologized. Then Edwina completed her sentence first.

'I gather you're keen on horses.'

I decided to risk the truth.

'Actually,' I said, with what I hoped was a confiding look, 'I'm scared stiff of them.'

'Really? But I thought...'

I nodded and out it all poured. It was Marianne who was – who used to be – the keen rider. She was very good, always given the most difficult pony in the stables and sent to canter ahead while I, clinging miserably to the pommel when no one was look-

47

ing, skulked at the back, wishing I did not exist. The mud flying, reins slapping and hot snorting so horrified me that sometimes I would hurl myself deliberately into the stinging nettles just so it would be over. Once I broke my wrist doing this but was so ashamed I got back on and kept quiet until the whole arm swelled so badly in the night I could not get my pyjama top off or on, and eventually had to go to hospital with the sleeves wrapped embarrassingly round my neck.

Edwina seemed very understanding about all this.

'What you need,' she said, 'is a quiet pony you could get used to by yourself.'

I agreed. To give up altogether would be an acknowledgement of personal weakness, the thing I most feared in myself and others. Weak people got left behind by strong people like Richard.

When Edwina and I said goodbye we smiled a lot and if I had been a boy we would have shaken hands. As it was I ducked my head in friendly farewell one last time and went out into the street hands in pockets. At the bus stop I found out what had happened to Odysseus – he survived the blandishments of the Sirens by stopping his ears with wax – and started on a James Bond.

Kay, Marianne and Edwina. One thing they all had in common was Richard as a focal point in their lives. And who was that actress with the kitten playing in a forest of black hair – he described her on the telephone, all husky and vibrant and come-and-see-me-soon – and the tall, fair one who was so beautiful and had a Swedish name? Would I ever meet the Indian lady who wooed him from his dark moods with solo performances of Bach on the violin or the one who bought him bedroom slippers and a dressing-gown, which made him run away?

No, that era was over. There would be no more commercials, no more pretty actresses, no more family holidays and no more after-supper rows. The dreams Richard had sketched when he visited me at St S—'s were now becoming realities. He did sail to Scotland but instead of buying a small croft to write in, which had been the original plan, he bought a hotel.

48

For a short period after Richard left I moved into an open residential unit on the advice of the Child Guidance people. The lady I had talked to about Chatter thought a supervised break from the home environment might ease pressures all round. Marianne was slowly recovering – physically at least – but things were difficult for Kay and my presence did not help. Once, after angry words, I banged the back door so hard all the glass shattered. Kay was convinced I had done this deliberately with my lacrosse stick which happened to be lying near by. The implication that I was being untruthful so enraged me that I smashed every piece of furniture in the Big Room and announced that *that* had been done on purpose but the back door was an accident. From that time on I slept on a mattress on the floor and found pleasure in the clarity of the empty room. Kay wept and raged at my behaviour but callously I ignored her. I could not help blaming her in some way for having let Richard go.

Then one day the call I had been waiting for came. It was always a special event when Richard phoned. Kay would speak to him first in her bedroom, then Marianne, huddled over the extension in the studio. Occasionally James would have a few words upstairs under Kay's eye and then it was my turn and I would stand in the hall and speak loudly so everyone could hear. On this occasion he said simply, 'Come,' and I said, 'Yes.'

Afterwards he and Kay talked for a long time and Marianne, who had been listening on the extension, told me they had been discussing the problem of my education. Apparently I was going to have private lessons and there was also mention of another school where I might board next year. I wrinkled my brow significantly at Marianne.

'I shouldn't worry,' she said. 'He sounded as though he was only saying it to keep Kay happy.'

Since Richard had gone she had begun calling Kay by name, but when she woke sobbing in the night the cry on her lips was always: 'Daddy, Daddy, Daddy!' She would be seeing him again after her term of private lessons had come to an end. For Marianne, too, had turned her back on conventional education. None of us knew then how finally the child in her had died.

Chapter Four

'Look.'

I looked.

Lead-coloured mountains pressed back in a bunch against the evening light, old and proud as veterans in a reunion pose. A still loch threw off a shallow glow, uneven edges soaking into bogland and waterlogged reeds.

Before, the landscape had been a dim, grand scene in the distance. But here, on the fifteen-mile single-track road leading to the coast, it was bang in front of us and all around. Our left front wheel mashed a tuft of yellowish fleece into a line of sheep droppings and Richard began to talk again.

It was late March, almost a year to the day he had visited me at St S—'s. This time he was driving a mud-spattered Land-Rover loaded with straw and sacks of animal feed, swinging it round blind bends on the Highland road with the same casual virtuosity he had handled the Bristol. March for him meant less than a month before the opening of the hotel. My imagination blinked as he made rapid verbal sketches of half-a-dozen already burgeoning schemes. He leapt from one topic to another – goat husbandry, kipper smoking, pig-pen building – creating an image of a hotel quite unlike any other I had seen. That was his vision too.

In the middle of an enthusiastic monologue on the virtues of producing methane gas from pig manure, he broke off suddenly and said, 'I want you to think of this place as home.' Then he was off again.

As we drove on with the glimmering loch on one side and rocks close enough to touch on the other, I hugged his words to me. That was what he was doing: digging, planting, building – he was making a home, something 309 had not felt like since I was too young to know the difference. A warm bubble of anticipation rose in me and I gazed out at the mountains and smiled. They were crazy shapes. The crazy shapes of home.

⋆   ⋆   ⋆

I had not expected there to be a car park or for the sea to be only two fields away. There were islands out there, dark hummocky clods like gingerbread spilled from a pan. Inland, beyond the row of houses straggled above the road like knots in a string – the hotel the biggest knot – there were mountains and sky, mountains and sky. We did not go into the car park – that was for when the guests came – but up a small side road with a sign at the top saying PUBLIC BAR. Richard swerved to avoid a fat puppy which waddled forward to greet us wagging its entire body.

'That's Caillach,' he said. 'She hasn't learned about cars yet.' The name means something like little old lady in Gaelic.

The kitchen door was open. Edwina stood before an enamel sink as long as a trough straining hot liquid through a triangular sieve. I had never seen a sieve that shape before. Nor had I ever seen Richard and Edwina kissing. I looked at the sieve. When they were detached, Edwina said a cheery hello and got on with what she was doing. Richard showed me to my room and told me that supper was at seven-thirty.

There were two single beds in the room. Automatically I chose the one nearest the window and looked out. There was not much to see: just a wall and a rickety sort of pen closed in at one end. I let the net curtain fall and set to unpacking. The room, which had looked dark and blank at first, improved as soon as my duffel coat and dressing gown were hanging on the door and my prune-stone and walnut necklace looped over the mirror. I was sitting on the bed dreaming of how I would gradually collect things to cover the blank surfaces when Richard's stride came along the corridor.

'Supper,' he called, drumming three fingers lightly against the door, and strode away again.

Soup was already on the table in the kitchen. There were five places set and as I hovered, wondering which was mine, two men in work clothes came in and sat down opposite a place which was clearly Edwina's, near the stove. I sat on the smaller of the two stools left and immediately wished I had not as it made me lower than everyone else. Richard came in last and ate quickly to catch up. Edwina had the main course dished up before the first soup spoon went down. Everyone had exactly the same on their plate and although I was not sure what it was, it was good. Richard said so and Edwina hrummphed absently. She was making notes in a large diary while she ate. The workmen responded with polite och ayes to comments Richard made concerning dwangs and spirit-levels. Otherwise there was no sound but the scraping of steel on china and occasional glops and rattlings from a pot on the stove. Edwina poured mugs of tea to go with pudding, which was a serious steamed affair, then the plates were collected and the table cleared. I was impressed by the efficiency of it all. Should I offer to do the washing up? But Edwina was already at the sink. The drying, then.

'Oh, I usually leave it to drain.'

Her arms plunged about briskly in the soapy water. It was clear she did not need any help.

Richard was at the back door, talking to the workmen. It was dark outside. Not knowing where else to go, I went to bed. I looked forward to becoming part of things so that I would not feel strange any more. After all, this was to be my real home.

In the middle of the night I was woken by a loud noise. It was a straining, pressureful sound, as though something of great weight were trying to rub its way through a barrier. It sounded close. Feeling for my torch I crawled to the end of the bed and cautiously pushed up the window. The beam shone on to a nude mountain of hairy flesh moving back and forth systematically and with evident pleasure. Embedded in the flesh was an ecstatically slitted eye fringed about with short blond lashes. Without interrupting the rhythmic rubbings of its body, the eye widened and stared unflinchingly into the light. I withdrew my head from the window but continued to watch, riveted. My neighbour, a pig bigger than I ever could have imagined, was clearly engaged in very private business.

A new sound added itself to the creaking and straining – a succession of low, hoarse breaths cut off sharply at the peak of each rise. I crouched motionless on the bed, staring at bliss and listening to agony. Until I realized the agony was bliss as well. The new sound came from indoors.

I dropped to the floor and crawled across to sit with my head locked tight against the door. Through the thin walls of the corridor between Richard and Edwina's room and mine the dragging gasps shuddered and swung. The volume rose and the seconds between breaths grew shorter until there was no space and one hoarse whoop crashed into the next, gathering at last to one continuous braying din. When I knew it could go no further, I felt my face flush and clapped my hands over my ears. Just too late to smother the final cry of 'Richard!'

Breakfast was punctually at eight. Porridge with thick Jersey cream, followed by eggs with yolks as bright as ox-eye daisies. Edwina had already milked the cows and fed the hens. I watched covertly as she moved around the big kitchen, mane of hair scraped back, tweed-covered hips businesslike. Her breasts, neatly harnessed under a dark sweater, did not swing as she worked. She wore the ultimate in 'sensible' shoes.

After whisking the table clear she gave her cheery smile and took me on a tour of the domestic facilities. Here was the place to leave dirty laundry and this was where the Hoover lived. Aprons were in a cupboard in the hall and all boots and outdoor shoes went into the drying-room. Clean linen was upstairs – please use only those sheets and towels marked Staff. I would find toothpaste and shampoo in the downstairs bathroom. Anything else I needed, I was to ask. Picking up a bucket and a can of paint-stripper, she strode away to attack a room. I thanked her disappearing back and plodded off to fetch my boots.

Richard was talking to the pig outside my room, scratching its back and muttering under the bristly flap of an ear. I went out to join them.

'It's huge,' I said, standing with hands firmly in pockets as the rude snout snuffed wetly at me through the chicken wire. I did not tell him about its performance in the night, because then he would know I had heard the other thing, too.

'He's called Hairy Hans,' said Richard. 'Come and meet the girls.'

We walked down past the bar and car park into the field below

53

the road. Wind rattled the gate behind us. I noticed the islands looked greener by daylight, and not so far away.

The three young sows were named Freeman, Hardy and Willis, after a shoe shop. Richard explained that it was the first shop he had passed when bringing them home.

'Willis is chief wife. She'll be the first to produce. The other two are more like concubines.' He tickled Willis's ear and she rubbed her long, slobbery jaws against his leg. 'When Hairy Hans turns into bacon next year we'll have to go on to AI.'

He noticed my questioning look.

'Artificial Insemination. I'm going to learn to do it myself. But you won't mind, will you, old friend?'

Willis did not look as if she would.

Richard introduced me to the cows: a big, buttery Jersey with pool-brown googoo eyes and a smaller one called the Heifer. There should be a calf in June. In another field were the goats, Linty and Emma. Emma nibbled his sleeve and playfully butted him with her small, snub-horned brow but when I stretched out a hand she backed away.

'They'll soon get to know you when you've milked them a few times. Watch Edwina this evening. She'll show you how to do the hens too. You'd like to have a shot at doing the animals, wouldn't you?'

'Yes.'

But I was sure I would never be as good as Edwina.

The animals were a crucial part of Richard's plans for self-sufficiency. He talked to them, scratched their backs, made houses for them and treated them as friends, but not one of them was there without a purpose. While learning to tend the animals I learned the relationship between field and kitchen, animal and man; while one hand kills to feed, the other feeds to kill. When the time came to test the culinary use of a hen which had gone off the lay, it was I who fed it, Richard who broke its neck and Edwina who cooked it. We all ate it and after the bones had been boiled for stock they went back to the hen field in the next feed bucket. Bonemeal was good for strengthening eggshells.

I did not mind squelching up to the hen field to scatter potato peelings and feel in the straw-lined beer crates for eggs; I had no objection to driving the dawdlesome cows from byre to field and back again; even Linty's tri-directional squirting teats did not bother me once I had mastered the art of keeping her back legs out of the milking bucket – but I would have given almost anything to avoid taking the swill down to Willis and Co.

The trouble began when Hairy Hans was moved in with the girls to perform his conjugal duties.

'Is he safe?' I asked Richard as I lifted the heavy buckets of swill.

'Of course he is,' said Richard, impatient at any sign of cissiness. As I set off he called after me with a grin, 'Just don't let him get on top of you!'

That was exactly what I was afraid of.

The minute they heard the clomp of my boots and the slop-slap of swill spilling into the tops of them, every pig in the field came charging towards the gate. Every pig except Hans. He was waiting by the trough and all I could see of him as I sloshed down the field, yelling at Freeman, Hardy and Willis as they shoved their faces into the buckets, was his long, pink, imperiously questing snout. As the distance between us narrowed I could hear above the squealing of the girls cosy, expectant little grunts rumbling up from somewhere in his huge gut. Then he would emerge.

The first time I saw his erect penis I dropped both buckets and ran. It was about two feet long, twizzled like a corkscrew and *multi-coloured*. I had to go back for another look. I wondered what sort of connection there was between his brain and the end of that thing to enable him to aim straight. It must be very difficult if Willis was not helpful.

After a few weeks a letter from the education authorities re-called Richard to the arrangements he had made for my continued schooling. This coincided with the arrival in dribs and drabs of ground and hotel staff, and when I returned from my first lesson I was not unduly put out to find Edwina going through the animal routine with a stranger. The new girl was huge and could handle seventy-pound feeding sacks with ease, but she still cried buckets when Hairy Hans bit her in the thigh one morning. I sympathized from a safe distance when Richard implied that it had only happened because she failed to understand the pig's character. It irritated all the staff that none of the animals ever bit him.

If efforts to re-channel me into conventional education had been half-hearted before, they now became token in the extreme. Once a week I went to the head of the local junior school for tuition in basic Maths, and a lady in a cottage above the fishing pier made patient attempts to civilize my French. There was talk of History and Geography but neither went further than a run-through of ground already covered. The most instructive study period came on a Sunday afternoon when I walked a mile to the house of a local lady artist and joined her for a session of painting and tea.

Her house, standing alone on a flat stretch of moorland, smelled cosily of mould and old coffee grounds. She was very English and very much a lady and her crystal-clear enunciation of every syllable delighted me. She waited for the kettle to boil with a faraway expression and ash from an expertly cocked cigarette flaking gently over mannishly cut trousers. Her eyes dropped in a sad lost way whenever she mentioned her late husband. I liked to think how happy the house must have been when he was alive.

We took our tea in the studio or in the garden if the weather were fine. I showed my appreciation of her excellent cake by eating a great deal of it. She paid me the compliment of talking as though, at fourteen, I were as much a woman of the world as any of her old companions at the Slade. We got on very well and I quite enjoyed the painting part too.

Initially, to avoid meeting people on the single village road, I walked to all my lessons over the hills. Feelings towards Richard among the local people were ambivalent. On the one hand he was admired for applying himself to the backbreaking task of transforming their modest old guesthouse into a uniquely self-sufficient hotel; on the other he was viewed with scepticism as an upstart Sassenach who would soon lose heart and go home to the soft South. As his daughter, I was looked upon as an extension of him who might provide interesting material for gossip. I found the frankly probing stares of Kirk-going women and watery-eyed old crofters hard to take, so I used the hills, which they only used for sheep, as a refuge. I did not know how readily their curiosity could turn to friendliness.

I had memories of long trudges in the Highlands, dating from the times Richard and Kay rented a holiday cottage near Lochinver. We went there several years running, accompanied by different au pairs, and sometimes Richard was with us and sometimes he was not. After the last time, when school had started again and everyone had to write essays on what they did in the holidays, I had to squeeze my imagination hard for impressions of Scotland other than chapped thighs and midge bites, Marianne being sick in the car and Kay getting in a rage because three-year-old James kept chanting 'fuckfuckfuck' with a beatific smile. He had learned the word from her when she dropped a tray on the cottage floor. Pressed for a description of scenery, I conjured up an image of a long, snaky road with a lot of squashed frogs on it and a high rock ledge over a sandy bay which Marianne dared to jump off and I did not. The fields were more brown than green and several had Aberdeen Angus bulls in them. The mountains were tall and brown and looming.

It took the secret joys and loneliness of puberty to open my eyes to the mysteries of that brown, looming land.

To begin with I kept my head down while walking to avoid twisting an ankle between tussocks. Even so I fell down often: town-bred limbs wobbling, stiff-booted feet sliding on the banks of hidden burns. Then my hands would fly out, clutching air, and I would land with a thump, momentarily winded, and lie still, feeling the black ground press its moisture through my clothes and hearing the soft crackle of heather stalks crushed against my palms. Sprawled like that, I heard for the first time the sound of sheep munching grass, the squeaky pull of stems breaking, the whispered creak of earth forced to yield. I lay and listened to it, idly tracing fissures in the black bog surface which had already began to crack under the first spring sun.

57

There was a rock part way to the lady artist's house from which, after the first few journeys, I could judge the timing of my descent accurately. The hill was strewn with rocks, as though some giant had crumbled the mountain tops and played a lonely game of marbles with the debris, but this one was special because it was the first stop from which no human habitation could be seen. There was just the sea before me, the sky above and an endless hinterland of brown valleys and grey hills. But gradually I learned that each of those vistas had only one constant, and that was change.

My nose became familiar with the warm smell of peat, my cheeks with the scratch of heather, my toes with the iron-cold kiss of a mountain burn. When I rubbed at the patterns of yellow-grey lichen on rocks, my fingers came away with an ochre stain. From other rocks the stain was bread-mould blue. Through trial and error, and sodden thighs, I learned to distinguish the alluring emerald of bog moss from the matt shades indicating firm ground. Many a time I lay prone at full-belly stretch to grasp a fistful of silken strands from a pink hummock in the centre of a treacly pool. I would slip and stumble yards up a rushing burn to press palms against the living resilience of tiny moss islands, dark and soft as moles. The damp brown hills were a feast for hands just beginning to learn the beauty of feel.

And as I walked a little further every day, my clumsy limbs began to strengthen. I grew confident about the width of burns to be taken in stride, challenged myself to leap others. Coming down the hills I learned to zigzag, running; flexing my hips to keep the pace light, swivelling my upper body with arms outflung for balance. I felt my young breasts jump and I laughed for no reason. Near the hotel the geese honked as I ran past their field and Caillach the labrador puppy squirmed up reproachfully to lick my hands. She had her walk in the evenings with Edwina, a never-changing tramp down the road to the postbox.

At that early stage in the evolution of the hotel, Richard and Edwina were experimenting on all fronts. Neither had worked in a hotel before and neither had smoked kippers or kept pigs. But they had a vision of what as guests they would like to see and their standards were uncompromisingly high. Edwina, naturally pale, acquired the blanched look of a prisoner who rarely sees the sun. I had never seen anyone work so hard and when I saw her arm snake over Richard's shoulder as he stood anxiously studying a list, or watched them together, digging foundations and shovelling manure, she seemed to me like a white Amazon beside whom anyone else would look small. It was impossible to resent the fact that under her thrall the hotel would flourish but never be a home in more than a mechanical sense for the three children of her lover. We were an overhang from the past. The luxury of regular meals and a meticulous laundry service hardly compensated for this, but it helped. And perhaps Edwina saw more than I knew for she gave me the means to explore deeper into my own developing personality, as well as the hill which I was growing to love. She gave me a pony.

Before anything alse, though, for every individual involved in the hotel, came work.

For a month my name was down on the duty roster for breakfast and dinner service, which included laying up the dining-room before and Hoovering and glass polishing afterwards. This left the middle of the day free, ostensibly for studies. Like all the other waitresses, I was equipped with a neat little Black Watch kilt and instructions to treat the guests as though they were special visitors in my own home. If, feeling more like a stranger in theirs, I saw any irony in this, I did not express it, concentrating all my attention on doing the job as well as, if not better than, the older girls.

Soon I learned how to tackle the two most daunting installations in the kitchen: the washing-up machine and the chef. Both were capable of giving vent to odious torrents if mishandled. The chef was a large, purple-lipped Liverpudlian called Gordon. He had an impressive chimney hat and an unpleasant habit of wheezing through his teeth while taking half-inch drags of cigarettes he was not supposed to have in the kitchen. His breath was strong and fishy and I avoided close contact with him, grabbing the dishes he set down with a forbidding expression which was transformed into a charming smile in the brief space between kitchen and dining-room.

Breakfast waitressing, I found, was more enjoyable than the dinner shift. The guests came wandering into the dining-room from seven-thirty onwards, blinking in sleepy appreciation of the morning-lit vista of sea and islands. Thermoses would appear on tables if the day looked promising and I would note down requests for boats on lochs and packed lunches, along with porridge and finnan haddies. It was a matter of pride to me that everyone got their order promptly and I took pleasure in the subtle rapport established with each table. It was funny how differently people behaved in the evenings, dressed up and talking with louder, less friendly voices, not always returning my smile. That all changed when Richard, keen to use any potential not going in an academic direction, carved out a special role for me which upped my status considerably. But that did not happen until after Dossan and I spent the best part of many a day 'studying' on the hill.

Dossan means fringe or forelock in Gaelic and because that was the first thing one noticed about my pony, that was what she was called. Her body was soft dun with a smudgy dorsal stripe running the length of a well-upholstered spine. Edwina had not forgotten that I was afraid of horses and had deliberately chosen one which was not too lively. But sure-footed and strong, Dossan was a true garron and Richard had his eye on her for hauling stags at the end of the season. By that time, however, she had unlearned most of her civilized ways, for I rode her bareback, unshod, and sometimes with only a rope in lieu of reins.

There was nothing miraculous about the transition from timorous pommel-clinger to bold bareback rider. Day after day I led Dossan out of sight of the hotel and often onwards for as much as a mile before I plucked up the courage to mount. I abandoned the saddle because of a recurrent vision of being dragged over the hills with one foot stuck in a stirrup. Also, without a saddle I could jump off easily and roll away, something I practised over and over again.

Two weeks, perhaps three, of cautious ambling and falling practice went by before the next breakthrough, which happened as a result of my being late for work. I turned Dossan's head in the direction of home and, perhaps sensing my feeling of urgency, she broke into a trot. Bouncing hectically I clung on with everything, including heels. Obediently her stride quickened and became a canter. The increased comfort of the movement came as such a relief that when I felt her slowing again I urged her on. Dossan delivered me, snorting a little after her unaccustomed leg-stretch, at our normal stopping place outside the byre. Richard and Edwina both happened to be in the yard.

'That was rather a grand entrance,' said Richard, smiling approvingly.

Edwina looked at my flushed face and fingers still knotted in the mane. I blessed her for saying nothing.

Next day I forced myself to do it again, only this time under control. With Dossan's head pointing straight up the hill I leaned forward, clove to her like a suction pad and told her to go. She went, and although it would be untrue to say we never looked back, the surge of exhilaration I felt as her body answered mine marked a turning point.

And, as often happens, one small personal triumph led to increased confidence in other fields. When Richard asked if I would like to have a go at some baking for the hotel, I embraced the idea as a brand new challenge.

It began with a few modest trays of shortbread for packed lunches and progressed swiftly to fancy cakes for afternoon teas. Recipes, I found, were easy to follow and improvisation amusing. The climax was a nightly extravaganza known as Lucy's Sweet Trolley. This last appeared on the dinner menu with asterisks round it like the star-turn in a cabaret and Richard stage-managed the whole performance with all his old film-directing flair. Every evening, on cue, I made a grand entrance, wheeling before me the most extraordinary collection of desserts ever to grace Highland cuisine. Most were of my own invention, all were of my own concoction and some – Jacobite Grenades, Mocha Genghis Khan and Goat's Milk Bavarois to name a few – were undeniably strange.

It was Richard's master stroke to deck me out to match my wares and make me stop at each table and recite the name of each dish. I did not have to be told to address my remarks principally to the head of table, for I was on the cusp of feminine awakening and I knew. Staring steadily from behind a curtain of long fair hair into the eyes of the nearest most impressive male, I gravely recommended cream-filled chocolate-covered Pretender's Balls. On more than one occasion a mouth fell open and deftly I would pop one in.

I loved the way Richard stroked my hair and looked proud when some parties of men asked for second helpings and kept me chatting at their tables. It was somehow less exciting when ladies asked for recipes.

Lucy's Sweet Trolley lasted all through that season and through all the changes of kitchen hierarchy. When Gordon left, taking his bad breath and wheezes back to Liverpool, and Gilbert moved in, my position was well established. It must have been strange for a fat Aberdonian chef, most of whose experiences, culinary or otherwise, had been picked up in the merchant navy, to share a kitchen with a nubile fourteen-year-old, who leapt around in jeans and scanty blouses during the day and appeared like the prize plum in a harem at night. A barman from Glasgow joined the team at the same time and when Marianne, stronger but still withdrawn, arrived part way through the season, she and I became the butt of many a ribald exchange between the two Scots.

It was unfortunate that Marianne should choose the barman for her first virginal crush. I was intrigued to know what she did with him and when I learned that things went further than salivary kisses felt I had to look into the matter myself.

On evenings when my performance with the sweet trolley had been a particular success I found it difficult to wind down. I would lie awake, covers kicked to the bottom of the bed, squirming restlessly until Marianne returned from her nightly visit to the barman. One evening, when she came in looking more flushed than usual, I asked her straight out if she would mind if I went and had a go. She sat on her bed regarding me dully. Neither her eyes nor her spirit had ever fully regained their lustre after her illness.

'I don't mind,' she said at last, bending to find her slippers under the bed so that I could see how thin the hair lay over her skull. 'Anyway he fancies you.'

'Does he?' I sat up with a jerk, entranced by the idea. 'How do you know?' 'Said so.' She swung herself under the covers and added, with eyes closed, 'But he reckons you're out of bounds.'

'What do you mean?'

'Too young.'

'But you're only fifteen months older.'

She was settling down to sleep, but before she turned over she said, 'Makes all the difference. Age of consent.'

I did not understand, had to go and find out immediately. As I pulled on my jeans I said to her still back, 'Are you sure you don't mind?'

Some part of me was distantly aware of how damning the change from prettiest, brightest daughter to sad shadow must have been for her. Her voice came out flat but I was too excited to care.

'I told you, I don't mind.'

The barman was getting ready for bed when I presented myself at his door. His shirt was off and belt unbuckled. I thought at once how disappointing his chest was.

'Lucy!' he said, broad Glaswegian accent full of surprise. 'What can I do for you?'

I insinuated myself into the room and faced him squarely. He was standing, back to the wash-hand basin, fingering his chin. I noticed on a shelf behind him a bottle of spot-clearing lotion. It obviously did not work.

'Is it true that you fancy me?'

His fingers stopped moving on his chin. He made a sputtery sound, well sprinkled with ochs, which I understood to be mostly positive.

'Kiss me, then.'

I suddenly found myself on his knee in the dressing-table chair. He was rubbing acne enthusiastically into my neck and muttering about jailbait. I held him away and said, 'Do it properly, like you do to Marianne.'

He immediately wanted to know what Marianne had been saying and did she know I was here and did anybody else know. I fidgeted impatiently. Talk was not what I had come for. Wriggling down lower on his lap I positioned myself so that his mouth was directly above mine. My jumper had risen a little and in a moment his hand was inside it and his face was rushing down towards mine in a blur. I closed my eyes and for a few seconds everything was strange and wonderful. Then all at once his tongue was in my mouth flailing about like a wedge of wet spam. I was so shaken that for a moment I could not react in any way. There was a quality of intimacy behind that raw, visceral invasion which brought a conclusion to my mind like a slap. For this to work you had to fancy them back. You even had to like their pimples.

I pulled my jumper down and wiped my mouth on a sleeve. The barman looked ready for another go but I was already off his lap and at the door.

'What's up? Did you no' like yer wee kiss?'

'Yes, thank you,' I lied, hand on the doorknob. 'But I don't want another one just now.'

I rushed off to report the disaster to Marianne. Years later she confided that the main reason she went to the barman's room was to escape the noises made by Richard and Edwina across the corridor. She did not think much of the wet spam kisses either.

Now that a large part of my time was taken up with the making of puddings, my hunger for the outdoors had to be satisfied with a quick run down to the sea each morning. The gorse shone brilliantly with stars of night rain and as I passed the bushes I stopped now and then to press one of the full flowers along its yellow or flame-tongued side. A tiny bunch of curled stamens would spring from a slit in the bulging pocket and hang there, trembling. Everything felt fresh and fine.

At the bottom of the first field was the ruin of a croft. The gable ends still stood, each irregular boulder slotted cunningly into its neighbour to form a solid, two-foot-thick blockade against the elements. Between them, pink-edged daisies grew beside tumbled stones and a pipit had made her nest in the rusty curve of a barrel hoop. In June I watched her flutter to and from the four chocolate-coloured eggs and rejoiced on the morning they hatched. I checked on them daily, amazed by the rapidity of their growth: how from helpless, floppy, damp things they blossomed suddenly into demanding little units of life with open beaks and pin-bright eyes. I mourned angrily when, before the end of the month, a predatory gull plundered the nest, leaving great gouts of shiny turd as evidence. It made me think how rich nature must be to afford to form and destroy life so fast.

I climbed over a makeshift gate to reach the sea, my weight stretching its orange string ties a little more each day. The stones at the top of the beach were large and loud to walk on. Below the tideline, strewn with bladder-wrack and plastic bottles, were smaller pebbles, a few among them flat enough to skim. Again, early in the summer, nature thrust itself under my eyes in the form of stray lambs bleating in exhausted bewilderment by the edge of the sea. I would pick them up and bleat with them until there came an answering cry. It pleased me to deliver them safely to their yellow-eyed mothers who came galloping to the call, simulated or real, of an errant offspring. I did not mind that the little ones peed down my front, glad that their bones were not destined to join the bars of grey, sea-sucked driftwood on the shore.

The hills were littered with carcasses of ewes at that time, making birth seem a lonely, hazardous process, death easy. Shards of bleached, ancient trees poking up through the bog like more bones told of other deaths, other times. But with the sundew and bog cotton growing up on the mulch of those compressed times, it was clear that what died only turned into nourishment for more life. Finality existed only in an individual sense, which made the individual both the most vital and the most dispensable thing.

But embryonic philosophies conceived in the course of my wanderings were hard put to match the reality of the hotel kitchen. Here, matters of life and death receded before the immediate drama of having the dinner ready on time.

Besides Gilbert, there were now two other members of staff in the kitchen. One was Lena, a fifteen-year-old lass with a top half lovely as a Dresden shepherdess and white hairy legs like a split parsnip. She was employed to do the washing up and stood before the trough sink hour after hour, dreamily running a brush round the same dish until Edwina bustled up and chivvied her on to the next. The other was Jeanie, a brunette, whose soft hips blotted amoebalike over two stools while she peeled battalions of vegetables into bowls which were always too small. Her husband was a fierce marionette-limbed character whose face was almost black from some disorder of the blood. The calm pink sea of Jeanie's bulk trembled when he was near and she found no respite from masculine tyranny at the hotel, for Gilbert kept both girls in a state of jittery subservience. He treated all staff, with the exception of the barman, with the same brand of casual sadism which makes grown men kick dogs. Marianne and I, as daughters of the boss, did not escape this treatment, but it was meted out to us in a subtly different way.

Gilbert was, I sometimes believed, the reincarnation of Hairy Hans, now interred in several deep-freezers. Man and pig shared the same not-quite-pink bristly skin, the same grossness of form and, above all, the same insidious threat of crude sexual power. As an instrument to dominate two adolescent girls, this last proved highly effective. All Gilbert had to do if either of us annoyed him was approach with one thick-fingered hand held out, palm cupped exactly to match the small, innocently blossoming protuberances on our chests. Marianne invariably fled, apologized or pleaded until a cool glaze of satisfaction jelled over Gilbert's small, blond-lashed eyes and the threat passed without contact being made. But I spat and fumed against the curious force of the gesture, flushing violently as he backed me against the shelves, against walls and once so that I was bent like a limbo dancer over the stove. My words, in a high, young voice, fluttered about uselessly, never succeeding in breaking the power I could not define.

In precise opposition to its unfolding to pleasure on the hill, my body learned to deny itself, to recoil: breasts, mouth, legs freezing at his approach. I knew now that between my legs could close up with disgust as well as squeeze inside itself with secret joy. That he could make this happen involuntarily was humiliating. It made me hate him. I did not learn until late on in the season that the perfect weapon against him was not denial, but a cunningly measured degree of 'come on'. Gilbert, by response and unconscious direction, taught me all I would ever need to know about the art of prick-teasing.

It began with casual observation of the effect produced by clothes and movement. Stretching and swaying was good, I found, for showing off the gap between the hem of a blouse and a trouser top, and a carelessly unbuttoned shirt, disappearing into an apron bib which slipped from breast to breast, never failed to produce results. But I discovered my master card accidentally one evening when my sweet-trolley caftan was in the wash, and I was forced to wear the only other dress I had, which was as short and shocking as the other was long and demure. Bending to get the cheese off the bottom of the sweet trolley had an interesting effect in the dining-room as well as on Gilbert and a gratifying backview response could be achieved by the simple act of reaching up to a high shelf for a bottle of wine. Gilbert got in a wonderfully bad temper and dropped two hors-d'oeuvres on the floor. He sweated and gurgled Aberdonian curses as, smilingly, I bent down and cleared away the mess. I knew that in this mood he would never make his threatening gesture because to do that he had to stare me in the eye, something he could not do when I was waving some other part of me at him. I did not know the dangers I was courting until two incidents, occurring on the same day, brought tensions to a frightening head.

It was a Saturday late on in the season. The wind which I had gulped during my brief dawn sortie had mellowed by mid-morning to a feathery breeze. I could see it from the kitchen window sifting lightly through Dossan's mane and tickling the leaves of a rowan tree. It was no time to be stuck inside. Thoughtfully, I licked a finger loaded with cake mixture and made a calculation.

Eleven minutes later the bases of six Mocha Genghis Khans were in the oven and I was up the hill. Made daring by the urgency of stolen moments I crouched low over Dossan's warm neck and hissed for her to go.

Go!

We cantered up and lolloped down the slopes her legs knew now as well as mine. We sprang across burns mowing down bog cotton, mud sucking at her fetlocks, black droplets spraying my knees. High up, where the crags began, the wind rose again and sun splashing on Dossan's teddy-bear coat turned it to gold. Jumping off for a moment, I spread myself flat below the wind and laughed with surprise when Dossan lay down too, squirming her soft striped spine into the heather, clods of bog flicking off her unshod hooves. I lay on, eyes travelling with the clouds, wanting to stop time. There was one cloud like a cuttlefish, another like an over-risen cottage loaf . . . Hah. Into my mind came the flat white face of the oven-timer, black hands ticking impassively round and round. I must go back.

There was no time to change spattered trousers, or brush the horsehairs from my arms. The timer was ringing as I ran in the back door. The cakes should not be burned if I got them out at once. I scanned the kitchen for the oven gloves. They were nowhere. A tea-towel then. But they were all damp. Then I saw the gloves. They were hanging from a string around Gilbert's cylindrical middle.

'Can I have the oven gloves a minute?'

'Yiu – can – not.'

His thick voice pressed out each word separately as his thumbs jabbed into a piece of dough. Check-trousered legs, buttocks wobbling through the thin cotton, blocked the oven doors. A landscape away beyond the marble table, Lena's back curved over the sink like a comma and Jeanie stemmed an avalanche of carrots with a reddened hand.

Gilbert went on pummelling his dough and the smell of cooked cake hung warmly in the air, its homeliness a sneer. Left another minute the Mocha Genghis Khans would be ruined. I stood rubbing a dusty elbow, feeling the weight of Gilbert's knowing challenge push me back from the oven. My face twisted at the thought of spoiled cakes, of failure. Edwina never wasted anything.

'Gilbert, my cakes are going to burn.'

He answered in the same slow, jabbing voice.

'Is – that – so?'

And squeezed the pastry like a thigh.

Deliberately I altered my stance, allowing one hand to fall casually on a hip while the other stroked back my hair with a movement that ensured my breasts were well raised. When I was sure that Gilbert had taken all this in I turned away abruptly and sauntered over to the sink.

'It's hot, isn't it?' I said to Lena, untucking the front of my blouse and fanning it over my belly.

She agreed, taking a hand from the dishwater and running a dripping wrist over her nose. Again I felt Gilbert's eyes flick over the length of me and again I turned away.

'Look,' I said, positioning myself between Lena and Jeanie, 'something bit me.' My fingers were parting the blouse just below my bra. The girls scrutinized the clear flesh, baffled. One of them murmured, 'Aye, is it the midges?'

I heard Gilbert move on the other side of the table. He was coming towards us. I knew he would.

Without warning, I dodged past him and quick as a pickpocket plucked the oven gloves from his waist. His fat hands humbled the air. In a second I was on the floor with the oven doors flung wide. Two, four, five cakes out, one more to go. Gilbert was saying all the rude words I had ever heard as though they were one. There was a gasp from Jeanie and I leapt up in the nick of time as a wet tea-towel cracked viciously in the air where I had just been.

'Come here, yiu little houri. Come here the nu and gi' me back them gloves.'

We were opposite each other, the table in between. I caught a glimpse of Lena staring, the washing-up brush frozen in mid-air. If it had not been for the one cake still to save I would have bolted.

Gilbert advanced and I scurried behind Jeanie's broad back.

'Let me just get that one cake out, Gilbert.'

'I'll let yiu do nothin'. Yiu gi' me back them gloves, the nu.'

I jumped up and down in frustration. The oven was still blasting out heat and I could smell the edge of a burn. Suddenly, ignoring him, I dashed round the table. My hand was almost on the cake when his damp fingers closed around the wrist. I was yanked upright and forced close to his aproned chest. His strange jellied eyes stared first into my own, then travelled slowly to the neck of my blouse, I wrenched away, the coquette in me smashed. But he still had hold of my wrist.

'I'm gonni' break yiur pinkie,' he said deliberately. He said it again, but until he started bending my little finger back, I did not know what he meant.

I held myself rigid, body averted from the captured hand, eyes compelled to watch. Gilbert's concentration was absolute, like that of a surgeon. The other oven-timer, the one he used, notched the half seconds between the ticking of the clock. Breath was held in the round o's of the girls' mouths. The tendon at the base of my bending finger was white and stretched like string.

'I'm gonni' break it,' repeated Gilbert and his voice broke the soft, cakey air.

I continued to stare, locked more in fascination than pain. I was convinced the tendon would snap before the bone.

There was another endless ticking hush. A black knot from my brain seemed to be trying to get out of my finger. As the pressure increased the knot became a ridge, sawing in unison with my pulse. The angles of the hand were mad. It did not look like a hand.

Then a small graunching crack, like wet wood or a chicken's wing. It fell into silence sliced almost instantly by the buzz of the timer. Gilbert released me and scooped up the gloves draped over my arm. He was at the oven door when a thud like a dropped flour sack made him turn. Lena had fainted on the floor.

At lunch Richard joked about the oversized thumbshield on my little finger. Burns were common in the kitchen. Gilbert was off duty and our voices were hidden from other ears by the din of the washing-up machine. I waggled my hand, experimenting for pain. Inside the thumbshield the broken pinkie lay snug in a splint of cocktail sticks. One of the waitresses, a nurse, had helped me fit it on. I decided not to mention the incident to Richard. The whole village could talk about it but he need never know. I feared that he would guess at once – and correctly – that something more than a petty battle for oven gloves had been going on.

The second incident, which took place in full view of all the staff coming on duty for dinner, could not be concealed.

Marianne at that time was in the odd-jobs position I had held at the beginning of the season. That evening it was her turn to perform stillroom duty. This entailed folding napkins, filling water jugs and winding fluted butter pats into chilled bowls. She had just started on the butter when I came in to add the final trimmings to the sweet trolley. We each sampled a meringue while I mixed the fillings for a gâteau. I had abandoned the idea of assembling the precarious edifice of a Mocha Genghis Khan with one finger out of action. Marianne knew about the broken pinkie and joined me loyally in sending wordless waves of hate through the stillroom wall to where Gilbert was stirring soup on the other side. We fooled around, making each other giggle, and Richard, not understanding our game but enjoying the high spirits, joked with us for a moment as he passed through. Marianne, busy with the coffee trolley now, hummed softly. She was always pleased when Richard paid her attention. My giggles sputtered out like a candle whenever Gilbert came into view. The sight of his blockish frame moving about casually filled me with fury.

The meringues being ready, I went into the kitchen to set them on the trolley. There was no swaying or shimmying as I walked past Gilbert. My body felt spiky as a mine.

'Will Modom be requirin' th' oven gloves this evening? Has Modom's tongue been stolen by the wee folk?'

I ignored his taunts.

The barman came in and leaned, hands in pockets, against the door. Since the failed kissing episode he had treated me with caution. Now, recognizing a weakness in my stiff bearing, he joined Gilbert in provoking me. The thought that they must have been discussing me – laughing about me – brought on a deep flush. Immediately they both commented on it. The flush grew deeper still.

'Will you look at the bonny face, Gilbert. I think the lassie fancies you. Isn't that right, hen?'

I made the mistake of answering, despising the silly tight sound of my voice as it wavered miles off the intended sarcasm.

'I don't fancy anyone.'

They laughed.

'Well, isn't that a shame and just when yer cherry's ripe too!'

'Oh aye, there's a ripe wee cherry there all right!'

Marianne came through from the stillroom. She lowered her eyes before the barman. Gilbert pointed at her with the spatula he was holding.

'And another one there.'

They joked for a moment between themselves, Gilbert saying something like: 'Thought you'd have done that job by now.'

Catching Marianne's eye I aimed a heavy hate glance at Gilbert's back. She giggled. I aimed another at the barman. Her lashes went down. It infuriated me that she should kow-tow before him. He was not worthy of her. The prim old-fashioned phrase repeated itself in my mind. Not worthy. I went back into the stillroom where there was the gâteau to finish. They went on teasing Marianne.

The cream filling I had made was not quite right. In the flurry of the morning it had been left out of the fridge and was insufficiently chilled. Because it was too late for anything else I spread the slack mixture over the first layer of sponge. It blobbed messily over the edges. Richard flashed through again.

'Hmm, that doesn't look like one of your best efforts!'

'You're not meant to see it at this stage.'

He disappeared and I fitted on the second layer, upset that he had seen. The voices in the kitchen took up their teasing again. Marianne's answering giggles grated. Why did she let them do it to her? Most of the cream filling squeezed out under the weight of the second sponge. I dumped on more. And as the voices grew louder, the giggles more uncontrolled, I stopped thinking what I was doing and dumped on spoonful after spoonful until the whole disaster was masked in wobbling yellow cream. There was not enough filling left for a third layer and feeling failure swell in me

72

like the taunts next door, I lifted the plate, balancing it on the flat of my injured hand, and was about to commit it to the rubbish bin when Marianne came in. She was moving backwards, jumping from side to side to avoid Gilbert, who capered in pursuit, trying to whip her bottom with a wet towel. She was grinning, playing the game, but I felt her distress.

'Piss off, Gilbert,' I said. 'Leave her alone.'

'Yiu mind yiur own business, yiu.'

There was a delighted chortle from the barman.

'Oh ho! What's that language I hear!'

Marianne was pink, giggling feebly. I had a sudden flashback to her first tinkly laugh after she had been in hospital.

With a mechanical motion I emptied the contents of all the nearest bowls on to the mess balanced on my hand. Strawberries, pineapple chunks, custard.

'Get back, Marianne,' I said.

Gilbert was less than two yards away. He must have realized my intention almost before I did, for his puffed, ugly features became a threatening mask.

'Yiu dare,' he said. 'Yiu just dare and it won't be yer pinkie that gets broken next time.'

Marianne's face appeared over his shoulder, eyes dancing. 'Throw it! Throw it!' she cried.

She urged me on. Gilbert threatened. His thick features were contorted, asking to be blotted out. My arm lifted and the dripping cake hovered in the air. Then, with full force, I flung it.

Gilbert ducked, although he need not have bothered. At the last minute I had changed aim. I saw Marianne's hands clench as though in spasm. Her lower lip, still somehow curved in a smile, shivered and then went still. Very slowly, like bits of opaque jellyfish, cream, custard and fruit slid down her poor, thin brown hair.

I ran out before the slipping sponge revealed her eyes.

My act did not go unpunished. In one way or another that summer I learned much about the strange, mixed powers of loyalty, pride, sex and shame.

When I returned from the second wild ride of the day Edwina sought me out and asked to talk for a few moments. Their room across the corridor was tidy but cluttered, containing all the personal accoutrements normally spread over a home. I noticed at once the same woven bedspread which had enriched the decor of her London flat. Only one or two things of Richard's lay in disorder: a tie dangling like a snake down the side of the dresser; a small mountain of books slipping from under his side of the bed. I found a focal point in the pattern of a dressing-gown and kept my gaze fixed on it while she groped for a balance between friendliness and authority. She found the key in the mention of Richard's name, for I wriggled involuntarily when she said, after briefly pointing out the unkindness to Marianne, 'It isn't easy, you know, for Richard. Having an intelligent – and attractive – daughter causing disturbances among his staff.'

She had not been oblivious to my experiments at coquetry.

'You know you are attractive, don't you?'

I moved around in the chair but said nothing. She continued.

'It isn't a good idea to lead people on.'

I knew that. The incident of the broken pinkie had quelled my flirtatious urges for a long time to come. I wondered if she guessed at the very different awakenings I experienced on the hill. She started to tell me – it sounded like a joke against herself – of her own behaviour as a teenager. With a laugh, she described it as outrageous. Although I was interested I did not like her playing big sister, confiding, so I failed to react. After a minute I said, 'I'll say sorry to Marianne.'

'Good,' said Edwina briskly, smiling as though something intimate had been exchanged. 'And no more nonsense like that, hmm?'

Humiliated by the word 'nonsense' I did not return her smile. As she opened the door to let me out, still, I sensed, hoping to establish a rapport, I was aware for the first time that even in this relationship there was room for a reshuffling of power. I could never be to Richard what she was to him, but by being blood of his blood, I was already something she was not.

Chapter Five

'Intelligent and attractive, full of potential.'

I was to get used to those words. They had been said at school and at the Child Guidance clinic. Now they were said by a man from the education authorities who came at the beginning of autumn to check how my studies were progressing. Luckily there had been a phone call in advance, time for Richard to get me into the lounge surrounded by exercise books. I nodded at all the man said, anxious to get back to the kitchen where I had a whole pig's head and a vat of rowan jelly on the boil.

Soon the words were repeated by a Sociology lecturer who interviewed me for a place at a London polytechnic. On the strength of that nebulous potential I was granted the place, even though, at fifteen, I was under the usual entry age and lacked the requisite number of O-levels. I made the move from the hotel back to 309 reassured by Richard's parting words: 'You can always come back.'

Although it had not turned out to be home in the sense I had hoped, a link had been forged between me and the land and this, coupled with my undiminished loyalty to Richard, made it a place to which I would inevitably return.

That year and in years to come, Marianne and I bounced north and south between our two non-homes like yoyos. James, too young to have been affected by my truant example, was a more conventional child of divorce. He spent termtimes and the shorter holidays with Kay and five or six weeks of the summer up at the hotel. The first Christmas after the divorce found me at 309, Marianne at the hotel. When our paths crossed the following spring we compared notes: hers had been a strained, mock-traditional affair, with Edwina cooking a lunch with all the trimmings which was consumed in virtual silence. Mine owed little to tradition but was a rite in its own way. The time had come for me to lose my virginity.

Being a student at the poly had advantages over being a school-girl, but was a far cry from the independence of working at the hotel. There, my efforts had been maintained by pride alone and needed no structure beyond a self-imposed routine. Now I was faced once more with being one of a crowd. The adjustment was not easy.

My fellow students were, with few exceptions, straight out of school and still mentally stuck behind the institution/victim barriers of the classroom. When a lesson was over they would sigh with relief and rush for the door. I hungered to find satisfaction in the learning process itself, aware that the choice to be there was entirely mine. Often I lingered after class, especially by the desk of the Sociology lecturer. His honesty about the limitations of the course was disturbing and when I asked why he did not change it, he said it would mean changing the whole system. We talked a lot about that.

Finding myself distanced from my classmates, I evolved a social life of my own outside the cultural parameters of the poly. It started one evening when I was given a free ticket for a local folk concert. I arrived early and was obliged to wait in a nettle and concrete garden until the doors opened. I had been sitting there for ten minutes, idly plaiting a chaplet into my hair, when out of the top window of the house floated a series of rich, obliquely human sounds. They came from a single instrument, a saxophone, but the breath behind it gave it the force of a collective cry. The notes clung together in the damp suburban air, a song from deeper than the diaphragm which had no need for words. I listened for a long time and when the folk concert started sat through one mournful dirge and then crept out into the garden again. The saxophone was no longer audible but a hand high above me played scales along the windowsill. I went inside and silently climbed the stairs.

The door of the top room was open. A young man, very slim and pale with black hair, stood at right angles to me. It was his hand on the sill. A girl with hair to her waist, figure hidden in a long, loose robe, squatted on the floor stirring a teabag in a mug. The saxophone sat on a high stool in the middle of the room, shining and complex amid the dust and bare walls. The young man, looking out of the window, was talking to himself in a low, wondering tone. He spoke a curious, old-fashioned English and after a moment I realized he was reciting a poem.

> 'And this is why I sojourn here,
> Alone and palely loitering,
> Though the sedge is wither'd from the lake,
> And no birds sing.'

The last phrase, so simple, rested on the air like its own echo. The girl looked up and saw me standing by the door. His glance followed, the pale and black profile turning full face. One long, catlike eye scrutinized me unhurriedly. The other was covered by a patch.

'And here she is, it seems. Is it you?'

Not wanting to break the spell I answered carefully.

'It is me.'

At once his pose changed and he swung away, stalking across the room to lean on a mantelpiece, cuff-booted ankles crossed like a pantomime lead.

'Hah! She knows.'

And he began to quote again.

> 'Pale warriors, death-pale were they all;
> Who cried: "La Belle dame sans Merci
> Hath thee in thrall!"'

The girl placed a mug of tea at his elbow and sat down to drink hers on the floor. I took a step further into the room.

'Yes, come.'

The saxophone was taking up the only stool so I leaned on the other end of the mantelpiece. The man and I stood looking at each other for a long time. From this distance I could see that the cheek below the eye-patch was roughened with pockmarks and there were thin razor scars on his chin. Gaps in his white shirt, a hard colour against the translucence of his skin, showed a scattering of dark hairs running together to form a shadowy line. Like Dossan's stripe, I thought, and wondered if they would be soft like the moss on the hill. It was the first time I had experienced the compulsion to touch another body. Every now and then I heard the girl take quick careless sips of her tea. The words 'his mistress' popped into my brain.

'Or are you a Maenad?' he said, as though continuing a thought out loud. His lips remained delicately parted after the last word and I had the same impulse to run my fingers over them as I had to stroke a leaf or a butterfly's wing.

'Was that you playing?' I asked.

He made a curious fluttering gesture with one hand and suddenly brought the knuckles to his teeth and bit them, looking right into my eyes.

'I am always playing,' he said with a short laugh and lifted up the saxophone. Facing the window he blew three, four, a dozen notes, energy seeming to pour up from his feet through his flat belly and hit the air in a curve. I hoped he would go on but he suddenly laid the instrument down and said huskily, 'I am thirsty for some whisky in my tea.'

He felt for money in his trouser pocket, widening a tear in the seat. I thought of the needle and thread I always carried in my bag. He did not speak to the long-haired girl as we went out, but this not speaking itself suggested the existence of a code. I wished she had not been there.

For his whisky we went to a pub across the road. It was a Friday night and the place was packed. Jem – for that was his name – inserted himself deftly between two sets of sprawled elbows. I stood back. It was the first time I had been into a bar, not counting the hotel's, which I had sometimes cleaned. Somebody made a loud joke about the seat of his pants falling out and he answered back in an identical Irish accent, making the whole bar laugh. I found the mixture of arrogance, sincerity, sham and fragile pride in him more and more appealing. Outside I told him about the needle and thread.

'You mean you're offering to . . .?'

I nodded. His good eye was nearest and the look he shot me through it was deep.

'But why? I am nothing: a gipsy, a stranger, a bad Catholic . . .'

78

I caught on to his poetic manner.

'It would give me pleasure.'

The look became warm.

'That, dear child, is something I should very much like to give you.'

'You'll have to take your trousers off.'

He swerved his eye away and I could not tell if his confusion was real or a game.

Jem took his trousers off in the room at the top of the grey house. The long-haired girl was nowhere in sight. He crouched in a corner with the silk rag used to polish the saxophone draped over his manhood and entertained me with a recitation of 'All the world's a stage'. It was strange to hear life so summed up, a predictable drama in seven acts, from the lips of one who seemed so raptly involved with the immediate.

From time to time my fingers on the needle paused as I took in the way short, silky hairs curled on his shins and one slender foot rubbed against the other. When I gave him back the trousers he turned away to put them on and again I was surprised by a hunger to reach out and touch. It was perhaps at this moment that the ambition to hasten my own passage from 'maiden' to womanhood took form.

But hastening did not necessarily mean now, and without knowing why, I suddenly felt I must go.

'I'm going,' I announced abruptly, as his hands still tucked in his shirt. My back was turned, first foot on the stair, when his voice came, low and with the mildest hint of a plea.

'How will I find you again?'

I hesitated. To be searched out, to be wanted by someone was something entirely new. It alarmed me a little.

'Oh,' I said nonchalantly, '*I'll* find *you*.'

It seemed to take hours to get down the stairs. When at last I stepped into the garden, thoughts still bound in the top room, a scrap of paper wrapped around a piece of rubble landed on the concrete by my side. I did not open it until I was out of sight of the house. Scribbled in a small, uneven hand the message read:

I cannot grow;
I have no shadow
To run away from,
I only play. (Auden)

And I'm only here on Fridays. (Jem)

I treasured the little ordinariness of the last line.

Back at 309 I revisited all the new feelings of the evening, smiling for no reason as I had sometimes done on the hill. When I went to bed I did not unplait the chaplet of my 'Maenad' hair and Richard's old poetry books lay scattered on the counterpane.

Those first intimations of desire, the nameless hunger which in Scotland had led me to cool my cheeks on lichen-covered rocks and press my body to the earth, transformed my outlook on the world of men. No longer did I see them through the clinical, disembodied eyes with which I had judged the unfortunate barman. The conclusion that I had drawn with him, that you had to 'fancy them back', now acquired real meaning. It was as though, through meeting Jem, a previously silent voice in my body had suddenly found its tongue.

The relationship developed erratically. The next time I saw him was loud with the presence of others. It was a free-for-all music night at the grey house and he stalked on between jigging folk bands and rosy-toned girl singers, breaking the easy chitchat of the audience with his forceful nose-to-toes blues. A six-foot-five Irishman, lanky as a scaffold, backed him for a couple of numbers on a double bass. He was introduced by Jem as McAllister, 'a better man than I and a good Catholic'. It was McAllister, as gentle and lugubrious as he was tall, who told me that Jem had once hoped to enter the priesthood. It was not difficult to conjure that pale face above a black soutane, even the eye-patch somehow fitted. I asked what had happened to make him change his mind.

'He could not keep the vow of chastity,' was the reply. And although he would have looked beautiful as a priest, I was glad.

It was not, however, until the third or fourth meeting that our intimacy – endorsed on my part by much poetry reading and listening to Charlie Parker in between – had a chance to blossom in any tangible way. Meantime, my revised vision of self as related to men exercised itself in another direction.

Once a week since moving back to 309 I spent an afternoon with a man called Mr F—. Kay, who had always been supportive of my musical inclinations, had been delighted when I hinted that I would like to take up another instrument. Wanting to make a change of direction clear, I blew a large chunk of my summer savings on a pretty blond guitar. (Richard, going by his own laws of justice as opposed to those of state, had paid me £3 a week at the hotel.) Thus equipped, I went down the list of teachers in the local paper. Mr F— was the only one able to start straight away, so I went to him. Richard agreed to pay for the lessons and Kay put the money in an envelope every week and gave it to me. I gave it to Mr F—, who immediately sprinted down the road and bought a steak with it – most of which I ate – giving the impression that the musical part of the afternoon was free.

I liked Mr F—. He lived alone in a small semi-detached house in Barnes and when he was not giving guitar lessons set polished stones in rings and painted portraits. His long hands, emerging from the sleeves of a comfortable old blue sweater, were clever and calm, the nails longer on the right for playing the guitar. I found this deliberate slip of symmetry appealing; the rest of him – ankles, ears and knees-through-his-jeans – was so even and clean. He made coffee using all milk and I liked the way a bit of froth he did not know about got caught in the hairs of his moustache. His eyes were brown and mild and, although I had no idea what he was thinking behind them, made me feel at ease. It was disturbing, therefore, to see him so differently after the encounter with Jem.

An observer would have found nothing different in the lesson with Mr F— that day. I sat across from him as usual and ran through the pieces I had practised during the week. The encouragement he gave was quiet and practical, as was his criticism. Much of his teaching was done by demonstration and sometimes he would treat me to an entire medieval air. He played the lute, too.

The routine with the steak had become established by now and he had already made his trip to the corner shop. At around 3 p.m. he put down his guitar and went into the kitchen to light the gas under the frying pan. We ate in the room where he taught, not bothering to move the piles of sheet music and jeweller's tools off the table, but finding perches for the cruet and mustard pots among them.

I watched Mr F— eat, the hands that rippled arpeggios and drew long, shivery vibratos from the guitar casually fitting themselves to the banality of knife and fork. Quite suddenly, I had a clear picture of those long fingers doing other things. I stopped in mid-chew, stunned, the image expanding. But imagination, curbed by inexperience, faded just where the curls of my pubic hair became more dense. It was a part of me I had only recently begun to explore.

'You all right?' asked Mr F—. 'You look a bit flushed.'

I stabbed a piece of tomato and pushed the meat I could not swallow into the pouch of one cheek.

'It's O K. I just need a sip of water.'

I went out to the kitchen, thankful for a moment alone. I was holding a cool glass alternately against one cheek, then the other, when Mr F— came in carrying the dishes.

'I was thinking,' he said, 'of going up to the Tate next week, which would mean cancelling your lesson. But perhaps you'd like to come? It's William Blake.'

This was an unexpected development and after saying yes – not too eagerly I hoped – I vanished into the lavatory to hide my rapidly re-reddening cheeks.

Before I left he said, 'Come a bit earlier than usual and we'll grab a bite of lunch up there.'

I was thrilled. It was going to seem a long time until next Thursday.

Sunday afternoon found me wandering by the Thames. Not many people were about as the day was cold. I rather liked the chill emptiness of the towpath, the age-worn cobbles near the bridge hunched together like tortoises and smooth miles of asphalt further on, stretching out by the bulging river like a flat grey hem.

I had been in the park watching a few wintry dressed couples pushing children on swings. Their faces were pinched and they did not speak much except to say, 'Whee!' occasionally or 'Oh, do come on.' It reminded me of Kay calling to me and Marianne when we were little. When Richard had come with us it was a special occasion and there were photographs and ice-creams.

I went and sat on a miniature island where my school friend Kate and I used to come before I ran away. Now that my legs were longer and more agile from all the tussock-hopping in Scotland, crossing the wobbly log to the island seemed easy. I trod down layers of wet leaves smelling like old newspapers and crouched among them for a while, hidden. The sky through a pattern of twigs was still one of my favourite views of the world.

Continuing my ramble on the towpath I passed the high walls of great houses whose gardens ran down to the river. Some of them had railings through which I could see clipped, empty lawns. If I lived in one of those houses, I mused, I would let the grass grow and make secret grottoes filled with Mr F—type music and statues of people like Jem.

On the bridge I stopped for a moment, gazing at the sparse-armed willows, the grey towpath and the broad brown water curving away below. When I looked up again, I saw Jem.

My first impulse was to run. The wind, which I had enjoyed before, was suddenly a menace rumpling my hair; the cold an enemy painting unattractive colours on my nose. But I did not turn round and the same force which drew my eager, reluctant feet on, raised that black-patched face to mine.

In contrast to my fluttering state, his composure was absolute. The dark hair lifting from his brow flopped softly in rhythm with his stride. He stared straight at me. It was only when the gap between us narrowed to less than a yard, and he staggered as though shot, that I realized he had not seen me at all before.

'You!'

The exclamation in his voice was flattering. His chin was flung high and his long throat, shadowed where he had not shaved far enough down, pulsed. Below us a wavelet broke over the stone bank and above, the clouds, which had been hanging low, gave like weary knees.

The rain was like a gift to us. Without a word we headed to the bottom of the bridge where the awning outside a skating shop offered shelter. There, staring into what I now knew to be the middle distance of his myopia, Jem said, 'Sweet child, I cannot bear to see you shiver. I have no right to offer, but will you do me the honour of stepping into the poor place where I rest my bones?'

His poetic manner verged on the ridiculous but I did not care. I followed him into the rain.

Jem's temporary abode was a small dry-docked cabin cruiser called *Angel II*. She was resting in a wooden cradle and to get into her we had to climb a rickety ladder. We had got into the boatyard through a gap in the fence. *Angel II* smelt of newspapers inside, like the wet leaves on my childhood island. The low ceiling made us stoop and he threw his coat over a mouldy seat and begged me to sit down. His own body he tossed like some lovely piece of rubbish on to the only bunk. Dirty portholes admitted just enough light to show the faded denim shirt he wore and his skin pale against rumpled blankets. One arm was flung above his head, fingers tapping lightly on a worm-chewed beam. Outside, the rain tapped a second rhythm against the boat's wooden sides and not far away the lapping of the river made faint accompanying chords. With a smile towards the quiet music of the Thames, Jem began to recite.

> 'Break, break, break,
> On thy cold grey stones, O Sea,
> And I would that my tongue could utter
> The thoughts that arise in me.'

He stopped and murmured, 'And how I long to know, child, the thoughts that arise in thee.'

I decided to tell him.

'Earlier, I thought of you as a statue – I thought how I would like to touch you like that.'

84

His fingers fell into a slower tapping on the beam and then were still.

'If that is what you want of me, then that is what I am.'

So saying, he straightened his legs, crossed his hands over his breast, and lay quite still like a knight in Westminster Abbey.

'Say that poem you wrote in the message,' I said. ' "I cannot grow ..." '

While he said it, I slid down between the exposed ribs of timber and knelt beside the bunk. His body stretched out before me was like a feast in a foreign country. I did not know where to begin. Finally my hand crept out and lay low on his belly between the high, articulate bones of his loins. He did not move under the touch but in the small sound he made, interrupting the poem, I felt a response.

'Go on,' I said, and his voice took up the words again. I laid a thumb lightly against his throat to feel the vibration. My other hand had found its way through a gap in his shirt and was stroking the soft, dorsal line of his body hair. I watched his lips, wondering if I would lean forward and kiss them when he came to the end of the poem: ' "... I shall never be/Different. Love me." '

I had not known that was the way it ended. His eye fluttered open as I hesitated, unsure of the next move. Then his hand was on my neck and that eye, drinking both my own, was drawing me down.

All at once there was a crazy explosion of sound outside. Hysterical barking. Jem wriggled a finger between us and laid it on his lips.

'Don't be afraid.'

I was not. I knew not many dogs could climb ladders. He said something else I could not hear and I leaned closer. The barking went on, high-pitched, a circus din.

Rr-wuff! Rr-wuff! Rr-wuff!

'You have the touch of a saint,' he murmured and laid his lips against my hair.

But I drew back. I could hear padlocks rattling on their chains and imagined the dog jumping up at the boatyard gate.

Jem's eye continued to pull at me but I would not be pulled. Now that thought had had a chance to intervene, I was flurried and unsure of what I had been about to do. I ducked from under his arm.

'But wait,' he cried, bewildered, as, on deck already, I pulled up my hood and prepared to climb down the ladder. 'I must give you something, a token.'

He plunged back into the cabin and when he emerged there were three things in his hands: a leather-covered bottle, what looked to be a rounders bat and a strange hairy bulb in a jar. 'These are all I have, please take one!'

By now I was on the ground. Our voices were raised against the dog's.

Rr-wuff! Rr-wuff!

'What's that thing in the jar?'

Jem stood above me with his treasures, offering them like sections of his soul.

Rr-wuff! Rr-wuff!

'It is my mandrake, my little man,' he cried. 'Here, take them all!'

I was by the fence, ready to dive through.

'Give me your shirt,' I called and within seconds it was in my hands, wrapped around the leather bottle, and I was through the fence and away.

We knew we would find each other again.

Monday went by, and Tuesday and Wednesday, and still I had not decided what to wear for my date with Mr F—. On Thursday morning, almost in despair, I rushed into Kay's room at seven, and demanded to borrow her curlers and best black top. Kay, still a little groggy from her sleeping pills, watched me fiddling at the dressing-table with a smile.

'You must think a lot of this Mr F— to go to all this trouble,' she said. 'How old is he?'

'I don't know,' I answered, ramming an obstinate hairpin this way and that. 'About thirty, I suppose.'

'Well, just you be careful!' she said, joking.

I had not told her about Jem.

The trip to the Tate exceeded my expectations. First Mr F—
surprised me by producing a wonderful car. It was a vintage
two-seater, slate blue, with a long rattling bonnet, ground-scrap-
ing chassis and huge close-together headlamps like crossed eyes.
I felt proud sitting in the squashy leather seat next to Mr F— as
we swept through Putney attracting envious glances.

Then there was lunch at the gallery, which we had straight
away. Mr F— left me to choose a table while he collected salad
and wedges of what he called 'kwitch' from the counter. Over
coffee he asked if I went to galleries often.

'Not very often.'

I did not want to admit that this was the first time since
Madame Tussaud's in a school crocodile.

'And has anyone ever done a painting of you?'

I laughed. 'No!'

His asking had made me strangely excited and I checked my
appearance in the cloakroom before we looked round the gallery.

At the entrance to the Blake exhibition Mr F— said, 'Feel free
to wander round at your own pace.'

So I did, and although I liked some of the thundery fairy-tale
creations of Blake, I strayed out into the corridor after a while
and became absorbed in a display of Hogarth cartoons. I spent
some time looking at other people looking at pictures too, fascinated by the dreamy, amoebalike splits and formations of couples
and groups, and the way everybody's limbs moved slowly as
though the air were full of invisible liquid.

When Mr F— came to find me to suggest it was time to go,
my head was swimming and the ordinary air outside, with people
moving at their usual pace, came as a shock. It was good to be
snug in the car again with Mr F—'s long fingers, clean and calm,
on the wheel. I was interested in London passing by outside the
window but my eyes kept coming back to his hands and before
we reached the outskirts of town I was blushing again. There was
no doubt left now: I badly wanted to stroke Jem, but I badly
wanted Mr F— to stroke me.

When he dropped me off at 309 I was cartwheeling inside. We

had agreed that during the Christmas holidays I would sit for some portrait sketches and in return he would give me some extra lessons, free.

Christmas was three weeks away.

Jem and I found each other again the following weekend. I saw him through the window of a pub near the grey house. Even through thick brown patterned glass that pale face cut by a triangle of black was unmistakable. I hovered, not sure enough of myself, or him, to go in. Then, as I watched his small hands talk through the mist of the pane, a plan took form: Kay was going out that evening. I could invite Jem to 309.

I hunted through my pockets for a piece of paper to write him a message but there was none. Only a penknife, some coins and a comb. The penknife gave me an idea. Slipping into an alley beside the pub, I loosened my hair and teased out a suitably wavy lock. Carefully, so as not to hack off a handful, I applied the blade. The lock looked a bit limp so I held it tightly wound round a twig for a moment, using spit as a setting aid. A scrap of torn lining from my cape made the perfect wrapping. I returned to the window, checked that Jem was still there, and accosted a stranger about to walk into the pub.

'Please, could you give this to the young man with the eyepatch?' I cast my eyes down. 'I can't go in myself, I'm under age.'

The stranger's mouth opened but I did not give him time to speak.

'Tell him,' I said, pressing the lock into a palm that could not flinch away because it was balancing a half-rolled cigarette, 'that She will be on the bridge at nine.'

I gave the 'She' Rider Haggardly emphasis and hoped it would be carried on with the message. Then, without waiting for a reply, I picked up my skirt and skipped off down the alley, emerging the other end on a road that led by a convenient back route to 309. On the way I ran into a shop that stayed open late and bought half a pound of mince and an onion. I was about to cook my first meal for a man.

Inside the house, having checked that Kay had gone, I slid the safety-chain on the front door, put on a jazz record and stepped out of my clothes. I planned to bath and change before fetching Jem. But then I saw the time. Nearly eight. How long did mince take to cook? I padded into the kitchen, shimmying to the music, and turned to the index of Kay's battered cookery manual. There were recipes for mince pies, minced collops, mincemeat, but no plain mince – and what on earth was a collop? I banged the book shut and lit the oven. I had watched Kay cook Saturday lunch mince for years, and it always started in a frying pan with an onion and ended in the oven with mashed potatoes on top. I slipped Jem's shirt over my nakedness and attacked the onion. It looked quite professional sizzling away with a little oil in a pan. And the addition of a cup of sherry and some ginger with the meat made it the right colour and texture. I put it in the oven to finish cooking while I bathed.

All clean and clad once again in Jem's shirt, with plaits wound into the chaplet his eye so admired, I went into the dining-room to look for a candle and some fruit for his pudding. The table around which Kay and I had sparred not so many years ago – she with a bread knife, me with my child's heartless words – had been moved since the household had shrunk, but the painting of Madonna and Child was still there. I switched on the small striplight above it and was about to draw the curtains when a noise in the passage alongside the house made me pause. Cats, I thought, dismissing it. But there it was again, a persistent little scrape, not uncatlike but not quite like a cat ... I leaned forward against the window, trying to see into the dark. There was one more scrape, firmer than the rest, followed suddenly by the bright yellow flare of a match inches from my nose. I stayed quite still, hand on the curtain, mesmerized.

Above the wavering flame two large black-rimmed lenses quested like the headlamps of Mr F—'s car. I could see nothing beyond them but there was a voice: ' "When I consider how my light is spent,/'Ere half my days, in this dark world and wide ..." ' It trailed off.

'That is Milton, child – "On His Blindness".'

89

His breath on the window made the thinning matchlight fuzzy, like a candle in a wet jar. There was a petulant 'Ouch!' as the light went out, then the deep voice resumed.

'It ends: "They also serve who only stand and wait." Madam, I have been standing and waiting a long time. The hour has come to serve. I beg you let me in!'

'Go round to the front door,' I said. 'But quietly.'

It would be awkward if Kay's elderly neighbours were roused.

I ripped the curtains to before he could reply and grabbed a pair of jeans off the back of a chair, dragging them on as I ran through to the front door. How had he found me? Why was he wearing glasses? Had he seen me looking up 'mince' with no clothes on? I took a deep breath before opening the door.

Jem stood a few steps back from the porch, chin raised. The patch was in place and his lips, a glisten of teeth between them, curved downward in a beautiful sneer. Had he been wearing a sword, his hand would have been on the hilt.

I stepped back without a word and in two strides he was in the porch, the door was closed, and I was backed up against Marianne's old bicycle with Jem blowing hot dragon's breath in my ear. His short black coat was open and his white skin gleamed very close. He smelled of whisky and night air. His arms, leaning against two walls, trapped me in the corner like a claw, and he was saying one word over and over again, dropping it from deep in his diaphragm on every outbreath so that it hit my neck in rhythmic thrusts: 'Bitch bitch bitch bitch.'

'Jem, I . . .'

He groaned as though hit in the stomach and flung away from me into the hall. As he looked around, half blind I knew, I gave a quick stage direction to the bishop's chair. Its grand carved back and arms formed a magnificent backdrop for him.

'Bitch,' he said again, floating the word on velvet waves to where I had plopped down, brain benumbed, on the edge of a long divan.

'Jem, I . . .'

'Don't speak!'

His eye closed and he held up a forbidding hand. There was

rather a long pause until, disobeying, I heard my own voice holding out the second verse of Shelley's 'To the Moon' like an offering:

> 'Art thou pale for weariness
> Of climbing heaven, and gazing on the earth,
> Wandering companionless
> Among the stars that have a different birth, –
> And ever changing, like a joyless eye
> That finds no object worthy of its constancy?'

He gave a deep, growling moan and threw himself upon me. I toppled back on the divan, Kay's white daytime handbag bumping my shoulders. His arm was under my back, clamping me to him. The hair was swept from my neck, teeth and lips sunk into my flesh, sucking, moaning, full of hot breath.

' "Companionless no more!" ' he muttered through mouthfuls of me. ' "O my America! my new-found-land!" '

I gulped, hands on his shoulders, half hugging him to me, half pushing away. His mouth was travelling lower, heat searing through the shirt which he dragged to one side in his teeth, chewing the collar with bearlike growls.

' ". . . Sweet disorder of the dress . . ." Gimme back my shirt.'

I had never felt such excitement but I was alarmed too. It was like when Richard used to tickle me and I loved it but thought I would die if he did not stop.

'Wait, please! Please!'

Jem's body was tight against me all over, pressing, undulating. I could feel the bones of his loins swivel over mine. My bare toes struggled feebly with his booted heels. A metal button at the top of my jeans caught on one of his, grinding. His hand went between us, ripping the buttons apart, then diving in where my inbreathed belly made a gap. I squirmed.

'Jem, really. Please!'

His mouth, fastened like an oyster to my chest, let go suddenly with a sharp sucking sound.

' "For Godsake hold your tongue and let me love." '

Now I pushed at his shoulders in earnest.

'Please be gentle. I haven't ... I haven't' – that mouth descended again – '*I haven't done this before!*'

Instantly he was still. After a long, long moment he sighed with his whole length and lifted himself from me. Hunched over, head in hands, he murmured, 'Dear God, what a fool I have been!'

I sat up, disengaging my hair from the handles of Kay's bag.

'Can you forgive me?' he said. 'I am nothing but a clumsy, loutish fool – and a little drunk.'

I knelt by him and patted his shoulder cautiously. A strong wave of meaty ginger vied with the dying cold-air smell of his coat.

'It's all right,' I said. 'Look, I've just remembered something. Wait.'

In ten minutes Jem found himself seated opposite me at the kitchen table. I had set out a glass of water with two aspirins, a cup of strong coffee, and a knife and fork. He drank the water and took the aspirins, but did not touch the coffee.

'Forgive me,' he said, this time not referring to his attack on my maiden state. 'It gives me heartburn worse than *l'amour*.'

I withdrew the casserole from the oven, hoping its contents would not do the same. In lieu of potatoes I had made little half moons of toast and put a slice of peeled pear on top as decoration. I thought how docile and endearing Jem looked with his fork poised.

'Is it *very* painful?' I asked, chin on hands, 'and is there *much* blood?'

The fork went down.

'Child, I cannot eat and discuss your virginity at the same time. Which do you want me to do?'

'Eat.'

Obediently his head went down.

'You did not make this ...' – he sniffed – 'this exquisite Eastern confection yourself?'

'It's not a confection,' I answered, offended. 'It's mince.'

'Madam,' he pronounced after the third mouthful, 'this delicacy is to mince what silk is to string.'

I laughed with pleasure. At least one part of the evening was going according to plan.

After he had finished eating, I offered him one of Richard's old cigars which I had found in the lounge. I parked him upstairs while I tidied up the kitchen. Kay would not question any of my doings so long as I did not leave anything messy for her to clear up.

Jem was ensconced on my mattress when I went up, leaning back behind a cloud of breaking smoke rings. He waved them away as I came in.

'Now,' he said seriously, 'come and sit by me and do not be afraid.'

He made a kind of speech, telling me that yes, he was a rake but not a scoundrel. No fruit fell unwillingly to his hands. He sensed in me, he said, 'a little well of sensuality, full of promise', and he said that whoever tapped that well would be honoured – but must also be honourable. He made me feel in possession of something rare and precious. I broadened the subject with a joke.

'People are always telling me I am full of promise – potential is the word they use. It makes me feel uncomfortable.'

'Ah, yes,' he said musingly. 'That was an accusation levelled at me once. It is a cruel one, at first flattering, finally threatening. It is hard to live up to. Potential, potential – potent shell. That is what I have become, a husk.'

'Why do you say that?' I demanded.

With his beauty and his music and his poetry he seemed quite the opposite, rich and full of value.

'I am a fretful soul,' he answered, 'black and full of flaws. I want things I cannot even name.'

There was a pause in which I moved closer.

'*I* want to see under your eye-patch.'

'Hell's teeth,' he said bitterly. 'You would find me out in all things.'

He turned his head away a second and when he turned back, the patch was gone. There was no burn scar, no glass monstrosity, but what there was I understood at once to be more painful to him than either of those would have been. His beauty, which rose above his pockmarks and his razor-nicked chin, was distorted by a squint.

'Thank you for showing me,' I said, and trusting him now, stroked his arm. After a few minutes we lay down together and quiet as a child he fell asleep in my arms. The cigar, lying in a shell where I kept my hair-grips, glowed until my cupped hand snuffed it out.

Some time towards midnight I heard Kay come in. Even though I knew she would not disturb us, I must have stiffened for Jem stirred. I whispered, 'Shh,' in his ear. When her door closed and the last light went out I relaxed.

'My mother,' I told him softly.

'And is your father downstairs?'

'No, he's in Scotland. Where's yours?'

'Ireland.'

It was easy to ask things in the dark.

'How old are you?'

'Nearly twenty. You?'

'Fifteen.'

His breath was warm on my face. His fingers found my cheek-bone.

'Can I kiss you now?'

'Yes.'

Right cheek, left cheek, forehead, lips. A benediction.

At six, standing in the cold drizzle on the front path of 309, Jem took a ragged silk scarf from his pocket, wiped it over his glasses and knotted it loosely round my neck. The bruises raised by his oyster mouth of the night before were tender, but he had not done anything to add to them in the night.

'Those marks of lust will fade, but the seal of amity I press upon you now will not.'

With that he kissed my forehead one last time and was gone, a black-coated figure in the dawn, measuring the distance between lamp-posts with long, catlike strides.

I took Kay her tea at seven-thirty.

'What does "amity" mean?'

'Something to do with friendship. Why do you want to know?'

'Somebody said it to me – a friend.'

'Mr F—?'

'No.'

I was irritated by her teasing tone and spoke without thinking. 'Mr F— isn't a friend like that – he's a man.'

It was only after the words were out that I understood the change that had come over my relationship with Jem, and when I looked up his word for it in the dictionary – 'Amity: friendly relations between states bound by mutual causes' – my feelings were confirmed. Marking the difference between our sexes with tenderness, Jem and I would meet in the future as comrades. Our youthful searchings were too closely matched and my sexuality too unformed for him to take me any other way. And for my part, now that I had held him unmasked in my arms, empathy had replaced desire. I needed the mystery of distance for my body to be roused beyond my mind.

Accordingly, I chose as my first man a friendly lover as opposed to a lovely friend. I will never know how things might have worked out differently in years to come had I chosen the other way round.

The day before Christmas Eve, Kay was still trying to persuade me to join her and James at an aunt's in Yorkshire and I was still saying no. I liked the way James, home from his first term at boarding-school, plunged the orderly dust of 309 into disarray by littering stairs, landing and hall with smelly piles of laundry and going through his rugger warm-up routine in the lounge. But even he, leaned on by Kay to put in a plea, could not change my mind. As far as I was concerned my aunt and uncle were strangers who went tight-lipped at the mention of Richard. James, more amenable, would lap up gifts and kindnesses without souring them with his own interpretations as I, unhappily, had done before. Besides I had my own plans.

They went off in the morning; James grinning and picking his nose, Kay waving anxiously and calling, 'You will ring, won't you?'

'Yes, yes!'

I closed the front door and leaned against it, revelling in the thought of four days of empty 309, each one of which I would fill with my own music and moods. Best of all was the knowledge that it would be empty to come back to - if I came back. The first portrait session with Mr F— was that afternoon.

Out of comradely loyalty to Jem - my passionate attraction to him was already material for nostalgia - I made no plaits in my hair but let it hang free for Mr F—.

One of the first things he said was: 'Would you mind putting your hair up somehow?'

As I had not brought any hairpins with me, I wound it over itself in a loose knot. 'It's slipping,' I said as he sat me on his chair in the music room and took my usual place himself, sketch-pad on knee.

'Doesn't matter.'

For the next hour the only sound was the soft scratching of lead on paper. I rested my gaze just above Mr F—'s head, focus blurring on the nondescript pattern of the wallpaper. My thoughts, released by the stillness, roved languidly like the visitors in the Tate, pausing now and then when they found a pleasing image. After a while I was only distantly conscious of being drawn.

'Coffee?'

'Mmm.'

'You can open your mouth, you know.'

I laughed and said I liked the quiet.

'Yes - you're a funny little thing, aren't you?'

I did not answer. It was the first time he had said anything so personal. After coffee Mr F— suggested I sit in his studio for the next sketch. The studio was upstairs, and in the middle of it was a large white bed.

'Music?'

'Mmm.'

A handful of slowly plucked lute strings fell into the quietness, then a man singing in a bell-clear Renaissance voice. Mr F— sketched, hidden behind an easel.

After half an hour the street lamps came on outside.

'Drat,' he said.

'Does that mean you can't go on?'

'Well . . .' He put down his pencil and stood with arms folded, regarding the sketch he had propped against the back of a chair.

'What time do you have to be home?'

'Oh,' I answered vaguely, looking at my toes, 'no special time.'

'Do you mind staying on a bit then while I set up some lights?'

'I don't mind at all.'

Mr F— began by pulling the curtains and turning on the main light. I noticed with a slight shock as he did this that half a woman's figure was painted on the wall and the light-switch was her nipple. I had a vision of Mr F—'s hands on my breasts and tried to imagine what it would feel like. I could not stop thinking about it and when he asked me to sit again - this time on the floor hugging my knees - I was more self-conscious than before.

'Move around until you feel comfortable,' he said, selecting a fresh cassette. 'The pose should feel natural, just as if you were having a little think to yourself.'

I nodded stiffly. 'I am.'

The new music was Elizabethan court dances. In my mind, Mr F— was dressed in doublet and hose.

'I wish I was wearing a long dress,' I blurted.

'It would be nice,' he said absently. 'I like girls in long dresses.'

Damn, I thought. I wanted him to like *me*.

'What-about-a-sheet?'

'Pardon?'

Mr F—'s head appeared round the side of the easel.

'A sheet,' I repeated. 'I could wrap a sheet round me like a dress.'

'What a good idea.'

He found a sheet of thin, soft material like muslin. I did not know if he expected me to take my clothes off there and then.

'You might like to sort yourself out in the bathroom,' he said, as though reading my mind.

I undressed looking at a mermaid he had painted in the bath. She had blue hair and a long green body winding all the way round the tub so that her fingers and the tip of her tail met at the taps. I imagined Mr F— lying in the bath with his head on her belly just where the skin became scales. The sheet was large and

97

wound round twice, giving me a sort of tail too. I tucked it under my arms at the side, but when I reached up to centralize the knot in my hair it fell down, showing my breasts. I touched the pale pink softness of the nipples and was surprised when they pinched up into tight, uneven little buds. They normally only did that in the cold. Retucking the sheet, I shuffled carefully back into the studio and stood by the door, holding up my tail.

'Do I look silly?'

Mr F— paused in his arrangement of pencils and brushes.

'Actually, you look rather charming.'

I coloured with pleasure.

The background he had made was stark: large sheets of white paper on the floor, a screen of white behind.

'Put your bottom about there,' he said, pointing to a space where some of the corners of the paper met. I was about to sink down, holding the sheet carefully round me, when he said, 'Hang on. Stay just like that.'

He left the room a moment and came back with a camera. I must have moved while he was setting it up because suddenly my hair fell right down.

'Oh!'

'It's all right, don't move. I'll fix it.'

Mr F—'s hand lightly steadying my skull as he combed my hair felt strange and intimate. His face was close and he was looking at me but it was as though he saw me from a long way away. Once, the comb touched my bare back and an involuntary shudder made the sheet slip lower. I knew if I took my arms away now it would fall down.

'Sorry, didn't mean to make you jump.'

He went back behind the camera and took several photographs before saying I could sit down. Then he sketched. After ten minutes he stopped and ran a hand through his hair.

'It's no good.'

He explained that the effect he was aiming for was one of curves and lines. The paper made the lines and my body was supposed to make the curves. But the sheet got in the way.

'It's like something fragile with soft contours – an egg, say –

98

against a background contrastingly flat and angular. I see you like that. Very egglike.' He looked at his watch. 'Never mind. Want to watch something on telly?'

I was disappointed that this picture had not gone well.

'What?'

'Old film. James Cagney' – he grinned suddenly – 'old cars.'

He lent me a dressing-gown and we sat side by side on the settee in the front room. Halfway through the film I went out to the kitchen to make us a snack.

'This is very nice of you, you know,' said Mr F—, popping his head round the door on the way to the lavatory.

I hoped he would not be long or the omelette I had made would go leathery. It had stuck to the pan anyway and I had to serve it in bits. I gave him the best bits.

'It's a scromelette,' I said. 'Cross between scrambled and ommed.'

'Great.'

He poured us each a glass of advocaat and wished me a Merry Christmas.

I snuggled deep into the settee beside him, my body in the warm dressing-gown feeling silky and snug. When the film ended Mr F— got up and switched off the T V.

'Well, I suppose I ought to take you home.'

'I was just wondering,' I said, inspecting a raised seam on the armrest beside me, 'if it would be better without the sheet.'

'Nude?'

Mr F— said the word just as if it were 'coffee?' or 'music?'. I nodded and he went on.

'Actually that's what I had in mind when I thought of the set, but didn't like to ask.'

'I'll do my best.'

It had got colder upstairs and Mr F— brought in an electric heater. He put on some music and said 'Ready?'

On a chair the sheet lay crumpled where I had left it. The dressing-gown joined it now.

'Fine. Not too cold?'

I shook my head, purposely making the hair fall forward. My

arms were shielding my upper body but it seemed to be my face I wanted to hide. My legs were straight and still; topped, from my view down, by a little ruff of goldy-brown curls. He took a photograph of my head and arms like that.

'Don't worry,' he said. 'I'm not going to take any pictures of your pubes.'

I had not thought about it.

The next pose, sitting down with my limbs folded, was a long one. The woman on the cassette had a strong, fluid voice and soon my mind flowed with the story of her songs. There was one about two sisters, one dark, one fair. The dark girl was jealous of her younger sister and pushed her into the sea. Some shepherds found her body and made a harp from the breastbone which sang the tale of the crime so that the dark girl was haunted by it forever. I wondered if Marianne had ever wanted to kill me for usurping her place in Richard's heart. I would have if I had been her.

'You look miles away,' said Mr F—, bringing me back. 'I've about finished. Want to look?'

My buttocks felt square from the hardness of the floor and squinting over my shoulder I saw two matching red blobs. Embarrassed, I tried to rub them out with my hands before going round to Mr F—'s side of the easel. The sketch he had done brought me up short.

'It's lovely,' I said wonderingly. 'But who is it?'

The face was nothing but the curve of a chin under a bell of hair.

'It's a young girl thinking a young girl's thoughts.'

'So, it's not really me at all?'

'Well, *you're* a young girl. Aren't you?'

Pride a little thrown, I reached for the dressing-gown. What he had said was interesting – a new perspective – but at the same time it robbed me of something. My reaction was lame.

'I'm not *that* young.'

He laughed and yawned.

'So, what now? It's pretty late and I've got a piece of jewellery to finish before tomorrow. You can kip down here if you like and I'll run you home in the morning.'

It was what I had been hoping he would say.

Mr F— went to finish the piece of jewellery downstairs and I climbed into the big white bed. After a few minutes in the dark, thinking, I got up and washed between my legs, being careful not to put soap inside as it stung. My eyes were shut but I was not asleep when Mr F— came in. I swore I would not jump when he touched me.

I heard his clothes fall to the floor, the clunk of his belt as it swung against a chair. Then he was beside me under the covers, cool and clean and smelling of toothpaste. I waited, yearning and dreading, but yearning more. So tense was every expectant inch of skin I thought the sheet must bristle.

But he did not touch me.

For the first three hours – the luminous dial of his watch clipped off the seconds less than a foot from my eyes – I lay ramrod stiff, unable to cancel hope. Then, after four o'clock, when I got up to go to the lavatory, the sap went out of me. He did not want me. I was blind, an idiot, had made a mess of everything. Thoughts darting about in angry confusion, I grasped at straw solutions in the dark. Jem had gone to Ireland for a while. I would go there tomorrow, find him, give him some whisky and make him do it out of comradeship. But my body betrayed me. Back in bed, to my horror, I started to cry. It was when I thought of the scromelette and how much I had enjoyed making it and watching James Cagney with Mr F—.

'Mr F—!' I said in a tiny, livid whisper, catching my lip. 'What a bloody silly name!'

There was a creak from his side of the bed.

'My name is Sebastian,' he said and, quietly rolling over, ran a hand from the crown of my head to my toes. And back again.

It was not too painful and there was not much blood. And all through the sweet, short sleep that followed I was aware of hugging the small torn tenderness inside me like a prize.

At nine-thirty on Christmas morning Sebastian – I had to remind myself not to call him Mr F— – brought me a mug of coffee in bed. He sat on the outside of the covers, blue eyes calm and kind.

'Feel all right?'

'Fine!' I said it so explosively that the skin on my coffee leapt out and hung over the brim. I felt very happy.

'Look,' said Sebastian and he paused and fingered his moustache before going on. 'I only did that because I thought you were expecting it.'

Thought I was expecting it. The coffee skin started to slide down the side of the mug.

'I'm engaged to a girl in Stockholm.'

Girl in Stockholm.

'But I want you to have this.'

He placed a little nest of cottonwool on the pillow and parting it with those long cool fingers which had so carefully parted me, revealed a small polished stone. Stripes on it ran softly into one another, white to lavender, lilac to mauve.

'I'll set it in a ring for you if you like.'

My hand set down the mug and closed over the stone. I thought of it at once as the Virgin Stone.

'No,' I said. 'I don't want a ring, but thank you.' And for all that he had only done it because I was expecting it, added, 'Thank you for everything.'

Chapter Six

The New Year brought a series of migrations. At the end of January Sebastian F— told me that soon he would be going to Stockholm. It was not a great blow but I would miss the quiet afternoons I spent with him, the unhurried education of my body in his hands. Jem, who reappeared at the grey house after Christmas, thin and coughing from rough days in Ireland, announced that he must take himself and his sax to warmer climes or both would die. Armed with a battered copy of *Don Quixote* and Hemingwayesque visions of the Spanish Civil War, he set off for Madrid from Richmond station one afternoon. Our farewell was tender and he vowed to write. I told him to use the Scottish address because I could not see myself at 309 or the poly in the spring. Marianne came south and I took the overnight coach from Victoria to Inverness. Nobody was surprised and Richard was pleased. Lucy's Sweet Trolley lived again.

Much had been learned from one season in the hotel. I heard Richard say to guests: 'Oh yes, in our first year we made an awful lot of mistakes.' By that he meant Gordon and Gilbert and other staff disasters. It was people who were mistakes rather than ideas.

Staff accommodation was short and the waitresses bunked together in a building at the back of the hotel called the Bothy. From my room near Richard's – the night noises had grown less frequent since Edwina had taken on the job of chef as well as everything else – I could just hear the music and revelry which started up when dinner service was over. There were no Jems or Sebastians among the local youths I saw trooping up the Bothy steps after the bar closed, half bottles sticking out of their pockets, hair tokenly slicked down, but nevertheless I was drawn to them. And their maleness, pungent in the ruddy body warmth and animal odour of damp Arran wool, was more immediate than that of the well-turned-out guests in the dining-room.

So I began to linger and chat with the waitresses, mostly university students from down south. One girl, Maxine, was particularly welcoming. She was the straw-blonde daughter of an old ballerina flame of Richard's. But she only spoke to me when there were no men present, because when there were, she curled up in a short skirt against a cushion and gazed into inner space, trickling smoke mysteriously through a gap in her front teeth. She told me that on the whole she preferred older men – 'wouldn't mind having a go at your old man' – but had recently got into waders and young fishermen. I was mildly taken aback by the mention of Richard as possible prey but found it intriguing too.

'I think you'd find he was too busy,' I said.

She gave me a smoke-blurred woman-of-the-world look.

'Men are rarely too bithy for thex,' she said with an oddly unchildish lisp. 'Ith love that buggerth up their routine.'

'What about women?' I asked, anxious not to let this mood of pearl-dropping go by without gleaning all I could.

'Thame thing, only they don't like to admit it.'

It was years before I made any but the most abstract sense of her answer.

My visits to the Bothy were doomed on two counts. First, when Richard found out that I was hobnobbing with the staff and locals he made it clear that he disapproved. Second, it became increasingly obvious that by being the proprietor's daughter – as well as *only just* not a virgin (Maxine's pronouncement after hearing about my non-orgasmic defloration) – I was cramping the waitresses' style. It was natural for the staff of a small hotel to discuss the management and awkward when I, a possible spy in their midst, made them feel obliged to watch their words. As soon as I realized this I reverted to my former solitary ways and once again the most constant companions of my free time were the hills, the wind and the sea.

But I did not forget Richard's disapprobation and inwardly I railed against it. The new relationships I had experienced with men left a gap that love for him alone could not fill.

A card came from Jem in Spain: 'ROOTLESS, BOOTLESS, FRUITLESS, STUMBLING THROUGH LORCA.' There was no address. I put my current favourite book in my oilskin pocket (Dr Desmond Morris's *The Human Zoo*), and did my stumbling on the hills. For all the success of the sweet trolley I felt as rootless, bootless and fruitless as Jem. Unanswered questions queued up at the back of my mind like fledglings anxious to fly.

Summer passed with the haze of heather fires, the bracken unfurling and fields crazy with thistles. Rain swelled the water in the hill lochs, and small trout rose in the reeds and flipped their bodies in brazen arcs through the air. Huge lilies, yolk-yellow and cream, sprung into being like mushrooms overnight. It was a fertile environment for a young girl thinking a young girl's thoughts to grow.

And on the crofts, the fruit of Richard's efforts burst through the wet black soil and filled trug after trug with abundant green mounds. His energy and enthusiasm seemed inexhaustible. Day after day he worked with both arms dug up to the elbows in the present but he never stopped thinking about the future. His plans for next year were extravagant; there would be a new staff house, a bakery, a darkroom, more cows, giant horticultural tunnels, quail ... It was impossible not to be swept along in the fierce current of his dreams but some part of me held back. His world was so full, so diverse, it was overwhelming. And while I continued to create and see demolished the gâteaux and pastries which were my small contribution to it, I clung stubbornly to the idea of a world of my own.

Once, at a low ebb in the middle of the season, I had turned my back on the hotel and hitched 350 miles down the road south before loyalty caught up and I turned round. Richard's only comment was: 'I should think so too' and we never discussed it again. Apart from guilt for threatening to leave him in the lurch, I felt ashamed of my own vagueness. Now that I was over official school-leaving age at last, the future awaited my own moulding, and the questions he did not ask I asked myself: Where was I going? What was the plan? There were still no satisfactory answers.

Because of this I agreed when Richard suggested that, instead of going south and starting something new at the end of the season, I should build on my one proven ability – dessert cookery – by taking a course in baking at a college in Inverness. Then I could run the new bakery he planned for next year. And if I did not choose to do that, at least I would have a recognized skill to make up for my lack of academic qualifications.

When autumn came and the hotel closed its doors, Richard hitched a horsebox full of pigs to the back of the Land-Rover and drove me to Inverness. Our goodbye was perfunctory because we expected to see each other again soon.

But it was over a year before we did.

*   *   *

I knew from the first day at the bakery course that it was not going to work. I was the only girl in a class of twenty-two boys, who as far as I could see were all miniature models of Gordon and Gilbert. They stole furtive looks at my legs from under lank swatches of hair and made obscene gestures with broom handles when they thought I could not see. The products we turned out – batallions of precisely matching, tasteless loaves – were things I would never cook for anybody and walking back to my digs past the River Ness, I tore them up and threw them to the gulls. I made my own brown rolls in a communal oven on the landing and ate them in bed with disks of hard goat cheese and pints of goat's milky coffee – my landlady bred goats and kept me generously supplied with their products.

I stopped attending the course at the end of the second week and spent my time mooching about the cold streets of Inverness, staring at the river and trying to decide what to do. I could not stay at the goat lady's much longer because sooner or later Richard would phone and I knew I would not be able to lie to him about giving up the course.

One morning, when I had walked up and down the same street five times and was considering a sixth, I saw an unusual figure emerging from a shop. He was dressed in long yellow robes of a chiffony material much too light for the weather and he was smiling into thin air. As he passed, the smile aimed itself into my eyes and he gave a sort of bow.

The shop from which he had come sold healthfood and I went in to have a look. Having established that their honey was twice the price of that in the supermarket, I was about to leave when I heard the women behind the counter discussing the stranger. They guessed he had come from a place out Kiltarlity way – 'one of those commune things'. I was curious. 'Commune' was a word I had heard Jem use, making it sound exciting and revolutionary. (He was in fact referring to the Paris Commune of the 1790s but I did not know that.) I had also heard the word used positively by a young couple I had met during the summer who were hitchhiking round the Highlands. Having nothing better to do, I decided to investigate, and that afternoon

I was on the road once more with my thumb wagging in the wind.

About sixteen miles outside Inverness, a truck with a cement-mixer on the back dropped me at the end of an unsignposted lane. Weeds sprung thickly from a muddy ridge running down the middle and I crossed from side to side to avoid potholes filled with puddles. It was a still day, the air damp and clinging cold. I hoped these people had a fire. I was not sure what else I was looking for.

The place was a tumbledown farm. Rusty hub-caps, broken roof tiles and a trail of yellow cabbage leaves littered the approach. A youth with a pudding-basin haircut was staring at a row of gone-to-seed Brussels sprouts.

'Excuse me, is this the commune?'

A white, spotty face bobbed and blushed beneath the ridiculous hair. Looking at the sprouts he said, 'It is the ashram of the Perfect Light Mission of Guru Kahan.'

'Oh,' I said, not sure where to go from here, 'is he in?'

The youth clutched at his shirt and said, 'He is in here. He is everywhere.'

I started to ask another question but was interrupted by the arrival of the man in yellow chiffon. He came at the head of a troupe, some similarly dressed, others in jeans.

'Brother Giles!' he cried excitedly, 'this is the sister I spoke of whose soul is already a ploughed field. Welcome! Come into our Master's house, come into our hearts!'

His speech was accompanied by beams, head-bobbing and wringing hands.

'Thank you,' I said, 'but I did not know you were religious. I think I'll . . .' My words trailed away at the flurry of hand-waving and denials.

'Come!' said the yellow man, bowing a path towards the farmhouse. And because I was curious and because I was looking for something, I went.

The Kiltarlity sect of the Perfect Light Mission took me to its bosom. They led me to a bare room with a spreading damp stain on the ceiling and announced that they were going to give me *satsang*, the first stage of initiation which would be completed when I received the Knowledge at the hands of the Master himself. *Satsang* consisted of talk.

I was told that I had come because I was searching and the Perfect Light had shown me the way. Had they not all been in the same position once? Ah yes, they knew, they knew. Each one had been led here by the questions in his heart.

They spoke rapidly, in turn, for over an hour, praising their saviour, Guru Kahan, and their simple way of life. I felt so benumbed by the constant bombardment of words that I found myself nodding. And whenever I nodded, they nodded with me. It was as though there were ten strings attached to the damp ceiling, nine belonging to them, one to me. Everything that had been in my head before seemed to be driven out by the flood of words. When I laughed shakily in a second's pause and said I felt dizzy, they said that was the power of *satsang* and after 'rice' they would give me some more. Too fuddled to resist, I nodded. And the nine heads nodded with me.

'Rice' came mounded in glutinous peaks in a plastic washing-up bowl. It was topped by a thin dribble of dhal. We held plates in our laps and dipped into the communal bowl. A lot of rice went on the floor.

As soon as the meal was over *satsang* began again. I was tired. I looked out of the window. It was dark. Where was the lavatory? What was the time? And then the singing began: 'Shri Guru Kahan! Shri Guru Kahan! Our Master, our Lord, our Master, our Lord!' The meaningless couplets went on and on. My head was beginning to throb. I shut my eyes and immediately, without their eager faces beaming in, felt relieved.

'Look at us, Little Sister! For *satsang* the windows of the soul must be open.'

'I'm sorry,' I said, 'I'm tired.'

They waved their hands solicitously but went on yet again to praise the wonders of the Knowledge, which all of them, except Giles, had already received. He was just waiting for a gift from home to help towards his contribution. Contribution?

'Yes, as a sign that we are truly prepared to accept the guidance of the Perfect Light, we willingly give what we can.'

The blessed Guru knew that many of his followers were humble so he accepted as little as £10. I looked at Giles's innocent, eager face and felt angry with myself for having allowed them to waste their *satsang* on me. They smiled and smiled out of eyes that were blinkered, shining with a light less divine than desperate. I lay down to sleep among them, unthreatened by their bodies ('we have no need of carnal pleasure'), but saddened and subdued. And in the half light of morning when I got up to go, I saw evidence of one type of passport to the Light. An arm, trailed out from a sleeping-bag on the bare boards of the communal room, was covered with needle tracks.

I thought when I left – thanking some other god that they were too bleary at that hour to attempt *satsang* – that I had seen the last of the Children of the Perfect Light. But the next day Giles stopped me in the street in Inverness. He gave me a long brotherly greeting and asked if he could travel with me as I had mentioned I was going south. He was on his way to get the Knowledge.

I was preoccupied. A letter forwarded to my digs that day had set me on edge with excitement. It was from Dr Desmond Morris, author and zoologist. After reading *The Human Zoo* I had written to him with vague hopes of a career working with primates. By now I had almost given up on a reply. But here it was, a fact in my pocket, complete with an introductory letter to a professor in London and the possibility of a job. And here was Giles, Child of the Perfect Light, on a mission of his own.

'Yes' I said, 'you can travel with me, but on one condition – not a single word of *satsang*.'

Hitching as a pair may be wise but it is far slower than travelling single-load. Giles's drooping presence felt like a severe encumbrance after two hours standing in a freezing wind without one car stopping, and eventually I resorted to the trick of hiding him behind a hillock so I appeared to be thumbing alone. A few drivers took exception to this, not believing the tale that Giles had been having a pee, but on the whole it worked and we arrived in London twenty-four hours later without mishap. Giles made a last attempt to lure me to the Mecca of Perfect Light but I shook my head, wished him luck and walked away. I wanted to find a Way – it was every young person's quest – but nothing would persuade me that Nirvana could be purchased tailormade for £10.

The good old 73 bus took me to Richmond and I walked over the bridge to 309 savouring the drab familiarity of the scene. Marianne and Kay made me welcome in their separate ways. There was no question of us all sitting down together; relationships in our family were strictly one to one. Marianne, who looked white and unhappy, brought me coffee in the studio and closed the door on Kay. Later Kay made tea which she and I took in the lounge. When these formalities were over I went upstairs, dumping my bag in the middle of the Big Room, and closed the door on them both. Allying myself more closely with Richard, I wanted to keep my life quite separate from theirs.

I found the number of the college mentioned in Dr Morris's letter and telephoned for an appointment. The professor I spoke to suggested I should pop in for a chat one afternoon next week. My heart sank at the number of days in between but I felt lucky to be seen at all. While waiting, I wrote long, diary-like letters to nobody and spent a great deal of time in the local library finding out what I could about monkeys and men. My secret hope was that the interview might lead to something like an apprenticeship with someone engaged in behavioural research.

It did lead to something, and quickly, but it was rather different to anything I had imagined. I was given the job of Monkey Keeper at Fircross Zoo.

Halfway through the first month I wrote to Marianne:

Marianne:

Zoos are not much different to towns with lots of separate racial communities. Keepers float about between them like servants of Big Brother. The monkey house is small but some of the cages are bigger than the room I've been boarded out in. After the first couple of days I was left in sole charge, which was nerve-racking, because the monkeys know the routine better than I do and if I do anything wrong they scream and glare and rattle the bars. *There is one tiny spider monkey who pisses in people's eyes – lucky for me he chooses only men. I think most of them (the monkeys I mean) have gone odd in the head from captivity but I get on with them better than I do with the people.*

All the staff have separate charges so we only overlap at mealtimes, all smelling of different animals. I never knew elephants smelled so strong. Those mealtimes are awful. My accent sticks out like a sore thumb – they're the sort who automatically think you're a snob if you say isn't instead of in't. The reptile man is the only one I like. I spend my lunch hour in the snakehouse standing like a tree with boas and pythons draped all over me while he cleans out the cages. It's a myth that they're slimy but they can certainly squeeze hard.

I don't know how long I am going to stick it out here. The ladies who run the place are definitely odd. They have head-mistress faces, dress in kind of drag, and have Sumo the gorilla in for tea every day. That gorilla looks just how I feel – fed up.

The truth was I was ready to leave after the first week. The professor had warned me not to expect too much but I suppose I was still hoping there might be more to the job than an endless round of feeding and cleaning. If it had not been for the seed of a travel idea, which was growing steadily, I might have persevered a little longer, but I was impatient. Before the end of three months I wrote: 'I've had it here. I'm going to save up enough for food and emergencies and aim to be off in the spring. Don't know where yet, but I'm going. And for quite a long time.'

My saving prospects at the zoo were poor and I knew I could do better working freelance from 309. I tried out the idea on Kay over the phone.

'Of course,' she said, 'but are you sure you'll be able to find work? There's so much about unemployment on the news these days.'

'Don't worry. I'll find work. You watch.'

And while working out my notice at the zoo, I set to devising ways of making this assurance come true.

YOUNG, STRONG, WILLING AND ABLE

Young people with good references available immediately for any part-time domestic work. Gardening, entertaining help and babysitting also undertaken.

Advertisements to this effect appeared in shop windows all over Richmond and Twickenham and in every corner shop in between. The response was swift and almost overwhelming. After a week I had to dash round taking out all the notices to stop Kay's phone ringing.

Inevitably, I double-booked myself one day and asked Marianne if she would mind helping out. She had been ill again and was not yet well enough to take on a full-time job, but the prospect of just a few hours' work appealed. It was my best-paid job, a thrice-weekly cleaning routine in a luxurious bachelor flat opposite the skating shop where Jem had once wooed me with antique phrases in the rain. The owner of the flat was never there. He had had a set of keys cut for me and left my wages behind a clock in the lounge. I handed the keys to Marianne with a list of the jobs to be done, and gave her a number where I could be reached if she needed to ask anything.

I was in the middle of scrubbing out Mrs Joanna Allerton's oven, up to the armpits in grease, when the phone rang. Mrs J. A. was reading *House and Garden* in the sitting-room. Her voice came floating through the hatch: 'Lucy dear, I think it's for you – rather a bad line.'

I lifted the kitchen extension gingerly between two dirty fingers.

'Marianne?'

There was an odd, muffled grunting noise on the other end of the line. Then a thick, whispered question.

'Can you come?'

There was nothing wrong with the line, it was Marianne's voice. Hurriedly, I transferred the receiver to the other ear so that the conversation was less audible to Mrs J. A. and threw her a wide smile through the hatch to make sure she put down her extension.

'What's the matter? Have you broken something?'

There was a funny little laugh.

'I don't *think* so.'

'Why do I have to come? I haven't finished here yet ...'

That weird laugh again.

'You'd better come,' she said thickly, and the phone went dead.

'Marianne?' I called foolishly down the dead line.

Mrs J.A.'s ears must have been stretching.

'Everything all right, dear?'

I replaced the receiver.

'Well, no, actually. I'm afraid I'm going to have to leave early.'

And I did, her bewildered voice pursuing me limply down the drive.

It was a fifteen-minute bus ride to the flat and there was often a half-hour gap between buses. I stuck out my thumb. There must have been something compelling in my attitude because the first car to come by stopped and the driver took me right to the door.

'You know why I stopped?' he grinned as I got out, already glancing anxiously up towards the flat.

'No idea.'

'Because you have the sweetest blob of black on your nose. Want to come for a drink later?'

'Piss off,' I said ungraciously, and smeared the blob of black up to my hairline.

On the landing of the second floor I heard singing. Soft, off-key, quavery: 'I - e vow to thee my cou - untry all earthly things a - bove,/Da da dar, de da de da da dar - the service of my love.'

Marianne's favourite. She used to sing it over and over between bouts of sobbing when Richard first left 309. Her voice after tears had an agonizing frailty which drove my head under three pillows. But she had not been crying now.

I knelt before the door and spoke through the letter box.

'Marianne? Open the door.'

The singing stopped. I called her name again. Could hear her listening in the pool of her own pause. I fastened my eyes to the narrow slit but could see nothing beyond a copy of *The Times*.

'For goodness sake, Marianne, let me in.'

I was afraid someone would see me there, grimy and hissing. There was a lift shaft just across the hall and the front doors of two other flats.

'That you, duck?'

Our old greeting.

'Yes, listen, let me in.'

The strange laugh I had heard over the phone grated through the thick door. It was small, distant, gently mocking.

'Can't,' she said, 'can't get up.'

'Are you hurt? Marianne *please*, what is it?'

'Dlunk.'

'What?'

'Dlunk.'

She laughed again and this time it was more of a giggle. I caught on. It was a peculiar game with rules I had to learn as we went along. I stretched my fingers through the narrow slit and tried to push the paper aside. I could not reach it.

'Look,' I said, beginning to feel angry because I was so helpless stuck out there, 'you can get to the door, can't you?'

She answered like a little girl.

'Are you going to be horrid? I won't let you in if you're going to be horrid.'

'I won't be horrid, I promise – just let me in.'

There was a skidding sound and the keys struck the door on her side. Somebody got into the lift on the ground floor. Running my hand along the bottom of the door, I scrabbled for the keys. I could just feel them. The lift was one floor below, the doors opening and closing. With a violent effort, mashing the skin on my knuckles, I got the keys and was inside less than a second before the lift arrived. I sent a silent prayer that it was not the owner of the flat and did not move until the footsteps had gone. Marianne was lying on her back in the corridor, smiling. Thin hair striped her forehead and through it her big brown eyes shone and shone.

'What have you been up to?' I asked, eyes sweeping the flat.

'Up to,' she murmured, beaming up at me.

The Hoover lay on its side in the kitchen. A spray can of polish sat beside the clock in the lounge. She had evidently tried.

'It's all the Hoover's fault,' she said, pouting. 'Dust coming out instead of going in. Tried to mend it but it wouldn't' – she found this extremely funny – 'it wouldn't. So had a little drink.'

'What drink?'

'There. Bit of each.'

She pointed to the lounge and pulled herself after me like a baby along the floor. The drinks cabinet stood open and the tops were off every one of the twenty-or-so bottles.

'Didn't want man to notice,' she slurred, propping herself against a chair to watch as I started mechanically to match lids to bottoms, 'so had just a little gollop from each. Won't tell Kay, will you? Try that cherry brandy. S'lovely.'

I looked at her to see if she was serious. She was. Smiling, encouraging, she was a total stranger.

My hands worked on. After I had gone through the lounge, dusting, straightening chairs, making it all just as usual, I carried on into the bedroom, then kitchen, bathroom, corridor. I used a dustpan and brush instead of the Hoover and left a note about needing a repair. And all the time this stranger followed me, shuffling, chatting aimiably, crawling sometimes. When I saw the tracks her knees made through the carpet I told her to sit still. She sat like an obedient doll.

'Sorry, duck,' she said once, and I stared at her. Did she know what she looked like with her white legs splayed like a cripple's under her rucked skirt and her hands, clumsy as paddles, pulling dimly at the twisted jersey over her chest?

'You won't tell, will you?'

'I won't tell.'

And through some childish, perhaps misguided, sense of loyalty, I did not. But from that time on, when Kay told me Marianne had had one of her 'giddy spells', after which she sometimes slept for as long as two days, my mind went curiously numb. The 'giddy spells' had been going on since Marianne's last summer in Scotland. She was just eighteen.

I was sixteen when, true to my plan, I took to the road in the spring of 1972. I intended to start by crossing the Channel and then go in whatever general direction offered itself with the first ride. Left would mean France and the Middle East; right, Spain and North Africa. I had thirty pounds in my pocket. It seemed plenty.

And besides, I mused, as I twirled round at the first hitching spot, testing the weight of a rucksack christened Beverly, the sun would surely not cost much.

PART TWO

Bruise

Chapter Seven

Rolling, tumbling, heart pounding, spine whacked in the grit every time I rolled again. Tar on bruise-blotched legs and in my hair. Rolling with mouth shut, tyres doing all the screaming as the white car wheeled and screeched away.

Beverly and I landed in a heap just over the unmade edge of the road. Fine dust scattered everywhere, making my brown skin matt, further staining already well-stained Beverly. After the giddiness went, I slowly brushed her down.

It was mid-afternoon. Below the road a shale slope stretched away under bright sun to acres of gravel wasteland. There was a building site in the distance – wire fences, red drums and rectangular slabs of cement. It was very quiet where I sat brushing Beverly, no cars coming along the tar-sticky road. The tyre marks made an overlapping zigzag pattern, a singular left to right and back again among otherwise straight lines. I knew that if they came back I would throw myself down the slope rather than get in the car again.

After a while my hands stopped moving on the rucksack and I sat quite still. My face was hot and dry, the skin sore where one cheek had scraped in the dirt as I fell. I sat on, vacant, until the sound of a vehicle approaching threw me, unthinking, into action. Grabbing Beverly, I slung her under a narrow ledge where the road gave into the slope and flattened myself beside her. The rumble of the motor gathered as it rounded the bend where the white car had disappeared. It passed by booming, shaking the stones and my hands, and receded finally to a distant, impersonal drone. I dared then to lift my eyes and saw the fading back of a lorry trailing twin streamers of dust. I stared after it a long time. It might have been going to Athens.

Slowly I clambered back on to the road. Stones disturbed by my feet bounded loudly down the slope, shale skittered. I remained motionless on hands and knees until the last stone stopped moving. The gravel bit into my palms. At last I stood up, one hand holding fast to Beverly's straps. As I bent to hoist her up, pain shot across the base of my spine, but I got her into position all right. Automatically, as they always did when Beverly was aboard, my feet began to walk.

The next car to come by was a silvery grey saloon. When it had almost passed and I had had a chance to see the driver's face, I jabbed out a thumb. He was not going to stop at first but a look in the rear-view mirror made him change his mind. I walked to where he had pulled up, opened the door and glared in. His head, thin on top, was ducked towards me, smiling. I glared harder.

'Athens?'

He nodded and made polite I-don't-speak-English noises.

'*Français?*'

'*Un peu.*'

As I got into the car I said loudly, in English, 'If you try anything on I'll kill you. I've got a knife.'

He shrugged helplessly to show he did not understand and leaned forward to help fasten my seatbelt. Flinching away, I did it myself. I did not look as we ran over the skid marks, past the shale slope and the distant red drums.

After a while he opened the glove compartment and took out a blue-spotted handkerchief.

'*Tenez. Essuyez votre visage.*'

I wiped. My cheek was tender but I rubbed hard. Blood came away with the grit and dust.

'*Attendez, je suis médecin. Etes-vous blessée ailleurs?*'

So he was a doctor. Was I wounded anywhere else? I hesitated.

'*Pas blessée, mais violée.*'

Violated. The word sounded theatrical.

'*Violée? Je ne comprends pas.*'

My French was becoming harder to find.

'Un homme disait qu'il peut me conduire à Athènes. Mais il arrêtait la voiture sur un tout petit chemin et il m'a violée. Il voulait faire l'amour mais pas faire l'amour.'

He wanted to make love but not make love. Did that make sense?

The doctor nodded.

'C'est bien ce que j'imaginais. Je vais vous emmener à l'hôpital.'

'No – to the police.'

He understood that but shook his head. Had I got the make and number of the car? No? Well then, he did not recommend it. As a girl hitching alone I did not stand a chance of being treated with any sympathy even if I was believed. It would be the man's word against mine and besides, he was probably miles away by now.

I shut up. If the man could not be caught at once, and preferably killed, I did not want to think about it any more. The thought of a physical examination was unbearable, so, against the doctor's will, I made him drop me as soon as we came to the main square in Athens. I knew that if we had not been speaking in French I would not have told him anything. The words I had used – *violé, faire l'amour* – seemed unconnected with the actual event, inhabiting a realm far removed from grit in the spine and gravel biting into palms.

Alone now with my body's private knowledge, my mind went numb. The aggression I had shown as I got into the doctor's car had evaporated. Without thought, without direction, I walked round and round Syntagma Square. As the pain across my lower back increased I began to limp, shifting the weight of Beverly from side to side. A long clump of sun-dried hair hung over one eye. After a while I did not bother to push it back any more.

It was late in the day now. Three times I had stepped over the shadow of a man reading a newspaper on some steps. Each time I came round the square again the shadow was longer. Seeing some young backpackers staring, I used a handful of hair to brush away tears which kept coming now. I wanted to brush away the stares. A man in a bright yellow open jeep stopped to talk to the young people, then drove on round the square. He slowed when he was level with me and hooted. I did not react, continuing my aimless, limping round. Cars behind blared for him to move on. He shouted at them angrily in Greek but shifted the jeep back into the main stream to go round again. This time when he came past he slowed almost to a halt and called out in English, 'Wait please, I want to talk to you.'

Again the blaring of the horns and his retort. The third time he came round, managing to bring the jeep closer, I started to yell, 'Go away! Go away!'

Careless of hoots, he leapt out and sprinted to where I stood backed up against a telephone booth. He was short and dark, dressed neatly in cream trousers and a casual shirt. His shoes, on which I concentrated, were of pale, expensive leather. He wore glasses, but not dark, like that other man.

'Listen,' he said, 'I have been watching you. There is something wrong I think. I would like to help.'

He was obviously in a hurry. The parked jeep was causing havoc.

'What do you mean help? I'm OK.'

He scratched his head energetically.

'Listen,' he said again, 'you are not OK. I want to take you home to my wife. You will come?'

'Hah! Your wife!'

My head felt as though it were stuffed with clouds, and the alien words which came out of my mouth like bits torn off them. them.

'Come, what do you think? I want to go to bed with you? Look!'

He pointed to my reflection in the glass of the telephone booth. I saw a scrawny, wild-haired figure in shorts with scarred and filthy legs. Mechanically I pushed the hair off my face. There were streaks of dirt all over it, smudges of dried blood and tears.

'If you can't trust me, we will telephone my wife. You can talk to her.'

He darted into the booth and picked up the receiver. Consternation creased his forehead and he worried at his short black hair with angry fingers. Pushing open the door of the booth, receiver still in hand, he shook it helplessly, a comic study in exasperation. I scowled.

'Come,' he said, banging the useless phone back on the hook, 'for a moment you must trust me. We go to find another phone.'

He ran to the jeep, soothing irate drivers with large, calming gestures. Opening the passenger door he beckoned. Reluctantly, still scowling, I approached. He held out his arms for Beverly but I swung her round and clutched her to my chest. Awkwardly, I scrambled into the jeep like that. There was another phone booth on the other side of the square but it was occupied. Letting go of the wheel he waved his arms expressively.

'OK,' he said, 'we can go to a hotel.'

Seeing my tight expression, he laughed.

'Not for bed, little silly one, for telephone!'

We left the square and he parked down a side street in front of a hotel. Telling me not to move, he ran in and spoke to the desk clerk. I watched as she lifted a telephone from behind the desk and he started talking into it. The conversation seemed to go on a long time and I lost interest, looking instead at a thin cat across the road. It was licking a back paw furiously, as though it would eat it. I had a headache and wanted a glass of water.

Then the man was beside the jeep and opening the door.

'Talk to her,' he commanded. 'Her name is Ursula – Uschi.'

Still hanging on to Beverly I walked past him into the hotel. I held the phone to my ear but did not say anything. Then a hesitant voice, German-accented, spoke in my ear.

'Hello? My name is Ursula. I am the wife of Costas, who is with you. Please will you come to my house? You can have something to eat and a bath if you like.'

Her English was formal, like a schoolgirl's. Costas made shooing gestures, round eyes encouraging behind his glasses. At last I said cautiously, 'All right.'

It seemed a long drive out to the suburb where they lived. Shadows of trees and lamp-posts sped by; a group of old women all in black; children playing catch with a pine cone outside white, flat-roofed houses. Costas pointed to where a small church stood on a hill. There were cypress trees planted close together in the graveyard.

'My place is near here.'

The jeep climbed the hill and just on the other side, we stopped beside a block of flats. Costas let me out while he went to park and I stood holding Beverly, looking up at the flats. A young woman leaning over a balcony waved.

'There, that is Uschi,' said Costas when he came back, and led the way up concrete stairs to the back entrance of the flat. Furious barking came from inside and Ursula's voice telling it to hush. When the door opened an excited Alsatian puppy bounded out.

'Down, Hector!' ordered Costas, and lovingly lifted him up.

I let go of Beverly to stroke the soft, deer-coloured ears. Uschi – she said I must call her that – led me into the sitting-room where the first thing I noticed was a bowl of strawberries on an elegant drinks cabinet. She disappeared for a minute and came back with a jug of iced water.

'Please,' she said, 'I think you are thirsty.'

She had a face like a lovely pixie.

While I drank, Uschi bustled about, lips compressed in concentration. She heaped an assortment of clothes and toiletries on a table before me. There was a white blouse, a pair of dove-grey trousers, a bathrobe, soap and a comb. Glancing at my dust-caked tangle of hair she took the comb away and brought back one with larger teeth. She showed me the bathroom and where I could sleep if I would stay the night. She hoped very much I would. Looking in at the small spare room, I remarked more to myself than to her that it was a long time since I had slept indoors. Laughing delightedly, she said that if it would make me feel more comfortable I could sleep on the balcony with Hector. She would arrange a bed for me there.

I was a long time in the bathroom. Uschi had given me cotton-wool, antiseptic and Elastoplast, and after I had washed my hair and thoroughly soaked my body – I could not bring myself to touch between my legs – I attended to all the minor cuts and scrapes. I had to cut the tar from my hair with scissors.

Back in the main room Uschi sat down with me and laid a hand very softly on my wrist. Her eyes, creased with concern, searched mine.

'Please, Eve' – that was the name I had given – 'tell me, are you all right? There was a man, yes?'

I did not look at her but answered her questions.

'Yes, a man. But I am all right. Could I – have you got a pair of knickers I could borrow?'

Mine, torn, were still somewhere up a mountain above Cape Sounion. She jumped up, small fists clenched by her sides.

'Of course. How stupid I am.'

They took me to eat at a place near the old port of Piraeus. We had *calamares*, followed by fresh fish with Greek salad. There was a bottle of chilled white wine but I had water instead.

Halfway through the main course I stopped eating. Costas and Uschi were talking together, laughing softly into each other's eyes. They had guessed, rightly, that I did not want to talk much. Watching them, liking them, I suddenly had a horrible vision of Uschi pinned in the same position as I had been, her pixie face distorted, hands scrabbling, body trying to snake itself into the ground. I looked away over the dark water. Light from paper lanterns in the restaurant shone on the surface in soft, crinkled beams.

We did not stay out late and Uschi made up my bed on the balcony as soon as we got back. She left me with a picture book of wild birds, another jug of water and some fruit in case I was hungry in the night.

At first I slept, comforted by the warm snufflings of the puppy and the familiar blanket of night air. When I woke it was with a jolt, heart pounding as it had when I was rolling in the grit on the road. I lay totally still, eyes wavering on the distant inner vision I did not want to see. It zoomed in closer and closer until I was right inside the scene, back on the hot road at Cape Sounion, waiting for the man in the diving-mask to take me to Athens.

It had taken the whole morning to climb up to the road from the tiny beach where I had been sleeping for the past week. I was hot and grubby and longed for a cool drink. The last of the water in Harold, my water bottle, was lukewarm and stale. I sat on Beverly, squinting up at the sun. We had agreed to meet at midday.

I had only seen the man twice before, both times when he had been snorkelling and surfaced in our bay. He seemed uninteresting: a white, middle-aged body bulging over a pair of black and yellow swimming trunks. He never took off his diving-mask. It was kind of him, though, to offer to take me to Athens. The Texan thought it a good idea too. In fact he wanted to come. But I knew if he did, I would never get rid of him in Athens. That was where he had latched on to me before. We had both been standing in a queue, waiting to board a boat to Haifa when we were told that it was already full; we could use our tickets for the next one in nine days' time. I had spent nearly the last of my money on the ticket, so there was nothing for it but to muddle through the next nine days, find a beach and eke out the spaghetti I had bought in Brindisi. Luckily I had a full jar of honey, too. The Texan, a thin, Jesus-bearded student, was in the same position and suggested we pool our resources. It had seemed a sensible idea but after a few days I found his company tedious. And all he had to contribute to the food kitty was one jar of Special Crunchy Kretschmer Wheatgerm. After the first day, when we scraped together enough between us for a loaf and some *feta*, we lived on spaghetti cooked in seawater with honey as a sauce and wheatgerm in lieu of parmesan.

On the beach the sun had been welcome, a brilliant white diffusion in a tall, blue sky. At any moment when the quartz-bright tingle of heat became too much I could plunge into the sea. Here, at the top of the cliff, heat and brilliance merged in a chalky glare from which there was no escape. I gazed for a while at the blank spot in the road which the car would fill when it came, then turned and watched small, fidgeting patterns of light on distant waves. When at last the white car drew up, I was miles away in a heat-hazy dream.

The driver's window was wound down. He put out his head and smiled. His eyes, behind smoothly curved dark glasses, were invisible.

'I'm glad you've come,' I said, climbing in beside him, 'It was getting very hot waiting there.'

The comment was wasted as we had no common language beyond a few words in French and German. 'Athens' and 'midday' had been easy enough to get across but conversation as we drove along was another matter. I wanted to know roughly what time we would arrive in Athens and tried framing the question several different ways. His shielded eyes stayed on the road but he nodded and shook his head to show he was trying to understand.

'Athens, ' I kept repeating. 'When? *Quand? A quelle heure?*'

He indicated the road ahead.

'Sounion,' he said. 'After, Athens. *Café trinken* in Sounion.'

Evidently there were one or two words he knew in English. Catching his meaning I said, 'Ooh yah!'

The thought of a cup of strong Greek coffee was very welcome. It did not matter if it took us a little out of our way.

I settled back to enjoy the ride, fluttering a hand in the breeze that came through the window. Before long the small, pillared temple of Sounion came into view, perched on a promontory overlooking sea blistered with light. We stopped at a tiny café, its three formica-topped tables spindly beside the splendour of ancient columns. We were served by a silent old woman who brought, along with the coffee and glasses of water, some thick yellow fingers of sponge. I ate one and the Greek, two. Out of habit I wrapped the remaining one in a paper napkin and slipped it into one of Beverly's side pockets. The Greek smiled. He was smoking a cigarette. Laughing, I refused when he offered one to me. I was sure not many Greek girls of sixteen smoked.

Back on the road, heading now the right way for Athens, we passed the spot where I had climbed up from the beach. I waved – as a small joke to myself – goodbye to another one of my many homes under the sky. I thought I might spend tonight on the Acropolis where I had stayed before. It was beautiful up there alone under the columns and the moon.

The car rolled on, the hot road stretching ahead like a panting grey tongue. I imagined that somehow if we drove far enough we would eventually disappear beyond that tongue, swallowed by the heat.

The Greek interrupted my thoughts by passing me something. It was a plastic wallet containing photographs of a plump woman and two little boys.

'*Mein Frau*,' he said proudly, '*und meiner Kinder*.'

I made suitably admiring noises. I was looking forward to reaching Athens; this man was not interesting company.

Then, out of the blue, he announced; 'We swim.'

'Swim?' I was puzzled.

'*Oui*, yah, swim.'

'But Athens, *nous allons à Athènes ...*'

'Yah, yah. Swim, swim' – he made swimming motions – 'after, Athens.'

'Swim where?' I asked. We had left the coast road.

He waved an arm inland towards the mountains.

'*Klein* swim. Good, nice.'

I frowned out of the window, wondering if I should get out now and try for a more direct lift. But there were no other cars about and besides, it would seem ungrateful. He had bought me coffee, after all, and would get me to Athens eventually. There was no reason why he should not have a swim *en route*.

A mile or so further on he turned off the main road and headed uphill along a meandering single track.

'Is it far?' I wanted to know.

He smiled and his dark glasses caught the sunlight.

'No far.'

The road we were climbing was steep and, as we went on, became rough. Large stones caught on the exhaust and made the car jerk; the tarmac, patchy at first, soon ended altogether. We came to a fork where a still smaller track joined the one we were on. Some warning bell told me that if he took that track there would be trouble. I looked carefully at his face. The smile was still there, the masked eyes the same black blank. There was no human habitation in sight now. Lower down we had passed a farm. An idiot boy had cooed as we drove by, thick droplets of sweat shining on a white, distorted face. Up here at the crossroads there was nothing but yellow-grey boulder-strewn land falling away on all sides. The sun seemed to clamp on to the roof of the white car. He took the small track.

The car lurched through sand and rubble. The Greek was concentrating now, leaning forward and steering carefully to avoid rocks and potholes. As we came to the brow of a hill he straightened up and pointed to the scene below.

'Swim.'

He wiped sweat off his face with the back of a large hand. Moisture glistened on a few black hairs below the knuckles. Below us was a lake, kidney-shaped, with a scattering of rocks at one end. It might have been a reservoir. He stopped, lumbering the car off the edge of the track, where it settled in a low cloud of dust, one wheel crushing a tussock of dried grass. I wound the window up part-way against the dust.

'You swim,' I said clearly. 'I will wait here.'

His eye-blank face turned towards me, broad mouth open with a half-smile expressing non-comprehension. I repeated what I had said, with gestures. He shook his head, grinning.

'Two swim,' he said slowly, 'me, you.'

As he said the last words he demonstrated by pointing first to himself, then to me. His finger was on a level with my chest. Still pointing, it came closer and poked experimentally. Through the thin cotton of my sleeveless top he touched my breast. I flinched and froze, the perspiration on my thighs suddenly cold. Then my hand flew to the handle of the car door. It would not open. I tried to wind down the window to get at the catch on the outside but accidentally wound it up instead. He sat back facing me and laughed, his big red mouth wide.

'OK,' I said, trying to play, pretending the touch had been a joke. 'Let's swim. Let's swim now.'

He laughed again and casually reached over a long arm. With the ends of his fingers he took hold of my left breast and squeezed it three times as if he were squeezing a motor horn. I tried to push him away. He shook his head, grinning, and I felt his free hand land heavily on my neck, the thumb curling round to the

129

throat. He swatted my hands away and the thumb played softly up and down.

'Naughty,' he said through his grin. 'No swim now.'

His other hand returned to my breasts. Every time I made a move to strike him away the grip on my neck tightened. He tweaked and twisted the nipples through the thin cloth and then pushed one shoulder-strap down. Taking the edge of the cloth in the very tips of his fingers, he peeled it slowly away until one frightened brown breast lay exposed. As he jabbed a thick, inquisitive finger into the tender auriole, I made a frantic move to pull the hand from my neck.

'Naughty,' he said again, this time louder. Letting go of my neck for an instant, he grasped both wrists firmly and pulled my hands down by my sides, indicating that this was where they should stay.

'No!' I cried, voice wavering, lost like the puff of dust from the car tyres over the brow of the hill. 'No!'

One hand closed over the lower half of my face, thrusting my head over the back of the seat. I tugged at the heavy, sweat-sticky palm and heard his gleeful laugh again.

'Oh naughty, naughty!'

While I struggled, he reached lazily into the back seat and lifted a long package on to his lap. It was his scuba gun. The metal tip of the spear caught bright asterisks of light through the plastic wrapping.

He removed the hand from my neck and wagged a finger under my nose.

'Naughty Fraulein.'

I sat rigid, back pressed into the hot plastic of the seat, thighs sliding with sweat. The smile still in place, but slacker now, he unwrapped the gun, keeping the curved rectangles of his blanked-out eyes on me all the time. He shifted his legs apart and unzipped his fly. Then, very carefully, he placed the tip of the spear-gun just above my heart. With the other hand he pointed to himself and pressed my chin down to make sure I was looking. His mouth was completely slack now.

His fingers parted the opening of his fly and dug out the heavy roll of flesh. It lay against one trousered thigh like a thick white slug. His fingers pulled at it but it remained limp. His hand came back to me.

Aware all the time of the pricking spear-point over my heart, I could not move. I watched helplessly as he undid my shorts and tried to tug them down. Hampered by holding the gun, he motioned impatiently for me to do it. Slowly my hands found the waistband of my shorts and stayed there, not moving. He shouted and made feints with the spear but it was no good, I was paralysed.

Sweat poured off him now. He flung open the door on his side and yanked me outside, landing me hard on my knees beside the car. He stood above me, the white slug dangling outside his trousers. I tried to stand up but he caught my hair and twisted my face up to look at him. He hit me on the cheeks and nose with the limp white thing. Then, bending over, legs straddled, he pulled my head back so that it almost touched the ground. I was still kneeling, so that my back was painfully arched and my pelvis thrust up to him. With short, angry jerks my shorts were dragged down and suddenly the whole world was great thick fingers digging into me. A noise like a bursting bubble of blood came from my throat. Pulling my legs down now and flinging the shorts away, he wedged one of my feet behind the front tyre of the car, pushing the other outwards. I felt the tendons of my groin pull like wires. My hands leapt down to protect but he grunted angrily and grabbed the spear-gun he had left in the car. Touching the broad arrow-head to my throat, he bent over and tore the flimsy cotton of my knickers to get them off. He gabbled at me in Greek and, standing with one foot grinding into my thigh to hold me wide, lowered the gun meaningfully. He took hold of himself with the other hand and, making harsh panting noises, pumped himself up and down. I turned my head and closed my eyes, hands digging into the sand; spine, shoulders, buttocks burrowing to get away.

Then the sweat and weight of him was everywhere and his fingers were pressing me open; thick fingers pushing and stretching, forcing a path unheeding as my whole being tried to close itself to him. I cried out loud as the white slug shoved in. Three times he thrust before he was fully inside and with each stab my

131

body convulsed, tried wildly to expel. But he was deep as a buried fist now, punching again and again on the same bruise. On, on it went and the sun was still shining and the earth would not give way. He got hold of my face and twisted it round to look at him.

'Laugh!' he ordered savagely. 'Laugh!'

The stretching inside deepened into a dark red flower of pain. Something small and hard was grinding into my chest.

'Laugh!' he shouted again, shaking my face. Then he gave a short double jump and flopped on to me, a damp dead-weight. There was wetness flooding inside and a new smell mingling with dust and fear. I looked up to where the sky beyond his sweat-sodden head stretched wide blue twinkling eyes over the sand and rubble and the lake, or reservoir.

Then I laughed.

He raised his head to look at me. Crushing the falter from my voice I laughed again. Slowly, his wet mouth slid into the old grin. It had all been a game then. It was still a game now.

'Good,' he said, starting to get up, 'good.'

The spear-gun was at my side. I did not touch it. The vision of it pointing into me had been in my head all the time. He must forget it now, pretend that it had been part of the game too. Leaning against the car, trousers already zipped, he took a pack of cigarettes and a metal lighter from his breast-pocket. So that was what had been grinding into my chest. I reached for my shorts and put them on before standing. Then, walking up to him, I held out my hand for a cigarette. I laughed again to cover my shaking as he lit it. He laughed too and making 'one' signs made me understand that he was asking if this was my first cig-arette. I nodded, wondering what to do with the bolus of smoke in my mouth. When I opened my lips it trickled out messily and I huffed to push it away. The Greek gestured to the scuffled patch on the ground where my body had lain and indicated 'not first'. I shook my head. My laugh was a bleat as I took another puff of the cigarette. Barnes, paintings, photographs and Renaissance music shimmered among the rubble for a moment.

Bored now, he looked at his watch.

'We go.'

He let me into the car and I kept my eyes averted as he slung the gun in the back. It was not easy turning on the rough ground and he muttered irritably in Greek. But when we were back on the larger track he began to laugh again and make what I assumed were jokes in his strange mixture of languages. I did not understand the words but laughed where it seemed appropriate. To cover the trembling of my legs I hoisted Beverly on to my lap and scrabbled in one of her pockets for a comb. I found a scarf instead and wiped at the sweat on my neck. We passed the farm with the idiot boy. He was still there, lolling like a broken puppet against the fence. He cooed again as we drove by. Beneath its distortion his face was gentle and wondering. Part of me wanted to leap out and scream in the dust at his feet.

When we reached the main road the Greek seemed to go into a world of his own, humming and tapping out bits of rhythm on the steering wheel. I could not look at those thick fingers. Once he said loudly, 'Laugh!' as he had done when I was under him. I laughed and his gleeful chuckle joined in. Under Beverly my legs shook and shook.

The road wound on and the sun winked off the car's white bonnet. Sometimes I could see the sea, sometimes just endless banks of high, yellow stone. We came finally to a garage next to a dump for old cars. The Greek pulled in. Leaning out of his window – both front windows were wound right down now – he shouted across to where a group of workmen sat in the shade smoking and reading magazines.

One of the men got up and strolled over. He was middle-aged with a creased complexion and dry, squinting eyes. All the men wore dusty blue overalls. This one had on a flat blue cap as well. He bent close as the driver continued speaking and I saw his eyes come over to me. Then he made a wide beckoning gesture with his arm and the four other men began to move. They folded their magazines and one stubbed out his cigarette in the dirt, grinding it flat with the toe of a workboot.

Then they were all in the car, squashed together in the back seat, voices loud, the smell of sweat-stained bodies strong. The tyres crunched on the gravel as the driver swung the car back on to the road. As he drove along his voice was merry and his hands waved airily towards the mountains. Towards the little road.

My hands on Beverly began to twitch uncontrollably. I could feel the attention of the men in the back on me as the driver held forth, describing something, laughing between phrases. The car went faster, swinging round curves in the glinting road. The sea was gone now. There was tall stone on one side, acres of gravel wasteland on the other. Tightly, tightly, I gripped Beverly, one elbow resting on the hot frame of the open window. There was a blind bend in the road ahead, the ground falling away sharply to one side. The car had to slow.

One hand left the rucksack and I hung it casually over the side of the door. As we drew near the bend the driver hooted and at the same moment my fingers found the outside catch. With all my strength I jerked it up and flung my weight against the door, bending up my knees. There was a rushing vision of grey, streaking road and wild voices in the car.

Then the rolling, tumbling, heart pounding, spine-whacked-in-the-grit every time I rolled again; tyres screeching like a crazed seagull, and the white car was gone.

Chapter Eight

The stars came gradually back into focus above Costas and Ursula's balcony. I noticed small, irregular mounds along a drainpipe. Swallows' nests. I counted them three times, each time getting a different result, before I slept.

Costas had already gone to work by the time I got up. Uschi said that she too must go out but would be back at midday. I was to help myself to anything I liked from the kitchen, 'do play some records', and was there anything I needed from the shops? I shook my head, smiling, and in a minute she was gone, a gay scarf tied over her chignoned hair.

She had left me a magnificent breakfast – including the strawberries I had had my eye on, even in yesterday's dazed state. After washing the dishes I decided to turn out Beverly. It would be the first time I had unpacked her properly since leaving England three months ago. I put on a record of South American flute music and stood listening to it for a moment in a wide rectangle of sunlight slanting through the balcony doors. Hector, chin on paws as he watched my every move, wagged his tail.

With her main part empty I attacked Beverly's pockets. In the front was my scarf and the comb I had not been able to find yesterday. My purse was there too, ancient and held together with an elastic band. It contained a boat ticket, a franc and five centimes, two Italian lire and a few drachmas. In a special recess inside was a one pound note. In the left-hand pocket was a tiny velvet bag of sewing bits – I was forever repairing Beverly and my shorts – and my all-purpose red-handled knife. The right-hand pocket usually held only two items: a coil of string and a matchbox with a butterfly painted on the lid. I kept the matchbox in my hand as I took out a third item.

Until now my mood had been light, busy, the music easy in the background, sun shining in. But as I held the napkin-wrapped object my hands began to shake. It was the thick finger of yellow spongecake I had taken from the café where the Greek bought me coffee under the Cape Sounion gods. Unwrapping it and screwing up the napkin I hurled it through the balcony doors. Hector was up like a shot, ears pricked, gauche puppy body leaping. His teeth snapped and it was gone. He sat down panting, crumby mouth agape, hoping for more.

Sitting down beside him in the sun, I opened the butterfly box. Inside, buried in a nest of cottonwool, was the Virgin Stone. I ran my fingers over its delicate, egglike smoothness, traced the white-mauve-lilac-lavender stripes. The music had stopped and my mind was reverting to the misery of the day before.

Then – it might have been minutes, might have been hours

later – I felt Hector's damp snout nudging under my arm. I gave him a hug and he darted long, doggy licks at my face. By the time Uschi got back Beverly was packed, Harold filled with water, and I was ready to go.

Uschi did not understand and neither, really, did I. My boat did not leave until tomorrow, I could have stayed another night. But something was telling me I must get back on the haphazard track of my own world before what happened yesterday took over and made me incapable of facing that world again. If I allowed Uschi and Costas to go on lulling me with their kindness any longer, the jolt back to my chosen brand of reality would be that much harder to bear.

As Uschi made a cool drink for us, a slight line of perplexity marked her pixie brow. I knew I could not explain, so I lied. I said I had friends to meet in Athens, people who were also going on the boat. Her face cleared. Of course, I had my own plans; it was selfish of her to have imagined I would be free to spend the weekend with them. But I would stop for lunch first, wouldn't I? She would walk me to the bus stop afterwards. I smiled, wanting to please her, and secretly hoped the odd change in my purse would cover the fare into town.

Hector came with us to the bus stop, bouncing along beside Uschi on the white pavement and stopping at every lamp-post and tree. When the bus came, Uschi jumped in before me and paid the driver my fare. Kissing me goodbye on both cheeks, she said, 'Eve, should I tell your parents? Do they know where you are?'

I shook my head and assured her that I was all right now. Just as the bus began to trundle away, there was a great shouting and barking. Uschi was running alongside banging on the window with her small hands. The driver stopped and wiped the sweat from his face good-humouredly as she handed in a carrier-bag. It was passed down the bus from hand to hand. As we moved off again I turned to wave. Uschi was smiling and waving and Hector was wagging his tail.

The bus lumbered unhurriedly past the church, the flat white houses and the groups of children playing. The last person to pass on Uschi's bag was a wrinkled old man with a bright smile showing toothless gums pink as a baby's. His eyes twinkled as he saw me peek into the bag. Uschi must have dashed round her kitchen at the last minute. There was pumpernickel, *feta*, three packets of biscuits and a grapefruit. The old man smiled again and bobbed his head up and down like a turkey as I held up one of the packets for him to admire.

By the time we reached the city it was late afternoon. I got out at the far side of Syntagma Square and headed straight towards Parthenon hill, back turned on the scene of yesterday's lost circlings.

As I made my way through the maze of small streets at the edge of town my pace evened out. Properly packed, Beverly was an easy, even load and my feet moved comfortably into their old stride. The pain across my back was almost gone. I came to a drinking fountain and stopped to take a long pull from Harold, topping him up afterwards. There was a white child's moon in the sky already. I looked forward to when it began to shine and I was lying in my sleeping-bag watching the stars form their clear, faraway patterns.

I found my sleeping place on the far side of the hill, a broad trough beneath a bank of stone. Before settling down I changed into my old shorts and ate a piece of the white, watery *feta* and some chocolate biscuits. A last band of sun haze flattened slowly into a brief gold-silver line and the bulging white columns of the temple turned black. I must have been wearier than I thought because my eyes were closed before I had a chance to trace the patterns of the stars.

Hours later, it seemed, sleep and darkness were pierced by a great beam of light. It swept like white rain across my eyes. For a moment I lay motionless with shock. Fear doubled my heartbeat.

Then it came again, a huge, dazzling eye sweeping right over where I lay. In a second I was on my feet and stuffing everything into Beverly. In my haste I dropped a packet of biscuits and when the light came round again, that was all it found. I was crouching out of reach on the darkest part of the slope. Looking up, I saw

137

similar beams moving all over the Acropolis and then there was sound as well. Slow, majestic music. Suddenly I realized what it was all about. It was not a police raid, not a visitation of the gods. I had been caught out on the night of the *Son et Lumière*.

Keeping well outside the sweep of the beams I slithered down the slope. The descent was long and dusty. Finally I emerged, worried and dishevelled, on a side road leading to the city. Reluctantly, not knowing where else to go, I followed it until I reached Syntagma Square.

It was a warm night and there were plenty of people about. Music came from the tavernas and the *souvlakia* stands were busy. There was a crowd of young people sitting outside a bar. Quietly, I slipped in among them.

I had been sitting there for some time, wondering where to go next, when a big girl with short blonde hair turned to me. She wanted to know the way to the youth hostel. Her voice was a little slurred.

'I have to go there and pick up some gear,' she said. 'I'm going to an all-night party.' Under the slur her accent was Australian. Sniffing the possibility of shelter for the night, I offered to show her the way.

'Great!'

We set off along the crowded pavement. She was large all over and walked with heavy rolling stride. Her name was Fred.

'Hey!' she said, 'this is really nice of you. Do you want to come to the party?'

'Well . . .' I hesitated. 'I'd like to but I'm all dirty.'

Fred gave a donkey's bray of laughter.

'You don't have to bother about that, it isn't a *smart* party.'

She was right about that.

When we had picked up her backpack at the hostel, we followed directions she had on a piece of paper. A signpost in blue and white told us we had arrived at the street where the party was meant to be. We checked with the Greek word scrawled on the paper and stood looking at the sign. It was the same, no doubt about it, but there was no street and no sign of a party. On either side of the unlit road ahead were the flattened remains of demolished houses. Only one or two low sections of wall still stood. Fred scratched her head and said, 'This is crazy!'

'Hold on,' I laid a hand on her arm. 'Listen.'

Very faintly, coming from the far end of the non-existent street was the sound of a guitar. Three long broken chords followed one another, then silence. Then another three chords. Every time the chords began, Fred and I moved forward. When they stopped, we stopped. All at once there was a shrill, yipping laugh ending on a long trill.

Fred's voice twanged loudly into the dark.

'Where *are* you guys? Is this the party?'

For a moment her words echoed limply. Then we heard whispering. Fred gripped my arm.

'Hey, they're here! Let's go! Let's go to the party!'

As she swung me jubilantly towards the sound, a gangling spectre loomed out of the dark. For a moment I thought it was the Texan off the beach at Cape Sounion. It had the same endless stringbean legs and huge feet in ethnic sandals.

'Fred!' it cried, 'you made it!'

We were taken behind a section of half-demolished wall. Crumbled stone steps led down into what had once been the basement of a house. There was a strong smell of brick dust and fried food. Light came from three tall candles in bottles on top of a packing crate. Beside them were other bottles filled with red and white Greek wine. Two young men sat by the crate on seats made out of bricks and a third lay full length on the floor, his hand clutching an empty tumbler. From shadows on the other side of the room came the guitar music, playing softly now. A large tumbler of wine was thrust into my hand.

As my eyes adjusted to the light I saw that aside from the crate and one chair there were two iron-framed beds in the room, one balanced drunkenly on three legs and strewn with backpacks, empty retsina bottles and the remains of a paper-wrapped meal. The gawky youth – who I had secretly christened Stringbean – swept an arm round apologetically.

'Sorry all the tucker's gone, ladies. There's a heap of retsina though, and Jock here' – he indicated the prone figure with a chummy kick – 'brought along some ouzo. We've been putting it in the wine to liven it up a little. Here, try some.'

A quantity of clear, strong-smelling liquor was poured into my tumbler. Fred knocked hers back.

'Phew! That's great!'

Tipping back the tumbler as she had done, I took a good mouthful. It was sweet, oily and acid all at the same time and brought back memories of aniseed balls and the school bus stop.

'Something for the music man,' came a voice from the corner.

'Sure,' exclaimed Stringbean. 'Let me introduce our host, Jorges.'

He filled a tumbler and taking one of the candles, crossed to where Jorges sat. The sputtering light revealed a small, dark figure sitting crosslegged with a large guitar on his knees. Huge wide-apart eyes like twin moons shone from under a mop of short, heavy ringlets fat as fir cones. A grin from almost negroid lips displayed superb teeth and a little catlike tongue. Jorges struck an introductory chord on the guitar.

'I greet you,' he said grandly. 'I will play for you.'

And he did, closing his eyes, and leaning his head against the wall. The palms of his hands were pinky brown like a monkey's and his shins under the big guitar were lean and full of knots. The candle was left by him as Stringbean returned to the rest of the party.

Fred was clamouring for a game. The man on the floor had been propped against the wall and there were cheers as he began to revive. He was ordered to stay awake and I was ordered to shell some peanuts, which Stringbean said were needed for the game. He poured a whole lot down on to the crate in front of me, and I set to work cracking the shells with my teeth. I was not sure where to put the kernels and, as if in answer, a large green beret sailed into my lap from Jorges' direction.

'Put them in there, little Queen,' he called over the music.

The rules of the game seemed simple enough. Taking it in turns, we would each demonstrate some action in dumb show which the others then had to copy. If they failed to do it properly the penalty was to drink a tumbler of wine. Fred insisted on going first. She shook my arm, scattering peanuts.

'You OK, you? I've forgotten your name. Just watch me.'

Lumbering to her feet she stood beside the crate, massive in the candlelight. She bent her carthorse knees, thrust out her arms in the shape of a giant caliper and leapt into the air. It was not clear what her feet did but she assured us that they 'changed' at least twice. The boys followed and I heard a bubbly giggle pop out of me as their hairy legs struggled to repeat the changements. Jorges did not join in but went on quietly providing an accompaniment. When my turn came I thought I did rather well but there were cries of: 'Your arms were wrong, your arms were wrong!'

I had held them above my head as I had been taught at dancing class. I got halfway through my penalty wine and lowered my tumbler. There were furious cries. The rules said you had to drink it all in one go and if you failed, the penalty was to have ten peanuts thrown at you which you had to catch in your mouth. I leapt about feeling idiotic but at the same time determined. I laughed, snarled, hiccoughed, biting on hands, nuts, air. Then I drank another tumbler of wine.

Recollections of how the game proceeded are vague. The happy, silly faces in the candlelight were flushed, the voices loud. I remember at one point tying my legs in a knot, an action nobody could repeat except Jorges, who came to join us then. He not only knotted his legs but stood on his head at the same time, skull cushioned by his extraordinary hair. I studied with rapt attention the vision of him grinning upside-down. I was not sure whether it was he or I who was the wrong way up. I threw a peanut and it bounced off his foreign little bump of navel. The brown skin creased and shook as he righted himself, laughing at the same time. He crouched beside me, shovelling peanuts into his wide mouth and occasionally popping one into mine. My mouth would not always shut when I meant it to and sometimes the peanuts fell out.

'You all right, little Queen?' he asked.

'Fine,' I said emphatically,' but I mustn't miss the boat tomorrow.'

'Where are you going?'

'Going on the boat, with Beverly.'

A thought struck: 'Where is Beverly?' I felt around with my hands and encountered Jorges' knee.

'Sorry. Oh, there she is'.

Beverly was leaning up against a bed-frame.

I smiled at Jorges and said confidingly, 'You know, Jorges, I only came to this party because of the *Son et Lumière*.'

I described it to him, waving my arms in the air to show the sweep of the arc-light beams. He shook his head and grinned and grinned.

'You were out there all by yourself?'

'No,' I said, 'with Beverly.'

There was an upheaval on the other side of the crate. Fred and one of the others were attempting to lift the man who had fallen unconscious again. A candle and one of the wine bottles, now empty, crashed to the floor. Jorges started to sweep up the broken glass with a piece of paper.

Thinking I might help him, I got to my feet. The room slid round and round and up and down. It was not unpleasant but I wished it would stop. I made an almighty effort and it wound to a halt, only to start sliding the other way. Fred's form wavered before me and I felt my head whack into some part of her big soft body as I fell.

'You know what?' I heard her say, slurred and warm, 'I reckon this kid's about fifteen years old.'

'I'm bloody not!' I retorted and slid into cosy oblivion, the shocks of the last few days blissfully, if only temporarily, expunged.

Like a ponderous daddy-long-legs the morning light climbed over my eyelids, but it did not react when I tried to swat it away. My mind groped, as it always did on waking, for the bones of the current plan. Israel via Crete and Turkey, that was it. On a boat. Today. Slowly awakening physical sensation pulled me back to the immediate. There was dust itching inside my nostrils and my

142

throat was dry as a husk. A peanut husk. It clicked. That ridiculous party.

Whose were those basso profundo snores so close by? Warily I opened one eye. And blinked. Bone and blubber like a beached whale, Fred lay sprawled across the three-legged bed. The snores were hers. From beneath her protruded an assortment of arms and legs and heads. Stringbean's head rested on one huge thigh, his thin fuzz of hair catching the sunlight that streamed down the stone steps. Brick dust rolled in the air. There was no sign of Jorges.

I looked at my own bedding arrangements. Hogging the whole of the only other bed alone, I was resting on a large striped poncho and my legs were modestly covered with a towel. Beverly was nowhere to be seen. Alarmed, I sat up and stared round the room. I hung over the side of the bed, searching, and remained hanging there. Jorges was underneath.

He lay straight as a ramrod on the stone floor, his head pillowed by his guitar. Looped across his feet were two straps, one belonging to Beverly and the other to a red backpack. But it was his eyes that riveted me. Without any doubt he was asleep, but his eyes were open. In their great wide-apart sockets they were rolled right up so that only the whites showed. With his negroid lips fleered back from his teeth and the curved bladed knife I saw resting under one hand, he looked like some devilish djinn. Just then his eyes closed for a moment and reopened, irises in place. He blinked at my face hanging down.

'Hi, little Queen. Did you sleep OK?'

'Very well, thank you. Jorges, tell me, was I very drunk last night?'

'In my opinion, which I would not hold to be of any great value, you were about as half-assed as anyone I've ever seen. I guess you're not accustomed to drinking retsina and ouzo.'

'That's true.'

'What time does your boat go?'

'Five o'clock.'

'Do you like cherries?'

143

'Yes.'

'Would you like to go with me to Ethiopia?'

'I don't know.'

The others showed no signs of stirring. I got up and splashed water from Harold over my face.

'By the way,' said Jorges, emerging from the dust, 'I want you to meet a friend of mine' – he pointed to the red backpack – 'Max.' I introduced him to Beverly and Harold and for once gave my real name, but he gave me a new one. 'Ivan,' he said, 'I think I'll call you Ivan.'

I spent the day with Jorges and Max on the Acropolis. Under the great white furrowed columns we sat in the sun and ate fat black cherries. Jorges seemed always to be smiling, the whites of his eyes and his perfect teeth shining. I showed him the bag Uschi had given me and watched as he sliced the grapefruit in two with his curved knife, using the tip delicately to free the segments.

'You coming to Ethiopia, then?'

'I'm going to Israel to work on one of those kibbutz places. I've run out of money.'

He considered, looking up at the sky and twisting the few dark hairs on his chin.

'Lemme see. Israel's kind of on the way. I could drop by and see if you'd changed your mind.'

'Mmn,' I said, not really believing him.

In the afternoon we dozed, Max and Beverly beside us, back to back against a column in the shade.

We said goodbye in Syntagma Square, Jorges executing a strange little bow, slender brown legs held straight together, shoulders stiff. Then he shook back his fir cone ringlets, smiled wide and departed. Beverly and I made our way down to the port alone once more.

Chapter Nine

The boat was overcrowded. I took up a firm position with my back against a great white-painted funnel and did not budge until we were past Crete. During the night I had plenty of time to regret my exclusivity. I had parked myself against the foghorn.

'Phwhaaaaaaaaargh!'

Silence for a moment. Just enough time for the hair to lie flat on my head after the first shock. Then again: 'Phwhaaaaaaaaargh!'

I lost count of how many times this happened. After a while the raw, gormless idiocy of the sound became familiar, welcome even. When morning came I was hardly well slept but felt strangely refreshed, as though everything in me had been thoroughly shaken up and then clicked quietly back into place. For breakfast I took a swig from Harold, and cracked another packet of Uschi's biscuits. I thought of Jorges and practised his djinn's grin. I did not imagine I would see him again.

Crete passed; the ferry ploughed on towards Rhodes. Abandoning the foghorn for a while, I made my way forward, and commandeered a giant coil of rope. A warm breeze blew wrinkles over the sea's fine skin and I drowsed, watching the skyline through slitted eyes and noting in the distance islands like lopped fangs appearing whenever the ferry rose on the highest point of a wave.

Without brooding on what had happened, I was aware that in a short space of time I had been the object of not one, but two extremes of human behaviour: the first remarkable for its ugliness, the second for its beauty. And resilient as my sixteen-year-old body and psyche were, the example of rare selflessness shown by Costas and Uschi occurring almost immediately after that contrastingly horrible event seemed in a way to cancel it out. It had to. I could not live with the memory of the rape, so, consciously or otherwise, I decided to live without it. It had not happened. It did not exist.

I was unaware then of how deep the bruise had gone; how

there are some things the body, if not the mind, can never forget.

At noon stark outlines of long hills and abrupt cliffs came into view; colours of hot earth, dust-yellow to terracotta, stippled with the misty grey of olive trees and the coarse green of salt-bitten scrub. We passed cliff faces with curved horizontal striations white as bleached bone and tall slabs of rust-orange stone scored with vertical lines neat as cross-section diagrams.

But my first hours in Turkey were coloured black. Stinking, viscous, clinging black.

It was hot, and welcoming the chance of an all-over wash I walked round to the far side of the tiny harbour where we moored and plunged feet first into the dark, choppy water. I landed heavily, straight on a squid.

Slime from a jet-shot stream rose in bubbles like farts in a bath and my feet churned deliriously. I flailed, gasping, and face squeezed lemon-tight, heedless of grazes, pulled myself clear. There was laughter. Men with narrow heads and elegant ankles curled their lips; pantalooned women hid titters behind bauble-tinkling scarves. I grabbed Beverly and scrambled clumsily over pitted shelves of rock to find another bay away from mocking eyes.

The bay I found was beautiful. Thyme grew wild in prickly abundance at the feet of carob trees and bands of wet weed, translucent and rubbery, gave off a sweet tang banishing the last of the ink-sac fumes.

I trod with clean, newly dusted feet among the fallen carobs and rustling herbs and stood for a long time watching a busy task force of ants striving with all their puny strength to manoeuvre the large, husklike carcass of a cricket. I wanted to know where they were taking it and when they got it there, what happened next. I never found out, for my dreamy observations were shattered by an all too familiar sound.

'Phwhaaaaaaaaargh!'

Like an old ewe gone hoarse calling for its lamb, the foghorn blared again, measuring the distance between me and it, the distance between a sea lane and the land. And for all that I might halloo and scramble, for all that I might dart and gibber and wave my arms, the ferry ploughed on aloof, first past, then gradually away, away, averted portholes winking in the sun.

I dashed at a rock-hopping run all the way back to the harbour. Beside the bollard where the ferry had been tied a glinty-toothed Turk stood picking warts on the palm of his hand. He flicked a sideways glance at me as I approached. It was a look I had seen before, casual, impenetrably foreign, registering only the fact that I was female. I changed direction, heading towards the harbour buildings. A group of children, silent and watchful as little gargoyles, stared after me.

The harbour office was a three-sided shack. Inside, a desk curved under the weight of a pair of uniformed legs. Their owner lounged back on a tipped chair, eyes half closed. Three other men were bent over a board game at a makeshift table. Lizardlike, the eyes of the uniformed man gazed through me. I dreaded the moment when the look would change and become that alien, bed-flesh-appraising stare. They would all look at me like that as soon as I spoke. Unable to face it, I walked on. The next boat was due in a week.

It was evening by the time I got back to the carob tree bay. I climbed on to a shelf of rock I had noticed before which jutted over the water just beyond the reach of the waves and curved into an anonymous roll of shadow against the cliff. Rolling out my sleeping-bag as a mattress I lay down, knife held tightly in my left hand. It was good to feel the big heart of the sea beating close by.

I might have stayed the whole week in the bay had it not been for the little girl who arrived on the second day. I was up in the scrub plundering the branches of a wild fig tree when I heard voices and saw a boat round the rocks into the bay. It stopped long enough to allow a small, bundled-up figure to jump ashore. Then the old man in the rowing seat pulled away. The small figure dragged its bundles into the shade of my rock shelf.

From my concealed eyrie I had a clear view of the beach. After a little while the child emerged from the shade and stood inspecting the rocks below the water. One small toffee-brown hand twitched impatiently on a long stick.

Squatting suddenly, she dived the stick into the water and prodded fiercely. There was a light grunt of satisfaction as her hand, covered with a cloth, swooped down to catch whatever she had poked free. A small pyramid of black prickly objects grew at her side. Sea urchins. When she had decided there were enough, she drew the four corners of the cloth into a hobo parcel and carried it, swinging, to where the rest of her things lay. She made a small fire and round the edge of it arranged four or five thin aubergines. The urchins sat on top, right in the flame.

One of my legs was cramped and I stirred, inadvertently sending a small avalanche of scree down the slope. The child's head swivelled on her neck like an owl's and she looked straight up at me, hands frozen in the act of peeling an aubergine. As I stood up slowly she leapt to her feet grabbing all her bundles.

'Don't go away,' I called.

But she had started to run.

She fled left and right, staggering to where the rocks began at both ends of the bay. Plum-coloured rags trailed from her, scarves and charred urchins scattered in her wake. She nearly fell under her load.

'Wait, don't run away!'

At last she stopped, panting through a gaping mouth, backed up and shrinking against the ledge where Beverly lay. Her arms clutched her possessions, eyes darting to the items which had fallen. I approached slowly and reached behind her for Beverly. As my arms went up the child cringed, hissing like a cat. Kneeling, I opened Beverly's front pocket and brought out a raisin bun, gift of one of the ferry's galley stewards. I offered it on an open palm as though to an animal. While her eyes, unblinking, stayed fixed on mine, one hand crept forward. In a flash the bun had disappeared among the ragged folds of her dress. Her pupils, unwavering, were huge.

I tapped my chest and said, 'Lucy. My name is Lucy.' Then I pointed at her, making a question of my eyebrows. Unwillingly her hand retrieved the bun.

'Elucy,' she murmured and offered it back.

'No, no!' I laughed, trying again with the name. She relaxed a little and hunkered down, placing the largest bundle beside her. I saw now with a shock that it was alive. No wonder it had been a struggle for her to run. Seeing me looking at the bundle, her face assumed a grown-up, world-weary expression. With a brisk movement she flipped back the piece of cloth covering its head. I caught my breath.

It was a tiny thing, a baby, and its features were almost invisible under an oozing crust of sores. Its mouth hung open but no sound came out. Inside the voluminous wrapping some part of it moved and the little girl replaced the shading cloth and sat back hugging her knees.

By now she had lost much of her fear. While I collected the scattered urchins, she poked up the ruined fire. We sat down side by side and from time to time one of us added a stick to the flames. When I went out into the sun to gather more wood she tut-tutted like a granny and loosened one of the baby's rags, indicating I should wear it on my head. Recoiling, I fetched my own scarf but when I put it on she frowned. It was incorrectly tied. I knelt for her to do it and the feel of her sure little fingers busily knotting and smoothing was very sweet. I gave her the last bun out of Beverly and in exchange she peeled me a roast aubergine. The baby lay between us, mute, unstirring, as if it might already be dead.

When the old man came to fetch the children, I went with them. The little girl spoke to him, eyes darting to me, and he nodded once, pulled a ribbon of phlegm from his throat with two fingers and rowed us out of the bay.

The journey was dreamlike and slow. The sea, deep turquoise with long indigo shadows as the afternoon smudged to evening, was very still. Only dark wave stains on white rocks revealed a sighing movement deep down. Heavy drops like silver oil ran off the old man's oars.

I was wondering if there was still far to go when the little girl gave a wriggle and waved towards a cluster of lights on the shore. 'Ooch Als,' she said. This was her village.

The glances that came my way at first were sharp; dark eyes raking from behind wheezing hurricane lamps, faces covered and turned away. But everywhere I went the little girl came too, shrill, exclaiming, chasing a shy welcome from the goaty-smelling shadows. Beverly was taken from me and placed on a cot in a hut whose roof showed every star in the sky. The baby was settled in the same room, bundled and dumb, and the little girl stroked a mat on the floor to show that this was where she slept.

Outside there were fires, and people were gathering on a rickety jetty. I was led to the cooking area where a lamp was held up proudly to show five barnacled shellfish tethered to a post. When jabbed with a stick they marched without moving. Their shells were mud brown and studded with blistered eruptions, reminding me of the baby's face. Further on I was shown a lamb, newly killed, hanging upside-down, and a bucket of fish cool under salt and weeds. In a corner a woman with cheeks as hairy as pig's ears patted ovals of dough between her hands. When I rubbed my stomach she ducked and bounced madly, hairy jowls flapping.

We sat late on the jetty, food appearing in slow relays. The men were served first. Women moved softly outside the light and children sat crosslegged on the wooden floor, scraps from their fingers falling between the planks straight into the mouths of tiny fish which glimmered in the water below. The fresh lamb seemed barely touched by the flame, tasting of smoke and mild, milky blood. The bread was spongy and warm, ballast against the fiery chillies that were the only vegetable. My tea was scented with half a stem of mint.

When I went to bed three small faces propped on hands watched me from a cot opposite. Their eyes and fingernails, more pinpoints of light among the stars, were the last things I saw before I slept.

Ooch Als. It meant Three Mouths, and I learned next day why the village had this name. Climbing at dawn to the crumbled honeycomb of a former citadel, I saw the sunrise gild the nipples of matching hills on two islets no more than half a mile from the shore. Channels on either side and one between the islets made three distinct approaches to the village from the sea: three mouths.

150

Turning round to explore further inland, I saw that I was not alone. Daylight gave mass to the outlines of shrouded figures lying on the cracked and potholed stage of an amphitheatre. One by one they stirred and sat up, hooded profiles like crows amid the rubble, centuries late for pickings from the last show. They hawked and spat and when they saw me, smiled. Stumbling sleepily past to get their first glass of tea in the village below, they pressed sprigs of thyme and carob pods into my hands.

I thought of letting the next ferry pass, for I liked Ooch Als. But the people were poor and I was an extra mouth they did not need. From the walls of the ruin I saw through the skimpy stick and leaf canopies of their homes and felt the coarse, precarious texture of their lives, a universe away from the standards of a child brought up in Richmond-upon-Thames. Standing by a wall draped with hanging gourds, breathing in air heady with the fermentation of trampled figs, I felt the incongruity of my own presence. Being a fly on the wall was a luxury these people would never know.

Twice I went out in the fishing boat and saw green-stained tombs hewn into the hills, and shorelines dotted with fat little sarcophagi. Ooch Als had its own minarets and a taped muezzin whose dust-wrecked voice scraped into the still hours like a nail on a blackboard. Once I looked over the side of the boat and saw the walls and corridors of a sunken city. Or was it that the water had risen? Ooch Als had known other patterns of sea and land.

I did not have to ask for a lift when the day came to return to the harbour. The women gathered on the jetty to see me off in the fishing boat and the little girl pushed her way to the front bundled up as on the first day. I still had not learned her name but knew now that the sick baby was her brother. The mother was dead, a fact conveyed through a chillingly dispassionate pantomime of death in labour. I was waiting for the little girl to join me in the boat when, without warning, she leaned forward, opened Beverly and popped the baby inside. Her hands pulled the drawstrings neatly. There was silence as they all watched to see what I would do.

At first I tried to make a joke of it, removing the baby with a creaky laugh and holding it out to the little girl. Expressionlessly, she took it from me and put it straight back, retying the strings. With gestures to breasts, heart and arms she made it clear that I was to be its new mother. Was this what she had hoped all along? The baby's face-covering had slipped and between swollen flesh and scabs flies were trying to squeeze under its eyelids. Unthinkingly, I brushed them away and at once there was a satisfied muttering among the women. Clumsily my fingers grappled with the knotted string and I lifted the small, silent body again and held it out to each of them in turn.

'I can't,' I said hopelessly, 'I can't. . .'

For hours, it seemed, they just watched. Then at last my anguish was acknowledged and an old woman took the baby from my arms. But the little girl cried out angrily and ground her fists into her eyes. Even so, as the old man made to cast off she stepped into the boat. I had let her down but was still her special charge.

I watched the coast all the way back to the harbour but saw nothing. All I could think of was the baby. At the carob tree bay the little girl shot me a glance but would not look again when I tried to talk. I knew that even if she could understand my words, nothing I could say would alter the fact that by refusing to shoulder the burden of the baby I had rejected them all. Their life and their problems were no business of mine. I found myself wishing that the baby had been dead, not dying, then I could have whisked it away and buried it under a stone.

The ferry was there, waiting to take me to another world. Just before the gangplank was raised, I ran down to where the little girl stood, pinched and alien, with a group of harbour children. I took her hand and placed in it the Virgin Stone. Her fingers closed over it and, expressionlessly, she pulled from her sleeve a gauze headsquare. It was new and white with flat gold disks sewn round the hem.

The ferry was about to leave, someone was shouting. Wrenching my old scarf off I knelt down, patting my head. The child understood at once and, tut-tutting like the little virgin grandmother she already was, deftly tied on the new scarf.

'*Tish'koor*,' I said – thank you – the only Turkish word I knew.

'Elucy,' she responded gravely, sum total of her English.

'Phwhaaaaaaaaargh!' A final, stateless wail.
And I was away.

Chapter Ten

At the port of Haifa I was given a choice of kibbutzim. I asked myself what I wanted besides a roof over my head and food.

'Are there any near water?'

In Scotland I had had the sea; in Richmond, the river. If I was going to stay here a while, I would like to re-establish links with that safe, non-human thread in my life.

'Galilee,' was the quick answer and I was put on a bus for Tiberias.

For a week I worked in the kibbutz kitchens swabbing floors and scrubbing out huge pots stained green with avocado. Alongside me, brown Swedish arms stacked crates of yoghurt, Australian accents twanged in syncopation with pinging cutlery, and sinuous Swiss thighs canoodled with hairy Canadian knees behind the fridge door. After work, mosquito screens were fastened in the communal cabins, guitars came out and American voices led the way in sing-songs that went on almost until it was time for the field workers to change into a fresh pair of shorts for the day. 'Good vibes' were everywhere; high spirits, fun times, the Beach Boys, John Lennon and *The Way of Zen*. I hovered awkwardly on the periphery, unable to pick up on the good vibes, and when a soldier came down from a *moshav* on the Golan Heights in search of volunteers, I went. The memory I refused to acknowledge was like an invisible barrier, cutting me off from my carefree cosmopolitan peers.

Ramat Hagolan, the Golan Heights. There was no road up to

153

moshav Ramot in those days, just a broad ribbon of sandy dirt crisscrossed by the tracks of canvas-covered army trucks and small, beetley tanks. Ploughing upwards through the dust, we stopped twice to pick up soldiers, one with a motorbike which was tossed into the truck and sat between me and him like a desk.

'You speak Hebrew?' he asked, in Hebrew. I recognized the phrase and shook my head. He switched to English.

'Stay long enough and you will learn.' He had a brown, handsome face and spiky black hair made matt by the dust. I had no idea if I would stay one week or one year.

'Is that your boyfriend?' asked the soldier, pointing to another volunteer.

'No.'

'Then maybe you will stay forever. Some of us are looking for wives!'

There was laughter and I found myself smiling too.

'Ramot,' he said, poking aside a canvas flap with his gun so I could see out, 'is a good place.'

On a hill ahead stood a cluster of red-painted triangles like pieces of Toblerone. Each one was a solid little house with an area of sand in front raked clean and clothes flapping on washing-lines in the yards. There were pot plants in the windows and a family of kittens played in the sun. The only things that gave away the vulnerable position of the *moshav* were the machine-gun placements at intervals beyond the washing-lines, and instead of hedges, low walls of sandbags around each house.

A girl soldier waved as the truck came in.

'Shalom! Shalom!'

This was Ayelet, who would show me around.

'Where are you from? What is your name?'

The questions I had been asked so many times since leaving Richmond.

'Ivan,' I said, sticking to the name Jorges had given me, 'from Scotland.'

'Well, Ivan, welcome to Ramot. We hope you will stay a long time.'

154

And I would have, if Cape Sounion had not gone before.

Day began at 3.30 a.m. when Uri, the foreman, padded across from his room at the top of our Toblerone house and shook my big toe. Lights would pop on all over the *moshav*, blocking out the grey cut-out forms of guards who shifted softly at their posts all night, silhouettes of guns pricking up over their shoulders like extra limbs. Sometimes, Ayelet told me, she smuggled one of the kittens on guard duty and kept it in her pocket to warm her hands when the night was cold.

At 3.45 a.m. the field workers assembled in the communal kitchen. We helped ourselves to strong black coffee from Thermos jugs and chipped sticky fistfuls of halva off a giant block in the fridge. At four our transport was ready. Ten bodies fitted into the trailer and the other five ranged themselves on the tractor: two perched on each massive mudguard and one behind the driver on the tow bar. Everyone held tight to something and the sleepy bodies bounced and thudded into one another as we lurched over the rough half mile to the fields. Galilee was quiet, a great grey lake lit in one place only by a thin rippled shaft from the moon. The hills of Ramat Hagolan crowded a blurred skyline, hiding the border not far away.

My first job was to help with irrigation. Lines of black hose-pipe, punctured at strategic intervals, wound through the sloping fields like veins. Stooping and straightening, soft-limbed puppets in the granular light, we lifted and repositioned the pipes, sandalled toes clogging with mud which would dry and crumble off soon after the sun rose. With the first breath of heat, kibbutznik hats popped out over brown faces like colourful pods, and strong-smelling insect repellent was passed along the lines. Uri, always smiling, directed operations without ever seeming to give an order. His short, compact figure moved about dispensing tenderness and enthusiasm to one and all. 'Come!' he would say persuasively when my hoe slipped inaccurately among roots and weeds, and the same 'Come!' to a watermelon as he gently turned it so that its pale whale's belly greened evenly in the sun. At nine o'clock, with the first sweat of the day running down our backs, we downed tools and headed back to the *moshav* for

155

breakfast. The small area of cultivation, growing daily, stood out like a green flag against the ochre and grey-blue of sand and sea.

Breakfast was a feast. Plates were filled and emptied and filled again. Health glistened from eyes and lips and in the laughter that bounded round the room. I sat with Ayelet and did not care that I could not understand all the jokes. I understood the language of hard work, hard play, determination and pride – it was the same language Richard spoke.

The second half of the morning was the most demanding, sweating away in the fields until the blissful moment when Uri cried 'OK!', and we all scrambled aboard the tractor to be dropped in a laughing, dust-blinded body right in the sea of Galilee. We played catch with one of the heavy round water-melons until somebody dropped it, whereupon it was pounced on and split. Earth-cracked hands clutched bottle-green rinds and lollypop-red juice dribbled down laughing chins.

'One day,' said Uri, waving a hand to encompass the whole of Ramat Hagolan, 'all this land is going to be green.'

I believed him.

'And there will be many houses at Ramot and many children.'

And hopefully, I added silently, no need for guards.

The knowledge that this fledgling community was launching itself in the face of constant threat left a deep impression. It made the struggles of my own world – truancy, family divisions, search-ing for causes – seem like idle self-indulgences, things for which these people would have no time. Here the issues were simple and profound: the land that was defended with blood was cher-ished with both hoe and soul.

But for all that I was drawn to the spirit of the *moshav* and swept up in the hard work and hard play, I could not ignore the messages of my own body. My period was nine weeks late.

Tel Aviv: dry heat, broad streets, girls with proud bodies, boys with proud eyes. I started my search on Ben Yehuda but knew as I wandered with Beverly past bright American-style cafés and the store fronts with famous names – Levi, Helena Rubinstein – that

156

I would not find what I needed here. What was Hebrew for gynaecologist anyway? And who could I ask?

Two months on the *moshav* had rounded out the hollows left by Greece and Turkey. I was tanned, skin and hair glowing, a picture of health. But my glowing legs dragged because inside I saw a dark shape slowly bloating like a tick in my womb. Ayelet thought I had gone quiet because it was 'that time'. She had given me a packet of sanitary towels. Uri had put an arm round me and tickled my feet to make me smile. But I could not smile and I could not tell anyone, so I left.

A good-looking soldier eating a pastry outside a café patted a chair for me to join him. When I shook my head he smiled anyway. I had never met men so friendly in their flirting as the *szabres*. Don't look at me, I thought. I do not want to see or be seen until this stain is removed.

I left Ben Yehuda for smaller streets and in a chemist's asked where I might find a doctor. The dispenser, an old man with white hair fluffed round his head in a halo, said kindly, 'There are many doctors in this city. What is the trouble?'

I looked without seeing at his cabinets. *I was raped. I think I am pregnant.* No.

'I have a headache.'

He gave me two aspirin – free – and two more wrapped in a piece of paper to take away.

'Stay out of the sun,' he said.

All afternoon I searched, and at last I found, on Rehov C—, a garden full of flowering cacti with a white plaque on the wall. Dr C. B. Wiedkowitz, Gynaecologist. I hid Beverly under a cactus and followed white arrows round to a door. A speaking-grille crackled when I rang and a man's voice said, 'Ken?'

'Excuse me, are you a doctor? I'm sorry, I don't speak Hebrew.'

'I am the doctor, yes, but it is not my hours. Come back after six o'clock and you can make an appointment.'

The speaker crackled off. An appointment. God. That could mean a week. Even the hour until six o'clock seemed too much.

Half a dozen houses on there was another white plaque, another name full of W's and Z's. A woman in a white coat answered the door. She looked me up and down out of heavily bagged eyes, said 'Vait' shortly, and disappeared.

It was hot on the doorstep and the sky, jigsawed by television aerials, seemed a very long way away. There were red flowers with black tongues drooping over the wall where Beverly was hidden. The woman came back.

'The doctor is busy. You are sick or vot?'

'Not sick, I ... I ... I ...'

'A baby or vot?'

'That's it. I'm afraid I ...'

'All right he vill see you. Vait zere.'

She was like something out of a bad film.

There were three chairs in the waiting-room. No magazines. Feet clomped upstairs and there was a loud masculine sigh. My thighs felt sticky on the plastic-covered chair, reminding me of the white car. I wished I had a long skirt, a sack to cover me to the ground. The woman's face appeared.

'Zis vay.'

The doctor's back was to me as I entered the surgery: broad, white-coated, sleeves rolled tightly over dumpy forearms. He was drying his hands on a towel.

'So,' he said, tossing the towel in a crumple on the draining-board, 'you think you are pregnant, yes?'

'Yes.'

He had round, rimless glasses which distorted the shape of his eyes. Wiry tufts of hair stood out around a bald crown. When he spoke again I saw that his teeth, set deep in a thin, mobile mouth, were evenly grey.

'You are what age?'

'Sixteen.'

'Nationality?'

'British.'

'Remove your lower garments and sit on that chair.'

The chair was large, like a dentist's, mounted on a solid metal swivel. Seat, back and arms were upholstered in green leather. The doctor tore a piece of paper off a white roll and spread it on

158

the seat before I sat down. Then he lowered the back so that I was lying almost flat.

'When was your last period?'

He made tut-tutting sounds when I told him, plump palms turning and pressing on my belly.

'You have had sickness?'

'I do feel sick sometimes.'

There was a rattling noise as he wheeled some sort of apparatus in front of the chair.

'Put your feet here.'

The apparatus was a tubular frame with two wide-apart stirrups on chains. The doctor, fingers looking like vacuum-packed meat in a transparent glove, waited, hand raised, while I inserted first one foot then the other into the stirrups. My knees flopped apart in the air and I concentrated on a spider's web of cracks beside the light fitting.

'Breathe deeply. This does not hurt.'

Nail-less fingers slid in. Soft slugs. A hand on my belly pushed down.

'Breathe!'

I gulped and my eyes rolled off the light fitting on to his bald crown where brown irregular moles merged together like amoeba. The hand slid out.

'Hmm hmm, well, something, I think.'

What? *Was I?*

'We will do a urine test. Step down.'

The chains on the stirrups danced as I withdrew my feet.

'Come for the result day after tomorrow. Goodbye.'

And within minutes I was on the doorstep again, looking at the red flowers with black tongues.

At six I went back to Dr Wiedkowitz, and when I explained what I had come about he agreed to see me straight away. I could not wait until the day after tomorrow.

His surgery was larger than the other, the gloves he wore thicker, but the chair was the same. He fired questions in a flat tone.

'Do you think you have venereal disease?'

159

I had not thought of that.

'I don't know.'

'Have you ever had an abortion?'

A-baw-tion. He made it sound very boring.

'No. I've never been pregnant.'

He was doing things with instruments on a trolley.

'You mean never until now.'

Oh God. I winced as cold metal touched my vagina and a long, rounded snout pushed in. There was a winding sound and the snout expanded into a thick cylinder. I pressed my fists to my eyes, saw a black tick, petals and tongues.

'Keep still.'

He went away for a minute, leaving the metal thing inside. It hung, dragging down at the opening, pressing up near the womb. When he came back he straightened it and put some other surgical instrument inside.

'I am taking a smear to test for infection. Might be problems, you know.'

This ceiling was magnolia and did not have cracks.

'Problems?' I said to it.

'Well, it depends' – he was busy now with pincers and cotton-wool – 'if you have disease and you go on with the pregnancy, might be problems. That's all.'

This business about disease flapped across my mind meaninglessly like a bat in fog.

'Why should I have disease?'

His answer was swift.

'Why shouldn't you?' He gave a grim little chuckle. 'If you can catch a baby you can catch disease! I don't think you are married, no?'

There was no need for an answer. The thick cylinder came out from between my legs with a sucking sound.

'You can get dressed now.'

While I pulled on my shorts – back to him – I said 'Do you do . . . abortions, here?'

He had stripped off the gloves and was washing his hands. Tel Aviv had become for me a white-coated figure washing its hands.

'So the father does not want to marry you, heh?' It was as though he were talking to himself. 'Yes, well, these things happen quite a lot nowadays and sometimes we can help and sometimes we cannot. It depends.'

Everything, I thought, depends. He went on chatting to himself at the basin.

'It is a pity you did not come earlier. It is not so easy at this stage.'

But can you do it? I did not say it aloud.

'... And time, you know, is not cheap. But of course you want it to be safe. Sure, I could promise you that. Quick, too.'

'When?'

'It would have to be before next week,' he said, because he was going away. Then he mentioned a sum. It was in lire. Hundreds. It did not matter to me whether it was one hundred or five. I had none.

'So come back and let me know.'

As he showed me out he pointed to the white plaque.

'By the way, that is not my name.'

I walked back towards Ben Yehuda and the bright American-style cafés. As I passed the spot where the smiling soldier had been I realized that my back, my arms were empty. Beverly was still under a cactus on Rehov C—. I went back to fetch her and knew that was the last time I would enter that garden.

Evening in Yafo: Jaffa, where the oranges get their stamp. People came up here for the view in the daytime, sat in cars at the top of the cliff and watched the sea beyond ancient walls. The walls looked golden and the water sparkling clean from here. In the daytime, that was. It was all glimmer and blackness now, slits and rectangles of light marking the streets lower down. I should go back down, try harder. I was only half drunk and it had failed, so far.

There were groups of young people around, generous with bottles of Maccabee beer. But beer was no good. All the old wives' tales spoke of the hard stuff. Gin and hot baths, shocks, falls, thumps in the gut. Israelis did not seem to go in for gin but there was brandy in the bars. Cheap stuff in straight bottles. Half a bottle should be enough.

But I got a whole one. Walked in and swiped it off the bar. In Beverly in a flash and me gone. A fat woman in a polka-dotted pinnie waddled out to serve the footsteps she had heard too late. Me plastered like a slap of bird dirt against the window of a shop two doors away. Beverly another lumpy outline beside a pile of litter bags. I drank before I ran.

Beside a river, I don't know where. Kneeling, retching, under a big fat moon. Song coming out of a window: something about another big fat moon and 'you won't regret it'.

Don't be sick.

Benches in the moonlight under trees. An Arab body on one, shrouded like at Ooch Als. Asleep or dead, been there years. I am not afraid. Break this bottle and twist it through the leather of his skin if he says one word. Black tick going to break away in red petals, *please* . . .

Oh God, give me arms around.

Oh God, make the black tick let go.

Leaning against the trunk of a tree. Smell of shit. Moonlight over the Arab's bare feet, cracked like elephant hide. Will it make a noise when it happens, suction breaking or a crunchy rip like Velcro? Laugh! Laugh!

Oh God, help me find the Greek. Stake him out on the same ground. Choke his thick fish mouth with the burst belly of the black tick. Grind his dark glasses into his eyes. And laugh, laugh, laugh as the boneless white slug shrivels in the sun.

Sliding down. Clipped grass on the bank cool as a drink. A wrist through Beverly's straps, hand on Harold. Sliding more. Trying-to-stay-open eyelids crimping off the moon like pinking shears. To unpeel, aeons later, on the stapled mesh of a litter basket and a sunlit close-up of a green stem tickling my nose.

I got up and walked. There are streets on the edges of towns that go on for miles. My head weighed and bobbed like an extra Beverly, a nugget of nausea knocking around to one side. But

I was hungry. If I could pinch a bottle of brandy I could do the same with a loaf of bread. Nearer into town there would be bakeries.

Nearer into town there was a sack of kittens in the road. Two were spilled out, flattened to bloody gloves. A third, covered by the sack, still moved. A car rolled by, oblivious, droning. More cars came. I stood on the kerb and watched as though five miles outside the scene. Then the kitten mewed. It was not a piteous sound but a small, strident announcement: *I am alive.* A head appeared, blind, swaying, four wobbling legs and a damp striped tail like an erect rudder pointing straight to the sky. The cry again, pale, tiny mouth opening wide and yelling yah-boo-sucks and here-I-am at the world. I ran out in front of the next car and scooped it up. Hoots and swearing. I swore back and so did the kitten. It settled in my bush-jacket pocket and every time it squawled I said shut up and every time I said shut up it squawled. I loved it for that go-to-hell sound.

We walked. Daytime on the big streets where the cafés had bread on outside tables, night-time in the shadow of half-made buildings by the grubby sea. On the third day I got the address of a clinic where you could sell blood. It was far, right the other side of town, and on the way I tried a dozen times to give the kitten away because I could not feed it and it was getting too lively for my pocket. At the clinic they said, 'You can't bring that animal in here.'

I looked for a place to leave it. When I set it down in a corner it tottered, blaring its small announcement of life, straight towards the road, towards dogs, cars and mashing feet. My life and the black tick's and the kitten's all seemed bound in the same nightmare vision. Moving within that vision I retraced my steps to the tourist part of town, booked into a hotel which did not ask for identification and stroked the kitten on the bed until it fell asleep, purring for the first and last time in its life. With the small red frying-pan I carried in Beverly, I cracked its skull and then held it in a sink full of water for ten minutes, staring through my own eyes in the mirror. I wrapped the wet body in a scarf – the white one with gold disks the little girl had given me in Turkey – and put it in my pocket. I believed that even if I had to wait nine months I would do the same with the legacy of the Greek.

Two hours later, with four words, my whole perception of the future changed.

'You are not pregnant.'

After selling my blood, I had found a place similar to a welfare clinic. I was not supposed to be there as I was not an Israeli citizen but a woman in the long gyny queue, whose child I held while she went to the lavatory, gave me her card. I think the doctor knew I was not Shoshana Ezra but he was kind.

'Why have my periods stopped then?'

He let me down from the straddle chair.

'It sometimes happens – travelling, a change of climate, some tension perhaps.'

It sounded so sensible, the amiable voice of reason dissolving the black-tick-glass-in-the-eyes dream.

I was heading out of the clinic, mind already flying ahead to the range of next possible moves, when a woman's voice, tight with exasperation, made me look round.

'Ee-un, Ee-*un*! Come 'ere when I tell you!'

Breaking into Hebrew she pushed her way through the crowd of waiting women.

'*Slicha, slicha*, excuse me.'

She was dank-haired with flabby arms and a bad complexion, but her figure was handsome and beneath the dank hair, her features strong.

'Ee-*un*!'

The cause of her annoyance was a golden-haired child of about two. He had toddled out of the queue and was quietly peeing under a chair. As she shoved her way towards him her number was called and in a panic she scooped up the child and slapped him so that he began to wail. As she passed me, snarling at him to 'stop that row', I held out my arms.

'Bless you,' she said, '*todah rabah*.'

Thrusting him at me she fought her way back to the front of

the queue. The golden-haired Ian hung limply over my shoulder. Gradually his wails dropped to a gurgle and he dozed.

The woman's name, I learned, was Glynis Weitz. Over coffee, which she insisted on buying me after her appointment, she told the full story of her married life.

'We was both workin' in Selfridges, see. He was in men's shoes and I was in 'aberdashery. He used to pass by me every mornin' and give me this lovely smile and then he'd blush and go all funny. I thought he was ever so nice. All the other blokes were just ordinary nudge-nudge, you know.'

She stirred more sugar into her coffee and went on.

'Anyway, one day I get moved up to 'osiery and he gets to pass my counter three times a day. I knew he was Jewish, and I'd never been out with a foreign bloke before, but I was dyin' for him to ask me. Gawd, though! I had to wait until the Christmas party before he got up the nerve.'

Ian dropped the bagel he had been tearing at and began to whimper.

'Don't you start,' said Glynis, swiping crumbs off his front, 'just when I'm feelin' relaxed for the first time in ages.' She turned back to me.

'So, well, we start going out. You know, the pictures and tea and that, and before I know what's happenin' he asks me to marry him. I dunno, it sounded excitin', movin' to Israel and that.'

She pronounced Israel, Iss-ray-ew.

'I even went Jewish and everythin' – took ages! – and we'd talk about what it was goin' to be like, livin' in Iss-ray-ew. And it *was* all right at the start. You know, everythin' different. But, oh my Gawd, these last two years! Stuck in the flat with the baby, no one to talk me own language to. I'm just about goin' round the bend!'

She finished her coffee with a gulp and looked at the clock on the wall. Moshe was supposed to be collecting her from the clinic.

'I suppose I'd better get back. He'll only be sittin' there with a face long as a coffin. Hey, you couldn't come back for a meal, could you? Save me from another 'orrible dreary evenin' with that long face?'

I said I would love to come and wheeled the pushchair back to the clinic for her.

Moshe was there, the long face unmistakable. It drooped like a wilted flower on a level with dozens of massive, milling female hips. He had saved a chair for Glynis. Her mouth gabbled at him angrily.

'Saved a chair for me? Whatever for? Do you think I want to 'ang around this place after I've been 'ere all afternoon? Anyway, we've got someone comin' 'ome to tea. This is Ann.'

Moshe propelled his long form forward and held out a hand. His eyes, wet and full above sharp cheekbones, were pained.

'I'm so glad you can come,' he said formally.

The Weitzes lived in a sand and tenement suburb forty minutes from the centre of Tel Aviv, and for the next month I lived with them. It was Moshe who, after a violent and apparently unprovoked tirade from Glynis that first evening, took me quietly to one side and asked if I could stay. Glynis, he explained, was going through 'a bad patch' and a bit of company would 'do her the world of good'. He uttered these stock phrases so hopefully and with such a plea in his sad eyes I could not refuse. And from a selfish point of view the prospect of free board and lodgings was attractive. I could use the flat as a base while looking for a paying position and it would also provide a limbo in which to recover my equilibrium after the little madness of the last few days. The doctor on Rehov C— who had lied in order to secure an abortion fee, the drunken retching and the kitten were all part of that madness. Gone now, a curtain across the mind.

But a limbo exists only in the imagination. From the moment of waking each morning to the cry of '*Avateea! Avateea!*' from the watermelon seller who trundled his barrow past outside, to the sigh of relief I breathed each night when poor Glynis's overwrought snarls were muffled by the slamming of her bedroom door, I was involved, physically and emotionally, in the world of the Weitz family.

Sometimes, as I wheeled Ian's squeaking pushchair to and fro

166

on hot suburban streets, I thought how I could have returned to the *moshav* and become involved in that world instead. But there was trouble on the Golan Heights, and one night I woke up soaked in sweat from a nightmare of Ayelet lying mashed at her sentry post like the kittens in the road and all the other *moshavniks* crawling around on their knees crying: '*I am alive! I am alive!*' I closed my eyes to that vision as I had to the reality of Cape Sounion. Another curtain across the mind.

And then Moshe returned very late from work one evening and reported with a blank face that over seventy innocent people had been killed when two Japanese with machine-guns opened fire in the middle of the airport. Glynis, who was always ready to hold forth on the disadvantages of living in 'this bloody country', started to make a scene. For once Moshe turned an indifferent back on her and that night slept in my usual place in the sitting-room while I, unhappily, shared with Glynis. Next day I went into town to put up some of my Young, Strong, Willing and Able adverts. I gave the contact address as the post office as I did not want Glynis to know I was going to abandon her soon.

Returning from that trip to town an incident occurred which showed that beneath a second superficial recovery from the Greek episode lay a mass of dangerously volatile feeling. The curtains I was pulling across my mind must sooner or later be torn down.

I was leaning up against a wall in the central bus station, waiting for a connection to the Weitzes suburb. I had already been there an hour and the heat and squalor of the place made every waiting second swell. A man with a urine stain down his trousers leered at me. I looked away. Loud cries and the smell of fried chickpeas were thick on the air.

In a neighbouring queue there was a convulsive surge forward as their bus arrived and a dithering old man was knocked down. A woman stepped on his head-dress, printing the mark of her heel in the cloth. There were cigarette butts clinging to the sleeves of his *djelebiya* when he sat up, mouth working, after the bus and the charging feet had gone.

A solid rail, the width of one person from the wall, was designed to channel those waiting into an orderly line. As I and two dozen others spied our bus nosing its way towards us, the line bunched up into a bulging worm of humanity. Sweat from alien legs oiled my own and the mesh cap of a wig in front bumped my chin. All around lips were clamped and eyes distant. Then two calm, deliberate hands and a third pressing presence moulded themselves to my hips.

I could not see the man but I could smell him, feel his breath like a sweating palm on my neck. My universe became a wig and two knowing hands. And amid the heat and pulse of that bulging human worm I became a stranger, as calm and methodical as those two hot hands, but cold.

In the carrier-bag I was holding was a notebook, an orange and my small, red-handled knife. Calmly, as the man's hands worked round, on my skin now, under the edge of my shorts, I reached into the bag and worked the serrated blade out of its homemade sheath. The handle tucked snugly into my palm and it was just a matter of waiting now until his hands came round to the front. I knew they would.

The bus, the hands and the third pressing presence nosed on.

Crushed against the wigged woman in front, I could not see. I would have to strike by feel. As the hands made a pouch over my groin and the breath slopped like soup behind my ear, I ran a hand over the back of the topmost hand. All the veins on it, like little pulsing animals, were raised. The man was working hard to finish before the bus, drawing in now, sucked his chance away. Memory of thick Greek fingers, harpoon tip pointing; soft, helpless lips pleading to expel.

The bus doors opened with the opening of the veins. There was a scream, a double jerking, fear smell and blood gushing, as the man ground back against bodies that would not give like the sand that had not given under my burrowing spine.

Small, terrified triumph as I felt the knife drop neatly back into the bag beside notebook and orange. My head turned as the queue, split now, absorbed another scream and a hand lashed under my chin. My scream now and blood from his hand lacing my throat. The woman with the wig raised a raucous female call-to-arms. The man, jaw shaking, clutched hand leaking, struggled to dive under the rail. His ducked head was beaten, women scrabbling in their shopping-bags for vegetable truncheons, while other hands guided me up the steps of the bus and voices, jabbing fingers and a ticket machine punched the air. The bus doors closed as he, lips curled back in panic, gained the other side of the rail and fled. A boy with curly hair in blue trousers who would never touch up a girl in a bus queue again.

Quietly, under cover of the bag on my lap, I fitted the knife back into its sheath. And the curtains, a little tattered now, drew back across my mind.

'So how you doing, little Queen?'

Jorges. And Max, the red backpack. We were in a train on the way to Jerusalem. I beamed at his moony, foreign face as at a white knight. He had found me, tracked me down somehow and we were going to eat cherries together again. I told him I was fine, just fine, because that was the way he made me feel. He sat crosslegged beside me in the carriage and peeled an orange with his big curved knife. His dark body rocked to the rhythm of the train and our knees bumped companionably. Through the segments of orange he sang:

> I rode through the desert on a horse with no name,
> It was good to be out of the rain.
> In the desert you don't remember your name
> Coz there ain't no one for to give you no pain ... ah ... ah.

It was an easy, clip-clopping rhythm and I liked the words.

'Let's go there,' I said, 'into the desert.'

'OK,' he said, heavy ringlets nodding, 'but I want you to let me buy you a dress in Jerusalem first. Because honey, one of these days those zazzy little shorts are going to get you into trouble.'

He dozed against the window after singing the desert song through again and I went on humming it, as the Weitzes, the massacre at Lod airport and the miniature horrors of the bus station receded further with each rocking bend in the tracks.

We passed flat fields of grapefruit and low brown rivers lined with bright weeds and humped with creamy dollops of scum. Everything, the golden weeds, the fruit, the scum, sparkled in the sun. Then all at once we were in the midst of hills blue with bracken and there were terraces of olives and flat-leaved cacti slumped over wire fences like saddlebags.

'..."I rode through the desert on a horse with no name ..." '

Jorges woke up in time to join in the last two verses and see the first white houses of Jerusalem glisten on tanned hills.

We put up in the Arab quarter in a room with one bed and eleven bodies and Jorges lay under the bed – me on it – with knife drawn, arms through Max and Beverly's straps and eyes rolled up, just as he had in Athens, my gentle djinn. He bought me the most beautiful dress in the market, hand-embroidered on black velvet with huge trumpet sleeves. We stocked up Max and Beverly with dates, halva and flat cakes of Arab bread and took the road south to the Gulf of Aquaba. One night at Eilat, the southernmost point of the Negev – and in those days little more than a Coke kiosk and four salt-water showers – then we moved into the Sinai where, deep in the wadis and in the laps of the dusty pink hills, we learned what 'in the desert' really means.

It was there, when sand had clogged my hair into a crazy Struwwelpeter thatch, dug its way under every toenail and filled laughlines I never knew I had, that I revisited the careless days of travelling before Cape Sounion. In the dunes of Nuweiba I conjured for Jorges nights of tramping the rainy autoroutes of France, days of lazing with the lizards in Pompei. And watching the moon rise over the Gulf, paring itself like a white peach from the skin of the sea, I spoke of how I had skipped naked on Corfu. How, scrambling for half a day, I had come upon a cove in the shape of a perfect horseshoe and danced, laughing for the sheer pleasure of being alive, until every inch of virgin sand had been churned.

'I felt like a goddess!'

'How do you know you're not?' grinned Jorges.

I liked the way he said that kind of thing and, in the desert, the idea seemed no more fantastic than the reality around us: raw bones of rock stacked face upon face, fading to pastel ghosts under the eyelid of a whitely sliding sun. I would wake up, a foot away from him on our double sunken mattress of sand – Jorges said that if you scraped away the warm surface-layer snakes were less likely to come – and not know whether it was summer or autumn or sunset or dawn. And not care.

Jorges told me that he was dodging the draft, running from a second stint in Vietnam. He showed me an angry strawberry-coloured stain around his groin, which had to do with days spent up trees in sweats of heat and fear. 'It was awful,' he said once, breaking off from stroking my back, something he liked to do for hours. He seemed to know without being told that I did not want him to go further than that. Somewhere beyond the pink hills, Vietnam, Sounion and Richmond Bridge existed. But it was hard to believe, in the desert.

At a waterhole in the heart of a maze of wadis we met a bedouin called Ayash. He was leading two camels, one of them lame. Jorges, who did not smoke, produced a pack of cigarettes and we sat with Ayash while he smoked three. I could not stop looking at his eyes which shone out from under his white head-dress like a beautiful woman's, rimmed with kohl. I showed how much I liked the effect and Ayash immediately offered to paint my own. We must come with him into the next wadi and meet his brothers.

Jorges and I rode on Ayash's good camel; the lame one carried Max and Beverly; Ayash, the cigarettes. First sight of the Bedouin camp was from above: white and grey figures in the dusk, squatting beside puddles on the cracked wadi floor or lying full length beside dung and palmleaf fires. Camels stood in twos or threes, long legs knobbled like jointed reeds. A young girl watching goats on the wadi bank drew her sleeve across her face as we passed, peeking shyly from the side. A group of boys ran to greet Ayash, rimmed eyes swooping up at us, brown hands vying to be the highest on the camel's rope. Beneath long *djelebiyas* small feet fluttered like birds. After protesting with a belly rumble our camel knelt and we were led away to sit by the biggest fire.

An old man lay sideways in the sand to blow up sparks and made tea in a tiny dented kettle. When it had boiled he lifted the lid, using his sleeve as an oven glove, and threw in four handfuls of sugar. It poured like syrup and glided sweetly over the tongue after the acrid invasion of hashish. I who did not take sugar and did not smoke dope, did both – in the desert.

We are roasted sheep's ribs and soft bread baked in the ashes. My eyes were painted four times until they wept with kohl. I fell asleep with the moon dilating in my brain and in my ears the chant of Jorges teaching the Bedouin the desert song: ' "In the desert, you don't remember your name/Coz there ain't no one for to give you no pain . . . ah . . . ah." '

Two nights later, when Jorges and I were alone again, I awoke to a pain like a red-hot needle in my chin. The same place where four years ago a cut from a wrought-iron gate had throbbed. I must have yelled for we both sat up at the same time and saw the culprit scrabbling away drunkenly over the sand. A scorpion.

'My God, Ivan, did it get you?'

Our voices – we – seemed insignificant in the massive silence of the Sinai.

'Yes,' I said, pointing to the pain, 'here.'

'My God, Ivan!' he gasped again, and dived.

He bit me so hard I screamed. Broad negroid lips welded themselves to my jaw and sucked and sucked until I felt the blood was being vacuumed from my toes. The stars swung round and round as Jorges, releasing me, turned away to spit.

'Shee-it!' he exclaimed weakly. 'Anybody ever tell you you need looking after?'

I have no doubt that Jorges would have looked after me all the way through Ethiopia and beyond, but it was not to be. Perhaps I knew even then that I was destined to go on a different kind of journey, alone.

172

PART THREE

Dangerous Bends

Chapter Eleven

It began on Richmond Bridge. I had made it, hitching without a penny through Greece, Yugoslavia, Austria and Germany, but on Richmond Bridge, I broke down and cried.

Kay was at 309, nothing changed. Marianne, between bouts of sickness, was away on a nursing course. James was at school. When I telephoned Richard he sounded pleased that I was back and asked what the plan was now. I said I did not know and the conversation trailed off. Nothing had changed.

For the next few months I was based in Richmond. I worked in a fish and chip shop during the day and cleaned out a grocery store at night. In between I went for long walks, avoiding sleep as much as possible because when I slept, I dreamed. And when I dreamed, although nothing would have made me admit it, I remembered.

The sleeplessness built up and soon I took to lying down on the ground during my walks and dozing. I found secret places all over the area: churchyards, deserted golf courses, people's back gardens. And nobody ever found me until the day I was so tired – tired of avoiding the past and no longer having any vision of the future – that I lay down right by the side of a motorway. When I woke up that time, I found myself in a mental hospital.

I had thought it would be like the place the Child Guidance people had sent me to after I ran away from school, but it was not. There I had had a room to myself and most of the other inmates were families. We had meals together and meetings. Nobody was really mad.

In this place the heat disturbed me straight away, a heavy,

airless fug which sapped the body and slackened the mind. I went round opening all the windows, none of which would go up more than six inches in case people tried to jump out. The whitecoats watched to see that I did not suddenly go wild and put a fist through. I never meant to, but their watching made me think about it.

I had a diary, a big one with room to draw pictures as well as write. I kept it with a fountain pen in a carrier-bag but was always having to change the bag because the pen made a hole in it and fell out. It was lucky the red-handled knife had not fallen out in Tel Aviv. I could not write during the day because there was no privacy, so the diary came out in the evening and I wrote in bed. Anger would boil in me if the night nurse switched off the light when I was in the middle of a sentence. I asked to be allowed to have one of the individual side rooms and my doctor agreed.

'So you write, do you?'

'Yes.'

'Would you like to show me what you write?'

'No.'

'Do you write about people?'

'Sometimes.'

'Do you write about me?'

'No.'

'Oh.'

But it was worse in the side room. There was a window in the door, a judas. At night when the staff made their rounds the light, a high naked bulb in the ceiling, would snap on without warning and an eye appear at the window. Once this made me so angry, I dragged the wardrobe into the middle of the room, climbed on top and unscrewed the bulb. I was moved back to the main ward.

I spent a lot of time wandering about the grounds where there were beautiful imported trees. Some of the other inmates, confined to wards, would ask me to fetch things from the canteen.

'Get me a packet of fags, love, just ten. Anything'll do.'

'Kitkat and a box of Smarties – 'I'll swap 'em with me tablets.' (Cackle.)

The canteen was in the middle of the grounds. To get there, I walked along the main drive where there was a big notice to visitors saying CAUTION, DANGEROUS BENDS. There were a couple of old men always patrolling the drive. They moved with identical shuffles and one of them sucked constantly on an unlit cigarette. When their paths crossed, one always touched a non-existent cap. The other ignored him.

Some people hung around the canteen all day. There was one woman, very fat, with bright orange lipstick painted on like a clown's mouth and hair dyed boot-polish black. She sat to one side of the canteen steps, legs apart under a short mauve skirt, asking everybody who passed for a cigarette. Once I saw an old man offer her two but he kept them just out of reach, bargaining. When I came back out on to the steps I nearly tripped over them. He was on top of her and she was smiling to herself, holding the cigarettes in one hand. One fat leg with a rheumatism bandage on the knee slapped against the step, up and down. Two white-coats pulled them apart and she screeched because one of the cigarettes got broken.

In those days I wrote in my diary:

Everybody here lives in their own world and they all believe that the world they live in is real and that there is only one real world and it is theirs. I suppose it is like that on the outside too. Sometimes I think reality is just a word.

More often I just jotted down things people did or snippets of conversation.

Overheard Stan talking to one of the other men about a new woman who came in today. She is a nun but in here they have taken away her habit and she has to wear a striped dressing-gown like everybody else.

Stan's friend said, 'Wouldn't mind defrocking her myself.'

'Nah,' said Stan, who is thin and rubs his hands together all the time, 'boobies on her like a coupla poached eggs, you can tell.'

Fat Michael, who often repeats the ends of other people's sentences, was there.

'Poach deggs,' he kept saying, 'poach deggs.'

The nun went twice a week for ECT. When she came back there were sticky patches in her hair where the pads had been and it took her a long time to recognize people again.

Judy asked to borrow my green dress today. She said her boyfriend was coming to take her out for a drink. Somebody gave her some make-up and she appeared at supper with the dress hiked into a mini-skirt halfway up her thighs. There was blue slapped anyhow over her eyes and great dobs of orange foundation on her cheeks. She had tied her hair into flaxen bunches like a little girl. She is about forty-five. She cried when her boyfriend did not turn up.

Botswana Steve has been put in the worst locked ward again. He said he had a flight booked back to his country on the fourteenth of this month. When he was told he had another six months to go he went berserk. It took six whitecoats to hold him down while they gave him an injection. I asked one of the Charge nurses if what he told me about himself is true. It is. In South Africa he was imprisoned as a political agitator of some sort. In the prison he was beaten up and his testicles were crushed with a hammer. When he was released he came to England, but he was caught drunk-driving one night and attacked the policeman who tried to arrest him. They put him in Broadmoor for two years where he had a breakdown, which is why he is here now. He is a half-caste with a beautiful speaking voice and permanently bloodshot eyes.

I used to smuggle in bottles of beer for Steve. He said it was the only thing he had to look forward to. I had a long Afghan coat with the pockets worn through and I could hold two bottles in each hand without being detected. All that came to an end one evening when I went joy-riding with a new boy.

The meals were trundled round to the wards on trolleys pulled by battery-operated trucks. When there were no trolleys on the back, these trucks could go quite fast. They were kept in a shed behind the kitchens, hooked up to chargers. The shed gates were padlocked but the new boy and I could just squeeze underneath. Expertly, he detached the wires from the charging apparatus and tested the thin planks of the gates to find the weakest point.

'Jump on,' he said, and I was reminded of a boy on a motor-bike saying the same thing to me when I was twelve. Again, I jumped on. The boy turned the key – he had stolen one earlier from a porter's pocket – and drove the little truck at the gates like a battering-ram. It went straight through, yard-long splinters flying everywhere. I was amazed that we were not caught on the way out, but there was no one on the drive except Larry the religious maniac who was addressing heaven in his pyjamas. I waved as we flew past and his gentle, startled face broke into a huge smile.

'Mary, Mary, mother of Jesus, you are so beautiful!'

We drove out of the main gate and on to the road. I had the money for Steve's beer in one hand; with the other I clung to the back of the driving seat like on the tractor at the *moshav*. I was standing on the platform where the trolleys were usually hitched, wearing a big black hat as disguise. A car passed at speed, its engine sounding loud beside the low whine of the truck. I noticed out of the corner of my eye that it was a white car and held on more tightly as we swung off the road down an alley. I had a dread of falling off to land in that rolling, tumbling, heart-pounding memory.

There was a pub just across the road as we came out of the alley. Behind it was a yard full of rubbish and cardboard boxes. The boy pulled apart some of the boxes to cover the truck. In the pub he bought me rum and blackcurrant and I bought Steve's beer. The place seemed to be full of faces split in grins. There was a woman with a front tooth missing and a dirty nest of bouffant hair. Hectic veins mapped big cheeks which forced her eyes out of sight every time she laughed. It was easy to see which of the customers came from the bin.

I tapped the boy's elbow after only a few minutes to let him know I was ready to go. Out in the yard he uncovered the truck and handed me a bottle of cider he planned to drink back in the ward after suppertime curfew. I crouched on the platform, cider gripped between my knees, beer wedged behind the seat.

In the alley again he tested the truck at maximum speed and, as we turned back into the road leading up to the hospital gates, told me to hold tight and jump when he gave the word. In the distance white-coated figures milled about near the gates. Four of them were getting into a car. One shouted. They had spotted us. A group of middle-aged patients from an open ward, all dolled up for the evening, cheered as we went by. The boy did not slow down on the main road. The whitecoats, expecting us to swerve, positioned the car ready for pursuit. I ducked down, glad of my hat disguise.

When we were just twenty-five yards or so from the gates and still going at top speed, the whitecoats realized we were not going to turn. Pouring themselves out of the car and yelling to their colleagues who stood by the porter's lodge, they spread themselves into a line across the drive. Shooting by, I caught a glimpse of the porter's eyes alive with excitement as he picked his teeth distractedly with a match. The boy drove straight on as though the line of whitecoats did not exist. They waved their arms and hallooed. In a second we were on top of them, the line cracked in the middle and the whitecoats fell back like skittles into the hedges on either side.

There was a ramp in the drive ahead and the CAUTION, DANGEROUS BENDS sign. As we lurched over the ramp the cider leapt from between my knees and bounded off the truck, smashing foam and glass in our wake.

'OK, get ready!' the boy shouted.

Where the hedge ended, there was a stretch of lawn. We were on it now and racing full tilt at a round flowerbed. I could hear above the truck's whine the jog-jog-jog of whitecoats in pursuit along the drive. I hated the businesslike clomp of their boots.

'Jump!' yelled the boy and as the truck careered through a

forest of rose bushes he leapt clear, on his feet and running as soon as landed, pale-shirted back flecked with earth.

I did not jump but stayed clinging to the back of the driverless truck as it plunged on, back on the grass now and belting towards a thick wall of bushes behind one of the wards. A picture of wrought-iron spirals and elegant fleurs-de-lis flicked across my mind like a slide, and before the snub nose of the truck slammed into a trunk in the heart of the bushes I had flung myself clear and was worming away flat to the earth, beer and the long Afghan coat abandoned.

There was music coming from the ward, a scratched record playing 'Jumping Jack Flash'. The weekly Social was on. Pulling off my hat, I used it to brush the dirt from my dress, then buried it under a clod of earth. The coat, as it was shared by a number of inmates, would not give me away.

By the time I got inside, the music had changed. 'My Boy Lollipop' was jerking out loud and clear. Most of the patients sat on chairs round the edge of the room smoking and drinking orange squash from paper cups. Judy was there in her flaxen bangs. Her eyes lit up when she saw me and she brandished a bag of Dolly Mixture. I chewed some quickly to mask the rum on my breath.

'Let's dance,' I said suddenly to an elderly man sitting next to her. He shambled on to the floor between the few individually jigging bodies and courteously extended a hand. At that moment there was a commotion at the door, voices of whitecoats firing excitedly in Chinese. Keeping my back to the door I accepted the proffered hand and was immediately steered into a rigid ballroom-dancing-school waltz. Staring fixedly over the man's shoulder I saw an old woman with a black eye and six handbags give me a wink and a thumbs up. As the eyes of the men at the door searched the room, I absorbed myself completely in the dance, heart thudding more rapidly than the staccato 'giddy up' of the girl on the record, feet moving in staid accordance with my partner's slow-slow-quick-quick-slow. After a few moments the Chinese voices faded and in my gratitude I saw the end of the record through with the gentle waltzing man and curtseyed when he bowed. Then Judy and I cleared the floor as we danced a wild can-can to 'Honky-Tonk Women'. Everybody clapped.

But Steve never got his beer and a week later he hung himself. It was fat Michael who told me.

''ung isself,' he kept repeating. 'Yes, 'ung isself from the lavatory chain.'

That was shortly before Addie came.

I knew at once that Addie and I would have much – or a great deal of poignant nothing – to say to each other. Because of his height and a strange combination of clumsiness and grace, I christened him at once the Heron. He had a diary too, in which he scribbled at length in a violent hand. He only wrote on the right-hand pages and worked from back to front of spiral-backed notebooks bought by the dozen.

For days neither of us said a word. He spent hours lying on his bed staring at the ceiling, but the whitecoats told him to get up and go into the dayroom, where male and female patients mixed. There we circled one another like cautious animals, acutely, excruciatingly aware of each other's presence and constantly avoiding a collision of eyes. We took to sitting close by, faces carefully averted. Then one day his large, bony hand strayed to the broad edging of my sleeve.

'That suits you,' he said quietly and I jumped as though shot. There was a long silence. Then he observed, 'You always cover your body completely.'

'Yes.'

I could feel myself blushing and wished his hand would come back to my sleeve. It did not. About a week later, when we had been sitting near each other all afternoon and he was making a mask out of summer burrs picked up in the grounds, I touched his foot. Days afterwards he said, 'I liked it when you touched my foot.'

That was how we were.

The hospital world around us – we called it the bin – seemed to recede on to another plane, distant and incidental like the backdrop of a ribald scene on the stage of a serious play. Obscenities could be shrieked, people could writhe in fits, women smash lavatory bowls and men shit on the floor: none of it touched us. The delicate structure we wove around ourselves was resilient. In our private shell, where the subtleties of communication were conveyed with few words and fewer touches, we were able to block out the crudities of other people's worlds.

Addie never asks why I am here. It is one of the reasons I am drawn to him, part of our unspoken pact. I like the way he moves so carefully and feel his self- and body-consciousness like my own. Everything he wears calls to be touched and yet he holds himself aloof as I do all the time. His heavy, knobbly hands poke out from the ends of his sweaters like clubs. There are holes in all his sleeves where he pushes his thumbs through. All my sweaters have holes over my belly button where I trace round and round with my forefinger when I am alone and thinking of nothing.

For a week or so pale, beautiful Imogen was included in our hushed world. She drank real coffee from a Thermos all day, sucking it in with hissing, desperate sips between lungfuls of smoke. Her face was like a bruised white valentine, a mobile abstract heart. She wore men's clothes, pullovers with sleeves she could hide in, and died all muddled up in her long black hair, Tchaikovsky booming from big sponge earphones. When they found her, the '1812' was just a thin, busy bleat on the air, the earphones having slipped off. I hardly knew her but the image of her face, alive and dead, stayed with me a long time. One of the battery trucks came to tow her away.

Beyond the hospital and the quiet twilit rim of the world I shared with Addie, I did not look. The bin was for me a limbo in which it was easy to believe the future was out of my hands. And when I was not with Addie, its inmates provided an endless source of distraction from thoughts I wanted to avoid. Like why I was there. My diary kept up a running commentary on goings on in the ward, but did not say much about me.

This place is all long corridors, red and white as a raw lamb chop. Beds laid out in blue-grey rows, a body here and there making a blue-grey lump. In the morning the lumps shift to the dayroom where they sag in plastic-covered chairs by the always, always too hot radiators.

Black Liza woke me with her ravings this morning. She saw me blink and came running, waving her handbag at the end of frantic arms, tubes and tissues falling everywhere, a lipstick rolling in a long oval grabbed, I noticed, by that big lump Jean. Black Liza talked so fast I couldn't hear the words. She'd got something special in the bottom of her handbag. 'It talks,' she gabbled, 'talking talking.' She emptied the bag on my bed and grabbed the talking thing.

There was a rhythmic vibration as the whitecoats came jogging in time.

It was the telephone receiver, yanked wires trailing. She pulled my head under her pink-sweatered bosom and jammed the phone against my ear. 'What's it saying? What's it saying?'

The jog-jog-jog came nearer. Curses and wailing as Black Liza and the telephone were taken away.

There are two or three on this ward who treat this place as a kind of holiday camp with free meals, free pills, free telly and pocket money from the State. They suck up to volunteer visitors knowing that because they are on the inside and their victims are from the outside, they will get sympathy whether they deserve it or not. There is one woman who cadges gifts of chocolate and cigarettes, hoards them up in her wardrobe, and has a business going with the inmates of the locked wards. The men suck up to the Charge nurses by a show of diligence over the ward chores. Their satisfied little world-weary sighs as they put their feet up and roll the 'nth cigarette of the morning are sickening. If I had been Hitler I would have tried to wipe out this lot, not the Jews, but some of them put on

184

*such a professional act it is hard to distinguish them from those
who are really trying, those who have hope and an aim.*

I could not escape my own criticism. In my own eyes, rape or
no rape, I was a failure. I was not sure that in the holocaust I
would mete out to those others I considered to be malingering,
I deserved to survive. Whatever the reasons for my being in
hospital, I was ashamed that I had not found some other way to
cope.

By now I was expert in the art of using the hospital. An old
file dating back to the days of truancy and connecting my name
with such terms as 'maladjusted', served as a sort of multiple re-
entry visa. But still I could not just announce that I wanted to
come in. I had to produce evidence that I *needed* to, something
forceful enough to bypass the usual waiting-list yet not so violent
as to get me locked up indefinitely.

One weekday afternoon, having walked for hours along the
Thames with no particular aim, I found myself within easy reach
of a large shopping centre. I did not know where I was going to
sleep that night – not 309 again with Kay's anxious, non-compre-
hending eyes – and this worried me. I knew before I left the
towpath and mounted the steps to the town that I was going to
do something which would take the worry out of my hands.

The streets were busy, milling with shoppers and office workers
hurrying on their lunchtime rounds. I held open the door of a
department store for a well-dressed woman and two others took
advantage of my portership to push through. I followed, entering
a bright, luxurious atmosphere designed to divert the weary shop-
per. Today, with a little assistance from me, they would be well
entertained.

I lingered for a while on the household goods and china floor.
There were tables laid up to display dinner services, apricot-
coloured napkins folded into tongued cones, stylish placemats
with elegant hunting scenes. In my mind I rearranged the settings, banishing the formality and making them warm and colour-

ful as I would want for a family of my own. I passed on into the clothes section, taking my time, finding sudden value in the last quarter of an hour of freedom. Before the mirror of a hatstand I tried on a wide-brimmed Garbo showpiece, tipping it down at the front so that only one middle-distance-gazing eye could be seen. Then I swapped it for a big Russian fur, drooping my mouth to look suitably proud and mysterious, and after that a Faye Dunaway beret, worn at a ludicrous slant. I liked hats for the clues they gave as to who I could be.

On the escalator to the restaurant floor, past lampshade and light fittings and long rolls of carpet, I stood behind two women discussing shopping problems. They were on their way to get their hair done but would stop for coffee first and 'a little something wicked to go with it'. I thought coffee a good idea too. My little something wicked would come afterwards.

The coffee shop was situated to one side of the main restaurant, surrounded by a low white rail. It looked out over the rest of the floor which housed the store's lavish display of lounge and bedroom furniture. It was a busy time and most of the tables were full. The women from the escalator joined the counter queue ahead of me and filled their trays with quiche and tinned fruit gâteau. The 'kwitch' reminded me of Sebastian F—, married in Sweden now. I bought my coffee and headed quickly for the one vacant table near the front. I needed to be near the front. There were dirty plates cluttering the table and I smiled at the overalled waitress who came to clear them away. She did not respond and gave the surface a perfunctory swipe, red fingers wielding a damp cloth. Memory of Kay. My head felt full of irrelevant little snippets of the past, each one pointlessly clear, as irritating as advertising jingles repeating themselves uninvited.

I watched the traffic at the counter. Talk ebbed and flowed all round. It seemed to me as if the words were unimportant; it was the nods, the affirmations which mattered. Each separate table was like a cog in a wheel of ritual reassurance. When one removed the mind a short distance, the voices were reduced to a few simple patterns of sound: animals signalling. I was back to being a fly on the wall again. When the coffee was finished my gaze wandered to the wider spaces of the room and rested on the rich drapery of an ornamental fourposter. There were modern bunk beds in bright colours, long walkways of thick carpet, a yellow velvet divan.

With me I had a bag containing comb, purse, toothbrush and a library book with the address of the hospital clearly marked inside. I stood up and politely interrupted two women at the next table.

'Excuse me, would you mind looking after my bag a moment?'

After a slight pause there were nods. I laid the bag on a chair, bending as I did so to slip off my shoes. Then I stood up straight and took a deep breath.

One, two, three. . . . Hup! Over the rail. Long diving somersaults down the nearest length of piles. Up on to feet with the last roll and three skips to the springboard of the yellow divan. Big leap and I'm on the Rest Assured mattresses, row of three. Spring! Spring! Spring! To land thunk among the jolly bunks and chintzy singles. Whumph! Air farting out as I hit a deep pink kingsize, satin bedspread all in a whirl. Short run up to a designer number, whoops-a-daisy it's on wheels – skid slide crump into a fat settee.

P-rrring! The bell. They're quick. Got to make it to the fourposter before they catch me. Come on run, short cut, dash towards the coffee crowd, brave it, brave it, oh look at their faces rolling back in a messy wave. Crash! A dropped tray. Yippee! Steady now for a big jump on to the final, the most inviting, row. Deep, satisfying springs, breaths. . . . Damn! They're coming at me from the other end. So what! They're going to get me anyway but not before I've had a bounce on that fourposter. . . .

We reached it at the same time. They came at me over the bed, one at the side and one at the end. Blue, this time, instead of whitecoats. At the last moment I dived under the valance to slide out unexpectedly the other side, dust up my nose and hands clinging trustingly to a pair of serge ankles. I kept my head down, mouth shut and went limp. Upside-down, dangling from their arms, I saw the pink satin bedspread crumpled like a bruised camellia.

What followed was always the same, a familiar treadmill of

formalities, the wheels of administration turning up Madame Tussaud copies of police, social workers and locum psychiatrists. I knew the reception routine at the bin by heart: clothes removed, taken away and replaced by the candy-striped dressing-gown, always too broad, always too short; forms filled in, nurses crackling around. Then waiting for the physical on hard, paper-covered couches in bare, cracked-ceilinged rooms. I hated those ceilings and those paper-covered couches, reminders of black ticks and red flowers in Tel Aviv – that other little madness I refused to connect with this.

A confrontation with a senior clinician did not occur until some days after admission when I would join a row of inmates in a draughty corridor examining the linoleum and red and white lamb-chop walls.

There was one doctor I rather liked. He was short and round with a perennial yellowish tan and a plump face like a kindly gnome. He had quick blue eyes which darted up sharply now and then from the notes he was jotting. Unlike other doctors I had seen, he seemed genuinely interested in signs that I had an active, if muddled, mind and he treated me like an adult, using technical expressions as though he assumed I would understand. I found this flattering and on one occasion when he used a term new to me did not like to admit it. We were discussing a phase of compulsive eating I was going through. I told him I had a thing about éclairs.

Dr: 'You know in some cases this type of obsession disguises a desire for fellatio.'

I was cagey.

'Really? Do you think that might be so with me?'

Dr: 'I don't know. Is fellatio something you enjoy?'

I was out of my depth but kept my eyes fixed steadily on his.

'Mmmm . . . *quite*, but I think I still prefer éclairs.'

When I looked up the word later – finding it only with difficulty – I was astounded. Nothing in my past had taught me about such things.

I was good at diverting myself, and others, from the deeper

causes of my 'maladjustment'. The curtains I had drawn across my mind to shut out Cape Sounion and Tel Aviv acted both as a protection against the violence of my own feelings and a barrier preventing other people coming anywhere near the centre of the problem. It never occurred to me to describe the white car episode to the doctor. Instead I threw out a trail of red herrings, behaving sometimes in a wild, extroverted manner and then withdrawing for days into a depressed shell. Being in the bin gave me a licence for lunacy and I used it to the full.

My use and abuse of the hospital system might have gone on indefinitely had it not been for a crisis one autumn weekend. It was a Saturday, Addie was on leave and I was at a low ebb and a loose end.

I had spent the afternoon wandering in a grove of trees. In the twisted intertwining of the branches I saw all the complexity of unwordable feelings spelled out. That the strong, smooth limbs of the trees should fold themselves into agonized knots, splitting, bleeding and developing strange growths, seemed synonymous to me of my own condition. I was half infatuated with, half horrified by, both the trees and myself.

Beyond the trees, in a meadow out of bounds to patients, I came upon Daphne, a great clumsy horse of a woman who did nothing but sit slumped in a chair all day, weeping and spilling tea. She did not see me coming and I crouched down in the long grass and watched. This was a different Daphne.

She had lost her slippers and her large feet, steadily trampling down the grass in a circle, were streaked with earth. She was humming to herself, her throat occasionally vibrating like a bird's so that the hum became a gurgling croon. Her eyes behind clear-rimmed glasses were girlish and happy. I had never seen her smile before.

After a while her feet stopped moving and she wriggled her shoulders out of her dressing-gown and let it drop to the ground. She stepped into the middle of the circle, back towards me, and the split down the back of the white gown showed her big innocent bottom wobbling. Her iron-grey head was thrown back, a lock of straggled hair waving in the breeze. The humming croon became a song and her heavy legs began to move rhythmically, knees lifting up and down. Her hand found the collar of the night-gown and she lifted it from her body, the ties at the back falling apart as she pulled. Naked, she moved with new confidence, singing louder, and as the beat of her dance quickened she raised blotched and flabby arms to the sky, her old breasts shook and her sagging belly flopped against her loins. In ecstasy the middle-aged thighs trembled and the veined calves glistened like bright columns brushed by the damp grass. A leaf was stuck between her toes. She was beautiful.

'Gawd! Come an' 'ave a look at this – the old twat's starkers!'

The porter's voice chopped into the still air like a shovel, crunching and clanging against Daphne's song. I ducked my head and kept quiet. Daphne did not seem to hear.

The porter's companion was a male nurse. From somewhere they found another, and the three of them strode purposefully into the field. Not until they were right upon her did Daphne understand that her moment of beauty was at an end. She went on singing and dancing, feet to the earth, face to the sky. When the hand of the senior nurse grabbed her shoulder she turned round and gave one low cry, eyes astonished behind glasses knocked askew. Efficiently they trapped her paralysed arms and bundled the dressing-gown around her. One of them had a cigarette in his mouth. All three moved quickly in case she should suddenly resist. But Daphne did not resist. They carried her limp, like a thick roll of carpet, and as they passed my hiding-place I saw tears slide silently out of her eyes.

Upset and disinclined to return to the ward, I wandered out of the grounds.

Before long a man in a car stopped and gave me a lift into the nearest town. This was not unusual. There were always hopeful cruisers in the area. Before I had grown wise to their hopes, I had allowed one to park in the corner of a pub car-park where he nervously tried to kiss me. My reactions had been rapid and, as in the bus queue in Tel Aviv, disproportionately brutal. I bit him viciously and gave him a hard punch under the eye. After this I made use of the cruisers for lifts whenever I wanted, quashing familiarity before they got further than the opening gambit by quoting their car numbers at them and threatening to turn them over to the police. Surrounded as I was by extremes of human behaviour, neither the men themselves nor my habit of using them as a convenient chauffeur service seemed peculiar at the time.

In town a lonely boy attached himself to me. He was also from the bin but unlike me, officially on leave. We strolled together and he told me about the unhappy hour he had spent visiting his mother.

'She's never been the same since me dad left.'

I said I knew what he meant.

As we passed a restaurant he commented that he was hungry. He had been meaning to go into a café but had felt too shy alone. I offered to go in with him and he said that would be great.

We sat in the window of a continental steak house and the boy chomped his way through a large mixed grill. I was not hungry but had a salad to keep him company. When he had his pudding I ordered a liqueur.

Halfway through a mouthful of chocolate cake and cream, the boy's jaws suddenly stopped working. Leaning across the table, too panic-stricken to swallow, his words came thickly through a mass of crumbs.

'I 'aven't got any money. I forgot I give it to me mum. She said I wasn't fit to look after it meself.'

His well-smeared lower lip shook. Whether it was the effect of the green liqueur or the way he said 'I give it to me mum', I don't know: I laughed. I did not have nearly enough money to cover the bill. We were going to have to do a bunk.

'Oh God,' I said, and laughed again.

The boy looked scared when I told him. I explained that the alternative was to give ourselves up and maybe have to go to the police station.

'No!' he said, 'me mum'd kill me. I'm scared!'

'Well, stop *looking* scared,' I snapped, and smiling at the waiter, ordered two brandies. The boy swallowed his in gulps as I out- lined what we were going to do. By the time he had reached the

191

bottom of his glass and had mine as well he was nodding enthusiastically. I made him repeat his lines and before he had time for
second thoughts told him to get up and say them straight away.
He pushed his chair back and lumbered to his feet, beginning
faultlessly.

'Sorry about this. I won't be a moment. I'm just going to . . .'

He dried up and stood there gormlessly with crumbs on his
chin.

'Yes, of course,' I said, 'your cigarettes. There are bound to be
some in the cinema down the road.'

I jerked my head meaningfully and he walked to the door,
opened it, and was gone.

I saw the waiter look my way. It was there, a hint of suspicion
round the eyes. Feeling reckless, stuck on the merry-go-round of
a situation I had not planned, I ordered another brandy. It came
and I drank. Immediately the taste brought back night in Yafo
and dead kittens. My cheeks were hot. I began to feel more fierce
than afraid, thoughts tumbling through my head like small
serrated-edged knives. By the time the drink was finished I was
wild, ready for anything; ready to run, fight, laugh, cry, rage.

I stood up while the waiter had his back turned and made for
the door. I was out before they saw me but in a second there were
two of them at my heels. Reflected in dark shop windows I saw
short red jackets flying out from white shirt fronts, shiny black
shoes pounding. Pounding inside and outside my head. Alcohol
and adrenalin lent speed but not direction to my feet and in the
doorway of a shoe shop I was caught. The grabbing hands and
excited faces maddened me and it took both of them to pin me
face down on the pavement as they shouted for a passer-by to call
the police.

The stranger they hailed did not run to call the police. He bent
down and looked into my face. I looked back, dumb, and heard
him say calmly, 'If she has not, as you say, paid the bill, I will
pay. There is no need to call the police.'

Now that he was standing, I could only see his trouser cuffs.
He had a kind voice. But they would not have it. I must not be
allowed to get away with it, it was the principle of the thing. The

192

kind voice was shouted down, jostled away by others, and I got away with nothing, for when at last I was passed from the hands of the police to the heavy gang on duty that night in the bin, I no longer had any self-control. I twisted away from the hands they laid on me and refused to speak. I was snarling and crying at the same time. When I understood that they were going to give me an injection I exploded. I did not kick or lash out for there was one on each limb, but I writhed and bucked with all the strength in my being. And I screamed all the way down the throat of the void as I felt the needle go in.

Chapter Twelve

On the fourth day, after the worst of the sickness was over, I felt a featherlight presence near my bed. Peering out of a slim periscope made of the sheet, I saw through blurred eyes a tall apparition waver and divide. As I struggled to concentrate, the figure became one again, still swimming and rippling but recognizable. A grey-sweatered arm with a thumb pushed through the sleeve was bent round a black box; a canvas bag stuffed with dog-eared notebooks hung over a bony shoulder. Addie. How he had managed to creep undetected up the back stairs to the far end of the female dormitory I will never know, but there he was, cautiously settling his long heron form on the perch of the bed. A wheeled screen and a locker closed us off from the rest of the ward.

'Are you awake?'

His low, slow voice was clear. I nodded the periscope.

'I've brought some music. Do you want to hear?'

I did not move. His strange club fingers pressed knobs on the black box.

'Play,' I murmured, and the word in my drugged mind was

huge and endless in meaning. He inched the box under the bed-clothes and I sucked it into my submarine.

At first nothing but the whirr of winding tape. Then, as though accidentally spilled over from some distant land where all was gentle order, came couplets of soft chords like a cat slowly knead-ing a rug by a fire. Lulling, but at the same time subtly insistent, the chords were overlaid by a melody of single notes taking me outside the window of the hearth scene to where calm water shone towards the end of day and wound into streams whose winking passage over moss and stones was a joyous hymn to life. It went on to conjure in my mind blue sky through a pattern of twigs when I was twelve; sun-warmed heather in the Highlands; the glow of the moon on pink desert hills.

'Good, isn't it?' said Addie quietly when the tape wound back to a whirr.

'Yes,' I said, groggy but sure and meaning far more than just the music, 'Yes, yes, yes.'

Coming at that time, when I was little more than an oblivion-bent lump of misery, that gentle music – it was in fact Satie's 'Trois Gymnopédies' – served as a reminder of all the simplest and most beatiful things I had ever seen. And it spoke of new things too. There were tendernesses there which made my body long to stray first with the sounds, uncurling from its denying ball, and then beyond, to open and grow, to give as well as re-ceive, create as well as respond.

The music and the feelings it aroused were poetic and senti-mental but neither sound nor feelings were frail. Those beauties existed. They were as real as darkness and pain, and as powerful. It seemed to me that I had a choice of ways to go and I must choose now. Looking and yearning, dreaming images from a hos-pital bed was not enough. It was time to get up, get out and say *yes* to life once more.

Experiencing a moment of profound personal realization is one thing. Acting on it is another.

During the months spent at 309, working and going for endless, aimless walks like a zombie, there were occasional moments of clarity in which I knew I must do something to break the frightening downward slide of my mind. In one of those moments I applied for membership of a club called Winners. The blurb said that the club existed for 'exceptionally bright' people who wanted to 'mix, learn and grow' with their own kind. 'Bright' was about the last thing I felt at the time but I needed something to convince myself that I was not as dim and incompetent as I seemed and membership of Winners was restricted to those who could pass a test.

Without telling anyone what I was doing – this was between me and me – I took a day off from the chip shop, washed my hair and caught a bus up to the West End. I arrived early, in time for a look at the other candidates. Whatever I had been expecting, I was disappointed. With the exception of one plump youth with a foolish grin, there was no one under forty. Dark jackets showed up uniformly sagging shoulders well dredged with dandruff. There were no other females sitting the paper that day. No one said a word while we waited and I, already marked apart by age and sex, felt too awkward to be the first to break silence.

However, when the test began, the others became irrelevant. I threw myself into it with a verve I had forgotten I had and finished twenty minutes before the final bell, feeling stretched and exhilarated. I sat idly until five minutes before the end when I thought I would have a last look at a question I had found too hard. I turned to the place and froze. No wonder I had finished before anyone else; two of the pages were folded together at the top, stuck. I had missed them out.

Feeling idiotic, I put up my hand to explain. The invigilator's response was acid.

'Young lady, you have come here to apply for membership of a club which requires of its members, among other things, exceptional intelligence. You cannot expect me to sympathize with such a stupid mistake.'

My mouth dropped open and then shut fast. Ignoring him and the plump youth, who giggled, I ripped the pages apart and worked through them like fire. When the bell rang I had not finished but was nearly there. I handed in my paper with the others and treated the invigilator to my stoniest glare. Infuriatingly, he smiled. When the results came through several weeks later I was tempted to go and wave my membership card under his nasty nose.

But then the bad dreams and the memories became too much, and it was not until I had been three months in the mental hospital that I made my first moves as a member of the club for Winners.

I had received several copies of the club magazine which listed activities available to members and I decided to make my début at a major gathering based in town and lasting a whole weekend. The gathering, for which I obtained special leave after two weeks confined to grounds following the injection, began with a party. It would be my first party – not counting the session with Fred and Co. in Athens – since the lie-down-and-grope affairs I had dallied with amidst all else that was happening at St S—'s. I took the opportunity to wear the beautiful dress Jorges had bought me in Jerusalem.

The main activities of the weekend were held in a large hall. I was daunted by its size and the hundreds of confident-looking, smartly dressed people milling through its doors. Most of them seemed to know each other and the hall resounded with squawks and growls of greeting. My loose hair, worn sandals and exotic robe felt out of place and I considered escaping before the party got under way. But I had not reckoned on the sociability of the lone academic female. A pair of broad, powdered, middle-aged shoulders bore down on me.

'Hello dear, whose little sister are you?'

I bridled. Sister, and little. It was assumed I was a tagalong. It had said in the party blurb that members were allowed to bring guests. I moved to a snacks table and scooped up a handful of crisps, crunching them before replying.

'Actually, I'm here on my own.'

Her eyes lit up behind donnish spectacles. She looked a little like Daphne with a perm.

'You mean you're one of us? But your pin, dear, where's your pin?'

I noticed then that everyone else had a small pink and white label pinned to their chests. Delighted to have an errand, the large lady dashed away to find me one. I was immediately approached by a smiling young man in a white rollneck sweater who asked if he could bring me a glass of wine. While he was fetching it another youth, with an eager, friendly face, started chatting amusingly. I giggled and chatted back. Suddenly it all felt easy and fun. The Daphne lady must have spread the word that I was new blood because a number of people came to say hello. My ego grew fresh buds every time someone squinted to decipher the name on my pin.

A Winners club jamboree is an unlikely occasion for a young girl to discover her social wings. There was no music, no dancing and the majority of people were much older and not essentially given to frivolity. But it worked for me. From a curled-up ball on a hospital bed emerged a happy butterfly insouciantly fluttering her wings in all directions. By the end of the evening I had made three dates, none of them of great individual significance but all adding to the proof positive that I was ready and able to start living again. I parried questions about 'what I did' with a fresh answer every time. I flirted, sparkled, giggled, glowed.

Then the next day something happened which knocked all the small pleasures of party games into a cocked hat. I fell under the spell of a man.

On the second afternoon of the gathering there were a number of events one could attend. There was a lecture, a self-hypnosis class, a discussion group on 'Winners in Business' and a tour of a printing works. I found out that the lecture had something to do with people and potentials and decided to give it a try. My 'dates' were opting for hypnosis and the tour.

Adrian Massell came as a shock. From the moment he walked on to the platform I was hypnotized. And it was not just his unusually green eyes and tall, confident form that captivated me, it was what he said. Here was a man I could listen to for days, someone who had much to say and who said it brilliantly. His words, swiftly chosen, firmly uttered, clipped away all the trimmings of an argument. With a light step and a quick, bright smile, he forged a path straight into the heart of my mind. He was positive without being fanatical, clever without flaunting his wit as a weapon, a man not only creating his own music but dancing to the tune. He shone, he burned, a strong, flame-headed, laughing-eyed god; arriving at precisely the point in my life when I most needed one.

And I was by no means the only one enchanted that afternoon. After the lecture a bevy of eager acolytes rushed to congratulate him, newly made admirers hanging shyly at the edge of the crowd. I remained seated, watching him handle their questions and praise, his mind operating like a dancer performing a faultless impromptu routine. Then I rose quietly and left. Outside the hall one of my dates was waiting. Damn. I wanted to be alone to think about Massell.

It was a while before I saw him again but the seed of the future had been sown. I learned that he was to hold a series of lectures in the New Year and telephoned to ask for a place on the course. He answered the phone himself, giving me the chance to print again on my mind that strong, sure voice. He could not put a face to my name as I had not introduced myself at the gathering but he was pleased to enrol me for the lectures.

I could hardly wait, believing that, through him, my whole life was going to find a new and positive direction.

Chapter Thirteen

Addie and I left hospital at around the same time. Our contact after that was sporadic, the empathy between us making meetings irresistible but stiflingly intense. I spent some days and nights at his mother's house and saw the cavern of a room where his journey from adolescent solipsism to a state of virtual catatonia had begun. The rest of the house was conventional and his gamine, vivacious mother imbued it with strident normality, but upstairs in the closed sanctum of Addie's room, the outside world ceased to exist.

I had not yet read Cocteau's *Les Enfants Terribles* or Huysmans' *Au Rebours*. Nor had I looked at the lives of Van Gogh, Rimbaud or a dozen other doomed and brilliant heroes. If I had, perhaps the atmosphere of Addie's room might not have seemed so unique.

Torn red velvets and creamy satins draped bed and walls, muffling and enclosing the occupant like a womb. Within that womb, ranged on bowed shelves beneath a permanently shuttered window and pinned with six-inch nails to the walls, were objects of timeless and macabre appeal. There were skulls of birds and snake's jaws; domed boxes like temples holding hair and blood-coloured stones; complex umbilical knots hacked from trees; pill-boxes, razors and a sinister row of surgical blades.

On a sloping table in a corner jagged half-bricks weighed down hectic columns of notebooks. Yarrow stalks, charcoal, paint-brushes and bones were jammed into jars like sheaves of straw on end. Propped on the floor was a stalagmite of mirror so spotted and green the reflection it gave of Addie's haunted eyes was not so clear as the pencilled self-portraits which rose in a ragged diagonal to the top of the wall, interspersed with prints of Munch's 'The Scream' and Da Vinci's bisected man. The mask of summer burrs made in the bin hung like a shrunken head on a nail and, beside the bed, sculptures taken from moulds of Addie's feet and hands held butts between the toes and ash in the palms.

In that narrow bed Addie lay like a cross between sleeping Endymion and liver-torn Prometheus, with me beside him not quite touching anywhere. It was sensitivity, not sensuality, that held the highest sway in our world. Nevertheless the meat we fed our minds on was strong. Head propped against a never-changed pillow, smoking needle-thin cigarettes and taking deep draughts from a mug of old, cold coffee, Addie read long extracts, in a low, mesmeric voice, from Nietzsche.

I listened, eyes closed, and before long that thin black book with the bone-yellow pages found its way into my shoulder-bag and accompanied me everywhere. On the tops of jolting buses I swallowed great tracts of Zarathustra's railings, often so absorbed I failed to alight at the right stop and ended up wandering bemused in Staines or Hounslow wondering what had happened to the funambulist and the serpent and the cave.

With the exception of my private future link with Massell and his contrastingly ordered world, there was a great deal of wandering and wondering and pondering and blundering in those days after the hospital. Finally those wanderings led to Mole's End.

It began with a rendezvous by the river with Julian, a friend from Addie's past. It was clear straight away that he suffered from none of the mawkish self-consciousness that we did. The first thing he did when he saw our two self-effacing forms approaching was, quite literally, jump for joy. He gave a deep, melodious whoop and sprang into the air like an exuberant Cossack. His costume, made entirely by hand, consisted of white sherpa boots over capacious breeches and a magnificent minstrel's jacket of almond green. Dark hair swarmed down his back and he had a long soft beard divided into three tapering plaits. The middle plait quivered expressively as he embraced Addie, his smile broad and glistening as a river in the sun.

The moment of ebullient greeting over, there was a pause in which I felt acutely the differences in our physical presence. When I was with Addie, my butterfly wings were closed in sympathy with his own. I moved at his pace which in those days was hesitant and slow. Julian was a startling contrast, a boy/man overflowing with *joie de vivre*. His wide-open eyes gleamed with health and body heat vibrated from him in an aura three feet deep. Beside him, Addie's ascetically fleshless form seemed more than ever like a stricken heron. I, aware by now of the chameleon flexibility of my own persona, took a step back from them both.

We sat by the wintry Thames, Addie smoking, hunched in duffel coat and half-a-dozen scarves, Julian apparently oblivious to the cold, drinking in and puffing out great lungfuls of vaporous river air and speaking in ardent, never-completed spasms of phrase which gradually died under the delicate steamroller of Addie's deliberate pronouncements.

'I wish we had a fire,' I blurted suddenly, 'a great big blazing fire to feed.'

'Mmmmmn,' breathed Julian in pulsing concurrence. And then, round-eyed as though amazed at the simplicity of the solution, he cried, 'Mole's End!'

I raised a quizzical eyebrow at Addie.

'It's a cottage,' he said, 'about half a day's hitch from here. I think you'd like it.'

And we decided there and then to go. I would hitch on ahead and as Julian, pressing my hands in temporary farewell, said, 'light a candle in the window'.

Sixty miles down the M4, following the boys' instructions, I crossed a bridge marked with a No Entry sign and found myself on a country road.

As I moved further away from the motorway, the hush of gently rising winter fields settled round my ears like a large, cool, unassuming hand. Remnants of magenta leaves clung to spiky hedgerows. Soft ridges of mud stood up in clodded curves where a tractor had turned in the road, and round a corner where a rabbit lay flat-ironed on the verge picture-book smoke rose from a red-bricked house on a hill.

A muddy van with chinks of road showing through the floor took me to the village of Renton. Here, children with cheeks the colour of crab apples pressed white noses against the window of a cake shop and a string of race horses with jockeys like frozen scarecrows unwound down the street. I walked on to a fork in the road where one sign showed clearly the way to Wetherbourn and another pointed mysteriously straight into the ground. On it was written Belleston Warren. Julian's directions, couched in a series of lopped, descriptive bursts, had been obscure from this point on.

'There's this long straight ... you'll see the barrows ... clump of trees on a hill ...'

Addie had tried to be more precise.

'You head towards Belleston Lisle, Lucy.'

Again Julian broke in confusingly.

Of course there's Belleston Bagpuize . . .'

'Belleston what?'

'Bagpuize, Bagpuize, Bagpuize!' His glistening mouth bounced and dandled the word.

'But do I want to go there?'

'To Belleston Bagpipes? Whatever for?'

I gave up. I would find the cottage somehow. And lo, as I set off along the fork away from Wetherbourn, there was the long straight dot dot dot, the barrows and the clump of trees on a hill.

Hills in broad slopes and billows rose and fell like muted green waves. A straggling circle of crows flapped clumsily between one slow swell and the next, raw cries splintering the silence, ragged bodies stippling the sky. That long straight stretch of road passed over a high tract of the Ridgeway and plunged, after a tidy four-way crossing, down the steep, humpbacked scarp of Blowing Stone Hill. Dark trees alongside the road became with the fading light one continuous columnar screen, seeming to lean inwards, forming a tunnel.

At the bottom of the hill a sign pointed the way to Belleston Lisle and a smell of cold cattle rose to meet me. Further on there was a village pub and opposite, a tiny cottage extension marked Post Office.

A squint SHUT sign on a piece of string told me that business was over for the day but I saw a figure moving behind a thin curtain and heard the gravelly clatter of a till. When I tapped on the door a woman's face appeared suddenly in a triangle of light where she had pulled back the curtain. One cheek bulged with something she was chewing and a bright eye goggled from beneath a wave of heavy brown hair. I smiled apologetically and the bolts were drawn back.

'Ye-es, what can I do for you?' A comfortable country lilt matched her cushiony figure and bird-sharp eyes.

'I wonder if you could tell me the way to a cottage called Mole's End?'

'Oh, going to Mole's End, are you?' She looked me up and down with interest. 'Well, you can't miss it.'

She pointed over my head to where the road led out of the village and gave simple directions. I thanked her and was about to go when, stepping back and shifting whatever she was chewing to the other cheek, she said, 'Is there anything you'll be wanting to take down? I've a pint of milk here . . .'

I saw now that the Post Office also served as the village shop. There were rows of old-fashioned sweet jars, bottles of soft drink, a block of yellow cheese and some bacon under a plastic dome.

'Well, perhaps some milk. That's very kind.'

She bustled behind the counter making a long business of finding the milk and as I hunted for change she said slyly, 'You're not that Orpheus's sister, are you?'

'Orpheus?'

'Well, that's what folk call him' – she grinned girlishly – 'going round the fields with that flute and them baggy trousies.'

I laughed. She must mean Julian.

'Be staying down there a day or two, will you?'

'I expect so.'

Again I was ready to go but before parting with the milk she looked me straight in the eye across the counter.

'You'd best use strong thread to sew up them baggy trousies – and it won't be before time!'

The grumbling affection in her voice was unmistakable.

The moon was rising as I launched into the last straight lap, softly lighting the wooded corner of a field where Mole's End lay. There were no other houses nearby and my eyes remained fixed on the little building as I walked, taking in its quiet square face, the twin sets of windows on either side of a porched front door. The cold had settled in hard now and I pushed on with a final burst of speed to get there quickly, light a fire, and set a candle in the window.

The key, on a long piece of linen tape, was old and bent and it took several tries to open the front door. The narrow entrance way, walled on either side, was for a moment pitch black. Ash and potato dust added themselves to a general scent of butt water and herbs. My hand went out and encountered something stiff which crackled, an ancient oilskin. Beyond, a window threw a broad lozenge of outside's dim visibility on to a square of tiles, to the left of which I could just make out the stepping diagonal of what appeared to be a gigantic set of pan pipes on the wall. A window-seat held a squat crock of spiky ferns whose shadows rose like clawing hands to a low, bulging ceiling. To the right was the main living area and after a quick glance at a spiral of triangular wooden stairs leading up into total black, I concentrated my exploration here; the first task being to discover a source of light.

On the mantel beam above the grey gape of a fireplace, my hands found a metal candle-holder with a box of matches at its rim. Damp had penetrated Mole's End's walls and five matches died before the candle would light. Then, faintly lit by the yellow flame, shapes came into view that over years would become as familiar as the knuckles of Addie's fingers and the warmth of Julian's breath. I found another candle to set before the largest window, a star to guide my boys.

Despite the damp, the fire I made took well and the hush which made the cold seem more intense was banished by the spit and scuffle of fast paper flame igniting twigs which in turn licked the belly of a damp log dry until a sudden burst of bright fire curled round and gripped it like a burning hand. I found water in jars beneath a church pew and filled a huge soot-blackened kettle which hung over the fire from three meat hooks dangling on chains.

In a trug on the floor were potatoes and onions and I made foil parcels of them to bake, enjoying the simplicity of little choice, few decisions. I was pottering contentedly with a candle, about to explore upstairs, when I heard singing outside.

It could only be Addie and Julian, one voice deep, flat and scowling, the other murmuring and round, innocent as a King's College choirboy. What detracted from the charm of the duet was the fact that each was singing a different song. Addie's voice tortured the lower rungs of a lyrical modern ballad and Julian fluted angelically through an *Agnus Dei*. The combined effect was bizarre, two dogs howling to separate moons. I was laughing as I ran to open the door.

Julian clowned as they came up the path, playing the bumpkin and doffing an imaginary cap.

'Ah, good lady, might there be room by your hearth for two strangers this cold night? We have travelled far and are wearied by our load . . .'

Addie's wry voice chopped into the flow.

'Wearied by our load is right. One guy refused to give us a lift when Julian told him that the sack was full of human hair.'

A large sack was dumped in the porch.

'For the garden,' said Julian proudly, 'or a pillow for you, my dear?'

Then, uncharacteristically, Addie burst out laughing.

'Talking of hair, Lucy, have you seen yourself?'

I put my hand up to my head and it came away gloved with cobwebs. We all laughed. It was a fine feeling to be so careless of appearance after the painful self-consciousness of recent months; to be a thousand miles away from the shrinking ghost on the hospital bed and the bright superficial doll at the club party. Here, isolated in the trough of a Berkshire vale, there were no standards to conform to or deny other than our own. There was no established order for Addie to rail against and nothing for me to run from except myself.

As the two of us stepped into the cottage, leaving Julian outside a moment bidding an elaborate good-night to the moon, I wondered how we would cope with the freedom to be ourselves in this quiet base in no man's land.

Once all three of us were inside, the contrasts in the boys' characters cluttered the place immediately with two distinct atmospheres. With the lavish endorsement of Julian's praise the small domestic moves I had made erupted into an extravagant paradigm of all that is homely and warm. The modest fire I had built became, with Julian kneeling before it and lovingly turning the foil parcels in his hands, a glowing heart for the room. Chairs were drawn up and rosemary-scented sheets draped to air, while bricks were heated to warm the beds. From the recesses of a long kitbag Julian produced a single enormous cooking apple. Holding it in both hands as I bent near he begged, 'You do it – you'll do it so beautifully.'

I took it and rolled its cool bumpiness against my cheek. He watched, pleasure flowing from him in gusty murmurs. From across the square hall I could hear Addie repeating in a sinister echo: '*Do it beautifully*', his voice loaded with the voluptuous innuendo of Hedda Gabler enjoining her lover to kill himself. Julian took no notice. While I wrapped the apple and made a place for it in the fire, he set an Aladdin lamp on the table and began carefully to trim it.

Addie sidled into the pool of light like a long black moth.

'What about a drink, Julian?'

Julian leapt up, conjuring from nowhere three mottled tumblers made of horn and a bottle of mysterious pinky-orange liquid.

'What is it?' asked Addie, flexing large nostrils over the rim of his horn.

'Rosehip,' cried Julian enthusiastically, 'pure rosehip.'

'Oh God,' said Addie, but took an obliging sip.

Julian swallowed his in huge gulps and bounded out of the door murmuring about turning on the water.

'Got any coffee?' Addie called after him.

'Dandelion roots,' came back a cry, 'whole bowl of them under the pew.'

'Oh God,' said Addie again, starting to roll a cigarette, 'no booze, no caffeine. What a set up.'

While Julian was outside, Addie lapsed for a moment into his old hesitant self-consciousness. I left my seat and quietly fed the fire.

'That suits you,' said Addie from behind his smoke, and I recalled the first time he had said that and wished it had been here instead of where it was.

'But look!' he demanded, suddenly fierce, and lifting his gangling length positioned himself before a pair of giant organ bellows to one side of the fire. He fiddled with a metal pipe under the logs and began to pump.

In the space of seconds the fire was transformed from a homely glow to a demoniacal blaze, violent orange forks of flame leaping up the chimney, wild sparks flying out on to the hearth like

206

glittering eyes. The sounds it made were like some panting bird-beast at bay, gasps and roars and the hysterical beating of wings. Even when it was obvious that the flames were feeding on their own blasting intensity Addie went on, making the crazed red tongues speak for his own directionless fire. When Julian came in, arms laden with logs, Addie grabbed them all and hurled them on to the blaze, pumping the bellows again but this time misdirecting the air so that ash flew about madly, dusting the hearth and kettle silvery-grey.

Half laughing, half in anguish, Julian scrabbled the burning parcels from the heat, reprimanding Addie like a naughty child.

'Oh Addie,' mocked Addie, flouncing away, 'wicked Addie.'

And he disappeared with a candle into the room across the hall and struck wild bursts of Rachmaninov from an ancient piano there.

While Julian was gentling the fire, I collected up the sheets, shaking off their hot dusting of ash. There were two doubles and a single sewn into a coffin-shaped tube. My candle threw a yellow semi-circle of light on each triangular stair as I moved upwards and lit up a spider straddling its mummified prize in a web under the bannister. A new, sweet smell met me at the top of the stairs and casting the light around I found its source – a small army of late autumn apples spread on the floorboards in rows.

Through a curtained doorway lay one bedroom with a low bed covered in a black plastic sheet. I lifted the edge and there was a muffled scrabbling followed by a soft plop on the floor and then silence. Mice. I was about to duck under the curtain again, hoping to find the other bedroom not so occupied, when I caught sight of a high shelf made of a single curved plank, the bark still on it. Ranged from end to end were books of all shapes and sizes. One end seemed to be all children's books: fairy tales, *The Water Babies* and anthologies of morality verse in old editions. I lifted one of these down and it felt both heavy and frail with age. Inside there were startlingly vivid pictures of 'The boy who would not eat his soup' and 'Basil who was eaten by bears'. Further along there were novels and books of short stories. I looked at the author's names: Sholokov, Fournier, Silone, Voltaire. Paperbacks were stacked at the end: Camus, Hesse, Hemingway, Sassoon, and, although I did not know it then, downstairs there were works of Chekhov, Anouilh, Plato and Donne. During the weeks I was to spend alone at Mole's End I caught up on a lot of the hours I had missed at school.

Beyond a corridor with a single bed under a window lay the master bedroom. Apart from a painted wooden chest, a huge, high bed was its only feature. An uncurtained window looked directly over coolly moonlit fields. This bed was also draped in black plastic but there was no evidence of occupants when I lifted it clear. Dried lavender and thyme were strewn over a striped horsehair mattress full of lumps and dips impressive as a mountain range. When I approached the chest, where Julian had told me the blankets were, my foot met the edge of a hatch on the floor. Curiously, I lifted it and was greeted with a burst of light from the fire below. This was Julian's central heating system. At that moment his upturned face appeared in the gap.

'Onions coming along beautiful, Ma'am,' he announced, and handed up three heated bricks wrapped in socks.

After making up the big bed I took the sewn-up single sheet into the small corridor room and laid it on the bed there, wondering whether it would be used by Julian or me. I knew in advance that one half of the big bed would be Addie's – unless he decided to sleep with the mice. I slipped in a brick to warm each place before joining the boys downstairs.

By now Addie had exhausted the more violent pieces from his repertoire on the piano and was producing a diverting version of the 'Trois Gymnopédies' from a homemade organ. Those shadowy pan pipes I had seen on the wall were attached to a keyboard. The higher register was perfectly pitched but some of the lower notes sounded like loud raspberries. Solemnly, lovingly, Addie thrilled and farted through that piece which not so long ago had reminded me of the beauties which made life seem worth embracing again. On the music stand, in place of a score, he had propped a picture of Salomé dancing with John the Baptist's head dripping on a plate. I found a triangle on a shelf and joined in with serious tings.

At suppertime Julian sat on the hearth dividing the vegetable parcels on to irregular blue-striped plates. The warm firelight and softly spoked beams of the Aladdin lit his face and his hands moving tenderly over the food. Addie glowered throughout the meal, head buried in a book. I sat between them revelling in the femininity which allowed me to glow, undivided, for both.

Addie smoked and brooded while Julian ran to fetch nightshirts from upstairs and I cleared the dishes. The nightshirts were thick and voluminous, patched but scrupulously clean. I changed in the shadow of a barrel that served as a bath and went outside for a pee. The air was brittle with cold now, the moon high and white flanked by chilly streaks of cloud. Shivering, I ran back inside, looking forward to snuggling into one of the brick-warmed beds.

The boys had changed before the fire, Addie keeping on all his clothes beneath the shirt, Julian proud and careless, unbuttoned to the navel, long feet flexing on the hearth as he lifted his flute and blew an impressive stream of saliva through the end. As I preceded them upstairs, commanded to warm the big bed all over, a high, clear melody rippled out, graceful as the shadows dancing from my candle on the wall. With the notes wafting sweetly through the central-heating hatch and faint pops and whispers coming from the fire, I fell asleep very soon.

But not for long.

I woke to see Julian tiptoeing round the end of the bed with a candle and a book in one hand, a pair of slippers, chamberpot and brimming mug in the other. His tongue was curled over his lower lip in the effort to hold on to everything and keep quiet at the same time. But the book was slipping. Pot, book, slippers and light tumbled to the floor, the chamber giving a resounding clang. I giggled.

'Oh!' came Julian's voice, all distressed, through the sudden dark, 'I've woken you.'

'Don't worry. I've got another candle here.'

I lit it and saw that, miraculously, he had managed to save the mug. This he gave me to hold while he searched under the bed for the book.

'Now that you're awake,' he said shyly, 'would you like me to read you to sleep again with a story?'

'OK.'

Perching on the edge of the bed he began to read the tale of 'The Little Mermaid', pausing every now and then to take a sip from the mug of hot milk we shared. I snuggled deeper in the bed, feeling very happy and about six years old.

'Aha,' came Addie's voice, as he clumped loudly up the stairs, 'story time, is it? Right Lucy, you're going to get two stories tonight.'

Climbing like a great cold spider into the bed he thumped down a massive volume on the pillow.

'Now then,' he announced, 'Wittgenstein!'

He opened it at any old page and began to read loudly in a doom-filled prophetic voice. Julian carried on with 'The Little Mermaid' as though nothing were happening. I lay for a long minute between the two of them, ears assaulted and hair on end, then wriggled up to a sitting position and cried, 'Enough!'

Because Addie refused to stop he was banished to the single bed where his droning bursts of passion continued as a backdrop to the adventures of 'The Little Mermaid'. Julian finished the story and after tenderly bidding me good-night, climbed into Addie's vacated place and fell asleep. His big, cuddly body gave out sighs of contentment and animal warmth in waves. At some point in the night they must have changed places because when I woke with the first stirrings of dawn it was Addie's familiar shape cupped in the dip beside me, long, chilly and concave as a razor shell. The casual proximity of those two masculine but undemanding bodies, in the atmosphere of Mole's End, did more to cure me of post-rape breakdown than any amount of treatment in mental hospital could have done.

The first day at Mole's End formed a pattern which was to repeat itself over and over whenever the three of us were there. I would come down first, light the fire and make porridge for Julian and myself. We breakfasted quietly, yawning and grinning in our nightshirts. Sometimes we plaited each other's hair. Then we would dress and go logging or walk for miles, picking up bits of edible fungus from the woods or climbing the hills to wander among the standing stones of Wayland's Smithy and watch winter set deeper in the valleys.

Addie never stirred in the mornings, lying silent as death with a black shirt wrapped over his face and blankets wound round him like swaddling clothes. We left him undisturbed, knowing that around noon or sometimes as late as three, he would emerge looking pale and exhausted, begging plaintively for coffee. After a while one of us usually remembered to bring some. Dandelion roots were just not the same.

When New Year came I was still under the Mole's End spell. I had gone back to London with Addie, hung around the old haunts for a day or so, then yielded to the quiet call of the Berkshire hills. Julian was there off and on, returning between trips to Canterbury where he was making a recording with some other musicians. My heart always lifted when I saw his cloaked figure striding through the dusk along that by now so familiar stretch of road, but I did not pine when he left again for I was equally happy alone.

Over Christmas – which I acknowledged absent-mindedly by eating nothing but Brussels sprouts out of the garden for three days – I started the reading that was to absorb so much of my time there. Between long sessions with a book before the fire, I went for dreamy walks over the snow-covered fields, picking up kindling and dragging logs on the way back.

I loved the simple rituals of Mole's End life: lighting the fire in the morning, white-faced and goose-pimpled in the cold, holding reddened fingers before the first hint of flame, watching the cloud of my breath grow fainter as the stone room gradually warmed. Sometimes, creeping down at some black, dateless midnight, I would suddenly throw myself on the bellows and blow up a wild blaze from the embers, pumping like Addie with my whole body until the walls were alive with crazy shadows and the roar of the fire filled the snow-muffled night with sound. Then I would dance through to the music room with two hysterically guttering candles and draw long, wheezing moans from the wood and canvas belly of the organ, triple-socked toes slipping madly as I pressed the pedals, chill fingers stiff on the silky smooth keys. When I stopped, and the fire quickly died, silence would close over once more, the little pebble of my actions sinking into the pool of night. Upstairs again, I would leap into the still body-warm cavern of the bed and squirm right down until I was totally enveloped by the lumps and ridges of mattress and bedclothes, snug in the dark as a pit in a prune.

On Christmas Day I climbed to the crest of White Horse Hill and sat there panting, snow melting on flushed cheeks, face up-turned to the sky. My pockets were filled with soft little apples and I bit the best from them one by one and spat the bright pips and crimson skins into the snow.

Julian came a few days later and the two of us climbed the hill again, fresh snow sparkling in his beard and building a rich fleece collar on the cloak I borrowed for the trek. At the top we sprawled full length, careless of the melting wet, and finally launched our bodies down the slope like human snowballs, loose sweaters gathering hard-packed layers of snow, boots filling, ears stinging with laughter and cold.

I knew more contentment than I had felt for a long time – perhaps ever – with the fire and the reading, the long, thought-careless walks and the occasional companionship of the boys. But I had not forgotten Massell, and in the second week of the New Year, when the snow had gone, I turned my back on Mole's End and headed towards London, happy and full of hope.

Chapter Fourteen

The first thing to sort out was accommodation. I could have stayed at 309 but too many times I had gone from that house in unhappiness, too many times returned to find unhappiness there.

I wanted to open myself to this new venture as a vessel unstained by the past.

As chance would have it, I bumped into an old acquaintance on Richmond Bridge – Ben, the boy from the bin, who had been the instigator of the runaway truck episode. He was less impulsive now, the horrors which had landed him in the bin having burned themselves out. He told me that he was living with his girlfriend and some others in a house near Felstead on the edge of the Downs. I was welcome to stay, there would be no rent to pay.

The house turned out to be a squat, quite grand on the outside, situated in an old-fashioned residential area, but inside it was little more than boards and rubble. A mattress was found for me and moved into a vacant front room.

The next thing to organize before the lectures began was work, and soon my Young, Strong, Willing and Able notices were pinned up all over the district. There were two replies on the first day, one from an agent looking for someone to shop and clean for an elderly lady, the other from a housewife needing a babysitter, meals provided. I secured both jobs, arranging to babysit at the weekend and do my first stint of shopping and cleaning that afternoon. The agent warned me that Mrs Browne 'could be a bit tricky sometimes'.

Mrs Browne lived in Canton, circa 1923, in a magnificent bungalow with scrolled turrets and ample accommodation for twenty-six servants and a peacock called Bluey. I learned all this within ten minutes of arriving at her third-floor flat in a crumbling block on the outskirts of Sheen.

'What would you like me to get you from the shops, Mrs Browne?'

'How should I know? What have they got today?'

She was a tiny, compressed figure, concentrating all her energy in her voice. My eyes moved cautiously round the flat, searching for clues as to how her daily life was run. She was waiting.

'Speak up, girl! What are you going to get, then?'

Her hands clasped and unclasped impatiently on the handle of a knobbly walking stick held between her knees.

'I expect you need some food. Does anyone – does anyone cook for you?'

'Cooks, you say? Terrible! Don't talk to me about cooks. Three of them, one after the other, pilfering the silver, forgetting to feed Bluey . . .'

There followed a tirade on the shortcomings of cooks, house-boys, gardeners and maids. I looked at her thin arms, the shrunken cheeks beyond the aggressively quivering chin.

'I'll get you some chicken and perhaps some tins to last until I come again.'

She nodded distractedly and waved me away. There was five pounds in an envelope marked SHOPPING on top of a string bag. I had no idea how long it was supposed to last. As I was glancing round the kitchen to see what basics were required she called, 'Don't forget my sweets, do you hear?'

It was no good asking what kind.

From a phone booth near the shops I rang the agent who had got me the job. Her reply was brisk.

'Look dear, I get this every time. We've been trying to get her into a home for years but she won't have any of it. We tried sending her meals-on-wheels and she told us to give them to the RSPCA. She's only got her pension so don't let her tell you to buy steak. You're the fourth person I've sent in a month.'

I put the phone down, feeling thoughtful. Surely Mrs Browne wasn't as bad as that?

Pleased with the sensible way I had eked out the five pounds, I returned to the flat in a confident mood. Mrs Browne was nowhere to be seen. I rustled the packages in the string bag to announce that I was back. She called out from the bathroom.

'*There* you are. Hurry up, I'm all ready.'

I thought she might need helping off the lavatory. Instead, I was confronted with the sight of her standing stark naked in a waterless tub trying to hook a shower-cap off the door knob with her walking stick. I handed her the cap. She thrust it back with irritable fingers.

'Put it on, you silly girl.'

It occurred to me that if I were to survive with Mrs Browne

214

any longer than my four predecessors something would have to be done about these rude commands. Stuffing up my hair, I nonchalantly put the cap on my own head. And curtsied. For a moment her whole scrawny frame froze. Even her shrivelled little witch's nipples managed to look furious. I remained demure.

'Cheeky hussy!' she spluttered, 'cheeky hussy!' But she cackled as she snatched back the cap and stuck it over her own wispy hair. While I was washing her, trying to treat her frail body naturally, as though this was something I had done a hundred times before, she told me how hers had been the most perfect, the most enviable, flapper figure. She told me in detail what she had worn, finishing with the triumphant line: 'It was nothing to me to wear stockings with sequins all the way up the seams – and don't think we didn't have garters to match!'

By the time she was dressed in her old grey cardigan and skirt and back in her chair in the sitting-room, she was so exhausted from talking she did not want to bother going through the shopping.

'Next time,' was all she would say. So I left out some obvious bits and pieces for her supper and said goodbye. Our worlds would cross again in two days.

I went to 309 before the first lecture. There were some clothes I wanted to collect and it was a good opportunity for a bath. There was no hot water in the squat.

Kay knew by the fact that I left my bag in the hall that I was not going to stay. When I came down with my hair loose and a 'new' skirt on, which I had bought in a hospital jumble sale, she asked if I was going to see Addie or Jem. I said no.

'And if they call, is there somewhere they can get in touch with you?'

'No.'

My rejection of 309 as a base was also a rejection of her. I was afraid of the lonely turn her life had taken after the divorce and was reluctant to connect my world with hers at all. I sent my love to Marianne but did not ask where she was or what she was doing. It was as if I did not dare learn, especially now, when I wanted only positive thoughts in my head to face Massell. I left with no indication of when I might be back or where I could be found. Still, illogically and with childish cruelty, I was punishing Kay for having let Richard go.

Since the last time I had spoken to him I had read two of Massell's books. One was a paperback on a self-improvement theme, the other a songbook. In the lyrics of one song he spoke of a rare kind of feather which made me think at once of a strange little amulet of woven feathers Botswana Steve had given me. I had it in the bottom of my shoulder-bag now and kept feeling for it as I sat on the bus, making sure it was still there. It was something very precious to me.

On a board in the foyer of the university building, crooked letters said: ADRIAN MASSELL RM 203 4TH FLOOR. I was a little early and I went into an empty classroom to tidy my hair. I did not want to look like a squatter.

I walked into 203 on the dot of 8 p.m. As it was the first day a register was being drawn up and students were queueing to hand in cash and cheques. I had no money and my fingers were clutching the amulet. When my turn came, Massell's head was bent over the register, hair in a brilliant red sweep across his brow. He was filling in the name of the student who had gone before. My back blocked off the space between us from the rest of the class and there was the smallest swish as I slid the amulet across the desk and quietly pronounced my name. For less than a second the hand holding the pen hesitated, then he looked up. Green, green eyes.

'Did you phone?'

'Yes.'

The next moves were so swift I hardly felt them happen. The amulet was in his pocket, my name written down and I was on my way to an empty desk at the back.

'I'll see you afterwards,' he had said with a smile.

That was all, but that was everything.

The hour of instruction raced, Massell never once allowing his audience's attention to slide. New words and new ideas were bounced at us in rapid succession and everything he said struck a ready chord in me. I had not been so enthralled since Richard had cuddled close and told me good-night stories when I was a child.

When the lecture ended there was a subdued shuffling as papers were stowed into cases, pens which had not had a chance to jot a line were recapped and the first chairs scraped back. The air seemed curiously flat now that Massell's voice was no longer in it. A number of students hung back to speak to him. I stayed by my desk taking a long time to put on my coat. Finally the group moved towards the door, Massell in their midst. He turned at the last minute.

'We are going for a quick Indian meal,' he said lightly. 'Coming?'

I had only enough money on me for the fare back to Banstead. Could I risk assuming I was with him?

'Yes,' I said, shaking back my hair, 'I'd love to.'

There were about nine of us in the restaurant. The atmosphere was low-lit and full of bustle after the white clarity of the lecture room. A waiter in a red jacket came to take our order, reminding me of the last time I had been in a restaurant – that time I had run out and got caught. It seemed a world away. We were at a long, narrow table, Massell at the head responding equably to the intense interrogation of a bearded young man. I sat on his left sipping a glass of *lassi*. Massell ordered for both of us. He had given back the amulet, saying, 'No need for that, we'll sort something out another time.'

I hardly spoke during the meal, intent on listening to and watching Massell. I liked the way he broke with confidence the soft, stuffed *parathas* and quested with his fork among the spiced gravies for the most succulent pieces of meat. Once our forks met in a dish of hot chillies and beef and he laughed, gallantly conceding the prime morsel. When he spoke, the muscles below his cheekbones worked gently and small creases appeared under his eyes. His image was printing itself indelibly on my mind.

Towards the end of the meal the young man opposite tried to capture my attention. It was after ten-thirty and he asked if I had far to go. When I said Felstead, he said I would be better to go early in the morning when the buses were more frequent. He offered me a spare room in his flat near by and I felt confused, half thinking it might be wise to accept but not wanting to cut myself off from Massell. He must have overheard for he said easily, 'There's always a couch at Bellington Road if you're stuck.'

It was awkward, the young man had offered first and was waiting for a reply.

'Thank you,' I said, 'but Holland Park would be handier for transport I think.'

I knew Massell lived in Holland Park, had read it somewhere in the club blurb. The young man accepted the thin reasoning gracefully. There was no competing with Massell.

The party broke up to cries of 'see you next week' and I found myself standing alone on the pavement with Massell. It was cold, but with the meal still warm inside and a thick sheepskin coat – another jumble sale buy – I was glowing. We set off towards the square where he had left his car, striding along fast, heads down.

'Brrr,' he shuddered, thrusting his hands into the pockets of his thin jacket. 'That's a good coat you're wearing. I could do with one like that.'

Without any hesitation I took it off and held it out.

'Have this one.'

We had slowed down. He laughed.

'Are you sure?'

'Yes.'

He shrugged out of the jacket and put on the big sheepskin. It looked good with his red hair, a fox in snow.

His car was dark green and low. Dynamic, I thought, like him. He drove with the same casual precision as Richard. I caught my reflection once in a side window and thought: you clever, lucky thing. He had not offered any of the other students a couch for the night.

His house was small but impressive, all white carpets and brown velvet curtains. There was a built-in sauna and shower unit as well as a sunken bath and a bidet. In the living-room was an open fire.

'Know how to light that?' he called, going upstairs.

'Yes,' I said with confidence, Mole's End rituals fresh in mind. Two young black cats played languidly around me and ran to rub against his legs when he appeared briefly in a short blue robe ready to take a shower. He was so at ease with his own body he somehow did not look undressed. His legs were red-downed and looked strong.

He was a long time in the shower and I was tired, so I undressed and arranged the cushions and blankets he had provided on a couch near the fire. I lay on my back, arms above my head, completely relaxed. He came down to say good-night, a white towel bunched under ears that glowed healthily.

'You know when you rang before Christmas?' he said, 'I thought you were one of those bespectacled old frumps from the club. It was quite a surprise matching your face to your voice in class.'

He paused, rubbing his neck with the towel, 'How old are you?'

'Nearly seventeen. What time do you get up?'

He stopped rubbing and smiled.

'Six-thirty. Breakfast at seven. What do you usually have?'

Feta in Greece, halva in Israel, porridge at Mole's End.

'A boiled egg,' I said firmly, 'and tea.'

'Right then, see you in the morning.'

I heard the bedroom door close and rolled over to gaze at the fire until sleep came. Both the cats had gone upstairs with him.

I was halfway through the titles on his floor-to-ceiling bookshelves when he appeared next morning at 6.45. My mind, awake for hours, was buzzing with questions. I began firing them straight away. Did he think the special diagrams he had shown us could be applied to the processes of thought and to emotions? Did he think he thought in words? Didn't it feel more like fast-moving images, clouds of thought reducing to puddles of words? Please could he recommend some reading?

'Good, good, yes, certainly,' he said, busy with the eggs. 'Try putting all this down. No reason the diagrams can't be used for thought processes. Excellent idea.'

I preened inwardly, feeling ready to attempt anything. All night, between short bouts of sleep, I had gone over everything he had said in the lecture. My brain this morning felt springy as an acrobat; it just wanted a trapeze to swing on.

I sat at the table tap-dancing a teaspoon over my egg. A pile of books accumulated by my elbow as we talked – Pavlov, Popper, Friedman, Illich, another by Massell himself. He said as I was leaving that I would be welcome to stay the night next week if it helped. I thanked him, bubbling over inside.

'But I don't know why,' I blurted. 'I mean I haven't got much to offer, have I? I don't know anything – anything!'

His green, green eyes rested on my excited face and the smile I had seen last night as he looked down at me under the blankets reappeared.

'That's just it,' he said, 'you have everything to offer, the greatest gift of all . . .'

I waited to hear what that was.

'. . . An open mind and an infinite capacity to learn.'

I danced down the street smiling at every lamp-post and stone.

Back at the squat that evening I covered the whole of one wall with a huge Massell diagram. It was ambitious, the central theme being the development of the individual in relation to outside influences from birth. It began with a clear picture of the main character propelled by hollow arrows marked Destiny and Desire, and ended by resembling a dozen spiders' webs inextricably tangled, with the 'individual' bound and gagged by the cords of influence and looking far less like a 'developed personality' than a hapless fly.

Standing back and regarding it critically, I decided it would look much better in colour, and not wanting to stint on materials for future efforts, I resolved to get a third job.

A notice next morning on the board where I had pinned my advert looked hopeful: BLIND GENTLEMAN REQUIRES YOUNG LADY TO READ TO HIM TWO OR THREE TIMES PER WEEK. REMUNERATION BY THE HOUR.

I would pop in on him after Mrs Browne.

A disturbing sense of time frozen closed around me as soon as I entered her flat that day. All was just as I had left it, the food

I had laid out for her supper untouched, a bar of soap which had slipped into the bath still skidded up against the plug hole. There was no evidence that anyone had been living there since Monday. I approached the living-room door with something like dread.

'Mrs Browne? Mrs Browne?'

Silence. I pushed and the door glided open noiselessly. I nearly slammed it shut again as two bloodshot eyes leapt at me with the ferocity of rats.

'Eeou!' came her voice, rasping with fury. And again, 'Eeou!'

She was alive, thank God, and bristlingly so.

Knobbly old spine forced straight as it would go, Mrs Browne was sitting right on the edge of her chair. She was kneading her walking stick so hard it had churned the rug at her feet into a sea.

''ook!' she commanded. ''ook 'ot 'ou've 'un!'

I gazed at her in idiot incomprehension, stunned by the intensity of her rage. What on earth was the matter with her mouth? My immobility increased her anger. Thud! went the stick on the pummelled rug. Thud thud thud! The last thud was so violent it dislodged the stick from her hand and sent it clattering down by the side of her chair. Glad of an obvious move, I bent to pick it up. In a flash she had grabbed it and before I could straighten up, her fingers were hooked under the collar of my jacket. I saw the stick lift out of the corner of my eye and ducked just in time so that it came down over my back and not my skull. Up it went again, with purpose. Grunts and sucking sounds issued from a throat drawn tight with effort. Down came the stick again in a series of astonishingly powerful whacks.

My hands leapt angrily to arrest the flailing arm, wavering in shock as they met the incongruous frailty of tissue-soft skin and baby-bird bones. For a moment we rocked together in a silent parody of combat. Then, for the second time, the stick dropped to the floor.

I stood up slowly. Her fingers were still imprisoned in my own, held together as though in prayer. I softened my hold, afraid she might crumble, but the shake in my voice was an echo of her own rage.

'Mrs Browne, don't you ever do that to me again.'

She would not be cowed. A trapped yellow talon dug into my wrist.

''ook!' she croaked, eyes and chin jerking towards the mantel-piece. I looked, and my mouth dropped open.

'Oh God, Mrs Browne, I'm so sorry . . .'

I felt her relax with satisfaction at my distress.

''ere, 'ou 'ee?'

'Oh I do see. I'm so sorry.'

The tableau on the mantelpiece told its own tale. After I had left on Monday, Mrs Browne had evidently looked through the shopping and decided to make a start on the chocolates. I imagined her sharp finger-nails ripping open the Cellophane, box balanced on bony knees. She must have thought they were good ones for she had ploughed in with a big, gleeful bite.

The big, gleeful bite, chocolate still clenched like a fat cigar butt between upper and lower molars, was exhibit number one on the mantelpiece.

Following this in order of experiment and rejection were all the other items she had attempted to feed herself on over the last two days. But the final word lay in six caramel-coloured blobs ranged on the metal cowl of the gas fire. Unable to gain satisfaction from mashing bread and cheese against her upper palate, Mrs Browne had returned to what was supposed to be her one reminder of luxury: the chocolates. Each melted, tongue-tortured lump added to the weight of accusation in her eyes. I fetched a knife and rubber gloves. It took twenty minutes just to scrape the dentures clean.

There was a tricky moment when I went to put her teeth back in. She still looked suspiciously fierce. I took a risk.

'Mrs Browne, I warn you, if you bite me I'll bite back.'

She mumbled the teeth into place and her hand twitched on the stick.

'You would too, wouldn't you, you cheeky hussy. Now get out of here and buy me some proper sweets.'

Later that week I made her some soft fudge on the squat's single gas-ring. The vision of her lonely chompings haunted me for years.

*   *   *

With Mr Geshner, the blind man, I felt I was on to a good thing. I had enjoyed reading aloud ever since making the discovery at school that a small pretence of religious fervour earned the privilege of spending cold breaktimes in the chapel, entertaining my friend Kate with random extracts from the bible. Then there had been the poetry sessions with Jem and later the lively Nietzschean recitations with Addie. Now I had the chance to get paid for it. But first I had to pass Mr Geshner's little test.

A table in his small flat was covered with old Sunday supplements. Mr Geshner felt for them with his hands and fluttered one on my direction.

'In zere,' he said in a strong, precise accent, 'is a pessage on contributions of ze Guggenheim family to art in ze United States. Read please from ze zecond peragraph.'

While I read Mr Geshner sat with his wiry grey head cocked to one side, rectangular eyebrows raised. On his nose rested a visor supporting two truncated telescopes which he referred to as his 'gedgit'. He interrupted halfway through the first paragraph.

'Zet's it, Miss Urfin, ze job is yours. You von't believe how many young ladies I hef hed to reject.' A nervous bubble of laughter popped in his throat. '. . . Ent all because of a zingle vord. To hear zem get it wrong has been driving me med, med! To me it is qvite simply a metter of stendards.'

The word in question was 'drawing'. If I had pronounced it 'drawring' I would have failed the test. I was grateful to Richard for imposing his 'stendards' when I was small. It was arranged that I should go to Mr Geshner twice a week and read articles on the Arab–Israeli war at 50p an hour.

The babysitting at the end of the week went satisfactorily and extended to cleaning as well which made it more lucrative. The only time I felt uncomfortable was when the lady of the house asked me about myself. Her questions were conventional: Did I live with my parents? Had I got a boyfriend? Where had I gone to school? I preferred coping with the idiosyncrasies of Mrs Browne and Mr Geshner, neither of whom was interested in my family or past.

Although my jobs were mere satellite occupations around the Massell lectures, it was impossible not to become involved to some extent with each of the different lives I was touching. After the initial hiccups, Mrs Browne decided that, for amusement value if nothing else, I was better than the usual domestics who tried to boss her into sensible habits. Why should she not eat her meals straight out of a carrier-bag or belabour the TV with a stick if someone she did not like was on? And I think she knew I did not listen to her tales of the past just to be polite. The world her reminiscences conjured delighted me. I was sure I would have enjoyed being a rich Canton flapper with a peacock called Bluey too.

Getting a foot in the door of Mr Geshner's world took a little longer.

Towards the end of the fourth or fifth session with him my throat felt dry. The piece I was reading on Moshe Dayan went on for another two pages and I knew I would become hoarse if I did not have a break. I asked if I might have a glass of water. Mr Geshner's attentively cocked head snapped upright and he made gobbling noises.

'My dear young lady, forgif me.'

Groping up from the chair he felt his way along the wall to a dresser where there was a jug and some tumblers. Stubby fingers tapped a tumbler rim to make sure it was the right way up before pouring. The twin black telescopes of his eye gadget quested in my direction and I spoke again to guide the outstretched hand. He hovered while I drank, looking strangely anguished.

'Shall I continue?'

'Fun moment Miss Urfin, I vont to explain.'

He scratched his grey head vigorously, hesitating, then his words tumbled out in a rush.

'My vife would never forgif me. Five times you hef been here and not vonce hef I offered you so much as a zip of water. But you see zere was ... an *inzident*.' He stopped and scrubbed at his hair again before going on. 'Always I used to offer ze young ladies a cup of tea - even ze ones with terrible accents! - but zen one day, over tea, a girl started to say strange zings ...' There was a long pause while he spread his hands wide in shock and gobbled, '. . . Ent zen she tried to remove my gedgit!'

The vision was clear as a film clip: Mr Geshner hopping helplessly round the table pursued by an amorous tart who said 'drawrin'. If it had not been for the look of misery on his face I would have rocked with laughter. There was more.

'Ent ven I asked her to leave she became abusive – such lenguage! She said vot did I expect advertising for young girls and inviting zem for biscuits and tea? So you see it has been a problem. I am not understood . . .'

His speech trailed off.

'Mr Geshner,' I said solemnly, 'I promise that if you were to offer a cup of tea I would not try to remove your gadget.'

A wild attack of gobbling dissolved into a shy giggle. Thereafter we always paused for tea halfway through the session and he made a regular little joke as he passed the biscuits.

'Look,' he exclaimed, 'none of zem has strings!'

His giggles became quite skittish.

The subsequent Massell evenings were no less riveting than the first and when he marked my homework with a flamboyant *excellent* in red I flushed from collar to fringe with pride. I did not mention that I had been playing with word diagrams on my own, wanting to get the wild scrawlings under more control before submitting them for criticism. The meal at the Indian restaurant after the lecture became a ritual.

'It's refreshing to meet someone with such an unashamed appetite,' he commented once as I soaked up the last of the meat juices with a *paratha*. 'Are you conscious of what you eat in a nutritional sense?'

I swallowed and a small burp escaped by accident. How could I tell him that in the life I led concern over nutritional value took second place to straightforward survivalist opportunism?

'Sometimes,' was my cagey reply and then on inspiration I gave him a rundown of some of the wholesome dishes I had prepared at Mole's End. He nodded approvingly and told me he was a great believer in always leaving the table before the appetite was completely satisfied. As I stuffed myself to capacity at every chance, I kept quiet.

The routine of day-to-day survival changed as my circle of acquaintances broadened. Fired by contact with Massell, I spent a lot of time hanging around libraries and ordering the books he recommended. One chilly evening, when the library was closed, I leant against the warm window of a café reading for so long that a man came out and asked if he could buy me coffee. He turned out to be a heavily Christian social worker who, interpreting my jumble-sale attire as a sure sign that I was on my way to the devil, was determined to save my soul. Unimpressed, I stared boredly over his earnestly bent head at a man opposite, who was covering the menu with fast-flowing handwriting. I laughed irritably at something the social worker said and the man looked up and caught my eye. His tanned face, under a flop of clean brown hair, was almost absurdly good-looking. When the social worker left – to return to his post at a vagrants' hostel in the East End – the man spoke. He had an appealing drawl, reminding me a little of Jorges.

'Seems you didn't have too much to say to that guy.'

I smiled and shook my hair back.

'He was dull. He said "have faith" so many times it sounded like an indigestion cure.'

He bought two more coffees and later drove me to his flat and gave me supper. He was Canadian, an art historian, and the first person I told about Massell. I did not understand what he meant when he said, 'The guy sounds like a real whizzkid type, better watch out.'

We talked for a long time, sitting several yards apart on giant tapestried cushions in his lounge. The room was full of interesting things: a fourteen-foot Mexican hammock, fetishes from Africa, Persian rugs and primitive paintings on the walls. I liked it and was interested in his books: Lowry, Neruda, R. D. Laing. In the long, comfortable silences between sentences we listened to an African Mass, the music beating softly from a concealed stereo.

I spent the night on a fur-covered water-bed in the spare room and his flat became another place where I was welcome to stay from time to time. Once, when there were other people using the spare room, I slept with him. In the middle of the night, with the moon shining in on the bed, he put his arms around me and gently lifted me astride his penis. But I must have looked doubtful because after a moment he said, 'OK' in his pleasant, easy way and put me down. His name was Michael.

Alf was another occasional doss-point. He was a figure I had seen around the Richmond area on and off for years but only met properly that winter. He styled himself as an actor and was always just off to, or just back from, Morocco or Algiers, where he played soldier number X439 in *The Charge of the Light Brigade* and other epics. But he was not *really* an actor, he told me, he was just an Alf. 'And you,' he said, cuffing me affectionately, 'you're just an Alf too.'

Until I had read Laurie Lee's *As I Walked Out One Midsummer Morning* I did not know what he meant, but as soon as I made the acquaintance of the lone wanderer under whose pan-rattling wing the young Lee was taken on his long walk from Slough to London, the parallel became clear. Alf was a gentleman of the road who took his ease wherever a pleasing hummock presented itself, the unhurried progress of his laceless boots guided only by the natural rhythms of the year; a being not so much outside society's law as beyond it, definable only as a feature of the countryside who in winter months temporarily became a feature of the town. He referred to himself and all other peripatetics as Alf and despised only those who had failed to hone their vagrancy to an art.

'The only difference,' said my Alf, 'is that your hummocks are people.'

And in this he was right. I drifted from person to person, world to world, perching on the periphery of half-a-dozen different lives. From the squat to Mrs Browne, to Mr Geshner, to Massell, I made my rounds. And in between there were Alf, Michael the Canadian, the babysitting people, Julian and Addie and 309. My days became even more crowded when I took to cramming all earning hours between Friday and Monday so that I could enjoy spring at Mole's End.

227

There I watched the hedgehogs emerging like tramps from their winter lairs, bumbling with straw still trailing from quills to cross paths with mice just vacating the mattresses. I wandered in woods where scrolled leaves shiny with the newness of birth sang out against wet black bark and my ankles brushed the waxy cups of crocuses. In the evenings I crouched, secure as an embryo, in the big barrel bath and watched camomile-scented steam uncoil among the low cottage beams.

And perhaps it was there, fed by tales of Julian's current romances, that I took to dreaming of a connection with my guru Massell beyond diagrams and a couch in his lounge.

The whole summer would go by, however, before I did something about those dreams, for suddenly a world which under the influence of all the others had lately grown distant, came abruptly back into focus.

Richard contacted me out of the blue.

'I need you,' he said.

It was infallible. My answer was instant.

'I'll come.'

PART FOUR

Blood

Chapter Fifteen

The short season I worked at the hotel that year seemed unconnected with the summers I had spent there before. Arriving several weeks after the rest of the staff made a difference. I was the new girl who had to ask where things were. But I learned quickly and soon had the routine off pat so that I could go through it mechanically, leaving my mind free to wander elsewhere.

Contact with Richard had been thready while I was away and the long, blank patch in the hospital was not something we discussed. Once, I had begun to tell him something of what happened in Greece but I was slow in my lead up and he had looked distant and vaguely disapproving. I was speaking of circumstances outside his world. I dropped the subject before reaching the point and never raised it again. Still loyal, I was back on his ground but this time preoccupied with visions of my own. I did notice, however, that his nails were down to the quick and that Edwina's previously girlish figure had gone very square. Things had changed in their lives as well as in my own.

Waitressing, baking, drying glasses and endlessly Hoovering the dining-room, I swung from dreamy recitations of Shelley to the bloodless repetition of Massell's mental agility exercises. Snatched hours off in daylight were spent on the hill overcoming my fear of a new, livelier pony, bought as soon as I had enough saved, and any spare moments before sleep were devoted to colourful entries in a dairy kept entirely in diagrams. I seldom wrote in words except in reply to letters from Kay. Addie and Jem were forced to grapple with cryptic messages in thought blobs. Julian and I limited our communication to postal exchanges of heather and Mole's End leaves.

The summer progressed with the familiar dash and grind of hotel life behind the scenes and the ordered, other-worldly passage of the guests. Richard was plotting again. When he was not shut up in the smokehouse with his kippers and terrines, organizing the guests' fishing rotas or guiding their choice of wines, he was down on the croft pacing out land for new developments. Incapable of treating the hotel simply as a business, he was forever throwing some new challenge in his own path. Life without a dream to realize was not worth living. And still, those who could not keep up were left behind.

News of Marianne was not good: talk of doctors, X-rays, temporary improvements, frequent regressions. Kay wrote bulletins of the physical ills but nothing was said about the pain in Marianne's mind, the still weeping child mourning the death of family. I skimmed the details of the letters, hanging on to the belief that Marianne would contact me when she was ready – in a space between her 'giddy' spells. Richard and I did not talk about what was happening to her. It was too difficult, too sad. We simply turned away and immersed ourselves deeper in the business of our own lives.

Halfway through the season a round postcard came from a Scandinavian town. Massell. The neatly printed message started in the middle and spiralled outwards like a catherine wheel. I twirled it round and round in my hands for a long time before putting it in a drawer with my diary. Apart from Addie's letters, which I only kept because he made such a point of hoarding mine, I generally threw away all correspondence as soon as it was read. Now, for everything that came from Massell, I set aside a large brown envelope marked M. In time, this became A, for Adrian.

Spring at Mole's End and the closeness of Julian and Addie had done much to break down the numbness I had where touch was concerned, but I still had a remote attitude to sex. The incident with Michael illustrates the degree of alienation: I was so far removed that it was almost immaterial whether he penetrated my body or not. But now, fired by an attraction already intellectually intense, mind, heart and body softened and changed.

In the evenings, when work was finished, I would creep upstairs to one of the guest bathrooms, a book wrapped in a towel under one arm. Warm water and secrecy, I had discovered, made the perfect environment for the development of fantasy. While one hand tickled gently at the floating curls between my thighs, the other flicked efficiently through the pages of Mrs Beeton. Memorizing lists of ingredients, weights, temperatures and timings for everything from Scotch broth to crab soufflé, I was teaching myself the art of cookery for two. For the fantasy was that I was Mrs Massell.

And it did not stop at recipes. I worked out minutely how my time would be divided between housekeeping, having babies and studying so that I could help Massell. I wrote poems now in the evenings, as well as the diagram diary, and his response was encouraging. Excellent! There was much potential there. That word again.

Cards came from all over the world. Then a score of song lyrics from London, part of a new book he was writing. I read through them twice but their message was beyond me, quite different to verses which came my way from another pen.

Alf had decided that, as fellow Alfs, we should join forces. His poems were flatteringly romantic and with one he even sent a red rose. Touched, although I could not return his feelings, I went to the hotel kitchen for a vase. Edwina handed me one without comment but Richard caught me in the corridor. He was wearing the smart jacket he used for mingling with guests in the evening. He noticed the vase.

'What's that for?'

'I've got a flower.'

His eyebrows rose in the slightly suave arch which told me he was already in his guest-mingling mood.

'Just one?' he asked teasingly.

'Yes, one.'

Catching his mood I rippled out a secretive smile and added, '. . . From a man.'

The arch went higher.

'Anyone – special?'

Suddenly I felt foolish. What was I doing messing about with Alf's rose? Of course he was not 'special'. I had not said a word about Massell. He was different. He *was* special. A triumphant scenario flashed through my mind: Massell driving me up to the hotel in his smooth green car; me getting out and making the introductions: 'Adrian, meet my father. Richard, meet my man.'

Later I blushed at my own temerity in thinking this. Apart from a disturbing confusion of faces and bodies in the picture, it was the first time I had called Adrian, Adrian in my mind.

Unconsciously I was taking steps away from Richard. Responding almost unthinkingly to his call: 'I need you', I had forgotten all that made life at the hotel uncomfortable: the non-position as daughter of the proprietor, neither a member of a proper family nor a proper member of the staff. Marianne had found the precariousness of identity intolerable and turned the pain inwards, inflicting yet more injury on an already injured self. Unlike me she had no perspective to draw on. I had been far enough away from the struggles of family and far enough into other worlds to know that the wealth of stances from which life could be led was infinite. The idea was daunting but I believed the choice of stance was largely up to me. Despite the complexities of influence, that was the message I read in the diagrams I drew. Comfort and distraction, but not a solution to oneself, might be found in others.

Poring complacently over those two-dimensional diagrams, I was blind to the roots of my own dreams. Passion, in my fantasies, was something very like salvation.

I grew strong that summer, working hard and spending all my time off outside. My body was taut and young, fit without effort, an easy vessel for joy. Carelessly proud, sure of my solitude, I angled every part of me to the sun. And as I stretched out beneath the casual splendour of the sky, the vague yearnings of earlier times were at last defined. I felt magnificent, invulnerable, and I wished Massell had been there, right then, to race me to the next valley and catch me as I fell.

Winter would be in London again and I must plan for it now. No vague job-hunting in shop windows, no return to doss points all over town. Both Mrs Browne and Mr Geshner had said they would like me back but this time I wanted one fulltime job. Initially I would stay at 309. Kay's letters had been welcoming and it was time to do away with adolescent antipathies. I waited impatiently for the newspapers which came once a week to the hotel and, scanning the columns, applied for a post as a receptionist in the West End. I wanted to be smart for Massell.

Before I left the hotel, Richard suggested I should take on the management of the café next year, have it as my complete responsibility. I was non-committal, off on a streak of my own. I wanted him to see that there were other things in my life besides the hotel – and him.

I did not recognize then how strong the blood attachment between us still was; how, in the impressive figure of Massell, I was secretly worshipping a Richard with whom I could make love.

Richmond, five months later.

Ah, but the plan had gone awry. Dreams-into-schemes were not so simple and now I was back on old territory, sliding rapidly downhill.

There was rain, no messing about. It streaked the lamp-posts, slanted at the shop fronts, puddled in the hoisted awnings and ran with the wine down Teddy's beard. Teddy was an ex-binmate; a mate, I had decided, more on my level than Massell.

We had one of those Spanish carafes you have to lift high, holding your mouth to catch the stream like a stone scallop under a fountain-sprouting breast. Jem was the only one who had got the hang of it. Even McAllister, all six foot five of him leaning over me with deadly concentration, could not get it right, spraying an ear by accident, soaking the front of my dress.

'Take it away!' I yelped, batting at his hands. It reminded me of when Kay and I had gone away for a week before the divorce. She in a stiff-cupped swim-suit being wooed by a Spaniard who had carafes like that in his bar. Me not knowing whether to encourage or condemn, finally pretending not to see. Jem started up again, jumbling Pyramus and Galahad:

'Oh night, oh night, oh grim-looked night
Oh night with hue so – *blood red and sliding down the blackened marsh
Blood red and on the naked mountain top . . .*'

He had been declaiming all afternoon; he had told the story of
Cain and Abel to the park railings, mumbled *The Rime of the
Ancient Mariner* into his pregnant girlfriend's hair and, now that
it was getting dark, struck poses before the swishing headlamps
of cars. Spotlit in the gutter, booed by hoots, he was now Zarathustra, now Hamlet, now Percy Bysshe. Rain streamed from his
eye-patch like tears and under his coat he hugged a stolen hassock
and a saxophone. We cheered him and ignored him by turns.
Teddy ignored us all.

But it was for me he had come. Big mad Teddy with his
Medusa snakes of sodden hair, broad body solid as earth and big,
wondering hands that held my face as he whispered strange, mad
messages to the Queen of France: 'Marie-Antoinette, the number
is not thirteen!'

I cleaned the wine and rain from the hollows of his throat with
my tongue, opened his heavy coat and pressed my head to his
chest. There was the distant pat-pat of his paw at the back of
my neck and McAllister's giraffe head shaking gloomily beyond,
motioning us on. We were about to cross Richmond Bridge.

I ran on ahead, holding up my long skirt, ducking my scarf-
swathed head against the rain. It was funny, wasn't it, that here
I was, crossing the same old bridge again? Only this time I was
with my cronies. Big Mad Teddy, my crony man.

'Come on!' I yelled, laughing at the bedraggled trail in the wet
lamplight: Teddy shambling in front, McAllister and Jem struggling for possession of the saxophone, pregnant Josie last, calmly
sucking Mackeson from a can. My teeth chattered as I licked in
rain. Teddy caught up and I took the carafe from him and poured
from the handle end, filling my mouth with sour pools.

*Hah! – and I had been so careful that evening after Scotland with
Massell, all dolled up in smart receptionist clothes, only taking tiny
sips of wine in case I slurred my words or said something silly. Better
if I had maybe, better than sitting there like a tongue-tied fool.*

And what a fool to think that the mess of adolescence could be

236

swept clean at one stroke, that 309 could suddenly become nothing but a convenient base.

I spluttered, carafe knocking against my teeth, as I thought of poor Kay with her trays of cold food in front of the television, adrift in the wake of Richard's life. And Marianne, slumped across the bed in the studio, hugging a puppy and a bottle. *Who the hell did I think* I *was?*

Teddy stood behind me, arms around, a cliff against the rain. Jem was tugging wildly at the saxophone, now being guarded by McAllister, who was being sensible, saying, 'Be careful, calm down.' I passed the carafe back to Teddy and it slipped through his fingers, shattering into curved shards on the road. With a final, twisting effort and dropping the hassock, Jem wrenched the saxophone from McAllister and ran to lean panting on the stone balustrade. Under the bridge the Thames swirled in a heavy, dimpled stream, reflected light shimmering in mud and water whorls.

'For heaven's sake!' shouted McAllister. But he was too late. Powering his throw with a wild, backward swing, Jem spun the saxophone through the air. There was a long second before it landed with a wet thwack just out of the reach of the river's pull. McAllister swore. Punctured, Jem tottered to the kerb, sat on his hassock and burst into tears. Josie walked straight past him, absently shaking the last drops of beer from her can. Teddy talked on softly to his voices.

'You're all mad!' ranted McAllister, long legs bounding down the steps to the towpath. Brandishing the saxophone below, he looked like a long, cold ghost in the rain. In the gutter Jem scratched daintily at his wrists and started on 'Death, the Leveller'.

'Let's go,' I said to Teddy, weary of the scene.

'Sure baby, go.'

We walked towards the Green, passing a house where one of my old schoolfriends lived. I had been to a party there once and wondered at the way her parents called everyone darling. She would be preparing for university now.

Teddy began to sing quietly in a deep voice full of tobacco ash:

'If Ah were a cat
Ah'd be purrin' right now
If Ah were a dawg
Ah'd be waggin' ma tail . . .'

I supposed we were going to sleep together, supposed we were looking for a bed. I wanted another drink.

We crossed the High Street, where I had shopped so sensibly in the first weeks back from Scotland: nipping round Sainsbury's on my way home from work, browsing among the fancy shampoos in Boots, reading the whole of *Jonathan Livingston Seagull* in Smiths. Because Massell had recommended it.

Past Alf's place – no light in the window – we roved on up the hill until we came to a pub Teddy knew. He had peddled coke to the barman there. We sat mind-drowned in rock, drinking tequila.

He had been so friendly, too, Massell. Interested to know what I was doing, telling me about a radio series he was making. Had I ever thought of working with kids, getting involved with education at its roots? Mustn't waste all that talent, you know, that potential. He smiled out of those green, green eyes and I just sat there blushing and blushing. I could not look at his face without recalling how I had touched it in my fantasies, could not speak for the bolus of saliva in my throat, could not eat.

'Where's that marvellous appetite gone?'

'I don't know.'

'Been writing any more of those promising poems?'

'No.'

Glowing with enthusiasm for his own plans he had asked, 'What do you see yourself doing five years from now?' Echoes of Richard: what was the plan? Numbly I answered, 'I don't know.'

There was more tequila, mine in a tall glass. No sunrise was ever that muddy. I gulped it down and reeled off to the Ladies. The face in the mirror was a mess.

'So much,' I hissed at it viciously, 'for Mrs Massell.'

At the name spoken aloud, I winced and my hands twisted involuntarily on my chest. But instead of feeling pain there, they met warmth, power, the strong, steady beat of a young heart.

Young, fit without effort, invulnerable. Remember? It was only the feeble mind that was floundering. The body was strong. It would not let me down.

A girl in leather hotpants jumped back against the wall as I shot past and through the saloon. There was a glass of whisky on our table which had not been there before. I downed it in one and spoke urgently to Teddy.

'Have you got change for the phone?'

His blurred, caveman's face broke slowly into a smile, the horizontal scar on his nose curving up like a third lip.

> 'Yeah, if Ah were a cat,
> Ah'd be purrin' and how,
> An if Ah were a dawg
> Ah'd be wag wag wag, waggin' ma tail . . . ,

I turned to a stranger at my side.

'Please have you got change for the phone?'

'You've drunk my whisky.'

'I know. Have you got change?'

He felt in his pocket and came out with several coins.

'Help yourself.' Then with a sidelong glance at Teddy, he indicated the empty glass, 'Like another?'

I nodded and went to find the phone.

My forefinger slotted itself confidently into the digit holes. No problem remembering the number. I held the coin poised, thinking I would scream if it was the ansaphone. It was. I did not scream, but beckoned to the whisky man. The message was that Adrian would be in later. *Adrian.*

'That bloke you're with,' said the whisky man, handing me a glass, 'is he all right?'

I drank quickly, and improvised.

'No, he's not. He's mad. Just out of prison for breaking into his ex-wife's house with an axe.'

'You're kidding.'

I shook my head.

The man's eyes travelled over Teddy's bulk and back to me.

'Want to go somewhere else?'

'Yes. Now.'

He had a car and we went to another pub. It was near the bus route for Holland Park. I checked before we went in.

'What do you do then, when you're not pinching other people's drinks?'

'I'm a char.'

Another failure. I had gone back to scrubbing floors.

'What, a cleaning lady? I'd have thought you'd be more like a secretary or receptionist.'

'Oh yes!' I said, startling him with my vehemence, 'I was. In fact I was *star* receptionist at the Wakeford Corvan fashion salon. But not for long.'

'Money' by Pink Floyd ground aggressively from the jukebox.

It all came back, the way I had come down from Scotland with heather in my hair and dreams in my heart and been transformed overnight into the Wakeford Corvan mould. The salon provided the clothes. Real silk blouses and swish tailored skirts. When I was sent out to buy stationery, I got whistled in the street. But I felt a million miles outside that world. Me an Alf, an ex-bin-mate, someone who stuck knives into people in bus queues.

Memories and whisky pricked hotly. Nothing would have mattered if things had gone all right with Massell. But I had blown it. Since that ridiculous tongue-tied evening there had been no spoken word. Only a distantly polite postcard in response to three of my own. I left the receptionist job and went to Mole's End. Neither Julian nor Addie was around, but Julian's parents were there and were so kind to me I could not bear it. I went to Felstead but the squat had changed and it was there, among the new batch of drifters, that I picked up Teddy, in whose schizo-phrenic presence I felt oddly at ease. He did not have any expectations. He never talked about potential.

And then I crossed the Channel with a new Beverly and hitch-hiked in the bitter cold as far as Pamplona. I did not know where I was going. Choking on chorizo in a gritty wind, I turned round and came back out of sheer funk.

'Sheer funk,' I said aloud to my companion who only got snippets of the reverie. 'But the worst, the stupidest of all' – here I stood up and faced him, draining the rest of my double – 'was Christmas back in the loony bin.'

Back came the drugged, suety faces mumbling and shovelling at the grey travesty of a Christmas meal. Judy, that same Judy, laughing with a sprig of burning holly in her hair.

People in the pub were gaping but I did not care. I said it again.

'Christmas back in the loony bin! And why? Why? *Oh, why not?*'

Shocked at my own bitterness and confusion, I slammed out of the pub and ran.

The rain had stopped. White markers on the road tapewormed away, gleaming, towards town. Up ahead was the red target of a phone booth. Lagging behind the hot drumming in my head, my knees blundered against flapping skirt. Wild with impatience, I ripped it to the thigh and ran on with hectic strides until I stood breathless within the steamy-windowed booth. I dialled and prayed. Hateful slow electronic burr.

'Hello?'

Him. Oh God, pips. Got it. *Now*.

'Adrian-I-want-to-make-love-to-you.'

There was a pause too brief for an eyelid to bat.

'That sounds nice. Why don't you come along now?'

'Right. On my way.'

My hand, while I was speaking, had made a wild scrabbling print on the window.

The 27 bus took me, locked in wooden astonishment, as far as Notting Hill. Then I was out in the wet streets again, whisky and tequila tangoing through my veins. I swung along fast, holding the torn ends of skirt through the liningless pockets of my coat – that same coat in which I had smuggled the beer for Botswana Steve. A taxi drew up at some traffic lights and I ran to ask the driver if I was heading the right way.

' 'olland Park? I'm running up there misself. Want to 'op in?'

'I haven't got enough for the fare.'

'Go on, 'op in. I told you, I'm goin' that way.'

I got in and fell back on the cigaretty-smelling seat. My eyes closed as we moved off and the after-image of the street lamps spun. I must have passed out for when I opened my eyes again we were there. Or so I assumed, because we had stopped. The driver was opening the cab door. I moved to get out but instead he got in. There was a smell of spearmint and the rough feel of his sleeve as it brushed my neck. He was opening my coat. His hand was on my knee.

Oh God. It was Tel Aviv all over again; Greece; the cruisers outside the bin. I lunged past him to the door and struggled with the handle. Behind me he swore and rough-sleeved arms tightened and hauled.

'Come on, you little 'ore.'

But I had got the door open and my feet were on the ground. I wrestled with the arms that would not leave my neck. He felt strong but I felt cunning. Deliberately, I sagged at the knees and then jerked upright hard. There was a crack as his head thudded into the roof. Gripping his arms now, and using the strength of my whole body to jerk up and down, I bashed the spearmint-breathing head again and again against the door frame. As I dived away in the dark, I felt with vicious triumph that I had scraped him off my back like a bit of dogshit off a shoe. Foul names bounced meaninglessly off my back as I zigzagged towards the nearest light.

The street was one I knew. There was the café where I had met Michael, the Canadian. I burst in through the door, drunkenly hoping he might be there. But all the faces were unfamiliar and the place had changed. Candles in chianti bottles, smell of patchouli and lasagne. I stood with one arm up clutching a hatstand, awareness of what was happening washing in and out in waves. A youth with an amiable grin stepped out from behind the cash register and adroitly grabbed the hatstand before it fell. I found myself seated, a glass of brandy in one hand and the youth and another man bending close, looking at me with listening eyes

Words fell out of my mouth in a lumpy patchwork, some of it woven from dreams. But they established where I was going and to whom. Shortly, when the restaurant closed, these young men

242

would walk me there. Meanwhile there was coffee, which I did not drink, and another brandy, which I did.

'Please,' I said, through a screen of bulging clouds, 'has anybody got a comb?'

The dressing-gown was different but the legs were the same. For a long time they were all I saw. From where I was propped by the bookshelf while he thanked the unknown youths; from behind a mug three times filled with weak tea; from under a towelling robe held out while he dinned in instructions about the showers I was to have, alternating with the saunas I was not to have too hot – legs, red-downed, padding about on short strong feet with clean pink spaces between the toes.

I stood in the shower with a hot monsoon flushing my brain, sat in the sauna panting beside a tray of fizzing stones. After the second wetting, moist billows rose until I did not know if it was me or the world steaming and reeling, body or mind enveloped in buffeting clouds. A voice intruded from another planet.

'O K in there?'

There was a distant briskness in the tone, like a vet handling an animal not quite clean.

'Mmmmmmmn.'

I was under the shower again, face right in it. It seemed unthinkable that I should open my mouth and make a hole in the spray. The door opened a crack.

'I said are you O K ?'

I nodded with my back to him, head still up.

'How many saunas have you had?'

I flipped a hand up by my bottom, two fingers raised then put down hastily. Rude sign.

'All right, stay just a few moments in the last one, then a cool rinse and out. Shampoo, if you want it, on the shelf.'

Back when the door was closed to the reeling and the steam. I breathed in deep, feeling heat tingle in my throat and separate the tiny hairs in my nostrils. Before the final wetting I lathered every inch of my body, swirling soap spirals over my belly, rubbing at

243

my scalp through a mountain of foam. Then I turned the cold on full blast.

'Yaaaaah!'

I had not meant to yell. There was a short laugh from outside. Moments later, turbaned and robed, I emerged. At once I was shepherded into the bedroom and told that now he was going to take a shower.

Slowly, I sank down crosslegged in the centre of the big bed; slowly combed and towelled my hair. With the alcohol receding, my mind felt blank. Stubbornly, cosily, my body glowed. I lay back yawning and wriggled between the sheets. The pillow was the palest green, smelling faintly of him. I gave it a deeply loving practice-kiss – and went out cold.

There were two thoughts in my head when I woke a decade of unconsciousness later. One, I was going to be sick; two, I had blown it again. Prompted by the urgency of the first, I groped a swift course to the bathroom and with one hand screwing back my hair, threw up, stifling the noise. It was not so easy to stifle the shame.

When it was over, I sat on the floor holding my toes. My feet were calloused from all the time I had gone barefoot abroad. Like all the rest of me they felt out of place in the clean, smoothly running world of Massell. I would leave now, never be seen by, never see him again.

I felt calm, beyond the little futility of despair. There would be no more drama, no more dreams.

There was a small blob of vomit on the lapel of the borrowed robe. Quietly, I washed the whole thing, hanging it over a towel rail to dry. I had only to find my clothes now and I would be away.

One of the black cats ran to wind its dainty body round my calves as, naked, I crept downstairs and searched the living-room. There was a blank spot in my memory over where I had undressed. Reluctantly, I concluded it must have been in the bedroom.

Upstairs again, very cautiously, I pushed open the door. Muted light from the landing trickled over the bed in a long bar. Massell lay in the centre, face in shadow. I could not see my clothes anywhere. What if they were in the wardrobe behind a loud, sliding door? I took a step further in and the cat, fur electric against my legs, trilled out a bright interrogative croon. I stooped to pick it up, to hush its noise, but too late. Massell stirred.

'Keep your claws in, Polydeuces.'

I straightened slowly, the cat's purring head warm between my breasts, its soft body dangling down mine.

'Bring him here.'

Massell was up on one elbow. I brought the cat close and sat down where he patted the bed. His hand reached out and stroked the furry head in my arms.

'Sleep all right?'

I nodded, head down. His fingers stroked low behind Polydeuces' ears. They were very close to my breast.

'Castor died, you know, so this fellow is a bit lonely now.'

A lock of hair fell forward and brushed his wrist. He lifted the strands and laid them half across the cat's fur, half across my skin.

'Nice combination.'

He must have felt my heartbeat under the back of his hand. A finger gliding lightly, almost accidentally, over a nipple, caused it to spring, tingling, into bud. Behind the curtain of my hair, my eyes closed. I felt him move up in the bed and gently detach the cat from my arms.

'Go and play, Polydeuces.'

My head rode on his shoulder, the rest of me rode in his hands. Hands playing over breasts, belly, thighs, stroking and moulding until my hips began to move in a rhythm of their own.

'Excellent. Keep doing that. Now touch here.'

Tentative fingers encircling. Power unfolding in my palm. Life pulsing, questing. Unexpected moistenings.

'Good. Now lie back and concentrate all your feelings here.'

There was a sudden soundless clamour, a little darting madness that licked at the soft edge of control. I bucked, half sliding away.

'Ha, found the spot, have I? Like it?'

'Nnnnnyes but . . .'

'But what?'

'I feel as though I'm going to explode!'

'That's the idea.'

And after I had come, I clung to stay. From his oh-so-welcome entry through the long crescendo of his rise, to the moment when I felt him soar, and a cool drop squeezed from his brow fell on my cheek, I could not hold him close enough. There was strength in my wrapping limbs and a new-found power inside that clasped him as the moist earth clasps the tree. I longed for him to spill deep into my ready womb.

But modern man responsibly withdrew and it was my navel that overbrimmed.

'I presumed you were not fixed up.'

'No.'

'Will I sort something out or . . . ?'

'I'll make an appointment today.'

I felt I could sort out the universe now that I was sure there would be a next time.

Within a fortnight I had moved into a flat less than two miles away with two jobs to pay the rent and save. To celebrate the installation of an intrauterine device I went out for a meal with Chris, the boy who shared the flat. As a flatmate he was conveniently self-effacing, although had he been otherwise I would not have noticed, for I existed on a tightrope five miles high, breathing in the rare altitude of bliss.

Whether it was weighing dried fruit in the healthfood shop where I earned my daytime wage or taking messages as a receptionist at night, I found pleasure in everything I did. Walking down the High Street was a joy; catching sight of myself in a shop window and pausing to readjust my new feminine glide. Every roll of the pelvis was a celebration of how good it was to be young, female and tinglingly alive.

'What do you think of that?' I would cry, prancing in to a startled Chris in some new exotic robe which, flung aside, revealed a clinging sheath of softest see-through stuff. I had suddenly become acutely aware of the subtleties of texture and wanted only to wear things which felt voluptuous against my skin.

Or else I was flourishing my latest culinary creation, which Chris was never allowed to touch until it was a day old, in case Adrian dropped by. Experimenting with homemade beauty aids, I suffered delicious terror that he might turn up when I had just daubed oatmeal and honey all over my face. Chris had strict instructions to employ delaying tactics in such an event.

Adrian. I hugged the name to myself, whispering it into the brush and pan as I worked to make the dreary little flat immaculate, kneading it into the wholesome loaves I baked – just in case. I longed to murmur it into his ear but the cries he drew from me were sounds without form, springing from regions of the woman in me that had no use for names.

Happiness was infectious. It made strangers in the street follow me with their eyes and broke through the suspicion of two elderly Russian sisters in the flat below. They heard me singing as I swept the communal stairs and invited me in for tea served from a samovar in an ornate silver stand. I brought them treats of halva and figs from the healthfood shop and liked the way they nodded significantly whenever I mentioned Adrian's name.

And safely out of the neighbourhood of 309, I found myself responding more sympathetically to Kay. Always shying from contact in the past, I now telephoned her regularly and chatted for hours without strain. As for Marianne, when I looked into her unhappy face, I ached to be able to offer some share in my joy. For a while we fell back on old patterns, with her thrilling vicariously to accounts of happenings in my life. The adventure now was a man.

It did not matter that I only saw him once or twice a week. I loved the urgent animal frisson which shook me when the phone rang and there was his brisk, sunny voice saying, 'Tonight?'

I had made sure the hours I worked in the evening were flexible. After he had rung there would be a frantic twenty minutes in which to bath and dress. Whatever I put on was for him to take off. Time and again I went over in my mind that moment of total trust, when I would stand before him naked, offered with

247

no holds barred from the crown of my head to the tips of my toes. The cool phrases he uttered while running eyes and hands over me echoed and re-echoed in my brain, heightening the pleasure of the fantasies which sustained me when he was not there.

If we met before nine-thirty in the evening he might take me out for a quick meal, but more often than not, he called me straight to his house. I ran to his call as surely as a turtle hatched in dry sand scuttles to the sea, and, absorbed as I was in the joy of everything newly roused in me that was physical, womanly, I paid scant attention to the further Massellian development of my mind. Echoes back to the days when lover Adrian had been mentor Massell had little meaning.

'You should think about becoming one of my lecturers. Once trained you could tour abroad – go all over the world.'

I shrugged the idea away and nestled closer under his arm. Why would I want to go lecturing abroad when I had him here? Procreation was the name of the only brilliant career I wanted; to be the perfect vessel for his seed.

Riding so blind, I could only be heading for a fall.

Chapter Sixteen

I felt all right. The dream backfired. But, as I had blocked off what happened in Greece, so damagingly and for so long, I blocked off what happened with Massell. Faithful to Richard in the idea of turning dreams into schemes, I had overlooked the fact that where other people's emotions are involved, one is no longer in control. It was Addie who got closest to pinning down the problem: 'So he just wanted to screw and you thought everything else was involved.'

I thought how I had fallen, head first, body last, heart some-where in between.

'Yes.'

'And you made a bloody fool of yourself?'

'Yes.'

'Well, you kept pretty quiet about it.'

'Not inside.'

No, the firecracker joys and pain I had learned through Massell would not end on a note of fizzle. But for the time being I pushed it all to that undefined region at the back of the mind where thoughts do not come in words. There it fermented dangerously, as the rape had done before I knifed the man in Tel Aviv.

And that year another major affair in my life came to a head. I gave up the flat in London and spent the summer in Scotland, half reluctantly back in Richard's world. With the end of the hotel season came the first painful opportunity to brood.

The old room near Richard and Edwina's had been made into an office and my accommodation now was a caravan, one field away from the sea. Because it stood up to the roughest batterings of the wind and was a small, pale oval nestling alone, I called it my egg-in-a-storm. Out of habit I still went down to the sea each morning, as I had all through the working months when it had been my only outside glimpse of day. I watched the islands change from sunlit brown hummocks to ice-blue clouds in an ice-blue sea and sky.

As a baffle to the ache I had brought with me from London, I had thrown myself at the challenge of managing the café with an all-absorbing will. And it had been a success. All the things I planned to display on the counter had appeared. Pride and in-sistence on doing all the cooking myself made the job formidable, but that was what I wanted – one demanding occupation to stretch me to the exclusion of all else; distraction from thoughts, memories, dreams.

There were times when from the moment the café doors opened until the last mackerel had been grilled for High Tea, there was no break in the flow of customers. Wanting to please, hating to say 'run out' to anyone, I worked and worked until, as Richard put it, my eyes hung out of my head like Davy lamps.

But others were stretched to the limit too. Up at the hotel Edwina never stopped. There was no such thing as time off for her. When there was work to be done she was busy and there was always work to be done. Although there was little communication between us, I admired her – it was impossible not to – and she must love Richard very much to work that hard. When, at the end of the season, faced suddenly with the shock of my own emptiness, I went badly to pieces, I even respected the way she washed her hands of me. In her world there was no room for weakness.

Weakness was cause for dismissal in Richard's world, too. People who fell in his wake became material for odd, nostalgic ponderings, nothing more. I had seen it happen to Kay and to Marianne. When it looked as though I were next in line, a solid nugget of determination set in my otherwise floundering mind. The woman in me, rejected by Massell, reverted to being an angry and frightened child.

That winter the storms were brutal. Boiling and massing, the sea sucked back to surge with hooligan violence on the land, slinging boats in splinters over the fields. The hotel speedboat was smashed to a blue and white nothing. Its dismembered parts lay with the sheep's bones and Squeezy bottles and I salvaged what was left of the seat to make stepping stones to the caravan.

Richard surveyed the havoc wreaked on his new horticultural tunnels with deadened eyes. He moved about as a distant figure, stooping in a field to wrestle a carrot from the frozen ground, building ramps to deflect the rush of water which would otherwise flood the hotel when the thaw came. Beneath the woolly rim of a bobble-less bobble hat his face was papery pale and there were thin grey feathers in his hair which had been so black. Edwina, duffel-coated, paler than he, carted the heavy buckets of swill down the pig field. Neither of them came to the caravan and we led very separate lives. Then, at the end of November, when Edwina went away for a fortnight, I went up to the hotel to housekeep for Richard.

The first few days went smoothly enough. Maintenance work was being carried out on the hotel and Richard was busy with his small labour force. In the evenings he was glad to slump into a deep chair in the smoke lounge with the dogs pressing around him in jealous adoration and a plate of supper balanced on his knees. I served him quietly, with a veneer of casual competence which belied hours of dithering indecision in the kitchen. The rest of my life was so bungled, it seemed quite probable that I would suddenly make a mess of a simple stew. And I did not want to keep asking Richard how Edwina did things.

Since the café had closed, all my confidence had gone. I knew I looked a mess but refused to care. Once, I had hung a cloth over the caravan mirror to dry and, intentionally or not, left it there. I lived in Richard's old pullovers and wore a scarf over my hair so that I did not have to brush it. I never wore it loose now or wrapped in soft phones around my ears as I used to for Massell. I looked forward to when Edwina came back and I could retreat once more into my egg-in-a-storm.

When the workmen stopped coming towards the end of the first week, Richard went back to his usual winter occupations of nail-gnawing and plot-hatching. I could tell how the plots were progressing by the way he moved: a heavy, knit-browed stride meant he was grappling with an awkward, possibly insoluble problem; a hesitant uneven step that he was teetering on the edge of vision; and a fine, upright swing that he had got there and had only to match the plan with action, which he always did in the end.

And although I had seen him look diminished beside the steam-roller of Edwina's earthy strength, had seen him lost and in the way in the heart of his own enterprise, I knew that he was still the life blood behind it all, the power that planted the seed. Feeling my old love for him revive, my own vapid wallowings seemed even more despicable. I was more directionless now than ever before, more than ever lacking in a plan.

I spent one afternoon swabbing the bar-room floor and was descending the concrete steps to the back door, armed with mop and bucket, when Richard's voice arrested me. He was standing by the animal steading, arms akimbo, brow crossed.

251

'Lude' – it was his old pet name for me – 'have you seen yourself recently? You look frightful.'

He said it again, shifting his foot almost as though he would stamp, 'Frightful!'

I set down the metal bucket and squeezed out the mop before putting it away.

'Well, it doesn't matter, does it, when I'm only cleaning out the bar?'

'It *does* matter. You look a disgrace. Why are you wearing that ghastly scarf? What's happened to you?'

I felt as though he had a pin stuck through me and was pulling off my wings.

'It *doesn't* matter. You're the only person who sees me.'

'But you look dreadful, frumpish, worse than I've ever seen you.'

'So what?' I was shouting now. 'I'm your daughter not your lover!'

'What's the difference?'

I had nothing to say to that. It was not so simple to dismiss his words as senseless. The question was one that had been simmering between us for years.

Later he was gentler, praising the supper I had prepared.

'Mmmmm, this turbot is very good, Lude.'

I felt myself preening, as Marianne would have done, at this titbit of a tribute to my efforts to please. I was frightened to see myself behaving like her.

Usually I went straight down to the caravan after clearing away. But tonight I was restless. I would go for a walk in the wind. Richard watched me pulling on oilskins.

'Going down already?'

'No. A walk.'

'I could do with a walk too.'

It was dark and damp and the moon was hiding so we walked on the road. If it was a wilder night than we had realized, neither of us said so. Heads bent to it we strode, moods and booted footfalls matching.

Where the road forked we turned inland and walked on with

252

the wind driving at an angle against our backs. The single-track road cut through flat bogland, rumbling away on one side towards the sea while on the other, close to in their blackness, the mountains crouched, nudging bony shoulders against the void. I would have liked to describe to Richard the way darkness fell at Mole's End. I knew he would like it. But somehow I never talked to him about those things.

The 'void' was on my mind. I liked the eggy vacuum sound of the word and the images it conjured – black, blank whirlpools of nothingness; oblivion. We tramped for a long time without speaking. It was a night for thoughts whirling down dark holes.

There was a loch to our left, black water trembling, so wind-whipped it lashed neither one shore nor the other but stood poised all over the surface in quiffs. Glimmers from a cloud-shredded moon caught a breaking wavelet here and there.

'Have you thought what you're going to do, then?'

Richard's words, the most dreaded, broke into the void.

I shook my head, but it was invisible within flapping oilskin hood and I had to call out loud.

'No!'

It sounded like a wail, against the wind.

'You can always do the café again next season. You didn't do badly for a first go.'

'No, I'll . . .'

'What? I can't hear.'

Why was his voice so clear and I had to shout? I jumped round to his other side.

'I said, no, I won't do it again.'

Now my voice was clear. His words came back wind-punched, vexed.

'Well, what *are* you going to do then?'

'I don't know! I don't know!'

I jigged around in a circle, let the wind box my other ear. We had reached the end of the second loch. Time to turn back.

Facing this way, it was impossible to talk. The wind shoved at our faces, worried our trousers round our legs like juddering leaves. We threw our bodies into it, sharing the exhilaration of

253

our two small strengths pitted against a far greater one. We caught our breath in gulps, bent almost double. Thought was blown away. Sheltered for a second in a dip before breasting the last wind-beaten lap, Richard gave the wild weather yowl I knew and loved. Our shoulders biffed together and he grasped my hand. Half running, hands tight, we charged all the rest of the way, only letting go at the top of the caravan field.

'Come up for a hot drink,' he mouthed, shrugging towards the hotel.

I beat him to the top of the bar road and stamped into the kitchen, puffed out and tingling from the wind. Caillach, the black labrador, thumped her tail on the floor, then laid her head back on her paws. She was missing Edwina.

Richard stood by the stacked chairs and tables in the dining-room looking out on to the roaring night through big picture windows. I came in carrying two mugs of coffee. He was ruffling his hair with one hand, a gesture which brought a sudden memory picture to mind: me and Marianne, each in possession of one knee and one side of his parting as he sat in the lounge at 309. She was putting in curlers, I was making Indian plaits. Kay was some-where off-stage cooking mince. It was a way we often spent Saturday mornings and what Marianne and I liked best of all was when the doorbell rang and Richard, unperturbed, got up and answered it as he was. We would hide behind the bannisters clutching one another and hissing to remind him to walk carefully or the pins and ribbons would fall out. He did not seem to have aged at all since then, except for the feathers of grey.

'I enjoyed that,' he said, meaning the walk. 'Need something like that from time to time. You look better for it too – less "blanched turnip".'

Richard had never been one to sacrifice a witty description for the sake of tact. Smarting inside, I moved nearer the window, blowing waves across my mug.

'You know, I've been thinking,' he said, taking short steps and pausing in the middle of the room, 'you could do a lot worse than spend another season in the café. You could use what you've learned from this year's experience to make improvements – might even organize yourself some time off.'

This last was said lightly. As family, I was not expected to want time off.

'I've already said I won't be doing the café again.'

Indoors the statement sounded different, as though I were taking a stand against him. He looked up irritably and I said defensively, 'There are things of my own I want to do.'

'Mmmm?' – he was prepared to listen – 'like what?'

The void was back in place. My words bounced feebly off its sides.

'I might go abroad again . . .'

'What, just bumming about?'

He tossed the expression at me like a dirty dishcloth. That was how my time in Greece and Turkey and the desert must have looked to him.

'No! I'd probably work for a while in London first.'

'Seems to me you don't do anything very serious there.'

No, I thought, floor washing and a bed scene with Massell flashing through my mind, *I don't do anything very serious there.*

Richard started walking about again, little finger neatly cocked away from the handle of his mug.

'You know, I've been watching you this winter, Lude . . .'

Rubbish. You've only just noticed me.

'. . . And I must say I have been surprised at the way you've let yourself go.'

The wind worried at the windows, Richard at his nails. He was saying he was disappointed in me. *Surprised and disappointed.*

'It's not like you to be lazy, but as far as I can see all you've done since the end of the season is sit around on your backside.'

My thoughts batted about angrily. How could he speak of what was or was not like me? He knew nothing of my other lives, my jobs, my travels, my friends . . . But the inner protests rang hollow. I saw all too clearly the fragmented mess of all my little lives.

'Oh, shut up!' I blurted – and it was 'not like me' to be rude to him – 'lecturing doesn't suit you and you're not telling me anything I don't already know.'

'Well, you need something, don't you, or do you mean to go on like this, wasting yourself, becoming a misery . . .'

He would have gone on but I cut him short, tension making my voice shrill.

'Do you think I like being like this? I wish I could just "pull myself together" but I can't. It's not as simple as that. Sometimes . . .' – I moved near enough the window to feel the rage of the darkness outside – 'sometimes I just feel like jumping off a cliff!'

It sounded pathetic, ridiculous, even as I said it, and I might have laughed if it had not been for his reply, which was instant and studiedly derisive.

'Oh God, Lude, you are beginning to sound like Kay.'

You shit, I thought, *you shit. Like Kay. Oh my God.* I had been relegated to the order of mistakes he did not have to live with.

It took four steps to cross the room to where he stood, four words to point the mockery of his promise of home.

'I hate this hotel' – the mug shook in my hand – 'and I hate you.'

And to stop another impossibly clever reply, I threw the hot coffee in his face.

I was frightened as soon as I had done it. But it was too late to regret or run away because Richard had caught the throwing wrist in mid-air and was propelling me backwards, wet slicked jaw rigid with rage. I did not see his right fist coming. It slammed in just below the browbone and I thudded full length to the floor.

Richard was on top, instantly pinning down legs and arms. I writhed, blind. It was familiar: Cape Sounion; the hospital. If he had let me go then, I would have attacked him with anything to hand. My heart seemed to be punching holes in my brain.

Then sudden still and his voice, very quiet, very full: 'Oh my love . . .'

I stopped moving and looked up to the echo of his words. His face hung above me, the skin under his eyes faintly lavender, trembling. As we looked at each other one tear popped out and slid away down a crease. I thought: he is older, after all.

There was a long, long moment before either of us moved

again. The storm outside went on raging as ours gradually died. When at last we drew apart it was as though, in breaking bodily contact, our visions of ourselves, which for a moment out of time had been without civilized judgement, animal blind, fled to the corners of the room. Dazed, we fumbled out way back to normal perspective, across the safe border of the everyday world.

I fetched a brush and bucket to scrub away the coffee stain on the carpet. Richard got out the best piece of steak in the fridge for my eye. Then we ate it, like a sacrifice, almost raw. But neither of us knew to what god.

The bruise had gone by the time Edwina returned and the era of the egg-in-a-storm was at an end. I said goodbye to the wind-scuffled hills and spent a last, long, goose-fleshed afternoon wedged in a rock crevice by the sea. Eight years of waves infinitesimally smoothing the sides of that crevice would go by before I came back to wedge myself there once more. And by then, I would have been seduced by another sea, and Richard would be a different man with a new love whose birthday fell on the same day as mine.

Chapter Seventeen

If ever I did any 'bumming about', it was that year in Bristol. I twirled a finger on a map of Britain and that was where I landed, exchanging the egg-in-a-storm for a cellar in the student quarter. Addie joined me shortly, at the end of some private era of his own. He arrived wrung out and haggard, climbed shakily into bed without removing his clothes, and stayed there for ten days, filling the air with stale farts and Dostoevsky.

During the weeks that followed, when he got heavily into West Country cider and Stockhausen and I hovered uncomfortably on the edge of the student crowd, we chewed the sap out of our relationship, finally reaching a stage where all we could say to each other was:

'Oh God, Addie.'

'Oh God, Lucy.'

'Oh God, Addie.'

It was Julian, bursting back into our lives with the first daffodils, who rescued us once again from ourselves.

He came from the Black Forest via Mole's End, carrying compost under his fingernails, dried mushrooms in his flute bag and a dozen new loves in his heart. Shy before us for a moment, he stood like a choirboy, one sherpa-booted leg shuffling against the other. Addie and I were more than ever effete pressed flowers before a field of shining corn. But it was Addie who opened his stringy arms.

'Julian,' he said, 'thank God. You don't know how badly we need you.'

That night all three of us slept in Addie's attic room. Julian rhapsodized about his latest love and we decided to go busking in the Antique Market next day so we could buy her a present. We did not know it then, but it would be the last time we would all be together for years.

The expedition got off to a prompt start. While Addie slept, I cooked porridge on a paraffin heater and Julian darned his breeks and plaited his beard. We left a note telling Addie to meet us at the Coronation Tap midday.

Julian and I walked with arms linked. We stepped lightly, feeling beyond the cool residue of night the promise of a sunny day. Stopping by my cellar, I collected a bright patchwork clown-suit and leather gaiters. I felt like dressing up.

The stalls of the Antique Market were set up and starting to trade by the time we arrived. Large women in holey cashmere served smaller women in Laura Ashley. Trivets and candelabra passed from hand to hand. Julian floated through the cluttered aisles absently bestowing and receiving smiles. We found a place for him in a section of the market devoted to paintings. Here, against a backdrop of sombre oils, all russet and wine, he ejected a streal of saliva from his flute, threw his head back, and began to play.

I stepped back, disassociating myself for the pleasure of watching people watch Julian. Within minutes a semi-circle formed, one, two, then three rows deep. Julian, eyes closed, played on oblivious to all but the heart of his theme.

At the end of the third piece, he paused. The audience had shuffled closer to make room for more at the back. When Julian opened his eyes, he blinked wide with astonishment and burst out laughing. Palpable droplets of merriment landed in a light spray on the shoes of the front row.

'Ooops, sorry,' he said, and bent to wipe it off with the hem of his tunic.

When he started to play again, coins tinkled at his feet and by the time he took his exit bow there was enough silver for half-a-dozen gifts. Julian expressed his pleasure by lifting me up and waving me around in my clown-suit like the fairy on top of a Christmas tree.

'It's funny I've never fallen in love with *you*,' he said suddenly.

'Don't be daft,' I said, hugging him hard, 'that would be incest.'

And truly that was how it felt. There was still no meeting in my mind between lovely friends and friendly lovers. Perhaps if there had been, I would have accepted more easily the end of the affair with Massell – and punished both him and myself less painfully.

We arrived at the Coronation Tap a little late. Addie may have thought we had deserted him. He was certainly cross. Emboldened by my own good feelings I wrapped my arms round him. It was like cuddling an iron spike.

'Oh God, Lucy, you smell happy. How sickening.'

'Not really,' I said to comfort him, 'just snatching a few sweet flowers before plunging into the abyss again. Are you drunk?'

'*Ish*,' he said, brows ferociously knit, 'drunk-*ish*.'

He hunched over to roll a cigarette and I noticed behind him a very large black bag. There was string in places, dividing it into irregular bulges.

'What's that?'

'It's not a what, it's a her. The new love of my life.'

I would not have put it past Addie to tie one of his girlfriends into a bag. He liked to feel in control.

'Can she breathe all right?'

'Doesn't need to. She's only got two functions in life. She screws and she sucks.'

Julian winced. He was always uncomfortable when Addie was in a black mood.

'Feel her. Go on. She won't bite.'

I reached past him and pressed tentatively.

'Harder.'

I increased the pressure and all of a sudden a loud, squeaky fart came out. I snatched my hand away but the fart went on and on, piercing as a cat's miaow. Every eye in the pub swizzled in our direction.

'Oh yes, I forgot,' said Addie loudly, 'she's pretty good at those as well.'

'What is it?' I hissed.

'*Her*,' he growled and his voice rose like a salesman's. 'The only woman in the world for me, guaranteed orgasm every time with the hiccup of a dying cow. What shall I call her, Lucy?'

'Jemima,' I said quickly, wondering if I could snatch her and get outside before he caught me. I knew he was going to start untying the bag any minute.

'I know! Let's play Tanks outside with Jemima.'

'She'll deflate.'

'Come on, we can try.'

I plucked the bag from behind him and ran to the door. Jemima emitted her protest from several directions. She must be well-endowed with orifices.

'Bitch! Traitoress! Coward!'

Addie clambered grimly over heads and tables, taking the shortest route. Behind him I caught a glimpse of Julian righting pint pots and staunching the flow of spilt beer. I was almost back at the Antique Market before Addie brought me down with a flying tackle. He landed on top of me and I landed on top of Jemima whose toeless plastic foot burst through the bag, splitting it open to her waist. Plump pink legs flew apart and stuck up in the air. I twisted my head round and gasped.

'Addie, she's dribbling!'

He panted, flushed face resting on my belly.

'Yes, well, I thought she'd make a handy water pistol, too.'

Julian cantered past, ignoring our tangle *à trois*.

'There's a fair,' he cried, 'with goats and everything, on the Green.'

Slowly we picked ourselves up and dusted off Jemima. To keep her under control we tied her legs together with string and plugged the poised 'O' of her mouth with a scarf as though she had toothache. I covered her bombnose breasts and gaping vagina with strips of the plastic bag; making a kind of bikini. Addie told me her history on the way to the fair.

'Found her in Leigh Woods, near where you go walking. She was stuffed into the hollow of a tree. But I'll tell you what was really peculiar. Beside her, all neatly wrapped up, was a gas mask, a duster and a little tin of polish. Put your imagination to that.'

I did, and decided not to go walking alone in Leigh Woods any more.

We spent the afternoon at the fair. Julian won a bottle of fizzy cider by hitting a weight with a hammer and ringing a bell. Addie cut the *ish* out of being drunk and insisted on having a game of Tanks in the middle of the fair. He held my ankles and I held his and we rolled head-over-back-over-legs-over-head making a giant human wheel. Julian found the tube from a Hoover and coaxed a range of musical notes from it to accompany us.

'Not so much Bach's Air on a G-string,' I said to the laughing onlookers, 'as Julian's air through a vacuum.' I was mildly tipsy too.

The sun went in and out and the day drew to a close. I waxed sentimental and told my boys I loved them. Addie burped and pressed a fart out of Jemima. Julian hugged me and said, 'Come to Mole's End.' All three of us went as far as the hitching point and then Addie slouched off with Jemima in a state of semi-tumescence under his arm. He said he was going to sell her for fifteen pounds and buy a scooter.

He did, but my life would turn a whole new set of somersaults before I had the chance to ride pillion.

Chapter Eighteen

It was good to be at Mole's End again, especially in the spring and with Julian. We played games, made music, planted herbs and danced. But beneath the superficial contentment I fretted; the old, old questions still floating around unanswered. Where was I going? What was the plan?

Then, tearing up newspaper to light the fire one morning, I saw the possibility of an answer, at least in the short term. Vacancies were being advertised for students on a fulltime contemporary dance course. Why not? In a way it hardly mattered what the course was, so long as it was something definite, with direction. And I had always enjoyed expressing myself physically.

Julian kissed me goodbye on the day of the audition and stuck a cowslip in my lapel for luck. Once more I headed up the M4 to London with high hopes for the future.

Five hours after the audition, which to my amazement I had passed, I lay chin deep in a warm, cosily lapping bath. Three strands of hair, subtly intertwined, drifted on the surface like a tiny ship. I imagined that the white marble sides of the bath were cliffs and the streaky red stains in the water reflections of a setting sun. Idly, I poked the hairs with the tip of a finger and they clung. His, not mine. I let my hand sink and the tiny ship bobbed up and floated away, crisp and brisk, just like him.

I had come to tell Massell the good news of my belated return to the rails. He would surely be impressed. But unfortunately he had not been in and I had had to break a little window to get into the house and I had cut my hand.

It is funny how coincidences can slide one into the other until they form a new entity unfurling slowly in the mind like a warning flag. Stop Go Stop. I saw the flag unfurl before I reached Holland Park, late and in the dark and rain, but I did not heed the warning on it and the pips on the public telephone obscured the message on the ansaphone. The same way womb wonder in me had obscured the message that he just wanted to screw.

'I'm sorry about this mess, though. I'll clear it up before I go.'

I said it aloud, even though he was not there. I felt like chatting to somebody and Polydeuces no longer seemed to be around.

When the pink bathwater began to cool I got out. I was dizzy so decided to fix something to eat before sponging down the paint-work. Breakfast at Mole's End was a long time ago. But perhaps I ought to take my shirt off first. Its white front was dyed scarlet from neck to hem and now it was dripping water as well. But my left hand, the blue woolly glove a black clot, would not go through the sleeve so I left it on, squeezing the worst of the wet into the bidet and running cold water to wash away the red. It was a nuisance about the glove, but it had been chilly when the rain began.

In the bedroom where I went to look for a robe – that sheepskin I had given him would do – I found instead a bright bikini. I took it off its hanger and held it against me. Red smeared the mirror where I tilted it and dripped in small amoebic blobs on the dressing-table. The bikini was about my size.

On the way he had been the old Massell to whom I was bring-ing the news of the rebirth of Lucy as potent shell. No more floundering or emotional nonsense. Briskly forward from now on like a positive arrow in one of his diagrams. But he was back to being Adrian now.

'*Look at that torso,*' *he had said,* hands appraising the velvety nipples as I sat astride his loins.

Now the stain there was turning from scarlet to brown. I felt light-headed but aware of a need to be practical. Must get a cloth to wipe the skirting and the light switches. Little blood goes a long way.

Downstairs I poured myself a glass of green Chartreuse. He had given me that the last time I was here, the time he had not invited me upstairs and I had lain all night on the old couch in the lounge staring at an art deco lamp. Coloured bubbles in it floated and rose, merged and fell apart.

'"All is vanity," ' I had thought, *misquoting Nietzsche*, ' "*vanity and coloured bubbles*".'

Comprehension had crept up slowly on my comfy couch in exile but it hit with the finality of a club. He did not want me any more. My body, my 'potential' even, had outgrown its appeal.

Drawing a diagram with my blood on the mirror I recalled how it had been once when I had come.

'*Do you remember? I wrote a miniature word song about it? And your fingers made it happen while I sang. And then your tongue.*'

Girl coming
    o
    m
    i
    n
    girl

    co-mingle   co-mingling
                         i
                        cling
                        k

                    Lick
                    l
                    i
                    n
                    g

'It wasn't very good, was it? But you were my lickling then, all right.'

I drank some more *Chartreuse* before going back into the hall. It was a shock to see what I had done to the door. No wonder they thought it was a crowbar at the trial. I kept saying it was a small grey umbrella but I don't think they believed me any more than Kay had over the lacrosse stick business years ago.

I had found the umbrella in a green litter bin attached to a lamp-post. The handle was broken but the spokes and canopy were fine. I had walked along twirling it, spinning off the rain. It had been disappointing to see no lights on in the house. Even though it was garbled by the pips, I had thought the message on the ansaphone said he would be back later. And I was not drunk this time.

As soon as I got in I had made a mental note to buy putty for the window and a seven-inch-square pane. I could not write down the measurement because of the pain in my hand. The glass must have got pushed in deep while I was making that great hole, deep into the soft mound at the base of the thumb.

It had been a surprise to find the inner door locked as well. The wood was tough, with a honeycomb of insulating material at the centre. I had to use my feet in the end to knock out a space big enough to crawl through. When at last I reached the other side, I could not remember why it had been so important to get there. I sat dripping for long moments on the thick white pile before thinking of the phone. Then I was in that little room where he had poured me the Chartreuse. He was wearing white trousers that day and a silky green shirt which I longed to put my hand inside. He stood with his back to me at the drinks cupboard, talking about a friend of his, a girl, who was gaining an important position in the world of contemporary art. It seemed that most of the people he mixed with were in important positions. I looked forward to the day he would introduce me to them.

There was a little red light on the phone. More, duller red lights when my hand had rested there a while.

The first time he had pushed my head down I had not known what to do. So I kissed him because I loved to kiss him anywhere and my breasts nestled around his thighs. He told me to take him in my mouth and as soon as my lips were round him it felt right. Wanting more contact still, my hand sought for his on the sheet, but it was not there. His arms were behind his head and his eyes were closed. So my tongue and lips made discoveries for themselves and I must have done something right for after a while my hands, massaging, felt a familiar tightening and, as though from another world, I heard the crow of his imminent come.

I was back through the hole now and opening the kitchen cupboards, looking for something quick and comforting. There were Japanese things in tins, cartons of Longlife milk, a whole crate of dried bananas. His pots and pans were in top-heavy stacks on the lower shelves. I would have arranged them better than that. I would have arranged them beautifully. While I sat there on the floor, feeling childish with the pans in my hands, echoes of Addie saying: '*Do it beautifully*' floated round the room.

I stood up, the liqueur chasing giddy spirals from belly to head. I emptied a can of abalone into a pan. It looked wetter than I expected and less appetizing. I tipped in another can, inadvertently adding a squirt of blood. The second can was a mistake, something white and glutinous like semolina, so I abandoned the idea of a meal and gnawed on a block of dried bananas. It amazed me that eleven of them could be so compressed. They would have made ideal Beverly ballast for the old days on the road. Then, when I crawled back through the hole again, leaving the bananas, I remember that I had forgotten to bring a cloth. But the most important thing now was to put on some music. I could do anything to music.

I knew now what I had done wrong but I did not understand at the time.

When I felt he was about to come I took my mouth away because I thought he would want to come inside me. I wanted him to come inside me. It was a bad mistake. The crow turned into a groan and then he shouted at me to grab him.

'*Grab him! Quickly!*'

Flustered, I took hold of him, hands forming a tunnel.

'*Tighter! Woa – not that tight!*'

It was the first time I was glad when it was over. When he came back from the bathroom he said, 'Why didn't you swallow it?'

I gaped at him from the pillow.

'I didn't know you could.'

What a fool. Didn't I remember that word the doctor had used in the bin? Éclairs?

I promised I would get it right in the future. And all the other important positions.

There was Handel and Beethoven but no Bruckner or blues. If I wanted something familiar it would have to be the 'Eroica' or the 'Royal Fireworks'. Both too grandiose. This was more like it: The Who. I recalled the lyrics of Tommy's most poignant plea and sang it while fiddling with the switches.

I put on the headphones because I could not work out how to make the sound come out of the speakers. The needle scored fresh leaks of blood in the grooves when I set it on the beginning of the track again. Pain yanked at my thumb and after a moment I pulled the phones off and let blood pool in the black padded cups of sound. I was not Imogen, had no plans to die to the '1812' – or The Who.

It was the vision of Imogen dead, cheeks translucent under the tangle of black hair, that brought me to my feet. I had to phone. The mess had gone too far, was too much for me to clear up alone.

The spattered staircase rippled upwards, the carpet seeming to dance my own red spots before my eyes. I stepped back, groping for solidity. Pain whistled through my teeth as my left hand hit the edge of something square hanging out from the wall. I turned round and held on to it, staring close up at softly symmetrical fusions of colour on canvas. Sliding carefully to the bottom of the stairs, I looked up and saw that blood destroyed the symmetry. In the lounge there was another painting. Somehow blood had got on that as well.

I crouched, animal still, as the phone in Michael's flat whispered cool couplets. Please, please be there.

'Hello?'

His Canadian accent was tousled with sleep.

'Michael? Michael? It's me. I'm sorry to bother . . .'

'Who is this? Do you know what time it is?'

'No, but I know it's late and I'm sorry to both –'

'Look, this really is not convenient. Could you call back another time?'

I held the damaged hand against my chest, knees drawn up close so that it only dripped into my lap. My eyes, skittering from the streaked carpet to a rainbow cascade on the wall, caught on the splintered wood in the hall.

'I've cut my hand.'

His voice, sleepy, unseeing, pressed from me a disjointed recitative in which the broken pane, Massell's name and a bloody umbrella stabbing through a hole featured like cryptic clues in a thriller. Michael said he was sorry I seemed to be in some kind of mess but it all sounded a little crazy and he really was not sure why I was phoning him. There was a pause before he pronounced the four short words which explained why he could not help.

'I am not alone.'

Again I apologized for bothering him. But now I was afraid. My own fragmented portrait of the scene in which I sat had brought it abruptly into focus. I saw the blood, I felt the pain. Weakly, I spoke again of the mess, saying – and feeling a numb kind of surprise at the truth – that the hand would not stop bleeding. He said maybe if it was that bad I should call an ambulance. It gave me a lead, something to think about when the phone went down.

I pulled myself over to the window and leaned my cheek against the pane. Outside the rain and the darkness seemed like old friends. But I could not go to them because my legs would not work any more.

And when it came, a long time later, to the rolling, tumbling, spine-whacked-in-the-grit and the wrought-iron spirals and the elegant fleurs-de-lis, there was no heart pounding and the grit was all in the palm of my hand.

Chapter Nineteen

It was a shock to see my old bush-jacket, with the wilted cowslip still in the lapel, in a polythene bag labled Prisoner's Effects. An officer from the CID interrogated me after the blood transfusion. Standing by the side of the bed – this scene was somehow familiar – he went straight to the heart of the matter.

'Why did you do it, then?'

'I don't know, really.'

'Now come on, Lucy. You go to a bloke's house at dead of night, break in and start laying about the furnishings with a crow-bar or something similar. Blood all over his nice carpet and half way up the walls. Not to mention a couple of paintings worth more than a couple of quid. And now you tell me you don't know what it was all about. Come on, girl, pull the other one.'

'I . . .'

'Sex, wasn't it? We get cases like this all the time. What did he do, throw you over? Well, you can't go round beating up private property just because it suits you. You, my girl, are in big trou-ble.'

I was. My ignorance of the value of the paintings was no defence against what the CID saw as an act of premeditated destruction. There remained only the question of whether self-destruction had been intended as well. I told the truth: I had no idea there was an artery in the base of the thumb. But I had called the ambulance, hadn't I? Surely that meant I did not want to die?

As to *why* I did it, the officer was, in his crude assessment, more or less right. Only I had not fully understood at the time that I was deliberately punishing Massell. And there was more to it than that. I was, once and for all, exploding a dream; crushing a misplaced ideal. Richard was a hero who turned out to be only human; so, in a different way, was Massell. I had to take my frustration out on someone and unfortunately the ideal sacrificial victim – the Greek who raped me – had long since got away. Now I had to face up to the consequences of my actions and, ironically, this turned out to be one of the best things that ever happened to me. It was a while, however, before this positive side of things became apparent.

The months before the trial passed like a summer in the dark. On bail of £500 I haunted the M4 between London and Bristol like a soul shuttling back and forth in the shadowy zone before judgement. Yet I had no sense of being damned, only an awareness that whatever happened at the trial, my immediate future would be structured by agents beyond my control. This knowledge produced a feeling of security not experienced since the days before I walked out of school. By a small act of chaos I had re-entered the world of established order where choices were clear and options limited.

Because no one knew about the dancing plan, no one said what a pity the trial was so near the beginning of term. But in the face of that black night of blood and all that followed, passing the audition now seemed no more than a pretty memory belonging to another place, another time. I let it go and looked coolly towards the prospect of prison instead. At the time, it seemed no better or worse than any other option.

My defence lawyer was hopeful of a light penalty on the grounds of diminished responsibility. The hospital to which I had been rushed in the early hours submitted helpful evidence of no recordable pulse. Sustained loss of blood was known to do strange things to the brain. I had no memory beyond the phone call to Michael. The lawyer advised me not to mention that I was conscious of what I was doing from the moment the artery was severed. The hospital said that but for my glove, which made the difference between swift spurt and slow leak, I would have passed out long before. And died. It horrified me to think that Massell might have come upon me like that, all leaked out on his white pile like a deflated Jemima.

As far as the police were concerned the case was simple: young woman with history of truancy and anti-social behaviour forces her way into home of ex-lover and wreaks bloody vengeance, committing a crime in the process liable to a two-year prison sentence. Hell hath no fury, etc. But as Massell did not press charges they were obliged to take me to court on a charge of common burglary, a label which covered the act of forced entry, even though it was acknowledged there was no theft intended.

Here, the lawyer warned me, was the stumbling block. Even if the court allowed that owing to loss of blood I could not be accused of malicious intent once inside the house, why had I broken a window in the first place, thus damaging both myself and the property? I had no satisfactory answer. So the lawyer delved into the past for material to support his case and as files appeared and psychiatrists were consulted, I felt myself sink further and further into an apathetic daze.

There was a time when I wanted to stand up and cry: No, this has nothing to do with the past. Don't take me back to it. Treat me as a criminal and punish me as such but don't saddle me with the burden of resurrected memory.

But I could not escape being me. And because I was me, I got off lightly. Two years' suspended sentence. There were, however, conditions. One, I must cease forthwith to be of no fixed abode. Two, I must consent to psychiatric treatment.

The matter of stabilizing my address was not difficult, although I felt choked with the irony of it all as I wrote down the number 309. It was like being sent back from Littlehampton all over again, back to what had made me run in the beginning. A term in Holloway would at least have been breaking new ground. But I knew it was for official purposes only and there was no reason why my independent meanderings should cease so long as I reported in from time to time. And Kay's unquestioning loyalty from the moment of her involvement on the morning after the crime made me feel ashamed of the offhand way I had treated her in the past. She said as we waited for the bail documents, 'I'll stand by you whatever happens.'

Richard would never have made such an unqualified statement.

On the way to 309 Kay had to stop the car twice to blow her nose, stifling sobs caused by a mixture of relief that I was alive and bewilderment at what I had done.

'*Bloody* man,' she said once, anger cracking the words through tears.

271

I was not sure who she meant – Massell or the aggressive C I D officer.

'That – whatever his name is – Adrian.'

I looked out of the car window.

'No,' I said, 'he's not a bloody man.'

I knew now that Massell was not to blame for anything. He was just a scapegoat; victim first of fantasy, then of reality. Kay was sobbing again.

'I don't care what you say, he *is* a bloody man. *All* men are bloody.'

Somewhere around Richmond roundabout I glanced at Kay, her hands nervous on the wheel, profile still pretty but lined, and imagined how she must have looked twenty years ago when she and Richard had run off to Ibiza and lived on love and rice pudding for six months before getting married. The legacy of that love was one daughter who was an alcoholic – Marianne's 'giddy' spells had at last been correctly diagnosed – another who had just been pronounced a criminal, and a son who was embarrassed by her because she turned up at his school plays dithery with nerves. Of all the family dreams, hers must have been shattered the hardest.

Strange that at such a nadir in my own life I felt big enough for the first time in years to look at my mother with genuine love.

The second condition set down by the court caused a private anguish from which there was no escape. That first day I reported to the psychiatric clinic is splurged on my memory like a nightmare Rorschach blot.

In dread of meeting any of my old Richmond cronies – Jem, Alf, McAllister – I went a long way round, eventually emerging on to the clinic road from under the fence of a golf course. I could see the patients going in from there and a bolus of nausea lodged between stomach and brain as I recognized the old gait, the unmistakable loony-bin shuffle.

Beyond the wheelchair ramp and the outer door was a short corridor painted ice-cream green. A receptionist screened off by a long glass window roved languidly among bays of stacked files.

I had to clear my throat several times before she came to the speaking grille.

'Yes?'

I spoke quietly, willing her not to be loud in return.

'I've come to see Dr S—. I have an appointment for one-thirty.'

Her face remained blank.

'Which department is that?'

My eyes darted to the end of the corridor where people were sitting in a row. Not bin types.

'Psychiatric,' I said, very low.

Her words jangled back like coins in a cash register.

'Psychiatric, did you say?' She ran a thumb-nail down a list. 'Oh yes, that will be Lucy Irvine for Dr S—. On your left and straight through. Take a seat and wait to be called.'

I hated her for her blank face and loud, uncaring voice.

On my left and straight through was a general waiting area. Two blocks of joined plastic chairs faced another green wall, this one crookedly patched with smoking cautions for pregnant women. I noted the slumped poses of patients in the farther block. That was my lot. None of the heads were up but I recognized two ex-binmates at once. One was a greasy-haired girl who had a phobia about hygiene, the other the unhappy boy who had been my partner in the restaurant meal escapade. That was four years ago but he looked exactly the same. I hoped I did not. There was a refreshment counter at the non-psychiatric end of the room. It was closed but I went and stood by it anyway, just to keep my head turned away.

At one forty-five a community nurse emerged from the glass cubicle separating the waiting area from the consulting rooms. He had a copy of the receptionist's list in his hand and was glancing over the patients. I covered the distance between us in four strides, grabbing his wrist before he could shout out my name. His face was familiar too. The whole scene, unchanged, perennial with its props of plastic chairs and slumped bodies horrified me. The only difference I could see was that the walls were green here instead of lamb-chop red.

273

The nurse greeted me casually as though I had been coming every week for the last four years. He said there was maybe an hour to wait before my turn, the doctor was a little behind today. Of course, the endless waiting was all part of the scene. Saying I would be back, I hurried away.

There were shops at the end of the road, one of them a bakery. I bought cakes, including three éclairs, and rammed them down my throat one after the other, staring at a fishless aquarium in a petshop. If everything was so the same, then I would be the same too. I was not going to talk to Dr S— about Massell. Let him grapple with the old red herring of compulsive eating and stick on the same old labels of insecurity and maladjustment. I stood in a telephone booth for the rest of the waiting time, chewing and choking furiously.

Beyond a loathing of the mechanics of the appointment, I was afraid the doctor was going to attempt to analyse my behaviour, and by defining it kill both the cause and all the feelings arising from it. For all the trouble it gave, I valued that dark region of the mind where thoughts did not come in words. It was the most fiercely living part of me.

But my fears were unfounded. I emerged from the clinic with a selection of pills designed to relieve current symptoms of distress and curb any further off-the-rails behaviour. Some I took, some I disposed of quietly on the underground market.

All I must do now to comply with the terms of the suspended sentence was be good for two years.

PART FIVE

Being Good

Chapter Twenty

And I was good.

After a while that suspended sentence became, instead of a sword of Damocles, a personal challenge, and when the two years were up, I continued to impose my own discipline from within. The age-old 'search for identity' was still on, but I now became very methodical in my approach to it.

I began by saying goodbye to 309 for the last time and finding myself a room. Wedged four flights up under the eaves of a narrow house overlooking a railway line, it streamed with condensation in the winter and turned into an oven as soon as the sun shone. But, cut off when I needed it to be from the rest of the world, it was mine and it was home.

Over the next four years I emerged from that room in a dozen different guises. As in the past I had tried on hats in a mirror, I now tried on a whole series of images. I recorded some of my experiences in a diary, this time with no Massell diagrams.

Sticking cautiously at first to a sexually anonymous role, I bought an all-concealing boilersuit and took a job as a stonemason's mate. This entailed lugging gravestones in and out of the back of a plaster-caked van and laying cables around churchyards for electrical tools. My boss cut IN LOVING MEMORY messages on the stones, adding the names of the newly dead to the old, but he was also a sculptor and one day, when we had had to call off work because of impossible weather, he asked if I would pose for him. Ready by then for a change of image, I said I would give it a try.

Dan has nearly finished the life-sized sculpture. It sits in the middle of the room, eyeless and nippleless but otherwise entirely me in grey clay.

When he is working I always look at the same tree outside the window. It was bare and spindly when he started, like the wire armature under the sculpture. Now it is gradually unfolding into a new soft shape, rounded out with hundreds of little leaves. When I go into a dream, Dan and the tree become blurs. It is a surprise sometimes when I come out of the dream to see that he has suddenly completed an ear or given me a navel. He has even got in my bunions and the funny way a bottom squares off sitting on a stool.

It disturbed me that from one side the face of the sculpture could almost have been Marianne's. Dan had never met her.

Thoughts of Marianne made me afraid. Her whole world, as far back as the days of divorce and anorexia, had been one of shadows, fantasy and pain. We had little contact now but the few words and gestures which did pass betwen us told me that beyond the baffle of exterior symptoms, Marianne was still the same proud, beautiful girl with whom I had shared every thought as a child. And that terrified me because essentially we were so the same. Every time I heard of some new manifestation of her despair – shameful alcoholic episodes, overdoses – I thought: There but for the grace of God go I.

And as if the injury to heart and mind was not enough, her body continued to betray her as well. While I was being sculpted – strong, whole and still, for all my ups and downs, an easy vessel for joy – her womb was being scraped away. Through the nightmare of the alcoholic void which followed she sent one message: *Scream. Long black howl.*

I resolved then that, should she ever claw her way back through that long black howl, I would one day carry children which in some way would be shared with her. I wanted a tribe, a great big close loving tribe, to somehow balance the splintered nucleus which had been our own experience of family.

Meanwhile, after one or two futile attempts to wrench her back by the imposition of my own will, I left her to fight on alone and went on creating and demolishing images in my own world.

Spent the day with Dan plastering the sculpture. We started by flicking the plaster on to the clay with brushes. Soon the whole room was covered in splashes like enormous seagull turds. Dan could hardly wait for the plaster to dry so that he could break off the moulds and get on with the final stage.

But something went wrong. All the moulds cracked. Dan just put his head in his hands when he saw the torso go and said, 'Oh shit. Shit shit shit shit.'

Half the semi-set clay had come off with the plaster. Half a face on the armature, half on the floor. One breast was sort of hanging. Dan sat there for ages with his head in his hands and I did not know what to do. In the end I picked up a piece off the floor and said, 'Never mind, at least you're left with a shoulder to cry on.'

He held the shoulder and I thought he really was going to cry but after a minute he giggled instead. So did I. We dumped the pieces into three big bags and took them all the way out to the Civic Amenities dump at Mortlake. There, instead of just leaving the bags, we took out all the bits and broke them against a wall. What was left of the head split quite neatly into four. Dan and I got almost hysterical laughing at the waste and madness of it all.

Trying out a new face – this time ministering angel – I went to work next in a Home for young disabled people. It was only temporary, filling in while someone was away, but it opened my eyes to a world I would never forget.

They call the things that dangle down their legs sporrans. I am always afraid to jog them in case the plastic tubes tear out from the other tubes inside. But the 'wheelies', as they call themselves, are quite matter-of-fact in dealing with their own bodies.

Once I nearly fell over William backing out of the lavatory with a soiled glove still on his hand. His face went red behind his glasses but his lips pulled themselves into a smile. Turning to face me, he held up the glove and waggled the finger like a puppet.

'Nasty, isn't it?' he said.

I suppose a proper nurse would have said: 'Oh, go on with you' or something. I just said, 'Yes.' William's neck was red too and the triangle of chest above his shirt, but the brown fingers went on waggling.

'Can you steer with one hand all right?' I asked. I thought he might want me to wheel him to the dustbins.

'Like Jackie Stewart,' he said. 'Haven't you noticed something?'

His eyes, big behind the glasses, were challenging me to understand. I looked at the waggling hand and its meaning suddenly clicked.

'Hey, that's great, William – the middle finger is working!'

He had not been able to move it independently of the others before.

'Yes, great, isn't it,' he said, spinning the chair away so fast that his withered pipe-cleaner legs slapped against the arm rest. 'Think what fun I can have now!'

We had a birthday party one day for Joyce, a quadriplegic. By four o'clock all the wheelchairs were assembled. There were seven 'wheelies' and three ladies from the Home committee at table. One of the ladies cut the cake and another opened Joyce's presents for her, blushing when William's fell out. It was a tiny pair of silk briefs with 'Where there's a will there's a way' stitched in crazy letters on the front. Joyce's face lit up and her boyfriend, in an electric wheelchair, clapped William on the back so hard his glasses fell off. While I was groping for them under the table I noticed that the stopper had come out of someone's sporran and a pair of smartly shod feet stood in a pool of urine. The youngest committee lady's face looked down as I looked up.

'Oh dear,' she said, embarrassed. 'I think someone has had a little accident.'

I could feel William smirk. As I emerged from under the table he said, in a polite tea-party voice, 'An accident, yes, but that's something we don't talk about much round here.' He paused, glancing pointedly at the assortment of twisted bodies around him, '. . . Do you think it was God, or the other fellow?'

The silence that followed was broken by some brave soul starting 'Happy Birthday'.

At six the party broke up and only a nucleus remained: Joyce, her boyfriend and William. The boyfriend produced a bottle of wine and insisted I stay to help them drink it. After a while Joyce and he stopped talking and just stared at each other. William said, 'Why don't you two disappear?'

It was clear that was what they wanted to do. I wheeled Joyce to her room and her boyfriend followed in his chair.

'Will you mind if we have to buzz for you?' he asked.

I told him of course not and left.

They did have to buzz. Twice, while William and I sat finishing the wine, I got up to answer their call. Wiliam's eyes behind his glasses watched me go and watched me come back. He smoked, sometimes missing his lips.

After the second time I came back – the two bodies still clear in my mind, the way his arm shielded her breasts so gently as I helped with their helpless legs – I accepted a cigarette. William leaned forward to light it, daring me to trust the flame in his dangerously flicking fingers.

'Come here and help find my cufflink,' he said. 'It's dropped down the side of my chair.'

As I bent down, William pulled the pin out of the leather slide holding my hair. He wheeled his chair forward as I drew back.

'Don't panic, this is hardly going to be rape.'

He had one arm looped round my neck and was reaching up with the other.

'Oh William . . .' I said feebly and remembered Addie mocking voices which were always saying to him: 'Oh Addie . . .'

The second arm was misbehaving. Each time he flung it up it

281

spasmed at the shoulder. If I pulled back now I would make him lose his balance altogether. If I yielded I would be clinched in his arms. I could picture already the small, hunched body pressed to mine.

'Do you realize,' he said angrily, 'what it's like to be a "wheelie" but still have the feelings of a man?'

By now he had both arms in place and all his weight was round my neck pulling me down like a giant human collar.

'William, I don't know what it's like to be a "wheelie" and I don't know what it's like to be a man but I do know what it's like to be a girl and you're making things impossible for me now.'

'Impossible, huh? You'd know what impossible meant if one day your legs packed up on you and you were suddenly reduced to a *thing* in a chair.'

The tops of his glasses were bumping my chin. Only his feet, little flopping things in shiny shoes, remained in contact with the chair. I had no idea what I was going to do.

Then, searingly loud, the buzzer went.

The urgency drained out of both of us like a pulled plug. He hung, a dead weight, and his lips curled wryly against my throat.

'Ha ha ha. Saved by the bell.'

'I'll have to go, William. Unwind.'

He let go slowly, feeling for the chair behind.

'Oh God,' he said, sagging into place, 'my heart is as full as my sporran.'

Both of us giggled.

Later that night when I came down to help Joyce pee, William called softly through his door.

'Hey – I've been thinking about you. Does that repel you? Where, oh where would man be without his dreams?'

My dreams these days were being kept firmly under control. I worked, went jogging every morning whatever the weather and spent my evenings alone, reading. I rejoiced in the self-imposed order of my days. Discipline was the keyword in my existence now and if ever I felt the old longings revive – to be tender and feminine, to hold and be held – I stamped on them hard. Things were going all right at the moment. I was being good. Passion, once associated with salvation, now looked more dangerous than alluring. After all, where had it led before?

The various jobs I took reflected the images with which I was experimenting. Back in a boilersuit, I worked for a while painting boats in Oxford. Then I became a nanny, taught conversational English to a Japanese and filled in any spare hours with life modelling. But, as the power of the suspended sentence came to an end, although I stuck unwaveringly to my own guidelines for discipline, the contrasts between the images became increasingly extreme.

WANTED: Caring and responsible person to look after elderly
disabled lady. Weekends only. £6 plus meals.

WANTED: Topless hostesses for gentlemen's luncheon club.
Earnings from £20 per session.

I took both jobs. My interest in learning to understand the problems of the disabled had continued and, in taking on the role of club hostess, I seemed in some way to be finally evening the score with the Greek and Massell. Now the shoe would be on the other foot. I would be the user, not the used.

I kept track of my progress in a tiny notebook which fitted as snugly into a stocking top as into the breast-pocket of my nursing overall.

An insignificant arrow in club colours pointed down an alley to a black door with a judas hole in it, just like those in the bin. Beyond the door a soft-carpeted stairwell led down into a red-illumined interior where a woman with dyed blonde hair whisked me into a booth. I had a quick glimpse of more booths and a small, dark bar.

The blonde woman handed me a bundle with a chit pinned to it saying New Girl. She smiled and said in a foreign accent, 'I ham Madame. Chour name is Zsa Zsa.'

The changing-room reeks of scent and hot bodies. Big Mona clouts people who get in her way with her enormous

283

*black breasts. Someone is always screaming for a Tampax and
everybody uses each other's make-up, lipsticky mouths muttering through hairgrips, painted eyes flashing signals in the mirror.*

*My tiny skirt keeps riding up over the flounces of my knickers
but Big Mona says, 'It's OK honey, it's meant to be that way.'*

*She told me to hide anything private down a boot because
Madame goes through our bags when we are out front.*

I liked Big Mona. She turned up every morning at the club in
an old white mac and flat shoes, looking like the cleaning lady.
But when she put on her wig and stockings and smoothed the
Kleenex-sized apron over her great rumbling belly, she was magnificent. Her breasts, with long purple stalks, seemed to boom
out in front of her like foghorns and her vast, jutting rump made
mincemeat of the tiny skirt, chewing it into a crumpled belt over
knicker flounces which barely spanned half her buttocks. From
time to time Madame scolded her for the disorder of her uniform,
but Mona just snapped a big bubble of pink gum in her face,
rolled her bulk languidly and answered, 'Anybody – Ah mean
anybody – can see Ah ain't *designed* for dis gear. Ya got any udder
complaints?'

Madame had not. Big Mona made her a lot of money.

Occasionally we would go for a meal together after the club
closed: Mona in her cleaning-lady gear again, steak and chips
vanishing between her broad lips like small change into a
carpet-bag. She told me she was just filling in time before taking
a cruise to Las Vagas.

'Won't that cost the earth?'

'She-oo! You green or what? Double trade all de way,
honey – crew for de short-times, first class for de dee-luxe
nights.'

I was green. It took me a week to realize that I was the only
girl in the club not 'going case'. While I was pulling in a steady
£20 a day – the fee a client paid for my company while he drank
champagne and I trickled it into the carpet – the others were

making assignations for after-hours which earned them anything up to £100 a throw.

This knowledge rolled around my head disturbingly as I looked after Dr Carew, the disabled lady, at the weekend.

> *She has to have four lots of medicine through the night and I turn her three times. Her poor body, each limb a greyish, powdery branch attached to a greyish, powdery trunk, is not always easy to shift, but she never complains. She just seems relieved when the TV programmes end and it is time for her first dose of oblivion.*
>
> *The last time I saw Jem he gave me a funny little poetry book called* Archy and Mehitabel. *In one poem a cat dances in the catacombs, describing the once-full lives of the bones that lie beneath and saying at the end of each verse:*
>
> *'All men's lovers come to this.'*
>
> *It's true. Dr Carew, Big Mona, Richard, Massell, me – that's all we really are in the end, bones.*

This distant and no doubt past-coloured way of looking at things made the issue of morality seem irrelevant, and with my habit of taking things to the limit it was inevitable that one day before leaving the hostess club I would try 'going case'.

It happened one Monday lunchtime. I was tired after a particularly painful night with Dr Carew. She had not been able to sleep and lay all night staring at the ceiling through pain-bright, exhausted eyes. Beyond the small promise of a grandchild's visit and tea in the garden when the sun came out, she was only waiting to die. As I shrugged out of my nursing overall and started to apply make-up for the club, I felt angry and confused at the seeming futility of it all. And by the time I had got up to town I was in a strange, hard mood, ready almost for anything.

He began by ordering a bottle of Krug. I sat across from him, face and upper body in three-quarter profile, which displayed me to advantage and at the same time allowed me to keep an eye on what was happening outside.

He said, 'Aha!' heartily as the cork, expertly thumbed off by

Madame, made a soft, steamy pop. We raised glasses and sipped.

'Mmmmmn,' I murmured appreciatively, 'my favourite.'

'Jolly good,' he said stiffly, looking at the wall a few inches from my breasts. 'Smoke?'

He offered a packet of Players and I refused politely. He lit one for himself, then waved it around awkwardly.

'I say, I'm sorry – do you mind?'

I had to decide quickly whether this shy formality was a pose or genuine. I tested.

'*I* don't mind, but it probably isn't very good for you, is it?'

He hesitated, a little startled, and eyed the cigarette shyly.

'I know I shouldn't really – but am I allowed just one?'

I was home and dry. Holding his eyes with mine and leaning forward deliberately, I passed a hand under the table and dribbled away the first glass of champagne.

'Oh, I might let you get away with that,' I said, '. . . if you are a good boy in other ways.'

His cheeks went pink and he gave a bashful smile. Definitely a case of spankypoos.

Two bottles of Krug later, my middle-aged schoolboy was looking more relaxed. His pure new wool tie was off centre and two fingers of mousy hair stuck straight up over his forehead like devilish horns. He was telling a long, complicated story about how he and someone called Crowther had once got lost in the backstreets of Cologne and ended up being taken in by an extraordinary woman.

'Ix-*straw*dinry,' he insisted, screwing up his eyes at the memory. 'Old Crowther and I had *such* fun.'

He was squeezing the cup of his champagne glass and twiddling the stem incessantly.

'*Stop fiddling* while you're talking,' I said sharply.

His eyes flew open and glanced guiltily at his hands. We both smiled and a warm palm came wobbling hopefully across the table.

'*Bad* boy,' I said, swatting it lightly just before it touched. 'Come here and let me straighten your tie.'

He began to shuffle quickly round the table.

'But wait a minute' – I held up the latest empty bottle – 'what about this?'

Madame caught the signal and bustled into the booth within seconds flourishing a new one. She wrinkled her nose at me delightedly. I was 'being good' at this game, too. When she had gone I moved up and straightened the man's tie. He had drunk a great deal very fast and there was a film of sweat over his face. As my breasts accidentally brushed his lapels he whispered breathily, 'I say, you are going to come with me, aren't you, and let me, let me . . .'

I gazed blankly for a moment at the curtain. Did it really matter, after all that had happened, what I did with my body now?

It did matter, it always would, but caught up as I was in this role, this game, I said, 'Yes . . . only with a friend.'

We arranged to meet outside the Café Royal, where he would have a taxi waiting. In the changing-room I made a deal with Suzanne, a thin, businesslike girl. We shared a chocolate bar as we walked to the rendezvous.

The man had already booked a hotel room by phone. Suzanne, muttering about having to be quick because she had to collect the kids from school, stripped down to stockings and suspenders and sat on the edge of the bed, thin legs apart, breaking open a packet of condoms with her teeth. She smoked a cigarette while I undressed as far as the club uniform and pushed off the man's coat. He stood dazed and grinning as I removed his tie.

'Drop your trousers,' I ordered.

He did so, staggering a little, and Suzanne's expert hands shot out to work on the half erection pointing up the cloth of old-fashioned Y-fronts.

'Bend over,' I said and he bent over, flushed face close to her lipstick-reddened nipples. Still working on him with one hand, Suzanne stubbed out her cigarette and spat on her fingers, moistening herself before hooking up a condom on a long red nail and rolling it on to him. He was still not fully erect and I gave an experimental whack with the flat of my hand. He lurched lower over Suzanne and the Y-fronts slithered down. His feet, in neat red-patterned socks, danced around at the edge of the bed. The whole scene was like something out of a third-rate film but someone had to go on directing it.

'Kneel here,' I commanded, smacking the bed between Suzanne's thighs and flipping up his shirt-tail to expose white, loose-skinned buttocks. My hand flashing down left a mark like a pink exploding star.

'Oo ow!' he cried, sounding like the villain in a Batman comic getting his come-uppance, and then: 'Oo oo!' as Suzanne pulled him into her. She grabbed a pillow from the top of the bed, whipped it under her bottom and clamping her legs high up on his back, sucked at him like a drain-plunger.

'I'll give you Oo,' I heard her growl between gritted teeth, 'fucking bastard, fucking prick.'

I peppered another series of slaps on his blotched buttocks as she went on drain-plunging, bony spine lifting clean off the bed in the effort to hurry him on. His hair was now little devil's horns all over, but the rest of him was beginning to sag.

One hand that had been trying to hold a breast fell off and groped for purchase on the counterpane.

'I'm afraid I've had a drop too much to drink,' he gasped.

Suzanne stopped in mid-plunge and unwound her legs. She was up and dressed before I had got the pillow out from where he had flopped and placed it under his head.

'Well, can't say we didn't try,' she said cheerfully, tucking away the fifty pounds I gave her off the top of the television. She blew me a kiss as she went out.

'Thanks for the biz, darl. I'll do the same for you.'

I sat on a chair before the dressing-table, slowly pulling on my clothes. The face on the pillow looked empty; the legs, still with socks on, white and sad. I thought he was asleep. Brushing my hair, I saw in the mirror the rest of the money on top of the television, another fifty pounds. I thought of the woman on the canteen steps in the bin opening her doughy legs for two cigarettes. The way she had screeched when the whitecoats dragged the man off and one of the cigarettes got broken.

'I say, you're not going, are you?'

The man was sitting up, pulling the counterpane over his legs.

'I must,' I said. 'Why don't you get into bed properly and have a sleep? You don't look too good.'

'Can't. Train to catch.'

He looked around him unhappily, taking in the rumpled bed, his tie and the Y-fronts on the floor.

'Did I – did you pay that other girl?'

'Yes.'

I went into the bathroom and came back with a glass of water.

'Try that.'

Looking at his embarrassed face I thought how happy and excited he had been chattering about his friend Crowther in the club.

'Do you still see Crowther?' I asked, peering curiously for a moment into his world.

'Crowther? Why, yes. Matter of fact I was supposed to be meeting him today. But he cancelled at the last minute. Can't think why.'

He looked disappointed now, as well as hungover and embarrassed.

'I say, I've made a nitwit of myself, haven't I? What a shambles.'

I went and sat beside him on the bed.

'Couldn't even . . .'

'Shush,' I said firmly and unbuttoning my dress took out a breast for him to lean on. As his hands came up to touch, mine went down to him. Somehow this experience, like everything else in my life, had to be seen through to the bitter end.

He came quickly and kept his arms around me until I gently pushed him away. I realized then with a shock that this stranger had touched me more tenderly than my onetime dream man, Massell, had ever done. It made the power of illusion – or self-delusion – seem stronger than even the crudest reality.

But once was enough. I never went back to the hostess club and the following week began work as a clerk in an Inland Revenue sorting centre.

289

From 8.30 a.m. to 4.30 p.m. I sit inside a giant shoebox built by Italian prisoners of war. Light hums from fluorescent strips ranged evenly over long, meccano-grey bays, each housing hundreds of lettered pigeonholes. Corrugations divide the meccano into blocks and in front of each block sits a man or woman in a high chair. If you wander up the bays during work hours all you can see are rows and rows of bent heads and pairs of arms moving up and down like sluggish pistons, each with a white slip of paper on the end.

Every now and then someone gets up and ambles to the end of their bay to fetch a fresh mailbag, settling back into position quietly, arms resuming the interrupted rhythm. There is the occasional cough but otherwise the only sound is the rustling of countless hundreds of letters about tax. If you close your eyes you can imagine it is the sound of surf riffling a shoreline of fine pebbles.

I stayed in that job for nearly two years, enjoying the role of being 'ordinary' for once. It was almost like sending myself back to school. I, who had rejected all early forms of structure in my life, now welcomed it, and the proof that I could stick to the tasks I set myself made me feel strong. The fight was after all not with the outside world. What I did was up to me.

But whatever I did, however immersed I became in one role, I could never escape the knowledge that there were a thousand other avenues open. Gazing beyond the pigeonholes in the Inland Revenue sorting centre, just as I had gazed out of a window in a Latin lesson years before, I knew that I was only waiting for another sunny day to walk out into the blue.

The time had come to go beyond all images, all roles.

At the beginning of January 1981 I started spending all my lunch hours in Richmond library, scanning lists of single airfares to places as far apart as Africa and Greenland. I wrote away inquiring about jobs in Leningrad, Peru and Singapore and looked into the possibilities of overlanding, joining the armed forces and crewing on round-the-world yachts. Some of the replies I got were encouraging but still I hesitated. What I wanted now was a personal challenge of such dimension it would almost be a case of kill or cure. Trying to pin down my desire, I had a vision of being dropped by helicopter into the middle of some nameless land and grappling the means to survive out of the earth. I wanted to scrape away the superficial layers of my environment – and of myself – until I was right down to the raw stuff of existence.

This dream, ironically, was probably easier to realize than any I had had before. All I had to do was answer one more advertisement: a writer was looking for a 'wife' to share a year-long survival exercise on an uninhabited tropical island.

I went.

Epilogue

Just before setting off for the island I went to see Marianne. At that time she was still in the grip of past unhappiness, hiding away in Richard's old studio at 309 surrounded by crumpled family photographs and vodka bottles.

'Hello, duck,' I said, using our old greeting. 'I'm going to live on an uninhabited tropical island with a stranger for a year.'

She smiled and settled back as though I were about to launch into one of Joey's adventures from our childhood game of Chatter. When I shrugged and said, 'That's all,' she asked seriously, 'Do you think you'll ever come back?'

'I don't know.'

She nodded, understanding everything.

'If you do, will you promise to tell what happened?'

'Yes.'

I kept that promise by writing *Castaway*. And while I was doing that, Marianne was fighting her demons. I am proud to say that she is now, among other things, a very special Auntie to the latest adventure in my life – a son. Kay, too, now leads a full life of her own and the unhappy days of family strife are long gone.

But real life, unlike fiction, does not wrap up neatly at the end of a chapter and it would take another volume to describe what has happened to all the others mentioned in these pages. As for me, the year on the island proved to be one of the richest and most instructive experiences of my life. It threw into new perspective all the ups and downs of my earlier years and when I came back I was humbler, stronger and more than ever aware of how good it is to be alive.

November 1985

The Germans
and Their Neighbors

EDITED BY

Dirk Verheyen and
Christian Søe

Westview Press

BOULDER • SAN FRANCISCO • OXFORD

Copyright © 1993 by Westview Press, Inc.

Published in 1993 in the United States of America by Westview Press, Inc., 5500 Central Avenue, Boulder, Colorado 80301-2877, and in the United Kingdom by Westview Press, 36 Lonsdale Road, Summertown, Oxford OX2 7EW

Library of Congress Cataloging-in-Publication Data
The Germans and their neighbors / edited by Dirk Verheyen and
  Christian Søe.
    p.   cm.
  Includes bibliographical references.
  ISBN 0-8133-8522-9 (hc) — ISBN 0-8133-1959-5(pbk.)
  1. Germany—Foreign relations—1990–   . I. Verheyen, Dirk.
  II. Søe, Christian.
  DD290.3.G47   1993
  327.43   dc20   91-38102
                                                                          CIP

Printed and bound in the United States of America

  The paper used in this publication meets the requirements
        of the American National Standard for Permanence of Paper
        for Printed Library Materials Z39.48-1984.

10   9   8   7   6   5   4   3   2   1

Contents

Acknowledgments

We would like to thank the contributors for their enthusiastic support of this project and for making its successful completion possible. We owe a special debt of gratitude to Edna Hastings for her superb typesetting work, to Dina Ng and the Loyola Marymount University library staff for their assistance in the preparation of the manuscript, and to Susan B. Mason and Steve Frye at California State University, Long Beach, for their research assistance. We are most appreciative of the professionalism of the staff at Westview Press, particularly Amos Zubrow, Susan McEachern, Alison Auch, Jennifer Watson, and Polly Christensen. Finally, we thank Louise, Nils, and Erik Søe for the good humor with which they endured our seemingly endless Westchester–Long Beach telephone conversations.

Dirk Verheyen
Christian Søe

Europe in 1993. *Source:* David S. Mason, *Revolution in East-Central Europe: The Rise and Fall of Communism and the Cold War* (Boulder: Westview Press, 1992). Reprinted by permission.

Introduction

Dirk Verheyen and Christian Søe

Except for the new Russia within its still mercurial geopolitical configuration, Germany has more neighbors than any other state in Europe. From its location in the northern middle of the Continent, Germany borders directly on nine countries, and there are many more slightly distant neighbors.[1] For each of them, Germany's proximity has long been a crucial fact of life. None of them can afford to be unconcerned about what happens in this centrally placed, powerful nation. All of them have been and will continue to be affected in important ways by the socio-cultural, economic, and political dynamism of Germany. All carry some memories and perceptions of intense past relations with Germany and the Germans. And all have hopes and anxieties concerning their future relationship with an enlarged and more self-confident Germany after the recent political upheaval in Europe.

Each of the 18 essays in this volume deals with the German factor from the perspective of a single country. A reading will underscore the conclusion that there is no single or simple story to be told about the Germans and their neighbors. Instead, there are multiple stories, both unique and overlapping in their complex mixtures of factors, themes, and dynamics. On one level, there are the most "practical" concerns about territory, trade and, increasingly, travel. On another level, one uncovers subtle connections between cultural sensitivity and economic dependence, traumas and traditions, memories and emotions. In no case is the bilateral relationship with Germany simple and straightforward. If there is one theme that is shared by the various essays, it consists of an underlying pattern of ambivalence, fluctuating between instrumental partnership, formal cordiality or pragmatic accomodation, and wary circumspection or even latent hostility.

In the final analysis, each country's relations with Germany and the Germans have been and continue to be unique, the product of special and distinct experiences and memories. Yet in any given period, all the countries included in this volume have had to deal, in a very basic way, with the same Germany. Even though they have all had to come to grips with their particular version of the "German Question," it is possible to detect important patterns and commonalities in the bilateral relationships. The observations that follow may assist the reader in standing back from the many individual case-studies and reflect more generally on the subject.

The "German Question" can usefully be analyzed as having four distinct yet related dimensions: (a) Germany's *search for a clear national identity*, (b) Germany's *pursuit of national unity* (both in the 19th century and after 1945), (c) the *impact of Germany's power* on European as well as global affairs, and (d) Germany's *quest for a commensurate role* in international politics and economics.[2] Many aspects of the relations between Germany and its neighbors are linked to one or more of these four dimensions of the German Question. In turn, the attitudes and policies of Germany's neighbors have been influenced by the following factors: (a) their size and power relative to Germany; (b) their proximity to or distance from Germany; (c) their general historical experience vis-a-vis Germany (with the two world wars as often decisive criteria); (d) their cultural and/or linguistic affinity with Germany; (e) the depth of their economic interaction with, if not outright dependence on, Germany; (f) the salience of border disputes (generally the result of ethno-cultural fluidity); and (g) the presence of ethnic German minorities in their national populations.

The German search for a clear national identity has had, and probably will continue to have, profound implications for several countries that share important cultural traits with Germany. This is especially so in cases of ethno-linguistic affinity, as illustrated in the essays on Austria and Switzerland. To a lesser extent the same is true for the Netherlands and the Flemish part of Belgium. In addition, the definition of German identity has been of obvious concern to those countries that contain(ed) significant communities of ethnic Germans, such as Poland, Czechoslovakia, Romania, and Denmark. These are countries that could find themselves subjected to special German influence or demands. The brutally aggressive definition of German identity during the Third Reich had terrible consequences for many other peoples in Europe, especially Jews and Gypsies as well as many Slavs.

Largely the same countries have had ample reason to be concerned about any German quest for national unity that might involve demands for territorial adjustments in order to reintegrate German minorities into a "complete" German nation-state. The very fluidity of German cultural identity and territorial expanse lies at the root of important historical border disputes between Germany and countries like France, Denmark, Poland, Czechoslovakia, and the Netherlands. Polish-German friction over the so-called Oder-Neisse boundary at the time of Germany's 1990 unification demonstrates the continued significance of this issue, as the essay on Poland will testify.

On a more subtle but nevertheless vital level, the German cultural impact has been mixed in many ways. There has been considerable cultural friction between Germany and several of its neighbors (Poland, France, or the Netherlands), frequently conducive to anti-German tendencies in those countries. At the same time, however, Germany has had a tremendous and often constructive cultural impact on many of its neighbors, ranging from philosophy or literature to music or the visual arts. Altogether, Germany's cultural radiance in Europe has been profound, often eliciting ambivalent reactions among its neighbors who feared a hegemonial German impulse. Such concerns increased after 1871, when Germany's political, military, and economic clout began to match its already considerable cultural influence.

The emergence of a powerful, united Germany in 1871 caused misgivings among near and distant neighbors about its role in international affairs. These misgivings were amply confirmed by both world wars. Germany was subjected to strongly punitive treatment at the 1919 Versailles Peace Conference, but allied policies proved incapable of preventing the Nazi disaster (and may have had a share in bringing it about). World War II and its aftermath appeared to recast the "German Question" in a fundamental way, with the division of Germany between 1945 and 1990 ostensibly transforming and diminishing the problem of the country's role and power in international affairs.[3]

During these four decades, when the provisional partition of postwar Germany seemed to become permanent, both German states found themselves integrated into opposing alliances. This predicament constrained their room for maneuver and ruled out a return to the independent exercise of national power associated with the German tradition of *Machtpolitik* and *Schaukelpolitik* (the tendency to "switch" or "float" between East and West as a centrally located great power). East and West Germans faced each other across the great political divide established by the Cold War. As a result, relations between the Germans and neighboring countries became differentiated, with alliance membership as a major determining variable. West Germany became closely integrated with its Western neighbors, economically, politically, and militarily, while its relations with Soviet bloc countries remained more limited. The reverse was true for East Germany.

The two neighboring German states were ruled by rival elites, separated by the competing power interests and ideologies of the Cold War. For a while, in the 1950s and 1960s, divided Germany could even appear to be the Cold War "cockpit" in Europe. Backed by its Western partners, the Federal Republic proclaimed itself to be the democratic representative of the Germans in both East and West, while the German Democratic Republic first pursued and then abandoned a symbolic commitment to a united socialist Germany in its own image. It was recognized that outright hostility between the two German states could have destabilizing consequences for the postwar order, and there was a shared interest between the two alliance systems in containing any *furor teutonicus*. At the same time, an inter-German rapprochement was bound to raise concerns in both East and West about the future of Germany and its place in the European system, even short of actual national reunification. The dilemma was resolved by the fact that, at least since the late 1950s, the Soviet Union seemed unwilling to agree to any terms of unification that would have been acceptable to the West. The fortified inner-German border and eventually the Berlin Wall symbolized an apparently unshakable will to uphold the country's political division. As a consequence, West Germany in the late 1960s abandoned the Hallstein Doctrine, with which it had tried to ostracize the rival East German powerholders. German unity remained on the constitutional and rhetorical agenda, but Bonn no longer campaigned actively for what appeared to be at best a distant goal with a reconstituted Europe of the future.

After 1969, a Social Democratic and Liberal coalition government in Bonn took decisive new steps in this policy of rapprochement toward Central and Eastern Europe. Willy Brandt's *Ostpolitik* included a special relationship with East Berlin under the formula, "one German nation, two German states." At first denounced by the conservative Christian Democratic opposition as a sell-out, the new approach was continued by its former critics, when they replaced the Social Democrats as chancellor party in 1982. Continuity was underscored by the fact that the liberal Free Democrats stayed on in the new coalition cabinet and continued, with Hans-Dietrich Genscher, to head the Foreign Ministry. By then, the "Genscherist" approach had gained wide acceptance at home as a pragmatic policy of seeking a *modus vivendi* with the GDR, in order to reduce international tensions and improve the living conditions in East Germany. "Genscherism" also evoked a positive response among many of the smaller European neighbors, but the reaction in the larger countries was more skeptical or even critical.[4] Despite the steady German-German rapprochement, however, the country's sudden political reunification in 1989-90 caught both the Germans and their neighbors by surprise.

Anxiety and misgivings concerning the power and role of a united Germany resurfaced, even if often muted through official statements of political approval and support. It is therefore not surprising that such concerns about German power constitute a recurrent theme in the essays that follow. Are there detectable patterns in the responses by elites and mass publics? They vary considerably, as already suggested, depending in part on such factors as a country's power and proximity relative to Germany as well as the former's economic dependence on and cultural affinity with the Germans. Public opinion polls taken between late 1989 and the end of 1990, in addition to press commentary, provide a vivid illustration of this complex pattern of reactions.[5]

As could be expected, an attitude of wariness seems to prevail in many quarters and at different levels in Russia, Poland, and Czechoslovakia, where individual and collective memories of the Third Reich and territorial concerns about the post-1945 settlement remain more acute than elsewhere. The

Netherlands also has special reasons to be troubled, given the shock of the German military invasion and occupation of this neutral country during World War II. The strong initial skepticism about German unification in Denmark is perhaps more difficult to explain, given its less traumatic experience during the war, but historical factors help clarify the small country's mixed reactions followed by a relatively quick accomodation to the new *status quo*. Three other small countries with direct boundaries to Germany (Austria, Switzerland, and Belgium) appear to have accepted German unification with greater equanimity, both at the elite and mass level. Hungary, another small neighbor, played a crucial role in facilitating the refugee stream from East Germany during the later summer of 1989, which triggered what became the revolutionary mass demonstrations within the GDR.

As major European powers, Britain and France also showed reservations, at least at the elite level in both countries, which presumably reflect concerns about the altered balance of power on the Continent. Other, more distant neighbors, like Italy, Spain, and Romania, appear to have reacted with considerable official and public support for German reunification, although there were reservations expressed here and there at elite levels, as in the case of Italian Prime Minister Giulio Andreotti. Reactions in Norway, Sweden, and Finland seemed to be more muted and low-key, perhaps reflective of their rather peripheral geographic location vis-a-vis Europe's dynamic and turbulent center.

More immediate experiences or memories of the Third Reich understandably played a crucial role, as the cautious reactions in the American Jewish community would underline, in contrast to the very positive response among much of the U.S. population. Countries that had fought against Germany or experienced German military occupation tended to be more skeptical than countries that had successfully remained neutral or that had been cobelligerents of Germany, although differences abound. Older generations have been generally more critical and concerned than younger cohorts, who have no individual experiences or memories of the Third Reich. On the whole, there has been more skepticism expressed on the Left, in the media and in polls, than on the Right.

When all is said and done, however, it is remarkable how relatively smoothly the formal political unification of Germany has met with international acceptance and support, as Andrei S. Markovits has also concluded in a systematic study of press reactions in EC countries.[6] This is not only to be explained in terms of an acceptance of what quickly became inevitable, once the basic condition of Communism's collapse in Europe had been fulfilled and Mikhail Gorbachev decided to play his "German card" while it still had some value. It cannot be overlooked that 45 years after World War II, Germany had lost many of its more fearsome aspects for many of its neighbors. One major reason was the country's division between East and West, and the close integration of a democratic West Germany into the Atlantic Alliance and the

European Community. The task of convincing Germany's neighbors that the merger with the GDR would not loosen those close ideological, economic, political, and military ties became a major feat of West German diplomacy in 1990.

The German Question can still be said to preoccupy Europe in the 1990s, even if in a vastly changed setting. The country has been formally unified, but its uncertain identity, its quest for true unity, its multifaceted power, and its prominent role in world affairs continue to shape the often ambivalent reactions of its many neighbors.[7]

The Germans themselves also have shown a continuous and unusual concern about their impact and image abroad, reflecting an abiding economic, cultural, and political interest in their diverse European as well as global "neighborhood." This has been a key issue in (West) German foreign policy since 1949, of course, shaping West German efforts at *Wiedergutmachung* (restitution and reconciliation) with a host of neighboring countries in Western Europe. Much of the *Ostpolitik* of the 1970s and 1980s was inspired by a similar German desire at political rehabilitation among the country's Central and Eastern European neighbors (especially Poland).[8]

Since unification, the German government and press have watched with considerable concern the reactions on the part of neighboring countries to a variety of developments in the "new" Germany.[9] The Commonwealth of Independent States and the new democracies in Eastern Europe expect extensive German assistance on the road to democracy and prosperity, while at the same time displaying a distinct fear of "DM-imperialism."[10] Some of Germany's Western neighbors are finding it difficult to accept that an already economically dominant Germany might now become an equally powerful political giant. The fact that some recent opinion polls suggest a noticeable reduction in German popular support for further European integration have only added to the growing uncertainty among Germany's EC partners, for whom such integration became a postwar method of restraining and "neutralizing" German political and economic power.[11] Thomas Mann's famous preference for a "European Germany" rather than a "German Europe" is frequently invoked, by German and non-German commentators and analysts alike.[12]

More recently, neighboring countries on all sides have begun to register growing concern about the proliferation of right-wing, anti-foreigner activity in German towns and cities, particularly in the new *Länder* of the former GDR. The fact that such right-wing violence also occurs elsewhere in Europe does not appear to diminish international anxiety about its presence in Germany, in view of the latter's Nazi past. In addition, observers frequently wonder whether the emergence of younger, postwar generations in Germany might bring about a change in values and orientation, tied to unfamiliarity with and forgetfulness about Germany's troubled past.[13]

In their present situation, the Germans must not only contend with frequently wary and anxious neighbors, but also with the problems of coming to terms with each other, after 45 years of acculturation in two very different societies and political systems. Furthermore, they must now adjust to a vastly changed European order, in which the disappearance of the Soviet Union and the immense task of reconstruction of Central and Eastern Europe, in addition to the violent disintegration of Yugoslavia, have changed much of the international agenda faced by what are often called the "New Germany" and the "New Europe."

All of the following essays suggest, either implicitly or explicitly, that the past, present, and future may not be quite so neatly separable for Germany or Europe. Each of the chapters provides a unique perspective on a particular country and its special relationship with Germany, before 1945, between 1945 and 1989-90, and, more tentatively, in the post-unification period. Inescapably, there is much that is sad and negative in the historical portion of these accounts, in view of Germany's disastrous course during the first half of this century. Yet none of these stories can be read as a morally simple tale concerning the well-meaning neighbor facing the ugly German. After all, many European nations have at times conveniently repressed the more unpleasant aspects of their own behavior during the Nazi era.[14] In any case, the past needs to be fully confronted, in order to base future relations on a foundation of honesty, understanding, and sensitivity. On such a basis, there is also reason for hope concerning a democratic Germany's constructive contribution to the difficult task of building a more stable, democratic, and decent post-Cold War order in a European setting of cultural pluralism and tolerance.

Notes

1. The significance and consequences of Germany's central geopolitical location in Europe are often stressed in scholarly analysis. See, for example, Renata Fritsch-Bournazel, *Europe and German Unification* (New York/Oxford: Berg Publishers, 1992), especially p. 123ff.; Renata Fritsch-Bournazel, *Das Land in der Mitte. Die Deutschen im europäischen Kräftefeld* (Munich: Iudicium Verlag, 1986); Renata Fritsch-Bournazel, André Brigot, and Jim Cloos, *Les Allemands au Coeur de l'Europe* (Paris: Fondation pour les Etudes de Défense Nationale, 1983); Dirk Verheyen, *The German Question: A Cultural, Historical, and Geopolitical Exploration* (Boulder, CO: Westview Press, 1991), especially chapters 1 and 4; David Calleo, *The German Problem Reconsidered* (Cambridge: Cambridge University Press, 1978); Günter Gaus, *Wo Deutschland liegt: eine Ortsbestimmung* (Hamburg: Hoffmann & Campe, 1983). See also Wolf D. Gruner, *Deutschland mitten in Europa* (Hamburg: Verlag Dr. R. Krämer, 1992)

2. This definition of the "German Question," and the discussion that follows, are based on Verheyen, *The German Question*.

3. The impact of Germany's Cold War division on the "German Question" is concisely analyzed in Wilfried Loth, *Ost-West-Konflikt und deutsche Frage* (Munich: Deutscher Taschenbuch Verlag, 1989). See also Michael J. Sodaro, *Moscow, Germany, and the West from Khrushchev to Gorbachev* (Ithaca/London: Cornell University Press, 1990); Eleanor Lansing Dulles, *One Germany or Two* (Stanford: Hoover Institution Press, 1970); Ferenc A. Váli, *The Quest for a United Germany* (Baltimore: The Johns Hopkins Press, 1967); Thilo Vogelsang, *Das geteilte Deutschland* (Munich: Deutscher Taschenbuch Verlag, 1980); Gebhard Diemer and Eberhard Kuhrt, *Kurze Chronik der Deutschen Frage* (Munich: Olzog Verlag, 1991); Wolfram F. Hanrieder, *Germany, America, Europe* (New Haven/London: Yale University Press, 1989), Part II.

4. For a discussion of FRG-GDR relations in the 1980s, and foreign concerns about developments in a still-divided Germany, see the essays in F. Stephen Larrabee, ed., *The Two German States and European Security* (New York: St. Martin's Press, 1989). See also Edwina Moreton, ed., *Germany Between East and West* (Cambridge: Cambridge University Press, in association with the Royal Institute of International Affairs, 1987).

5. Relevant polling data and commentary can be found in "One Germany: U.S. Unfazed, Europeans Fret," *Los Angeles Times*, January 26, 1990, pp. A1, A10; "Survey Finds 2 in 3 Poles Opposed to German Unity," *The New York Times*, February 20, 1990, p. A8; "From Germany's Neighbors, Respect and Then Acceptance," *The New York Times*, September 27, 1990, pp. A1, A6; "They like it and they fear it," *The Economist*, January 27, 1990, pp. 29, 32; *Eurobarometer* (Commission of the European Communities), No. 33, June 1990, pp. 36-40 and No. 34, December 1990, pp. 18-20.

6. See Andrei S. Markovits, "Die Deutsche Frage — Perzeptionen und Politik in der Europäischen Gemeinschaft," in Ulrike Liebert und Wolfgang Merkel, eds., *Die Politik zur deutschen Einheit. Probleme, Strategien, Kontroversen* (Opladen: Leske & Budrich, 1991), pp. 321-41.

7. A vivid illustration of this fact can be found in the various essays in Ulrich Wickert, ed., *Angst vor Deutschland* (Hamburg: Hoffmann & Campe Verlag, 1990), especially Parts II and III.

8. See, for example, the views of Germany's neighbors collected in Manfred Koch-Hillebrecht, ed., *Das Deutschenbild* (Munich: Beck Verlag, 1977), Günter Trautmann, ed., *Die häßlichen Deutschen: Deutschland im Spiegel der westlichen und östlichen Nachbarn* (Darmstadt: Wissenschaftliche Buchgesellschaft, 1991), and Hans-Helmuth Knütter, *Deutschfeindlichkeit — Gestern, heute und morgen. . .?* (Asendorf, 1992).

9. See, for example, the discussion in "'Das häßliche deutsche Haupt'," *Der Spiegel*, Nr. 6, 1992, pp. 18-24.

10. A Czech joke maintains that "the only thing worse than being dominated by the German economy is not being dominated by it." Quoted in Robert Gerald Livingston, "United Germany: Bigger and Better," *Foreign Policy*, Nr. 87, Summer 1992, p. 168.

11. Interestingly, a recent analysis suggests that "fears of a powerful Germany have been used as important arguments both for and against ratification" of the 1991 Maastricht Treaty in referenda in countries like Denmark and France. See "Germany's New Strength Awakens Europe's Old Fears," *Wall Street Journal*, September 24, 1992, p. A13.

12. Foreign Minister Hans-Dietrich Genscher frequently evoked Thomas Mann's dictum in his speeches and essays. See, for example, his "Wir wollen ein europäisches

Deutschland, nicht ein deutsches Europa," in Wickert, ed., *Angst vor Deutschland*, pp. 317-24.

13. See Stephen F. Szabo, ed., *The Successor Generation: International Perspectives of Postwar Europeans* (Boston: Butterworths, 1983).

14. See Tony Judt, "The Past is Another Country: Myth and Memory in Postwar Europe," *Daedalus*, Vol. 121, No. 4, Fall 1992, pp. 83-118.

PART ONE

Neighbors to the West

1

France, Germany, and the New Europe

Anne-Marie LeGloannec

The demise of the Soviet Empire has transformed the divided European continent and, particularly, the country that this division partitioned: Germany. Cut in two by a front-line on which both superpowers met, Germany in a sense epitomized the predicament of the European continent. The implosion of the Soviet Union and the partial withdrawal of the United States from Europe have brought about the twin reunification of Europe and Germany and have changed the nature of German power. Reunited Germany has become both sovereign and central. It has become sovereign, both legally and politically, as it no longer needs to "import" its security from the United States. It has become central as it returns to its position as the geopolitical core of Europe without ceasing to be one of the main pillars of Western European institutions.

German reunification caused concern among Germany's neighbors and partners. In France, François Mitterrand displayed reluctance vis-a-vis the process, if not opposition to it, while trying to put a brake on the reunification process. Generally speaking, French elites wondered whether a united Germany would follow a national path, rather than a European one. At the EC summit in Maastricht, in December 1991, Chancellor Kohl certainly proved to be one of the best Europeans. Yet the recognition of Slovenia and Croatia, a little ahead of the eleven other members of the European Community, seemed to indicate that the German government was ready to use its clout.

As French suspicions were raised, the question arose whether this German diplomatic assertiveness was a passing, exceptional phenomenon or whether the pattern of Franco-German relations had been profoundly altered by changes in

Germany's status, as Valéry Giscard d'Estaing, François Mitterrand's predecessor, suggested in 1990. Had not a number of commentators stressed in the past that Franco-German cooperation was based on misunderstandings?[1] After looking first at the balance of French and German interests in the past and at the way they were met or not by Franco-German cooperation, we will try to analyze the changes brought about by reunification, and the fears and answers they generate.

From de Staël to de Gaulle

Over the centuries, strife and war, misunderstanding and mutual hatred have shaped Franco-German relations more than entente and cooperation. Certainly Germany in the past was not always perceived as an enemy striving for domination over Europe. The Germany Madame de Staël encountered after being sent into exile by Napoleon was politically weak, divided into a myriad of territories and devoid of patriotism: "Germans," she wrote, "have too much consideration for foreigners and too little national prejudice."[2] While she thought political fragmentation fostered cultural creativity and individual thriving, she assumed that "only political institutions can shape the character of a nation."[3] Yet hardly had Madame de Staël written those lines when the German states began throwing off the yoke that Napoleon had wanted to impose on them. In 1836, the historian Edgar Quinet suggested that the idyllic Germany Madame de Staël had thought to perceive was ridden by deep currents of change. An era was closing — that of Goethe and Hegel, Lessing, Klopstock, Schiller, Kant, Fichte, and Herder, those heroes of a German renaissance. Rightly worried, Quinet wondered what the new era was to bring.

Quinet's fears later turned out to be well-founded, as two elements coalesced that accounted for France's distrust of Germany. One was a German *Sonderweg*, a particular, rather illiberal development; the other was the achievement by force of German unity. In other words, France and Europe feared Germany's domestic political order as well as its foreign policy inclinations. In 1848, French Foreign Minister Jules Bastide suggested that "Germany's unity, which is presently starting to take shape, will turn this 40 million people into a power much more terrifying than today's Germany; therefore I do not believe that it is in our interest to call for unity, let alone to press for it."[4] The 1870 Franco-Prussian war that led to France's defeat and to the creation of the German *Reich* enticed French intellectuals to ponder the causes of German power — a number of them held industrial development and eventually scientific and academic achievements to be the very engine of German expansion — while public discourse, primary education, and even some scholarly publications spread the grossest anti-German clichés that persisted well into the next century.

During the first half of this century, the German drive for hegemony over Europe went hand in hand with the glorification by Germans of their *Sonderweg*, a notion more ideological than scientific, which praised the peculiarities of Germany's development as opposed to those of the British and French democracies. This led those who fought against Germany during two world wars, French as well as others, rightly to think that both Germany's internal constitution and her position in the international system had to be dramatically altered to bring about peace on the continent. The tragedies of this century also led them sometimes to believe that these German evolutions or revolutions they had not always understood, let alone forecast, reflected something evil. Thus Jacques Bainville, a well-known historian and disciple of Maurice Barrès and Charles Maurras, wrote in 1933 that the history of the two peoples "presents at this turning point the awful fact that never have the French understood the Germans so little. Their reasoning and their feelings escape us. Their intellectual and their emotional world is not ours. Never perhaps have they been so different from us. Even in the arts there is a wealth of misunderstandings."[5]

The end of World War II ushered in a new Europe and a new Germany. The division of Germany became in a way the very condition of the Federal Republic's integration in the Western community of states. It allowed the imposition of democracy on Germany and an opening to Western values. In other words, it firmly rooted the rump state in the West, whereas a united Germany might have been tempted to achieve a balance between East and West, maybe seduced by illiberalism, just as the Weimar Republic had been. The westernization of the country fostered both Germany's political rehabilitation and economic development, promises and achievements that almost no one in the Federal Republic actually thought of discarding for the sake of reunification. The division of Germany also allowed a reconciliation between former enemies, and the creation of a community of Western European states with a rough balance between France and Germany, Italy and the Benelux ensued: both vanquished and partitioned, Germany could no longer be a source of trouble.

However, this was not enough to convince French politicians, General de Gaulle first and foremost, that a German danger had been eliminated. Toward the end of the war and in the immediate postwar era, de Gaulle had aimed at controlling a weakened Germany, a policy supported by the public and pursued by his successors during the first years of the Fourth Republic. He sought to hold Germany in the pliers of the 1944 Franco-Soviet treaty. He wished to fragment it, following the policy Richelieu had implemented with the Treaty of Westphalia in 1648, and to annex territories bordering on France. "No more centralized *Reich*" became the watchword. In its occupation zone, France dismantled industrial plants, objected to the immigration of refugees, and treated the Germans harshly. In other words, the most adamant of the three Western powers, France tried to duplicate the policy pursued at the end of World War I. De Gaulle and his successors, however, missed these points: the Franco-

Soviet treaty quickly became moribund; fragmentation of Germany encountered the other three Allies' opposition; and out of the projected annexation of the Ruhr and Saar came nothing but a special status given to the latter and terminated in 1957 by a local vote following a Franco-German agreement.[6]

The Cold War allowed a Franco-German reconciliation in two ways. First, French politicians and public opinion came to realize that the Soviet Union, not Germany, was the foe. Voices were raised pleading for reconciliation with German democrats and advocating both the recreation of a Franco-German Union that Charlemagne had embodied and the federation of Europe. De Gaulle himself came to that conclusion toward the end of the decade. While in the opposition in 1950, he favorably replied to Konrad Adenauer's appeal to foster a Franco-German Union. Second, as it extended its protection to Western Europe, the United States acted as an "equalizer," as a balancing power between former enemies now deprived of the means and the necessity to compete for supremacy. The European Community was, to that extent, the fruit of the Cold War, of both Soviet threat and American protection. In 1950, the first stone of the Western European house was laid, that of the European Coal and Steel Community.

An Alliance Based on Misunderstandings?

By turning Franco-German reconciliation, rapprochement, and integration into the cornerstone of a Western European community (which was, in turn, to facilitate relations between the two former enemies), French and West German politicians altered the pattern of intra-European relations. In the past, these had been shaped by hostility between France and the House of Austria and later Prussia, alone or in alliance with other states. The pattern was now different. France and West Germany were allied against the Soviet Union and in order to promote its own relative position in the system, each of the two countries was resorting to cooperation with the other instead of waging war against it. As the history of Franco-German relations in the first four decades of the postwar era proved, each of the two countries would draw benefits from its alliance with the other.

To some extent, both France and West Germany shared common interests and objectives, in particular that of strengthening the Western community through their own alliance, "the alliance within the alliance," which served as a motor of European integration.[7] In turn, integration within the Western community of states was deemed necessary by both the French and West German governments in order to prevent the return of a tragic past and instead to further democracy in Germany by opening minds and markets to Western influence and to make war impossible by pooling resources. But each also pursued particular interests as a consequence of its geopolitical situation and of its aims within the Western community, in the East-West dimension, and/or world-wide.

For West Germany, reconciliation with France was crucial in the pursuit of moral rehabilitation, while cooperation allowed it to play a political role in Europe, although leadership was not the name of the game. For various reasons, the Federal Republic could not pretend to play a leading role in Western European affairs.[8] While it was at first too weak politically and still feared for its past policies, Germany's division and integration into two antagonistic military blocs later perpetuated its inability to seek dominance. As part of a divided country, a potential battle-field in case of war where Germans, East and West, would have fought against one other, the Federal Republic had to "import" its security from the United States and to rely upon its North American and European allies to protect its interests and to defend its existence. As such, it could only be an eternal second to the United States, also on the European continent. This had a twofold consequence: as the Federal Republic depended on the United States, its sovereignty and political margin of manoeuver were limited and, as it tried to widen that margin from the 1960s onward, it came to rely increasingly on France, with Franco-German relations looked upon as "a convenient substitute for leadership."[9]

In both cases, France's status was enhanced. On the one hand, while the Federal Republic depended on the United States for its security and its political concerns, France could claim to be one of the victors of World War II, responsible for Germany's reunification and for the defense of Berlin. As if to underline the differences in status between France and Germany, General de Gaulle, who came back to power in 1958 to assist in the creation of the Fifth Republic, pursued the development of an independent nuclear capability, a policy that had actually been embarked upon by the Fourth Republic, and he asked for equality of treatment together with the United States and Great Britain, a policy more timidly pursued by his predecessors. As the United States rebuked his demand, he ordered France's withdrawal from the integrated military command of the Atlantic Alliance.

On the other hand, de Gaulle supported Adenauer in his search for increased autonomy from the United States. The 1963 Elysée Treaty was devised to provide the foundation for Franco-German cooperation in numerous areas, including the military field. To that extent, the Franco-German partnership was presented as an alternative to what could be looked upon as American dominance over the Federal Republic. While this was the very reason why Adenauer agreed to the treaty, it was precisely the reason why a majority of representatives in the West German Parliament deemed it necessary to stress, in an addendum, the importance of their country's links with the United States: Germany's role was embedded in the Atlantic Alliance. Conversely, Germany served France's interests. The Franco-German treaty was devised by de Gaulle as a bench-mark on the road towards the Europe he wanted to build. It was meant to be a continental counter-weight to the combined influence of Great Britain and the United States, that is, as an instrument of France's independence and power. Later again, when France pulled out of NATO's integrated military network, it could do so because Germany served as a buffer between France and the Warsaw Pact. Protected by a Federal Republic that would have been defended by an allied coalition in case of attack, France could act both as a protector of Germany — being still part of that coalition — and as a free-rider within the Western Alliance. However, as persistently as the French government sought to maximize its gains, it could not avoid unwanted outcomes: France's withdrawal from NATO, which was designed to increase its leverage both vis-a-vis the United States and the Federal Republic, boosted the latter's role and influence within NATO. While, in the early 1960s, the French government had sought to attract the Federal Republic in its attempt to build a more "european" Europe, it reinforced the latter's position in the Euro-American dimension a few years later.

In their relations with the Soviet Union, both countries did not share the same interests either. While both looked upon the USSR sometimes as a threat, sometimes as an opponent, the Federal Republic had greater interests at stake than did France. As a divided nation, deprived of territories and populations on which Moscow had imposed an illegitimate system, and as a potential battle-field in case of war, the West German government was, together with the United States, the most fiercely opposed to Communism and most committed to defend Western Europe against a Soviet threat, especially in the first two decades after World War II. From the 1960s on, however, it attempted to reach a *modus vivendi* with Central and Eastern European states, prodded by the American and French examples.

While Washington and Paris dropped their earlier position, which had made Germany's reunification a prerequisite for detente, and sought accommodation with Moscow, Bonn feared isolation and estrangement from its Western partners and lack of any contacts with the East. To prevent isolation, it designed its own policy, very similar indeed to what de Gaulle had foreseen. In a 1959 press conference, de Gaulle had stated that "until this ideal [of reunification] is reached, we believe that the two separated parts of the German nation should be able to multiply the ties and relations between themselves on all levels. Transportation, mail services, economic activity, literature, science, the arts, the comings and goings of individuals, and so on . . . would be the objects of agreements that would bring the Germans closer together domestically and benefit what I would call the 'German matter' [*la chose allemande*], which they share in common, after all, in spite of the differences in regimes and conditions."[10]

De Gaulle did not suggest any practical steps, however. Although he had in a way imagined what *Ostpolitik* was going to be all about, the West Germans were to define and pursue it while remaining firmly rooted in the Western

Alliance. France, meanwhile, was not driven by the same obligation to succeed: due to its geographical position, it could ignore the East. Certainly de Gaulle did travel to Eastern Europe and certainly he dreamt of reunifying the continent. However, the East-West stalemate, obvious in Czechoslovakia in 1968, rendered his plans irrelevant. When, soon after the demise of the Prague Spring, all Western countries emulated one another in establishing ties with the East, the USSR chose to address the Federal Republic first, as the richest and most powerful country on the continent, the main pillar of both NATO and the EC, and as the country closest to Eastern Europe.

Signed between Germany and USSR

Too Weak or Too Strong?

The French were then — and still are to some extent — haunted by the Rapallo trauma, that is, a sudden reversal of alliance as happened a number of times in German history, be it Tauroggen (1812), the treaty of Rapallo in 1922, or the Hitler-Stalin Pact of 1939.[11] De Gaulle's successor, Georges Pompidou, betrayed a deep-seated distrust of German intentions in Eastern Europe. Willy Brandt's *Ostpolitik*, his treaty policy (*Vertragspolitik*) vis-a-vis Eastern Europe — which eventually acknowledged Soviet hegemony over that part of the continent — and his unannounced trip to the Soviet Union in the summer of 1970, prompted Pompidou to look for support in the West and to allow Great Britain into the European Community. De Gaulle had sought West Germany's assistance to balance Anglo-American preeminence. Pompidou aimed at reversing this policy even though it was the West Germans rather than the French who advocated Britain's EC membership.

In the 1980's, French distrust flared up once more as the West German Left opposed the stationing of Pershing II missiles on German soil lest the Soviet Union retaliate politically (by freezing German-German relations, for instance) or militarily (by deploying counter-weapons and by firing these weapons on Germany in the event of a war). Was the Federal Republic or, at least, were parts of public opinion and some political leaders about to "finlandize" themselves (to use a catchword)? Were they, in other words, submitting to Soviet pressure for the sake of preserving, if not a European detente, at least a German-German detente? In a now famous speech delivered in the *Bundestag* in January 1983, François Mitterrand called upon German representatives to deploy the American weapons on their soil: "For the first time in the history of the Fifth Republic, the President of France has, in effect, asked West Germany to be a reliable and strong ally of the United States."[12]

Behind French fears lay the specter of Rapallo. As Jacques Huntzinger, then in charge of international relations within the Socialist Party, bluntly put it: "Formerly, we feared German militarism, now we fear pacifism."[13] Yet, while West German opposition to stationing Pershing II missiles in the Federal

Republic might have entailed political costs for the Atlantic Alliance by weakening both political and military links between the German and European theater and the United States, those in France who feared an eastern drift of Germany (*"une dérive à l'Est"*) chose to ignore the essence of the postwar system.[14] Whereas in a society of nations, Germany and Russia (or the Soviet Union) were able to strike an agreement at the cost of other states that had isolated them, such a deal could not be reached in the postwar system.

First, a deal would only have pertained to Germany's reunification and the Federal Republic was not ready to pay a high price for it, such as the one Stalin had demanded in his 1952 note and which Chancellor Adenauer had actually rejected. Second, the nature of the system itself did not allow a German *Sonderweg*, as the Federal Republic was tightly embedded in a community of states and societies and benefitting from it. What was actually to be feared was rather the definition of German special interests, for instance the introduction of security discussions in Soviet-German and German-German bilateral relations. Special interests that would have been advocated not only by West German opposition parties and the public but also by the Federal government might have diluted West Germany's commitments within the Atlantic Alliance.

In any case, *Ostpolitik* and public protest over the deployment of new missiles on German soil were both interpreted by part of the French political elite as threats to the Franco-German relationship because they were deemed to loosen Germany's anchorage in the Western community. As an answer to what was perceived as German weakness, Mitterrand looked to reinforcing both the European and Atlantic communities in order to strengthen France's role and to prop up the Federal Republic's commitments. The strengthening of Franco-German relations, European integration, and the reinforcement of Atlantic ties went hand in hand. While the European Community was hammering out the Single European Act, Mitterrand played a crucial role in putting it forward and in reconciling French minds and markets with a European opening: in 1983 in particular, he put an end to France's socialist experiment, a first step towards Europe. In 1983 as well, he called upon West German representatives to deploy Pershing II missiles on German soil, stressing the necessity to recouple European and American security as the French government felt it was facing the possible scenario of a faltering Federal Republic as a consequence of intense external pressures and internal tensions."[15]

Other decisions followed, aimed at strengthening Franco-German military cooperation, which was reactivated as early as 1982. In October of that year, a joint commission on defense and security was set up, to be convened four times a year and consisting of three working groups on arms production, military cooperation, and strategic and political matters. The creation of a Rapid Action Force (RAF) was agreed upon in 1984, to supplement the First Army wherever needed, that is, to play a decisive role in the forward defense of the Federal Republic if necessary. In September 1987, the Bold Sparrow exercise was held, where major units of the RAF came under the operational control of a West German commander. Also in 1987, the creation of a Franco-German brigade was proposed. These and other steps were evidence of a deepening Franco-German "security community."

By reinforcing the Atlantic Alliance and by propping up West Germany's commitments within it, Mitterrand aimed at binding the latter to the United States while strengthening France's role, as an umpire or an on-looker, astute but distant. In other words, he thought NATO would bind West Germany while France could remain outside the integrated Alliance. In the European Community and in the Franco-German dimension as well, he sought to bind his country to West Germany in order to bind the latter to France, while at the same time devising a major role for France. This generated a dilemma that has never ceased to haunt French politics since the 1950s. As Stanley Hoffmann put it: "How could the desire to anchor West Germany in the West be reconciled with French refusal of integration and insistence on military autonomy?"[16]

Public protest over the deployment of Pershing II missiles was accompanied by developments that were perceived as weakening the West German economy.[17] At the beginning of the 1980s, French economists (the CEPII in particular) and, a little later, West Germans themselves, began to wonder — though not for long — whether the West German miracle was not fading away, as a result of having concentrated since the 19th century on machine tools and now ignoring the third industrial revolution in the production of numerical command machines (NMC) and in other areas.[18] With the ecological movement, along with the trade unions (which were fighting unemployment), nourishing opposition to technological development and innovation, the Hudson Institute's dramatic predictions in the 1960s of impending French economic superiority and West German decline seemed at least partially confirmed. Yet this could not cause much satisfaction in France considering the broader geopolitical context.

France was not only concerned about Germany's relative position in the East-West and transatlantic dimensions but also about the latter's domestic conditions that might have tilted the Franco-German balance. More often than not it was thought that West Germany's increasing power rather than its weaknesses might have altered the relationship — at France's expense. Actually, there was some evidence to support this kind of argument. In the immediate postwar era, France was certainly weakened, both politically and economically, yet it was a victor thanks to de Gaulle's — and Churchill's — determination to treat France as such. Soon, however, from the 1950s on, an economically buoyant West Germany seemed to out-trump it. The last days of de Gaulle's government brought the differences to light, as if to shatter the political edifice built by the grand old man. Bonn's refusal to revaluate the D-Mark before the federal elections of 1969, in spite of intense speculation and France's subsequent devaluation, ushered in a succession of monetary crises, repeated devaluations,

and widening inflation differentials for years to come, which the institutionalization of the so-called "snake" and, in 1979, of the European Monetary System
(EMS) were intended to bring to an end.

The EMS in particular was the product of a Franco-German initiative, a rare
instance indeed of West German initiative within the EC. Chancellor Schmidt
and President Giscard d'Estaing, who shared a common past as Finance
Ministers, a common language (English), and, on the whole, similar outlooks,
worked together to overcome "Eurosclerosis," designing pragmatic schemes.
Thanks to their mutual understanding, they promoted closer monetary cooperation and later admitted to having envisaged a closer military cooperation. The
establishment of both the "snake" and the EMS were made necessary by the
monetary turmoil that a weak dollar and the consequent termination of the
Bretton Woods agreement had caused, and they were facilitated by the strength
of the D-Mark and the *de facto* existence of a "DM zone" in Europe. The result
was the creation of an area of stability in Western Europe somewhat isolated
from monetary upheaval and a reinforced West German dominance vis-a-vis its
partners.

Thirty years after the end of World War II, the Federal Republic had become
an "*économie dominante*," exercising a structural pre-eminence within the
European Community. Industrial production, export growth, and an increasing
surplus ensured prosperity in the Federal Republic, in spite of successive
revaluations of the D-Mark that should have affected exports and put a brake on
growth. Based on a "virtuous circle," the German economy seemed to defy the
classical laws of economics.[19]   German industry had specialized in the
production of capital-intensive high-quality products such as machine-tools,
chemical products, and so forth, which could meet an exacting demand at almost
any price. As a number of analysts showed, external growth and domestic
stability complemented one another: domestic stability — wage moderation, slow
growth, and an inflation that was kept under control — allowed exports to grow
while export growth, combined with monetary revaluations, strengthened both
purchasing power and domestic stability.[20]

The German growth model exercised a constraint on its environment. As
Western European economies increasingly depended upon one another and
especially on the Federal Republic as the main supplier, as monetary policies
became more and more intertwined within the "snake" and the EMS, West
Germany imposed its economic and monetary choices on its partners, even
though these choices were not necessarily compatible with the others' national
interests. This notion of a West German "model," which became popular in the
1970s, was to be understood in a restricted sense.[21]   Rather than an example
to be emulated, the West German model was seen as a particular mode of
organization, constraining others, and as such it came to be criticized, both at
home and abroad.[22]

In France, criticism came from different sources and took different forms. The French Communist Party went so far as to oppose the EC as "Helmut Schmidt's Europe" while, in an effort to counterbalance or reverse West Germany's structural dominance, French Finance Ministers dubbed what they considered the "obsession of the *Bundesbank* with price level stability" as an "obstacle to lower interest rates in France and to more rapid growth . . . in Germany" and criticized the "unilateral and surprise decisions by the *Bundesbank* to raise its discount rate."[23]   Giscard d'Estaing himself toyed with the idea of increasing French conventional forces as a counterpart to the *Bundeswehr* and repeatedly stressed France's economic aim of overtaking the Federal Republic by 1980.

While the Giscard-Schmidt working team had in a sense masked the growing imbalance between France and the Federal Republic of Germany, the Mitterrand experiment unveiled it in the 1980s. The attempt to "build socialism in one country" while ignoring international constraints ended in 1983 when the French president rescinded his previous policy and decided to maintain the French currency in the EMS, that is, to impose austerity measures on the French economy. France was economically weakened and had to lower its profile worldwide. Certainly the dangerous complexities of civil wars, in Chad or Lebanon for instance, where France had special interests, partly account for French restraint. Both public opinion and political parties in France wondered, however, whether France was still a great power.[24]

"I Love Germany So Much . . . ": Reunification and After

Considering the care with which French politicians tried to balance the Federal Republic by binding it into the West while trying to boost France's status without weakening or strengthening Germany, making the latter a partner that would be strong enough to match Soviet influence and to prop up Western Europe but not strong enough to cast a shadow on France, one might wonder whether France's political elite ever really supported the idea of German reunification.

On the one hand, the question seemed to lose relevance after a while, towards the beginning of the 1960s at the latest. The Germans themselves — West Germans at least — considered that it would take place in a distant future, if at all. On this particular point, the Franco-German dialogue seemed to lose touch with reality. Never, for instance, had a phrase been so often quoted by both peoples as François Mauriac's: "I love Germany so much that I am happy that there are two of them." For the French, the phrase was pronounced sometimes as a confession, often in jest; for the Germans, it exemplified French opinion. Conversely, while a number of German intellectuals and politicans held reunification to be irrelevant and even obsolete in a post-modern world, some in France would actually suspect that the Germans were pursuing precisely what the Basic Law of the Federal Republic claimed to aim at: German unity. In other words, the Franco-German dialogue on that particular question lacked clarity, not least of all because the Germans themselves were confused.

One may, on the other hand, try to figure out what were the preferences of French politicians. Though de Gaulle attempted to prevent the resurgence of German power at the end of World War II, he did acknowledge later that reunification might be possible under certain conditions, including first and foremost the recognition of all postwar borders as definitive. However, de Gaulle sometimes referred to reunification and sometimes to confederation. At times he spoke of the German people and at times of the Saxons and Prussians, as if to underline the distinctiveness of the German states. Stanley Hoffmann labelled France's policy "byzantine:" "Paris assured the West Germans that it stood up for this ideal of reunification, so that the case would never happen where a disappointed West Germany risked entering a separate dialogue with Moscow. At the same time, France indicated to the other Western powers that it had everything under control: no reunification could take place, at least no reunification within a mighty, neutral state."[25]

While de Gaulle's successor, Georges Pompidou, suspected that the Kiesinger and Brandt governments were pursuing reunification under the cover of *Ostpolitik*, Giscard d'Estaing was probably less moved by defiance than by an ahistorical vision of international relations: for him, the German Question was settled once and for all. However, both leaders carefully insisted on France's rights in Berlin, the former during the negotiation of the 1971 Quadripartite Agreement, the latter when he visited Berlin in 1979 and the Federal Republic in 1980.

As a leader of the Socialist Party, François Mitterrand had at times had strained relations with the Federal Republic and with the German Left as well. In the 1970s in particular, the French Left expressed unease at West Germany's professional restrictions designed to bar Communists, or suspected Communists, from holding federal or local positions, including menial jobs. It also sharply criticized some aspects of the anti-terrorist campaign, such as prison conditions in the noise-proof cells of the Stammheim jail. The famous, if not infamous, writer Jean Genêt even sided with the Stammheim inmates of the Baader-Meinhof gang in an extremely controversial article published by *Le Monde*.[26] The French Socialist Party, at that time in the opposition, went so far as to create a so-called "committee for the defense of human rights," even though the issue of human rights in the GDR did not attract such attention.[27]

While Mitterrand was trying to rally the southern European Socialist parties around him as a counter-weight to West Germany within the Socialist International, his criticism gave the impression that party-to-party dialogue between the PSF (French Socialist Party) and the SPD (German Social-Democratic Party) would no longer be sustained and that nothing short of public controversy could ever bring the West German comrades to revise their positions on and respect for human rights along French lines. The tension illuminated some deep-seated misgivings and misunderstandings between the French and the German Left, the former reproaching the latter for being too respectful of state institutions and authority. This very criticism flared up again in the 1980s over the Polish question. While West Germans sent thousands of care packages to Poland, the French demonstrated in favor of Solidarity. The former favored humanitarian practicalities, the latter humanistic principles, each highlighting the other's insufficiencies.

When he came to power in 1981, however, Mitterrand followed the political rules of cooperation and established a close relationship with SPD Chancellor Helmut Schmidt and, a year later, with his CDU successor Helmut Kohl. Very early, he underlined the necessity of "overcoming Yalta" ("*sortir de Yalta*," Yalta symbolizing, even though inaccurately, the partition of Europe) and in his 1983 *Bundestag* speech, he expressed understanding for the tragedy of partition: "For having lived in occupied France, I deeply feel what the Germans — divided as they are — may feel. For having known a devastated Europe, I feel what dispersed people may feel."[28] Contrary to his predecessor Giscard d'Estaing, Mitterrand went so far as to invite Chancellor Kohl to (West) Berlin when he visited the former capital in October 1985, a significant symbol of Franco-German togetherness in the divided city. In the summer of 1989, well before reunification took place and even before the German revolution, he called unity a legitimate concern of all Germans, without suggesting, however, that it had a renewed significance.

Meanwhile, public opinion in France increasingly welcomed a possible reunification, maybe as a result of the decades-long policy of reconciliation at both governmental and societal levels. While at the end of the 1970s, the French still expressed concern at this possibility (36 percent thought it would be detrimental to France and to other European countries as well), six years later a remarkable majority of French people (59 percent) felt that Germany's reunification would be fully legitimate and only 20 percent dismissed it as undesirable. A majority of the French people advocated a French involvement in the defense of Germany, were the latter to be attacked. Some even went so far as to say that France should not interfere if reunification took place. In any case, most looked upon their German neighbors as France's best friends.[29]

Neither public opinion nor political elites nor governments, in Germany, in France, or elsewhere, could have guessed that reunification would come so rapidly and so suddenly. Certainly, as early as 1987, the GDR had entered an era of turmoil while Poland and Hungary were, in their own ways, striving to overcome Communism and to build more Western-style democracies. Certainly, too, East Germans, particularly the young, had started to flee their country in the summer of 1989, emboldened by the opening of the Austro-Hungarian border. Yet it was the opening of the Wall on November 9, 1989, which accelerated the decomposition of the East German regime and state. Even then, however, few understood that the opening of the Wall was to have such dramatic consequences. Though on the second Monday after the opening demonstrators in the streets of Leipzig demanded Germany's reunification, most French politicians and commentators did not believe in such an eventuality — just as few of their German counterparts did.

More than others, however, more than the Germans and the Americans, the French government wanted to believe in an East German solution and, once it became obvious that reunification would take place, Paris thought that it could and should be slowed down. In other words, Mitterrand attempted to put a brake on reunification and maybe to prevent it. A series of steps ensued, designed to cement the *status quo*: in Athens on November 29, 1989, where Mitterrand stressed that reunification could only be peaceful and democratic, taking into account not only the right of Germans to self-determination but also that of Germany's neighbors to determine the process; in Kiev on December 10, where the French President tried to win over President Gorbachev to his views; on December 21 and 22, when visiting the GDR, he praised its cultural identity; and in the spring again, when the French government sided with the Polish government, both a little late and a little too loudly, while the question of the Oder-Neisse border was being settled.

This conservative policy was paralleled by another, bold one, the pursuit of European integration. In Paris, on November 18, 1989, and in Strasbourg, where the European Council met on December 8 and 9, 1989, Mitterrand, together with other European heads of state and government, advocated increased integration within the European Community. In April 1990, both he and Chancellor Kohl took the initiative of calling for a political union, involving a deeper cooperation among the Twelve on foreign policy and security issues, matching the economic and monetary union that was to be achieved in the coming decade.

One may argue, in a sense, that both policies were conservative, designed to consolidate the *status quo*. The first one was to reassert the rights of Germany's neighbors and, first and foremost, those of the four former victors of World War II, responsible for Germany's unification and Berlin's status. The second one was intended to strengthen the European Community to embrace Germany, divided or united. Yet both policies expressed different perspectives. The first one was to cement the Four Powers' domination in a Europe of nations. Nineteenth century Europe was its geopolitical map. The policy of European integration was, on the contrary, designed to pursue the construction of this new political and social community of nations, started after World War II. The former was directed against Germany's reunification. The latter took both Germanys, divided or united, into consideration. To that extent, the former almost marred the latter though the latter eventually triumphed over the former.

Behind Mitterrand's policy lay the concerns of many political leaders who in the weeks and months between the opening of the Wall and Germany's reunification voiced their fear of a German political and economic dominance over Europe. One foresaw the "come-back of Bismarck's *Reich*," of a "*Großdeutschland*."[30] Paradoxically, as Ingo Kolboom points out, the business world was much less preoccupied than were politicians. Moreover, French public opinion, which, in the 1980s, had increasingly favored Germany's reunification and advocated support for that country in case of war, turned out to judge the East German revolution and the Germans' reunion quite positively.[31] According to opinion polls conducted in 1990, a constantly high percentage of French people (between 61 and 73 percent) approved of unification, among which the young more than the old supported developments in Germany. At the same time, however, about half of the population questioned expressed its concern over a dominant Germany, a smaller proportion, however, than those in Poland and Great Britain who feared reunification.[32]

A Pivot, a Model, a Power

Paradoxically, both approval of and opposition to reunification may have stemmed from the same evaluation of Germany's role and influence in Europe, particularly in Western Europe, and of the changes that reunification entails at both the economic and political levels. West Germany already played a central economic role in the European Community before the five *Länder* of the former GDR joined the Federal Republic. It produced 27 percent of the Community's Gross National Product and accounted for a quarter of total intra-Community trade. The world's major exporter, the FRG was the main source of imports for all Community members except Ireland. According to major German and foreign institutes, unification will have both short-term negative and long-term positive effects on the FRG's position within the Community. Diminished at first, the overall performance of the German economy in the EC will later be fostered by the reconstruction of East Germany: assuming that the share of both Germanys accounted for 25 percent in 1985, the Industrial Bank of Japan reckons that it will reach 28 percent in 1995 and 30 percent in the year 2000.[33] After subsiding in 1991, trade should also expand.

In other areas as well, both functional and geographical, the Federal Republic has proved to be a core country, well before German and European unification took place. In such areas as investments, tourism, student exchanges or migrations, West Germany was before 1989 "at the center of [a] network of multiple flows and [it took] part in all types of movement, often with a prominent role."[34] A pivot country for all EC members, it also became increasingly a pivot for the EC periphery of both Northern and Southern

Europe, as Western Europe grew more cohesive, as its relations with the North and South grew more dense, and as ties with Eastern Europe were reconstituted. After the upheavals of 1989-91, Germany's pivotal role will only increase.

The growth in Germany's export and import capacities, in terms of goods, capital and labor, the integration of the EC with the completion of the Single Market, the Schengen agreement and the Maastricht Treaty, and, last but not least, the development of relations of all kinds between the EC and the former members of the Soviet bloc, all point in this direction. Even in terms of demography, the Federal Republic may turn out to be much more dynamic than is often assumed. Though the united Germany accounts for only 23 percent of EC population (as compared with 19 percent accounted for by West Germany before unification) and though its natural population growth is modest, to say the least, it attracts numerous migrants (migrants of German origin and asylum-seekers).

As the pivot of the European Community, the Federal Republic continues to exercise a determining influence over economic and monetary policies in other member countries, particularly in those which, like France, have come to accept the "German model" as an example. Whereas, as earlier indicated, the notion of "model" referred in the 1970s and 1980s to a specific mode of organization, certainly dominant yet inimitable, it is now understood in France as an example of macro-, micro-, and socio-economic organization worthy of adoption and adaptation. Political leaders such as Roger Fauroux, Minister of Industry in Michel Rocard's government, and Edith Cresson, Michel Rocard's successor, have praised the synergy between banks and industry, vocational training, or consultations and co-decisions that gather employers and trade-unions around the same table. In other words, the Federal Republic has become an example not so much because of its values but rather because of the way in which those values are being produced and propagated.[35]

At the same time, when Germany is presented as an example because of its micro-economic policies, its political organization is also increasingly conceived as a kind of blueprint for the European Community. The future European Bank has been designed on the pattern of the *Bundesbank*, and the German system where monetary policy is decided by monetary authorities in Frankfurt, thus escaping political control, should be applied to the Community. Through vertical organization and subsidiarity as the rule of power devolution between *Bund* and *Länder*, Germany's political organization seems to foreshadow the structure of tomorrow's European Community as well, or at least to match it and to fit in neatly — even though the problems accompanying unification have strained Germany's federalism.

A pivot of the European Community and of pan-European relations and a model for a country like France, the reunited Germany has also seen its political status enhanced: compared with the old Federal Republic of Germany, the new one is not only mighty, it also regains both sovereignty and geopolitical centrality. The old Federal Republic had indeed gained in power over the years. Though mighty, it was nevertheless constrained by limitations on its sovereignty. Legally minimal, these limitations were politically powerful, compelling it to import its security from the United States and to look for accommodation with the Soviet Union. With the demise of Communism and the end of Cold War bipolarity, the new Federal Republic becomes sovereign and therefore mightier as the gap between power and sovereignty closes. As it hardly needs to import its security from the United States any longer and as it no longer depends on its victors for a future reunification, it ceases to be an eternal second to the United States or to France on the European continent. Finally, the new Federal Republic is returning to the heart of Europe, a neighbor of Poland and of the successor states to the Soviet Union. While the old FRG lay at the margin of a divided center, the new FRG regains its central position, at the core of the continent.

Of course, power, sovereignty, and geopolitical centrality are all mitigated by Germany's international commitments, first and foremost by the most binding of all, the integrating system of the European Community. The EC, as a system and a process of increasingly supranational, transnational, intergovernmental and inter-societal interdependences of all kinds (economic, financial, industrial, political, and social), restrains Germany's power and sovereignty. Germany's power has also been temporarily weakened by the extraordinary financial and political burden of having to rebuild eastern Germany and to restructure many of its institutions.   *GERMAN RELATIONS WITH EASTERN EUROPE*

As to the third qualification, Germany has undoubtedly resumed a geopolitically central position on the continent: the demise of the Warsaw Pact has brought about the end of bipolarity, while the break-up of the Soviet Union and its erstwhile Eastern European empire have created a power vacuum and an area of considerable instability. As a consequence, Germany has become the dominant economic and political power in Central and Eastern Europe. It cannot, however, regain the central position that it used to have prior to World War II, that is, that of a *Wanderer zwischen den Welten* ("wanderer between the worlds"), between East and West, both because it cannot assume alone the enormous task (financial, political, and social in terms of immigration) of restructuring the Central and Eastern European economies and because it could not and would not give up the advantages that it has gained from its anchorage in the Western community. The majority of German public opinion, German political elites, and, last but not least, Chancellor Kohl himself, all share the basic conviction that Germany must never go it alone again, voluntarily or not, as it did from the latter half of last century to the end of World War II.

Public opinion, political elites, and present and future governments may, however, want to convert this increased power into a policy of high profile. According to opinion polls, in particular, German public opinion displays an increased desire to have Germany play a greater role in Europe. Whereas in

1990, merely 29 percent of Germans in East and West advocated a greater role for their country, 43 percent pleaded for it a year later. Though Germany's membership in NATO and EC is advocated, support for a continued U.S. military presence has eroded and enthusiasm for a European Economic and Monetary Union, Political Union and a European defense identity has abated.[36]

At the governmental level, too, certain moves made by Kohl or his associates since 1991 amount to muscle-flexing: the request to increase German representation in the European Parliament; the desire to turn German into an official language of the European Community; the decision taken by the *Bundesbank* to further increase interest rates just after the signature of the Maastricht Treaty; the demand to install the future European bank in Frankfurt at a time when the government intends to turn the city into a major financial center and to create a fully developed financial market thanks to sweeping reforms; and, last but not least, Germany's attitude during the Serbo-Croatian war from the beginning of the hostilities up to the recognition of both Slovenia and Croatia. All these steps, as legitimate as they may have been individually, raised concern, inside Germany and even more so abroad, over a so-called new German assertiveness.[37]

Do these changes in Germany's status and, to a certain extent, in public mood mean that the Franco-German axis belongs to the past? In July 1990, former President Giscard d'Estaing suggested that the Franco-German "tandem" would never again play the same role it had in the past.[38] President Mitterrand may have shared these views. In the summer of 1990, he stated that France would withdraw all its troops from German territory, a rather unexpected announcement that by-passed the bilateral agreements concluded in the 1960s and 1970s and contrasted with the declared wish to further a European defense identity. The president apparently deemed it wiser to withdraw troops before a German government would ask the French to do so, a demand that would inevitably be made. One may wonder, however, whether it was not actually an attempt to underline France's independence. In a similar vein, Mitterrand in 1991 called for a meeting of the four nuclear powers in Europe to discuss security questions, leaving out the German government.

Franco-German cooperation nevertheless proves to be resilient. In spite of the French temptation to withdraw, Kohl and Mitterrand in October 1991 proposed the building of a Franco-German military unit as the core of a future European defense, the composition and mission of which were hammered out in 1992.[39] The reason for this resilience may be fairly simple: it lies in the closeness and intricacy of Franco-German ties and in the complexities of Europe's architecture. While Mitterrand and his other EC partners, including the European Commission, wanted to further the Economic and Monetary Union to tie in Germany, Chancellor Kohl insisted on fostering Political Union. A prerequisite to deeper economic convergence, political union may also be a channel for German influence as the Federal Republic tries to promote the democratization of the EC and to influence the European political agenda. In any case, this *quid-pro-quo* between Germany and others is crucial in the promotion of European integration.

The complexity of security issues in Europe after 1989-91 also accounts for an increased Franco-German cooperation. Even more than the Gulf War, the EC's inadequate response to the violent disintegration of Yugoslavia demonstrated the diplomatic impotence of the Community. One of the missions assigned to the future "Euro-corps," to be set up by 1995, would involve, among other things, peace-keeping operations as well as humanitarian efforts. Since the Federal Republic does not have the financial clout or the military means or the political authority to provide answers to the new questions and problems — problems that no single country can or should tackle alone — Franco-German cooperation may find increased substance and purpose.

Notes

1. See, for example, Wilfried Loth, "Vierzig Jahre deutsch-französischer Verständigung? Realität oder Mythos?," in Deutsch-Französisches Kulturzentrum Essen, ed., *Deutschland-Frankreich. Höhen und Tiefen einer Zweierbeziehung. Ergebnisse eines dreitägigen Symposiums im Februar 1988 in Essen* (Essen: die blaue eule, 1988), pp. 203-217; Michel Tatu, "Aussenpolitik zwischen Ost und West," in Robert Picht, ed., *Das Bündnis im Bündnis. Deutsch-Französische Beziehungen im internationalen Spannungsfeld* (Berlin: Severin und Siedler, 1982), pp. 69-92.

2. Germaine de Staël, *De l'Allemagne* (Paris: Garnier-Flammarion, 1968), p. 56. For an overview of French perceptions of the Germans, see Joerg von Uthmann, *Le diable est-il allemand?* (Paris: Denoël, 1984); Franz Herre, *Deutsche und Franzosen. Der lange Weg zur Freundschaft* (Bergisch-Gladbach: Luebbe Verlag, 1983); Manfred Koch-Hillebrecht, *Das Deutschenbild. Gegenwart, Geschichte, Psychologie* (Munich: Verlag C. H. Beck, 1977).

3. de Staël, *De l'Allemagne*, p. 63.

4. Quoted by Herre, *Deutsche und Franzosen*, p. 148.

5. Jacques Bainville, *Histoire de deux peuples continuée jusqu'à Hitler* (Paris: Librairie Arthème Fayard, 1915 and 1941), p. 251.

6. See Wilfried Loth, "Die Franzosen und die deutsche Frage 1945-1949," in Claus Scharf and Hans-Jürgen Schröder, eds., *Die Deutschlandpolitik Frankreichs und die französische Zone 1945-1949* (Wiesbaden: Franz Steiner Verlag, 1983), quoted in Ernst Weisenfeld, *Welches Deutschland soll es sein? Frankreich und die deutsche Einheit seit 1945* (Munich: Beck Verlag, 1986), p. 30; Anne-Marie LeGloannec, "France's German Problem," in F. Stephen Larrabee, ed., *The Two German States and European Security* (New York: The Institute for East-West Security Studies, 1989), p. 247, from which this paragraph is reproduced.

7. See Tatu, "Aussenpolitik zwischen Ost und West," pp. 69-92. As to whether the Franco-German tandem actually served as a motor to European integration, see the essays in Robert Picht and Wolfgang Wessels, eds., *Motor für Europa? Deutsch-*

französischer Bilateralismus und europäische Integration. Le couple franco-allemand et l'intégration européenne (Bonn: Europa Union Verlag, 1990).

8. Other reasons accounted for German abstinence, for example, limits on chancellorial authority; sectorization of policy responsibilities; *Bund* vs. *Länder* dynamics; and, last but not least, party politicization, a process Simon Bulmer and William Paterson describe in *The Federal Republic of Germany and the European Community* (London: Allen and Unwin, 1987), pp. 20-22.

9. Helen Wallace, "The Federal Republic of Germany and Changing Coalition Habits. The Paradox of Partnership," in Wolfgang Wessels and Elfriede Regelsberger, eds., *The Federal Republic of Germany and the European Community: The Presidency and Beyond* (Bonn: Europa Union Verlag, 1988), p. 280.

10. Charles de Gaulle, *Discours et Messages: Avec le renouveau: 1958-1962* (Paris: Plon, 1970), p. 85.

11. On this question, see, for example, Renata Fritsch-Bournazel, *Rapallo: Naissance d'un mythe. La politique de la peur dans la France du Bloc National* (Paris: Armand Colin, 1974).

12. Stanley Hoffmann, "Mitterrand's Foreign Policy, or Gaullism by any other name," in George Ross, Stanley Hoffmann, and Sylvia Malzacher, *The Mitterrand Experiment* (Oxford: Oxford University Press, 1987), p. 298.

13. Quoted by the weekly *Stern*, April 26, 1984.

14. See, for example, Alain Minc, *Le syndrôme finlandais* (Paris: Le Seuil, 1986).

15. See André Adrets (pseudonym), "Les relations franco-allemandes et le fait nucléaire dans une Europe divisée," *Politique Etrangère*, nr. 31/1984, p. 651.

16. Hoffmann, "Mitterrand's Foreign Policy, or Gaullism by any other name," p. 296.

17. See, for example, polls published in the weekly *L'Express*, January 27-February 2, 1984, pp. 12-19.

18. CEPII is the Centre d'Etudes Prospectives et d'Informations Internationales. Quoted in LeGloannec, "France's German Problem," p. 251. This paragraph is taken from that earlier work.

19. To use Bernard Keizer's expression, "Le modèle économique allemand. Mythes et réalités," *Notes et études documentaires*, (Paris) nr. 4549-4550, December 31, 1979.

20. See, for example, Christian Deubner, Udo Rehfeldt, and Frieder Schlupp, "Deutsch-französische Wirtschaftsbeziehungen im Rahmen der weltwirtschaftlichen Arbeitsteilung: Interdependenz, Divergenz oder strukturelle Dominanz," in Robert Picht, ed., *Deutschland, Frankreich, Europa. Bilanz einer schwierigen Partnerschaft* (Munich: Piper, 1978), pp. 91-136; Michael Kreile, "West Germany: The Dynamics of Expansion," in Peter Katzenstein, ed., *Between Power and Plenty: Foreign Economic Policies of Advanced Industrial States* (Madison: University of Wisconsin Press, 1978), pp. 192-224; Michael Kreile, "Die Bundesrepublik: eine 'économie dominante' in Westeuropa?," *Aus Politik und Zeitgeschichte*, July 1, 1978, pp. 3-17; Keizer, "Le modèle économique allemand."

21. Several books had this title. See, for example, Eduard Pester et al., *Das Deutschland-Modell. Herausforderungen auf dem Weg ins 21. Jahrhundert* (Stuttgart: Deutsche Verlags-Anstalt, 1978); Istituto Gramsci (a cura dell'), *Modello Germania. Struttura e problemi della realta tedesco-occidentale* (Bologna: Zanichelli editore, 1978).

22. For a longer development on this question, see Anne-Marie LeGloannec, "Le sens de la puissance allemande," in Zaki Laïdi, ed., *L'ordre mondial relâché, sens et puissance après la guerre froide* (Paris: Presses de la Fondation Nationale des Sciences Politiques et Berg, 1992), pp. 45-67.

23. Christian de Boissieu and Hans-Eckart Scharrer, "Accord and Conflict in French-German Cooperation," in Picht and Wessels, eds., *Motor für Europa?*, pp. 187-209, in particular p. 199.

24. See, for example, the polls published in the weekly *L'Express*, January 27-February 2, 1984, pp. 12-19.

25. Stanley Hoffmann, "Verlobt doch nicht verheiratet. Frankreich zwischen dem Wunsch nach Einbindung der Bundesregierung und eigener Unabhängigheit?," *Die Zeit*, March 2, 1985, as quoted in Weisenfeld, *Welches Deutschland soll es sein?*, p. 112.

26. Jean Genêt, "A propos de la Rote Armee Fraktion. Violence et brutalité," *Le Monde*, September 2, 1977, pp. 1-2.

27. Certainly most in France ignored the GDR, mainly for political and ideological reasons, which led them to view the FRG as the sole legitimate representative of Germany. Those who had relations with the GDR were led by (reverse) political and ideological considerations, be it the Communist-affiliated Société France-RDA, which supported the East German regime, or the Codène, a pacifist movement that had chosen to back the independent East German peace movement. For further discussion, see LeGloannec, "France's German Problem," p. 244, on which these paragraphs draw extensively.

28. François Mitterrand, *Réflexions sur la politique extérieure de la France. Introduction à vingt-cinq discours 1981-1985* (Paris: Fayard, 1986), p. 208.

29. *L'Express*, March 17-23, 1979, pp. 84-85; *Le Nouvel Observateur*, February 10-16, 1984, pp. 1-2; Claire Tréan, "La France doit garantir la sécurité de la RFA," *Le Monde*, June 28, 1985, pp. 1-2; *Le Figaro-Magazine*, November 11, 1988, p. 108. All these polls are quoted in Ingo Kolboom, "Vom geteilten zum vereinten Deutschland. Deutschland-Bilder in Frankreich" (Bonn: Forschungsinstitut der Deutschen Gesellschaft für Auswärtige Politik, Arbeitspapiere zur internationalen Politik, April 1991), pp. 23 and 31.

30. See Georges Valence, *France — Allemagne: Le retour de Bismarck* (Paris: Flammarion, 1990).

31. Kolboom, "Vom geteilten zum vereinten Deutschland," p. 50.

32. See, in particular, the polls published in *The Economist*, January 26, 1990; *Libération*, February 19, 1990; *L'Expansion*, February 22, 1990. All cited in Kolboom, "Vom geteilten zum vereinten Deutschland," p. 31.

33. Research Department of the Industrial Bank of Japan, *Effects of the German Economic Union* (June 1990), cited in "Regards sur l'économie allemande," *Bulletin économique du CIRAC*, nr. 1, March 1991, p. 13.

34. Federico Romero, "Cross-border population movement," in William Wallace, ed., *The Dynamics of European Integration* (London: Pinter Publishers for the Royal Institute of International Affairs, 1990), pp. 188-89.

35. See, for example, Michel Albert, *Capitalisme contre capitalisme* (Paris: Le Seuil, 1991), a book that elaborates upon the German example and has been a best-seller in France. As far as the analysis of the notion of a German model in the 1990s is concerned, see LeGloannec, "Le sens de la puissance allemande."

36. Renate Köcher, "Aufwind für die Bonner Koalition. Die Europabegeisterung der Deutschen kühlt sich ab. Der Allensbacher Monatsbericht," *Frankfurter Allgemeine Zeitung*, January 15, 1992. The Rand Corporation has published some roughly similar findings. See Ronald D. Asmus, "Germany in Transition: National Self-Confidence, International Reticence," Statement made before the House Foreign Affairs Committee, Subcommittee on Europe and the Middle East, January 29, 1992.

37. Daniel Vernet, "Le retour de la 'question allemande'," *Le Monde*, December 22-23, 1991; Joseph Fitchett, "Mood Shift in Germany. Growing Nationalism is tracked by poll," *International Herald Tribune*, January 30, 1992. On the consequences of Germany's unification for Western Europe, see Anne-Marie LeGloannec, "The Implications of German Unification for Western Europe," in Paul B. Stares, ed., *The New Germany and the New Europe* (Washington, DC: The Brookings Institution, 1992), pp. 251-78.

38. Interview with *Le Figaro*, July 30, 1990.

39. Henri de Bresson and Claire Tréan, "La création d'un embryon de défense européenne: Paris et Bonn protestent de leur fidélité à l'OTAN," *Le Monde*, May 22, 1992.

2

The British and the Germans:
From Enemies to Partners

Anthony Glees

Britain and Germany before May 1945:
Anglo-German Relations as a Cultural Phenomenon

Relations between Germany and Britain have been close for over a century in the sense that each has regarded the other as important. They have been reasonably warm for the past 25 years. Yet over the decades the relationship has been a tortured one, because in 1914 and then again in 1939, it broke down completely, leading to war, to mutual hatred and to defeat for Germany. The history of their culture suggests that Anglo-German relations can never be ordinary.

Relations between countries are not always the same as relations between the regimes of those countries. There is a continuity about the former that can transcend inter-governmental tensions, and the severing of relations is caused exclusively by the latter. Britain's relations with Germany did not collapse because the Kaiser existed or because Hitler gained power in 1933. Rather, they disintegrated because the actions of the imperial and Nazi regimes inflamed an already existing relationship.[1] Relations between countries are in many ways like relations between individuals. They can be motivated by self-interest or genuine affection and admiration for the other. They can also collapse without any regard to the financial or human damage that ensues. As we shall see, the Anglo-German political relationship has been the outcome of the interplay of many factors, hard-nosed self-interest as well as more nebulous concerns like admiration, envy, and above all competitiveness and rivalry.[2] The cultural roots of this relationship lie partly in geopolitical considerations (Germany and Britain are neighbors, albeit across the North Sea; they are European states; they have even shared the same royal families). Yet they also stem from the fact that the political classes of both countries perceive the other to be very similar. Indeed, competition and rivalry can only exist where states see themselves as both different *and* similar: sufficiently different to make the one fear being outclassed by the other, sufficiently similar to make their competition real. That war broke out in 1914 and 1940 was the consequence of political disasters within the German political system. The imperial British government of 1914 was certainly not shy of fighting but the war with Hitler was generated wholly by his and the Nazis' radicalization of Germany.

Even when the two governments were on good terms with each other before 1914, public opinion in each country tended to regard the other with hostility. The reasons that have often been given for this have to do with differences in national character. But at least one author has pointed to other explanations, for example, the different pace of economic and political modernization in the two countries.[3] Indeed, Mommsen has argued that the British and the Germans have more in common with each other than with any other nation, with the exception of the Americans and the British, a statement truer, perhaps, in hindsight than it seemed before Britain joined the European Community in 1973. There had always been members of the British political class who had felt closest to Germany (just as there had been those who had looked to France and Italy), but the pre-1945 links with the white Commonwealth probably outweighed those with Germany.

Before 1933 and then again after 1945 until the 1970s, it was usually the Germans who envied the British. Britain had an empire on which the sun could not set, and at home it had a firmly established liberal political system (highly prized by thinkers like Dahlmann and von Gneist).[4] It was wealthy and had a way of life and leisure that seemed eminently desirable. The British for their part found relatively little to envy in the German kingdoms. They had supported the formation of a German nation under Prussia, although they were worried about what might prove to be a destabilizing German nationalism. Subsequently, they tolerated Bismarck even if they displayed anxiety from time to time about aspects of his foreign and domestic policies.

By the end of the 19th century, in economic terms, the British and Germans were becoming increasingly dependent on each other. In about 1900 Germany overtook Britain as a producer of iron and steel, chemicals and electrical goods.[5] It can even be argued that this economic competition is by itself sufficient explanation for what was by now a burgeoning political rivalry, bringing with it a menacing arms race. The notion that economic dependency of itself promotes a desire for cooperation is probably a post-1945 invention, imposing on natural competition between states a logic that only two world wars could establish.[6]

At any rate, by the turn of the century there was clear evidence of virulent (and popular) anti-British feeling in Germany (particularly during the Boer War) and anti-German feeling in Britain. In the German case, this feeling was often associated with a sinister contempt for liberalism, and it seems plausible to believe that since German liberals tended to look to Britain as a model, German anti-liberals were disposed to use Britain as an anti-model. The name of Werner Sombart springs readily to mind with the distinction he drew between *Händler* (merchants) and *Helden* (heroes).[7] These became the stereotypes bandied about during the Third Reich. We cannot, of course, know what the non-Nazi political class thought about them, although a number of leading anti-Nazis definitely looked to Britain as a source of hope and, after 1940, of ultimate victory over the Nazis. For Hitler and his aides, the British Empire (but not Britain itself) continued to be a source of admiration and, it appears, they might have been prepared to divide the world between themselves and a Nazi Britain. Dunkirk had demonstrated, as Hitler put it, that Britain had been chased out of Europe.[8] At the same time, British bombing policy (seen, not wholly inaccurately, as the bombing of people and cities rather than factories) did much to cement the Germans to their leaders and apparently increased their hatred of the British, though to what precise extent is hard to say. We should not forget that by 1945 (according to the BBC's German Service 1988 report) some 12 million Germans were risking their safety by listening to the BBC's German Service.

The defeat of the Third Reich once again changed the terms of Anglo-German competitiveness. The British found it hard not to despise the Germans and treated them, in some ways, as if their country had become a colony and they colonial subjects. Even in the early 1990s, it seemed clear that the ghosts of World War II had still not been laid to rest, and it could be questioned whether the hostility and the rivalry between the two countries had truly been banished for ever. There were good grounds for believing that they had, not least thanks to the partnership that common membership in the European Community had produced. At the same time, historically speaking, the period from 1945 to 1989 has represented an exception in Anglo-German relations rather than the rule. One could argue that in the event of any elimination of the preconditions for the vastly improved relations between Britain and Germany — Germany's integration into the Western world, Britain's declining insularity, and the bonds of the European Community — relations between the two countries could again deteriorate. Good relationships must be made to work; they do not simply happen.[9]

British and Allied Policies in the Years 1945-49:
The Punitive and Colonial-Constructive Paradigms

The origins of Britain's postwar relations with the Federal Republic — and indeed with the German Democratic Republic — are clearly to be sought in its occupation policies.[10] These policies had a number of distinct sources. First, the ideas and attitudes about Germany developed in Britain during the war. Second, the general agreements made by all of Germany's victors and, following the outbreak of the Cold War, the agreements reached by the Western Allies. The third source of occupation policy was the specifically British dimension that emanated from Britain's position as one of the four occupying powers.

Postwar policy, whether the outcome of Britain acting together with its Allies or of Britain's own particular policy style, fits into one of three distinct paradigms: the punitive, the colonial-constructive, and the partnership paradigm. Not surprisingly, the first model was most in evidence during the period immediately following Germany's capitulation, the second appearing after statehood in 1948 until the early 1970s, and the third visible from the time Britain sought entry into the European Community until the present.

Yet each paradigm could also co-exist with the others in that even during the punitive phase, there were authoritative individuals who sought to be constructive rather than destructive. Conversely, as late as 1992, certain British papers and members of Britain's political class could be heard attacking what they alleged were traditionally dangerous German ambitions in Europe. Anti-German sentiment, as we shall see, continued to play a not insignificant role in British political life, fueled in part by history but also by the heavy emphasis the British and West German media place on stories about the Third Reich.

Post-1945 policy was not decided upon during the war. With one or two exceptions, the reverse was the case: Churchill had insisted that nothing about Germany's future was to be fixed until it had unconditionally surrendered.[11] Before Churchill became Prime Minister, the British government had sought to differentiate between Germans and Nazis, with the war depicted as a struggle between liberal democracies and Fascism. Churchill and his cabinet, however, developed the line that the war could only be successfully waged if the Germans themselves were to become the target, both literally and metaphorically, with the result that wartime policy-making was to be confined to destroying the Third Reich and developing (but not fixing) only those postwar plans designed to destroy the old German order.[12]

British occupation policies have been extensively described and analyzed elsewhere.[13] The aim here is simply to outline the most important aspects of these policies as they illuminate the nature of the Anglo-German relationship from 1945 to 1949 and the transition in British thinking about Germany from the punitive to the constructive-colonial model. The policies were based on the agreements or protocol reached at the Potsdam conference which defined the broad framework of Allied policy towards Germany. It produced quick consensus on the need for demilitarization, de-Nazification, disarmament, democratization, and decentralization. Local self-government on democratic lines was to be introduced speedily. Indeed, the Commander of the Soviet Zone in his "Order no. 2" of June 10, 1945 had already permitted the formation of four political parties.[14]

Economically, it was decided to treat Germany as a single unit. Although neither the Americans nor the British would agree to the Soviet demand for reparations from their zones, there was agreement that the Allied Control Council in Berlin would take unanimous decisions on all matters affecting Germany as a whole (even though within their own zones, the military commanders-in-chief had full authority). This, combined with the economic decisions, showed clearly the desire to retain the element of an all-German government during the period of military occupation. Finally, the Potsdam agreement established a Council of Foreign Ministers (including the French foreign minister) which was to meet at regular intervals. It was charged with special duties for the process of making peace in the future, especially with the future German state. The Potsdam protocol signed on August 2, 1945 thus laid the basis for the political and economic control of Germany under occupation. In the event, its writ was to disintegrate within two years.

Britain's attitude towards Germany's division was wholly shaped by Allied policy as outlined at Potsdam. It was a consistent policy that continued even during the period of uncertainty surrounding Stalin's 1952 "notes" on German unity and the 1955 Geneva conference. It held until unification in 1990. The official British view was that the German state had ceased to exist but that in due course another unified German state would be established, and that the form this process would take would be the subject of inter-Allied decisions.

Britain's commitment to German unity both after the war, and more recently, has often been doubted. A distinction must be drawn, however, between policy and the utterances of individual politicians. While the latter have voiced anxieties about the nature of Germany from time to time, British policy has consistently demanded the restoration of German unity by means of a peaceful and democratic process. The allegation that the 1944 decision to divide Germany into zones of occupation was, in fact, a decision to dismember German national unity is inherently implausible and contradicted by the agreements reached at Potsdam.[15] No fixed British plan for dismemberment existed after the war, and wartime thoughts on dismemberment were ideas to be put into the melting pot and did not constitute firm policies.

In fact, all of Germany's victors had every interest in seeing Germany unified (an interest that the Russians seem to have finally abandoned only in the early 1970s). Each wanted the creation of a single German nation that would conform to its own social, political, and economic system. It is worth noting that in his celebrated speech at Fulton, Missouri, Churchill spoke of the "iron curtain" as existing to the east of the Soviet zone of occupation (from "Stettin on the Baltic"). Yet both blocs, realizing that they could, for the time being, not have this, preferred to see a Germany divided along ideological lines instead of a united Germany that might conflict with their own systems.

Throughout 1946 there were agreements and also disagreements among the Western Allies as well as between them and the Soviets. Britain, for example, made it plain that it opposed the French policy of seeking to separate the Rhineland and the Ruhr from the rest of Germany.[16]   Germany's future division was in effect sealed by the failure of the Moscow meeting of the Council of Foreign Ministers from March 10 to April 24, 1947. Yet it is important to realize that this was more of a negative slide into keeping Germany divided than a positive one, despite increasing friction between East and West. The greater the certainty that the Soviets would never relinquish their hold on eastern Germany, the more determined were the British and the Americans to build a West German state and transform their policies towards Germany.

In the initial postwar period, the punitive paradigm in British (and Allied) occupation policy was by and large predominant. Sir William Strang, the chief political advisor to the British Military Governor, stated plainly that "the primary purpose of [our] occupation is destructive and preventive."[17]   The British thus set about destroying Nazism and its effects. The chosen means were the trial of war criminals and de-Nazification. The process was realized both at an all-German and at a zonal level. The Nuremberg Tribunal specifically produced 13 separate trials involving 177 people and passed 20 life sentences, 25 death sentences, and 35 acquittals. The British dealt with the second count, crimes against peace.[18]   Figures supplied by a Canadian government report stated that in 1946 Britain had 5900 active war crimes files in its zone and a list of 1085 suspects; it had passed 240 death sentences (more than the French but less than the Americans).[19]   By the end of 1946 the British had interned 64,000 "dangerous Nazis," the Soviets 67,000, the French 19,000, and the Americans 100,000. Britain, like America and France, in due course passed de-Nazification procedures to German officials and courts.

British (and Allied) economic policy can also be analyzed from the perspective of the punitive paradigm. Although severely damaged, the German economy was not totally devastated. Recovery was always thinkable. It was true that in 1945 coal production was but one-tenth of its 1939 level. But the coal was in the ground and all of Germany's victors saw it — quite rightly in a pre-oil era — as the cornerstone of the German economy. By January 1946 coal production had been increased five-fold. Yet this coal was to be *used* for the benefit of the victors rather than the Germans themselves.

The German economy was affected by punitive measures in other areas as well. One of the most dramatic ways was through the dismantling of German industrial plants (demontage),[20] some 262 of which were in the UK zone. As we have seen, Britain had perceived Germany to be its chief economic rival, and occupation superficially gave the British the opportunity of stunting the German economy. In the event, it was soon realized that a weak German economy was not in the British interest, and even where there was initial enthusiasm for taking over a German industry (as, for example, in the case of Volkswagen) it soon evaporated.   The British did not believe there was a market for the curious beetle.[21]   Yet none of the Western Allies wished to repeat the mistake made at Versailles of taking more than was economically or politically sensible.   A growing fear of the Communists who were thought to benefit from economic distress contributed to a milder approach.

A shift thus took place to a colonial and constructive attitude, which affected both economic and politico-constitutional affairs.   The British and the Americans soon decided to try to put the western German economy on a sound footing. They set up the Bizone, to be run by an Economic Council (a pseudo-parliament) in Frankfurt.   Final agreement on this was reached on June 17, 1947. The aim was to create economic unity between the U.S. and British zones, to restore the German economy, to minimize the expense of occupation, and to transfer virtually all the occupation costs from Britain onto America.   It was widely believed in Britain that by making it impossible for the Germans to feed themselves, the British people were suffering a lower standard of living than they would otherwise have, and that they were paying reparations to the Germans instead of the other way around.

In order that Germany should be able to participate in Western recovery, real money had to be restored to western Germany.   This was done in a series of four laws, of which the most obvious was the German currency law of June 18, 1948 (to take effect on June 21, 1948).   On June 23, 1948 (the day after the western currency reform) the Soviets instituted their own reform.

As East-West disagreement over the treatment and disposition of Germany deepened, plans to create a separate West German state gathered momentum in Western capitals.   As early as April 1946, Foreign Secretary Ernest Bevin said the British should do what the Soviets had already done in their zone, namely establish a "German government."[22]   On May 3, 1946, the British Cabinet was given a paper produced by Bevin discussing the merits of a unified but federal Germany versus a western German state "more amenable to our influence" to be set up in view of the "Russian attitude and the danger of Communist domination of western Germany."[23]   By 1948, the Americans and the British felt they could openly develop western Germany into a state that would be part of the Western community.

America and Britain took the lead in initiating a constitutional dialogue with western German officials and intervened over a myriad of issues in order to ensure that West Germany would have a constitution guaranteeing "a federal form of government which adequately protects the rights of the respective states and which at the same time provides for adequate central government."[24]

Meanwhile, developments in eastern Germany further escalated the East-West standoff over Germany's future.   On March 17 and 18, 1948, a people's congress with 2000 delegates was convened in East Berlin, claiming for itself the sole right to represent Germany (indicating, yet again, the Soviet interest in German unity), announcing a plebiscite on unity, and recognizing the Oder-

Neisse line. It established a people's council (*Volksrat*) led by Wilhelm Pieck of the newly established eastern German Communist Party (SED), Otto Nuschke of the eastern Christian Democratic Union (CDU), and Dr. Külz of the German Liberal Democratic Party (LDPD).[25] Accordingly, on March 20, 1948, General Sokolovsky, the military commander of the Soviet zone, walked out of a meeting of the Allied Control Council in Berlin in protest at Western policies. The four victorious Allies were not to meet again in this fashion for another 42 years, but meet again they did, and this time it was to unite Germany rather than divide it.

At the beginning of 1948, the Soviets began interfering with transports from western Germany to West Berlin. On June 24, in an attempt to prevent the transfer of the western D-Mark into West Berlin, Soviet forces imposed a complete blockade on western land traffic to Berlin. As a result, America and Britain began the Berlin airlift of food and fuel on July 7, and within a few days 3000 tons of supplies were flown in. There could have been no more basic or emotional illustration of the Western commitment to the German people than an airlift whose purpose was not military but to keep people alive and to prevent them from being blackmailed. Berlin's political significance was never to evaporate. The very truth that those who had three years previously been the mortal enemies of the West were now treated as its allies escaped no one in the West or the East. The blockade came to an end on May 12, 1949.[26]

Let us return now to our analysis of the UK's occupation policies. The British, as was perhaps to be expected from an imperial power, were determined to take occupation very seriously. The British Element of the Allied Control Council was headed by Field-Marshall Montgomery. His deputy, General Sir Brian Robertson, succeeded him in 1947. In October 1945 a Minister for Germany, John Hynd, was appointed (his real title was Chancellor of the Duchy of Lancaster) and almost 55,000 people were employed by the Control Council (29,000 of them in the UK Zone). By early 1946 this was costing £80 million per year.

The cost of occupation was one factor concentrating British minds. They were already aware of the implications of the precariousness of British finances as a result of the war that had just been fought and an over-ambitious domestic plan for the socialization of important parts of the British economy. Another factor was the growing perception that the Soviets were intent on extending the power of Communism. Strang, the advisor to the British Military Governor, now defined British tasks as being first and foremost concerned with food, coal, displaced persons, and public safety. Politics, he believed, could wait.[27]

At this point, it is necessary to note the role played by Konrad Adenauer in the British occupation zone. It is hard to overestimate his contribution to the creation of what became the Federal Republic.[28] Interestingly, Britain's behavior towards him was fraught with anger and resentment. Since Adenauer's personal position was so significant, it is necessary to analyze his treatment by the British as a vital aspect in the Anglo-German relationship. From the British point of view, Adenauer was simply another anti-Nazi German political leader, a leading member of what might be termed the "reserve team" of German politics, but essentially an old man with provincial rather than national credentials. From the West German perspective, Adenauer did have a national reputation and Britain's attitude towards Adenauer mirrored its attitude towards western Germany as a whole, demonstrating a transition from punitive to colonial-cooperative and then partnership models.

On June 21, 1945, the British assumed control of Cologne and friction with Adenauer, who was the city's mayor, was not long in coming. As early as September, Adenauer delivered the first of many attacks on British occupation policy.[29] As a result, on October 6, 1945, he was dismissed by the British military governor, General Barraclough, and banned from further political activity. Whether justified or not, his dismissal could only sour Adenauer's view of Britain. He quickly saw that the prime mover in western Germany would be America (he said as much in 1948) and that America could therefore not be crossed but that England was a lesser mover and therefore a far safer target to hit. Adenauer was soon permitted to resume his political life, however, and continued to attack British policy, opposing, among other things, the planned socialization of industry and what he claimed was British colonialism towards Germany.[30]

It can be argued, however, that these brushes with the British were tactical rather than deep-seated. Adenauer certainly got on well with individual members of the British military government and found Frank Pakenham (Lord Longford), Minister for Germany in 1947 and 1948, especially sympathetic. It is plain, however, that the accusation by Social Democratic leader Kurt Schumacher that Adenauer was the "chancellor of the allies" rather than of the Germans was quite untrue as far as Britain was concerned.

The situation facing the British in Germany was, like that which faced its Allies, one of complete and utter chaos. People were starving. The food shortages were dealt with by the continuation of the Nazi system of food rationing. Twenty-five percent of food production had been lost with the lands east of the Oder and Neisse. The British laid down a food norm for Germans of 1550 calories per day, although the League of Nations limit was 2400.[31] By 1946 the incidence of TB was four times the 1938 figure and the Allies realized they would have to modify their stance on the importing of their own food. Although the Labour government was reluctant to use its own much-needed dollar reserve to purchase North American wheat, by January 1946 it was not only forced to do so but also to make no distinction between the German people and others with regard to food supplies.

The British had toyed with the idea of the socialization of parts of German industry. Bevin ordered that the Ruhr mines be taken over by the authorities on December 21, 1946 to "eliminate the present excessive concentration of economic power" as well as to show the Ruhr miners that the British were committed to bringing about socialism in their zone.[32]

Political parties had been permitted to establish themselves under license since August 6 in the UK zone. On the whole, of all the occupying powers, the British seem to have given least thought to this particular matter. As we have seen, it was felt that food came before politics. While this may have been true for the ordinary German, Germany's prospective leaders took a different line. For them, politics were as basic as food. Incidentally, the notion that the British Labour government might have had a natural affinity towards the German Social Democratic Party (SPD) is wholly misconceived. In particular, Bevin distrusted the older generation of German Socialist leaders.[33]

Britain's rather colonial attitude towards Germany may also be seen in its attempt to form a new German political identity by the formation of a Rhine-Ruhr "super" *Land*, North Rhine-Westphalia. The British planners believed that a new *Land* that would include the Ruhr, whose industries were to be nationalized, might be a model for other German *Länder*, either as part of a federal set of units or indeed as a separate German state.

Plainly, but with some justification, the British felt that they knew better than the Germans how the British zone ought to be governed, and although this may have appeared to the Germans as a simple demonstration of arrogance, it was hard for the British to get it right. Studies of British occupation in individual areas of their zone illustrate this point well. There was a serious conflict between military and civilian government, between the desire to purge Nazis from the civil service, the police, and industry while at the same time preserving the continuity of society's vital functions.[34] British attempts to reform the civil service in their zone were subject to exactly the same constraints.[35]

Britain and German Unity

The issue of German unity proved to be a major theme in Anglo-German relations. All-German affairs, of course, were the preserve of all the wartime Allies, so that the Soviet Union as well as the West had a decisive role to play (a state of affairs that was to endure until unification in 1990). The Allies' role was most important from 1945 until 1951 (when the Federal Republic was allowed to establish a Foreign Ministry) but still decisive until 1955 (when the High Commission, set up in 1949 under the Occupation Statute, was finally dissolved).

Both in western and in eastern Germany, the states that were set up were more than simply the creation of Germany's victors and reflected, far more so, it is true, in the pluralistic society of West Germany, a variety of ideas and beliefs that were German, and not American, British, French or Russian.

On November 3, 1950, East German premier Otto Grotewohl had sent a letter to FRG President Theodor Heuss offering a return to the Potsdam process, the demilitarization of Germany, and a Four-Power summit on German unity. He also agreed to create a provisional all-German government and hold a plebiscite on its policies. Adenauer was implacably opposed to what he rightly regarded as a Soviet ploy to gain control of all of Germany.

Matters became more complex following the receipt by the Western Allies of the celebrated Stalin "notes" of March 10 and April 9, 1952, offering unity on apparently favorable terms, provided Germany remained neutral, like Austria. The Allied High Commissioners now decided to put pressure on Adenauer to adopt a more positive line. The latter felt vulnerable, not least because he faced a federal election and the opposition SPD was also pressing him to respond positively.

The death of Stalin on March 5, 1953 appeared to put an end to the Soviet initiative on German unity. But in fact it introduced an element of uncertainty into East-West relations. For one thing, the dictator of Russia was dead and his personal rule therefore over. For another, the East German people decided to exploit this apparent seachange by staging a revolt. Although it did not succeed, the uprising of June 17, 1953 showed that the East German Communist government was highly unpopular. Neither the Western Allies nor indeed the West German government believed that there was anything that could be done to assist the rioters. Indeed, British Prime Minister Winston Churchill was at first inclined to be very hostile to them. In addition, he argued that Stalin's death might help rather than hinder the cause of German unity.[36]

Speaking in Parliament on May 11, 1953, he praised Adenauer generously ("the wisest German statesman since Bismarck") but privately drew up a memorandum on the subject which said that in terms of security against any future German aggression, a West Germany of 55 million inhabitants was no less dangerous than a united Germany of 70 million. He predicted that the European Defence Community (EDC), which was under discussion at that time, would fail and that with or without Adenauer "nothing will turn the German people from unity. . . . However the election goes, all parties will be ardent for unity. We must face the fact that there will always be a 'German problem' and a 'Prussian danger'."[37]

Although Adenauer was deeply unsettled by all of this, he was quickly able to overcome his fears, partly because the East German uprising was put down by Soviet tanks, which destroyed Communism's political credibility with some force, and partly because Churchill suffered a major stroke on July 6, 1953, which put him out of commission.

On April 18, 1951, the treaty for the establishment of the European Coal and Steel Community (ECSC) had been signed. Adenauer called it the foundation stone for European Union and prophesied that other countries would wish to join it one day. Britain, however, had refused to do so, chiefly for fear of losing its sovereignty. Yet it is clear that Britain thereby began a move away from West Germany (which was to last for more than a decade) and that the intensity of Anglo-German relations could only diminish as a result.

In September 1954, following the rejection of the proposed European Defence Community by the French National Assembly, the six EDC states joined with the US, Britain, and Canada and admitted West Germany into NATO. The British played a key part in the success of this enterprise yet they remained anxious about Adenauer's firm refusal to recognize the Oder-Neisse line between Germany and Poland. It was a British NATO chief, Lord Ismay, who coined the *bon mot* that NATO's purpose was to "keep the Russians out, the Americans in and the Germans down."

At the same time, the Occupation Statute was abolished and the High Commission dissolved. West Germany became a sovereign state in almost every regard, the chief exception being its acceptance of the rights of Western Allied forces in West Germany and Berlin and their right to determine the circumstances of German unity. The treaty (which was finally ratified in May 1955) has always been known in Britain as the Relations Convention and in Germany as the *Deutschlandvertrag*.

Meanwhile, on May 14, 1955, East Germany was admitted into the Warsaw Pact. In some sense, these events appeared to settle the political division of Germany for the forseeable future. In reality, however, not only did they simply confirm a state of affairs that Soviet policy towards Germany had made inevitable, but without West Germany's integration into the Western world, unity in 1990 under conditions of peace and liberty would not have taken place.

Anglo-German Relations, 1966-89

By the time of his retirement in the autumn of 1963, Adenauer was 87 years old.[38] He had lost his touch. The British saw him as too old and rigid in his attitudes towards the Soviets, and his support for what was to be de Gaulle's first veto of Britain's EEC membership application caused understandable bitterness. Consequently, Britain had high hopes for the Grand Coalition (1966-69) and the government led by Willy Brandt (1969-74). The British believed that the Federal Republic would now actively support British membership in the European Community and be more ready to pursue policies of detente with the Soviet bloc.

Thus, although the Anglo-German relationship had lost much of its political immediacy in the period from 1955 to 1965, the emergence of Willy Brandt and his *Ostpolitik* after 1966 did much to reinvigorate it. Brandt was seen as a dynamic new force in German politics and he had very many British admirers.[39] He had been an active and courageous anti-Nazi, had helped transform the German Social Democratic Party into a party of government, and his foreign policy, too, showed an ability to be both highly imaginative and reassuring. By virtue of its rights and obligations as a victor over Germany, Britain was actively involved in West German security affairs and, in particular, with the position of Berlin, which was taken especially seriously.

Brandt was a firm believer in the European Community and strongly supported British EC membership although it was only after de Gaulle left office in 1969 that this could be achieved.[40] Brandt wryly recalled the comment made by George Brown, then British Foreign Secretary: "Willy, you must let us in so that we can take the lead."[41] Brandt also strongly supported European political union. He wanted employment, trade and industrial policy issues to be jointly managed. He also favored a common European foreign policy.[42]

Yet Brandt often found the British hard to please. In April 1971 British Prime Minister Edward Heath visited Bonn, and expressed what were to become oft-rehearsed British fears about the power of the Brussels bureaucracy and the need for heads of governments to excercise firmer control over it. Yet the two leaders reached agreement on a European monetary union by 1981 and a reformed European Parliament that was to be based on the West German model. At the EC summit meeting of heads of government in Paris in December 1974, it was indeed decided that in 1978 there should be direct elections to the European Parliament.

Britain's interest in Brandt's *Ostpolitik* centered on the British desire for detente in Europe. It is true that it appeared to run counter to Britain's support for unity because it was constructed on West German acceptance of the status quo in Europe (formally expressed in the Soviet-West German Treaty of 1970) and thus the existence of two German states and their borders. Yet the British took the line that if this did not upset West Germany, it should not upset Britain.

While an agreement between the two Germanys and Germany's victors could in theory lead to German unity and also to a renegotiation of existing borders, in practice it was inconceivable that the Soviets and their East German puppets would ever agree to this. They wanted recognition precisely because they figured it would ensure the continued existence of a Communist German state and a Communist Eastern Europe. Adenauer had always refused to countenance any recognition of either the GDR or the Oder-Neisse border for this very reason.

Brandt's own position on unity was somewhat equivocal. Within his party, his realism was seen as the alternative to his predecessors' total commitment to German unity. Yet, paradoxically, Brandt's acceptance of the existence of two German states helped create the conditions under which unity could eventually occur, both because West Germany had ceased to be a threat to the GDR and because the contacts between the citizens of both states that were a core part of his policy helped strengthen the inter-German cultural linkage.

As far his rhetoric went, neither as Foreign Minister nor as Chancellor did Brandt ditch the aim of unity; he simply came to the conclusion that it had ceased to be an achievable aim. By 1969, he argued that he was "enough of a realist to know that the self-determinaton of the German people does not stand on the agenda of practical policies."[43] In February 1968 Bonn had sent the Soviets a memorandum offering detente and closer relations between "both parts of Germany." The two German states, he also said, would never regard each other as "foreign" but there could be two German states in one German nation.[44]

Britain was not only concerned with the GDR but also with West Germany's relationship with other Eastern bloc states. London felt that it was finally time to accept the facts created by the defeat of the Third Reich. It began to plan actively to establish a British embassy in East Berlin. In November 1969 Brandt offered to begin negotiations with Poland. The Poles demanded the recognition of all existing borders. At first, Brandt refused. Later, the Poles dropped their demand for the full recognition of the GDR and insisted only on the recognition of the Oder-Neisse line. On December 6, 1970, Brandt went to Warsaw to complete the agreement (the treaty with the USSR had in any case meant that Poland's western border would be recognized by West Germany). These moves were seen as highly positive and innovative by the British. Without doubt, they believed that detente lessened the risk of war in Europe and in the world. It seems likely, too, that they believed that, in practical terms, the German Question had been solved.

Brandt's line on the GDR predicated an agreement with the Soviets. This closely mirrored the Western interest in concluding a Four-Power agreement on Berlin. The FRG-USSR treaty was signed on April 12, 1970. West Germany and the Soviet Union agreed to abide by the existing frontiers in Europe and renounce the use of force. Brandt insisted that "the goal of German unity by means of self- determination was not affected by the treaty."[45] On September 3, 1971, a Four-Power agreement was reached on Berlin: the Soviets committed themselves to not changing the situation in Berlin unilaterally and visits were made easier.

The Basic Treaty governing relations between West Germany and the GDR was signed in East Berlin on December 21, 1972. It created the preconditions for further negotiations. The GDR government was also handed a letter on German unity stating that West Germany had the "political objective to work for a state of peace in Europe in which the German nation could recover its unity in free self- determination."[46] Both states were to seek membership in the United Nations (gained in September 1973). Permanent representative missions (but not embassies) were to be set up in Bonn and East Berlin.

Brandt himself concluded that the treaty "did not directly bring us closer to the goal of German unity."[47] For East Germany, however, national unity did cease to be a political goal: it now defined itself as the "Socialist state of the German nation" and later as the "Socialist German national state" (although it could never find a substitute for the word "German"!). Brandt had firmly come to believe that "there could be no return to a nation-state on the 19th century pattern, even if the nation would live on under differing political systems, because nationhood is a matter of awareness and resolve." He stated that his aim had always been to keep the "cultural nationhood" of Germany intact without precluding West Germany's "search for a wider political home" in the Western community of states.[48]

Britain was delighted at all of this. West Germany had divested itself of any appearance of revisionism and had built a solid bridge to Eastern Europe. East Germany had been brought into the diplomatic fold. Britain felt that the GDR occupied an important position within the Soviet system and hoped that diplomatic recognition would produce a considerable increase in British exports to the GDR. The British knew that Western credits were essential to the regime in order to buy the materials it needed for its industries. The East German growth rate was believed to be rather higher and the East German economy healthier than was in fact the case.[49]

Helmut Schmidt, Brandt's immediate successor, seemed less interested in *Ostpolitik* than his own Christian Democratic replacement, Helmut Kohl. Schmidt was much admired in the UK for his economic expertise. Britain was going through a desperate slump and its political, economic, and social crisis contrasted strongly with growing West German prosperity. In addition, Schmidt joined with Prime Minister James Callaghan to urge NATO's INF ("Euromissile") double-track decision on an initially reluctant President Carter. Britain and West Germany shared identical security concerns and the extent of their agreement on the remedy — in effect, the re-arming of NATO — bespoke an increasingly close relationship. This was further underscored by Britain's success in selling the Tornado jet-fighter to the Germans against considerable odds.

Both Schmidt and Kohl shared the same Foreign Minister, Hans-Dietrich Genscher, yet Kohl's interests in Eastern Europe and in German unity were much stronger (even though many observers discounted his seriousness). The historian and occasional Kohl aide Michael Stürmer noted: "The operative aim of Deutschlandpolitik under . . . Schmidt 1974-82 and then of the new CDU/CSU-FDP coalition of Chancellor Helmut Kohl . . . was not reunification on Western conditions or neutralism on eastern conditions. German unity through free self-determination remains a historical objective but the agenda of international politics today is different. . . . Ostpolitik and Deutschlandpolitik remain part of the Federal Republic's central European responsibility, essential to its identity and self-esteem. . . . [They] continue to depend on the Atlantic Alliance and on European integration." Stürmer even queried whether West Germany had not said a "final goodbye to the German question."[50]

Britain and Germany after 1989

Although no one could know it, 1989 would be the last complete year in which two German states existed and, at year's end, would bring one of the most testing times for Anglo-German relations. Yet it was also the 40th anniversary of the founding of the two German states. It was an obvious time to take stock of Anglo-German relations.[51]

By 1989, British and West German foreign policies were running in tandem (something in which the British and German foreign ministries took great pride). British and West German diplomats took seconded posts in each other's foreign offices; the German official in Whitehall would even read the British dispatches about his country. The Konrad Adenauer Foundation established an office in London and did remarkably well in promoting contacts with the British Conservative Party (the head of the London office was seen as more influential than the German ambassador and worked closely with Chancellor Kohl). These good political relations were complemented by good cultural ones. State institutions like the British Council and the Goethe Institutes worked hard in each other's country. The *Deutsch-Englische Gesellschaft*, founded in Düsseldorf in 1949 by Lilo Milchsack and her husband, promoted contact between leading West German and British opinion-leaders in its Königswinter conferences.[52]

Yet there existed serious policy disagreements on the future of the European Community. British Prime Minister Margaret Thatcher argued (most clearly in Bruges in 1988) for a looser Community which upheld national sovereignty and sought to include other European states. West Germany, however, remained committed to the supra-national element in the Community and pressed for a closer political and economic union among existing members.

In April 1989 the British ambassador to Bonn spoke publicly about the Anglo-German relationship and Britain's policy on German unity.[53] This was, of course, after Gorbachev's reforms had transformed the Soviet Union but before it had become clear that the Kremlin would accept the disappearance of the GDR. His views fully reflected the Anglo-German partnership paradigm. He stressed the warmth of relations and his government's consistent support for unification.

Britain's bilateral relations with West Germany were conducted around two very potent multilateral institutions: the European Community and NATO. It was not insignificant in 1989 that the British chose to emphasise the latter in their dealings with West Germany. NATO and deterrence, the ambassador declared, had been a "remarkable success."

He added that Britain continued to support strongly German aspirations for unity. It regarded the Berlin and German questions as interlocked and it was determined to continue to play its part in these matters. The 1955 Relations Convention upheld the three Western Allies' rights in Berlin and over German unity. The ambassador then listed some of the major declarations of support for unity. He noted the three Western Powers' statement of May 12, 1965, calling for a solution to the German Question in the interests of the German people "who desire unity." In December 1972, NATO members had affirmed their support for the efforts of the Federal Republic to work for a condition of peace in Europe in which the German people could, through self-determination, achieve their unity. In 1980, on the 25th anniversary of the Relations Convention, Lord Carrington, then Foreign Secretary, repeated these aims. In May 1984 Mrs. Thatcher had said that real peace in Europe would be hard to achieve if the German nation remained divided against its will. Britain continued to be committed to Berlin with a presence of 3000 troops and was very critical of the GDR's violations of human rights. It wanted the Berlin Wall to be taken down. Yet, the ambassador concluded, Britain could see no signs that Moscow was prepared to change its German policy. The Soviet Union ostensibly still believed that its interests were served by the division of Germany.

It is impossible to doubt that this assessment was a genuine one and much evidence suggests that Britain was indeed taken by surprise when Gorbachev indicated his willingness to see the GDR disappear. Yet the very fact that the unity issue was clearly on the ambassador's agenda in April 1989 may indicate that behind the scenes some diplomatic observers were already beginning to speculate that it might come about as a by-product of the changes taking place in the Soviet Union.

The more inevitable unity seemed, however, the cooler Mrs. Thatcher became. There had certainly been personal frictions for some years between Mrs. Thatcher and Chancellor Kohl. She considered him loquacious, he considered her domineering. She had serious reservations about Germany's future position in Europe. Some Germans even believed, in view of her attitude on German unity, that British support for it was predicated on the belief that it would never occur. Yet this was not the view of the Foreign Office, which argued that unity was in Britain's interest. Not surprisingly, tension between Downing Street and Whitehall on Germany grew considerably. It was resolved only by the departure of Mrs. Thatcher and her replacement by John Major.

While the discord in Anglo-German relations of the late Thatcher years was not the chief reason for her resignation, it was certainly symptomatic of the extent to which her policy style was out of joint with that developed by her wider government. At this time, the partnership paradigm was, from the British end, to revert briefly to something more akin to the colonial one. Mrs. Thatcher, in her own rather exciting way, appeared to want to follow Lord Ismay's dictum.

Although Britain had been committed to the idea of a united Germany, this had not until now seemed a real prospect, despite indications of serious opposition to the East German regime since 1985.[54] British academics and

media observers certainly had failed to predict unification.[55]   In December
1989, when it was clear that the Wall would be breached, Mrs. Thatcher said
that German unity was not on the agenda nor would it be for a long time to
come.   Britain's line was that a popular move for unity in Germany might
destabilize Gorbachev (although it was hard to see how, since Gorbachev
himself supported change).   On February 6, 1990, she told Parliament that a
"lengthy transition period" would be needed before unity could occur.   On
February 18, 1990, she suggested to the Board of Deputies of British Jews that
German unity would be of "particular concern" to them.   A few days later she
once again criticized the rush to unity: "We dare to talk the sense that other
people are fearful of saying. . . .   You cannot just ignore the history of this
century as if it did not happen and say 'we are going to unify and everything
else will have to be worked out afterwards'.   That is not the way."[56]   She also
opposed East German membership of the EC, arguing that this would be "much
worse than taking in Belgium, Denmark and Ireland combined.   It means taking
in a state that has either been Nazi or Communist since the 1930s."   Finally, she
used German unity as an additional stick to beat the notion of a federal EC: "It
would be by far the most powerful country in the federal state and everyone
else's freedom . . . would be diminished."[57]

On March 24, 1990, a meeting on Germany was held at Chequers which
took the line that Germans were either "on their knees or at your throat," as one
participant recalled.[58]   The aim of the meeting was to decide what a united
Germany would be like.   It would be important to get the balance right between
the "lessons of the past and the opportunities of the future."   The meeting then
rehearsed the "characteristics of the Germans:" their "insensitivity to the feelings
of others, their obsession with themselves, self-pity, aggressiveness, bullying,
sentimentality and a capacity for excess," to name but a few.   Yet the meeting
did conclude that "today's Germans are very different from their predecessors
. . . 1945 was a sea change" and that Britain need have no worries about the
new generation of Germans.[59]

However, Mrs. Thatcher said in New York on October 2, 1990 that
"Germany will be very dominant in Europe, so it will be up to the rest of us not
to allow it to dominate. . . .   I thought some time ago that the transition of two
Germanies to one should be taken in slower time so we could get things sorted
out more easily."   On June 18, 1990, she had said that "many people in Britain
were a little bit apprehensive" about a united Germany and that she herself was
"worried" because of the "history of this century which we cannot ignore."
Although West Germany was a "very good democracy," its parliamentary
tradition was "just a few years old" when compared with Britain's.[60]

There were indications that Mrs. Thatcher's anti-German line (for this is
what it was) was not without weighty support.   One of her closest advisors in
the Cabinet, Nicholas Ridley, was equally outspoken about Germany in an
interview in *The Spectator*, published on July 14, 1990.[61]   He said that

European monetary union was a "German racket designed to take over the whole of Europe." Germany, he claimed, was "uppity" and already running most of the EC. "Being bossed by a German would cause absolute mayhem in this country." He made no apology for having his views colored by the war, saying that it was "useful to remember" Auschwitz and Czechoslovakia.

Ridley had to resign as a result of this interview (although he was not dismissed) which called into question his sense of balance. But the incident was not quickly forgotten. John Major's selection as Prime Minister introduced a new dynamic into Anglo-German relations for although he, too, was sceptical about the German concept of European Union, he was anxious to stay on good terms with Chancellor Kohl and his government. He made his first speech abroad in the *Adenauer Haus* in Bonn (and praised the work of the Foundation in bringing Conservatives and Christian Democrats together). He received a personal message of congratulation after his election victory in April 1992 (made public by the Germans). His close advisor, Chris Patten, was on excellent terms with the CDU and its leading younger member, German Defense Minister Volker Rühe (who had campaigned with him in the 1992 British general election).

There could be no doubt that the Major-Kohl friendship had decisively put an end to the ill-feeling generated by Margaret Thatcher's line. Indeed, as Britain assumed the presidency of the European Community for the final six months of 1992, there were signs that Britain's policy on Europe was striking chords with German public opinion. Britain wanted to see a widening of the Community to include, in time, the new states of Central and Eastern Europe. It also declared its support for the EC's "deepening," not by means of a transfer of more power to Brussels and the European Parliament at Strassbourg (which Kohl had wanted), however, but by the greater use of the principle of subsidiarity. Many Germans appeared to feel happier with British ideas than with Kohl's more idealistic (and imaginative) concepts of closer political union within Europe. There was even talk of joint British and German embassies in the new states of Central and Eastern Europe.

Yet the future of Anglo-Germans relations was not wholly settled in 1992. Britain under Prime Minister Major and Foreign Secretary Douglas Hurd (who became the senior European foreign minister after Genscher's resignation) seemed to lack the imaginative vision of Kohl. Britain's European policy appeared to be motivated solely by economic self-interest, in the view of many Germans, whereas Kohl's commitment to European federation was dismissed by many Britons as "windy rhetoric" (the phrase was Hurd's). Germany wanted a Europe that was wider before it became deeper, whereas Britain seemed increasingly to hanker for a Europe that was simply a free trade area. There were other real differences between the two countries that caused ripples in the relationship, such as initial disagreement on the policy to be pursued regarding the break-up of Yugoslavia (where the German policy of recognizing small new national units had seemed precipitate but was reluctantly, and perhaps unwisely, supported by Britain). Germany's wish to pull out of the European Fighter Aircraft project caused considerable dismay as well. There was also a strand of public opinion that was becoming anxious about the new German Right and the Bonn government's inability to act against it.

Finally, the furor over the 1991 Maastricht Treaty in the fall of 1992 showed a potential for even greater tension between Britain and Germany. Having refused to accept the full treaty, Prime Minister Major nevertheless recommended it to the British public. When doubts began to surface that the French voters would favor the treaty in a national referendum scheduled for September 20 (they eventually did, but only by a very small majority), the British Pound faced growing pressure in the European Exchange Rate Mechanism (ERM), and Major found himself under attack from those Conservatives who had never liked either the ERM or the Maastricht Treaty. The British government had to remove the Pound from the ERM and accept a *de facto* devaluation. For political reasons, it was decided not to explore the domestic British causes of the Pound's shakiness but to blame the German *Bundesbank* for its policy of keeping German interest rates high in order to counter the inflationary pressure brought on by high unification expenses. Chancellor Kohl strongly rejected this criticism and was clearly angry about it. While Britain found itself ensnared once again in its historical quarrel with the vision of a supranational European Community, there was increasing evidence that the Germans and the French, supported by the Benelux states, wished to press ahead with the ratification of the Maastricht Treaty, even if Britain were to end up in the second tier of a two-tier Community.

Many observers argued that Britain had bizarrely painted itself into a corner with its anti-German stance, but that the Germans had also exhibited a lack of sensitivity regarding Major's domestic difficulties. New bridges needed to be built. Yet even if the relationship between Britain and Germany has become more problematic, there remains the clear political will to ensure that it should be a beneficial one. Not least because of the necessities of working together within the European Community, it could, by 1992, no longer be denied that out of competition, rivalry, and war, a pragmatic partnership had been fashioned.[62]

Notes

1. Paul M. Kennedy, *The Rise of Anglo-German Antagonism, 1860-1914* (London/Boston: Allen & Unwin, 1980).

2. Wolfgang J. Mommsen, *Two Centuries of Anglo-German Relations: A Reappraisal* (London: German Historical Institute, 1984).

3. Mommsen, *Two Centuries of Anglo-German Relations*.

4. Mommsen, *Two Centuries of Anglo-German Relations*, p. 11.

5. Mommsen, *Two Centuries of Anglo-German Relations*, p. 16.

6. Anneliese Poppinga, *Konrad Adenauer: eine Chronik* (Bergisch-Gladbach: Luebbe, 1987), pp. 68-69. See also Hans-Peter Schwarz, *Adenauer: der Aufstieg* (Stuttgart: Deutsche Verlags-Anstalt, 1986).

7. See Werner Sombart, *Händler und Helden: Patriotische Besinnungen* (Munich/Leipzig: Duncker & Humblot, 1915).

8. Alan Bullock, *Hitler: eine Studie über Tyrannei* (Düsseldorf: Droste, 1960), p. 596ff.

9. David Calleo, *Legende und Wirklichkeit der Deutschen Gefahr* (Bonn: Keil Verlag, 1980), and Karl Kaiser and Roger Morgan, eds., *Britain and West Germany: Changing Societies and the Future of Foreign Policy* (London: Oxford University Press for the Royal Institute of International Affairs, 1971).

10. Angelika Volle, *Deutsch-britische Beziehungen. Eine Untersuchung des bilateralen Verhältnisses auf der staatlichen und nichtstaatlichen Ebene seit dem Zweiten Weltkrieg* (Doctoral dissertation at the University of Bonn, West Germany, 1976), and Alfred Grosser, *Germany in Our Time* (New York: Praeger, 1971).

11. For a different view, see Lothar Kettenacker, *Krieg zur Friedenssicherung: die Deutschlandplanung der britischen Regierung während des Zweiten Weltkrieges* (Göttingen: Vandenhoeck & Ruprecht, 1989).

12. Anthony Glees, *Exile Politics During the Second World War: the German Social Democrats in Britain* (Oxford: Clarendon Press, 1982), pp. 145-65; Anthony Glees, *The Secrets of the Service: British Intelligence and Communist Subversion, 1939-51* (London: Cape, 1987), pp. 25-62.

13. Dennis L. Bark and David R. Gress, *A History of West Germany*, 2 volumes (Oxford/New York: Basil Blackwell, 1989); Winfried Becker, ed., *Die Kapitulation von 1945 und der Neubeginn in Deutschland* (Cologne: Böhlau, 1987).

14. Henry Ashby Turner, *The Two Germanies since 1945* (New Haven: Yale University Press, 1987), p. 16.

15. Kettenacker, *Krieg zur Friedenssicherung*.

16. Anne Deighton, *The Impossible Peace* (Oxford: Clarendon, 1990).

17. M. Pelly and G. Bennett, *Foreign and Commonwealth Office (FCO) Historical Branch Occasional Papers* (London), no. 3, November 1989.

18. Hilary Gaskin, *Eyewitness at Nuremberg* (London: Arms and Armour, 1990).

19. Tom Bower, *Blind Eye to Murder* (London: André Deutsch, 1981); Anthony Glees, "The Making of British Policy on War Crimes: History as Politics in the UK," *Contemporary European History*, vol. I, no. 2, 1992, pp. 171-97.

20. Turner, *The Two Germanies since 1945*, p. 12.

21. Ian D. Turner, ed., *Reconstruction in post-war Germany* (Oxford/New York: Berg Publishers & St. Martin's Press, 1989).

22. Pelly and Bennett, *FCO Historical Branch Occasional Papers*, no. 3, November 1989.

23. Pelly and Bennett, *FCO Historical Branch Occasional Papers*, no. 3, November 1989.

24. Grosser, *Germany in Our Time*, p. 111.

25. David Childs, *East Germany* (London: Benn, 1969).

26. Ann and John Tusa, *The Berlin Blockade* (London: Hodder & Stoughton, 1988); Wolfgang Krieger, *General Lucius L. Clay und die amerikanische Deutschlandpolitik, 1945-49* (Stuttgart: Klett-Cotta, 1987).

27. Pelly and Bennett, *FCO Historical Branch Occasional Papers*, no. 3, November 1989.

28. See Schwarz, *Adenauer: Der Aufstieg* and Hans-Peter Schwarz, *Adenauer: Der Staatsmann, 1952-1967* (Stuttgart: Deutsche Verlags-Anstalt, 1991).

29. Schwarz, *Adenauer: Der Aufstieg*, p. 469.

30. Schwarz, *Adenauer: Der Aufstieg*, pp. 469-70.

31. Becker, ed., *Die Kapitulation von 1945*, p. 100.

32. Pelly and Bennett, *FCO Historical Branch Occasional Papers*, no. 3, November 1989.

33. See Glees, *Exile Politics During the Second World War*.

34. Barbara Marshall, *The Origins of Post-War German Politics* (London/New York: Croom Helm, 1988).

35. Ulrich Reusch, *Deutsches Berufsbeamtentum und Britische Besatzung* (Stuttgart: Klett-Cotta, 1985).

36. Anthony Glees, "Churchill's Last Gambit," *Encounter*, vol. LXIV, no. 4, April 1985, pp. 27-35.

37. Glees, "Churchill's Last Gambit," pp. 27-35.

38. Poppinga, *Adenauer*, p. 138.

39. Turner, *The Two Germanies since 1945*, p. 148.

40. Willy Brandt, *Erinnerungen* (Frankfurt: Propyläen, 1989).

41. Willy Brandt, *People and Politics* (London: Collins, 1978).

42. Brandt, *People and Politics*, p. 247.

43. Terence Prittie, *Willy Brandt* (London: Weidenfeld & Nicolson, 1974), pp. 199, 208.

44. Prittie, *Willy Brandt*, p. 242.

45. Brandt, *People and Politics*, p. 332.

46. The text of this letter has been reprinted in many sources. See, for example, *Ratifizieren oder nicht? Die großen Reden der Debatte über die Ostverträge im Bundestag 23.-25. Februar 1972* (Hamburg: Hoffmann und Campe Verlag, 1972), p. 11 (version of the letter given to the Soviet Union); *Dokumentation zu den Innerdeutschen Beziehungen. Abmachungen und Erklärungen* (Bonn: Presse- und Informationsamt der Bundesregierung, 1989), p. 26 (version of the letter given to the GDR).

47. Brandt, *People and Politics*, p. 396.

48. Brandt, *People and Politics*, p. 397.

49. Turner, *The Two Germanies since 1945*, p. 184ff.

50. Michael Stürmer, "Deutschlandpolitik, Ostpolitik and the Western Alliance," in Kenneth Dyson, ed., *European Detente* (London: F. Pinter, 1986), pp. 135-36, 151.

51. See Roger Morgan, "The British View," in Edwina Moreton, ed., *Germany Between East and West* (Cambridge/London: Cambridge University Press & the Royal Institute of International Affairs, 1987). For an earlier assessment of Anglo-German relations, see Winfried Böttcher, *Deutschland aus britischer Sicht, 1960-72* (Wiesbaden: Humanitas Verlag, 1972).

52. Ralph Uhlig, *Die Deutsch-Englische Gesellschaft* (Göttingen: Vandenhoeck & Ruprecht, 1986).

53. Sir C. Mallaby, "Die deutsche Frage aus internationaler Sicht: der britische Standpunkt" (Bonn: Forschungsinstitut der Friedrich-Ebert-Stiftung, 1989).

54. See *Zurück zu Deutschland*, edited by the *Rheinische Merkur* (Bonn: Bouvier, 1990).

55. See, for example, David Marsh, *The Germans: Rich, Bothered and Divided* (London: Century, 1989); John Ardagh, *Germany and the Germans* (New York: Harper & Row, 1987).

56. *The Sunday Times*, February 25, 1990.

57. *The Sunday Times*, February 25, 1990.

58. *The Times*, July 17, 1990.

59. *The Independent*, July 17, 1990.

60. Anthony Glees, "Portraying West Germany to the British Public: British high policy towards Germany on the eve of unification," Brunel University, Department of Government Working Paper no. 11, 1990.

61. *The Spectator*, July 14, 1990, pp. 8-10.

62. In spite of the new partnership, the weight of history and its traumas continues to be an occasional factor of considerable significance in Anglo-German relations, as evidenced by the uproar over the dedication in Britain in the spring of 1992 of a statue honoring Sir Arthur Harris, the chief of Britain's bomber command during World War II, and the subsequent sensitivity and symbolism of the visit to Dresden by Queen Elizabeth II in October 1992.

3

The Dutch and the Germans:
Beyond Traumas and Trade

Dirk Verheyen

In late 1987, West German Chancellor Helmut Kohl made a diplomatic visit to the Netherlands. Ostensibly not an earth-shaking event. Yet, as *The Economist* reported at the time, Kohl's visit marked "only the third time in a quarter of a century that a West German chancellor had made a formal trip to next-door Holland." Rational explanations by officials for this "dearth of top-level meetings between Holland and West Germany" notwithstanding, the British magazine quite correctly noted that "[t]he real reasons for the economy of contact have more to do with emotion and history. The Dutch have a harder time forgetting the second world war than most Europeans because they live squarely in Germany's cultural, political and economic shadow."[1]

In just a few words, *The Economist* managed to give expression to much of what is often referred to as the "German factor"[2] in Dutch foreign policy. Relations between the Dutch and the Germans are deeply ambivalent, and not just as a result of the trauma of wartime occupation. For reasons of political culture, economic sensitivity and vulnerability, profoundly unequal military capability, historical identity, and psychocultural orientation, relations between these two countries have always been marked by problems, mixed feelings, and burdens.[3]

In the following pages, several major dimensions of Dutch-German relations will be explored. First, we shall examine some selected features of the pre-1945 period. In doing so, we will note the significance of various themes and facets that have continued to play a significant role in the years since 1945, and that can be expected to have continued relevance in the future. Second, we take a

closer look at the first decade after the war, when Dutch-German relations had
to be conducted in a context of rapidly changing international conditions,
particularly the collapse of the wartime Grand Alliance and the onset of the
East-West Cold War with the integration of a German state into each "camp."
Third, we analyze the place of West Germany in postwar Dutch security policy.
Fourth, we focus on the profound importance of Germany for the modern Dutch
economy. And fifth, we examine official and public Dutch attitudes with respect
to German reunification and the outlook for the future.

The Legacy of the Past

In 1989, Dutch historian Maarten C. Brands explored some of the develop-
mental contrasts between Germany and the Netherlands and suggested that

> [s]ince at least as far back as the 17th century, Dutch history has almost been the
> opposite of German history. The year 1648 encapsulates this contrast. For the
> Germans it was a year in which a catastrophic war was ended by a humiliating peace.
> For the Netherlands the peace of Westphalia was the conclusion of a long war of
> liberation in which the small Dutch republic had gained its freedom from Spanish
> centralism. The Dutch territories were no longer part of the Holy Roman Empire.
> As later German historians have put it: the Netherlands withdrew from that very
> creative *compositio oppositorum* that was to become the mighty heart of Europe, the
> German *Reich*. With the Danes and the Swiss, the Dutch were doomed to
> marginality and impotent neutrality.[4]

Consequently, Brands notes that "the main difference between the German
and the Dutch lines of development is to be found in the field of political
culture." Unlike Germany, with its strong feudal legacy, its "Reich tradition,"
its "continental expansion" tied to an "Eastward orientation," its unsuccessful
attempt at revolution, and its heritage of *Realpolitik* and *Machtpolitik*, "from the
outset the Netherlands was a bourgeois republic, with strong minorities and a
weak central government." In the course of the 19th century, the Netherlands
"made a successful transition to liberalism" and developed a foreign policy
characterized by a maritime orientation, colonialist prowess, and moralistic
inclinations that were not atypical for a small European power animated by a
well-developed Calvinist ethos.[5] Brands adds that, in contrast to Germany, the
Netherlands "experienced a very long peaceful 19th century which lasted till
May 10, 1940."[6]

As noted, Dutch foreign policy historically contains a markedly maritime,
non-continental political and psychological orientation. Until the 1860s, German
developments could be easily ignored, since the disunited individual German
states could hardly be seen as an explicit military threat. However, the
emergence of Bismarck's Prussian-dominated *Reich* transformed Holland's

security environment. The rise of this new European power immediately to the east necessitated inescapable adjustment. Many facets of the "German factor" in Dutch foreign policy have their origin in this transformed set of geopolitical circumstances.[7]

It is important to note, however, that some of the political and psychological aspects of Dutch-German relations predate the rise of the Second Reich, as the statements by Brands suggest. According to Friso Wielenga, the decline of the Dutch Republic at the end of the 18th century, followed in the 19th century by the Belgian secession from the Dutch kingdom (1830) and domestic constitutional difficulties, amounted to a serious "national identity crisis" in the Netherlands by the mid-1800s. At the same time, the Germans' Romanticized sense of national superiority began to blossom, leading to some German suggestions that Holland "return" to the old Germanic Reich. Rather condescending German attitudes toward what Goethe had called the *Wassermänner* ("water-men") in little Holland, this stingy, bourgeois people with their "tulip-fields, little garden houses, wooden shoes, cheese, butter, and porcelain," became quite noticeable.[8]

Many Germans were inclined to see the Dutch as not-so-distant relatives, particularly because of the closeness of Dutch and German as languages. In fact, it has not been uncommon for some in Germany to consider Dutch a "*plattdeutsch*" dialect rather than a completely separate language. In addition, Holland's image among the Germans (and elsewhere in the world) has been intricately connected to its small size and hence its presumably limited cultural and political significance. Compared with the Poles and the French, for example, the Dutch have in many ways simply not been an important neighbor for the Germans. At the same time, however, it is appropriate to note here that all Dutch monarchs in the 20th century have (had) German husbands, a fact that is indicative of the close yet sensitive relationship between the two nations.

Over time, positive and negative elements came to characterize much of the German image of the Netherlands. The Dutch have generally been seen as hospitable, (too) tolerant, egalitarian, Calvinistically stingy and narrow-minded, unromantic, unnecessarily self-critical, often overly moralistic, commercialist, thoroughly bourgeois, and usually pacifistic.[9]

The fundamental Dutch ambivalence vis-à-vis Germany acquired very definite contours after the 1860s, when the new German Reich had arisen on the European diplomatic scene.[10] There was a clear Dutch liberal-bourgeois distaste for the way in which German unity was "imposed" from above by feudal, expansionist Prussia, although some have suggested that there was more fascination with German political institutions and ideas in the Netherlands during the 19th century than is often admitted.[11] In addition, as Wielenga points out, the danger of getting geopolitically caught in the Franco-Prussian rivalry generated an increased sense of vulnerability. The result was a renewed emphasis on neutrality and passivity in Dutch diplomacy. A continued preoccupation with maritime-commercial and colonial interests reinforced a fundamentally non-continental Dutch orientation in foreign affairs.

As German industrialization proceeded, Dutch-German economic interaction intensified. The German Reich became a crucial *Hinterland* for Holland's export-oriented economy. Thus, Wielenga reports that on the eve of World War I 48 percent of Dutch exports went to Germany, while more than 28 percent of Dutch imports originated in Germany. Cultural and scientific links also expanded.[12] As we shall see, Holland's economic dependence on Germany has remained fundamental ever since.

The increased German-British rivalry that preceded the outbreak of World War I again caused the Netherlands to re-emphasize its neutralist orientation in foreign policy. An orientation that entailed an unmistakable "moral arrogance," tied as it was to a Dutch inclination to claim a superior diplomatic vocation as model of political and legal rectitude in a jungle of international power politics.[13] Since it was the joint interest of the warring Great Powers to respect this Dutch neutrality (even if not its concomitant moralistic pretentions), Holland escaped the carnage of the war.[14] Dutch relations with the subsequent Weimar Republic were largely uneventful. Holland's financial assistance to the fledgling German democracy was by no means negligent, however, and as the 1920s progressed a resurgent Germany could resume its role as a vital economic partner.[15]

The consolidation of Nazi rule after 1933 became an obvious source of political, military, and economic concern, although Dutch governments generally went out of their way to adjust to the new circumstances.[16] The Third Reich's predilection for economic autarky, plus its increased economic ties with Italy and southeastern Europe, generated clear limitations on Holland's ability to maintain (let alone expand) its trade with its primary export-market. Agricultural exports especially declined. Politically, special efforts were made to avoid unnecessary friction with the short-tempered Hitler regime, largely to safeguard whatever beneficial economic relations remained. In addition, a policy of quiet passivity was expected to enhance Holland's security amid the mounting tensions of the late 1930s. If war came, neutrality might thus yet again enable the Dutch to remain aloof and survive unscathed.

Yet the emergence of pro-Nazi Fascist movements in Holland (especially the NSB) complicated such a posture of intentional political aloofness. Prewar Dutch government "cooperation" with the Nazi regime in the apprehension and extradition of left-wing refugees from the Third Reich, as well as government concern about potentially undesirable consequences of anti-German reporting in the Dutch press, provide further evidence that a policy of strict aloofness became increasingly illusionary. In addition, the articulation of unmistakable anti-Nazi sentiment by various sectors and segments of Dutch society, such as the Social Democratic Labor Party (SDAP) and a number of labor unions, suggest that the notion of aloofness did not preclude active concern and wariness. However, Holland's options remained limited, especially since potential allies like Britain and France were (also) dedicated to a policy of appeasement. When war came to Holland, in May 1940, all illusions of neutrality and aloofness in world affairs would be forever shattered.[17]

After War and Occupation:
Neither Revenge nor Reconciliation?

According to Brands, Holland's "democratic tradition" formed the "basis of a strong sense of autonomy and of being different from neighbouring countries." In his opinion, "[t]his partly explains the trauma of 1940, when that immunity from history suddenly ended. Unlike Belgium, the Netherlands had not experienced the violation of its territorial integrity in its recent history." Other aspects of the war experience were highly traumatic as well. "[T]he Netherlands was treated more severely than its [western] neighbours in many respects: it was ruled by the SS instead of the *Wehrmacht*, a higher percentage of Jews were deported, Rotterdam became a symbol of massive destruction in Europe and so on. Moreover, for most of the country the war or occupation lasted longer than it did in Belgium and France." The psychological impact of the war experience turns out to have been so severe that "for many the war is still a yardstick of good and evil in present-day Dutch society."[18]

As Brands, Wielenga, and others have pointed out, Dutch governments faced a fundamental dilemma in the first 5 to 10 years after the end of the war.[19] On the one hand, the war experience had left behind major traumas, and the desire to punish the Germans and exact heavy reparations, possibly including annexations of German territory, was correspondingly strong. On the other hand, the inescapable reality of Dutch economic dependence on German economic recovery required that a policy of punishment be strictly limited. This need for German recovery was soon enhanced by the onset of the Cold War between the West and the Soviet Union, since it heightened concern that a prostrate Germany constituted a dangerous power vacuum in the heart of Europe, open to Soviet expansionist adventures. During these initial postwar years, the basis was laid for Dutch-German relations for the next four decades.

Despite an obvious Dutch desire to play a role in the shaping of Germany's future, actual Dutch involvement would turn out to be strictly limited, however, since the Germans' fate was placed primarily in the hands of the victorious Great Powers with occupation rights, namely the U.S., Great Britain, the Soviet Union, and France. It was they who would decide on such issues as reparations, territorial annexations or corrections, and general economic recovery policy. Like the other smaller European states, the Netherlands could only affect the course of events in a marginal way, and largely remained a diplomatic spectator as Germany's Cold War division into two competitive republics unfolded.   Initial Dutch claims for reparations and territorial compensation would be scaled down with the passing of time, due to both Great Power resistance (especially at the 1948 London Six Power Conference) and a growing desire to give priority to German economic recovery.[20]

In his study of these early postwar years, Wielenga notes that Dutch governments faced the difficult task of effecting the necessary diplomatic and political normalization with the new Federal Republic, while at the same time maintaining a focus on a list of unresolved issues stemming from the war period.[21]   In addition, public opinion could not be expected to adjust overnight to the need to consider the Germans allies in the growing EastWest confrontation, although it is rather remarkable that the percentage of Dutch people who had a "friendly" view of the Germans went from 29 percent in 1947 to 54 percent in 1954.[22]   In view of the war's traumas, how "normal" could any normalization with the FRG really be?

In addition to strengthening the West German economy, the need to create adequate Western European security structures also came more clearly to the fore by 1948-49.[23]   The tradition of neutrality and aloofness was clearly abandoned by Dutch policy-makers, but the strong desire to ensure full British and American participation in any future European security arrangement was striking evidence of Holland's continued maritime, Atlanticist orientation. Hence the Dutch dislike of an EDC that might have excluded the UK and the U.S.   Furthermore, the Dutch government sought to enlarge its international diplomatic clout in the formation of the West European Union (1948) and the North Atlantic Treaty Organization (1949) by coordinating its policy more closely with Belgium and Luxembourg in the newly created Benelux.

In the wake of the outbreak of the Korean War in 1950, the likelihood of West German rearmament appeared explicitly on the international agenda.   As was true of its other alliance partners, a reluctant Holland consented to such rearmament in the context of NATO in order to strengthen the Western defensive bulwark vis-a-vis the USSR while maintaining strict controls over Germany's independent military potential.   As Wielenga puts it, it was a matter of "security *with* and *against* Germany."[24]   In order to turn the FRG into a reliable ally, the Dutch government favored as sympathetic a treatment of West Germany as possible, focused on "positive" integration of the West Germans into the Western community rather than a merely "negative" integration based on a crass calculation of Western manpower needs in a military confrontation with the East.[25]

The idea of "positive" integration was further promoted by Dutch and other allied fears of a potential "Rapallo II," in view of the fact that Soviet control over the GDR held the major key to any German reunification. A dissatisfied and unfairly treated West Germany might be attracted by Soviet suggestions for a reunited, neutralized German nation. As a result, the Western allies supported the West German claim of *Alleinvertretung* (sole representation) and refused to recognize the East German republic. Reunification was not considered likely, but support for the West German government's notion that Western integration linked to a policy of strength would ultimately bring it about was seen as the best way to ensure the FRG's diplomatic reliability. Yet Dutch worries about the potentially destabilizing West German desire for reunification would continue.

Wielenga cites some public opinion data from those years to illustrate the fact that for most Dutch people the FRG really was "a partner of necessity."[26] In November 1950, 31 percent of the population opposed West German participation in a European army, while 49 percent supported the idea. In August 1951, 49 percent supported West German membership in NATO, 14 percent opposed the proposal, but a rather high 37 percent claimed to have "no opinion" on the issue. He suggests that this relatively high indecisiveness was indicative of the unease and wariness with which much of the Dutch population reacted to the notion of German rearmament in a context of Cold War crisis. A variety of groups, organizations, and movements in Dutch society actively opposed the resurgence of German military might under any circumstances, but their efforts could not prevent the occurrence of what was more and more seen as inevitable.

The fundamental importance of Germany to the Dutch economy has already been noted at various points. It became clear very quickly after 1945 that German recovery would be vital for Holland's economic resurgence.[27] Once again, Wielenga shows the Dutch public's keen awareness of this inescapable Dutch national interest. For example, a survey conducted in 1947 found that a lopsided 77 percent of the public favored renewed trade and other economic cooperation with the Germans, while a mere 11 percent was opposed and 12 percent had no opinion. In the very same survey, however, only 29 percent professed a "friendly" attitude towards the Germans, while 53 percent harbored "unfriendly" sentiments. Even among those who had "unfriendly" feelings, a clear 66 percent still favored renewed Dutch-German economic interaction.[28] A more obvious mixture of economic pragmatism and psychological traumatization would hardly be possible to find.

Acting upon this explicit Dutch economic self-interest, the government of the Netherlands strongly favored German recovery in the larger context of the Marshall Plan in 1947 and beyond. As a result, Dutch-West German economic interaction intensified rapidly after the conclusion of trade agreements in 1949 and 1950, and earlier concerns in some Dutch circles about possibly uncontrollable German economic power largely vanished. These developments were further enhanced by the settlement of a number of outstanding Dutch-German questions in the West's *Generalvertrag* (general treaty) with the FRG in 1952. But while economic "normalization" proceeded rather rapidly, the opinion data cited above suggests that other aspects of the Dutch-German relationship could hardly be considered "normal" yet.[29]

Wielenga points out that West German political, military, and economic integration into the Western "camp" after 1949 was accompanied by persistent allied concerns about *internal* West German political and ideological developments.[30]   For the Netherlands and the other neighbors of Germany, the so-called "German Question" was not just a matter of German power and its potential abuse by a revisionist German government.   The concern about "power" was inevitably connected with sensitivity regarding Germany's domestic political course, particularly a potential neo-Nazi revival.   Would the Bonn republic turn out to be another Weimar Republic, and what ought to be done to prevent this from happening?   As the years passed, West German democratic stability and predictability became key Dutch concerns.   Wielenga describes the general Dutch attitude as one of distrust and watchfulness.[31]

Despite the solidification of the FRG's liberal-democracy, these concerns have persisted in various guises,[32] and have resurfaced in the context of German unification and its possible politico-cultural consequences.   Particular sensitivity has been shown toward any manifestation of renewed German nationalism.   Dutch perceptions of domestic German political developments continue to be influenced by the kinds of stereotypical images of the Germans that many in Holland have held since at least the late 19th century.

It is on this more psychological level of Dutch-German relations that Wielenga notes "a gradual relaxation" by the mid-1950s.[33]   He argues that Dutch perceptions of West Germany's realities became more "nuanced," although stereotypical elements persisted.   An increased openness in Dutch-German contacts became noticeable, for example reflected in patterns of tourism.   A variety of Dutch organizations, including the churches, endeavored to promote reconciliation between the two nations, while some of them also added German "re-education" to their activities.   The latter element was of course a clear outgrowth of the Calvinist, moralist bent in the Dutch "character."   Altogether, the psychological relationship would remain burdened for some time to come, and "for many the need to accept the previous enemy as a true partner was too trying."[34]   The road from enmity to alliance was difficult indeed.   And the fact that the FRG faced many greater challenges in the years after 1949 than the relationship with little Holland only enhanced West Germany's inability to come to grips fully with the legacy of wartime traumas that continued to haunt the Dutch.[35]

By the mid-1950s, a number of issues remained to be settled between the Dutch and West German governments, including some border disputes (especially in the northeast), financial claims dating from the war years, and the status of German war criminals in Dutch jails.[36]   The Dutch government sought to gain maximum West German concessions, whereby frequent (public) reminders of German guilt were employed, but in view of Holland's growing economic and political inferiority to a resurgent Federal Republic the Dutch negotiating position was subjected to unmistakable erosion as the years passed.

The West German government for its part resisted what it saw as unacceptable concessions, and refused to accept the idea that all issues could be tied to a question of German guilt. It was not until 1960 that many of these issues were finally settled in a Dutch-West German *Ausgleichsvertrag* (treaty of settlement). In doing so, Holland turned out to be the last of Germany's small Western neighbors to conclude such a final settlement with the former enemy, following Denmark (1955), Belgium (1956), and Luxembourg (1959). And it would take about three years until the Dutch parliament finally ratified the treaty. But some of the border questions remain unresolved, and the problem of German war criminals in Dutch jails would persist into the 1980s. This latter issue would also serve as a periodic reminder that the psychological climate between the Dutch and the Germans continued to be burdened by the traumas of war and occupation, despite additional improvements in the course of the 1960s and especially during the Brandt/Heinemann years.[37]

A Sensitive Security Relationship

The foregoing discussion makes clear that issues of security and economics form the two areas of principal Dutch sensitivity, if not vulnerability, in the Dutch-German relationship, both today and in the past. In the postwar setting of East-West Cold War, West Germany's position and role in the Western alliance became a central concern for the Dutch and for all others in Europe.[38] With direct military confrontation between Germany and Holland now highly improbable, each country participated in NATO on the basis of a broadly shared security interest vis-a-vis the Warsaw Pact, although the FRG's special concern with the GDR and the possibility of reunification always implied at least a partial divergence of outlook and induced a permament wariness in Holland (and other Western countries) about the solidity of the FRG's political and ideological commitment to the Western "camp."

In view of Germany's pivotal Central-European location and its political and military weight, it is fair to say that the German-Dutch security relationship is characterized by inescapable Dutch dependence on German policy developments. One area of significant German security dependence on the Dutch involves the latter's strategic importance as maritime gateway to the German hinterland, especially focused on Rotterdam and the Rhine.[39]

Broadly speaking, the Dutch and the West Germans have evinced similarly ambivalent reactions over the years to NATO's defensive strategies.[40] While the governments of both states fully supported NATO's flexible response doctrine and its forward-defense planning, Holland and West Germany frequently joined other European NATO members during the Cold War years in questioning the credibility of the American extended nuclear deterrent. In view of the Warsaw Pact's conventional superiority, both countries' govern-

ments tended to place greater emphasis on deterrence and consequently on a
low nuclear threshold to enhance that deterrence, unlike the American
preference for a higher nuclear threshold tied to a greater reliance on conventional defensive efforts. To the Dutch and the West Germans, the American
approach might (unintentionally) lead to a devastating conventional and/or
limited nuclear war in Europe. In addition, high levels of public spending for
the maintenance of generous Welfare State programs in Holland and the FRG
would tend to preclude even the fiscal and political feasibility of greater
conventional defense expenditures: hence a heavy reliance on a cheaper nuclear
deterrent strategy. Yet, unlike the French, for example, the Dutch and the West
Germans, along with the Belgians, the British, and others, have always stressed
the importance of the Atlantic link in their security policies, particularly the
involvement of the U.S. in European security affairs, despite frequent calls for
greater Western European security integration in the overall NATO context.

In addition, both the Netherlands and West Germany have been the scene of
extensive and often influential peace movements, with the Protestant churches
playing an especially prominent role in both cases.[41]   In both countries,
evidence of "neutralism" could be found during the Cold War years. In the case
of the FRG, such neutralism was generally connected with the notion of a
neutral, reunited Germany, while in Holland such sentiment was reminiscent of
older traditions of neutrality and aloofness in foreign policy, tied to an absolutist
Calvinist moralism.[42]   The activity of the peace movements was especially
strong (but unsuccessful) during the early 1980s when both governments decided
to implement NATO's double-track INF decision of 1979 and permit the
installation of American medium-range nuclear missiles on their nations' soil.

As was true for other Western European NATO members as well, Dutch
security interests were directly affected by the change in West German foreign
policy that resulted from the more active and "positive" *Ostpolitik* and
Deutschlandpolitik pursued by Brandt, Schmidt, and Kohl during the 1970s and
1980s.[43]   The new initiatives in the FRG's international behavior were, on a
broader level, reflective of West Germany's increased prominence and
independence as an international power. Such developments highlighted the
reality of Dutch security dependence and vulnerability, a reality that had been
obfuscated in earlier postwar years by the FRG's highly constrained room for
diplomatic maneuver. Insofar as West German policies did not undermine
NATO's cohesion and survival, they were fully supported by all Dutch
governments. The seemingly more stabilized inter-German *status quo* that
resulted from the *Deutschlandpolitik* between FRG and GDR, embedded in the
framework of the Conference of Security and Cooperation in Europe (CSCE),
was fully appreciated. Yet the Dutch government was caught as unprepared as
all other European governments for the sudden collapse of the GDR in 1989 and
the totally unexpected reappearance of the German reunification issue on the
international political agenda.

A Vital Economic Relationship

Aside from the crucial security relationship between the Netherlands and (West) Germany, the economic interaction between the two countries is of the utmost importance, particularly for a Dutch economy that is so heavily oriented toward exports and services. The influential 1982 Dutch report on Dutch-West German relations cited above placed particular emphasis on the importance of the economic sector, and noted that "if one ranks all bilateral trade relationships in the world in terms of volume, the Dutch-West German relationship places fourth on the list."[44] This is not just a postwar development, however. Even before World War II, Germany already was Holland's most important trading partner.[45] Exports to West Germany as a percentage of Dutch national income are now twice as high as was the case with exports to prewar Germany. A great deal of this change is the result of Holland's much greater export-orientation since 1945.[46]

The report noted that about one-third of Dutch exports of goods is destined for the Federal Republic, while these exports constitute 12 percent of West Germany's total imports.[47] However, only 10 percent of all West German exports go to Holland, but those exports make up 20 percent of Holland's total import picture. Of all Dutch exports of goods to fellow EC countries, some 57 percent consists of trade with the Federal Republic.[48]

Dutch exports to the FRG have been focused primarily on agricultural products and energy (especially natural gas), while Dutch imports from the Federal Republic consist especially of investment and consumer goods.[49] In fact, some 40 percent of Dutch agricultural exports have tended to go to the FRG.[50] The report warned that the rather one-sided nature of Dutch exports forms a built-in economic weakness for the Dutch economy. This point was re-emphasized by G. J. Koopman and C.W.A.M. van Paridon in 1989, when they suggested that "the product composition of Dutch exports is less and less compatible with the product composition of West German imports."[51] Trade between the Netherlands and West Germany has been concentrated particularly on the areas of North Rhine-Westphalia, with about 50 percent of Dutch exports going to this region in 1986, and Lower Saxony, which received about 35.5 percent of Dutch exports in 1986.[52] This again is a potential source of weakness, since West Germany's economy has shifted its relative weight in a southward direction, where Dutch trade activity is much less well-developed, amounting to only 14.6 percent of Dutch exports in 1986.[53] The 1982 report noted that these and other developments have led to a loss of market share in West Germany for Dutch exporters.[54] In addition, the unification of FRG and GDR can be expected to occasion a relative eastward shift in German economic activity, again in a direction that is not particularly favorable for the Dutch economy.[55]

Dutch-West German relations have also been especially crucial in the service sector. A full one-third of Dutch exports of services is focused on the FRG. Of all goods that are loaded in Holland for export or transit, one-half has the FRG as destination, according to the 1982 report,[56] and two-thirds of this involves transit, especially sea-land transit with Rotterdam and surroundings as a most vital economic region, since 90 percent of Dutch transit activity is located in that area. Of goods transported from Holland into the FRG, 75 percent originates in the Rotterdam area, while 75 percent of West German transports into the Netherlands tend to come from the highly industrialized Ruhr area. A well-developed infrastructure of roads, railways, rivers, canals, and pipelines connects Holland and the western part of Germany. Furthermore, the 1982 report indicated that some 6.7 percent of West German investments abroad is made in the Netherlands, while the FRG has been the target of about 16.3 percent of Dutch foreign investments.[57] It is also worth noting that by the 1980s, about 43 percent of expenditures in Holland by foreign tourists were made by West Germans.[58]

An additional area of very close Dutch-West German interdependence is the monetary sector.[59] The Dutch guilder and the German mark have been very tightly linked, especially since 1979 within the European Monetary System, which in turn succeeded the so-called "snake" arrangement for the management of floating exchange rates that had been set up among EC countries in the wake of the collapse of the Bretton Woods system in the early 1970s. In this monetary relationship, the D-mark has clearly played a leadership role, with Dutch central bank policies, particularly in the area of interests rates and money supply, closely following the German *Bundesbank*. One consequence has been that the level of inflation in both countries has tended to be fairly similar, and due to conservative monetary policies generally equally low. The rate of unemployment has tended to be higher in Holland than in the (pre-unification) FRG, however. Both countries have relied heavily on "guest-workers" from southern Europe and North Africa during the decades of high growth, and both must now deal with anti-foreign sentiment in some quarters of their societies in a context of slower growth, higher unemployment levels, and general fiscal crisis of the post-industrial Welfare State.

In conclusion, it is fair to say that "the Federal Republic is Holland's engine. . . . Holland has become more and more dependent on the FRG. . . . Aside from the Federal Republic itself, no country has derived as much profit from West Germany's postwar *Wirtschaftswunder* as [Holland]."[60]

Dutch trade with the former German Democratic Republic was much more limited, amounting to only a few percentage points in the total Dutch economic picture.[61] The value of Dutch exports to the GDR increased from 289 million guilders in 1983 to 465 million guilders in 1987, while the value of Dutch imports from East Germany dropped rather significantly from 660 million guilders in 1983 to 400 million guilders in 1987, with various kinds of manufactures being the most important segment in the import picture. In 1988, the overall trade volume between the Netherlands and the GDR amounted to about 2.9 billion D-Mark, which was roughly comparable to the GDR's trade volume with countries like Yugoslavia, Cuba, or France.[62] Altogether, the balance of trade between Holland and the GDR moved clearly in the former's favor in the course of the 1980s. Prior to the 1970s, Dutch trade with the GDR was even more limited, which was of course partially due to an absence of official diplomatic relations in a context of Cold War.

A United Germany: Old and New Dutch Questions

The rapidity with which the unification of FRG and GDR suddenly appeared on the international agenda and was completed caught the Dutch as unprepared as all of Germany's other neighbors. The initial relative silence in Holland about the profound changes in its mighty neighbor to the east was quite revealing, signalling a mixture of unarticulated unease, a sense of uncontrollable inevitability, and quiet hopefulness. This rather passive Dutch reaction to some extent fits a larger pattern, however: despite its importance, both positive and negative, Germany does not appear to be much of an every-day concern in the Netherlands, except when certain events manage to trigger painful reminders rooted in wartime traumas and long-standing anti-German popular stereotypes. Such traumas and stereotypes also resurfaced prominently among certain segments of the Dutch population during the spectacular events of 1989-90.

In these final pages, an attempt will be made to sketch the Dutch reaction to German unification on two levels. On the one hand, the psychological level, where we encounter stereotypes, prejudices, fears, and traumas. On the other hand, the policy level, where certain political, military, and economic questions emerged that the Dutch government has had to respond to.

In February of 1990, a survey was conducted to register popular Dutch attitudes regarding German unification.[63] The FRG-GDR merger was supported by 52.4 percent of the sample, while 23.2 percent opposed unification and 24.4 percent was undecided or had no particular feelings on the subject. Some 10.2 percent professed to be "very strongly" in support of German unity, while about 8 percent considered itself "very strongly" opposed.

Political and generational contrasts in opinion were especially interesting. Supporters of the Dutch Christian Democratic Party favored unification by about 62 percent, while opponents of German unity could be found particularly among supporters of the Labor Party (26.6 percent) and the environmentally oriented Green Left coalition (26.1 percent). Among those who experienced the war as a child, moderate and fervent opponents of unification ranked at 27.1 percent and 15.3 percent, respectively. In the 65-and-older age group, 12.6 percent were moderately and 16.8 percent were strongly opposed. The pattern of opinion was also interesting among those between 18 and 24: just under 47 percent favored German unity, 30 percent had no particular opinion, and a rather high 23.2 percent opposed unification (compared with 13 percent opposition to unification among those between 25 and 44). Of those in the interview sample who opposed German unity, 35.7 percent related their opinion to the experience of war and German occupation, and 32.9 percent indicated that a united Germany would wield too much power in Europe. Also interesting was the fact that 48.5 percent of the sample felt that Holland's role in Europe would not be affected one way or the other by German unification, while 21.9 percent even felt that German unity might help enhance the Dutch position in Europe. Finally, the enduring traumas of the past were dramatically reflected in the fact that only 1.6 percent of those questioned believed that one should "forget" World War II because there now is a new generation alive in Germany.

Also noteworthy is the study *Niederländer über Deutsche*, which appeared in the spring of 1990, and which documents attitudes toward Germany and the Germans among the Dutch public. When asked to "describe" the Germans, 45 percent of those interviewed for this study responded with exclusively negative characteristics, while 17 percent provided a mixture of positive and negative characteristics. The Germans were described as "pushy" and "loud" (or "noisy"), arrogant and proud, disciplined and business-like, ambitious, domineering, materialistic, sober, and thorough.[64] The historian Wielenga sees in this Dutch "Germanophobia" a continuation of an already old tendency, going back to the days of Bismarck. After 1871, "the Netherlands became economically dependent on Germany and the German hinterland. The structurally low pain threshold that we have vis-a-vis the big neighbor already emerged in the [19th] century. For more than a century now we [Dutch] try to maintain our identity against [the Germans'] supremacy."[65] In popular Dutch culture and everyday life, for example in the context of the always sensitive games between the Dutch and German national soccer teams, it seems to be hardly ever unacceptable to express anti-German attitudes.

Recent research has shown, however, that anti-German sentiments in Holland are also surprisingly strong among many of the country's most prominent politicians. The kinds of sentiments expressed by British government minister Nicholas Ridley in the summer of 1990, leading to his resignation amid an uproar of controversy, are by no means absent in the Netherlands, even though they are rarely so explicitly articulated. According to Jan Hoedeman, "the five years of occupation [during World War II] have left deep marks on Dutch society. They have become part of the national consciousness."[66]

A survey conducted among members of parliament yielded some telling results. According to Hoedeman, "the most important conclusion that can be drawn [from the survey] is that a great majority of the polled MPs displays a sense of wariness regarding the current and future developments in the FRG and the GDR."[67] Among the highlights of the findings were the fact that 65 percent of the sample admitted to at least occasional "anti-German feelings," 68 percent asserted that the memory of World War II plays a role for them in the question of German unification, 90 percent of the polled MPs assumes that the reunited Germany will be economically expansionist, 63 percent expects a German political expansionism after unification, and no less than 36 percent would not preclude the possibility of renewed military expanionism by a united Germany. The continuing significance of World War II in Dutch political life is perhaps best expressed in the fact that 95 percent of those polled insisted that commemorations of the war should continue beyond the year 2000, 79 percent supported continued prosecution of those who might have committed war crimes, and 85 percent claimed that the World War II experience factors into their consideration of human rights issues.

As is true of the general Dutch public, the members of parliament also display attitudinal variation based on political party affiliation and generation. Members of the Labor (PvdA) and conservative Liberal (VVD) parties proved more likely to express anti-German sentiments than members of the Christian Democratic Party (CDA). Of the total sample, 77 percent expressed basic support for German unification, 12 percent had no particular opinion, and only 8 percent was against. These opponents of unification were primarily to be found among the members of the Labor, the Liberal, the left-liberal Democrats '66 (D66), and the ecologically oriented Green Left parties. Labor MPs were most likely to express worries about the potential revival of radical-nationalist movements in a united Germany, while Christian Democrats professed to be least concerned about such a development. Generational contrasts are also revealing. More than half of the MPs born after 1950 claimed to have "occasional" or "frequent" anti-German feelings. Of those MPs who were born before 1940 or during the war-years, about two-thirds admitted to "occasional" anti-German feelings. Most significantly and interestingly, a full three-quarters of the MPs born between 1945 and 1950 claimed to experience anti-German feelings. In addition, two-thirds of the opponents to German unification among the MPs were born after 1945, and more than three-quarters of the MPs born between 1945 and 1950 assumes that a reunited Germany will be politically expansionist.[68]

As far as the Dutch policy response to German unification is concerned, it is noteworthy that the initial response was characterized by considerable passivity. In the words of one journalist, the precipitous rush toward German unity had "hardly caused a ripple on the cosy Dutch pond."[69] Some responded with quiet wariness and a sense of fatalistic inevitability to the events, while others sought to identify likely sources of economic benefit for Holland in the emergence of a unified Germany. Some even suggested that such Dutch passivity reflects a realization of dependence on the powerful Germans, while still others added that the Netherlands is locked into such a maritime and Atlanticist diplomatic orientation that it has proved incapable of developing a more activist kind of continental *Ostpolitik* (independent of the German pattern) in response to the spectacular changes in Central and Eastern Europe.[70] Dutch Foreign Minister Hans van den Broek sought to justify such passivity by suggesting that "it is not the Dutch role to add yet another [blueprint] to the multitude of [existing] plans and ideas [for Europe]."[71]

More generally, the relative lack of active Dutch involvement in the process by which Europe was being transformed in 1989-90 is quite reminiscent of the early postwar years, when Dutch governments proved unable to affect the decisions that divided Germany and Europe into two Cold War "camps." In addition, recognition of Germany's economic importance to the Netherlands appears once again to outweigh reservations and concerns in the collective Dutch psyche. It all created the impression of a remarkable Dutch nostalgia for a supposedly obsolete tradition of aloofness in foreign policy.[72]

Behind this facade of passivity, however, some clear policy elements have been quite visible.[73] Two of the most important pillars in postwar Dutch foreign policy have been the Atlantic alliance and European integration, and it is in these contexts that the Dutch government has sought to respond to the unification of Germany and the demise of Europe's Cold War division. As far as the security status of the united Germany is concerned, the responses by the MPs in the survey discussed earlier provide a clear picture. While only 10 percent favored a neutral Germany, a large majority of 70 percent insisted that both FRG and GDR ought to be integrated into NATO, coupled with the demilitarization of East German territory.[74] In addition, the Dutch government has made it quite clear that the proper place for the united Germany will continue to be in a steadily integrating Europe, whereby the modalities of European Union ought to be managed in such a way that the status and rights of smaller countries like the Netherlands are adequately safeguarded. According to Foreign Minister van den Broek, the solid integration of Germany into both NATO and the EC would help prevent "the return of the German problem, that is, the political and psychological homelessness [of Germany]."[75] The bottom line, from the Dutch viewpoint, was that German unification was not just of concern to the Germans, but that all European nations ought to have a proper degree of input in the decision-making process.[76] Nevertheless, it is also obvious that Dutch input has been very strictly limited.

Due to Holland's great economic sensitivity vis-a-vis Germany, the economic implications of unification have received particular Dutch attention. For example, the Dutch government insisted that the FRG-GDR monetary union, which went into effect on July 1, 1990, be closely coordinated with other EC member-states, in order to avoid undesirable economic and monetary consequences (including further progress toward a full-fledged European Monetary Union).[77] One of the issues of debate in the Netherlands has been the extent to which Dutch interest rates should be set more independently of German policy decisions, unlike the current close association of German and Dutch interest rates based on a rather tight guilder-mark linkage.[78] The projected expense of German unification, and its resulting pressures on German interest rates, are clearly an area of Dutch policy concern. At the same time, the commercial possibilities inherent in the enlarged German market have been the subject of extensive discussion and analysis.[79]

A working-paper produced by the Dutch Central Planning Bureau (CPB) in February of 1990 sought to outline some of the economic consequences of German unification for the Netherlands. The report suggested that expanded pressures for consumption and investment in a resurgent eastern Germany would open up export possibilities for the Dutch economy, although high German interest rates would also affect the Netherlands.[80] Also noteworthy was the sudden East German interest in closer economic relations with Holland, apparently out of fear, according to a spokesperson at the Dutch Ministry of Economic Affairs, that "West Germany [would] roll over the GDR like a steamroller." He added that "the East Germans [wanted] to broaden their future economic base."[81]

Conclusion

The prospects for Dutch-German relations in the 1990s and beyond must inevitably be considered in a context shaped by (traumatic) historical memory, psychological sensitivity, and economic as well as geostrategic closeness. The traumas of history may weaken as the generations pass, yet they have been absorbed into the larger Dutch syndrome of uneasiness vis-à-vis the powerful neighbor that was examined above. As a result, their effect can be expected to linger for many years to come. Any Dutch-German friendship, if at all possible, will require careful nurturing and an honest mutual examination of a very difficult relationship.

However, Dutch feelings about Germany are more ambivalent than merely negative. This ambivalence was perhaps best captured by the title of a 1983 study of Dutch-West German relations between 1945 and 1981: *Wariness and Profit*.[82] We have amply noted Germany's vital economic significance to the Netherlands, and there is absolutely no reason to expect any major change in this regard. In fact, there are many in Holland who see great commercial possibilities as a result of the FRG-GDR merger.[83] Even before unification, Dutch exports to the FRG in 1990 had risen 8.6 percent in value compared with 1989, although subsequent statistics do suggest a less spectacular growth in Dutch-German economic interaction in the next few years. The only difficult item on the Dutch-German economic agenda might be the question of the Dutch guilder's close ties to a clearly more inflationary post-unification German mark. At this point, however, no decision has yet been made in Holland to "de-couple" the two currencies in any formal way. In addition, discussions on cross-border pollution (acid rain and the condition of the Rhine's water quality) can be expected to continue and perhaps intensify.

Finally, in the area of security, Germany and the Netherlands, along with the other members of NATO, will face the task of reaching out through an unraveled Iron Curtain in order to fashion a new security order for Europe and formulate a satisfactory policy response to the Soviet Union's imperial breakdown as well as Eastern Europe's socioeconomic and ethnopolitical upheaval.[84] In the process, maritime Holland will have to come to grips with a neighbor whose policies will more than at any time since 1945 be shaped by the logic of its continental, Central-European location. While history's traumas will linger, the hope is warranted that the very remembrance of the tragedies and calamities of this century will encourage the development of a new Europe, and a transformed Dutch-German relationship, in the next.

Notes

I wish to thank Erna Verheyen-Loeff, Charles Verheyen, Wim van Dijk, and Rosita de Vos for their valuable assistance in locating some of the source material cited in the notes.

1. "Goodbye, and keep in touch," *The Economist*, December 12, 1987, p. 54.

2. See Sam Rozemond, "Nederland en de Duitse factor," in S. Rozemond, ed., *Het woord is aan Nederland: thema's van buitenlands beleid in de jaren 1966-1983* (The Hague: Staatsuitgeverij, 1983); Friso Wielenga, *West-Duitsland: partner uit noodzaak. Nederland en de Bondsrepubliek 1949-1955* (Utrecht: Het Spectrum, 1989), p. 21ff.

3. A recent book that presents an excellent overview of Dutch-German relations, with particular attention to aspects of political culture, is Horst Lademacher's *Zwei ungleiche Nachbarn: Wege und Wandlungen der deutsch-niederländischen Beziehungen im 19. und 20. Jahrhundert* (Darmstadt: Wissenschaftliche Buchgesellschaft, 1990).

4. Brands, "The Federal Republic of Germany and the Netherlands: contrasts and complementarity," *Internationale Spectator*, vol. xliii, nr. 11, November 1989, p. 690.

5. Ever since, "peace, profits, and principles" have been central categories of thought in Dutch foreign policy. See J.J.C. Voorhoeve, *Peace, Profits and Principles: A Study of Dutch Foreign Policy* (The Hague/Boston/London: Martinus Nijhoff, 1979), especially chapter III. In 1830, Dutch prime-minister J. R. Thorbecke remarked that "[t]he Dutch polity, being itself free from lust for power, is the most impartial judge of other nations' lust for power." Quoted by J. C. Heldring in his "Between Dreams and Reality," in J. H. Leurdijk, ed., *The Foreign Policy of the Netherlands* (Alphen aan den Rijn, 1978), p. 310. See also Lademacher, *Zwei ungleiche Nachbarn*, chapters II and III.

6. Brands, "The Federal Republic of Germany and the Netherlands," p. 690. For an interesting discussion of Dutch-German differences, focused especially on elements of continuity rooted in factors of divergent political culture, see Hermann W. von der Dunk, "Holländer und Deutsche: Zwei politische Kulturen," *Beiträge zur Konfliktforschung*, nr. 2, 1986. The prewar legacy in the Dutch image of Germany is ably discussed by Horst Lademacher in his essay "Der ungleiche Nachbar," in Günter

Trautmann, ed., *Die hässlichen Deutschen?* (Darmstadt: Wissenschaftliche Buchgesellschaft, 1991).

7. Consequently, much in Dutch-German relations can be "understood" as more typical difficulties between a large and a small country. See Lademacher, "Der ungleiche Nachbar," esp. pp. 184-86, and in his book *Zwei ungleiche Nachbarn*, see chapter III.

8. Wielenga, *West-Duitsland: partner uit noodzaak*, p. 22ff. See also the discussion in Joachim F. E. Bläsing, *Niederländer und Deutsche über sich und den Nachbarn* (Bonn: Kulturabteilung der Königlichen Niederländischen Botschaft, n.d.); W. L. Brugsma, "Was ist ein typischer Deutscher?," in *Nachbarn. Der 10. Mai 1940 − 50 Jahre danach* (Bonn: Königliche Niederländische Botschaft, n.d.). On German stereotyping of the Dutch, see Lademacher, "Der ungleiche Nachbar," esp. pp. 187-88, and in his *Zwei ungleiche Nachbarn*, see chapter I.

9. An excellent discussion of Dutch-German mutual stereotyping can be found in Will van de Ven and Bart Vink, "Dominees en handelslieden," *Intermediair*, vol. 25, nr. 16, April 21, 1989, p. 27ff.

10. The following discussion is especially indebted to Wielenga, *West-Duitsland: partner uit noodzaak*, chapter 2, pp. 22-34. See also Lademacher, *Zwei ungleiche Nachbarn*, chapter III.

11. See H. A. van Wijnen, "Pro-Duits in Nederland," *NRC Handelsblad*, November 18, 1989.

12. Wielenga, *West-Duitsland: partner uit noodzaak*, p. 26.

13. Wielenga, *West-Duitsland: partner uit noodzaak*, p. 27. See also Hermann von der Dunk, *Die Niederlande im Kräftespiel zwischen Kaiserreich und Entente* (Wiesbaden: Franz Steiner Verlag, 1980).

14. On Dutch-German relations at the time of World War I, see Lademacher, *Zwei ungleiche Nachbarn*, chapter IV.

15. Wielenga, *West-Duitsland: partner uit noodzaak*, p. 28.

16. See the discussion on Dutch-German relations during the Nazi era in Wielenga, *West-Duitsland: partner uit noodzaak*, pp. 29-34.

17. On Dutch attitudes toward Nazism, German-Dutch relations during the interwar years, and the events leading up to World War II, see Lademacher, *Zwei ungleiche Nachbarn*, chapter V.

18. Brands, "The Federal Republic of Germany and the Netherlands," p. 691. The centrality of the war experience in the Dutch image of Germany and the Germans is emphasized by Lademacher in his essay "Der ungleiche Nachbar." See also the various essays in *Nachbarn. Der 10. Mai 1940 − 50 Jahre danach*, and Lademacher, *Zwei ungleiche Nachbarn*, pp. 177-78.

19. Brands, "The Federal Republic of Germany and the Netherlands," p. 691; Wielenga, *West-Duitsland: partner uit noodzaak*, chapter 3. See also Lademacher, *Zwei ungleiche Nachbarn*, p. 194ff. On the general topic of Dutch-German relations in the early postwar years, see also Horst Lademacher and Jac Bosmans, eds., *Tradition und Neugestaltung. Zu Fragen des Wiederaufbaus in Deutschland und den Niederlanden in der frühen Nachkriegszeit* (Münster: Regensberg Verlag, 1991). This book examines five key domestic policy themes in each country from a comparative perspective (the restoration of democracy, the reconstruction of the party systems, the return of market

economies, economic organization, and policies on youth), as well as some themes in the area of foreign policy.

20. Wielenga, *West-Duitsland: partner uit noodzaak*, pp. 34-42, 525-26. On the issue of possible Dutch annexations of German territory after 1945, see Herman A. Schaper, "'Wij willen zelfs niet Mönchen-Gladbach!'," *Internationale Spectator*, vol. xxxix, nr. 5, May 1985. On the issue of annexations and border corrections, see also Lademacher, *Zwei ungleiche Nachbarn*, p. 213ff.

21. Wielenga, *West-Duitsland: partner uit noodzaak*, pp. 69-70. See also the discussion in H.J.G. Beunders and H. H. Selier, *Argwaan en Profijt: Nederland en West-Duitsland 1945-1981* (Amsterdam: Historisch Seminarium van de Universiteit van Amsterdam; Amsterdamse Historische Reeks, nr. 6, 1983), chapter I.

22. Data cited by W. L. Brugsma in his Foreword to Wielenga, *West-Duitsland: partner uit noodzaak*, p. ix.

23. On the following, see especially Wielenga, *West-Duitsland: partner uit noodzaak*, chapter 4. See also the discussion by Albert E. Kersten, "In de ban van de bondgenoot," in David Barnouw, Madelon de Keizer, and Gerrold van der Stroom, eds., *1940-1945: Onverwerkt verleden?* (Utrecht: HES Uitgevers, 1985).

24. Wielenga, *West-Duitsland: partner uit noodzaak*, p. 185.

25. On Dutch policy regarding West Germany's integration into the Western security and economic communities, see Lademacher, *Zwei ungleiche Nachbarn*, p. 240ff.

26. Wielenga, *West-Duitsland: partner uit noodzaak*, pp. 191-92.

27. See Wielenga, *West-Duitsland: partner uit noodzaak*, chapter 5. See also Lademacher, *Zwei ungleiche Nachbarn*, p. 198ff.

28. Wielenga, *West-Duitsland: partner uit noodzaak*, p. 225.

29. Wielenga, *West-Duitsland: partner uit noodzaak*, pp. 271-72.

30. Wielenga, *West-Duitsland: partner uit noodzaak*, chapter 6. See also Brands, "The Federal Republic of Germany and the Netherlands," pp. 692-94.

31. Wielenga, *West-Duitsland: partner uit noodzaak*, p. 315.

32. See, for example, Jürgen C. Hess and Friso Wielenga, "Veertig jaar na dato: voltooide Nederlands-Duitse normalisering?," *Internationale Spectator*, vol. xxxix, nr. 11, November 1985, especially p. 692ff.

33. Wielenga, *West-Duitsland: partner uit noodzaak*, p. 363 and chapter 7 generally.

34. Wielenga, *West-Duitsland: partner uit noodzaak*, p. 367.

35. See the discussion in Hess and Wielenga, "Veertig jaar na dato: voltooide Nederlands-Duitse normalisering?"

36. Wielenga, *West-Duitsland: partner uit noodzaak*, chapter 8.

37. See the discussion in Beunders and Selier, *Argwaan en Profijt*, chapter II. Discussions on the evolving Dutch-German political and psychological climate in recent years can be found in Jürgen C. Hess, "Het Nederlandse Duitslandbeeld. Enkele actuele overwegingen," *Internationale Spectator*, vol. xxxiii, nr. 8, August 1979; Hess and Wielenga, "Veertig jaar na dato." The sometimes difficult relationship between the Dutch and West German Social Democratic parties is discussed in Harry van den Bergh, "De PvdA en de SPD," in Marnix Krop, ed., *Burengerucht: Opstellen over Duitsland* (Deventer: Kluwer, 1978); Hess, "Het Nederlandse Duitslandbeeld," pp. 467-69; H.J.G. Beunders, "De PVDA, de horzel van de SPD," in M. C. Brands, H.J.G. Beunders, and H. H. Selier, *Denkend aan Duitsland* (The Hague: Staatsuitgeverij, 1983;

Wetenschappelijke Raad voor het Regeringsbeleid, Voorstudies en achtergronden, nr. V36).

38. In connection with this brief discussion of the Dutch-German security relationship, see chapter 3 in the report entitled *Onder invloed van Duitsland* [Under the influence of Germany], produced for the Dutch government in 1982 (The Hague: Staatsuitgeverij) by the advisory Wetenschappelijke Raad voor het Regeringsbeleid [Scientific Council for Government Policy]. See also Beunders and Selier, *Argwaan en Profijt*, chapter IV.

39. *Onder invloed van Duitsland*, p. 100.

40. See the discussion in *Onder invloed van Duitsland*, p. 102ff.

41. *Onder invloed van Duitsland*, p. 108. See also Beunders and Selier, *Argwaan en Profijt*, chapter X; H. H. Selier, "De kerkelijke vredesbeweging in Nederland en de Bondsrepubliek," in Brands, Beunders, and Selier, *Denkend aan Duitsland*.

42. See J. A. Emerson Vermaat, "Neutralist tendencies in the Netherlands," *The World Today*, vol. 37, nr. 12, December 1981.

43. See *Onder invloed van Duitsland*, p. 109ff. See also Beunders and Selier, *Argwaan en Profijt*, chapter III.

44. *Onder invloed van Duitsland*, p. 91.

45. See, for example, the study by Joachim F. E. Bläsing, *Das goldene Delta und sein eisernes Hinterland 1815-1851. Von niederländisch-preussischen zu deutsch-niederländischen Wirtschaftsbeziehungen* (Leiden: H. E. Stenfert Kroese BV, 1973).

46. *Onder invloed van Duitsland*, p. 25.

47. *Onder invloed van Duitsland*, p. 91. See also G. J. Koopman and C.W.A.M. van Paridon, "De economische betrekkingen tussen Nederland en West-Duitsland," *Economisch Statistische Berichten*, vol. 74, nr. 3714, July 5, 1989, p. 645.

48. *Onder invloed van Duitsland*, p. 92.

49. *Onder invloed van Duitsland*, pp. 30-33.

50. *Onder invloed van Duitsland*, p. 51.

51. "De economische betrekkingen tussen Nederland en West-Duitsland," p. 646.

52. *Onder invloed van Duitsland*, p. 41ff.; Koopman and van Paridon, "De economische betrekkingen tussen Nederland en West-Duitsland," p. 646.

53. *Onder invloed van Duitsland*, p. 37; Koopman and van Paridon, "De economische betrekkingen tussen Nederland en West-Duitsland," p. 646.

54. *Onder invloed van Duitsland*, pp. 41, 47ff.

55. Nevertheless, figures for both 1989 and 1990 continued to show very significant levels of Dutch-German trade. After a few years of sluggishness, Dutch exports to the Federal Republic accelerated again in 1988, even leading to record-levels of trade in both 1989 and 1990. For further discussion, see "1988: Trendwende im deutsch-niederländischen Warenaustausch," *Handelspartner*, nr. 3, 1989; "1989: ein Rekordjahr für den deutsch-niederländischen Aussenhandel," *Handelspartner*, nr. 3, 1990; "Nederlandse export bereikt recordhoogte," *NRC Handelsblad* (Weekeditie voor het Buitenland), January 29, 1991; "Deutscher Importsog sorgt für gute niederländische Exportergebnisse," *Handelspartner*, nr. 3, 1991; *Export Magazine Special*: BRD, 1991, pp. 2-5.

56. *Onder invloed van Duitsland*, p. 93.

57. *Onder invloed van Duitsland*, p. 75. Recent data shows a basic continuation of this pattern, although it is still too early to calculate the long-range impact of German unification in this area. In 1989, the Dutch share of foreign investments in the FRG

stood at 13 percent (following the U.S. with 33 percent and Switzerland with 15 percent), while the West German share of foreign investments in the Netherlands was approximately 8 percent (which put the FRG in fourth place, after the U.S., Great Britain, and Switzerland). For further discussion, see "Über Handelsströme und Investitionsbäche," *Handelspartner*, nr. 3, 1991.

58. *Onder invloed van Duitsland*, p. 62.

59. *Onder invloed van Duitsland*, pp. 82-91.

60. Dirk-Jan van Baar, "Op de vleugels van de Bondsrepubliek," *Intermediair*, vol. 25, nr. 16, April 21, 1989, p. 41.

61. See the figures provided in *Export Magazine*, March 11, 1989, p. 32.

62. See *Handelspartner*, nr. 3, 1990, p. 36.

63. *NRC Handelsblad* (Weekeditie voor het Buitenland), February 27, 1990, p. 1.

64. See the discussion in Connie de Jonge, "Zij van hiernaast," *Elsevier*, May 5, 1990, pp. 82, 84.

65. Quoted in de Jonge, "Zij van hiernaast," p. 85.

66. Hoedeman, "Anti-Duitse gevoelens in de Tweede Kamer," *Elsevier*, April 7, 1990, p. 36.

67. "Anti-Duitse gevoelens in de Tweede Kamer," p. 37. The following summary of the survey among Dutch MP's is based on Hoedeman's article.

68. An interesting collection of editorial essays from Dutch newspapers on German unification and its (perceived) implications can be found in *Meningen over Duitse Eenheid* (Amsterdam: Uitgeverij NPA, 1990).

69. Huib Goudriaan, "Duitse eenheid maakt nog geen rimpeltje in Nederlandse vijver," *Trouw*, February 16, 1990.

70. See, for example, Jan Zielonka, "Nederland heeft behoefte aan eigen Ostpolitik," *De Volkskrant*, January 24, 1990; Wio Joustra, "Het dilemma van een Ostpolitik," *De Volkskrant*, March 17, 1990; J. M. Bik, "Tijd is rijp voor Hollandse oostpolitiek," *NRC Handelsblad*, February 21, 1990; W. H. Weenink, "Den Haag staat aan de zijlijn bij debat over toekomst van Europa," *NRC Handelsblad*, April 4, 1990; Detlev van Heest, "Rol Nederland in Europa taant," *Het Parool*, February 3, 1990.

71. Tweede Kamer, *Handelingen* [records of parliamentary debates], January 25, 1990, p. 32-1590.

72. See the interesting analysis in Henri Beunders, "Beter zedelijk dan machtig," *NRC Handelsblad* (Weekeditie voor het Buitenland), February 27, 1990, p. 7.

73. See H. van den Broek, "Nederlandse betrokkenheid bij het vormgeven van een nieuw Europa," *Internationale Spectator*, vol. xliv, nr. 8, August 1990; *Rijksbegroting 1991*, Hoofdstuk V: Buitenlandse Zaken (Tweede Kamer, vergaderjaar 1990-1991, 21800 hoofdstuk V, nr. 2, pp. 5-24).

74. Hoedeman, "Anti-Duitse gevoelens in de Tweede Kamer," p. 43.

75. Tweede Kamer, *Handelingen*, January 25, 1990, p. 32-1585.

76. See, for example, Herman Amelink, "Eén Duitsland is zaak van alle Europese naties," *NRC Handelsblad* (Weekeditie voor het Buitenland), February 20, 1990.

77. See the letter to parliament by the Dutch Finance Minister of February 16, 1990, and the subsequent discussion with selected MP's (Tweede Kamer, vergaderjaar 1989-1990, 21-458, nrs. 1 and 2).

78. In this context, see also A. Heertje, "Germany on the Monetary War Path," *Internationale Spectator*, vol. xliv, nr. 11, November 1990.

79. The reader might wish to consult the following material in this regard: *Export Magazine*, May 1990 (which contains a special section with analysis of the export opportunities for the Netherlands vis-à-vis the enlarged Germany); *Handelspartner*, nr. 3, 1991, esp. pp. 25-29, 58-60, 63.

80. Centraal Planbureau, "Gevolgen van de Duitse economische eenwording," Werkdokument nr. 34, February 1990, pp. 11-12. See also P. A. Boot, "Economische aspecten van de eenwording van Duitsland," *Internationale Spectator*, vol. xlv, nr. 1, January 1991, esp. p. 44.

81. See "DDR lonkt naar investeerders uit Nederland," *NRC Handelsblad* (Weekeditie voor het Buitenland), March 20, 1990. See also "Kansen op de Oost-Duitse markt — DDR-Seminar in Amsterdam," *Handelspartner*, nr. 4, 1990; "Topdelegatie Treuhand naar Nederland," *Informatieblad*, Nederlands-Duitse Kamer van Koophandel Berlijn, Jaargang 14, 1e kwartaal 1991. Yet, the so-called *Treuhandanstalt*, charged with the supervision of the privatization of eastern German enterprises, in the fall of 1991 lamented the striking lack of Dutch interest in the economic opportunities available in the former GDR. By the end of November 1991, the *Treuhandanstalt* reported that it had sold 4,337 former GDR companies to new owners, which included 210 companies sold to 142 foreign investors. Investors from France had bought 42 companies, followed by the Swiss (33 purchases), Great Britain (23), the Netherlands (19), and Austria and Sweden (17 each). Data reported in *The Week in Germany*, November 29, 1991, published by the German Information Center in New York.

82. Beunders and Selier, *Argwaan en Profijt*.

83. In a recent article, Arend Jan Boekestijn of the University of Utrecht has suggested that the Netherlands today is essentially a "contented" country, and that Germany's increased leadership in Europe is ironically the major factor contributing to this "contentedness" ("Nederland vaart wel bij Duits leiderschap," *NRC Handelsblad, Weekeditie voor het Buitenland*, March 31, 1992).

84. At the end of 1992, the Dutch and German governments announced plans for a fully integrated Dutch-German army corps, similar to the French-German brigade. While the ultimate fate of this proposal was uncertain when this manuscript was finalized, the implications of such an initiative, particularly in light of the Netherlands' traumatic experiences with Germany in the not-so-distant past, are obviously quite profound.

4

Belgium and Germany: An Enigmatic Relationship

John Fitzmaurice

Belgium, like most of its neighbors, has suffered much from German expansionism. It was neutral and yet was attacked by Germany in two World Wars, suffering total occupation in both wars. Yet, its relations with Germany have never been simple, never black and white.

As a small, vulnerable nation, with an open economy and indeed as the leader of the industrial revolution in continental Europe and hence an exponent of freer trade, Belgium has always been pragmatic in its approach to its powerful neighbor. The most striking example of this pragmatism was Belgium's rapid post-war abandonment of neutrality and espousal of the cause of European economic and political integration, which inevitably and necessarily included Germany. At the same time, Belgium has been at the economic, cultural, and intellectual crossroads of Europe since its establishment as a neutral, independent state in 1830.

Hostility, Indifference, or Reconciliation?

It is the central thesis of this essay that the effect of Belgium's actual historical relationship with Germany has been to create a degree of indifference and "disengagement." On a deeper level, relations between the two countries are less important than one might expect.

Three main reasons account for this fact. First, the essential political, cultural, and initially even economic frame of reference for the new post-1830

Belgian state focused on France and, subsidiarily, the Netherlands and Britain. Belgium turned South, West, and North, not East. Certainly, by the late 19th century, Germany assumed first place in Belgian trade[1] and still retains that position, and indeed has strengthened it, but that has not altered Belgium's fundamental orientation.

Second, Belgian national identity has always been weak. Regional identities have tended to be stronger. Relations with Germany and perceptions of Germany have generally been distorted through the prism of regional — Flemish or Walloon — consciousness. Indeed, relations with Germany have often been weapons in an internal struggle, having little to do with Germany itself. Those espousing regional interests, and German occupiers as well, have made use of the opportunities this presented. Thus, dislike of the Belgian unitary francophone state was sufficient to lead many Flemings who were certainly not National Socialists (at least not initially) to enter into a tactical collaboration with the Nazi occupiers who, in their eyes, had the merit of having destroyed that francophone Belgian state.[2]

Third, the Belgian approach to political issues is essentially pragmatic, consensual, and problem-solving, rather than ideological.[3] Compromise is the pivot of Belgian political life. This way of thinking is deeply anchored in the Belgian mentality. The basic starting point is that virtually any issue can be resolved, by a "splitting-the-difference" type of compromise. Divisive issues are filtered out and sidelined.

Belgian political leaders, such as Paul-Henri Spaak, were already thinking of far-reaching forms of European integration while in exile in London (1940-44). It was their unspoken belief that any such construction would have to include Germany on a more or less equal basis. A European embrace, including, in their view, Britain, and closely allied with the United States, would both rehabilitate and contain Germany. As an examination of parliamentary debates, public speeches, and press commentary of that time makes clear, this approach owed nothing to any particular sense of kinship with Germany or reconciliation. Rather, it was based on hard-headed pragmatic realism, based on Belgian experience in the 20th century.

Certainly, there remain a residual anti-German feeling and a vague sense of distrust, but such hostility as does remain has no relevance at all to political discourse, let alone action. Belgium's position is clear: it strongly supports the development of a European Union with a united Germany as an active and equal partner, not in the German interest, but in the Belgian interest. As a result, there is a certain indifference and disengagement that square the circle of contradictory considerations.

The origin of this Belgian approach to Germany is deeply rooted in Belgium's own history and in the history of its tormented relations with Germany in this century. It is this intense historical experience that has produced the weak national identity, the bifurcated regional consciousness, the consensual political system, and the strong commitment to European integration that characterize modern Belgium and determine its predisposition toward its German neighbor.

Early Links with the Germans

Before we turn to an analysis of the relations, positive as well as negative, between Belgium and Germany, it is important to examine briefly some selected aspects of Belgian history. How did the Belgian nation originate in 1830, and how has it evolved down to recent times? At several points, the history of the Belgian lands has crossed the path of Germany and the Holy Roman Empire, to which all the different feudal lands that now make up Belgium belonged at some point in their history. It should also be remembered that Belgium is one of only four countries in Europe in which German is an official language, alongside French and Dutch. In the south-east corner of the country, there is a small German-speaking community with its own political institutions.

The Belgian state, founded by the revolution of 1830, arose on the overlaid sediment of numerous regimes and occupations in the Low Countries. The present language boundary between the French- and Dutch-speaking communities, running slightly south of Brussels, deviates little from an earlier demarcation line that represented the maximum extent of northern and eastward penetration of the Roman legions. In the Middle Ages, the Belgian lands were a patchwork of feudal duchies, principalities, and ecclesiastical states.

During the Burgundian period (1382-1477)[4], the various provinces of the Belgian lands were gradually unified into a single unit. These lands came under the rule of the Holy Roman Empire, and with the abdication of Charles V in 1559, the Netherlands passed to the Spanish Habsburg branch and became known as the Spanish Netherlands. As a result of the revolt in the Spanish Netherlands between 1559 and 1609, the Spanish Crown recognized the independence of the Northern Seven Provinces, later to become the United Provinces (today, the Netherlands). The United Provinces were recognized by the European powers at the Peace of Westphalia (1648), which concluded the Thirty Years' War and recast the European Continent. The southern, Catholic provinces eventually preferred, essentially for religious but also for economic reasons, to reconcile themselves to the King of Spain. This became the basis of the separation between the modern Netherlands and Belgium.

In the dynastic and political conflicts of the early 18th century, known as the War of Spanish Succession (1701-1713), the Spanish (southern) Netherlands passed to the Austrian branch of the Habsburg family. For the remainder of the Ancien Régime, down to the 1790s, the Belgian lands were ruled from Vienna.

The period of Austrian rule in the Netherlands was not particularly oppressive, nor did it leave a very strong mark.[5] Public business was, as in the past, conducted in French and not in German. The influence of Imperial German ideas was marginal. Indeed, the Empire was, by the 18th century, if not earlier, a purely nominal structure. The links among the various territories were tenuous, and the power of Imperial institutions was very slight. Government was mostly carried on by local and traditional means. There was no missionary Germanizing or centralizing effort, which explains the very small impact of "Germany," itself then only a "geographical expression," on the Low Countries.

Indeed, toward the end of the century, there were two distinct democratic, Enlightenment influences. The crushing of the democratic revolt in the northern Netherlands by Prussian troops in 1787 brought a large influx of political refugees with radical democratic ideas to the Austrian Netherlands. Even earlier, the new ideas of the French philosophers had gained considerable currency, circulating in publications such as *Le Journal Encyclopédique* (1756-99) or the *Journal Général de l'Europe*. Political opinion in the Austrian Netherlands was divided into two opposed tendencies: those who sought to maintain and defend the customs and privileges of the Low Countries against Austrian reformism, and a more radical reformist group, which wanted bourgeois democratic reforms. Political thought was certainly not at this period influenced from beyond the Rhine.

As part of the Austrian possessions, the Austrian Netherlands were involved in the revolutionary wars with France. French forces defeated the Austrians at Jemappes in November 1792 and proclaimed the "liberation" of the southern Netherlands. The Austrians returned for a brief period after their victory at Neerwinden in March 1793, but were defeated at Fleurus on June 26, 1794. After a military occupation of a year, the Austrian Netherlands, Liège, and the Duchy of Bouillon were incorporated into France by decree on October 1, 1795.

The French régime was anything but popular. It was boycotted by the voters, and there was resistance to conscription, taxation, and the continental system that blocked trade with Britain. Yet, the importance of the French period, however unpopular, should not be under-rated, and was much greater than the Austrian/German period. It laid the foundations of the modern Belgian state, and created the basis for the rapid spread of the industrial revolution. Belgium was, in fact, the first continental country to undergo the industrial revolution. The French language became even more clearly dominant as the administrative and political language.[6]

As a result, by the beginning of the modern period, the French language, French administrative methods, French law, and French thinking were entrenched and not greatly influenced by the post-Napoleonic Dutch régime (1815-1830). Belgium was therefore predisposed, as it were, to lean toward its French rather than its Dutch or German neighbors, though, as we shall see, this became in itself a matter of controversy, as the Flemish movement developed in the later part of the 19th century.

Belgium in the 19th Century — Independent and Neutral

There was hope in the southern Netherlands, after the defeat of Napoleon, that an independent state might at long last emerge. Although the Treaty of Campio Forno (1797), by which Austria had recognized the loss of the Austrian Netherlands, was clearly void, and despite a general tendency of the peacemakers of the Congress of Vienna to restore the *status-quo-ante* where that was possible, there was no attempt to restore Austrian rule. Allied interests, as ever, were concerned with making all of the Netherlands a neutral barrier against expansion, French expansion in this case. It was therefore agreed to create a buffer kingdom of the United Netherlands, under the Dutch Orange dynasty. But the United Netherlands had little support in the south. With a much larger population, the southern provinces had only equal representation in the States General (national parliament). Religious conflict, lack of political influence, the undemocratic nature of the kingdom's institutions, trade and economic issues, and pressure to extend use of the Dutch language fueled opposition and after 1827 threw southern Catholics and Liberals into an alliance that became known as Unionism.

The year 1830 was a year of revolutions throughout Europe (France, Belgium, Poland, Italy). In the southern Netherlands, a French-speaking middle class led and organized the revolution against the Union. By the autumn, Dutch troops had left, an independent Belgian state had been proclaimed, and a Congress (Constituent Assembly) was elected. Independence was unanimously affirmed on November 18, 1830, and the Congress approved the Constitution on February 7, 1831. On February 3, 1831, the Congress elected the Duke of Nemours, second son of Louis Philippe, as King. The offer was refused under pressure from the Great Powers. On June 4, 1831, Leopold of Saxe-Coburg was elected King and accepted. This solution was acceptable to the Great Powers.[7]

In the meantime, the conflict had become internationalized, as the King of the Netherlands had formally requested military assistance from the Congress of Vienna powers (Prussia, Austria, Russia, and Britain). Prussia and Russia were opposed to Belgian independence: Russia opposed revolution, and Prussia feared French expansion and supported the Netherlands. Indeed, had Russia not been otherwise occupied with the Polish revolt, the Czar would have sent troops to assist King William to crush the revolt. Prussia backed off as Britain sought to organize an international compromise. Liberal Britain supported the Belgian cause. The international settlement involved a general recognition of an independent and permanently neutral Belgian state. Belgium was to defend its neutrality, which was guaranteed by the Great Powers, including France. Luxembourg was divided, as was Limburg. Northern Luxembourg would become a Belgian province, while the southern part became a Grand Duchy in a personal union with the Netherlands until 1890 and also a member of the German *Bund* (Confederation) until the latter's dissolution in 1866. Eastern Limburg with Maastricht went to the Netherlands but was also a member of the German *Bund*. Relations with the Netherlands remained poor, while relations with Prussia and the German powers had not been close. Belgium had received no support for its independence from the German states. Its patrons were France and Britain. It leaned culturally and diplomatically toward France, and looked to Britain for diplomatic support. Economic ties were also closest with France and Britain.[8]

Belgium was established as a liberal constitutional monarchy. Political power, with a limited franchise, was in the hands of a French-speaking aristocracy and a liberal, entrepreneurial middle class. Until 1847, the Unionist alliance of Liberals and Catholics that had brought about the revolution remained solid and consolidated the new state. French was firmly in place as the language of the state, with possible local use of Dutch or German as the maximum concession to linguistic pluralism. Indeed, the "founding fathers" opposed any significant language concessions. For them, French was the natural official language. They wanted to establish a centralized, unitary state, applying French administrative traditions and law in the French language, with a significant degree of intervention in economic life. Indeed, creation of such a system was a major economic and political goal of the revolution. Obviously, despite the nationality of the King, the ruling élite would not seek to develop close ties with the "Germanic" states, as they considered the Orange enemy to be both in the Netherlands and the nearby German states. Although, paradoxically, France constituted the main threat to Belgian independence, down to 1870, official and intellectual Belgium looked almost exclusively to France, especially after 1848.

Once the Belgian state had been fully established and the industrial revolution had begun to take hold, the small protected Belgian market based on pump-priming intervention by the state became too small. Thus, in the 1860s, Belgium espoused free trade, signing agreements with Britain (1862), France (1861), the Netherlands, and the German *Zollverein* (1863).[9] Belgium became, as it was to remain, an open, trading economy, but with considerable intervention in economic life. Free trade seemed to be an obvious parallel to political neutrality. The way was opened for Germany to become Belgium's premier trading partner, although this new economic orientation had no major political implications.

In the early period of the history of independent Belgium, down to the Franco-Prussian War of 1870, relations with France were ambiguous but intense. Cultural and economic relations were well developed and almost familial, whereas political relations had to be kept, as it were, at arm's length. Belgium was, after all, an artificial creation of the Great Powers, especially Britain, as a buffer against French expansion. The feeling (was it a fear or a hope?) that France sought to absorb Belgium was never completely absent in this period. Neutral Belgium did not and could not play the Victorian balance of power game. Consequently, no rapprochement with neighboring Prussia or later Germany was ever sought. Belgian defense policy consisted of a credible defense of the Sambre-Meuse barrier, and holding a fortified Antwerp as a sally port for friendly forces of the other guarantor powers of 1839 in the event of aggression. Closer economic relations with France, based on an 1840 trade treaty that France actually sought to use as an economic and political lever, and later conflicts over the control of railways in southern Belgium and in the Grand Duchy of Luxembourg, led to reactions by the other Great Powers. Both the revolutionary France of 1848 and the Second Empire of Napoleon III at times seemed to threaten Belgium. In 1848, an armed French revolutionary force of over 2,000 men invaded Belgium at the evocatively named village of Risquons Tout, and were routed by Belgian forces. Napoleon III discussed secret territorial changes in Luxembourg, Limburg, and even in neutral Belgium with Bismarck in the late 1860s.[10]

Significantly, in the light of much later events, Bismarck seemed to regard Belgian neutrality very lightly, as of no consequence to Prussian interests. Following the defeat of Austria in 1866 and its exclusion from German affairs, Napoleon III sought territorial compensation for the relative weakening of his position in Germany vis-à-vis Prussia. The Rhineland, Luxembourg (then in the *Bund*), and Belgium were discussed. Bismarck wrote: "I do not consider Belgium a viable state in the long run and thus, we could tolerate the increase of French power in French Belgium . . ."[11] Was he perhaps already contemplating a division of Belgium at some future time? In any event, it illustrates how low Belgium came in the German scale of priorities.

Britain obtained effective commitments to respect Belgian neutrality from both belligerents during the Franco-Prussian War of 1870. After the defeat of France, Belgium was no longer under any French pressure. Now, pressure came from Bismarck, as during the *Kulturkampf* of the 1880s, when Catholic circles in Belgium led the attack on Bismarckian anti-clericalism. Again, despite some limited concessions, Belgium maintained its independence and liberal stance on press freedom. Neither Prussia nor later Germany presented as apparently pressing a threat to Belgian independence in the late 19th and early 20th century as France had done in the first half of the 19th century.

Wallonia, Flanders, Brussels: The Language Question

After the emergence of the Flemish movement in the course of the 19th century and the achievement of universal suffrage, Belgian political life came to be dominated by the language issue. Indeed, these issues were intensely linked at the end of the 19th century, as a wider suffrage and proportional representation brought Flemish speakers into political life. The Flemish movement began to make an impact from the mid-1840s on, with a large-scale petition to Parliament in 1840 leading to the establishment of a so-called "Grievance Commission" to examine Flemish concerns. The use of Dutch in Parliament was legalized in 1893. In 1898, the two languages were given an equal "national status" through revision of the Constitution. In 1930, the Flemish goal of a fully Flemish University (in Ghent) was realized. A series of language laws passed in 1932 and 1935 established a "linguistic frontier" and laid the basis of the later principle of full territoriality in the use of languages, a key demand of the Flemish movement.[12]

As we shall see, the complex and emotive issue of the relationship between the German occupiers in two World Wars and the Flemish movement seriously muddied the debate about the language and national issue, and set back the progress of the Flemish movement, especially after World War II. It did not recover its dynamic development until the late 1950s when a new Flemish party, the *Volksunie*, made an impact in Parliament.

The post-war Flemish movement not only demanded the full application of the territoriality principle, but also a degree of political autonomy for Flanders and rights for Flemish speakers in Brussels. The issue of the return, or not, of King Leopold III after the War (the so-called *Question Royale*, focused on his controversial behavior during the German occupation) had a major impact on Flemish consciousness. In the 1950 national referendum, the King obtained a favorable majority in the country as a whole (in Flanders, over 70 percent), but was forced to abdicate due to near revolutionary opposition in Wallonia, led by the Socialists. A Flemish majority had been overruled by the Walloons. There were quite different sensibilities in the two regions, and no Belgian national unity or solidarity seemed to exist. Flanders clearly needed its own political means of expression. As the Flemish movement developed, a defensive and more left-leaning Walloon movement emerged for the first time.

After the conflict over the future Louvain University in 1968, the struggle entered a new phase. The national political families began to disintegrate, and ten years later, the three traditional "national" parties (Christian, Socialist, and Liberal) had become six independent parties. A centralized and unitary state was becoming ungovernable, and the road to a hesitant, reluctant, almost furtive federalism was opened. So far, there have been three major constitutional revisions, each pushing the process one stage further forward (1971, 1980, and 1988). Given the complexity of the problem of bilingual Brussels, the need for different boundaries for language and cultural questions and socio-economic issues, and the existence of three somewhat unbalanced language communities (Flemish, French, and German), a simple geographical federalism was not a viable solution. Creative, complex, and even untidy solutions were evolved over a period of a decade.[13]

As a result of these reforms, there is now a national government, with competencies in foreign affairs, defense, European policy, and economic and monetary policy necessary to maintain the unity of the Belgian economic system, and a minimum social solidarity in areas such as social security. Almost all other policy areas have been wholly or partially devolved to regional or community authorities.

There are three Regions: Flanders, Wallonia, and Brussels, each with a regional Executive (government) and Assemblies. These regional authorities exercise socio-economic powers over regional economic policy, planning, environmental policy, control of local government, and transport. Strict geographic federalism was not possible due to the bilingual nature of the Brussels region. Beginning in 1970, two Communities were established, responsible for language and cultural legislation, then so-called "personalisable" matters, such as health, social provision (but not social security) and, since the 1988 reform, education. The Flemish Community was from the start fused with the Flemish region, whereas in Wallonia, there is a French Community as well as a region with separate Executives and Assemblies. There is also a German Community with its own institutions.

The Brussels reform of 1988 introduced some special "cultural institutions" and provisions for cross-delegation of powers in the Brussels area. The six governments (national government, the Flemish Executive, the other two community Executives and two Regional Executives) sit together in a "Concertation" Committee to coordinate policy and resolve differences. An Arbitration Court was established in 1983 to hear cases involving conflict between the various layers of government. The community Councils have the sole right to conclude international agreements within their own (domestic) areas of competence. This right has been most extensively used by the Francophone community Council to conclude agreements with French-speaking countries such as France, or Quebec, but is equally open to the other communities.

Outstanding problems concern issues of financing (for example, the French-speaking community can only bear the cost of its education functions with some regional assistance); tidying up of competencies; external competencies and representation; rights in international organization; and above all the question of further devolution of matters such as social security or agriculture. The creation of independent, free-standing, directly elected Assemblies will create real federalism, capable of representing the genuine political pluralism of the various regions and countries.

In sum, Belgium is in the process of becoming institutionally federalized, whereas it has long been spiritually federalized. Jules Destrée, the Walloon Socialist leader wrote, as early as 1913, in his famous open letter to the King, "Sire, il n'y a pas de Belges!" This was, even then, scarcely new.[14]

As the foregoing discussion makes clear, Belgium has never really developed a strong sense of national identity. Instead, strong and antithetical regional identities have emerged, which the new federal structure of the state seeks to accommodate. The regions have often held dramatically different attitudes toward Germany. Even in times of severe crisis, such as the two occupations (1914-18 and 1940-44) by Germany, there was no common attitude, as will be shown presently. Yet, while no group or region has ever looked automatically or unreservedly toward Germany, much of Belgium's cultural élite in both Wallonia and Flanders has, almost as a reflex, looked toward France.

The German-Language Community in Belgium

Belgium has a small German-speaking community of currently about 66,000 persons in the Eupen-Malmédy-Sankt Vith area, near the German border, southeast of Liège. The so-called "Cantons de l'Est" only became Belgian under the Treaty of Versailles in 1920. There can be little doubt that had there been a genuine test of opinion, the inhabitants would have opted to remain German. In the 1930s, there was a considerable degree of Nazi agitation in the region, though many remained loyal to Belgium. After the German invasion in 1940, these areas were formally annexed to the Reich and remained so until the liberation in 1944, when they were again returned to Belgium. The position of the inhabitants had been very difficult. The area was rural, perhaps even backward, isolated and strongly Catholic. It was an extension of the Eifel. Its people felt themselves to be German, though they may not have been supporters of National Socialist ideology. They may well have felt that the transfer to Belgium in 1920 had not respected Wilsonian principles. As German citizens, according to the German occupation authorities, they were subject to German law and the obligations of citizens of the Reich, including naturally the obligation to serve in the *Wehrmacht* during the war. Some 8,700 so served, whereas others escaped service by going underground. The same tensions developed here as in Luxembourg and Alsace-Lorraine between those who served voluntarily or involuntarily, and those who refused to serve. Their situation was tragic. Not surprisingly, after the liberation, they were regarded with suspicion and some 3,000 — a large number in a total population of only some 60,000 — were convicted of various crimes during the *épuration* of 1944-49.

The 1932, 1935, and 1963 language laws had established the right of usage of German in administrative matters, not only within the German-speaking areas, but also in correspondence with provincial and central authorities, provision of local services in German, the use of German in the courts of the region, and schooling in German (but in all cases with some French minority provision, as an exception to the otherwise basic territoriality principle).

The 1970 reform of the Constitution established the principle that Belgium is made up of three language communities. In 1983, article 59bis of the Constitution regarding linguistic communities stipulated that the German language community was equal in its powers and status to the other two. Since

1973, it has an elected 25-member Council and, since 1983, a 3-member Executive with the same powers as the other communities, including education, international relations, the use of languages, and broadcasting. The Executive of the German community usually has two Christian Democratic (PSC) members and one Liberal or one Socialist. Elections take place on a four-year cycle, beginning in 1986. Although the region is rural and Christian-Democratic in tendency, there is a separate German community party (*Partei der Deutsch-sprachigen Belgier*, or PDB), founded in 1972 as a dissident segment of the PSC (*Parti Social Chrétien*). It has managed to obtain up to 24 percent of the vote, but has not yet achieved representation in the Executive. It is not a separatist party, seeking only to defend the specific interests of the German speakers. At the time of the 1983 constitutional revision, the German community demanded some socio-economic powers, such as environmental protection, normally reserved for the regions. This was not granted, but as a compromise, the Walloon region may delegate such powers and has done so in some matters.

There are usually one or two PSC national MPs who are German speakers elected in this area. A special German-language broadcasting body, the *Belgisches Rundfunk und Fernsehzentrum* (BRF), was established in 1977 under community control and broadcasts (radio only) over 70 hours weekly, a very significant increase in the modest 20 minutes per day in 1945. There is also one daily paper, *Der Grenz Echo*. However, the links between this area and Germany have remained limited and the German community has almost no impact on national consciousness in either country.[15]

Incidentally, the presence of Belgian troops in Germany since 1945, first as occupiers and then as a NATO contingent, involving many thousands of national servicemen over the years, has had equally little impact on national consciousness.

Belgium and Germany in Two World Wars

Although some pan-Germanists in Germany had been early supporters of the Flemish movement, this did not influence official policy on either side, nor did it make much impact on public opinion. It was only in the two World Wars that the complex triangular relationship between Germany, Flanders, and Wallonia came to center stage. Belgium was rapidly overrun by German troops in August 1914. German military plans (the Schlieffen plan) had long intended to pass through neutral Belgium, in order to give the extra curvature to the scythe movement into northern France. After the German defeat on the Marne, the war settled into a static pattern of trench warfare, with the front line in northern Flanders close to Ypres. Belgium only held a small salient of its own territory. Throughout the war, the King and the government operated from St. Adresse, near Le Havre in France. Belgium declined to join the Allied Powers formally, but did sign on to joint declarations to the effect that it would not conclude a separate peace with Germany or other Central Powers.

The German occupation authorities, led by General von Bissing, saw an opportunity to split Belgian opinion and eliminate opposition to the occupation, at least in Flanders, by pursuing an active *Flämenpolitik*.[16] This "Flemish policy" involved actively favoring the demands and interests of the most radical Flemish groups. The Flemish movement split into three groupings: the Frontists, who were active within the Belgian army on the Allied side, moderate nationalists, and the "activist" group. It was this third group that was the most amenable to collaboration with the German occupation authorities.

The Germans applied existing language laws in a strict pro-Flemish sense, and split the Ministry of Arts and Sciences responsible for education and culture into Flemish and Walloon sections. In 1917, the occupation authorities, which, in the absence of a government, assumed more and more direct decision-making power, ordered an administrative separation into a Flemish administration based in Brussels and a Walloon administration. An attempt was also made to reverse the Francization of Brussels. The most spectacular gesture was the reopening of Ghent University in 1916 as a wholly Flemish institution, thus realizing a major dream of the Flemish movement, much of which was prepared to accept such a victory, even at the hands of the occupiers.

Going beyond the administrative separation, the most activist elements promoted a Council of Flanders in which intellectuals, teachers, and officials sat. This body had no direct popular mandate, but was at first broadly representative of the Flemish movement. It sought to establish a provisional government and declared the political independence of Flanders in December 1917. This extreme move caused the more moderate elements to leave the Council, which came more and more into conflict with the German authorities, who had not intended it to go so far. The practical implications were small, but for the first time, political independence was put on the agenda of the Flemish movement. The movement was to enter a more institutional phase, which would lead eventually to the federalist thinking of the 1960s. That was the long-term, positive consequence. The short-term consequence, which was to last for most of the inter-war period, was to taint the Flemish movement with treason and make it easy to ignore, criticize, and even to ridicule its demands. Thus, the creation of a Dutch University at Ghent was reversed after 1918 and, under various pretexts, the promise of the exile government to act on this issue was postponed until 1930.

After World War I, Belgian opinion was naturally very anti-German. At the Versailles Conference, Belgium was in the hardline camp with France when it came to measures aimed at placing permanent restraints on Germany, not only through the collective security approach of the League of Nations favored by most other small nations, but also through more direct and severe measures. Belgium, therefore, strongly supported provisions that limited German military and industrial power, such as reparations and the demilitarization of the Rhineland and occupation of the Ruhr, in which it participated with France in 1923. Its own specific demands at Versailles, apart from reparations, were directed at neutral Holland in relation to control of the Meuse, or, insofar as they were aimed at Germany, were quite modest. It received the Eupen-Malmédy area that had been part of the Prince Bishopric of Liège before 1815 when it had gone to Prussia. It was a German area, and its culture remained and remains quite clearly German.

Importantly, the imposition of neutrality in the 1839 Treaty was removed. At least for a short period, Belgium moved closer to France. A form of military alliance was concluded in 1920 and Belgium both joined in the occupation of the Ruhr and was a signatory to the Locarno Pact of 1925 by which Germany freely (unlike at Versailles) accepted its western frontiers, in particular with France and Belgium. Yet, the French-Belgian military alliance was never developed further. It was always unpopular in Flanders, and probably too controversial domestically. Belgian policy was allowed to drift, as a half ally of France and a supporter of the League, until well after Adolf Hitler had come to power and began to undermine the stability of Europe. Indeed, the military alliance, though purely defensive, was abandoned in 1936, for domestic political reasons. Flemish and Socialist opinion had never favored the close ties with France that the alliance was intended to inaugurate. The remilitarization of the Rhineland by Nazi Germany, and the failure of the Locarno powers to do more than protest verbally, was a dramatic breach in the Versailles/Locarno system. Worse for Belgium, it meant that for the first time since the end of the Great War, German forces were at its border. Domestic political reaction dictated a form of appeasement of Germany.[17]

As a consequence, Belgium dramatically reverted to its former policy of neutrality in 1937. This was supported by a curious coalition of King Leopold III, the Socialists, the Fascist Rexist Party of Leon Degrelle, and the Flemish movement, especially its most radical elements in the *Vlaams Nationaal Verbond* (VNV), led by Staf Declerq. Such a policy was, of course, militarily and internationally disastrous. It prevented any effective Franco-Belgian coordination in the run-up to World War II and made a German attack on Belgium in the event of a war between Germany and France almost inevitable. The policy was based on the illusion, common to many of the smaller neighbors of Germany, that the Nazi monster would somehow ignore or respect weakness and submission. But more importantly, it was unfortunately the only foreign policy that could command a sufficient degree of domestic consensus under the circumstances of the 1930s. Thus, when World War II broke out in September 1939, Belgium at once declared itself to be neutral, but mobilized its armed forces. There were persistent rumors of a German attack and some plans were even captured when a German plane came down in Belgium.

On May 10, 1940, as in 1914, German forces opened their western offensive by violating Belgian neutrality. This time, the German attack also included the Netherlands. Belgian resistance only lasted 17 days before the King, in a much disputed decision, surrendered the army, leaving a serious gap in the northern end of the Allied lines. In the period of chaos that followed defeat, with the King refusing to follow his government and continue the war from exile, and with the government itself after a period of confusion reaching London in October and joining the Allied cause, the various strands of opinion hostile to the pre-war order sought to benefit from the new situation. At first, the King tried to nominate a new government that would have supported a policy of collaboration. This attempt failed both because he could not form a government and because the Germans were not favorable to the idea. The King and his circle of rightist, Catholic advisors who favored a more authoritarian political system, possibly with more power for the King himself, but in any event with less power for Parliament and the political parties, then sought to take charge of the Administration, which came under the tutelage of the German *Zivilverwaltung* and effectively ruled Belgium.

Old and new authoritarian movements tried to fill the political vacuum and obtain a monopoly of political action for themselves. These movements were in themselves disparate and varied in their objectives. In Wallonia, *Rex*, under Leon Degrelle, and rightist Catholic groups sought to establish an authoritarian Belgian state, or in the longer term, a "Burgundian" state, in close alliance with Germany as part of the New Order.[18] Degrelle went so far as to pronounce that the Walloons were "Germanic." The old Socialist Party, under the leadership of Henri De Man, became an authoritarian corporatist movement, which led many of its members and leaders to leave and join the resistance. The only legal trade union was the *Union des Travailleurs Manuels et Intellectuels* (UTMI), a corporatist body modelled on the Nazi *Deutsche Arbeitsfront*.

In Flanders, the Flemish movement was split into various strands. Even within the dominant *Vlaams Nationaal Verbond*, there were those who supported an authoritarian Flanders, while others favored annexation to the Reich or creation (as did the purely cultural VERDINASO movement) of a so-called "Dietse" (Netherlandish) state. All those political movements, whatever their aims and whatever their initial attitude to the German occupiers had been, found themselves in a similar situation. All came under increasing pressure to collaborate more and more fully and unreservedly with the Germans. These pressures came from the occupier, from potential competitors for the favor of the Germans, who alone could bestow a political monopoly and eliminate rivals, and from within the movements themselves, as their adherents demanded "benefits" from the collaboration policy.

As the war progressed and Belgian society polarized, with the development of an active resistance movement that not only attacked the occupier but also the collaborationist movements, the latter were forced into even closer collaboration. With hindsight, it is clear that the Germans never intended to establish any form of equal political relations with the collaborationists, nor to make any genuine political concessions to them. They sought to use and dupe them, and to divide and rule. These movements were useful since they divided public opinion, made the occupiers look "moderate," provided armed militia to do the Germans' dirty work for them, and provided docile recruits for the *Waffen SS* in the crusade against Bolshevism after June 1941, as well as volunteers to work in Germany.

Leaders such as Staf Declerq and later Elias of the VNV and Degrelle of *Rex* had to enter into demeaning and pathetic forms of competitive overbidding in terms of political and material support for the Nazi cause, cutting themselves off even more from all but the most fanatical, especially after the tide of the war turned in 1943. Even then, the SS leadership was not satisfied with the VNV and kept VNV volunteers under a tight and demeaning scrutiny within the SS, denying them any form of Flemish identification, and unleashed a competitor in Flanders, the *Deutsch-Flämische Arbeitsgemeinschaft* (known as DEFLAG), under full SS control.

The King, for his part, sought to reach a political arrangement, guaranteeing the future of Belgium in the New Order by meeting Hitler. The meeting was a failure. No political guarantees were offered. All concessions to the Flemish prisoners of war (released without their Walloon compatriots) and on the language issue were aimed at sowing division and nothing more. Indeed, such plans as existed for the future of Belgium after a German *Endsieg* probably involved dismemberment.

Not surprisingly, political and public opinion in Belgium over these terrible events remained divided, to some extent along regional lines. The King was forced to abdicate and the post-war repression against collaborators took on a distinctly inter-communal aspect and put the Flemish movement back a decade. It was as if "the Flemish idea" itself was being hunted down, as indeed had happened after World War I. Probably, the percentage of collaborators committing serious crimes such as murder or torture was not greater in Flanders compared with Wallonia, but there was a somewhat higher percentage of the Flemish population convicted of collaborationist offenses (0.73 percent in Flanders, 0.56 percent in Brussels and 0.32 percent in Wallonia).[19]

The Post-War Pragmatic Reconciliation

Already during the war, the Belgian government-in-exile had begun to rethink Belgian foreign policy. Neutrality had failed it twice in 30 years. Belgium joined the Allied cause, subscribing to the Atlantic Charter in 1941 and becoming a member of the United Nations. It was an early convert to the idea of a united Europe and permanent collective security through regional defense pacts. It joined with the governments-in-exile of Luxembourg and the Netherlands as early as 1944 to sign the Benelux Treaty, a prototype of the later European Communities. It was a signatory of the 1948 Brussels Treaty, a mutual security pact that was a purely European precursor of NATO, which it also joined in 1949 as a founding member.

This radical rethinking of Belgian policy during the years of exile in London emerged from a think-tank-style operation conducted between 1941-44 by the "Commission pour les Etudes d'après-Guerre" (CEPAG)[20], established in January 1941. CEPAG examined the whole gamut of Belgian domestic and foreign policy, in the light of the likely situation at the liberation. The analysis was clearly based on broad, international and European conceptions. Belgium no longer saw itself in isolation. The foreign policy Sub-Committee was led by Socialist Foreign Minister Paul-Henri Spaak.

Spaak, who, it should be noted, had been the main architect of the 1937 neutrality switch, was now convinced that a new and more cohesive and hence primarily European collective security arrangement was needed. In his view, this meant not only a high degree of economic integration, but also political integration. As early as 1941, he said: "We must organise strongly those groups with a close affinity; that means in particular Western Europe and Atlantic Europe. We must establish a whole series of obligations in the military and political areas. Such a plan would not be possible if based *only* on economic agreements."[21] He was clearly thinking of a long-term, permanent organization, which was not merely a temporary anti-German move: "Solidarity in war, but isolated in peace is not valid now or ever can be again . . . The idea of a European Order is not an artificial creation of Germany but a necessity."[22] In the same speech, he moved toward "reconciliation" with Germany. Past errors must not be repeated and a place for a new, but different Germany must be found in the new Order: "We must do more or less the reverse of what was done at Versailles. . . . Our ideal must be a Germany participating in the prosperity of a new World, but whose beak and claws have been drawn and broken."

Back in liberated Belgium, though the war was still going on, Spaak gave the government's first major "post-war" foreign policy statement to the House of Representatives on December 6, 1944. Here, he sketched out his theory of the levels of organization of the new World Order: collective security through the new United Nations Organisation; a European alliance, initially to be based on the Anglo-Soviet Treaty; and regional agreements, of which, of course, the Benelux was an early example but in which Germany might later be included.[23]

At this point, before the onset of the Cold War, Spaak believed that an Anglo-Soviet alliance could be the basis of security and containment of a Germany that would in time find its place in the new Europe. In any event, he believed it to be essential to involve Britain and Scandinavia in the organization of the new Europe.

As the Cold War became inevitable in 1947, containment of the new Communist threat came to take precedence over the need to contain Germany. Spaak then began to promote the idea of a Western European Community Organization for security and economic and political cooperation. Central to his thinking was the need to involve Britain and then the United States in a wider European-Atlantic Community. The Marshall Plan, the OEEC, and the Brussels Treaty (later the Western European Union, or WEU), in which Belgium and Britain played leading parts, were all elements in this overall strategy of accelerated European economic and political recovery and containment of the Soviet Union, which culminated in the establishment of NATO in 1949.[24]

A series of threatening events, especially the Prague Coup in 1948, the Berlin Blockade that same year, and the outbreak of the Korean War in June 1950, forced the German problem onto the agenda earlier than anyone had foreseen. A solution was required that permitted Germany's rearmament and re-industrialization and tied it to the West, resisting Stalin's neutralist siren song, but in such a way as to be acceptable to its former victims. Here Spaak, ever the realist, had seen the possibility of a need to integrate Germany very early. He had openly expressed this requirement as early as February 1947 in a major speech to the Belgian House of Representatives. By 1950, he was referring to the need for "the explicit integration of Germany."[25]

The solution lay in what came to be called the functionalist or Monnet approach (after Jean Monnet).[26] More radical federalist approaches could not win the support of governments, but faced with the concrete problem of reintegrating Germany, European functional integration was accepted. It worked with the Coal and Steel Community (ECSC) in 1950-53, but the European Defense Community (EDC) in 1954 was "a bridge too far!" With the establishment of the EEC and EURATOM in 1958 the process was back on track. A Germany bound into a whole complex of European and Atlantic bodies such as WEU, NATO, OECD, the Council of Europe, and the European Communities was sufficiently controlled that its rearmament could be accepted. Belgium supported the ECSC and the other European bodies strongly after initial opposition from coal-mining interests. It was, in a sense, the fulfillment of Spaak's vision. Germany and Belgium were bound together in the European adventure, not alone but with other partners.

Economic and Cultural Links

Belgium's economic links with Germany have certainly always been important, but perhaps less significant than one might expect. Germany, itself then still divided, did not play any major part in the 19th century Belgian industrial revolution, though the choice of Malines (Mechelen) as the center of the Belgian rail network was in part dictated by the interest in linking Antwerp and the Rhine.   The Belgian industrial revolution occurred early, and its inspiration, as well as many of its active exponents and machinery (such as the Cockerill family), came from Britain. The most important early markets were France and the Netherlands, to which the Belgian lands were variously politically linked between 1792 and 1830, the formative period of the industrial revolution. Nor was foreign capital an important element in the industrialization of Belgium, representing well under 10 percent of total investments in the formative period before 1860.[27] It was only later that the German market became important, surpassing France as Belgium's main trading partner only in 1890 (Germany 22 percent, France 21 percent, Britain 19 percent in 1895). However, this German lead had risen to 26 percent in 1910, against 20 percent for France. In 1873, France had represented 31 percent and Germany only 22 percent (18 percent in 1845). In reality, it was more a question of a decline in the French share than a rapid rise in the German share.[28]

The German economy was undoubtedly more important in the second (post-1890) industrial revolution, based on technology, electricity, and the internal combustion engine. Today, Germany is again almost Belgium's major trading partner, after the vicissitudes of the two world wars. It provides 24.3 percent of Belgium's imports, equal to one-third of all EC imports and equal to all non-EC imports. Receiving 19.8 percent of Belgian exports, it is in close second place to France (20 percent) and is followed by the Netherlands (15 percent).[29]

Today, Belgium is the most open economy in the EC with 70 percent of GDP exported, compared with an EC average of 27 percent. The openness of its economy and the dominant position of Germany within its trade, both on the export and import side, have led to an inevitably close economic relationship. Its economic policy and basic economic indicators such as inflation rates and interest rates cannot diverge from German rates. The Belgian franc (BFr) is in the Exchange Rate Mechanism (ERM) of the European Monetary System (EMS), applying the narrow range of fluctuation against all other ERM member currencies. Belgium's economic ties with Germany are so strong that it has tied the BFr to the D-Mark in a decision taken on June 15, 1990. [30]

Culturally and politically, as we have seen, there has always been a natural tendency for the Belgian French-speaking élite to look toward France. This tendency was also present for much of the Flemish or bilingual intellectual élite. At the most basic level, it was a matter of language. German was not much used or taught in Belgium. From the 1830s on, German academics no longer used Latin or French. There were few contacts until the 1860s, and even then they were quite limited. Belgium was, in effect, an intellectual outpost of France.   Writers such as Henrik Conscience, Maeterlinck, Gezelle, and Verhaeren were European intellectuals or looked to France or to the Flemish historical tradition. Even in science, mathematics, history of literature, painting or sculpture, the source of intellectual inspiration was more France, Britain or the Netherlands but rarely Germany or the German cultural tradition.[31]

The Belgian intellectual renaissance that in Flanders gravitated around the *Revue van Nu en Straks* (1892) and in Wallonia around the *Revue Jeune Belgique* (1881-97) likewise was tied to a broader European and in particular French movement. As almost a second capital of modernism and Jugendstil, Brussels was connected to the Viennese turn-of-the-century cultural scene. With the distinctive urban landmarks of Victor Horta (for example, the Maison Solvay or the Maison du Peuple) and Hoffman (the Stocklet House), Brussels has a justified claim to belonging to that tradition, which also seems to "belong" to Brussels as it belongs to Vienna. This, however, does not represent a strong cultural link with Germany. It was interesting to note that the Austrian Europalia[32] in 1988 (the first non-EC country to be included) seemed to strike a chord in Belgium, with a return to a modernist common heritage and even to the short period of 18th century common history when Belgium constituted the Austrian Netherlands. There would probably be no more commonality with Germany and possibly even less.

In post-World War II Belgium, despite political reconciliation and European integration, there would seem to be a degree of cultural indifference (no longer hostility) to the large German neighbor. To take but one important indicator — the study of languages among students in French-language schools — English was the third or fourth language for 99.4 percent of students and German for only 50.8 percent at secondary school level. In Dutch schools, it was 100 percent for English and 89 percent for German. English was even the "second" language (being preferred to Dutch/French) for 12.9 percent in French-speaking schools and 6 percent for Dutch-speaking schools. A survey of national servicemen has shown that 31.6 percent had a good knowledge of English, and only 12.7 percent of German. From the early period when Paris was the reference point for all Belgians, through the conflictual period of the rise of the Flemish movement, foreign cultural influences in Belgium have acquired a greater degree of pluralism, but German influence still remains small. The small German community is marginal and isolated. Though extremely favored from an institutional point of view, its impact on overall national consciousness remains negligible.

The Current Situation

Belgium remains, as it has been since the late 1940s, strongly committed to European integration, in which its neighbors (France, Luxembourg, Germany, and the Netherlands), as well as Britain, are firmly embedded. This, in the Belgian view, is the best guarantee for peace, stability, open frontiers, and economic prosperity. Fear and hostility toward Germany, particularly strong in Wallonia, have gradually, over 40 years of cooperation in the building of Europe, been replaced by excellent cooperation, at first suspicious and wary, but now much more wholehearted. There is a new respect for German democracy, stability, and the German *Wirtschaftswunder*. It is thus revealing that, when the Berlin Wall came down in November 1989 and German unification became first feasible and then urgent and unstoppable, there were almost no negative voices in Belgium.

The sudden possibility of German unification took Belgian leaders and public opinion as much by surprise as everyone else. Opinion was strongly favorable and remained very much so throughout the process. When asked whether they were in favor of unification or opposed, the response of Belgians was: 71 percent in favor, 15 percent opposed, and 14 percent "no opinion" (November 1989); 61 percent in favor, 19 percent opposed, and 20 percent "no opinion" (Spring 1990); and 69 percent in favor, 16 percent opposed, and 15 percent "no opinion" (Autumn 1990).[33]

This is very similar to the pattern of opinion in the Netherlands and represents a middle position in the European Community as a whole. In the spring of 1991, Belgians were asked whether they were hopeful or fearful about the consequences of German unification for their own country and for the EC in general. As far as the consequences for Belgium were concerned, 50 percent were "hopeful," 31 percent "fearful," and 18 percent had "no opinion." Regarding consequences for the EC as a whole, 57 percent were "hopeful," 32 percent "fearful," and 11 percent registered "no opinion."[34]

This pattern is not dissimilar from other small, immediate neighbors, where surveys also show that between a quarter and a third of public opinion is "fearful" regarding the impact of unification on their own country and on the EC (33 percent and 38 percent in Denmark being the peak). It suggests, for Belgium, an acceptance of unification as, in principle, a good thing because it is linked with the end of the Cold War, but also with potentially worrisome implications both for Belgium and the EC. Those worries could concern the severe problems of integrating the former GDR and hence recession in Germany, with its inevitably negative effect on Belgium (though for the moment reunification has led to an increase in Belgian exports to Germany of more than 10 percent[35]), the instability of Central and Eastern Europe, the flow of refugees, and above all the strength of Germany's commitment to continued European integration. Belgium has always viewed with concern any diminution of Germany's priority *Westbindung*. It would not wish to see any reduction in Germany's willingness or capacity to embrace economic and Monetary Union as well as Political Union.[36]

German unification and the emergence of a new united Germany with a population of almost 80 million has been viewed as a catalyst for accelerating moves toward European union, to anchor the new Germany economically and politically firmly into the West. The Belgian-German relationship should now no longer be seen in isolation, but as part of the wider development of Europe and as a relationship between two people sharing a common membership of the

European Community, permitting a more confident and less conflictual or fearful relationship between large and small peoples.

Notes

1. See Jean Gadisseur, "Le Triomphe Industriel," in *L'Industrie en Belgique: Deux Siècles d'Évolution* (Brussels: Crédit Communal, 1981), p.93.
2. For an account of collaborationist movements, such as the *Vlaams Nationaal Verbond* (VNV), VERDINASO, and *De Vlag*, see Jean Stengers, "Belgium," in Hans Rogger and Eugen Weber, eds., *The European Right: A Historical Profile* (Berkeley: University of California Press, 1966).
3. On the Belgian "method," see John Fitzmaurice, *Politics in Belgium: Crisis and Compromise in a Plural Society* (London: Hurst, 1983), Chapters 4 and 5.
4. For the early history, see Fitzmaurice, *Politics in Belgium*, Chapter 1.
5. Xavier Mabille, *Histoire Politique de la Belgique* (Brussels: CRISP, 1986), pp. 23-27.
6. On the impact of the French period, see Mabille, *Histoire Politique de la Belgique*, pp. 55-70.
7. On the Belgian Revolution, see Mabille, *Histoire Politique de la Belgique*, pp. 87-97. For a Flemish "reading," see Th. Luykx, *Politieke Geschiedenis van België* (Amsterdam/Brussels: Elsevier/Kluwer, 1964/1968/1973/1974), Vol. 1, pp. 45-60.
8. On Belgium's international position, see R. Dollot, *Les Origines de la Neutralité Belge* (Paris: F. Alcan, 1902).
9. On Belgian economic policy in this period, see J. Pirard, *L'État et l'Industrie Belge, 1848-1913* (Brussels: Crédit Communal, 1981).
10. W. Carr, *The Origins of the Wars of German Unification* (London/New York: Longman, 1991), pp. 155-61.
11. Letter to Golz, August 8, 1870, in *Bismarck; Gesammelte Werke* (Berlin: Verlag für Politik und Wissenschaft, 1924), vol. 6, 539.
12. On the development of the Flemish Movement and its gains in the 19th and early 20th centuries, see Th. Luykx, *Politieke Geschiedenis van België* (Antwerp/Amsterdam: Elsevier/Kluwer, 1973/1985), pp. 113-19, 160-62 and 191-93; Mabille, *Histoire Politique de la Belgique*, pp. 125-30.
13. For a discussion of the recent communitarian conflicts, see Fitzmaurice, *Politics in Belgium*.
14. For a brief analysis of the Belgian political system and parties, see John Fitzmaurice, "Belgium," in F. Jacobs, ed., *Western European Political Parties* (London: Longman, 1990).
15. André Méan, *Comprendre la Belgique Fédérale* (Brussels: La Libre Belgique, 1990), pp. 24-26.
16. See "German Policies in Belgium and Collaboration," in Mabille, *Histoire Politique de la Belgique*, pp. 213-22; on the *Flämenpolitik*, see José Gotovitch, "Wallons et Flamands: le Fossé se Creuse," in H. Hasquin, ed., *La Wallonie, le Pays et les Hommes* (Brussels: Renaissance du Livre, 1982), Vol. 2, p. 297. For a Flemish view, see Luykx, *Politieke Geschiedenis van België*, pp. 270-75.

17. On Belgian foreign policy in the inter-war period, see J. K. Miller, *Belgian Foreign Policy between the Wars* (New York: Bookman Associates, 1951), and J. Willequet, "Regards sur la Politique Belge d'Indépendance," *Revue de l'Histoire de la Deuxième Guerre Mondiale*, 1958.

18. On wartime collaboration, see Luykx, *Politieke Geschiedenis van België*, pp. 383-400.

19. J. Gilissen, "Etude Statistique de la Répression de l'Incivisme," *Revue du Droit Pénal et de Criminologie* (Brussels), 1951.

20. See B. Henau, "Shaping the New Belgium," in M. L. Smith and Peter M. R. Stirk, eds., *Making the New Europe: European Unity and the Second World War* (London: F. Pinter, 1990).

21. Quoted in *La Pensée Européenne et Atlantique de P. H. Spaak* (Groemaere: Textes Réunis, 1980).

22. P. H. Spaak, speech to the Institut Belge in London on April 9, 1942, in *La Pensée Européenne et Atlantique de P.H. Spaak*.

23. P. H. Spaak, Débats Parlementaires, Chambre des Représentants, December 6, 1944.

24. On Belgium and NATO, see Mabille, *Histoire Politique de la Belgique*, pp. 264-74.

25. Débats Parlementaires, Chambre des Représentants, February 11, 1947 and Débats Parlementaires, November 29, 1950.

26. M. Burgess, *Federalism and European Union* (London/New York: Routledge, 1989), pp. 43-61.

27. P. Lebrun, "La Révolution Industrielle," in *L'Industrie en Belgique: Deux Siècles d'Évolution* (Brussels: Crédit Communal, 1981), pp. 30-32.

28. Gadisseur, "Le Triomphe Industriel," p. 93.

29. M.-O. Riquet-Marchal, *Histoire Economique de l'Europe des Dix* (Paris: LITEC, 1985), and EC Commission, "Impact of the Internal Market by Sectors," (Belgium), in *European Economy* (Brussels/Luxembourg: European Commission, 1990).

30. EC Commission, *European Economy*, 1990, p. 121.

31. On the late 19th century cultural revival and its international links, see G. H. Dumont, *La Belgique* (Paris: Presse Universitaire de France, 1991), pp. 71-78.

32. Europalia, a cultural festival focusing on one particular country, is held every two years and organized on a lavish scale in Brussels.

33. *Eurobarometer*, nr. 34, December 1990.

34. *Eurobarometer*, nr. 35, Spring 1991.

35. See *L'Économie Belge en 1991* (Brussels: Ministère des Affaires Économiques, 1991).

36. See E. Arnold, "German Foreign Policy and Unification," *International Affairs*, Vol. 67, nr. 3.

PART TWO

Neighbors to the North

5

Denmark and Germany: From Ambivalence to Affirmation?

Christian Søe

Denmark is the only Scandinavian country that is physically attached to Central Europe and thus located directly in the hegemonic shadow of Germany. It has served for centuries as the main bridge for the movement of people, goods, and ideas to and from the rest of the North. The intermediate geographic location has brought the Danes closer than their more isolated northern neighbors to the rest of the Continent. As a result, Scandinavians tend to regard the small country as the most "European" member of the Nordic grouping of nations. Yet Denmark is located near the European periphery in more than a physical sense. While it has maintained an active international trade policy, in which Britain and Germany have long been balanced off together with Sweden as major markets, Denmark decided relatively early to withdraw from the power politics of Europe, after a long string of poor performances. Many Danes continue to display an ingrained preference for their country's tradition of political detachment, even in a time when the role of bystander may no longer be possible. Their reputation for a "certain half-heartedness" of commitment within both NATO and the European Community derives from the historically developed partiality for the sidelines of international politics.[1]

Germany is not only the nearest, biggest and most dynamic neighbor, but also the only nation with which Denmark shares a land frontier. While the Danes have derived both material and cultural benefits from the proximity of Germany, such gains have sometimes come at a price. A prominent Danish politician raised some eyebrows a few years ago when she bluntly described her country's political and economic position as an extension of "the North German lowlands."[2] From an economic and geographic perspective, at least, it would be difficult to disagree. On closer examination, there is also evidence of a continuing Danish political dependence on Germany, even after World War II. The historically constructed reality, however, differentiates the two nations considerably and has complicated their political relationship as well.

The most basic factor that influences Danish-German relations is the enormous asymmetry in size and power between the two nations — economic, cultural, political, and military. These differences were compounded by the divergent paths of political development taken by the two nations from the middle of the 19th century until the middle of the 20th century. Long before Germany emerged as a powerful nation-state in 1871, however, Danes worried a great deal about the insecure southern gate leading into their "fair garden."[3] The centuries-long border struggle became a *Leitmotiv* in Danish national mythology, much of it created by historians of the 19th century. To be sure, the notion of a German threat was not entirely a figment of the imagination. It was confirmed by the wars over Schleswig-Holstein in 1848 and 1864 as well as the German military occupation of Denmark between 1940 and 1945.

These more recent experiences served to reinforce, rather than create, a modern Danish identity that to a considerable degree came to define itself by a conscious self-differentiation from Germany and the Germans.[4] While modern Denmark adopted a foreign policy posture of cautious accomodation toward the giant neighbor to the south, public opinion exhibited considerable resistance against what might be perceived to be German ways or influence. In the intellectual and cultural sphere, where ties had once been very strong, they became increasingly weaker in this century and were in some cases almost severed after World War II.

Despite the problems of Danish-German history, the political and economic relations between Denmark and the Federal Republic of Germany have been excellent. By 1977, the latter had replaced Britain as Denmark's most important trading partner. Danish and West German troops trained together as alliance partners and formed a joint NATO force in the Baltic. The border question was settled long ago, as a result of Northern Schleswig's reunification with Denmark in 1920 and the Danish government's prudent territorial abstinence in the aftermath of World War II. After many years of strife, the remaining minorities in the border region have developed a harmonious *modus vivendi* that receives considerable structural and financial support from the respective governments. Diplomatic relations could hardly be better. But the general socio-cultural distance appears to have remained until recently, with Danes tending to establish mainly pragmatic contacts with their southern neighbors.

Germany's own reunification of 1990 at first appeared to encounter more reservation in Denmark than in most other Western European countries. The Danes quickly seemed to come to terms with the new situation, however, and began to find ways of profiting from it. There are even signs of at least a modest revival of interest in German society, which once was the main point of external orientation in Danish intellectual and cultural life.

Danish Reservations about a Larger Germany, 1989-90

Like other Western Europeans, the Danes were completely taken aback by the great political earthquake of 1989-90. No observer had prepared them for the rapid collapse of the established Communist systems in Central and Eastern Europe. Least of all had they anticipated Germany's swift drive toward unification after forty years of division into two states, ruled by rival elites who subscribed to the competing ideologies of the Cold War. Although much of the political landscape in Europe is still unsettled, it has been irrevocably altered by the crash of the imposed postwar regimes. Germany's new dominance in the center of the continent will presumably be reinforced by the decline and disintegration of the Soviet Union. By now the Danes, like other neighbors, have no doubts about the need to adjust to a new international reality in Europe, in which Germany will be the key player.

The political implications of the great upheaval were not immediately apparent in late 1989, when the postwar *status quo* began to totter. The opening of the Berlin Wall in November evoked as much popular excitement and enthusiasm in Denmark as anywhere else in Europe. Immediate television coverage gave everyone an opportunity to experience the reunion of Germans from East and West. It was not clear at first that the onrush of events would also bring political unification to Germany. Indeed, political analysts in Denmark, like their counterparts elsewhere, initially focused on reasons why the two German states would likely continue their separate existence in order to preserve the balance of power established in 1945.[5] Perceptions began to change when East German protesters in late 1989 added to their democratically appealing assertion, "*Wir* sind das Volk," what seemed to be a more national claim, "Wir sind *ein* Volk." It took another half year before international negotiations cleared the way for Germany's unity, but some of the first Danish reactions to the idea itself seemed far less positive than the many years of ritual support for German self-determination would have suggested.

A widely observed note of caution was struck by the Danish prime minister in reaction to Helmut Kohl's early and (in retrospect, at least) relatively modest ten-point plan for a confederal union of the two German states. The Chancellor presented his plan on November 28, 1989, apparently without prior consultation with his own foreign minister or the Allies. When questioned on the topic, the conservative Danish Prime Minister, Poul Schlüter, told journalists that he could not imagine, nor did he wish, a German reunification.[6] The very next day, Foreign Minister Uffe Ellemann-Jensen issued a clarification that explained away the Prime Minister's statement and reiterated the official policy of support for

German self-determination. Nevertheless, Schlüter was widely thought to have
spontaneously expressed his own preference for the continued division of
Germany or, at least, his personal reservations about its unification. His
reaction was duly recorded as "somewhat critical" by Chancellor Helmut Kohl's
foreign policy advisor, Horst Teltschik.[7] And there were indications that
Schlüter's initial skepticism or ambivalence reflected a more widespread attitude
in Denmark.

The press reaction generally resembled that to be found among many of
Germany's other neighbors, but it displayed some   particular points of
sensitivity.[8] Like their colleagues elsewhere, Danish journalists sometimes
played on emotional assocations by referring to the larger Germany as a "new"
or "fourth Reich." Cartoonists had a field day with stereotypical impressions
of Germany and the Germans, including the inevitable caricatures showing brash
D-Mark tourists or an overweight Chancellor Kohl in traditional German dress
or uniform.[9] In a much-discussed case of willful hearing, a German-speaking
Danish journalist informed the intellectual readership of the left-wing newspaper,
Information, that the members of the Bundestag had sung "*Deutschland über
alles*," after the opening of the Berlin Wall. Many older Danes know that the
first verse of Hoffmann von Fallersleben's national song appears to make
German territorial claims up to the Danish straits leading into the Baltic. In
fact, West German parliamentarians had adhered to protocol by singing only the
liberal-democratic words of the third verse of the *Deutschlandlied*, whose call
for justice and freedom in a setting of German unity — "*Einigkeit und Recht und
Freiheit*" — has been the official anthem since the early 1950s.[10] Danish public
opinion was understandably irritated when the nationalist West German party,
the *Republikaner*, issued a map that showed the southern part of Denmark as
belonging to Germany — as though the end of Germany's division were now to
be a license to question the results of Denmark's reunification seventy years
earlier.[11]

Danish opinion polls also registered considerable public hesitation about
German unification. In fact, the Danes appeared to be least supportive among
all the members of the European Community. *Eurobarometer* polls showed that
78 percent of all EC respondents were in favor of German unification in
November 1989, falling to 71 percent in a differently conducted poll of
March-April 1990, whereas the corresponding figures for Denmark alone were
59 percent and 56 percent, respectively. Several other polls confirmed that it
was difficult for many Danes to support the idea of a fully united Germany.
One of the earliest polls, taken by the Danish *Observa* institute at the beginning
of December 1989 for *Der Nordschleswiger*, the newspaper of the German
minority in Denmark, received considerable press attention. It showed that
when given the choice, Danes overwhelmingly preferred "a form of unification
in which the two states retain a certain form of independence." This preferred
"solution" to the German Question received the support of 62 percent of Danish

respondents and was opposed by only 18 percent. The alternative of "a full reunification" was supported by only 20 percent and opposed by 54 percent.[12]

The fact that most Danes, including the Prime Minister, appeared to prefer some way of continuing the existence of two not fully integrated German political systems did not, of course, mean that they approved of the East German party-and-police state. Danish relations with the German Democratic Republic (GDR) resembled those of other Western nations. The timing and manner of formal recognition had been carried out in full coordination with West Germany's *Ostpolitik*, and the later relationship had never been more than formally correct. The volume of trade was very small, primarily because the GDR lacked hard currency to pay for a high volume of imports and, after 1982, pursued a general austerity policy in importation from the West. Although many of its own products were not highly competitive in delivery time, price, or quality, East Germany's exports to Denmark (as to many other Western countries) henceforth outpaced its imports — in the Danish case, by four to one in 1986. But the flow of trade with the GDR never became an important or stable component of Denmark's economy.[13]

The Danish media generally reflected liberal-democratic dismay over East Berlin's repressive policies. There had been a major embarrassment a couple of years earlier, in September 1988, when the Danish Embassy in East Berlin had released eighteen East Germans who had sought asylum there to the GDR authorities. The embassy apparently had acted without the knowledge of either the Danish Foreign Minister or Prime Minister, but it had negotiated with GDR representatives and believed (incorrectly) that no legal actions would be taken against the refugees. The incident put a dent in the Danish self-image. It was particularly embarrassing in view of the fact that it took place just a few days before a long-planned journey by Poul Schlüter to East Berlin, the first state visit to the GDR by a Danish prime minister.

The GDR had done its best to improve its image in Denmark and the rest of Scandinavia.[14] Even before the arrival of diplomatic recognition, it had worked in all of these countries through its cultural institutes and friendship societies as well as the German-Nordic Society (*Deutsch-Nordische Gesellschaft*), founded in 1961. Between the late 1950s and the mid-1970s, the GDR organized an annual week of festivities in Rostock, directed toward the Northern neighbors, under the slogan that "the Baltic Sea must become a Sea of Peace." With the onset of detente, the GDR had used additional forms of public relations in the attempt to improve its image in Scandinavia. When East-West tensions returned in the late 1970s and early 1980s, East Germany registered with some satisfaction that Denmark (and, to some degree, Norway) tended to play a moderating role within NATO on questions concerning a new military build-up as well as stricter trade boycotts with Eastern Europe.

On the whole, the result of the GDR's efforts had been modest. In Denmark, as in most other Western countries, there was a widespread conviction that the German division was a political reality with which one had to deal constructively. Willy Brandt's *Ostpolitik* had been welcomed in the early 1970s, and Hans-Dietrich Genscher's continued "mini-detente" toward the GDR was seen as high statesmanship. Danish politicians had pragmatic encounters with East German party and state officials, and there were similar links at the professional and cultural level. But sympathy for the Communist regime in the GDR was essentially limited to a very small portion of the political Left. It comprised people who, for either partisan or idealist reasons, were able to accept, overlook or romanticize political realities in the GDR. Most often, these admirers seem to have been impressed by the East German state's claim to represent a socially "progressive" and determinedly "anti-fascist" position in postwar Germany.

The initial Danish ambivalence about the prospect of German unification is readily understandable as the preference of a small country for a not too large neighbor. Modern Denmark's political relationship with Germany can be understood in large part by reference to two factors that have shaped both experience and perceptions. The first, as previously mentioned, is rooted in the geopolitical reality that these two adjacent countries are enormously different in size and strength. The second factor is cultural: it consists of the historical contrast in dominant political values, governing style, and state behavior of the two countries for a period of approximately one hundred years. Denmark became a constitutional monarchy in 1849 and evolved into a liberal parliamentary democracy by the beginning of this century, whereas Germany undertook dizzying political swings which ended in the Nazi dictatorship and World War II. The contrast of political culture was still felt in Denmark for many years after the collapse of the Third Reich, although close observers knew that a liberal democracy had gradually become rooted at both the mass and elite level in the Federal Republic of Germany.

The first of these factors, the difference in size and power, continues to be significant. In the last year of the German division, Denmark's population of five million people was less than one-twelfth the size of West Germany's (62 million) or only about three-tenths the size of East Germany's (16.5 million). Today, the population of reunited Germany (80 million) is approximately sixteen times as large as Denmark's; it lives somewhat more cramped in an area that is about eight times larger.[15] The relative economic strength of the two countries approximates their demographic ratios.

The asymmetrical relationship is fundamental for practitioners as well as theorists of Danish foreign policy. Both will inevitably resort to a well-articulated Danish version of "small state theory" in explaining their country's ambivalent relationship with Germany.[16] Many other Danes who are less inclined to formal geopolitical analysis will show an intuitive understanding of the basic power relationship and frequently, in an almost Chaplinesque manner, flirt with the advantages of being "*lille*" (little).[17] Even when presented with the coy self-irony that foreigners often seem to observe and find attractive in Danes, it would be difficult to deny that at times the self-comparison with the large neighbor to the south also reveals a touch of national smugness.[18] The lesson from history, however, is that Denmark can neither block nor ignore the political will of its giant neighbor.

Danes and Germans before 1864: No Thousand-Year Struggle

The Danish multinational state (Denmark, Norway, Schleswig and Holstein) lost its position as a major regional power in the course of a series of unsuccessful wars against Sweden between 1523 and 1720. It thereupon adopted a neutral status, but became involuntarily drawn into the Napoleonic Wars in 1807, when it received rival French and British ultimatums to become an ally or be treated as an enemy. The Danes only chose the side of France after the British had bombarded Copenhagen and seized the large Danish fleet. At the end of this unpleasant experience with a Hobson's choice in foreign relations, Denmark also lost Norway to its old Scandinavian rival, Sweden, which had chosen camp more wisely and ended up on the winning side.[19]

It is remarkable that in the 19th century, Danish historians were able to create a patriotic history in which Germans largely displaced the Swedes in the role of the traditional enemy (*arvefjenden*). As contemporary scholars have pointed out, once the idea of a national conflict with the southern neighbors had become established, Danish historians would sometimes anachronistically read this relationship back into a much earlier history, to a time long before strong national identities had emerged.[20]

According to the national historians, the Danish kingdom had, for about one thousand years, been threatened by invasions from the south but had repeatedly fended off the German danger. Until some time after World War II, every Danish school child learned about the patriotic deeds of such heroes as Uffe, who slew two Saxons "dead as herrings" in a mythical duel over the Danish realm, or Harald Bluetooth's mother, Thyra Danebod, who built the very real wall of Danevirke to keep out intruders from the south. A heroic role was also assigned to Niels Ebbesen, who helped to save his mortgaged country from arrogant German moneylenders by killing the giant Count Gert — "a hard man, as steel and iron" — in his residence at Randers.[21] In recent decades, this kind of national romantic history has disappeared from the school curriculum. However, there were telling echoes of its main theme in some Danes' opposition to the Federal Republic's entry into NATO in the early 1950s or to Denmark's entry into the Common Market two decades later.

Recently, the popular Danish author and critic of his country's European integration, Ebbe Kløvedal Reich, has drawn upon the same theme of a centuries-long struggle between Danes and Germans.[22] Indeed, this version of history can cite a venerable if largely unreliable antecedent in *Gesta Danorum*, the politically commissioned work of Denmark's first historian, Saxo Grammaticus.   The historical reality has been considerably more complex, as Uffe Østergård and other contemporary Danish historians have pointed out.[23] There were indeed many conflicts over the centuries, but they were not always or mainly against Germans. Nor were they fought in the name of national ideas before the 19th century. They included Danish-led invasions southwards, and the "Danish" armies regularly included German-speaking officers as well as numerous foreign mercenaries. Moreover, the commercial rivalries and political or military conflicts between Germans and Danes were offset by a good deal of reasonably peaceful and mutually beneficial interchange. In the late Middle Ages, the Hanseatic trade in the Baltic brought closer contact between the two peoples. The German influx into Denmark was large from this time on, with many merchants and craftsmen settling in the towns, above all in Copenhagen. Some Danish craftsmen in turn worked for a time in Germany. After the Reformation, Danish theology students often attended German universities, and German ministers preached in their own language and churches in the Danish capital.   Furthermore, the Danish royal house and aristocracy contained numerous members of German descent and cultural orientation.[24]

The cosmopolitan experience was restricted to a relatively small part of the population, to be sure, and it did not go unchallenged. In the uneven course of bourgeois Danish identity formation during the 18th and early 19th centuries, the relationship with Germans and their language took on a crucial and increasingly negative importance. Indeed, "German" came to serve as a point of contrast and self-differentiation for the Danes.[25]

The increasing interest in and cultivation of Danish as a distinctive language in the 1700s was the occasion for a growing patriotic emphasis on greater linguistic purity.   Ludvig Holberg, the great 18th century Norwegian-born playwright who struggled to make Danish a respectable literary language, was the best known of several writers who made fun of "affected" foreign and especially German borrowings in the speech and behavior of their contemporaries in Denmark. Collections of proverbs, sayings and popular songs from this time contain a conspicuous element of linguistic and national polemic against the foreigner, who more often than not was German. Indeed, the Danish word *tysk* ("German") often became a general label for anything "foreign," simply because the German presence in Denmark was considerably greater than that of other cultures. Ironically, as Vibeke Winge has pointed out, many of the negative traits that Danes began ascribing to Germans (such as "arrogance") were quite similar to ones that Germans for their part had tended to attribute to the French. She concludes plausibly that both were cases of defensive reactions by people who felt their identity threatened by a culturally vigorous and assertive neighbor.[26]

In the second half of the 18th century, the socio-cultural tension intensified and took aim at what an increasingly assertive Danish bourgeoisie felt to be undue German influence and, no doubt, competition. One highly visible, if temporary, target was Johann Friedrich Struensee, a German physician to the mentally ill Danish King. In a short period, from 1770 to 1772, he had used his position not only to carry on a widely rumored affair with the Danish Queen, but to gain control of the monarch's absolutist powers. He used them to introduce some highly enlightened reforms before he was overthrown, tortured and executed. The Struensee episode served as catalyst for an emerging Danish identity linked to a growing anti-German sentiment.   This development represented a potential threat to the culturally pluralist character of the state (Danish, Norwegian, and German). One result was a novel attempt in 1776 to defuse the growing Danish-German tension by restricting high public service posts to persons born *within* the multinational realm. Germans who were born outside Denmark were henceforth shut out of the public service, but not those native to Schleswig or Holstein. In 1789-90, however, the national confrontation came to a head during the so-called "German feud" (*tyskerfejden*), triggered by bourgeois Danish enthusiasm for the French Revolution.[27] It became the occasion for an unprecedented storm of verbally aggressive Danish nationalism in Copenhagen, directed against German-speaking fellow citizens of the realm. In the next half century, Danish writers and historians would raise the patriotic sentiments to a more literary level, projecting the new national confrontation far into the past. At a popular level, anti-German feelings would continue to find a less elevated expression.

If nationally awakening Danes harbored negative images of the Germans, the reverse was certainly also true. To be sure, Denmark was usually of marginal significance to most Germans, but the struggle over Schleswig and Holstein from the 1840s on gave a new prominence to the northern neighbor, who claimed sovereignty over these duchies with their high proportion of German inhabitants. Thus Denmark served as a frequent target of nationalist outpourings during the German constitutional debates of 1848 in Frankfurt's Paulskirche.[28] The occasion was the first of two wars for political control of the duchies, and Denmark's eventual success in the first conflict did not solve the underlying problem of national self-determination in Holstein (which was largely German in language and sentiment) or Schleswig (which was more culturally divided).

Apart from the occasions provided by the Schleswig-Holstein issue, Denmark appears to have received a relatively modest share of the nationalist condescension bestowed by assertive Germans on their many neighbors. Some unusually sarcastic remarks about the backward condition of Denmark and the "rest of the North" came from the young Friedrich Engels, himself no celebrator of the German way of life. In a letter of 1846 to his new friend, Karl Marx, he described the whole area as a "really piggish mess" (*eine Sauerei*): "Such a miserable fullness of morality, guild-cliquishness and snobbery exists nowhere else any more."[29]

Yet during this whole time of an emerging national assertion and self-differentiation, the German cultural area continued to be a major source of inspiration for Danish intellectual life. As already mentioned, the Reformation had established strong and continuing theological links to Martin Luther's homeland. The flowering of German art, literature, and philosophy in the 18th century and later continued to draw many Danish artists and intellectuals southward. In the 19th century, it was as natural for Søren Kierkegaard, Hans Christian Andersen, and (a generation later, in the 1880s) Georg Brandes to make longer stays in Germany as it is for Danish writers, artists, and scholars of today to cross the Atlantic in search of higher learning or cultural inspiration.[30] German was still the most important foreign language in Denmark at that time, and there were many lesser lights who tried their minds on German forms and ideas. Presumably Friedrich Engels was referring to such literary encounters in his diatribe, when he described Denmark as a backward cultural dependency of Germany with a literature that was no more than a "dull imitation" (*matter Abklatsch*).[31]

Later in the century, the nascent labor movement and Social Democratic party developed personal, political, and cultural links to their counterparts in Germany. The resulting network facilitated some ultimately unsuccessful efforts by Danish and other Scandinavian Social Democrats to promote peace initiatives during World War I.[32] The contacts continued during the Weimar Republic and have never been entirely broken, although the ties to Sweden later became more important for both Danish and German Social Democrats. In these circles, there seems to have been a genuine internationalist orientation, with mutual respect and sympathy among people committed to a shared vision of progress.

Denmark's German Problem: 1850-1945

Politically, Denmark became permanently preoccupied with Germany and the Germans after the first war over control of Schleswig-Holstein at mid-century. The concern was given a telling expression in the title chosen by Troels Fink for his lectures on Danish foreign policy during the following century, *Deutschland als Problem Dänemarks*. He could hardly have stated the thesis more succinctly: for Danish foreign policy during this period, "the relationship to Germany was *the* problem" (*das Problem*).[33]

In the first of Bismarck's three wars leading to German unification, Prussia in alliance with Austria easily defeated Denmark and annexed Schleswig-Holstein in 1864. For Denmark, the conflict had been as long on idealistic fervor and anti-German nationalism as it was short on rational prudence and modern artillery. The disastrous outcome, in which Denmark lost about one-third of its territory, led to much troubled self-scrutiny in the humiliated nation.

The defeat necessarily had foreign policy implications for Denmark. There were some desperate political hopes that an eventual French victory in the Franco-Prussian War of 1870 would lead to a restoration of the Danish role in Schleswig. But the government pursued a cautious line, and the relatively swift German victory over France ensured that the popular sympathies found no official expression in Copenhagen. Danish foreign policy-makers drew the lesson that henceforth their small country must abstain from illusions and adopt a policy of avoiding conflict with the powerful neighbor. Their strategy of going out of the way to accomodate the Reich would often run into criticism from patriots who derided "the German orientation" (*Tyskerkursen*). But they were unable to suggest a plausible alternative.

If Denmark's foreign policy henceforth would be closely attuned to Germany, its internal socio-cultural and political development took another direction. One important result of the loss of the two duchies, just fifty years after the cession of Norway to Sweden, was that Denmark (excluding Iceland and the Faroe Islands) had almost completely lost its former multinational character. The truncated country had been reduced to one of Europe's culturally most homogeneous nation-states for the first time in its history. That may have made it easier for the Danes to turn their strongly developed sense of national identity in a constructive direction and infuse it with liberal-democratic values.[34]

Denmark did not give up the hope of reunification with Schleswig, although there seemed increasingly little reason to expect a move in that direction by Germany. The national goal could also be expressed plausibly in democratic terms of self-determination, given the province's considerable Danish population. However, the irredentist longing was tamed and never given a chance to dominate national politics in these years. Instead, the country adopted a pragmatic approach for coping with the loss, as reflected in the popular slogan of the time: "What has been lost externally, must be won internally."[35]

It would be hard to exaggerate the impact of N.F.S. Grundtvig on the Danish outlook in this period. During his long and prolific life (1783-1872) as a patriotic priest, poet and educator, Grundtvig gave expression to a sense of Danish national identity that included a good portion of the romantic self-differentiation from the Germans. In Grundtvig's case, however, it also carried a peculiar democratic, voluntary, and non-excluding spirit.[36] His ideas on education led to the formation of the folk high schools (*folkehøjskoler*), a unique Danish institution in which a new generation of small farmers gained a rudimentary literary, historical, and social awareness, learned democratic skills, and in some cases emerged as budding political leaders. In combination with the growth of farmers' cooperatives and the broadly based movement of small farmers for political reform, the folk high schools were an important element in the process that led to a rapid democratization of Danish life during the last half of the 19th century.[37]

In other ways, Denmark began a significant westward intellectual and socio-cultural reorientation. There was a marked turn toward Britain, with a growing Danish appreciation of that country's more empirical approach to inquiry and more liberal way of handling social relations and conflicts. Grundtvig himself had set an example by his early visits to Britain for inspiration. The English language began to be studied more widely and stays at British universities came to be far more frequent than previously. The cultural ties to Germany were not abandoned, but they appear to have been gradually loosened during the decades around the turn of the century and thereafter.

A parallel economic shift had set in already before the turn of the century. Trade patterns began to change away from the traditionally strong orientation toward Germany, partly as a result of Bismarck's tariff policies in favor of German agrarian interests. But this trend came about also because of the inability of Danish farmers to compete in the international grain trade with such new exporters as the United States and the Argentines. As a result, there was an important adjustment of the whole Danish agricultural sector toward the making of meat and dairy products — bacon, ham, eggs, cheese — for export to the large English market. A new harbor town, Esbjerg, was built on Jutland's otherwise relatively barren west coast, to provide an important sea link with Britain.

This revamping of Danish agriculture was supported by the growth of modern dairies and slaughterhouses. These were often cooperatively owned and became an important source of political skills in the rural population, just as the network of folk high schools imparted a strong sense of democratic patriotism. Thus Danish society underwent a rapid modernization encompassing the development of human beings as much as the material infrastructure. In almost perfect historical timing, the new westward-oriented trade could also take advantage of a significant expansion of the country's railway system. Even Friedrich Engels might have been impressed!

Throughout World War I, the Danish government adhered to its careful course toward Germany, while maintaining official neutrality. Popular sympathies in the country lay overwhelmingly with the Western powers, but the government in Copenhagen went out of its way to be more than correct in its dealings with Berlin. It even acceded to Germany's wish to have the sea entrances (the Belts) to the Baltic mined against possible intruders. The latter were most likely to have been British, but London indicated its understanding of Denmark's action. It was widely understood that if the Danes had not mined the waters, the Germans would have done it "for them."[38]

An important consequence of the peace settlement for Denmark was the opportunity to re-open the Schleswig Question. After plebiscites in a northern and southern zone of the province, with three-quarters of the vote going to Denmark in the former and four-fifths to Germany in the latter, the northern part was returned to Denmark in 1920. This limited reunification was not an easy compromise for Copenhagen, although it conformed to the country's ingrained policy of avoiding (future) trouble with Germany as well as a democratic respect for majority sentiments. The government in Copenhagen resisted strong irredentist pressures from a Danish lobby that, with some French encouragement, wanted to go for a larger slice of what had been lost over half a century before. It is worth noting that the official Danish reluctance to take advantage of Germany's temporary weakness would be repeated after 1945, when the opportunity to make demands for another piece of Schleswig came up again. Then, as in 1920, political disagreement led to a government crisis, but it took a much milder form the second time around.[39]

As a result of the 1920 border settlement, there remained a minority of people with Danish identity in the part of Schleswig that stayed German, while the return of the northern part of the province to Denmark gave the latter a German-identifying minority.[40] The solution to the Schleswig Question thus left dissatisfied groups on each side, but it seemed to pose no serious problems during the Weimar period, when the German and Danish governments had relatively cordial relations.[41]

There was a marked change after Hitler's accession to power at the beginning of 1933. The Third Reich had its own policy of conciliation with the Scandinavian states and carefully refrained from casting official doubt on the border arrangement. Nevertheless, its fundamental opposition to the Versailles settlement made Denmark uneasy. The Danish minority in North Germany came under chauvinist social pressure after 1933, and some members of the German minority in Denmark took encouragement from the nationalist turnabout south of the border to agitate for "help" from the new rulers in Berlin.[42]

The strongly German-oriented Schleswig Party had consistently won only between 0.6 and 0.8 percent of the vote in Danish parliamentary elections since 1920, but that was based on around 15 percent in the North Schleswig region alone. Following Hitler's international breakthroughs, the party had reason to anticipate a considerable regional growth in the parliamentary election of April 1939. Moved by the fear that irredentist consequences might result from a sharp increase in the pro-German vote, the established parties worked together to mobilize the "Danish" vote in North Schleswig or, as the Danes usually say, South Jutland. The result was an impressive regional voter turnout of 92.4 percent (against 79.2 percent in the country as a whole). The Schleswig Party garnered 15,000 votes, but this was only 15.9 percent of the regional vote (marginally up from 15.5 percent in 1935) or a mere 0.9 percent of the total popular vote in Denmark. It was just enough to recapture the party's usual one seat in a *Folketing* that had 149 members.[43]

A Danish Nazi Party (DNSAP) had been founded already before Hitler's rise to power, but it never drew more than flimsy support. Under the leadership of Frits Clausen, a physician, it won 1.0 percent or 16,000 votes (no mandates) in 1935, and rose to 1.8 percent or 31,000 votes (three mandates) four years later, on the eve of World War II. To be sure, this was not the whole story about ultra-right politics in Denmark. A small Farmers' Party (*Bondepartiet*), which showed increasing Fascist leanings, received 3 percent of the vote in 1939, giving it four seats in the *Folketing*. In other words, these two extreme right-wing parties together garnered almost 5 percent of the total Danish vote in that year.

There were some other relatively minor spasms of ultra-right politics in Denmark during these years, most notably within the Conservative Party's youth movement. A number of intellectuals and artists expressed an interest in abandoning the parliamentary form of politics in favor of some vaguely conceived national redirection or "renewal." Not only were they few and without effective political organization or influence, but some of them would go out of their way to distinguish their search for a "third way" from what was going on in Germany. All in all, then, Denmark seems to have been considerably less affected by the radical Right during the 1930s than several of Germany's other neighbors.[44] This conclusion is supported by the results of an election held four years later, at the height of World War II, which will be discussed below.

During the second half of the 1930s, the official Danish policy of accomodating Germany went unusually far. In 1935, Denmark abstained as a Council member from voting on a resolution of the League of Nations that condemned Germany's unilateral decision to remilitarize. Four years later, Denmark was the only Scandinavian country that felt obliged to accept the German offer of a non-aggression treaty. Denmark had only a skeletal defense force by this time. This was itself a result of the widespread belief at both the popular and elite level that the country was indefensible and should stick to its policy of neutrality.[45] In May of 1939, therefore, Denmark and Germany formally agreed not to invade each other.

The German Occupation, 1940-45

At the outbreak of World War II, in September 1939, Denmark reaffirmed its neutrality and hoped once again to remain outside a great European conflict. Its policy was not based on a naive faith in German respect for Danish sovereignty, of course, but rested on the long ingrained conviction that the country could only be preserved if it avoided war with the hegemonic neighbor. The policy of accomodation was designed to convince Germany that there was little to gain by taking direct control of Denmark. In line with this strategy, the

Danish government took no major defense precautions during the entire period of "phony war" that followed the defeat of Poland, even after it received warnings about an imminent German move in early 1940. On April 9, the *Wehrmacht* occupied Denmark within a few hours, meeting only token military resistance.

In a sense, the Danish strategy might have worked if Denmark had not been a stepping stone as the Germans moved north to Norway, their main military objective. In contrast to Denmark, Norway had taken some defense preparations, and its king and government could escape when the German naval task force was delayed by combat actions before reaching Oslo. As a result, Norway resisted the German invasion and later carried on the war from outside the country. Throughout the war, Danes were very much aware of the contrast between the repressive military occupation of Norway and their own much less violent experience with the Germans. For some, the Norwegian example of resistance was a constant moral reminder of an alternative to the Danish policy of accomodation. Supporters of this policy, however, saw one of its main goals as avoiding what came to be known as "Norwegian conditions."

The German occupation of Denmark was highly peculiar in that the country's government stayed in office and pronounced its independence. The cabinet continued to be headed by the veteran Social Democrat, Thorvald Stauning, who expanded his coalition cabinet to include both Conservatives and Liberals. The Germans had declared that they were simply protecting the country's neutrality and would not interfere in Danish internal affairs. Although Danish independence was fundamentally a pretense, the government pursued a pragmatic course designed to protect Danish interests by restraining German influence within the country and maintaining a democratically elected government. Popularly known as "the policy of negotiation," it has been described by a sympathetic observer of Denmark as "a supple policy of . . . dragging out issues, of watering down the persistent German demands, and of keeping as much control in Danish hands as possible . . . ."[46] Henrik S. Nissen, a Danish historian, has pointed out that, "despite striking and at times humiliating concessions," the policy should be distinguished from collaboration "by the fact that it never linked Danish interests to the ultimate victory of German arms." Instead, he adds, the policy of negotiation sought to "protect Danish interests, often by finding solutions that accomodated German desires, but never in such a way that an advantage for Denmark became a consequence of a favor to Germany."[47] It was clearly a difficult balancing act that aimed at minimal cooperation with a potentially violent intruder.

There can be no doubt that the Danish government sometimes conceded very much in the hope of "preventing worse from happening." It followed a German request to intern Danish Communists and gave in to Berlin's pressure to sign the Anti-Comintern Pact after the German invasion of the Soviet Union. German demands for concessions increased as the war continued, but the *Wehrmacht* could also be pragmatic in its recognition that it derived advantages from having a well functioning Danish administration continue in office. The relatively cooperative responses from Erik Scavenius, the Foreign Minister who succeeded Stauning as Prime Minister in 1942, increasingly became a subject of controversy that would intensify after the war. Scavenius later defended his actions in terms of what might be called a Danish situational version of "the ethics of responsibility" (*Verantwortungsethik*), but his critics have assessed the political and moral dilemmas somewhat differently. The often equivocal policy of the wartime Danish government appears to have found a growing understanding, but understandably no great approval, among contemporary historians.[48]

It is remarkable that Denmark held its regular parliamentary election in March 1943, while under German occupation. There was a record turnout (89.5 percent) in response to the established parties' call to show support for democracy. The reality of German occupation undoubtedly reduced the range and depth of campaign debate, and the banned Communist Party could not participate. However, there were no outright manipulations or other irregularities in the election.[49]

The outcome was a strong support for the four government parties, which together received over 90 percent of the vote (almost one-half of it, 44 percent, was cast for the Social Democrats). This show of support for the established parties was matched by the electoral disaster of the radical Right. The strongly collaborationist Farmers' Party, which had received 3.0 percent of the vote in 1939, sank to only 1.2 percent (two seats) The Danish Nazi Party, which had received 1.8 percent of the vote in 1939, rose slightly to 2.1 percent or 43,000 votes (keeping its three mandates).[50]

It is striking that the Danish Nazis continued to perform so poorly, even in 1943 when the Schleswig Party did not compete as a separate party. Any explanation of the relative immunity to National Socialism in Denmark would have to include a consideration of the movement's radical rejection of the liberal-democratic values that had become ingrained in the modern Danish political tradition. But it would also be necessary to weigh the disadvantage of the DNSAP's close association with the Germans as well as its incredibly unattractive and fragmented Danish leadership. In a historical assessment written some two decades later, Malene Djursaa could fairly conclude that Danish Nazism "had no roots and left no traces."[51]

The Danish resistance movement also had few members and relatively little support in the early war years, but by the summer of 1943 the tide had begun to turn. There were strikes and demonstrations, as well as increasing sabotage activity. The Germans demanded strong counter-measures, but the government decided to resign at this point rather than agree to death penalties and other repressive measures. Two years earlier, the leading Danish politicians had agreed among themselves on three non-negotiable items in dealing with the Germans: (1) the parliamentary basis of the government; (2) Danish participation in the war; and (3) special legislation for the Danish Jews.[52] The Germans had refrained from exerting pressure on any of these points, but their demand for a violent crackdown on the resistance movement in effect turned out to collide with another non-negotiable position.

For the rest of the war, the internal administration of Denmark was largely in the hands of top civil servants, who stood in close contact with political leaders. The policy of negotiations with the German occupation authorities continued, but the room for Danish maneuver had been reduced with the departure of the elected government. After August 1943, the Germans took brutal steps of their own to deal with the resistance, although they never resorted to the extreme savagery used in other occupied countries.

In October 1943, Berlin ordered that the small Jewish population of Denmark, about 7,000 in number, be rounded up and sent to concentration camps. During the first three and a half years of German occupation, the Jews had been protected by Danish law and suffered no persecution. Their civil status had been one of the non-negotiable positions of the Danish government. Now almost all Danish Jews managed to escape the destruction intended for them. Their rescue was made possible by a number of circumstances, including the actions of Germans who provided an important advance warning or practiced connivance. In the last analysis, however, the escape depended upon the active part played by the Danish resistance movement and many individuals, who helped the Jews go underground and later flee by fishing boats to Sweden. Not every helper was moved by the purest of motives, but the rescue of Danish Jewry is nevertheless a story of many small acts of decency and moral courage in a time that was woefully short on both.[53]

In the last twenty months of the war, there was increasing conflict with the occupying power. The Germans dissolved the very small Danish army and navy as well as the police force. Many policemen were sent to concentration camps, but most went underground. Members of both the armed forces and police joined the resistance movement, which grew rapidly as the end of the war approached. It now received broad support from a population that had become increasingly critical of the policy of accomodation. A Freedom Council had been founded in September 1943 to coordinate some of the resistance activities and fill the authority void left by the absence of a national government. Its members were drawn from the resistance movement, and they favored a more oppositional strategy from the beginning. This probably helped them advance their diplomatic aim of gaining Allied recognition of Denmark as a co-belligerent against Germany. By early 1945, there was an underground resistance army in Denmark and a better trained Danish brigade in Sweden, but they were not required to fight.

The German capitulation in early May 1945 spared Denmark the direct experience of land warfare. The small nation emerged from five years of occupation with remarkably little physical deprivation, destruction of property, or violent loss of life.   There can be little doubt that Germany had treated Denmark far better than the other occupied countries.   It is likely that racial ideology played a role in the German behavior, but pragmatic considerations probably weighed more, as the disparate treatment of both Norway and the Netherlands indicates.   After all, the Danish policy of negotiation had only been possible because it also served some important needs of the conqueror.

Although relatively mild, the wartime experience had been traumatic for the Danish people.   Like other countries, Denmark soon developed something of an exaggerated resistance legend that a later generation would appropriately feel justified in questioning.[54]   In dealing with its active collaborators, Denmark appears to have been relatively strict, compared to some countries where the problem was far more widespread.   There was a special problem in South Jutland (North Schleswig), where support for the occupying power had been quite high among members of the German-speaking part of the population.[55] Some irredentist Danes wanted to take advantage of Germany's defeat to raise the Schleswig Question once again, but the established political parties and most of their leading politicians opted against such action.[56]

The Post-1945 Period: Relations with West Germany

The Cold War division of Europe and Germany after 1945, following closely upon Denmark's experience of military occupation, resulted in a sharp break with the country's traditional orientation in international politics.   The official policy of an almost defenseless neutrality had lost much of its appeal and there was no immediate reason for seeking to accomodate a prostrate and divided Germany.   The prime concern shifted to the Soviet bloc.

In the late 1930s, the Scandinavian countries had considered forming a Scandinavian security system, and they returned to the idea more seriously after 1945.   Once again, however, the plans came to naught, suggesting that there was only a weak basis for such a common Nordic undertaking.   Thereupon Denmark somewhat reluctantly followed Norway in 1949 to become a founding member of NATO.   Here it soon gained the reputation of being a footdragger, in budgetary and military terms.   From a broader perspective, however, it is remarkable that Denmark, however reluctantly, has moved away from its neutralist tradition and joined such a military defense pact at all.   Its membership gave NATO control of the strategically important straits to the Baltic as well as air bases in Greenland, even though Denmark like Norway consistently refused to allow the stationing of nuclear weapons on its soil.

NATO membership also meant that Denmark after 1955 found itself in a new multilateral partnership with the Federal Republic of Germany.   There was vocal opposition in Denmark, primarily on the far Left but also among some national conservatives, to the rearmament of the West Germans.   Their later participation

in joint training exercises in Denmark also triggered anti-German demonstrations. Such opposition has subsided long ago. Over the years, the
German-Danish naval cooperation in the Baltic sea (with little more than a token
force supplied by Denmark) appears to have functioned smoothly. The same is
true for the rotating command of the joint defense forces. That in itself is a
considerable achievement, even though public relations officers may have a role
in producing such positive impressions.

The vexing border question has been settled because of a number of formal
and informal developments that might be a valuable study object for other
nations. The ghost of irredentism was laid to rest as a result of the plebiscite
that led to Northern Schleswig's reunification with Denmark in 1920 and the
Danish government's prudent decision for territorial abstinence after World War
II. Ten years later, the Bonn-Copenhagener Declaration of 1955 provided a
formal basis for a better co-existence of Danes and Germans in the border
region. A special electoral provision has even made it possible for a Danish-
oriented minority in Schleswig to be represented by an elected representative in
the state's *Landtag*, although this party cannot pass the 5 percent minimum
otherwise necessary for parliamentary representation. Since 1979 the German-
oriented minority in South Jutland has not been electorally strong enough to elect
a representative to Denmark's *Folketing*. However, its interests are now
channeled through a special office in Copenhagen, headed by an outspoken
representative, Siegfried Matlock, who also uses his newspaper, *Der Nordschleswiger*, to articulate special concerns. Most important, perhaps, the
relations between Danes and Germans in the border region have improved
because of the dedicated efforts of many individuals and groups on both sides.
Within Europe, there is probably no border region outside Scandinavia with
more harmony than this one.

Economically, Denmark and Germany have re-established and strengthened
their temporarily disrupted ties. During the occupation, Denmark had lost its
British market and instead become a well-stocked pantry for Germany. When
international trade began to regain momentum after 1945, Britain and Sweden
returned to their position as Denmark's most important trading partners. In the
second half of the 1950s, Denmark followed the lead of the U.K. in joining the
European Free Trade Association (EFTA) rather than the Common Market
(EEC). Before long, however, the fast growing West German economy put
Denmark under increasing cross-pressure to consider the economic advantages
of membership in the Common Market. The resolution of the dilemma came
in 1973, when Denmark was able to follow Britain into the EEC. It was a
purely economic decision for most of the Danish supporters, since the idea of
a European political union would have found relatively few backers in a country
with such a tradition of international detachment.

Already by 1977, the Federal Republic had become Denmark's best trading
partner. The (West) German lead over Britain soon became unprecedented for

peace time trade in this century. In 1989, the last full year before reunification, West Germany provided 22.2 percent of Denmark's imports and received 17.5 percent of its exports. The corresponding figures for Danish-British trade were 6.9 percent and 12.1 percent respectively.[57] This reversal is remarkable, especially if one considers Britain's considerable headstart after World War II. By 1989, Sweden had also moved ahead of Britain, providing 12.1 percent of Denmark's imports and taking 12.2 percent of its exports.

Denmark's Relations with the United Germany

The initial ambivalence with which many Danes greeted Germany's rush toward unity was tied to the many uncertainties raised by the abrupt conclusion of the Cold War. Clearly a larger Germany would play a greater role in European politics, after the Soviet retrenchment and a partial withdrawal of the United States. Yet a restoration of Germany as the dominant power in central Europe was not an attractive vision to many.

Against this background, it is remarkable how quickly the new reality of a larger Germany became an accepted fact of life in Denmark and elsewhere for many who had at first expressed reservations. Even before the first and last free *Volkskammer* elections in East Germany, on March 18, 1990, when GDR voters left no doubt about their overwhelming preference for a rapid merger with the Federal Republic, polls began to show a shift in Danish opinion toward greater acceptance of what appeared to have become both democratically legitimate and politically inevitable.[58] There were some generational and ideological differences in the degree of acceptance, with older people and those furthest to the Left tending to show somewhat greater apprehension.

Uffe Ellemann-Jensen, former Foreign Minister Genscher's veteran Danish counterpart, personal friend and fellow Liberal, was near the top of the list of leading European politicians who strongly supported the changes in Germany. Prime Minister Schlüter went out of his way to correct his early skeptical response and to welcome the changes in Central Europe.[59] Other cabinet ministers followed suit. In the major opposition party of Social Democrats, the prominent and outspoken foreign policy expert, Ritt Bjerregaard, adopted an almost pedagogical role in trying to wake up her party and the country to the important challenges and opportunities presented by the new developments. Ambassador K. E. Thygesen in Bonn came close to breaking with a tradition of diplomatic reticence, in his enthusiasm for a similar educational mission to his country. The current situation suggests a near consensus in the foreign policy elite on this question. After Poul Schlüter's initial misstep, there have been no incidents in Denmark comparable to the Ridley affair or the Chequers incident in Britain, where apparently more deeply seated apprehensions in the political class regarding German unification found expression.

German unification no longer preoccupies the quality press and the mass media in Denmark. But all of the serious newspapers now carry relatively informed background stories and analyses on German culture, economics, and politics in what appears to be a tacit acknowledgement that the southern neighbor is important and has been neglected too long. The fiftieth anniversary of the invasion of Denmark, April 9, 1990, was understandably the occasion for historical reflections on the German-Danish relationship. Yet if one considers what *could* have been made of the occasion, the Danish press was remarkably restrained in avoiding easy polemics concerning a "Greater Germany."[60]

There are a number of reasons for the relative equanimity with which Denmark now appears to regard German unification. First, of course, the Danes have a long practical training in making the best out of foreign realities that they cannot change. Here their "small nation" experience comes into its own. Second, the importance of the West German market is well known in Denmark, and this made it simpler for the country's press to turn attention to the new market opportunities in the eastern part of Germany.[61] The Ministry of Economics has contributed to such speculation, which runs from reports on a possible new flood of guests from eastern Germany in Danish summer houses to the new demands for Danish technical equipment in the revamping of the economic infrastructure of the former GDR. Recent trade statistics bear out some of this optimism, for while Germany in 1991 continued to account for 22 percent of Denmark's imports, the Federal Republic had risen sharply in just two years from 17.5 percent to 22.4 percent of Denmark's total export trade.[62]

Third, there is also considerable anecdotal evidence, backed up by some polling data, that many Danes have begun to have a more positive, or at least much less negative, image of Germany and its people. Numerous conversations with Danes on this topic support the impression that there has been an informal process of image-correction. In part, the shift is generational, as polls indicate. To be sure, it is possible to cite counter-evidence as well, as has been emphasized by some concerned observers who point to the prevalence in Denmark of negative images and stereotypes of Germany.[63] In any case, there can hardly be any disagreement about the conclusion that Danish views of Germany only rarely display a close understanding of the neighbor. Here decades of cultural ostracism have produced a pervasive ignorance in a country whose intellectuals and artists used to flock to Germany for inspiration.[64]

But even if Danish views of the southern neighbor may well begin and even end with superficial impressions based on quick tourist passages through Germany or fleeting meetings with German vacationers in Denmark, the perceptions gathered from such encounters cannot but weaken the hold of stereotypes concerning the "typical German." Danes are frequently surprised by their "discovery" that contemporary Germany is a federally organized, highly pluralistic society that in many ways bears little resemblance to the centralized, authoritarian image of the past.

In a fourth and more political category, the long postwar development of the Federal Republic has on the whole provided a record that can only bolster its image as a stable liberal-democratic society, at both the elite and mass level. It would be a mistake to underestimate the importance of the confidence-building measures of German foreign policy over the years, even if they reach the average citizen only in the form of somewhat vague images. At the elite level, Hans-Dietrich Genscher and other leading Germans have adopted a political style that does not appear threatening or offensive to their small neighbors. Federal President Richard von Weizsäcker, who once attended the German school in Copenhagen, has turned out to be a great asset for public relations in Denmark as well.

As much as anything else, perhaps, Danes were impressed in 1989-90 by a fifth factor or, really, a significant "non-event," namely the absence of a wave of national enthusiasm in Germany when unification became a possibility and a reality. Chancellor Helmut Kohl did provide an opportunity to fret and protest, when he seemed to suggest that the Oder-Neisse boundary might not be permanent after all. But here too there was a reassurance, first when his position met with obvious embarrassment and criticism at home and then when it was definitively abandoned.

There has been a far stronger Danish concern about some later and more serious nationalist deviations in Germany. The recent electoral growth of neo-nationalist parties and, worse, the outbreak of right-wing violence, especially among German youth, have met with strong condemnation in Denmark. There probably would be considerable understanding in Denmark for official steps to alter the Federal Republic's liberal asylum provisions for the purpose of reducing the very high number of non-political refugees who seek to take advantage of German generosity in this respect. It is the widespread violence and the tardy official responses that have amazed and disturbed public opinion in Denmark.

Here too, however, there is a bright side. The Danish press has begun to pay more attention to the many Germans who publicly and privately express dismay over these actions and sympathy with the victims. Richard von Weizsäcker's speeches on the subject could have been crafted with a Danish audience in mind. The small country is not without its own social and political tensions linked to the influx of economic or political refugees, and one encounters expressions of xenophobia there as well — whether in the more indirect, "polite" form or the direct, verbally more aggressive variety. Both the problem and the response may eventually bring more Danes to realize that the civic culture of the two countries has become much more alike than they realized.

All these factors combine with a spreading awareness in Denmark that while Germany's size and proximity will continue to be major factors in the relationship, their impact can be modified or even used to advantage. This is a view often expressed by prominent Danish officials or politicians, like Uffe Elleman-Jensen or Ritt Bjerregaard, and it appears to have been picked up by at least some Danes. They see a more integrated Europe less as a loss of sovereignty than as a means of binding the larger Germany into the transnational framework — a view that has also been strongly promoted by leading members of the German political class.[65]

Nor should one overlook yet another factor, the widespread expectation that a united Germany could have an important, constructive role to play in the political and economic rebuilding and stabilization of Central and Eastern Europe. Here expectations were at first so high in Denmark and elsewhere that some disappointments were bound to follow. But once again, the perceptions of the German role in a changing Europe tend to be rather positive.

There are signs that some informed Danes have begun to rethink the cultural relationship with the southern neighbor. As already pointed out, Denmark's increasingly westward orientation can be traced back to the late 19th century, but the severance of cultural links with Germany is mostly a product of World War II. Today it is relatively rare to meet younger Danes who have studied seriously in Germany or in some other way gained a good understanding of the country. It will take time to bring about a significant reorientation in this area, but the circumstances for such a change appear more favorable than they have for many decades. Ritt Bjerregaard may have set an early example among leading politicians when she decided to use a part of her summer vacation in 1990 to brush up on her German — something that she admits would never have entered her head a year earlier! Characteristically, she also made sure the public found out.[66] Newspapers have reported a strong new interest in learning German among Danish gymnasium students.[67] Per Øhrgaard, the Copenhagen *Germanist* who writes astutely on German history and politics, may find that his calls for more cultural attention to Germany will finally meet with a response.[68]

Danes might then agree that the rediscovered neighbor can be much more than their main trading partner. They would even encounter an unusual respect for and interest in their own small country. There appears to be a greater awareness of Scandinavian culture among Germans than one finds in the United States, Britain or France, and there is a widespread admiration for the northern neighbor's supposedly more attractive "way of life." Sympathetic Germans may exaggerate the social achievements and perhaps even the gentle charms of Denmark, but this is a welcome change from the past, when both Left and Right in Germany tended to look upon Denmark as a place of petty bourgeois banality. One needs only reread the sarcastic remarks made by Friedrich Engels concerning Denmark and all the other Scandinavian countries to appreciate the polite manner in which Helmut Schmidt, in the second volume of his memoirs, comes close to an expression of love for the small neighbor.[69]

There may be a revival of Danish concerns about the German factor, of course. The dismay over right-wing political activities has already been mentioned. In the spring and early summer of 1992, warnings about Germany played a prominent role in the national debate that preceded Denmark's third referendum on the European Community. Proponents of each side on the Maastricht Treaty used the emergence of a more powerful Germany as a reason for backing their respective positions. By voting yes, some supporters argued, one would help to tie Germany into a larger European framework. A no vote, opponents suggested on the contrary, would keep Denmark at a distance from a German-dominated Europe. Such considerations, however, do not appear to have been foremost in the minds of the voters. According to a Danish poll, only two percent named the German argument as a major factor in their decision on the day of the referendum.[70]

The slim majority (50.7 percent) that voted against the proposed move toward European monetary and political union can be explained without invoking a lingering Danish fear of German domination. The outcome took the political class by surprise, but it represented a broad populist anxiety about rules and directives imposed from "the outside and far away." Since the Danish referendum, it has become increasingly clear that this EC-version of the center-periphery dimension in politics is not restricted to Denmark but has parallels in some other Western European countries, including the Federal Republic. It cannot be ruled out that such fears could end up centering as much on Bonn or Berlin as on Brussels, if Germany does not continue to play a relatively moderate and understanding role in dealing with sensitive neighbors like Denmark.

Notes

I wish to thank the many people in Denmark and Germany who found time to discuss the subject of this essay with me, and who often provided me with additional written materials. A special note of gratitude goes to Louise Søe, as well as Glenn Hansen and Nils Søe, for checking my original manuscript and to Anne-Marie Foged, who helped me locate relevant Danish library sources. My research was supported by a grant from California State University, Long Beach.

1. This is the basic theme developed historically and analytically by Carsten Holbraad in his superb study, *Danish Neutrality. A Study in the Foreign Policy of a Small State* (Oxford: Clarendon Press, 1991).

2. Ritt Bjerregaard in *Politiken*, November 17, 1988.

3. The reference to the unhinged garden gate is contained in a still sung verse, "Danmark, dejligst Vang og Vænge," written by the clergyman, Laurids Kok, and first printed in 1695.

4. This is a recurrent theme in the four-volume study, *Dansk identitetshistorie*, edited by Ole Feldbæk (Copenhagen: C. A. Reitzels Forlag, 1991 and 1992).

5. A typical example would be Niels Nørlund's article, "Skyggen fra Potsdam," *Berlingske Tidende*, November 11, 1989, p. 10. It reviews the historical origins of the postwar division of Germany and concludes that this state of affairs will continue because it reflects the shared interest of the victor powers in European stability. Nørlund is one of a handful of Danish journalists who specialize in explaining Germany to their country-people.

6. Poul Schlüter's spontaneous remarks have been quoted or paraphrased repeatedly in the Danish and German newspapers as well as other sources. There appears to be some disagreement about the formulation and interpretation of what he said. For an early Danish report, see Jan Bo Hansen, "Tysklands bekymrede venner," *Weekendavisen*, December 1, 1989. For a later German commentary, see Freddy Gsteiger, "Geister, die Kohl rief," *Die Zeit*, March 16, 1990, p. 13. An early analysis of this and other Danish reactions was provided by Bodo Crenzien, "Dänemark und die deutsche Frage," in Klaus Benjowski, Bertel Heurlin, Gregor Putensen, and Hakan Wiberg, eds., *Endzeit für Deutschlands Zweistaatlichkeit — Konsequenzen für Europa*, protocol of a symposium held in Copenhagen on May 3-4, 1990, pp. 7-13.

7. Teltschik later recorded his impression that the Danish prime minister and his Italian colleague, Giulio Andreotti, had been "somewhat critically inclined" about German unification until an EC summit meeting on April 28, 1990, when they both showed themselves to be "very constructive." See Horst Teltschik, *329 Tage. Innenaussichten der Einigung* (Berlin: Siedler Verlag, 1991), p. 211.

8. For an insightful comparative analysis of press reactions in all EC countries, except Denmark and Luxembourg, see Andrei S. Markovits, "Die Deutsche Frage — Perzeptionen und Politik in der Europäischen Gemeinschaft," in Ulrike Liebert und Wolfgang Merkel, eds., *Die Politik zur deutschen Einheit* (Opladen: Leske & Budrich, 1991), pp. 321-42.

9. The following newspapers have been examined for this study: *Politiken*, *Berlingske Tidende*, *Information*, *Morgenavisen* (*Jyllands-Posten*), and *Weekendavisen*.

10. See *Information*, November 11, 1989, p. 6, and the later discussion of the *Deutschlandlied* in this and other Danish newspapers. *Information* had its start as an underground newspaper during the German occupation of Denmark.

11. Both incidents were widely discussed in the Danish press. See Bernd Henningsen's insightful essay, "Der Deutsche wird nie ein guter Däne. Zum Bild der Deutschen in Dänemark," in Günter Trautmann, ed., *Die häßlichen Deutschen?* (Darmstadt: Wissenschaftliche Buchgesellschaft, 1991), pp. 167-80.

12. See *Eurobarometer* (Commission of the European Communities), No. 33, June 1990, pp. 36-40 and No. 34, December 1990, pp. 18-20. See also the Gallup Poll report, *Berlingske Tidene Magasin*, February 1, 1990. Siegfried Matlock has kindly provided me with the results of the *Observa* poll commissioned by his newspaper, *Der Nordschleswiger*. This poll gave special insight into Danish reactions, because it presented the respondents with an alternative to "full" reunification. The results were widely reported in Denmark.

13. For a useful overview of economic, cultural, and political relations, see Marcel Bulla and Karl-Heinz Rabe, "Die Beziehungen der DDR zu den nordischen Staaten Schweden, Dänemark, Norwegen, Island und Finnland," in Peter R. Weilemann et al., *Die Westpolitik der DDR* (Melle: Verlag Ernst Knoth, Forschungsbericht 66 der Konrad-

Adenauer-Stiftung, 1989), pp. 191-220. The trade statistics for 1986 are summarized on p. 214.

14. On the cultural and party political "outreach" activities of the GDR, see Bulla and Rabe, "Die Beziehungen der DDR," pp. 216-20.

15. Statistics from *The 1989 Information Almanac*.

16. A very good survey of the discussion, with reference to works in both Danish and English, is Hans Branner, *Danmark som småstat* (Copenhagen: Gyldendal, 1990). A standard work by a Danish scholar in English, which includes a long analysis of Denmark's "Finlandization," is Hans Mouritzen, *Finlandization: Toward a General Theory of Adaptive Politics* (Aldershot: Avebury, 1988). See also Nikolaj Petersen, "Adaptation as a Framework for the Analysis of Foreign Policy Behaviour," *Cooperation and Conflict*, vol. 12, 1988, pp. 221-50.

17. The self-flirtation with being *lille* but *hyggelig* or "cozy" is evident in almost all Danish reflections on national identity. It begins for many with the little verse learned as a child about the "big, big world" out there: "*Verden er så stor, så stor.*" Ritt Bjerregaard characteristically used this line as title for her published correspondence with Sven Burmester, *Verden er så stor, så stor. Breve mellem Maj 1987 og September 1990* (Copenhagen: Gyldendal, 1991).

18. See Henningsen, "Der Deutsche wird nie ein guter Däne." The author reviews the Danish reactions to reunification and puts them into perspective, by historically surveying what might be called Danish "German-bashing."

19. See Holbraad, *Danish Neutrality*, chapter 1, and Uffe Østergård, "Feindbilder und Vorurteile in der dänischen Öffentlichkeit," in Trautmann, ed., *Die häßlichen Deutschen?*, p. 148.

20. For examples, see Østergård, "Feindbilder und Vorurteile," pp. 145-66.

21. Even during World War II, a country teacher could steep his pupils in this dramatic version of Danish history, as I have briefly related elsewhere from my own experience. See my chapter in David Childs and Jane Wharton, eds., *Children in War* (Nottingham: Institute for German, Austrian, and Swiss Affairs, University of Nottingham, 1990), pp. 160-70. Østergård gives a broader perspective and includes the lines cited from N.F.S. Grundtvig's romantic verse descriptions of these heroic feats, "Feindbilder und Vorurteile," pp. 153-54 and 161.

22. Ebbe Kløvedal Reich is an unusually prolific essay writer, and the "German" theme crops up repeatedly in his writings. See for example his most recent collection of articles, *Kontrafej af den danske ånd* (Copenhagen: Vindrose, 1992), especially p. 94f.

23. See Østergård, "Feindbilder und Vorurteile," p. 146f., as well as his recent collection of essays, *Europas ansigter* (Copenhagen: Rosinante, 1992), pp. 29-83.

24. According to a census taken in 1699, twenty percent of the population of Copenhagen was German-speaking. This figure included subjects from the king's duchies, Schleswig and Holstein, as well as people from various German states. See Vibeke Winge, "Dansk og tysk i 1700-tallet," in Feldbæk, ed., *Dansk identitetshistorie*, vol. 1, *Fædreland og modersmål, 1536-1789* (Copenhagen: C. A. Reitzels Forlag, 1991), pp. 91-92.

25. The following discussion draws selectively on the first three volumes of *Dansk identitetshistorie*.

26. Winge, "Dansk og tysk i 1700 tallet," pp. 109-10.

27. See Ole Feldbæk and Vibeke Winge, "Tyskerfejden 1789-1790," in Feldbæk, ed., *Dansk identitetshistorie*, vol. 2, *Et yndigt land, 1789-1848*, pp. 9-109.

28. See Günter Wollstein, *Das "Großdeutschland" der Paulskirche. Nationale Ziele in der bürgerlichen Revolution 1848/49* (Düsseldorf: Droste Verlag, 1977), pp. 23-97. This and some other points are covered by Wolf D. Gruner, *Deutschland mitten in Europa* (Hamburg: Verlag Dr. R. Krämer, 1992), pp. 393-97.

29. See Karl Marx/Friedrich Engels, *Werke*, vol. 27 (Berlin, DDR: Dietz Verlag, 1963), pp. 71-72. The letter was sent by Engels from Paris to Marx, dated December 1846. Less than two years later, he writes in the *Neue Rheinische Zeitung*, Nr. 99, dated September 10, 1848, that Denmark is economically, politically, and culturally completely dependent on Germany, adding that "it is well known that the real capital of Denmark is not Copenhagen but Hamburg." He confidently predicts that Germany will one day "take" Schleswig, based on the historical "right of civilization over barbarism, of progress over stability." Marx/Engels, *Werke*, vol. 5, p. 394.

30. See Per Øhrgaard, "Offizielle Anpassung und inoffizielle Distanz — das Verhältnis Dänemarks zu Deutschland in den letzten 150 Jahren," in Øhrgaard, ed., *Die Bundesrepublik Deutschland in der heutigen Welt 1989* (Copenhagen: Akademisk Forlag, 1990), p. 124-26. The following part of the chapter has drawn on the insights in Øhrgaard's spirited and thoughtful essay.

31. Marx/Engels, *Werke*, vol 5, p. 394. He does grant a single exception. It is, as one would expect, Ludvig Holberg.

32. See Martin Graß, *Friedensaktivität und Neutralität* (Bonn-Bad Godesberg: Verlag Neue Gesellschaft, 1975), on the subject of the unsuccessful Scandinavian Social Democratic efforts to promote an early peace, between 1914 and 1917.

33. Troels Fink, *Deutschland als Problem Dänemarks. Die geschichtlichten Voraussetzungen der dänischen Außenpolitik* (Flensburg: Christian Wolff Verlag, 1968), p. 7. See Øhrgaard, "Offizielle Anpassung und inoffizielle Distanz," pp. 120-21, who adds that the former Danish Foreign Minister, Per Hækkerup, used to tell his diplomats that Denmark had three main problems, namely "Germany, Germany, and once again Germany."

34. The topic has been brilliantly explored by Uffe Østergård, "Peasants and Danes: The Danish National Identity and Political Culture," in *Comparative Studies in Society and History*, Vol. 34, No. 1, January 1992, pp. 3-27.

35. "*Hvad udad tabes, det må inad vindes.*" The phrase became widely used with reference to the loss of Slesvig or Schleswig. It is attributed to Enrico Dalgas, who played a central role in the cultivation of Jutland's barren heathlands in the 19th century.

36. This point is stressed by way of contrast to German nationalism by Leni Yahil, "National Pride and Defeat: A Comparison of Danish and German Nationalism," in *Journal of Contemporary History*, Vol. 26 (1991), pp. 453-78.

37. See Østergård's discussion of Grundtvig's ideas, in "Peasants and Danes," pp. 13-16.

38. Hans Branner, *Småstat mellem stormagter. Beslutningen om mineudlægning August 1917* (Copenhagen: Munksgaard, 1972), p. 130ff. Branner, who is one of the foremost Danish users of small state theory, shows here that Denmark was basically written off by Britain as lying within Germany's sphere of interest.

39. See Bjarne W. Frederiksen, *Danmarks sydslesvigpolitik efter det tyske sammenbrud i 1945* (Copenhagen: Munksgaard, 1971).

40. The members of the minorities are today identified by their own subjective preference (*Gesinnung*) rather than by such "objective" traits as the language they speak in the home.

41. This summary draws upon Lorenz Rerup's excellent article, "Dänen und Deutsche," in *Beiträge zur Konfliktforschung*, No. 3, 1987, pp. 54-55.

42. Rerup, "Dänen und Deutsche."

43. Data from the table, "Folketingsvalg 1913-1945," in Niels Finn Christiansen, Karl Christian S. Lammers, Henrik S. Nissen, *Tiden 1914-1945*, vol. 7 of Søren Mørch, ed., *Danmarks historie* (Copenhagen: Gyldendal, 1988), pp. 478-79. Additional data from Erik Rasmussen, *Velfærdsstaten på Vej*, vol. 13 of John Danstrup and Hal Koch, eds., *Danmarks historie* (Copenhagen: Politikens Forlag, 1971), p. 492.

44. See S. J. Woolf, ed., *Fascism in Europe* (London: Methuen, 1981), with its country chapters, including Malene Djursaa, "Denmark," pp. 237-56.

45. See Holbraad, *Danish Neutrality*, pp. 59-85, for a fine discussion of Danish "defenceless neutrality" between 1920 and 1945. The author links the development of a more idealist notion of neutrality and disengagement in Danish foreign policy to the democratization of the Danish political system.

46. John Fitzmaurice, *Politics in Denmark* (New York: St. Martin's Press, 1981), p. 19. For a longer informed discussion, see Henrik S. Nissen, "Adjusting to German Domination," in Henrik S. Nissen, ed., *Scandinavia during the Second World War* (Minneapolis: University of Minnesota Press, 1983), especially pp. 111-15.

47. Nissen, "Adjusting to German Domination," p. 114.

48. The subject is brought up by several contributions in Nissen, ed., *Scandinavia during the Second World War*. See also Hans Kirchhoff, *Kamp eller tilpasning* (Copenhagen: Gyldendal, 1987), with its sensitive discussion and helpful bibliographical references, pp. 200-208.

49. Aage Trommer, "Scandinavia and the Turn of the Tide," in Nissen, ed., *Scandinavia during the Second World War*, pp. 222-24.

50. Rasmussen, *Velfærdsstaten på vej*, pp. 388-89.

51. See Djursaa, "Denmark," p. 237.

52. Nissen, "Adjusting to German Domination," p. 114.

53. See Leni Yahil, *The Rescue of Danish Jewry. Test of a Democracy* (Philadelphia: The Jewish Publication Society of America, 1969). Also, Leo Goldberger, ed., *The Rescue of the Danish Jews. Moral Courage under Stress* (New York: New York University Press, 1987). For a number of different perspectives on the moral and political significance of the Danish case, see the exchange of letters in the *New York Review of Books*, March 29, 1990, September 27, 1990, and April 25, 1991. The whole discussion was touched off by Istvan Deak's letter of December 21, 1989.

54. On this general topic, see Tony Judt, "The Past is Another Country: Myth and Memory in Postwar Europe," *Daedalus*, Vol. 121, No. 4, Fall 1992, pp. 83-118.

55. See the extensive study of the purge of the Danish collaborators after World War II by Ditlev Tamm, *Retsopgøret efter besættelsen* (Copenhagen: Jurist- og Økonomforbundets Forlag, 1985), vol. 1 , pp. 408-10. The English summary of the author's findings brings the main statistics and arguments together, see vol. 2, pp. 789-94. The total number of people arrested as suspected collaborators reached about 40,000. Of the approximately 13,500 persons who were sentenced as collaborators, about 3,000 appear to have been members of the German minority (p. 792), or about one quarter of its male

population. The great majority were sentenced for having served in some military or paramilitary body of the occupying power.

56. For a study of the problem, see Fredriksen, *Danmarks sydslesvigpolitik.*

57. *Denmark, Iceland. Country Profile, 1991-92.* (*The Economist* Intelligence Unit, 1991), p. 24.

58. *Politiken,* February 25, 1990, p. 8. For a second Gallup Poll that shows a significant shift between late January and early March 1990, see "Ændret holdning til et samlet Tyskland," *Berlingske Tidende,* March 11, 1990, p. 4. The percentage of respondents who felt German unity would have positive effects for Europe grew from 26 to 37 percent, while those who felt it would have negative consequences fell from 51 to 33 percent. The trend has continued, and German reports now bear such indicative headings as, "Deutsche Einheit erfreut die Dänen," *Frankfurter Rundschau,* June 13, 1990, or "Allzugroß ist die Angst vor einem zu starken Deutschland nicht," *Stuttgarter Zeitung,* August 20, 1990. Both of these articles were written by Hannes Gamillscheg, a well-informed foreign correspondent in Copenhagen, whose occasional reports to several German and Swiss newspapers are a good barometer of the remarkable shift in Danish views on German unification. At the beginning of the year, he had emphasized the anxiety with which Danes viewed German unification, as indicated in another heading, "Viele Dänen haben Angst vor einem vereinten Deutschland," *Hannoversche Allgemeine Zeitung,* January 25, 1990.

59. For just one example, see the long interview, "Die deutsche Vereinigung sehe ich ohne Sorge," in *Die Welt,* April 27, 1990. Here Schlüter describes German unification as "the natural consequence" of the end of Communist rule. Other Danish politicians and officials have also used the press to spread their views. See, for example: Uffe Ellemann-Jensen, "Tysk enhed og Danmarks interesser," *Politiken,* February 3, 1990; K. E. Thygesen, "Tysk samling er en gevinst," *Weekendavisen,* March 9, 1990; Ritt Bjerregaard, "Danmarks nabo mod syd," *Politiken,* February 4, 1990.

60. The fiftieth anniversary of the occupation also saw the publication of a new set of informed contributions to the Danish historical debate for the broader public. See the articles in the journal published by the Centre for Peace and Conflict Resolution in Copenhagen, *Vandkunsten,* No. 3, 1990, "Historie og myte. Et liv med den 9. April."

61. For one of many possible examples, see Morten Løkkegaard, "Dansk milliardgevinst ved tysk genforening," *Jyllands-Posten,* March 4, 1990.

62. *Denmark, Iceland. Country Profile, 1992-93.* (*The Economist* Intelligence Units, 1992), p. 26.

63. The publication, *Grenzfriedenshefte,* regularly publishes articles that emphasize one or the other of these interpretations. There is truth in both positions, as the editors of this excellent little journal clearly understand. It is published by the *Grenzfriedensbund* in Flensburg.

64. See Øhrgaard, "Offizielle Anpassung und inoffizielle Distanz." Also many articles in *Grenzfriedenshefte,* such as: Eckhard Bodenstein, "Hilfe, die Deutschen kommen!," No. 4, 1983, pp. 222-43, Bodenstein, "Der ewig häßliche Deutsche?," No. 2, 1987, pp. 67-80, and Elin Fredsted, "Dein Nachbar, das unbekannte Wesen," No. 3, 1985, especially p. 157f.

65. See the various writings by Morten Kelstrup and Ole Wæver on this subject, including their co-authored analysis, "The German Problem," originally published by the Centre for Peace and Conflict Resolution, Copenhagen, *Working Papers,* 8/1990. Other

political analysts who stress this argument include Tøger Seidenfaden, *Et helt Europa* (Viborg: Spektrum, 1991), especially pp. 120-38, and Nikolaj Petersen, *Tysklands enhed — Europas sikkerhed* (Copenhagen: SNU, 1991). Petersen's concluding chapter is devoted to a Danish perspective on German unity and European security.

66. See her published correspondence with Sven Burmester, in which she mentions her efforts to brush up on the German language through summer studies in Stuttgart. Bjerregaard, *Verden er så stor, så stor*, p. 177.

67. See Leif Ahm, "Wir lernen Deutsch som aldrig før," *Politiken*, March 11, 1990.

68. He has written frequently on the subject. In 1985, he and three other Danish *Germanisten* presented a parliamentary commission on education with data in support of a plea for more attention to the German language in the Danish schools. The following points were supported with quantitative data: (1) Denmark exports more to West Germany than to any other country; (2) West Germany is the country that creates most jobs in Denmark by importing Danish products; (3) Denmark imports more from West Germany than from any other country; (4) Denmark has a higher letter correspondence with West Germany than with any other country; (5) West Germany ranks second, after Sweden, in the number of telephone conversations made with Denmark; (6) West Germany is (by far) the country from which Denmark receives the most tourists. See the recommendation and supportive data, *Til folketingets uddannelsesudvalg og undervisningsministeren*, October 21, 1985. I am grateful to Professor Øhrgaard for making these materials available to me.

69. See Helmut Schmidt, *Die Deutschen und ihre Nachbarn. Menschen und Mächte II* (Berlin: Wolf Jobst Siedler Verlag, 1990), pp. 375-82. The former Federal Chancellor ends his impressions with the conclusion: "I regard the Danes as a happy people" ("In meinen Augen sind die Dänen ein glückliches Volk"), p. 382.

70. See Maria Eysell and Bernd Henningsen, "Dänemark. Politik, Wirtschaft und Gesellschaft diesseits und jenseits von Maastricht," in *Aus Politik und Zeitgeschichte*, No. B42/92, October 16, 1992, p. 5. For a report on the role of the German factor in the Danish campaign for and against the Maastricht Treaty, see "Dänemark. Historische Chance," *Der Spiegel*, May 25, 1992. It is based in part on a longer Danish article by Niels Krause-Kjær, "Det tyske spøgelse," *Jyllands-Posten*, May 17, 1992.

6

Norway and Germany: Changing Relations between Europe's Periphery and Center

Trond Gilberg and Jens Drews

Introduction

Norwegian-German relations have always revolved around several major issues, namely those of national security, economics, and historical memory. Throughout the centuries, the two countries existed inside their respective international and interstate systems, and this had a profound effect on the evolution of their bilateral relations. From the 14th to the early 20th centuries, Norway was first a member of the Danish and then of the Swedish security system. During that period, the German states were part of various empires and involved in numerous alliances, all of which enhanced or stymied their interests in the North. Basically, the early relations were structured by trade and other economic interactions through the Hanseatic League. This produced a legacy of economic predominance in the relationship that lasted well into this century. By the time Germany was united, Norway was already a committed neutral, trying to stay out of alliances. In a nutshell, these were the broad developments and factors that dominated bilateral relations until April 9, 1940, the day German troops invaded Norway.

The ensuing occupation left a lasting historical legacy that is felt to this day. The experience of invasion and occupation became the first breakpoint in Norwegian-German relations in this century. This and each of the subsequent breakpoints defined and redefined the extent and character of the relations between the two countries. The second breakpoint occurred in 1949, when Oslo abandoned its longstanding policy of neutrality and became a founding member of NATO. A resurgent Federal Republic joined the Atlantic Alliance in 1955. In other words, less than a decade after Germany and Norway had faced each other as occupier and occupied, both countries found themselves as comrades-in-arms in the same military-political alliance.

In 1972, Norway had to decide whether to join the European Community in which West Germany was already the major partner. Its decision not to become an EC member constituted the third breakpoint because it reduced Norway's presence in Europe. As a direct result, it figured less as a factor in a West German foreign policy that aimed at further European integration. And now, in the early 1990s, bilateral relations have reached their fourth breakpoint. After the Soviet Union has exited the world stage, and the Cold War has come to a rather unexpected end, many political axioms that have guided Norwegian and German foreign policy for more than four decades are in need of reassessment. Because reunited Germany's status as Europe's dominant political and economic power is undisputed, Oslo is once again forced to reconsider its relationship with Europe in general and Germany in particular. And as has been the case in the past, the next phase in Norwegian-German relations will be defined on the basis of security and economic interests as well as in the context of the history that is shared by the two countries.

Historical Background

Norway and Germany are two of Europe's "belated nations." Nevertheless, relations existed between them long before they were able to establish themselves as modern nation-states in 1871 (Germany) and 1905 (Norway). A thousand years earlier, Norwegians had been christianized by missionaries from Northern German bishoprics. In the 12th century, the Baltic city of Lübeck, *capud et principum* of the more than seventy towns organized in the Hanseatic League, forged lasting commercial, trade, and cultural relations with Norwegian seaports such as Christiania (today's Oslo) and Bergen on the Atlantic coast. Thus, peripheral, isolated, sparsely populated, and poor northwestern Europe became part of a common economic space that linked the Baltic area with England and the commercial centers of continental Europe. And in the wake of the traders, the German guild system, German construction methods and architecture, and German forms of local government were introduced in Norway.[1]

After the 14th century, the height of Hanseatic power, Norway's international orientation remained directed towards Germany in the South and towards England in the West. In this matter, the forces of economy and geography joined in establishing a lasting pattern because "links across the sea were more convenient and . . . became more important than land links."[2] Despite the fact that all Nordic people had the same religion, spoke similar languages, and followed comparable legal principles, Norwegian relations with its immediate neighbors on the Scandinavian peninsula were relegated to a secondary status. The primary orientation towards the British Isles and Germany survived the decline of the Hanseatic League and the end of Danish rule over Norway that lasted from 1380 to 1814. And with Norwegian independence, won after the peaceful dissolution of the union with Sweden in 1905, the country came to rely even more on its powerful neighbors to the West and South, as historical economic statistics have shown.[3]

Throughout the centuries, England, Germany, and, increasingly so, the Scandinavian countries were more than just natural trading partners. They also provided significant political, cultural, and social impulses for Norway's nation-building process. This was important because the country had "little in the nature of native institutions upon which to build," and, therefore, an effort was made to "transplant to Norwegian soil a body of political forms and usages calculated to produce a high order of popular government."[4] The latter proved to be quite successful: despite the fact that regional, cultural, and, later, socioeconomic cleavages divided the ethnically highly homogeneous nation, the Norwegians were able to create and maintain an exemplary democratic system at a time of rapid economic and political change. Contrary to what happened in Germany, Norway's democratic development was neither impeded by existing divisive issues (urban versus rural, pietistic versus secular, and so forth) nor by encumbering legacies that dated back to the period before independent statehood. Quite the opposite: because Norway "entered upon modernity with a very broad and very flat social hierarchy," without an "indigenous aristocracy," and with a "lack of resources," the "tasks of national development and integration" fell almost naturally to the state and its civil servants.[5] The state, in cooperation with strong political parties and well-organized sectional interests (workers, farmers, fishermen, traders), succeeded in its tasks remarkably well. And because it did so without sacrificing the welfare and prospects of any of society's groups, modern Norway evolved as a nation that was characterized by a "culture of equality, solidarity and pro-statism."[6]

Throughout the process of nation-building, Norway remained open to outside influences. For example, the country's powerful traders, merchants, and shipowners were by and large anglophile and advocates of strong links with Great Britain, the leading maritime power. The country's labor movement, however, was greatly influenced by the left wing of German Social Democracy with its Marxist political theory and Karl Liebknecht's and Rosa Luxemburg's political practice. As for the rest of Norwegian society, it looked to these two and other countries for inspiration and innovation, especially in the fields of industry, arts, and sciences.

Norway's relations with the outside world in general and Germany in particular were by no means unidirectional. Artists like Ibsen, Grieg, Hamsun, and Munch won early critical acclaim in Germany. Indeed, many Norwegian writers, painters, composers, and scholars saw Germany as their second *Vaterland* (fatherland), admired for its great *Bildung* (learning) and *Wissenschaft* (science).[7]

As multifaceted German-Norwegian relations developed over the centuries and as they intensified in the 1800s, a peculiar pattern emerged: Norway looked with great interest at certain aspects of German political, economic, social, and cultural life. For example, social policies, bureaucratic procedures, educational structures, the country's *Dichter und Denker* (poets and thinkers) as well as the achievements of the workers' movement, all contributed in one way or another to Norwegian development.

At the same time, however, Norwegians were deeply apprehensive about the excesses of Wilhelmine Germany that manifested themselves in aggressive foreign policy postures abroad and a lack of democracy at home. Both aspects of Germany's national development reflected a predominance of attitudes and values that were quite alien to Norwegian political culture. In addition to an imperturbable commitment to democratic procedures, this political culture was characterized by a genuine belief in the principles of neutrality and peaceful resolution of international conflicts. Consequently, there was little common ground that Norway and Germany shared in matters of "high politics." An example of the two countries' different approaches to politics was the method by which both nations achieved statehood: Germany by means of *Blut und Eisen* (blood and iron) in a series of wars, and Norway through a series of plebiscites. First the Norwegian people approved the dissolution of the union with Sweden, then they rejected a republican form of government and selected a member of Denmark's royal family to be the country's king.[8]

Clearly, this procedure stood in marked contrast to the authoritarian ways of Wilhelmine Germany. As a result, respect for Germany's accomplishments was mixed with fear to what ends it might use its rapidly increasing power, and how its drive for "a place in the sun" would affect Norway. Its strategic location and its long, rugged coastline (which was ideally suited for naval operations in the Atlantic) made the country necessarily a factor in Germany's *Weltpolitik* (world policy). Therefore, Norway strengthened its ties with Great Britain, a country that had a much more compatible approach to politics and that was not perceived as a threat to national independence and security. But despite the country's strong pro-British sentiments, Norway continued to pursue a policy of neutrality, as did all Scandinavian countries.

During World War I, Norway resisted pressures by the British and the Germans to take sides. Nevertheless, "half of the Norwegian fleet was being directly employed by the Allied nations, and Norwegian shipowners made large profits. But the cost was high: between 1914 and 1918, 663 vessels totaling 1.1

million tons were lost."[9] Only in the last year of the war did Norway begin to mine its waters in response to German submarine activities that were responsible for most of these losses. It did so without entering the war officially, and it did not participate in the Versailles Peace Conference.

After 1918, Norway viewed active membership in the League of Nations as a natural extension of its policy of neutrality and as the most promising way to guarantee its national security. Although "the war brought a setback to Scandinavian unity,"[10] cooperation among the Nordic countries continued to preserve a zone of peace, democratic stability, social progress, and relative prosperity unlike any other region in Europe.

The rise of National Socialism confirmed these Norwegian fears about Germany that had existed since before 1914. Because of its violence in form and content, Nazism was distasteful and unacceptable to most Scandinavians with their different political-cultural traditions. Norway's Labour government, in power since 1935, did not conceal its antipathy and granted asylum to many German refugees. Nevertheless, the country stood by its policy of neutrality once World War II began in September 1939. The antipathy did not go so far as to override the desire to stay out of the latest round of Great Power conflict. But just as the League of Nations could not prevent the war's conflagration, so was Norway's policy of neutrality rapidly overtaken by events. Great Britain and Germany were equally determined to deny the enemy control over Norway and access, via Narvik, to the strategically important iron-ore mines in northern Sweden. As a consequence, neither side could accept Norwegian neutrality as the stakes rose, and, inevitably, Norway was drawn into the war.

In order to gain a base for submarine operations in the North Atlantic and to forestall British efforts to mine Norwegian waters, German naval and airborne troops invaded the country on April 9, 1940, in the *Aktion Weserübung*.[11] After two months of fighting, the Norwegian forces capitulated, a British expeditionary corps withdrew, and the royal family and the legitimate government went into exile in London. For the duration of the war, Norway remained under German occupation, ruled by a German *Reichskommissar*, Josef Terboven. Hitler's proconsul could rely on a collaborationist government led by Vidkun Quisling, a Norwegian National Socialist who had personally already offered his loyalty and service to Hitler in December 1939. Quisling's political party, the *Nasjonal Samling*, never gained more than 2.2 percent of the vote (1933), and its share fell to even less than one percent in the local elections of 1937.[12] This is evidence that the "Aryan" Norwegians were largely immune to the precepts of National Socialist ideology.

An active underground, the Homefront, was among the best organized resistance movements in occupied Europe. It helped many members of Norway's small Jewish community escape to neutral Sweden. Despite the Homefront's efforts, 760 Jews, that is, 40 percent of all Jews living in Norway in 1940, perished in Nazi concentration camps.[13] In response to sabotage and other forms of resistance by the Homefront's *Militaer Organisasjonen*, the new authorities retaliated brutally against the civilian population. During the war, "the resistance suffered a total of 2,089 fatalities, including 266 women. Some 35,000 were imprisoned — from a population of 2.8 million."[14]   These repressive measures further frustrated efforts to convert more Norwegians to the National Socialist cause, and only 57,000 of them joined Quisling's *Nasjonal Samling*. In comparison, more than 300,000 Germans were stationed in Norway and Denmark throughout the war.[15]

After five years of occupation, Norwegian sovereignty was restored when King Haakon returned from his London exile. The new democratic government was led by the Social Democrat Einar Gerhardsen, who had just been freed from a German concentration camp. Under his leadership, Norway faced the task of redefining its place and function in the region, in Europe, and in the world. Many conflicting internal and external factors and forces had to be considered and balanced over the coming decades. Torn between isolationist, regional, Atlanticist, European, and global sentiments, Norway has since tried to pursue a foreign policy that has faced the following tasks: to prevent renewed threats to its sovereignty and territorial integrity while at the same time to meet those unprecedented challenges that an evolving complex and increasingly interdependent international system posed.

Norway and Germany, West and East: Setting the Stage after 1945

The management of Norwegian-German relations was an issue that required special attention as Norway took a new look at foreign policy. Memories of invasion and occupation were too fresh simply to resume normal bilateral contacts. Indeed, the years 1940 to 1945 constituted the first and decisive breakpoint in the relationship between the two countries. The war has left an indelible mark that since has faded but not disappeared. At the same time, geographical proximity, obvious disparities in population size, in industrial strength, and in economic and political power forced Norway to interact with a resurgent West Germany. Therefore, Norway had little choice but to overcome historically well-founded apprehensions and fears and to engage its neighbor to the south in a wide range of economic, political, and other activities. These included military cooperation after the Federal Republic joined NATO in 1955. But in all of these endeavors, wartime experiences remained a factor. For example, it was not until February 1990 that a large contingent of German soldiers could participate in NATO's winter maneuvers on Norwegian soil.[16]

However, the resumption of relations was facilitated by the fact that Norway's postwar foreign policy underwent a fundamental reassessment. It took into account the country's peripheral and precarious location in northwestern

Europe, the lessons learned from history, as well as an appreciation of the new geopolitical realities of the Cold War. As a result, the following tenets were formulated to guide Norwegian foreign policy beyond the late 1940s. They provided a broad framework in which relations with Germany (West and East) have to be placed.

First, and most importantly, a return to the prewar policy of neutrality was no longer possible for Norway. World War II and its offspring, the Cold War, precluded it as a viable option. Realizing this, Norway became a founding member of the North Atlantic Treaty Organization in 1949. Its motives for joining were shared by all other continental European NATO members of the first hour — to keep the Soviets out, the Americans in, and the Germans down, as aptly summarized by Lord Ismay, NATO's first Secretary-General.[17]

Second, in addition to membership in NATO, Norway reinforced its Atlantic ties by rebuilding its traditional relationship with Great Britain and by extending it to the new Great Power of the West, the United States. Political affinities, geographical realities, and historical memories led Norway to define itself as an Atlantic country first, and as a European nation second.

Third, for the same reasons, Norway also strengthened its role in Nordic affairs. Through a series of bilateral and multilateral agreements with Denmark, Sweden, Finland, and Iceland, it helped Scandinavia establish itself as a distinct entity with its own voice in international affairs. This was done in a manner that avoided interference with conflicting international obligations (Sweden's neutrality, Finland's special relationship with the Soviet Union, and Denmark's, Iceland's and Norway's NATO membership) but rather complemented them by creating a specifically Nordic security balance that benefitted all parties.[18]

Fourth, relations with continental Western European states consequently remained problematic. For Norwegians, Europe always meant Germany, an identification that reinforced the self-assessment of being an Atlantic country. This was an important reason for shunning membership in the European Community in 1972. Twelve years earlier, Norway had joined the European Free Trade Association (EFTA), whose original membership (Austria, Switzerland, Portugal, Great Britain, Ireland, Denmark, Sweden, and Finland) and limited purpose were more palatable to the Norwegian people.

Fifth, relations with the Soviet Union, a country that shared a common border with Norway, and with Eastern Europe, were maintained and developed on the basis of Norway's Atlantic ties, its NATO membership, and its regional identity. The latter allowed Norway to serve as bridgebuilder between East and West in the 1960s, and again in the early and mid-1980s when the smaller states of NATO and the Warsaw Pact sought to overcome the impasse caused by deteriorating relations between the superpowers. However, the country never forgot that its common border with the Soviet Union, the "suffocating vicinity of . . . power,"[19] was one of the main reasons for its membership in NATO.

To this day this geographical factor continues to shape Norwegian attitudes towards the Atlantic Alliance and Russia.

Sixth, Norway also became a leader in dealing with North-South issues, challenging the industrialized countries to play a greater and more constructive role in the Third World's economic and social development. Since the days of Fritjof Nansen and the League of Nations in the 1920s, such a globalist perspective, rooted in some highly moralistic and deeply religious aspects of the country's political culture, has always influenced Norwegian domestic and foreign policies.

Seventh, at the same time, there continued to be a strong isolationist sentiment that was also fed by a strong undercurrent in Norwegian political culture. The presence of such attitudes made itself felt during the "fierce, savage, and vitriolic debate"[20] over EC membership in 1972. Since then, the rise of the populist Progressive Party and the debates over immigration policies have shown that isolationism is still a force to be reckoned with.

Since the end of the war, these have been the basic orientations that determined the direction of Norwegian foreign policy, including the resumption and development of relations with the two German states. In other words, Norwegian-German relations have been a function of Oslo's perception of, and response to, the postwar world order. This order, however, no longer exists, and new foreign policy accents will have to be set. Above all, the Norwegian people face the issue of their participation in the process of European integration with renewed urgency. And it is precisely within the framework of European integration that Norwegian-German relations have gained a new salience and reached their latest breakpoint. Even before reunification, Germany was the continent's hegemon, and since then Bonn — or should one say: Berlin? — is in a position that will allow it "to dominate Europe to the degree (if not in the manner and the same purpose) intended by prior generations."[21] Undoubtedly, this will continue to be a weighty factor in Oslo's future foreign policy.

Even more than Norway, Germany had to regain statehood before foreign policy initiatives could even be considered within the narrow confines of postwar realities. These realities were created by (a) the victorious powers' occupation of Germany, (b) the country's national division into two antagonistic states with incompatible political and economic orders, (c) the horrendous legacy of the National Socialist regime, and (d) the Cold War as the new defining international issue. All of these factors circumscribed the foreign policy options of both German states as they arose from the rubble of the Third Reich under the auspices of their respective occupation powers.

In the case of the Federal Republic, it meant that all foreign policy was to be based on an unconditional commitment to the West, its political and economic institutions and structures, and its concomitant socio-political values. In practical terms, it required close cooperation with its democratic neighboring states in newly created institutions such as NATO, the West European Union

(WEU), and the Common Market after a "probationary period" (1949-55) during which West Germany regained much of its sovereignty. The Federal Republic's political class came to accept the axiom that Germany could only rejoin the community of civilized states if it subordinated all national aspirations, and especially the desire for reunification, to the demands of democracy, peace, and stability. Bonn was aware that it was no longer in a position to pursue foreign policy *Sonderwege* (special paths): its fate rested *in* the West and *with* the West. Only on this basis, the country was able to re-establish relations with its neighboring states, including Norway, that had been victims of German military aggression only a few years earlier.

The German Democratic Republic was not given the chance to establish itself as a foreign policy actor in its own right: until 1989, it remained under Soviet tutelage. Therefore, its domestic and foreign policy margins were closely circumscribed. In short, the GDR existed only because the Soviet Union wanted it to exist, and only as long as the USSR was willing and able to preserve the western-most member of its bloc. Naturally, East Germany's rather hapless position in the international system had consequences for its relations with its non-fraternal neighbors, including Norway.

However, by the early 1970s, the increasing importance of the FRG in the Western alliance and of the GDR in the Soviet sphere affected Norway's relations with both German states. Briefly put, the leaders in Oslo had to deal with each of them on the basis of their impact on Norway's national security vis-a-vis the Warsaw Pact. Furthermore, the Norwegians had to reckon with the two German states in economic matters. West Germany was Europe's powerhouse, accounting for more than 25 percent of the EC's economic activity by the early 1980s, and the GDR, Comecon's most productive member, was also considered to be a potentially important partner in foreign trade. However, national security and economic aspects of Norwegian-German relations continued to be overshadowed by historical legacies. It took about a quarter century before historical memories receded into the background and national security and economic interests could become the main operative factors that shaped the course of interstate relations. But even as a dormant issue, history continued to be of importance and especially so whenever Norwegian-German relations reached a breakpoint after 1945.

For most of the 1950s and 1960s, Norway's relations with the Federal Republic were based on the foundation of NATO membership, which provided a reliable anchor that prevented the Norwegian ship of state from drifting helplessly between the shores of the Great Powers. On the basis of this newly won security and certainty, Norway announced the formal termination of the state of war with Germany in July 1951. In 1953, Norway's occupation force of 6,000 soldiers was withdrawn from northern Germany, and only two years later, the Norwegians and West Germans became allies in the Atlantic Alliance. This allowed the intensification of bilateral relations because Oslo was reassured that West German political, economic, and military power would be integrated in a strong network of Western, democratic institutions. But despite common membership in a multilateral organization such as NATO, bilateral relations could only be further normalized after West Germany met several preconditions. One of the more important requirements was the ratification of a *Wiedergutmachungsabkommen* (restitution treaty) with Norway. It formally acknowledged West Germany's responsibility to compensate the victims of National Socialist occupation. This was largely a symbolic act, since monetary payments could certainly not undo the crimes and injustices committed during the war years. After the treaty was signed in August 1959, the road was open for intensified bilateral relations inside and outside of NATO.

In March 1965, Prime Minister Gerhardsen was the first Norwegian head of government officially to visit West Germany, and the following year Federal Chancellor Erhard came to Oslo. During these visits, relations between the Common Market and EFTA, various NATO issues, and the two countries' policies towards Eastern Europe were discussed. Erhard wanted to receive assurances that Oslo would not recognize East Germany. Their talks on substantive issues were overshadowed by memories of the recent past. As a West German observer pointed out, "relations between Germany and Scandinavia can only develop with the greatest of circumspection. It will take a long time before the after-effects of the war will be effaced."[22]

A decisive improvement in Norwegian-West German relations occurred when Willy Brandt was elected Chancellor in 1969. He had come to Norway as a young political refugee from Hitler's Germany, joined the anti-Nazi resistance, married a Norwegian woman, acquired citizenship, and returned to defeated Germany as a Norwegian foreign service officer in January 1947. He resigned his commission as a press attaché (with the rank of Major) after one year in order to begin his rapid ascent in German Social Democratic politics.[23] However, his attachment to Norway remained very strong, and Brandt's election created a great deal of confidence in the new Germany that he seemed to represent. His official visit to Norway in 1970 was widely seen as a "sign that the past was being overcome."[24] Later in the same year, President Gustav Heinemann was also able to represent a better Germany to the Norwegians. Openly discussing what had been done to Norway in the name of Germany during occupation and war, the Social Democratic "citizen president" won the sympathy of his hosts because of his anti-Nazi credentials and his strong Lutheran background. During that state visit King Olav V confirmed that relations with West Germany had indeed been improved and that no unresolved bilateral problems existed.[25] In 1973, the king visited Bonn as well as some state capitals, and his warm reception indicated that German-Norwegian relations had been normalized to the extent that this was possible at that time. From the early 1970s on, the number and frequency of high level contacts increased, and talks focused more on current issues that were of mutual interest, and less on the bitter history that was shared by the two countries.

Despite these positive developments, relations reached their third breakpoint in 1972 because of Norway's self-imposed absence from the European Community. After a popular referendum blocked membership, bilateral relations did not really develop and intensify much further. As a result of Oslo's decision not to participate in an organization that was widening its membership and deepening its cooperation throughout the 1970s and 1980s, the spheres of Norwegian and West German foreign policy did not intersect in this crucial area. Thus, while the Federal Republic emerged as a European leader, Norway remained a geographically and politically peripheral country. Had it not been for Norway's membership in NATO, relations would have been even more overshadowed by the dynamic processes that took place south of the Skagerak.

As a consequence of Norway's absence from the European Community and because bilateral relations were routinized, largely problem-free, and, in general, had reached a self-sustaining level, West Germany's public, press, and politicians showed little interest in Norwegian affairs. For example, in his more than one thousand pages of memoirs, former Chancellor Helmut Schmidt devoted less than seven pages to the *schweigsamen Norweger* ("taciturn Norwegians").[26] Only President Richard von Weizsäcker's trip to Norway in 1986 led to a brief moment during which Norwegian-German relations received some more attention. As he had done at many other occasions before, von Weizsäcker used his visit to remind the Germans of their past, and to reassure his hosts that the Germans were aware of their historical responsibilities.[27] But his state visit did not change the overall pattern of a relationship that was friendly, stable, and predictable but not very dynamic.

By all accounts, Norwegian relations with the other German state never reached such a level. The contentious issues of the present (Cold War), even more than the problems of the past (World War II), stood in the way of normal bilateral relations. Norway recognized the German Democratic Republic at the height of detente and only after Bonn had given the "green light" in 1974. Subsequent official contacts remained limited to the ministerial level, and they were not as frequent as the Honecker regime would have liked, as it sought to expand political relations for two main reasons. First, East Germany recognized that "despite its limitations," Norway's "ruling class" belonged to those elements among the "internationalist monopolistic bourgeoisie" which advocated "realistic policy positions" vis-a-vis the socialist states.[28] In other words, the East German leadership believed that Norway along with the other Nordic countries would be responsive to their political overtures, especially on the issues of war and peace. Second, each high level interaction with a NATO member had an intrinsic value for East Berlin. The promotion of such contacts was part of East Germany's strategy to overcome its handicap of being, literally and metaphorically, the second German state. The goal was to gain international legitimacy by being a more active participant in the East-West dialogue. Therefore, each visit by a Norwegian official was prominently covered in the official Communist Party daily *Neues Deutschland* in an attempt to reassure the East German leadership and people that the GDR had indeed become a valued player in the concert of Europe.

Norway, of course, did not need to worry about its international credentials, and it viewed its relations with East Germany in the context of Norway's responsibility for a peaceful management of the East-West conflict. Oslo also continued to remind the Honecker government of the importance of human rights, and, especially, of the principles of the 1975 Helsinki Accords, which demanded "a freer flow of people and ideas across borders."[29] Outside the realm of high politics, relations were virtually non-existent, and even the volume of trade between the two countries was by and large as negligible throughout the 1980s, as earlier, more optimistic expectations did not materialize. In a rare moment of what might pass as self-criticism, this was even acknowledged by the East Germans themselves.[30]

As far as economic relations between Norway and West Germany were concerned, they were an indication of the extent to which relations had been normalized since the end of World War II. Historically, Germany and the United Kingdom had always been Norway's most significant trading partners. Today, they are only surpassed by neighboring Sweden. Between 1969 and 1989, West Germany constantly ranked second as an exporter of goods to Norway. As the Scandinavian country's trade relations broadened, the share of imports from West Germany fell from 14.9 percent in 1969 to 12.5 percent in 1989. Looking at the destinations of Norwegian exports, the United Kingdom still ranks as the number one importer, although its share has fallen from more than 36 percent in 1979 and 1984 to 26.8 percent in 1989. West Germany ranks third behind Sweden, and in 1989, 11.2 percent of all Norwegian exports went to the Federal Republic. This figure is down from the 1970s, but up from 1984 when less than 10 percent of all Norwegian goods were imported by West Germany. Not surprisingly, Norway does not figure as prominently in German foreign trade statistics. In 1989, only 1.4 percent of all West German imports originated in Norway, a share that was down from 2.5 percent in 1981. As a market for German products, Norway is even less important. In 1971, about 1.5 percent of all West German exports went to Norway; by 1989, this number had fallen to only 0.8 percent.

Vehicles and other kinds of transport equipment, electrical and general industrial machinery are the most important commodities that Norway imports from Germany. In 1989, these types of products accounted for 40.3 percent of all imports from Germany. At the same time, Norway's exports to Germany consisted mainly of raw materials and other natural resources. In 1989, the five largest commodity groups that were imported by West Germany were non-ferrous metals (22.5 percent), gas (17.6 percent), oil and petroleum products (12.7 percent), iron and steel (6.3 percent), and paper and paperboard (5.2 percent). Over the last decade, natural gas has lost much of its importance as a trade commodity. In 1978, it accounted for 43.4 percent and in 1984 even for 49 percent of all Norwegian exports to West Germany. Its relative decline was largely due to falling prices and the fact that the Soviet Union had entered the international natural gas market and established brisk trade relations with West Germany.[31]

Norway, Germany, and a Changing Europe

The development of bilateral trade relations should be discussed in the larger context of Norway's refusal to join the European Community. Ever since the 1960s, the West German government had not concealed its support for Norwegian membership in the Common Market. This issue, along with NATO and other security matters, has always topped the Norwegian-German agenda. When Great Britain showed renewed interest in opening talks with Brussels in 1967, the Norwegian government followed suit. It assumed that without British (and Danish and Irish) membership, EFTA's effectiveness as an *ersatz* (substitute) EC would be greatly diminished. Oslo signed a treaty of accession and submitted it to the people for approval in a referendum. As it turned out, the government's logic for joining the EC was not generally shared by the population. A powerful coalition of well organized groups and associations emerged, an *ad hoc* movement that had the single goal of preventing Norwegian entry into the Common Market. Especially the trade unions, the farmers, and the fishing industry were opposed because they feared that their particular sectional interests would suffer.

In their fight against EC membership, these interest groups had the advantage of being able to assert pressure at two levels. First, they could exploit the fact that Norway's political system was, and is, highly corporatist. In terms of foreign policy making this meant that those "groups most directly affected by a prospective decision are invited to take part in its preparation."[32] Second, opponents of the EC were successful in appealing to the isolationist and neutralist segments of the Norwegian population. The opposition's efforts boosted a grass-roots campaign, and when the special referendum on Common Market membership was held in 1972, 53 percent voted against it. Before the government resigned in response to this defeat, it terminated further talks with Brussels.

Aside from economic fears, many Norwegians had other reasons to vote against closer European integration. Indeed, rejection of EC membership was based on a broad range of concerns that included the worry of how powerful Germany would be vis-a-vis Norway, fears of economic exploitation and of environmental degradation, and more general political-cultural apprehensions about having to alter time-honored Norwegians ways. Fears of losing one's identity and of becoming a cog in an alien political and economic machinery were also voiced. Further contributing to the negative vote on the referendum were tendencies of isolationist introversion as well as the hinterland's skepticism about the morally corrosive influences of urban centers, be they Oslo or Brussels. Willy Brandt summarized Norwegian political-cultural idiosyncracies, which he knew well, quite sarcastically when he wrote that "the Norwegians were haunted by a pietistic tee-totaller's nightmare that the Common Market might oblige them to become regular wine-drinkers and that their girls would be carried off by swarthy southerners."[33]

The rejection of EC membership had lasting, almost traumatic, consequences for Norway and its people. In the words of one observer, "it almost ripped the country's fabric apart."[34] True enough, in a country that prides itself on its consensual form of democracy and decision-making, the aftermaths of the "hardest fought political issue which has occurred in Norway this century"[35] were not easily dealt with. And that is what has happened since 1972: not many leading politicians have dared to reopen the dormant question of Norwegian EC membership. For example, after Prime Minister Brundtland met with Chancellor Kohl in Bonn in 1988, they insisted that the issue of possible Norwegian membership in the Common Market had not been raised. To this Kohl added that he did not want to interfere in internal Norwegian affairs.[36] This, however, was the last time that both governments could deal with this matter in such a discreet way. Only one year later, the issue of EC membership gained new salience as Europe's longstanding political premises and paradigms were overturned.

Until the *annus mirabilis* of 1989-90, Norway could afford to be aloof as the twelve Community nations accelerated their economic and political integration. While this process gained momentum, Oslo continued to remain on the periphery of events, satisfied that its links with continental Europe were guaranteed through its participation in NATO. All members of the Atlantic Alliance, many of which also belonged to the EC, were aware of Norway's strategic location and its control over the "North Atlantic lines of communication."[37] Because this was an important factor in the security of the Alliance, Norway was given a voice in European matters. This special Cold War consideration compensated, at least partially, for some of the influence it lacked as a result of its absence from the Common Market.

Yet, after four decades the Cold War ended and the Soviet/Russian fleet ran, quite literally, out of steam. As a consequence, the traditional problems of national security were receding into the background. New issues such as Western Europe's economic and political integration under the terms of the soon to be signed Maastricht Treaty, and the East's problems of transition, instability, and ethnic violence were topping the Continent's agenda. Given the nature of these issues, Norway's importance, which was largely based on its strategic location vis-a-vis the Soviet Union, was diminished, and Oslo found itself isolated from the mainstream of European politics. In other words, Norway began to face a similarly defining moment in its history as it did in 1949. Then, a changing world led Norway to a cross-road at which a fundamental choice had to be made that would shape its foreign policy for the coming decades. In 1949, Oslo made the decision to forgo its policy of neutrality. Overruling popular objections, the government recognized the need to join other states on both sides of the Atlantic in creating NATO. This was a momentous decision that came as much as a response to the past (German invasion and occupation) as in anticipation of a more uncertain and dangerous future (Soviet threat).

It appears that joining NATO was the extent to which Norway's postwar governments were able to break with the country's foreign policy traditions of neutrality and noninvolvement in Great Power conflicts. But these political-cultural predilections continued to exert some influence even after 1949, and they help to explain why Norway put unilateral restrictions on the terms of its NATO membership and, more generally, why it held a distinctly Nordic perspective on East-West relations. Thus, it was an early advocate of opening a dialogue with the Soviet bloc in the 1960s. For example, Foreign Minister Halvard Lange suggested to the Bonn government in 1964 to take a more realistic approach to the "German question," to abandon the Hallstein Doctrine, and to pursue its national goal of reunification through a policy of *Entspannung*.[38] And as overall international conditions deteriorated into a last round of Cold War in the late 1970s and early 1980s, Norway was especially adamant to keep detente alive. It was during those years of "damage limitation" that contacts with the smaller Warsaw Pact states, including East Germany, won new importance for Norway. While some saw this as evidence that Norway was in pursuit of "semi-neutrality,"[39] others conceded that Oslo had little choice in light of its "domestically driven foreign policy."[40]

The question is whether the changes that were brought by the end of the Cold War, German unification, and the apparent momentum for further European integration will change the country's foreign policy postures. In other words, is Norway's period as a "reluctant European" coming to an end? In many respects, an answer to this question is tied to Oslo's perception of its own and of Germany's role in Europe and the world.

It is in this context that Norwegian-German relations have reached their fourth breakpoint. The question is whether Norway is prepared to accept German leadership in a Europe in which it is fully integrated. As has been the case throughout the postwar period, the legacy of history continues to influence strategic and economic considerations. This explains the Norwegian fear that Germany is filling the power vacuum left by the collapse of the Soviet Union and a reduction in the American presence in Europe. Germany today already is Europe's most powerful polity and economy, and it is trying to set the pace and direction of European integration. Furthermore, German initiatives on how the EC should respond to the break-up of Yugoslavia as well as the *Bundes-bank*'s high interest rate policy have shown that Bonn/Berlin is willing to use its political and economic muscle in dealing with Paris, London, and even Washington. Although the German government might argue convincingly that its goal is not the creation of a German-dominated Europe but of a "European Germany" that is committed to the "ideals and fundamental values of freedom, human dignity, and democracy,"[41] the reality of being a Great Power might follow its own logic.

At this point, it is useful to take a look at how Norwegians responded to Germany's unification. The results of two opinion polls indicate that a great majority was in favor. In April 1990, 64.1 percent of a sample expressed a positive attitude, 14.9 had a negative attitude, and 21.1 percent had either no opinion or was not sure what to say about Germany's possible unification.[42] In response to a differently worded question, 77.1 percent of those interviewed supported German unification at the time it actually happened in the fall of 1990.[43] The second Norwegian survey copied a question asked in a *Euro-barometer* poll that was conducted on behalf of the EC Commission during the same time period. A comparison of the data indicates that the level of Norwegian support was within one percent of the EC average. The level of support in Norway was even higher than in Denmark (69 percent) and the United Kingdom (72 percent), traditionally two of Norway's closest allies in the EC.[44]

Public opinion data such as this can be interpreted as a vote of confidence in Germany's future, and it is largely in Germany's hands whether or not its Scandinavian neighbor will retain this positive outlook. More precisely, Norwegians will watch closely how Germany conducts itself in two of Europe's most important institutions, NATO and EC. Both are rapidly approaching the next phase of their existence, and this will affect Norway greatly. Despite setbacks and second thoughts, the European Community still is poised to implement its ambitious Maastricht program which, if successful, could be a crucial step towards the eventual creation of a United States of Europe with Germany at its center. NATO, however, might enter into its last phase, as strategic planners begin to look at alternatives such as a purely European defense system, a rejuvenated Western European Union (WEU) led by France and Germany, or a strengthened CSCE with expanded defense and security tasks. In any case, Norway as a country with a distinctly Atlantic identity will be disadvantaged: it is not a member of WEU, and American influence would be diluted among the fifty-plus members of the CSCE. Therefore, one can expect Norway to remain a strong proponent of present NATO defense arrangements and of continued American engagement in European security matters.[45]

Already, there have been highly visible disagreements between Norway and Germany over a restructuring of NATO arrangements. In response to changing political and military realities, the German government proposed to dissolve

NATO's Northern Command at Kolsas, Norway, which oversaw Norway, Denmark, and the German state of Schleswig-Holstein. Germany wanted NATO's command boundaries to be redrawn in order to bring Denmark and Schleswig-Holstein together with Belgium, the Netherlands, and the rest of Germany under NATO's Central Command. The Norwegian government called this plan "unacceptable," and the Norwegian Parliament's Defense Committee Chairman stated that if German plans were implemented, "a new barrier between Norway and Europe will have been created. That is a situation which would be almost impossible to live with."[46] At a NATO meeting in November 1991, Germany carried the day, and Norway found itself virtually isolated on this question. Neither Denmark nor the United States, but only Great Britain supported the Norwegian position. This led a commentator to conclude that "models for security policy from earlier periods of history are emerging."[47] This conflict between Germany and Norway was reminiscent of their dispute over the appointment of a new NATO Secretary-General in 1987. Then, the German government was able to prevail with its own candidate, Manfred Wörner, over Norway's Kaare Willoch who had the support of Denmark and other smaller NATO members. This episode left many Norwegians and others concerned about the not-so-subtle way in which Germany exercised its power in the Alliance.[48]

Despite these and other experiences with Germany's assertion of its newly won power, Norway will soon be forced to make a decision on whether or not to participate in the process of European integration. Several external factors are effectively limiting its choice, eventually directing it towards full membership in the EC.

First, the country's strategic importance is greatly diminished as a result of the demise of the Soviet Union. The rest of Europe is no longer concerned about a Soviet military threat to NATO's northern flank, which gave Norway an important role in the Alliance, and by extension, in other European affairs as well. Furthermore, the reduced threat level will have an impact on America's interest in Norway. As the sole remaining global power, it is going through a process of trying to define the extent and purpose of its might. Regardless of the outcome of the stocktaking, it is likely that the levels of commitment to Europe and Norway will be reduced.

Second, EFTA is in danger of expiring. To date, Austria, Sweden, and Finland have applied for full EC membership. It is highly questionable whether Norway could refuse to follow its most important trading partner, Sweden, into the Common Market. Indeed, the creation of the European Economic Area (EEA), the West European free trade area combining EC and EFTA, in the fall of 1991 can be viewed as a step towards EFTA's eventual incorporation into the European Community.

Third, as a country located on Europe's periphery, Norway can ill afford to be excluded from decision-making in Brussels. As the EC is preparing for political union, complete with a common foreign and security policy, it will become even more influential in international affairs, whereas NATO's future is rather uncertain. Thus, by continuing to stay on Europe's sidelines, Norway will put itself at a disadvantage. Norway's Defense Minister Holst pointed that out when he said that "for small countries marginalization and isolation always present dangers in foreign policy."[49]

In other words, changing strategic considerations and economic dependencies seem to dictate that Norway join the EC sooner rather than later. However, as has always been the case in its foreign policy, the decisive factor is whether or not Norwegians themselves want to join the process of European integration or remain at its periphery. The European Community can function without Norwegian membership, but can Norway continue to prosper economically once its oil and gas riches are exhausted, or when it has to compete with a much more productive Russia for the same European energy markets? It has to be remembered that similar arguments were made in 1972 when reality seemed to require that Oslo join its two close allies, Great Britain and Denmark, in entering the Common Market. Then, the Norwegian people disagreed with this political logic, and the "We-are-different-from-the-rest-of-Europe" sentiment is still very strong.[50] Although polling data showed a slight majority favoring EC membership (38 percent for, 33 percent against, 28 percent undecided) for the first time in October 1990, these numbers reverted to the old pattern only two months later (34 percent for, 41 percent against).[51] In other words, the picture is far from clear, and more recent polls have not been much more conclusive.

Clearly, Norway's EC membership will depend on whether the Norwegians can be convinced of the benefits of such a step. The current Social Democratic government has begun to make the case for it by saying that Norway needs to follow its Nordic neighbors to Brussels.[52] However, Denmark's rejection of the Maastricht treaty in June 1992 has given new support for the *Nei til EF* ("No to the EC") movement. Despite the active support of Prime Minister Brundtland, Foreign Minister Stoltenberg, and Defense Minister Holst for Norwegian membership, their Social Democratic Party has not made up its mind on this question. Its decision, *pro* or *contra*, will be an important indicator as to how the country will vote in a referendum that will have to be held. At this time there is no guarantee that the country will be spared the agonies of 1972, which left lasting scars on the Norwegian body politic. It cannot be guaranteed that the opposition to the Common Market will be able to reassemble its powerful *ad hoc* coalition. It is thus up to Norway's political class to use the coming years to open the debate and to try to shape public opinion on this crucial issue.

However, what can be said with certainty is that in this "fight for the soul of the people,"[53] any outside intervention will be counterproductive, especially if it comes from Germany. Recently, Chancellor Kohl predicted that all EFTA states will have joined the EC by 1995.[54] Such an assessment can turn into a powerful argument against EC membership because it is likely to resurrect historical fears about the influence that Germany, as Europe's leading power, would have on Norwegian affairs. Kjell Eliassen has aptly summarized such concerns: "The task of convincing Norwegian trade unions that it is in their interest to join a political system, in which within a European Monetary Union the *Deutsche Bundesbank* decides on Norwegian wage increases, is extremely difficult."[55]

Therefore, much will depend on the Norwegian perception of Germany's conduct in Europe. Only if the Norwegians are assured that Germany does not pose a threat, will it be possible for the country to move from Europe's periphery to Europe's center. And there is no guarantee that this will happen now that the euphoria and joy of 1989/90 are gone. Instead, Europe's impotence in dealing with the human tragedies in former Yugoslavia, quarrels within the Atlantic Alliance over the usefulness of a French-German military corps, second thoughts about the Maastricht provisions throughout the EC, and, last but not least, the growing social unrest in Germany's new states, complete with pictures and slogans reminiscent of the 1930s, will influence the further development of Norwegian-German relations, inside or outside the European Community.

Notes

The authors would like to thank Mr. Melvin Westerman of the Pennsylvania State University's Pattee Library for assisting us with our research. We also would like to thank Mr. Bjug Boeyum of the Norwegian Social Science Data Center, Bergen, for providing us with polling data from the NSD's archives. Neither the NSD nor the polling agencies are responsible for the interpretation of their figures.

1. E. M. Anderson, "Hanseatic League," in Byron J. Nordstrom, ed., *Dictionary of Scandinavian History* (Westport CT: Greenwood Press, 1990), p. 261.

2. Paul F. Knudsen, "Norway: Domestically Driven Foreign Policy," *The Annals of the American Academy of Political and Social Science*, vol. 512, November 1990, p. 102.

3. See B. R. Mitchell, *European Historical Statistics 1750-1970* (New York: Columbia University Press, 1975), pp. 544-46.

4. Frederic Austin Ogg, *The Governments of Europe* (New York: Macmillan, 1913), p. 579.

5. William M. Lafferty, "The Political Transformation of a Social Democratic State: As the World Moves in, Norway Moves Right," *West European Politics*, vol. 13, nr. 1, 1990, p. 81.

6. Lafferty, "The Political Transformation," p. 85.

7. "Ein symbolischer Besuch in dem Städtchen Elverum," *Frankfurter Allgemeine Zeitung*, September 29, 1986.

8. Ogg, *The Governments of Europe*, p. 577f.

9. A. Thowsen, "Shipping — Norway," in Nordstrom, ed., *Dictionary of Scandinavian History*, p. 533.

10. Frantz Wendt, *The Nordic Council and Co-operation in Scandinavia* (Copenhagen: Munksgaard, 1959), p. 30.

11. See B. H. Liddell Hart, *History of the Second World War* (New York: G. P. Putnam's Sons, 1971), pp. 51-63.

12. Wolfgang Wippermann, *Europäischer Faschismus im Vergleich (1922-1982)* (Frankfurt: Suhrkamp Verlag, 1983), p. 169f.

13. Michael R. Marrus and Robert O. Paxton, "The Nazis and the Jews in Occupied Western Europe, 1940-1944," in Francois Furet, ed., *Unanswered Questions: Nazi Germany and the Genocide of the Jews* (New York: Schocken Books, 1989), p. 195.

14. G. S. Gordon, "World War II — Norway," in Nordstrom, ed., *Dictionary of Scandinavian History*, p. 657.

15. Lothar Grundmann, *Der Zweite Weltkrieg: Kriegführung und Politik* (Munich: Deutscher Taschenbuch Verlag, 1982), p. 60.

16. See *Foreign Broadcast Information Service (FBIS)*, WEU-90-006, January 9, 1990, p. 1, and *FBIS*, WEU-90-041-S, March 1, 1990, p. 86.

17. Lord Ismay as quoted in Francois Heisbourg, "The Future of the Atlantic Alliance and European Security," *Security Policy Library of the Norwegian Atlantic Committee*, No. 2, 1992, p. 12.

18. Helga Haftendorn, "The Changing European Security Context and the Nordic Region: A View from Germany," *The Annals of the American Academy of Political and Social Science*, vol. 512, November 1990, p. 183.

19. Johan Jorgen Holst in a conversation with G. R. Urban, in Urban, ed., *Detente* (New York: Universe Books, 1976), p. 128.

20. H. Peter Dreyer, "Scandinavia Faces Europe," in Peter Christian Ludz et al., *Dilemmas of the Atlantic Alliance: Two Germanys, Scandinavia, Canada, NATO and the EEC* (New York: Praeger, 1975), p. 78.

21. Andrei S. Markovits and Simon Reich, "Modell Deutschland and the new Europe," *Telos*, vol. 24, nr. 3, 1991, p. 46.

22. "Nachbarn im kühlen Norden," *Frankfurter Allgemeine Zeitung*, August 27, 1966; this and all subsequent translations are the authors'.

23. See David Binder, *The Other German: Willy Brandt's Life & Times* (Washington DC: The New Republic Book Company, 1975), p. 114f.

24. "Brandt Besuch in Norwegen Zeichen neuen Vertrauens," *Frankfurter Allgemeine Zeitung*, April 24, 1970.

25. See the coverage in *Frankfurter Allgemeine Zeitung*, September 9 to 11, 1970.

26. Helmut Schmidt, *Die Deutschen und ihre Nachbarn: Menschen und Mächte, Band II* (Berlin: Siedler, 1990), pp. 369-75.

27. "Der Bundespräsident in Norwegen," *Frankfurter Allgemeine Zeitung*, September 25, 1986.

28. Institut für Internationale Beziehungen an der Akademie für Staats- und Rechtswissenschaft der DDR Potsdam-Babelsberg, ed., *Nordeuropa — Positionen zur Entspannung* (Berlin: Staatsverlag der DDR, 1979), p. 64.

29. Foreign Minister Thorvald Stoltenberg as quoted in *Neues Deutschland*, March 8, 1988.

30. *Nordeuropa — Positionen zur Entspannung*, p. 72.

31. The percentage figures are based on data from the annual editions of the *Yearbook of Nordic Statistics* (Stockholm: The Nordic Council, 1972ff), *Statistisches Jahrbuch für die Bundesrepublik Deutschland* (Stuttgart/Mainz: Kohlhammer Verlag, 1976ff), and *Statistisk Arbok* (Oslo-Kongsvinger: Statistisk Sentralbyra, 1970ff).

32. Knudsen, "Norway: Domestically Driven Foreign Policy," p. 113.

33. Willy Brandt, *People and Politics: The Years 1960-1975* (Boston/Toronto: Little, Brown, 1978), p. 165.

34. Derek W. Urwin, *The Community of Europe: A History of European Integration* (London/New York: Longman, 1991), p. 143.

35. Kjell A. Eliassen, "Nordic EC Membership — The Question of When," *Aussenwirtschaft*, vol. 46, nr. 1, 1991, p. 8.

36. "Frau Brundtland wirbt für bessere Beziehungen," *Frankfurter Allgemeine Zeitung*, November 29, 1988.

37. Haftendorn, "The Changing European Security Context," p. 184.

38. Karl E. Birnbaum, "Die nordischen Staaten und das kontinentale Europa," *Europa Archiv*, vol. 26, nr. 16, 1971, p. 574.

39. Dreyer, "Scandinavia Faces Europe," p. 85.

40. Knudsen, "Norway: Domestically Driven Foreign Policy," p. 101.

41. Address by Hans-Dietrich Genscher, Minister for Foreign Affairs of the Federal Republic of Germany, to the the Foreign Relations Committee of the French National Assembly, Paris, November 19, 1991, as documented in *Statements and Speeches* (German Information Center, New York), vol. 14, nr. 12, 1991, p. 1.

42. The NSD provided this data to the authors from an Opinion A.S. poll conducted in Norway in April of 1990.

43. Data provided to the authors by the NSD from an opinion poll conducted by Norges Marketsdata on behalf of the NSD in the fall of 1990.

44. *Eurobarometer*, No. 34, December 1990, p. A26.

45. See Marten van Heuven, *Europe 1991: A Scandinavian Perspective* (Santa Monica CA: RAND, 1991), pp. 5-7.

46. See *Foreign Broadcast Information Service (FBIS)*, WEU-91-174, September 9, 1991, p. 28f.

47. See *Foreign Broadcast Information Service (FBIS)*, WEU-91-242, December 17, 1991, p. 40.

48. See "Oslo and Bonn at Odds on New NATO Chief," *The New York Times*, November 25, 1987, and "Norwegian Withdraws, Enabling German to Hold Top NATO Post," *The New York Times*, December 1, 1987.

49. Johan Jorgen Holst, "The New Europe: A View from the North," *Den Norske Atlanterhavskomite*, nr. 143, 1991, p. 18.

50. See "Anders als der Rest Europas," *Süddeutsche Zeitung*, June 13-14, 1992.

51. See Eliassen, "Nordic EC Membership," p. 10f.

52. See "A sea of change," *The Economist*, March 14, 1992, p. 55f.

53. Eliassen, "Nordic EC Membership," p. 10.

54. See "Kohl: EFTA-Staaten bis 1995 in die EG," *Süddeutsche Zeitung*, March 6, 1992.

55. Eliassen, "Nordic EC Membership," p. 14.

7

Sweden and Germany: Forgetting the Past and Restoring the Future

Steven S. Koblik

Sweden's relationship with Germany historically and in a contemporary context can be classified as intimate and important. The development of modern Sweden and modern Prussia/Germany followed parallel yet different paths. The ties between the two countries became especially strong in the period after German unification. Sweden's modernization process was linked indelibly with Germany's spectacular rise to Great Power status. Yet in the wake of the Nazi experience, Sweden deliberately cut much of its cultural and political ties to Germany and practiced a form of historical self-delusion. The Swedes have viewed the rise of a reunified Germany in 1990 with mixed emotions and a certain distance. Today Sweden faces an interesting and difficult dilemma with regard to its relationship with Germany and Europe. As a result, the "German Question" has become an issue in domestic Swedish politics.

Lübeck, Luther, and the Birth of Modern Sweden

The birth of modern Sweden occurred in 1523 when a Swedish noble, Gustav Vasa, led a revolt against the Danish king who ruled all of Scandinavia. Partially financed by the German Hansa merchants of Lübeck, Vasa established a sovereign state with himself as king. Vasa's debt to the Hansa merchants, combined with fiscal demands, led him to see the Catholic Church in Sweden as a potential source of monarchial wealth and power.   His rejection of Catholicism, confiscation of all church property and other forms of wealth, and the subsequent development of a Lutheran state church were one of the best 16th century examples of political and economic concerns driving royal religious behavior. At the same time, his actions affirmed the close affinity between the nascent Swedish state and the Protestant states of Germany.

For an extended period of time, Swedish religious figures took their religious and much of their university training in Protestant Germany. The ties between Swedish and German Lutheranism thus forged remained intimate throughout the next 350 years. Even though Swedish Lutheranism developed its own high church forms in the 17th century, established an independent base in Sweden, and experienced strong dissenter traditions within the church, especially in the 19th century, Lutheran figures on either side of the Baltic remained within a broad, common intellectual tradition.

Conversion of the Swedish populace followed more slowly after the policy initiatives of the monarch. By the end of the 16th century Sweden truly became a Lutheran bastion. Once the state church was established, religious tolerance remained at low levels. While Jews received rights of residence and religious practice in the late 18th century, and Catholics also got limited freedoms, laws protected Lutheran control over all official facets of Swedish life. For example, members of the government were required to be members of the Swedish Lutheran state church until the early 1960s!

There is no doubt that Sweden is a Lutheran country, although most Swedish Lutherans have little idea about Luther himself or the difference between their formal beliefs and those of other Christians. At an intellectual level, the ties between German and Swedish Lutherans remained active until the end of World War II. Yet the rigidity of the state church meant that most Swedes experienced religion as a series of rituals and/or local customs that bound the community together. Their understanding of the religious context of Lutheranism was minimal. As a former prime minister, Thorbjörn Fälldin, recently said, when referring to the suggestion that the state and the Lutheran church separate, "Then the church would be left only as a religious movement."

Most contemporary Swedes are unaware where their ethical values come from. Already in the 1930s church attendance began to drop; by the 1970s, sociological studies indicated that Sweden registered the lowest "belief in God" and church attendance of any European country. Cultural figures such as Ingemar Bergman who represent the dominant historical linkage in religious-ethical terms between Germany and Sweden are oddities in contemporary Sweden. Most Swedes, for example, are hostile to Catholicism yet would be hard pressed to explain why, except in terms of a general dislike of any religion. Tage Erlander, prime minister from 1948 until 1968, more than once reflected that his ambivalence about Sweden joining the European Community depended upon the fact that Sweden would have to work intimately with Catholic countries: "The French are Catholics, you know." The absence of an understanding by the broad Swedish populace of their own religious-ethical tradition and especially its connections with German traditions is not a unique phenomenon. Other similar linkages have become part of a by and large ignored past.

Construction of the modern Swedish state began in the late 16th century. Modern Prussia evolved slightly later and borrowed many Swedish innovations in modern statecraft. During the 1600-1720 period, Sweden was the primary imperial power in the Baltic. Its empire at its height included much land in northern Germany from Bremen through Pomerania. In fact, Sweden was very much a "German power." The differences between the two countries are important, however. The social structures of the two societies were dissimilar. The peasantry in Prussia was enserfed and bound, while in Sweden, serfdom never existed and the peasantry had its own cultural and political traditions that influenced the broader pattern of Sweden's development. All Swedes had common legal rights, while Prussia differentiated between social classes.

The nobility's land-holding and general political power was much stronger in Prussia than in Sweden. A late 17th century Swedish king, Charles XI, reclaimed significant portions of noble lands granted by previous monarchs. No Swedish equivalent to the authority of the Prussian army developed. After the 17th century, Sweden was far more homogeneous in religious and cultural terms. It experienced nothing like the influx of Huguenots into Prussia or the impact of large numbers of Jews at the beginning of the 19th century. While Swedish economic development lagged behind Prussia's, the state-building process that occurred in the years between 1610 and 1718 saw a conscious interaction between the two.

The Hohenzollerns and the Vasas faced the same dilemma of how to construct a state in regions that were relatively poor economically and had no distinct geographical boundary. Both achieved an effective alliance between the royal house and the nobility, including the older, powerful noble families. In Sweden, the Vasas also managed to maintain a close relationship with the free peasantry. A cabinet system of statecraft developed in the 17th century which, while nominally establishing the absolutist power of the monarch, assured the nobility of authority and influence. The exercise of military power was, of course, the obvious expression of the success of the state-building process. Under Gustav Adolph II, Sweden expanded around the entire eastern and southern Baltic, save Denmark, and as far south into Germany proper as Munich. Charles XII invaded Russia just as Napoleon and Hitler would do in the following centuries.

Sweden's Great Power status lasted only from 1610 until 1718. Nonetheless, it was critical to the country's modern development. The formal organization of the state was created, and in general terms, despite constitutional revisions, the outline of modern Sweden was established. The bureaucratic traditions that were to serve the welfare state, the recruitment of talented non- nobles into the bureaucratic elite, and the commitment to honesty and efficiency were all established during the Great Power period. Prussia was as much victim as anything else during this period and no doubt this fact led the Hohenzollerns to build their own unique entity — often borrowing formal institutional structures from Sweden.

After the collapse of the Habsburg dynasty in the 17th century, France became the leading power in Europe. Especially in the area of culture, France established a dominant position. The Swedish nobility and educated classes were often drawn to French examples and influence. All read and spoke French. They participated in the intellectual debates we now call the Enlightenment. A French lawyer and field marshal, Bernadotte, established the modern Swedish dynasty at the end of the Napoleonic wars after the collapse of the Vasa dynasty.

While Russia became the primary northern European power in the 18th century, Prussia succeeded in establishing itself as the second Great Power in the region. Sweden quickly became a political backwater. Indeed, by the reign of Frederick II of Prussia (1740-1782), the Great Powers attempted to manipulate domestic Swedish politics through bribery and more than once contemplated dividing the Swedish state much as they divided Poland in the later part of the century. Sweden's economy stagnated relative to the dynamic growth in Western Europe. It played a marginal role in the Napoleonic wars — losing Finland to Russia while gaining Norway from Denmark.

The slow emergence of a united Germany during the 19th century was viewed critically in Stockholm. Various monarchs and cabinets attempted to make alliances with anti-German forces on the continent and with Great Britain, but these efforts stopped short of participation in military conflict. The unification of Germany in the 1860s found Sweden an interested but retiring bystander. The spectacular economic growth of Germany after 1870 pulled Sweden into the modern industrial age. The linkages between the two countries grew. In economic, political, and cultural terms, Sweden fell more and more into the late 19th century Germanic world.

The Period of German Hegemony

In broad historical terms, late 19th century Europe divided between two cultural-political tendencies. The conservative tradition emphasized established values, community, order, and hierarchy. The progressive tradition demanded democracy, equality, individualism, and often encouraged challenging established truths. All the industrializing countries experienced both tendencies but one or the other appeared to dominate in specific localities. Great Britain and France perceived themselves as representatives of the progressive tradition, while Germany took pride in defending the traditional order. We should be careful not to misrepresent the realities of these countries — the first two were far more traditional and imperial than they claimed, and Germany more progressive than it wished to acknowledge. Nonetheless, there evolved a sense of difference that can be found in the late 19th century political dialogue, in literature, and in the arts.

The main currents of Swedish cultural and political developments followed Germany's, and so did its economic growth. Conservatives, liberals, and socialists in Sweden drew inspiration from and often sought contact with their Germanic brothers. Only rarely, as in the case of the liberal leader Karl Staaff, did a pro-English or pro-French official surface. The new royal family, the French Bernadottes, quickly married into Germanic royal houses and identified themselves with the German cultural mission. Traces of these connections can be found throughout the Nazi period. The impressive rise of the German university system no doubt contributed to Sweden's growing connection with Germanic culture.

As the modern educational system evolved in Sweden, German was the primary foreign language. Aspiring professionals — doctors, dentists, clergy, engineers, and so on — spent time in German schools. Swedish businessmen linked their activities with counterparts on the southern shores of the Baltic, while Swedish literature and the arts operated within the German cultural tradition. Rare exceptions drew inspiration from France and even more rarely from Great Britain and the United States, despite the huge numbers of Swedes who emigrated to North America. Those in control of Swedish institutions remained loyally pro-German.

Parliamentary democracy came slowly both to Sweden and to Germany. The final phases of democratization occurred at the end of the Great War, after the defeat of Germany. Sweden had practiced a policy of benevolent neutrality toward Germany during much of the war. Fear of Russia, combined with skepticism toward the Entente, reinforced the natural pro-German attitudes of Sweden's political, economic, and cultural elites.

Swedish-German ties remained strong throughout the 1919-1933 period. Germany found great sympathy in Sweden for its view that it had been unfairly treated by the victorious powers at Versailles. German arms manufacturers gained control over Swedish companies and used their Swedish plants to test weapons that were forbidden to Germany under the terms of the Versailles agreements. The flowering of culture in the Weimar period provided ample inspiration to virtually all cultural elements in Sweden.

Both countries established parliamentary democracies in the 1920s. The "Versailles *Diktat*" tainted the entire German political spectrum, saddling the progressive parties with an unpopular peace and encouraging the conservatives to seek to overthrow the extant political order. In Sweden, the conservatives made a remarkable transition into democratic processes and became staunch supporters of the parliamentary order.   The accompanying violence and emotionalism in Germany was not prevalent in Sweden. Germany continued to be prominent in a number of major sectors of the Swedish economy. Yet political ties with Germany across the entire party spectrum were no longer as strong, with influences from the Western democracies becoming more visible.

The impact of the Depression led to dramatic changes in both countries. In Germany, it generated economic misery and the collapse of the Weimar political system. Adolf Hitler came to power and by the summer of 1933 had established a one-party state.   The Depression's impact on Sweden was less severe. Unemployment at its worst was less than 20 percent. The crisis did, however, produce great tension and threatened the political system. The result was a strengthening of Swedish democracy and shortly thereafter a significant improvement in the Swedish economy.

The striking difference in the way the Depression affected Sweden and Germany is worth a more careful analysis.   The strong political ties of the prewar period and the linkages in their economies and culture can lead one to question why Germany became a dictatorship while Sweden affirmed its democratic traditions during the crisis of the early 1930s. There are undoubtedly many factors that contributed.

Two quite different political parties benefitted from the political unrest in each country: the Nazis in Germany, and the Social Democrats in Sweden. Unlike their counterparts in Germany, the Swedish Social Democrats were not associated with the established order, which carried responsibility for both the economic chaos and political malaise. They had faced their first major crisis in 1928 when they lost electoral support for the first time.   As a result, they tempered their classical socialist doctrines and began advocacy of more "Keynesian" policies. As a party whose electoral base had become more and more anchored in the working class, their new leader, Per Albin Hansson, recognized that the Social Democrats would have to find political partners who would provide a firm parliamentary base for an active governmental intervention in the economy.

The elections of 1932 were a clear victory for the Social Democrats but left them without a working majority in the parliament. In 1933, Per Albin struck an agreement with the traditionally most conservative party, the Farmers (or Agrarian) Party, which guaranteed a parliamentary basis for the minority Social Democratic government he headed from 1933 until 1936. In effect, the deal was based on a concession from the Social Democrats for higher food prices and from the Agrarians for an active labor market policy to combat unemployment. Some Liberals also gave parliamentary support to the minority government.

Sweden's economy recovered quite quickly. Unemployment had dropped significantly by the end of 1934. The Social Democrats claimed that their policies had been responsible for the recovery. More likely, the recovery was a result of the previous government's timely decision to take the Swedish crown off the gold standard and the economic recovery in Germany under Schacht, which in turn stimulated the most important economic sectors in Sweden. Whatever the reasons, the economic recovery in Sweden benefitted the Social Democrats just as it benefitted the Nazis in Germany. Further Social Democratic gains in the 1936 election led to the establishment of a formal coalition government between the Social Democrats and the Farmers party, the first majority government in Sweden since the early 1920s.

The traditionally close cultural ties between Sweden and Germany began to show strains after Hitler took power. For the pro-German cultural elite of Sweden, Hitler at first appeared both as a restorer of the rightful place of Germany and as a rather vulgar individual who needed instruction on proper behavior. A number of prominent Swedes, led by King Gustav V, visited Berlin and offered advice to the new chancellor on his comportment. Needless to say, the advice was neither well received nor effective. What appeared to have bothered Hitler's Swedish visitors most were his active anti-Semitic policies, which had attracted much public attention in 1933-34.

Hitler's anti-Semitism was a radical form of a well- established strain in Western culture. In Sweden, anti-Semitism could be found in the state church, much of the literature, within some of the political parties, especially the Agrarians, and at the universities. The Jewish community in Sweden was small (approximately 5,000 individuals) and quite differentiated in terms of religious opinion, political affiliation, economic well-being, and educational background. Of course, a few Jews had achieved prominence and seemed to serve as useful spurs to an ingrained hostility to Jews. The most famous of these Jews, the Bonniers, controlled a large percentage of the press, and were frequently the specific target of Swedish anti-Semites. Actually most of the Bonnier family, originally Jewish, had converted to Lutheranism, but this fact was of no import to the anti-Semites.

Although Sweden had its own anti-Semitic traditions, anti-Semitism never took a prominent place in the political or cultural life of the country. Hitler's anti-Semitism appeared raw and crude to the Swedes who visited him. When Hitler demanded that the German Lutheran clergy swear loyalty to the Third Reich and its principles (Oath of Barmen, 1934), the Swedish church supported the anti-oath faction which came to be called the Confessional Church. The Swedish Nazi party found little or no support politically. Meanwhile, the Swedish government tried to find solutions through the League of Nations to what was called "the refugee problem." Public criticism of Hitler was widespread as the decade progressed. The criticism came primarily from the middle and left parts of the political spectrum.

Swedish attitudes toward Germany in the 1930s need to be balanced with Swedish perspectives on Russia. A strong antipathy to Russia had deep historical roots. The success of the Bolsheviks only strengthened these anti-Russian feelings, especially among Swedish conservatives whose ancestors had colonized extensive parts of the Russian Baltic shores. Germany was viewed as the only balance to a Russian-dominated Baltic. Increasing international tension after 1937 left the Swedes with little choice but to declare their intention to remain neutral in a forthcoming conflict and to hope they survived intact. One of the first episodes of World War II that actually reinforced these traditional attitudes was when the Soviet Union attacked Sweden's neighbor, Finland. While individual Swedes volunteered to fight for Finland in the Winter War, the government provided supplies but declined to send the military support that Finland wanted.

The dominant factor in Swedish-German relations during the war was geographic. From 1940 until 1944, Sweden existed in a German-controlled region. Germany's occupation of Denmark and Norway, combined with German-Finnish co-belligerency and German control of the southern Baltic, meant that Sweden's real freedom of action was limited. On a strategic level, the credibility of Sweden's defense capacity was dubious. The coalition government tended to follow the line of least resistance, especially after June 1940. Important concessions were granted to Germany, violating international understandings of neutral behavior. The more important of these was the transshipment of troops on Swedish railroads (both the reinforcement of Germany occupation troops in Norway and the movement of an armed German division from Norway to Finland), and permission for German air and naval units to use Swedish territorial space. Still, these activities brought little condemnation from the Allied powers at the time, since it was recognized that Sweden had little choice.

For Germany, the importance of Sweden was primarily economic. There is little or no evidence that Germany ever planned or seriously contemplated an attack on Sweden. Sweden's neutrality served German interests in the short run and left the longer term till a later date. Germany needed iron ore, ball bearings, and other Swedish products. Since Sweden was effectively cut off from its traditional Western markets, trade between the two increased accordingly. The relationship did, however, cause growing difficulties for Germany's enemies as they attempted to strangle the German war machine.

The attempt by the Western powers to limit and then to eliminate Swedish trade with Germany remains one of the most fascinating subjects of the war period. Britain and the United States moved slowly to convince Sweden to cut back its trade. Applying more serious pressure in the spring and summer of 1943, the Allies eventually won Stockholm's agreement to stop all trade on January 1, 1945. Many Swedish scholars have seen these concessions as a balance to those made to Germany at the start of the war. In some sense they were, but such an interpretation ignores the importance of how slowly Sweden responded to Allied requests, and why, and the dilemma faced by Swedish policy-makers.

Key figures in the Swedish government and in the business community were well aware by the winter of 1942-43 that Sweden would find itself in a very different situation after the war than at any time since 1870. Germany would lose the war; the Soviet Union would extend its control westward; and no democratic European country would be strong enough to provide a counterbalance to Russia. Sweden faced the prospect of a postwar northern Europe totally dominated by the Soviet Union. The last two years of the war saw Sweden focus its attention more and more on this dilemma and, within the confines of the few opportunities offered to small neutrals, balance policies that responded to wartime circumstances yet looked to the postwar future.

The elements of this balancing act were fourfold: try to protect a place in the postwar order for a non-Nazi Germany; encourage Finland to break its relationship with Germany and seek reconciliation with the Soviet Union; seek to establish a new relationship with the United States; and find some way of assuring the Soviet Union of the good intentions of a non- aligned, capitalist Sweden. What is striking is how consistent Sweden managed to be in balancing these elements. A real place for a democratic Germany in the postwar order was the only long-term hope for a Great Power balance in the Baltic. Sweden's attempts to mediate a peace, its efforts to remind the Western powers of the importance of issues related to the postwar order (Willy Brandt and Bruno Kreisky, among others, were refugees in Sweden and spent much time writing Washington about how a democratic Germany and Austria should be included in the Allies' plans for the postwar world), and a reluctance to isolate Germany economically or diplomatically — all reflected this critical focus on the postwar order.

Sweden obviously had little impact on the relations among the Great Powers or on the treatment of defeated Germany. Nonetheless, much in Sweden's postwar Baltic policies can already be identified in the last years of the war. Nor is this a surprising phenomenon. It represents an attempt by Sweden to restore a Great Power balance in its regional area so that Sweden might maintain its own independent position. At the same time, a deep popular antipathy to Germany had developed as German atrocities in Norway and against the Jews became more widely understood. Sweden offered a safe haven for as many as 180,000 refugees at a time from the Baltic area. It is also worth noting that the Swedish Communist Party polled higher electoral support in 1944 and 1946 than previously, which undoubtedly reflected an appreciation of the role the USSR had played in defeating Nazi Germany.

Forgetting the German Connection

In the first three years after the war, Sweden moved to re-establish its peacetime role in the postwar order. It joined the United Nations and it participated actively in postwar relief efforts. It acceded to Soviet requests to return Baltic refugees whom the Soviet Union claimed were Fascist exiles, provided significant aid to the part of Germany occupied by the Western powers, and tried to work toward some form of regional, Nordic cooperation. The division of Europe in 1947-48 forced the Swedes to make difficult decisions. Sweden chose to remain non-aligned in terms of military alliances but to affirm its economic relationship with the Western capitalist countries. The Norwegian and Danish decision to join NATO appeared at the time to be a defeat for Sweden's attempt to establish a non-aligned Nordic Defense Union. In reality, Scandinavia's inclusion into NATO provided the strategic balance that Sweden had sought in the Baltic and guaranteed the continued viability of Swedish non-alignment.

In terms of Sweden's relationship with Germany, the immediate postwar period saw one of the most remarkable and dramatic shifts in what had been a long-standing and important set of connections. Decisions were taken in Sweden to eliminate much of Germany's cultural influence. The school system adopted English as the country's second language, while individuals who had been closely identified with German culture lost their prominence. New leaders arose whose ties with the Western democracies were clear. Things Germanic quite suddenly were not to be discussed. Of course, Germanic intellectual traditions continued to play a major role in Swedish life, but predominantly through those Swedes who had been educated before the war and thereby influenced by earlier traditions. The postwar generations of educated Swedes would grow up with considerable ignorance concerning the historical ties between the two countries.

The peculiarity of this development is worth further reflection. Since it has not been the subject of any serious investigation by Swedish scholars, my thoughts can therefore only be viewed as speculative. There was a widely felt sense of shame among adult Swedes for their perceived failures during the war. Certain prominent figures — most importantly the "men of 1940" (King Gustav V, Christian Gunther, the foreign minister, Arvid Richert, Swedish ambassador to Germany, Sven Tunborg, chair of the Information Board, and so forth) — were identified as "responsible" for an overly servile Swedish policy toward Germany. The prime minister, Per Albin Hansson, was whitewashed. The governing Social Democrats found the exorcism of certain officials useful to their own postwar fortunes. The dominating role of the United States in Western Europe in the postwar period also contributed to the disappearance of things German from Sweden.

Sweden received Marshall Plan aid, established the Swedish Institute to foster cultural relations primarily between itself and the transatlantic countries, and sought to benefit from the American-driven postwar economic boom. Scholars who previously would have studied in Germany now crossed the Atlantic, and intellectual fashion shifted westward. Young Swedes growing up after 1945 were not informed of past traditions. Even the Lutheran ties dissipated as the Swedes themselves lost interest in and knowledge of religion.

If Germany's cultural influence declined drastically and its political role remained marginal, in the economic area the close prewar ties were retained. Even a truncated Germany after 1950 remained an important market for Swedish companies. The intimate ties between the two countries continued, indeed expanded after the full recovery of the Federal Republic in the 1960s. While the general Swedish public was unaware of it, Sweden's own remarkable economic and social progress after 1950 was to a considerable extent dependent upon a free-rider effect of the Western European economy led by West Germany.

How could nearly all postwar generations of Swedes ignore the close historical and continuous economic ties with Germany? In a country that has strong traditions of intellectual conformism, of elite governance, of corporate representation, and of Lutheran guilt, combined with a desire to deny linkages between the Germany that produced Hitler and the budding new Swedish Welfare State, it proved remarkably easy. Like so many other European countries, Sweden found it convenient to look to the future rather than consider its past. Sweden's evolution as a welfare state provided an exciting and internationally impressive demonstration of its capacity and will to offer cradle-to-the-grave security for its citizens, to democratize the workplace, and to play a constructive, progressive role in world politics.

The division of Europe between NATO and the Warsaw Pact led Sweden to opt for non-alignment in peacetime with a desire to remain neutral in case of war. Its non-alignment in the 1950s took the character of a traditional suspicion of Great Power politics, and a strong defense combined with an active international policy to serve world peace. An authoritative Swedish civil servant, Dag Hammarskjøld, as Secretary-General of the United Nations, served as a symbol of that active internationalism. Sweden was not neutral in any conventional sense of the term, however. Close ties with the West, not just in economic and political terms, were firmly established. While the full extent of these ties was not made public, they included shared development of weapons and other military equipment, cooperative military planning in case of a Soviet attack on Sweden, and a sharing of sensitive intelligence information.

There were a few Swedes who, recognizing the dependence of Sweden on NATO and the fledgling Common Market, argued for the elimination of Sweden's traditional non-alignment and for membership in NATO and the EEC. Most prominent among these was Professor Herbert Tingsten, Professor of Political Science and editor of *Dagens Nyheter*, the most influential newspaper in the country. Tingsten argued that Sweden should play an active role in the evolution of a postwar democratic and integrated Western Europe, including defense planning. Tage Erlander, the Social Democratic prime minister from 1946 until 1968, took primary responsibility for rejecting Tingsten's views and suggested that Sweden should remain on the sidelines of the Cold War and seek alternative ways of aiding world peace.   In domestic political terms, the governing coalition parties during the 1950s, the Social Democrats and the Agrarians (renamed the Center), supported the traditional Swedish policy, as did the Communists, while the Conservatives (renamed Moderates in the 1960s) and some Liberals opted for the Tingsten position. By the late 1950s, non-alignment had become a popular symbol of Swedish independence. It served as a useful weapon for the Social Democrats in their domestic struggles with the Conservatives and Liberals.

The successful canonization of non-alignment — for example, the refusal of the Social Democratic government in 1959 to allow the leader of the Conservative Party, Jarl Hjarlmansson, to take his traditional place in the Swedish UN delegation because he "weakened the credibility of Swedish non-alignment" — contributed to a decline in the quality of discussion in Sweden concerning the country's foreign and strategic policies. Politicians and scholars alike learned through the 1960s and 1970s that to raise fundamental issue with Sweden's traditional policy was not possible.

The elevation of Olof Palme to prime minister in 1969 changed little in this regard. Palme was to serve as chief of government from 1969 until 1976 and again from 1982 until 1986. Undoubtedly Palme was more interested in international issues than any of his predecessors. He was at home internationally, fluent in German and French as well as English. He had close ties with European leaders such as Willy Brandt and Bruno Kreisky and was deeply interested in the major strategic issues of the day. Yet his fundamental Europeanism found little place in his political activities or public utterances.

Palme seems to have accepted the pro-NATO attitude of Willy Brandt and to have followed his lead in German affairs. He supported Brandt's *Ostpolitik*, and Sweden recognized the GDR in 1972, though relations were quite formal. Despite efforts by the East German regime to develop close ties along the lines of Swedish-German relations prior to 1933, Stockholm showed little interest in anything but normal diplomatic arrangements.

Palme's strong concerns about the Third World and his criticism of American policies in Vietnam and elsewhere dominated his agenda.   He affirmed and extended the non-alignment tradition by establishing neutrality as the unassailable heart of Swedish foreign policy. The Swedish public was led to believe that what mattered most to Sweden were events in Vietnam, Chile, Nicaragua, and South Africa.   That Sweden's fundamental security and economic interests were tied tightly to NATO and the European Community was rarely discussed. Hardly anyone paid attention to the emerging strength of the Federal Republic and the relative decline in the power of France and Great Britain, even of the United States in an economic perspective.

The two periods in which Swedish attention focused on Europe were the early 1960s and early 1970s. The cause of this attention was the decision of a number of EFTA countries, especially Great Britain, Denmark, and Norway, to seek membership in the European Community. The potential departure of Sweden's most important EFTA trading partners into the Community forced a discussion of Sweden's relationship with the EC. The first of these debates ended abruptly with de Gaulle's veto of the UK's application in 1963. The second discussion lasted nearly two years and resulted in a trade agreement with the Community and the retention of Sweden's traditional non-alignment. The latter discussion, while quite extensive in terms of its length and its coverage by the press, did not affect domestic politics in any fundamental way. Moreover, the discussion centered on the implications for Sweden's neutrality and the potential loss of sovereignty, rather than on Sweden's responsibilities in Europe or the specifics of the potential institutional development within the EC itself. The changing nature of Europe, especially the success of the Federal Republic, was all but ignored. Swedish international attention remained focused on issues beyond Europe and reflected rarely on Sweden's most pressing economic and strategic interests.

Twenty-five years after the end of World War II knowledge of Germany, interest in Sweden's southern neighbor, and recognition of Sweden's continuing linkages with that country continued to weaken. The generations educated into the German cultural world were dying and the Swedish school system seemed determined to ignore the past. English came to dominate the comprehensive school and even at the upper secondary levels the number of students studying German declined. Standards of living were rising throughout Western Europe and, among other things, encouraged greater and greater travel. With some exceptions — Berlin, the Black Forest, and so on — Germany was a transit station as Swedes used the *Autobahn* on their way to vacations in the Alps, Spain, Italy, Greece, and France.

Of course, Germany did not completely disappear from the Swedish cultural "radar-screen." Yet, German television programs, for example, were infrequently shown on Swedish television. Compared to the variety of American programs that flooded the country, they were truly a "drop in the bucket." The fact that Sweden's leading cultural figure, Ingemar Bergman, sought refuge in Munich after a tax scandal in 1976, underscored the historical cultural linkages but had little impact in Sweden itself. American and British culture continued their dominance and Swedes often talked of themselves as the most American of all Europeans.

What is difficult to explain, but nonetheless a fact, is that genuine Swedish culture remained closely tied to Germany. Some young writers and other cultural figures found stimulation in cultural trends of Sweden's southern neighbor. Most Swedes, however, simply did not understand the historical evolution of their own values or their linkages with another larger culture. Germany remained in the popular mind the source of Hitler and Fascism. To be called a "fascist" in Swedish was to be labeled the worst possible thing — the term's usage was similar to "communist" in the United States.

Strangely, Sweden's governing elites in both business and politics were fully sensitized to the continuing importance of Sweden's linkages with Germany. Germany remained one of Sweden's largest trading partners, and the rising importance of the D-Mark and the growing role of the German central bank in European affairs did not go unnoticed. By the early 1980s, the business community was engaged in a campaign to eliminate domestic restrictions on capital movement, especially from Sweden into the European Community.

The economic policies of the Reagan and Thatcher administrations, which were followed to a degree by the Kohl and Mitterrand governments, changed the nature of the Western economic world. "Deregulation," lower taxes, controlling inflation, less government interference, and free trade became central goals for all the major Western economies and the basis upon which the EC could extend its range of activities in the later part of the 1980s.

Most of these ideas ran counter to the conventional wisdom that dominated Swedish Social Democratic thinking. The Social Democrats won a resounding victory in the 1982 election and claimed that they intended to follow a neo-Keynesian "Third Way." Nonetheless, under the leadership of the Minister of Finance, Kjell Olof Feldt, the government began to "temporarily" remove restrictions on the free flow of capital in 1984, and Sweden glided slowly toward integration into the European Community. In addition, the economy seemed to deteriorate at an ever-increasing rate. Feldt now advocated a more Community-like mix of economic policies, which was rejected by the labor unions. He left the government in 1990, triggering what was called a governmental crisis.

In 1991, Feldt published a memoir of his years as Minister of Finance. For the first time, a leading Social Democrat underscored how central Europe was to the health of the Swedish welfare state. Although the book stops far short of a careful analysis of Sweden's broader foreign policy, it leaves no doubt that the Minister of Finance felt that it was time to admit that Sweden was indeed a European state.

What is so interesting about this turn-about in Social Democratic thinking was that it was not accompanied by much understanding among the broader Swedish public. The terms of discussion about foreign policy remained for nearly all the 1980s locked in the neutrality dialogue that had dominated the Palme years. If Feldt adjusted Swedish economic policy in the direction taken by the major Western economies and therefore began a new phase of integration of the Swedish economy into those of its most important trading partners, he did so quietly and without a political debate about its ramifications.

Rediscovering Germany

The new initiatives undertaken by the European Community in 1987-88 on the so-called EC'92 project stimulated a renewed discussion on Sweden's relationship to the Community. Key business figures, most prominently Per Gyllenhammer, president of Volvo, pushed for Swedish membership in the new Europe. Swedish investments in Europe grew dramatically now that currency restrictions had been all but eliminated. Swedish corporations, desperate to establish a foothold in the Community, invested more in Europe than in Sweden. The Moderates led by Carl Bildt and some prominent Liberals also argued for active Swedish participation in the Community. On the eve of two of the most momentous changes in modern European history, the reunification of Germany and the collapse of the USSR, stirrings of a new climate of opinion in Sweden could be measured.

The latter period of Feldt's tenure had been one of dramatic change in European affairs. Most crucial was the liberalization of the Soviet Union's domestic and international policies under the leadership of Mikhail Gorbachev. While welcoming the end of the Cold War in Europe, the Social Democratic government clearly found itself in a somewhat awkward position as champion of a neutrality policy that seemed obsolete.

This awkwardness was most strongly demonstrated as the Baltic states tried to re-establish themselves as independent nations. Ties between the Baltic states and Sweden had been frozen after 1940, and neither Palme nor any other prime minister risked Sweden's relations with the USSR to support Baltic independence. The Swedish Foreign Office initially reacted to events in the Baltic with considerable deliberateness and caution, sometimes reflecting publicly that it would be unwise for those in the Baltic states to seek freedom. These comments proved highly unpopular in Sweden and the public reaction led in turn to a shift in policy and an active support of Baltic independence.

The Baltic question provided the non-Social Democrats with the first major foreign policy question in decades where they were in the dominant domestic position and the Social Democrats on the defensive. There was great advantage for the non-Social Democrats, especially the conservative Moderates, to press the question for domestic gain. Just as the Neutrality Doctrine had served the Social Democrats, independence for the Baltic peoples served the non-socialists.

The Soviet liberalization policies also made the reunification of Germany possible. Sweden was completely unprepared for this process and somewhat stunned by its speed and totality. Germany had continued to be ignored in what had become traditional postwar Swedish style. Initial comments about the possibilities and ramifications of German unification in 1989 were cautious. In particular, there were few Swedes willing to comment upon the possible ramifications for their own country. The requisite positive comments were made by the government and leading politicians, but no general discussions in the popular media about the implications for Sweden developed. Public attention remained focused on developments in the Soviet Union, particularly the soon-to-be independent Baltic countries.

The implications of German reunification for Sweden are hard to exaggerate. The nature of Swedish security, its economic interests, and, in all likelihood, its cultural development will all be fundamentally affected. Yet the combination of postwar public ignorance of things German and Sweden's intimate economic relationship with Germany made an understanding of these implications all the more pressing and, simultaneously, unlikely to occur.

The collapse of the USSR meant that a unified Germany would be the dominant force in northern Europe. Policy-makers within the Social Democratic government and within the opposition parties, particularly Carl Bildt for the Moderates, clearly understood the importance of these changes and the need for a significant Swedish response. The exact nature of their internal discussions and reflections is not currently available; however, they must have served as the basis for one of the most dramatic shifts in modern Swedish foreign policy.

With little public discussion or preparation, the Social Democratic government, supported by its historical non-socialist rivals, announced in October 1990 that it would seek full Swedish membership in the European Community, provided that neutrality could be maintained. For a country whose entire modern history had centered on avoiding entangling alliances, the change was stunning and for most of the Swedish electorate unexpected. Since the Moderates had already been engaged in a pro-Community campaign, the interesting aspect of this announcement was the attitude of the Social Democratic government.

The government's explanation of its change of direction was hardly convincing, especially to its own constituencies. Citing changing strategic, economic, and social realities, it made the case that Sweden's general welfare would be endangered if it remained outside a post-1992 integrated Europe. As the parliamentary election campaign of 1991 had already begun, the issue remained strangely isolated because all the major parties supported the initiative to join the Community.

To Capture or Join Germany

Despite broad elite support for the Community application, there existed strong differences between and within the parties about the nature of the initiative. Clearly one of the major issues remained how to respond to a stronger, unified Germany. As in many other international issues since Palme's death, Carl Bildt seemed to capture the initiative. He published an autobiography, *Hallaning, Svensk, Europee* (1991), as part of the election campaign. Bildt made a forceful case for full Swedish participation in the Community, including eventual acceptance of joint defense and foreign policies. He further argued that Sweden must draw closer to Germany and affirm the historical ties long since established but too often ignored since the war. Bildt sees a natural affinity between the northern European states within the broader European context and the need to develop effective cooperation between these states in order to insure that their views have pre-eminence within Community policies.

Bildt's perspective represents a sophisticated and integrated notion of Sweden and Europe. He realizes the likely divisions within a future expanded Community and seeks to establish natural political linkages from the outset, with an appreciation of the connections among economic, social, and strategic policies. He believes that close cooperation with Germany will achieve the kind of Europe most Swedes would support. In a sense, Bildt wants to join Germany to establish a progressive if conservative domination of Community institutions.

The Social Democratic perspective is not, as yet, as well developed. There is, however, some indication that one of the motivations for their commitment to Community membership is much like that of France's attitude toward Germany since 1950 — to capture Germany within the web of the Community's institutions. The Social Democrats remain skeptical of German behavior and of their reliability in terms of the basic values that the Social Democrats hold dear — democracy and equality. When they talk of active involvement in EC institutions, they talk of traditional political divisions — left/right conflicts — rather than geographical splits. Bildt's enthusiasm for cooperation with Germany is not shared by many Social Democrats.

An Unclear Future

What has now become clear is that Sweden has once again found itself confronting a powerful and massive state to the south. To the east, it remains to be seen how Russia will reconstitute itself. Sweden has entered a new period of international politics in which its old visions and policies are outdated. How Swedes will create a new vision is not clear today. The new non-socialist government headed by Bildt presses ahead to join the Community. At the same time, there is much discussion in Sweden about how the public will be allowed to participate in the process. There is an agreement among the major parties that a binding referendum on the EC application will be held. However, the "when" and the "how" of that referendum are still unclear.

Meanwhile, opposition to EC membership has grown particularly within the Social Democratic party. The failure of all political elites to keep the Swedish public informed about the realities of Sweden's international position during the past four decades is now coming back to haunt policy-makers. The Neutrality Doctrine is so deeply engrained in the Swedish mind-set that membership in the Community, particularly of the type advocated by Bildt, seems a rejection of a proud past. The Social Democratic leadership is struggling to control a protest against its own policies that could cause a real split within the party and weaken it for a decade.

Ideas about Germany, at least up to this point, remain fuzzy. Despite Bildt's clarity, the public has not yet really been exposed to any sustained debate. It is not clear that Bildt's vision will have much appeal in Sweden anyway. One is tempted to argue that so long as Russia remains viable as a military great power, the average Swede will instinctively think in traditional terms. To become reacquainted with Germany in any fundamental way will be a long and difficult process. To be fully active in Europe, as Bildt and some others demand, also seems something for the distant future.

Yet, who, if anyone, would have predicted in 1985 that by 1992, Germany would be united, the USSR gone, and the European Community on its way to a much more meaningful integration? We live in a rapidly and dramatically changing time. Sweden, as all others, is going to have to adjust its traditional ideas, identify its interests, and pursue the opportunities that present themselves.

Bibliographical Essay

The preceding interpretive essay on Sweden's ties with Germany reflects the thirty years of research and writing conducted by the author on modern Swedish history. Time limitations did not permit the construction of a complete set of references or extensive bibliography. Readers will have to draw their own conclusions about the power of the author's arguments.

For novices to this topic, the best place to start is Franklin D. Scott's *Sweden: The Nation's History* (Minneapolis: University of Minnesota Press, 1977). The number of works in English on Swedish foreign policy is growing. Among those worth consulting: Nils Andren, *Power-Balance and Non-Alignment: A Perspective on Swedish Foreign Policy* (Stockholm: Almqvist & Wiksell, 1967); Wilhelm Carlgren, *Swedish Foreign Policy during the Second World War* (New York: St. Martin's Press, 1977); Paul Cole and Douglas M. Hart, eds., *Northern Europe: Security Issues for the 1990s* (Boulder: Westview Press, 1986); Ebba Dohlman, *National Welfare and Economic Interdependence: The Case of Sweden* (Oxford: Clarendon Press; New York: Oxford University Press, 1989); Harto Hakovirta, *East-West Conflict and European Neutrality* (Oxford: Clarendon Press; New York: Oxford University Press, 1988); Barbara Haskell, *The Scandinavian Option: Opportunities and Opportunity Costs in Postwar Scandinavian Foreign Policies* (Oslo: Universitetsforlaget, 1976); Donald Hancock, *Sweden: The Politics of Post-Industrial Change* (Hinsdale IL: Dryden Press, 1972); Johan J. Holst, ed., *Five Roads to Nordic Security* (Oslo: Universitetsforlaget, 1973); Steven S. Koblik, *Sweden: The Neutral Victor. Sweden and the Western Powers, 1917-1919*, Vol. III of the *Lund Studies in*

International History (Stockholm: Läromedelsförlagen, 1972) and *The Stones Cry Out* (New York: Holocaust Library, 1988); Milton Leitenberg, *Soviet Submarine Operations in Swedish Waters, 1980-1986* (New York: Praeger, 1987); Geir Lundestad, *America, Scandinavia, and the Cold War, 1945-1949* (New York: Columbia University Press, 1980); Bengt Sundelius, ed., *The Committed Neutral: Sweden's Foreign Policy* (Boulder: Westview Press, 1989), *Foreign Policies of Northern Europe* (Boulder: Westview Press, 1982), and *The Neutral Democracies and the New Cold War* (Boulder: Westview Press, 1987); and Herbert Tingsten, *The Debate on the Foreign Policy of Sweden 1918-1939* (London/New York: Oxford University Press, 1949).

Studies in Swedish are more extensive. Many are, however, likely to be superseded by new work that reflects the end of the Cold War and the reunification of Germany. Much of the existing Swedish scholarship has been influenced by Sweden's contemporary policies and restrictive access to documents. New studies on Swedish-Soviet relations and Sweden's relationship with Europe in general can be expected. Some of the above-mentioned works offer bibliographical references to studies in Swedish.

8

Finnish-German Relations and the Helsinki-Berlin-Moscow Geopolitical Triangle

Alpo Rusi

Introduction

Although Germany is primarily a Central European power and Finland lies along Europe's northern periphery, both countries have often shared similar kinds of security concerns. These commonalities are the result of the significance of the Helsinki-Berlin-Moscow geopolitical triangle for both Finland and Germany. The dynamics of that triangle have tended to bring the two countries closer together, in times of war as well as peace, than their respective geographic location might lead one to expect.

In addition, the Baltic Sea has served as an important economic and even cultural link, turning Germany and Finland into neighbors in a variety of ways. In the course of history, cultural, economic, and political influences and innovations have reached Finland not only from Sweden but also from Germany. In fact, one could say that Finland is a Nordic country with strikingly Germanic aspects in its overall character.

Imperial Germany, for example, rather than Sweden, played a crucial role in strengthening the Finnish independence movement in the latter's efforts to win Finland's full independence from Russian rule during the final phase of World War I. Until 1917 Finland was an autonomous Grand Duchy within the Czarist empire. Many young Finns volunteered at the time for training in Germany as infantrymen in the army of Russia's enemy, and these Finnish troops in turn formed the military backbone of the nationalist movement that fought for Finland's independence in the Civil War between January and May of 1918. As a result, many Finns subsequently saw Germany as a potential ally against any renewed (Soviet) Russian expansionism.

The destiny and independence of Finland were dramatically at stake in the course of World War II, with Germany playing a crucial role throughout. As a result of the secret protocol of the August 1939 Molotov-Ribbentrop Pact, Stalin considered Finland to be part of an envisioned Soviet sphere of influence. However, since the Red Army significantly underestimated the capability and morale of the Finnish forces, Stalin was unable to secure his complete "share" of territory, as originally designated in the Pact, during the so-called Winter War of 1939-40.

Between 1941 and 1944 (known in Finland as the Continuation War), Finland fought with Nazi Germany as a co-belligerent, primarily in order to regain those areas it had been forced to cede to the USSR, rather than in support of the Germans' broader war aims. In fact, the Soviet Union had again emerged as a historic threat to the Finns immediately after the end of the Winter War in March 1940. It proved impossible to establish anything resembling normal relations with a Soviet Russia that had occupied some 10 percent of Finnish territory and caused heavy human casualties in the course of the Winter War.

Under these dire circumstances, Finland made active political and military overtures to Nazi Germany. During the months leading up to the outbreak of war between the Third Reich and the Soviet Union, Finnish military leaders secretly negotiated a plan for joint action with their German counterparts in case of a Nazi military offensive against the USSR. The German government also began using Finnish ports as stop-over points in its deployment of troops to Norway in August 1940. The joint German-Finnish military plan was ready for execution when the German army launched its Operation Barbarossa against the Soviets in June 1941. Throughout the remainder of the war, German military assistance was of vital significance to the Finns. In fact, it is not inaccurate to conclude that this very assistance enabled Finnish forces to resist the USSR's massive counter-offensive in the summer of 1944 and forestall a Soviet conquest of Finland.

When World War II ended, German-Finnish relations had entirely collapsed. In view of Germany's traditional importance in Finland's foreign trade, major efforts at revitalizing the economic relationship were undertaken in 1947 and 1948, in spite of continuing political difficulties between the two peoples. Such economic ties were particularly quickly restored with the Western-occupied sections of Germany.

During the ensuing Cold War, Finland pursued a policy of neutrality between East and West, which also affected its relations with the newly established Federal Republic of Germany and German Democratic Republic. Neutrality enabled the Finnish government to thwart undue Soviet pressures. The policy did have its price, however, because it forced Finland to apply a certain political, if not moral, symmetry in its relations with countries in both East and West. As a result, Finnish neutrality was frequently met with skepticism, and even dismay, in many Western nations, particularly in West Germany. The pejorative notion of "Finlandization" originated in the Federal Republic in the early 1960s, connoting a neutralism based on *de facto* subservience to Soviet domination.

Although West Germany became one of Finland's most important trading partners, it is not inaccurate to say that Helsinki maintained a calculated political distance to both German states during most of the Cold War. The initiation of a new *Ostpolitik* by the Bonn government after 1969, however, enabled the Finnish government to recast its own policy vis-a-vis Germany. As a result, both German states received Finnish diplomatic recognition in November 1972. From the mid-1970s onward, and more dramatically in the wake of Germany's recent reunification, German-Finnish relations entered a new era.

The united Germany has rapidly become Finland's most important European partner. This development is the result of two fundamental factors. First, Germany now is indisputably Finland's primary trading partner. As a consequence of the almost complete collapse of trade with the former Soviet Union, which earlier had amounted to about 25 percent of Finland's foreign trade, Germany's role as foremost trading partner has been enhanced even further. In 1991, imports from Germany constituted 17 percent of Finland's total import volume, while exports to Germany represented 15.4 percent of all Finnish exports.

Second, as a result of Finland's March 1992 application for membership in the European Community, Germany is clearly looming as one of Helsinki's most crucial partners in a future European Union. Shared membership in such a European Union would reinforce the traditionally and geopolitically close Finnish-German relationship. Europe has changed a great deal since the 1930s, of course, but the historical linkage between Germany and Finland constitutes a political and strategic factor whose importance should not be underestimated in the new Europe of the future.

Neighbors across the Baltic Sea

Finland is a Nordic country that shares important cultural and religious characteristics with its Scandinavian neighbors. Many of its social and political institutions resemble those of Sweden, Denmark, and Norway. While Finland is largely western from an ethnographic perspective, the eastern roots of its language provide a striking contrast with all its neighbors (except Estonia). There is a small Swedish-speaking minority living in some of the western parts of the country. More permanent human settlement in the area now known as

Finland resulted from the Viking expeditions between the year 800 and the 12th century. Consequently, studies have shown that a considerable portion of Finland's population is of Germanic origin.

Finland found itself under Swedish rule for about 700 years, followed by incorporation into the Russian empire as an autonomous Grand Duchy between 1809 and 1917. By means of the Treaty of Tilsit of 1807, Czar Alexander I of Russia and Napoleon had come to an agreement on their respective spheres of influence, opening the door to Russia's conquest of Finland. Due to its proximity to St. Petersburg, the Czar's government considered Finland to be of strategic importance.

During this period of Swedish and then Russian rule over the Finns, the Holy Roman Empire and then the emerging Germany of the 19th century gained cultural, political, and especially economic influence in Finland. From the 12th century onward, the famous Hanseatic League, a trading network among port-cities in the Baltic Sea region, had an important springboard on the Finnish coast, particularly via Tallin. Although the Swedes maintained political and military control over Finland, the Germans increased their grip on Finnish trade relations by means of certain privileges. It appears that the Germans were also interested in serving as peace-makers in various Swedish-Russian conflicts, for example in the case of the Treaty of Pähkinäsaari in 1323. This treaty was particularly significant because its constituted the first peace settlement between Russia and its northwestern neighbor that involved an attempt to establish a specific boundary line.

From the beginning of the 13th century onward, Finland experienced a change of decisive importance, as a merchant, city-centered culture with a strong German flavor emerged. The Church of Rome lost its erstwhile influence and the Lutheran Church became by far the most dominant religious institution in Finland. In addition to Finnish and Swedish, German was spoken rather widely in a number of southern Finnish port-cities, such as Wiborg on the Karelian isthmus, beginning as far back as the 16th century, as a consequence of Finnish participation in the Hanseatic League.

The influence of German culture in the development of Finland may have been most decisive in the context of the emergence of Finnish nationalism during the 18th century and beyond. A major role was played here by Johan Vilhelm Snellman (1806-1881), who was regarded as one of Hegel's most brilliant students in the early 19th century. Influenced by the Idealism of Herder and Hegel, Snellman studied at the University of Tübingen in 1839-41, and became the most influential Finnish politician of his time. He was a leader in the *Fennoman* nationalist movement, and wrote frequently about Finland's identity and about the role of small nations in the world. It is important to note this German inspiration behind the *Fennoman* movement, considering the much smaller Hegelian influence in Sweden, for example.

Snellman held significant political positions for some twenty years, and as Director-General of the Bank of Finland created a special Finnish currency (*Markkaa*), in spite of continuing Russian rule. In addition, he introduced what would turn out to be key concepts in Finnish foreign policy, particularly based on considerations of political "realism." It is also worth noting that the most influential Finnish political parties, the Conservatives, the Agrarians, and the Social Democrats, emerged at the end of the 1890s and in the early 1900s in the spirit of Snellman's *Fennoman* ideology. In sum, Germany's philosophical Idealism, along with its unification process and the Lutheran factor, clearly rank as the most important foreign formative influences in the genesis of Finnish nationalism, with Lutheran Protestantism particularly noteworthy for its promotion of national consciousness among the poor in rural areas.

Germany and the Emergence of an Independent Finland

The last phase of the Finnish struggle for independence occurred under difficult international and domestic circumstances in December 1917, towards the end of World War I. The Finnish declaration of independence, proclaimed on December 6, triggered a brief but traumatic civil war (January-May 1918). Although Finland had never experienced feudalism and although the country had had a single-chamber parliament based on universal suffrage since 1906, there was a clear division within the population along socioeconomic and political lines.

As a result, the Civil War pitted two distinct groups against one another. On one side, there were the so-called "Reds," revolutionary socialists from the Social Democratic Party who had a clear link with revolutionaries in Russia. Opposing them were the "Whites," who had particularly strong ties with Imperial Germany. The latter played a decisive role in the conflict.

As noted earlier, Germany had already tried to promote rebellion in Finland at the outset of World War I by providing for the training of groups of Finnish volunteers as light-infantrymen. With the assistance of the German army, a 12,000-strong division of "White" freedom fighters, led by General Carl Gustav Mannerheim (1867-1951), succeeded in defeating units of the former imperial Russian army stationed in Finland as well as the forces of the pro-socialist "Reds." This victory of the "Whites" all but guaranteed the demise of any possible revolutionary "spill-over" from Russia into Finland. When the Civil War ended, some German troops stayed behind on Finnish territory, and German generals were invited to help organize the armed forces of the newly independent Finland. Thought was also given in Finnish army circles to the possibility of a formal military alliance with Germany. For its part, Germany attempted to tie Finland firmly into its sphere of influence. A number of

Western countries believed that Germany had, in fact, occupied Finland as a result of the operations of its forces there during the war.

A large group of politicians who had favored an active Finnish pro-independence policy, including the use of military force, moved to establish close political ties with Imperial Germany. Prior to the actual conclusion of World War I these pro-German politicians decided to elect Prince Friedrich Karl of Hessen, the German Kaiser's brother-in-law, as King of Finland. However, this plan failed as a result of Germany's defeat in the war. Furthermore, the government in Helsinki abandoned its economic and military alliance with Berlin in November 1918.

Ironically, General Mannerheim, leader of the "Whites," was not really known for his pro-German attitudes, having served in the Russian Czar's elite troops. After the end of the war, he became Regent, and under his leadership Finland turned more fully to the Western world. On July 17, 1919, Finland's present constitution was ratified, and its relations with foreign states were normalized. Under a peace accord with Russia, signed at Tartu in 1920, the area of Petsamo in Lapland was added to Finland's territory, which meant that the country now extended to the Arctic Ocean. However, Finland would lose this area again under an armistice in 1944.

Finland's Interwar Foreign Policy

During the 1920s, foreign relations were cultivated primarily with the neighboring Nordic countries, the Baltic states, and Great Britain. Soviet Russia continued to be seen as an adversary, making good or even normal inter-state relations difficult to achieve. This basic fact constituted a fundamental geopolitical point of orientation in Finnish foreign policy.

The initially pro-German orientation in Finnish foreign policy essentially ceased after November 1918. Nevertheless, the former "Whites" in Finland, particularly the Conservatives and the Agrarians, continued to harbor a distinct gratitude toward Berlin, even though Imperial Germany had lost the war and was assigned responsibility for its outbreak in the Versailles Peace Treaty. As postwar Finland turned toward the West, especially Sweden, Great Britain, and the United States, the feeling persisted in Helsinki that some form of cooperation with Germany was vital in order to adequately balance a perceived Soviet Russian threat.

During the Civil War, the Finnish Social Democratic Party had been dominated by pro-Russian, revolutionary hardliners, whose policy had been a key cause of that war. The more moderate wing of the party, which had developed strong ties with the Swedish and German Social Democrats, had been unable to block the revolutionary frenzy of the radical wing. After the complete defeat of the "Reds," however, the moderates were able to build a new Social

Democratic Party, from which all pro-Russian Communists, most of whom fled to the new USSR, were thoroughly purged.

In 1922 a distinctly negative change occurred in Finnish-German relations as a result of the conclusion of the Rapallo Treaty between Germany and the Soviet Union. The Helsinki government perceived the treaty as inimical to Finland's security interest because it helped strengthen the international position of what was still considered to be a hostile Communist giant on the other side of the Baltic Sea. Consequently, the Rapallo Treaty prevented a further improvement in Finnish-German relations during the remainder of the Weimar era. At the same time, however, no major negative sentiments against Germany emerged in Finnish cultural and military circles. The influence of German language instruction, for example, was considerably enhanced in the Finnish school system during the 1920s. In fact, Germany in general and Berlin in particular had become key centers of cultural and scientific life, for the Finns as well as for many others in Europe. A large number of trade treaties was also signed by the German and Finnish governments during these years, with imports from Germany amounting to one-third of Finland's total import volume.

Against this general background, it is perhaps not a major surprise that some Finns almost welcomed Hitler's rise to power in 1933. After all, Hitler gave expression to anti-Communist sentiments that, from the Finnish point of view, served to counterbalance the Soviet threat. Thus, German National Socialism could count on a certain degree of support in Finland during the 1930s. At the same time, however, the Finns succeeded in resisting the totalitarian temptation at home more effectively than many other nations in Europe during that fateful decade.

Yet, the earlier, more positive attitudes vis-a-vis Nazi Germany vanished rather quickly. A trade war erupted between Berlin and Helsinki, causing the Third Reich to lose a prominence in Finland's overall foreign trade that it would never regain.

The subsequent radicalization of German Nazism, along with an increasingly aggressive German posture in foreign affairs, ruined any potential for closer Finnish-German political relations. The Germans' occupation of Czechoslovakia heightened the anti-German mood in Finland and was widely condemned by both the press and the country's political elite. It became clear to most Finns that Nazi Germany's aggressive policies were turning into a clear and present threat to their own nation's security. These feelings of national insecurity were enhanced by the fact that the Soviet media and the USSR's diplomats in Helsinki left little doubt, from 1937 onward, that the growing German menace would compel the Soviet Union to safeguard its strategic interests in the Baltic region. Finnish politicians did not ignore these signals, and they recognized that it would be well-nigh impossible for Finland to avoid getting caught in the middle in case of a conflict between an expansionist Nazi Germany and a Communist Russia.

The Winter War

In August 1939, several months before the Soviets launched their attack on Finland, the USSR and Germany concluded a non-aggression pact that included a secret protocol relating to Finland, the Baltic states, and Poland. The protocol assigned most of these areas to the Soviet sphere of influence, thus setting the stage for the intense drama that was to follow. In the early 1930s Hitler had already seen Finland as a possible ally against the Soviet Union. However, he did not regard Finland as an integral part of Germany's *Lebensraum*, and was thus prepared to leave that country outside the German sphere of influence at the time the secret protocol was signed.

Moscow triggered the first act of the drama by pressing the Baltic states and Finland one by one into negotiations. Immediately upon receipt of what was a *de facto* Soviet ultimatum, the Finnish government ordered a full national military mobilization. The Finns were determined not to accept any Soviet demands for border changes. Using hindsight, some Finns have debated whether the ensuing Winter War with the USSR could have been avoided if a more flexible approach to the Soviets' demands had been adopted. It is true that a disagreement did exist among Finnish political leaders on how best to deal with Moscow.

In spite of appeals made by pro-German Finns and Swedes, Hitler left Finland to its own devices. When the war broke out on November 30, 1939, Germany refused to mediate between Moscow and Helsinki and took the position of a "friendly neutral" toward the USSR, even offering assistance to the Soviet fleet by servicing Russian submarines that were involved in a blockade of Finland. This blockade turned out to be extremely harmful not only to Finland but to Germany as well. In fact, the Germans were far from unanimous in their policy vis-a-vis Finland, and when it became obvious that the Finns were able to mount a successful resistance against the Soviet attack, the mood in Berlin underwent a noticeable change.

Although the Finns were able to defeat the attempt by the USSR to conquer their nation during these winter months of 1939-40, Finland's survival certainly hung by a thread. The Finnish army's successful resistance contrasted sharply with the fate of the neighboring Baltic states, which were brutally subjugated after acceding to the Soviets' threats and demands.

During the Winter War the Finns stood alone in their fight against the expansionism of the Soviet Union. Although some Western states, like France and Britain, contemplated the possibility of intervention, these plans never materialized, due to Sweden's unwillingness to have its territory used for purposes of transportation and logistics. At the same time, the Winter War offered Hitler an opportunity to launch his offensive against Norway and Denmark earlier than he had originally planned. Perhaps more importantly, the Winter War did much to determine the timing of Nazi Germany's attack on the

Soviet Union. It may also have misled Hitler into believing that Stalin's closed society would be an easy target for Germany's rapidly moving military forces. If that is so, hindsight would suggest that this misperception on Hitler's part ranks as a key factor in his overall underestimation of the Soviets' ability to resist an all-out invasion.

Upon the conclusion of the Winter War, in which it had lost about 10 percent of its territory (including Karelia) and in which some 21,000 Finnish soldiers had been killed, Finland was confronted with a tragic dilemma: a) to try to live between two enemies, the USSR and Nazi Germany, or b) to join Germany as a co-belligerent, not as a true ally but in order to regain the territory of which it had just been deprived.

The Continuation War, 1941-44

The end of the Winter War saw Finland in a seriously deteriorated strategic position. Territorial losses left the country with a virtually unfortified land frontier, while both civil administration and military organization had been badly disrupted. In addition, the Gulf of Finland was now firmly under Soviet control. Considering the circumstances, it was hardly surprising that Finland joined in Germany's attack on the Soviet Union in June 1941. As noted earlier, the Finnish military leadership had been preparing plans for joint German-Finnish military efforts in a possible German invasion of the USSR ever since the end of the Winter War. These plans were kept secret throughout the war and were, in fact, not publicly revealed until fairly recently.

As the Continuation War got underway, Finland was able to recapture Karelia, yet all additional objectives were subject to close coordination with Germany's own war aims. Discussions between Finland's political leaders and the German government created a kind of non-declared political commitment, if not alliance, between the two countries, even though the war as such had not really been initiated by Finland. In the final analysis, all of Finland's war aims were dependent on a defeat of the Soviet Union by Nazi Germany, leading the Finnish foreign minister to caution that "you don't skin the bear until you have killed it."

Finland paid a heavy political price for its pro-German wartime orientation. Britain, at that point an ally of the Soviet Union against Germany, broke diplomatic relations with Helsinki, while the U.S. decided to freeze its ties with the Finnish government. However, Finland encountered no major problems in its relations with Sweden, which was of utmost importance to the Helsinki government, especially since many a peace initiative aimed at the USSR passed through Stockholm.

For its part, Finland attempted to emphasize the separate nature of its own war effort by refraining from participation in the German siege of Leningrad.

In addition, Finnish authorities refused to allow even a single member of Finland's small Jewish community to be deported to Germany, even though the German government persistently tried to get the Finns to change this policy. More generally, the Germans appeared to have considerable doubt regarding the Finns' real motives during the war. German diplomats in Helsinki exerted pressure on the Finnish government and even tried to change the latter's censorship policy in order to gain a greater degree of Finnish ideological commitment to Germany's war aims. There is little doubt that such efforts did pay off in some cases.

By 1944, with the tide having turned on the eastern front, the Soviet Union appeared to be close to conquering Finland. In order to obtain badly needed German assistance, Finnish President Risto Ryti signed a political agreement with the Nazi government, known as the "Ribbentrop Agreement," in June 1944. With German military support, the Finns were able to halt the massive Soviet offensive during July. Upon the replacement of President Ryti by Marshall Mannerheim, Finnish-Soviet peace talks began, leading to a September 1944 armistice agreement that obligated the Finns to fight against the Germans in Lapland for two additional months in order to remove German troops from Finnish soil by force.

The conclusion of the armistice with the USSR, in addition to the accompanying break in diplomatic relations with Germany, marked the abandonment by Finland of what had been a key component in its foreign policy, namely the search for security guarantees vis-a-vis the Soviet Union. In addition, the requirement in the armistice that Finland act to clear its territory of any remaining German forces necessitated the Finns to go to war again, for the third time within a five-year period. As German resistance stiffened, the conflict escalated.

Although most of the fighting in Lapland had ended by early November of 1944, the last German forces did not depart from Finnish territory until April 1945. Having lost some 70,000 men during the Continuation War, the struggle with German troops in Lapland cost Finland another 4000 casualties, of which almost 800 were killed in actual combat. As they withdrew into Norway, the German troops destroyed most of Lapland. The close but peculiar wartime Finnish-German relationship had come to an end.

Finland between East and West

World War II took a heavy toll on Finland. The country lost 2.3 percent of its population and some 10 percent of its territory. Compared to many other European nations, however, Finland still emerged from the conflagration relatively intact. At no point was the country actually occupied by the Soviet Red Army. Nonetheless, the Finnish economy had been severely damaged, and the armistice with the USSR involved the payment of considerable war reparations by the Finns.

Even though Finland emerged from the war as an independent, functioning parliamentary democracy, the outbreak of the Cold War and the growth of Soviet power cast a dark shadow over the country's future. The Red Army swept through Eastern Europe, and Soviet-style client regimes were established throughout the area, behind what would become known as the Iron Curtain. Finland did manage to stay on the Western, democratic side of Europe, but until 1955 it was compelled to accept the presence of a Soviet naval base on Finnish territory about 12 miles west of Helsinki. In the first decade after the war, Finns had to come to grips with two fundamental problems: the reconstruction of their war-ravaged economy and the containment of Soviet expansionism.

In the immediate aftermath of the war, the Finns tried to fulfill the conditions of the 1944 armistice. For example, they were required to prosecute all those politicians who had shown pro-German sentiments during the Continuation War. Altogether, fourteen Finnish wartime leaders, including former President Ryti and several government ministers, were tried and received sentences ranging from two to ten years in prison. The verdicts deeply hurt the Finnish people's sense of justice.

Finland faced a serious likelihood of "easternization" until at least 1949. The country's Communist Party attempted to stir up domestic unrest by extra-parliamentary means in order to facilitate the expansion of Soviet influence in Finnish politics. One of the Communist leaders suggested in 1948 that "the road of Czechoslovakia is also the road of Finland." However, these destabilization efforts during what are now called the "years of danger" (1945-48) largely failed.

The Finnish government's policies during the postwar years aimed at a harmonization of three strategic objectives. First, the development of a strategic compromise that enabled Finland's political leaders to provide the Soviet Union with guarantees that the latter's reasonable security interests would, under all circumstances, be taken into consideration by the Helsinki government. Second, the creation of an adequate response to the economic realities facing Finland. This involved a fundamental recognition that, in the long run, a small country's economy could not develop and prosper without an infusion of foreign capital and technology and without access to foreign trade. The third objective was essentially ideological, and entailed a determination not to let cooperation and good relations with the Soviet Union obscure the fundamental ideological differences between the two countries. In other words, Finland would be committed to preserving its parliamentary democracy, its basic civil rights, and its market economy.

During these postwar years, and especially after the conclusion in 1948 of the Treaty of Friendship, Cooperation and Mutual Assistance with the USSR, Finland embarked on a new orientation in foreign affairs, at first called the

"Paasikivi line" and later renamed the "Paasikivi-Kekkonen line."* This policy centered on the maintenance of good relations with the Soviet Union and caused a distinct diminution of Germany's role in Finnish diplomacy. The 1948 treaty, signed primarily at the request of the Soviets, identified Germany as a *de facto* adversary, which could only have a complicating impact on the future of Finnish-German relations. These relations had to accomodate themselves to the spirit, even if not the letter, of the Soviet-Finnish treaty. As recently as September 1990 the treaty's articles relating to Germany were still essentially unchanged.

By 1951, Finnish exports were restored to their prewar level. The Helsinki government's trade policy aimed at striking a balance in trade with both East and West, while showing a recognition of Moscow's determination to keep Finland outside the Western European integration process. Finland voluntarily turned down the Western offer of Marshall Plan aid, and such foreign aid as it did receive was strictly state-controlled and bilateral in nature until 1956.

Although Germany was divided into two antagonistic states at the end of the 1940s, Finland had already tried to rebuild its traditionally close trade relations with occupied Germany during 1947-48. In order to facilitate Finnish-German commercial interaction, Finland set up formal trade delegations in Frankfurt and East Berlin, while the two German states established similar delegations in Helsinki in 1953.

Finland's Cold War Crises

For more than two decades after 1945, the "German Question" constituted one of the most difficult problems in Finnish foreign policy. In accordance with its status as a neutral, Finland was determined to stay outside East-West conflicts of interest and power, and this had obvious consequences for the country's policy toward the two German states. By and large, the Helsinki government maintained a clear political distance between itself and both the FRG and the GDR. Although ideological and economic considerations would have made Finland a more natural partner for West Germany than for East Germany, the Finns' precarious position between East and West seriously inhibited the development of any such partnership. The Finnish commitment to neutrality had an inevitably negative impact on commercial relations with the Federal Republic, for example, particularly during the 1950s and early 1960s.

---

* Juho Paasikivi (1870-1956) was Prime Minister in 1918 and from 1944 until 1946, and then President from 1946 until 1956. Urho Kekkonen (1900-1986) served as Prime Minister during 1950-53 and 1954-56, and as President between 1956 and 1981.

Soviet pressure on Finland reached a climax during a series of critical Cold War junctures, especially when the German Question was at stake and the USSR appeared to be convinced of a heightened German "threat." The so-called "note crisis" of late 1961 turned out to be one of the most serious crises faced by Finland in the course of the postwar era. It involved an October 30, 1961 note, from the Kremlin to the Helsinki government, requesting urgent consultations, based on the 1948 Soviet-Finnish treaty, in order to discuss the possibility of joint military preparations in the face of what was alleged to be growing West German militarism.

The debate continues in Finland today as to whether the note was the result of an actual deterioration in East-West relations or whether it was issued for domestic political consumption in Finland, where the re-election chances of President Kekkonen had become uncertain and might be boosted by this kind of Soviet rumbling. Whatever the truth may be, it is impossible to fully understand the note without taking into consideration the growing concerns of Soviet military leaders about the Warsaw Pact's ability to cope with an accelerating arms race. In addition, the note may have been the result of a Soviet interest to link Finland more closely to the Warsaw Pact's air defense system.

Having won re-election, President Kekkonen did support measures to strengthen Finland's defense capability, including the acquisition of anti-aircraft missiles. In order to do so, he secured the consent of the signatories of the Paris Peace Treaty of 1947, which, next to the 1948 Soviet-Finnish treaty, constituted the second fundamental postwar document regulating Finland's international status. In 1961, the Swedish government proposed the creation of a bloc of nuclear-free countries in northern Europe, and in 1963 Kekkonen matched this idea with a formal proposal for a Nordic nuclear-free zone. These proposals were at least in part aimed at reducing possible Soviet fears of (nuclear) militarism on the part of NATO in general and West Germany in particular.

The Debate about "Finlandization"

In retrospect, it is not surprising that West Germany had difficulty accepting Finland's neutralist policy during the Cold War. This was in part the result of the way in which the question of neutrality had affected the Germans themselves. After all, there had been several postwar efforts to arrange a reunification of the two German states on the basis of neutrality. For example, Stalin had floated a proposal along these lines in his famous "note" of 1952. West German governments had rejected any plan along these lines, however, since they were deeply convinced that the FRG's foreign policy should be firmly based on Western European integration and West German participation in

Western security structures. As a result, the terms "neutrality" and "neutralism" acquired a distinctly negative connotation in the Federal Republic.

The debate over "Finlandization" was, perhaps not surprisingly, triggered during the early 1960s in West Germany in connection with the Berlin crisis and the construction of the Wall. It accelerated further when SPD leader Willy Brandt introduced the outline of a new *Ostpolitik* vis-a-vis the Soviet bloc. Critics of the USSR and of Brandt's policy suggestions employed the term "Finlandization" to suggest that any policy of ill-considered accomodation toward the Soviet Union would risk a surrender of basic Western freedoms and amount to *de facto* subservience. Finland was not a direct issue in this West German debate. Rather, the term was used to describe what his critics saw as Brandt's "softness" in the face of Communism, and Finland's Cold War neutrality was treated as symbolic of such "softness." One of Brandt's major opponents, former Defense Minister Franz-Josef Strauss, stressed that Moscow aimed at a permanent division of Germany, undiminished Soviet control over the GDR, and a "Finlandization" of the Federal Republic. The "Finlandization" debate faded considerably during the 1970s, however, although the term continued to enjoy a notable popularity in conservative circles, especially during the 1980s, in the context of NATO's "Euromissile" crisis.

Finland and the German States in the 1970s and 1980s

Largely as a result of West Germany's *Ostpolitik* and the general climate of East-West detente, Finland was able to revise its policy vis-a-vis both German states. In fact, by the early 1970s Finland was the only European country that did not have formal diplomatic relations with at least one of the two German states. The Helsinki government was one of the main supporters of the idea of a Conference on Security and Cooperation in Europe (CSCE), and it felt that Finland would have little chance of hosting the conference unless diplomatic recognition were extended to both the Federal Republic and the German Democratic Republic. While the Finnish government was satisfied that its Cold War policy of neutrality and consequent non-recognition of FRG and GDR was accepted by both superpowers, such acceptance or understanding seemed to be often absent in both German states.

The government of Finland decided that recognition of West and East Germany should occur simultaneously, based on parallel negotiations. Not surprisingly, the Bonn government resisted this approach, since it implied a fundamental equality between both Germanys. However, President Kekkonen publicly stated that the existence of two separate German states was an obvious fact of life, and thus Finland did extend simultaneous recognition to both German states on November 24, 1972.

When the formal process of recognition had been completed in January 1973, the German Question appeared to have been solved, at least for the forseeable future, as far as Finland was concerned. However, the Finnish government continued to pursue a balanced policy vis-a-vis the two Germanys on the basis of its Cold War neutrality. For example, Finnish presidents were careful to make symmetrical state visits, rather than giving in to more natural Finnish interests that would have suggested a preferential treatment of the FRG.

Relations between Finland and the GDR followed a distinctly peculiar path. On the surface at least, the Finns had accepted the *de facto* existence of two separate, sovereign German states, necessitating normal relations with both. Yet reality was different, and East Germany never succeeded in becoming a "normal" state among other states in Finnish diplomacy.

In their separate ways, both Finland and the GDR were interested in good relations with the Soviet Union, and this partial convergence of interests at times found notable reflection in their respective positions on certain international questions. For its part, East Germany tended to "showcase" its relations with Finland as a model for its relations with Western countries generally, and displayed a clear interest in using Finland in order to shore up its own international status. In 1975, the two countries signed a consular agreement, whereby the Finnish government recognized the existence of a separate East German nationality (an act that clearly contravened the West German insistence on a single all-German nationality). Finland in turn tried to use this as an opportunity to obtain East German recognition of Finnish neutrality, but that effort failed.

The Helsinki government initially believed that good economic relations with a "model" socialist country like the GDR would be possible. Those expectations were never really met, in spite of the conclusion of a number of trade agreements with East Berlin. Finnish-East German economic relations remained very shallow, and trade with the GDR never amounted to more than about 0.5 percent of Finland's overall foreign trade. However, East Germany did succeed in maintaining fairly good relations with various left-wing Finnish parties. In addition, certain groups and individuals on the Finnish cultural scene were eager to treat the GDR as a model country in the socialist bloc, and did not hesitate to criticize their own government for doing too little to promote closer Finnish-East German relations. This became most noticeable in the late 1970s and the 1980s, when some Western (including Finnish) left-wing parties expressed frequent appreciation for support given to various peace movements by socialist countries.

Finland, Germany, and the End of the Cold War

President Kekkonen died in 1986 and thus did not live to see the Berlin Wall crumble. In less than 20 years after the Finns had recognized both German states, international reality had undergone an almost unprecedented transformation. The traditional Finnish policy of equidistance vis-a-vis the FRG and GDR had already been eroded in the course of the 1970s and 1980s. During these years, the old Cold War *status quo* had changed, particularly as a result of a CSCE process within which Helsinki and Bonn were collaborating increasingly closely.

While in many ways the formal *political* relations between Finland and each German state remained very much symmetrical until the late 1980s, no such symmetry existed in *economic* relations. Finnish trade ties with the Federal Republic became more and more vital, while, as noted above, the GDR failed to become an important trading partner.

The collapse of Communism and of the GDR came as a shock to much of the political elite in Finland. There can be little doubt that Finland had in certain ways benefitted from the Cold War division of Europe, at least economically. The neutral Finns had been able to develop extensive trading relations with both "camps," and the economic relationship with the USSR had become significant. It appeared that much of Finnish-Soviet trade had been "politically" motivated, enabling Finnish businesses to make considerable profits. The end of the Cold War and the disintegration of the Soviet Union clearly undermined what had been an advantageous Finnish foreign trade position. Clouds of a deep recession now appeared on Finland's economic horizon.

Finland found itself ill-prepared to adjust to the end of the Cold War, and the country did slide into a serious recession during 1990-92. Trade with the Soviet Union, which had amounted to some 25 percent of Finland's total foreign trade, disappeared almost overnight, and the Finns ended up paying a high price for their good-neighborly relations with the former USSR. The many ways in which Finland "benefitted" from Europe's Cold War *status quo* might thus explain the cautious and uncertain reaction of the country's political elite when they received the news about the Berlin Wall's collapse.

The rapidly advancing reunification of Germany triggered a debate in Finland about the geopolitical consequences of German unity for the small Nordic neighbor. Some observers suggested that the traditional Helsinki-Berlin-Moscow triangle, which had been such a source of trouble for centuries, would now re-emerge as an even more threatening configuration. However, the majority of Finnish analysts and commentators expressed the conviction that the disappearance of Europe's Cold War division would help strengthen not only Finland's international position but also the country's political and economic relationship with the new Germany.

In the fall of 1990, the Helsinki government undertook a more active revision of Finnish foreign policy. On September 21, it declared that several stipulations of the 1947 Paris Peace Treaty were no longer relevant, with the exception of the prohibition of Finnish possession of nuclear weapons. Finnish authorities asserted that with Germany no longer limited in its sovereignty as a result of the so-called "two-plus-four" negotiations, any constraints on Finnish sovereignty based on the 1947 treaty could no longer be justified. Helsinki proceeded to inform the Soviet Union and Britain of its determination in this regard.

The collapse of the Soviet Union in 1991 entailed the *de facto* demise of the 1948 Soviet-Finnish treaty. As a result, Finnish-German relations were now finally freed from some of the burdens and consequences of history, opening the way for a new beginning. In what amounted to a major change in its postwar foreign policy, Finland applied for membership in the European Community on March 18, 1992. The unification of Germany enabled Finnish political leaders to argue convincingly that the division of Europe had ended and that, consequently, Finnish EC membership had become both possible and appropriate.

The Federal Republic has been a key supporter of Finland's membership in the EC for some time, arguing that, after a decade of southward Community enlargement, the time has come to admit the Nordic states and other members of the European Free Trade Association (EFTA). Finland's entry into a prospective European Union will be a historic turning-point in Finnish-German relations.

The Future of Finnish-German Relations

The future relationship between Finland and Germany will depend primarily on five factors. First, the reunited Germany again lies in the European continent's geostrategic center. Throughout most of modern history, Germany has been either too strong or too weak to constitute a stable pivot on the continent. The "new" Germany faces the challenge of playing an increasingly significant role as a stabilizing agent in European affairs.

Second, the collapse of Soviet power has led to a Russian withdrawal from Central and Eastern Europe and from the Baltic states. However, the military-strategic importance of northern Europe remains considerable and may even grow. As a result, the maintenance of general stability in the Baltic region amounts to a significantly shared Finnish-German security interest.

Third, the European Union, as envisioned in the 1991 Maastricht Treaty, will be a new kind of international actor, neither a United States of Europe nor a traditional alliance of states. This European Union will bring the member states closer to something like a "union of peoples," sharing increasingly similar interests and perspectives in international affairs. If, in the longer run, this

Union assumes a more important role in the area of defense, for example by means of a common defense system, such a development would have very fundamental consequences for Finnish-German relations as well.

Fourth, the establishment of the European Economic Area (EEA), comprising the EFTA and EC countries, as of January 1, 1993, has produced the world's largest single market. The united Germany has already become Finland's most important trading partner, a development that will certainly intensify as a result of the EEA.

Finally, the international system continues to undergo profound changes, with new geopolitical realities constantly emerging. Europe's Cold War division has disappeared, yet no new unifying structure has so far taken its place. This process of systemic transition will most likely take years to run its course. Russia will be a somewhat reduced factor in the overall balance for at least a generation, and currently appears to be withdrawing in a geopolitically northward direction. This is bound to have an impact on Finnish-German relations in the 1990s and beyond. At the present time, Finland and Germany seek to harmonize their respective security interests and perceptions primarily within established Western European (EC), pan-European (CSCE), and transatlantic (NATO) cooperative structures. All this does not mean, however, that the old Helsinki-Berlin-Moscow geopolitical triangle has completely lost its erstwhile meaning and significance. During the remainder of this century, and into the next, it will continue to exist as a major source of challenge for both Finland and Germany. Yet the fact that both countries now share the same values and interests in facing this challenge constitutes a profoundly hopeful sign.

Selected Bibliography

The views expressed in this essay are those of the author. They do not necessarily represent the official views of the government of Finland.

Roy Allison, *Finland's Relations with the Soviet Union, 1944-84* (Oxford: Macmillan Press, 1985).

William Copeland, *The Uneasy Alliance: collaboration between the Finnish opposition and the Russian underground, 1899-1904* (Helsinki: Suomalainen Tiedeakatemia, 1975).

Ian M. Cuthbertson, *Redefining the CSCE. Challenges and Opportunities in the New Europe* (New York & Helsinki: Institute for East-West Studies and Finnish Institute of International Affairs, 1992).

John Hodgson, *Communism in Finland: a history and interpretation* (Princeton, NJ: Princeton University Press, 1967).

Martti Häikiö, *A Brief History of Modern Finland* (Helsinki: University of Helsinki, Lahti Research and Training Centre, 1992).

Max Jakobson, *The Diplomacy of the Winter War* (Cambridge, MA: Harvard University Press, 1961).

Eino Jutikkala and Kauko Pirinen, *A History of Finland* (London: William Heineman, 3rd. ed., 1979).

D. G. Kirby, *Finland in the 20th Century* (London: C. Hurst & Co., 1979).

D. G. Kirby, ed., *Finland and Russia, 1808-1920: from autonomy to independence: a selection of documents* (New York: Barnes & Noble, 1976).

Matti Klinge, *A Brief History of Finland* (Helsinki: Otava, 1987).

Keijo Korhonen, *Autonomous Finland in the Political Thought of Nineteenth Century Russia* (Turku: University of Turku, 1967).

Hans Peter Krosby, *Finland, Germany, and the Soviet Union. The Petsamo Dispute* (Madison, WI: University of Wisconsin Press, 1968).

John Lukacs, "Finland's Vindication," *Foreign Affairs*, Vol. 71, Nr. 4 (Autumn 1992).

George Maude, *The Finnish Dilemma. Neutrality in the Shadow of Power* (London: Oxford University Press, 1976).

Kari Möttölä, Oleg Bykov, and S. Korolev, eds., *Finnish-Soviet Economic Relations* (London: Macmillan, in association with the Finnish Institute of International Affairs, 1983; New York: St. Martin's Press, 1983).

Tauno Nieminen, *Flank or Front. An Assessment of Military-Political Developments in the High North* (Helsinki: War College, 1991).

Jakko Nousiainen, *The Finnish Political System* (Cambridge, MA: Harvard University Press, 1971).

Rene Nyberg, *Security Dilemmas in Scandinavia: Evaporated Nuclear Options and Indigenous Conventional Capabilities* (Ithaca, NY: Cornell University Press, 1983).

Juhani Paasivirta, *Finland and Europe: international crises in the period of autonomy, 1808-1914* (London: C. Hurst, 1981; Minneapolis: University of Minnesota Press, 1981).

Tuomo Polvinen, *Between East and West: Finland in International Politics, 1944-1947* (Helsinki: Werner Söderström Osabeyhtiö, 1986; Minneapolis: University of Minnesota Press, 1986).

Hannu Rautkallio, *Finland and the Holocaust. The Rescue of Finland's Jews* (New York: Holocaust Library, 1987).

Th. Rein, *J. W. Snellman* (Helsinki: Otava, 1928), 2 vols.

Tomas Ries, *Cold Will: The Defence of Finland* (London: Brasseys's, 1988).

Alpo Rusi, *After the Cold War: Europe's New Political Architecture* (London & New York: Macmillan Press and St. Martin's Press, 1991).

Alpo Rusi, *Lehdistösensuuri jatkosodassa 1941-44* [Press Censorship in the Continuation War 1941-44] (Helsinki: Suomen historiallinen seura, julkaisuja nro 118, 1982).

Alpo Rusi, "Finlandization without Finland," *Yearbook of Finnish Foreign Policy* (Helsinki: Finnish Institute of International Affairs, 1987).

Anders Sjaastad, "The Changing Geopolitical Environment," J. J. Holst, K. Hunt, and A. C. Sjaastad, eds., *Deterrence and Defence in the North* (Oslo: Norwegian University Press, 1985).

Anthony F. Upton, *Finland in Crisis, 1940-1941: a study in small-power politics* (Ithaca, NY: Cornell University Press, 1965).

Anthony F. Upton, *Communism in Scandinavia and Finland* (London: Weidenfeld & Nicolson, 1973).

Pekka Visuri, *The Evolution of Finnish Military Doctrine 1945-1985* (Helsinki: Institute of Military Science, Finnish Defence Studies, 1990).

Pekka Visuri and Thomas Forsberg, *Saksa ja Suomi* [Germany and Finland] (Helsinki: WSOY, 1992).

David Vital, *The Survival of Small States: studies in small power-great power conflict* (London: Oxford University Press, 1971).

John H. Wuorinen, *Nationalism in Modern Finland* (New York: Columbia University Press, 1931).

Raimo Väyrynen, *Stability and Change in Finnish Foreign Policy* (Helsinki: University of Helsinki, Department of Political Science, Research Reports, no. 60, 1982).

Yrjö Väänänen, *Finlandia Bonn* (Porvoo: WSOY, 1991) [memoirs of a former Finnish ambassador to Bonn].

PART THREE

Neighbors to the East

9

Moscow and the German Question

F. Stephen Larrabee

The unification of Germany, the external aspects of which were codified in the "two-plus-four" agreement signed by the four original occupying powers in September 1990, ends an important period in East-West relations — and in Soviet diplomacy. For the Soviet Union, the German Question — how to treat Germany — was *the* problem of European politics during the postwar period. The basic Soviet objective after 1945 remained constant: to prevent the resurgence of a powerful Germany and to maintain as much control over developments in Germany as possible.

This essay traces the evolution of Soviet policy toward Germany in the postwar period. In particular, it examines the various shifts in Soviet policy and the factors that prompted them. The central focus of the essay, however, is on Gorbachev's policy and its consequences for East-West relations. What were the main objectives of Gorbachev's policy toward Germany? To what degree did his policy represent a break with the past? Did he anticipate, even desire, the unification of Germany or was unification an unintended by-product of his policy? A final section looks at the implications of the collapse of the Soviet Union as an integral state for future relations with Germany.

The Historical Legacy

Strictly speaking, the German Question arose as the result of the inability of the anti-Hitler coalition to agree upon a common policy towards Germany after the collapse of the Third Reich in 1945. Yet in assessing postwar Soviet policy towards Germany, it would be well to bear in mind the historical dimension of the problem. Over the centuries an ambivalent love-hate relationship, perhaps unique in the annals of international politics, has prevailed between the two countries. On the one hand, as Walter Laqueur has pointed out,[1] there has been no country that Russia admired more and no country that has had a greater impact on Russian intellectual life. On the other hand, there has been no country that Russia has feared more.

The Russian fear of Germany has deep roots. In part it is traceable to the experience of a large influx of foreigners, many of them Germans, at the time of the Petrine reforms. While the Germans were needed and admired as technicians and specialists, they were resented and scorned by the Russian aristocracy for their bourgeois values and lack of elegance. There was, as Victor Frank has noted, an almost irrational sense of superiority on the part of the Russian upper classes, a social hostility that took the sting out of the envy for the material achievements of the Germans.[2] In the 19th century, Westernizers and Slavophiles disagreed on most things; in their dislike and fear of Germans, however, they were at one.

Until the 1860s, anti-German feeling was primarily a domestic problem. With the emergence of Germany as a major actor in European politics, however, anti-German sentiment took on a new dimension. Germany began to be regarded with increasing anxiety as a potential political rival. While Tsarist Russia under Foreign Minister Alexander Gorchakov pursued an essentially pro-German policy, much of Russian public opinion was anti-German. This anti-German feeling was in part rooted in the fear that a powerful Germany would attempt to claim the Baltic provinces and restore an independent Poland. It was reinforced by the growing economic competition between the two countries after 1870 and the protectionist policies adopted by both governments. After Russia was shorn of its gains in the Balkans at the Congress of Berlin (1878) at which Chancellor Otto von Bismarck presided and attempted to act as an "honest broker," Germany came to be regarded in many circles, particularly among Pan-Slavists, as the main obstacle to Russian expansionism.

The collaboration between Russia and Germany in the early years after World War I represented less a change in Russian attitudes than a marriage of necessity forced on the newly established Soviet state by the harsh facts of international life. Internally, Russia lay in ruins, its economy devastated by six years of foreign war, revolution, and civil strife. Externally, it was an outcast, a renegade state without allies. Moreover, with the suppression of the Spartakus uprising in Berlin in January 1919, Lenin's initial hope that a revolution in Germany would spark a world revolution began to fade.

Under such conditions, Germany became the logical focal point for Soviet diplomatic initiatives. Germany was the major industrial power in Europe. Relations were not burdened with the problems of prewar debts, and the punitive policy pursued by the allies — above all, France — made the prospect of cooperation with Russia attractive, regardless of ideological differences. Weak and isolated, each saw in the other the chance to gain diplomatic maneuverabili-ty. The cooperation that arose, particularly in the military field,[3] was undertaken purely for reasons of expediency: it allowed the Germans to evade some of the provisions of the Versailles Treaty regarding rearmament. At the same time, it offered the struggling Soviet state a means of obtaining help in rebuilding its military industry and training the new Red Army. The economic cooperation also gave Moscow a source of much-needed machinery and industrial goods with which to rebuild and expand its industrial base.

The interwar cooperation was symbolized by the Treaty of Rapallo (April 1922), which provided for the establishment of diplomatic relations between the Soviet Union and Germany as well as the regulation of war debts and the expansion of trade. It was not an alliance, but an act of expediency by two international pariahs seeking to escape diplomatic isolation. From the Soviet point of view, its importance lay in the fact that it split the West and kept Germany at odds with France and England. For Germany, it offered an opportunity for more flexibility in diplomacy. In the West, however, it aroused fears of a degree of cooperation that neither existed nor was to develop. Once German Foreign Minister Gustav Stresemann succeeded through skillful diplomacy in regularizing relations with the West, relations between Germany and Moscow cooled.

The same sense of weakness and desire to avoid isolation impelled Stalin to conclude the infamous Non-Aggression Pact with Nazi Germany in 1939. Like Rapallo, the Pact was an act of expediency. Its prime goal was to buy time and keep the Soviet Union out of war. And like Rapallo, it was motivated by economic and military weakness. Stalin appears to have calculated that the Soviet Union was too weak to fight a war. (That Stalin himself was largely responsible for this weakness is another matter.) When the Western powers showed themselves too weak and indecisive to prevent Hitler's growing power, a pact with Hitler must have seemed the best means of keeping Russia out of war and buying time.

Viewed against the background of the Soviet Union's economic and military weakness, the Pact is less of a *volte face* than it initially appears. The issue from Stalin's perspective was survival — his own and that of the Soviet state. A war risked the collapse of both. A pact with Hitler bought time and allowed Stalin to equip and rebuild the Red Army, which had been decimated by Stalin's purges. Stalin's main mistake was not in concluding the Pact, but in trusting Hitler and not recognizing that the Pact for Hitler was also an act of expediency that would be broken as soon as it no longer served Hitler's interests. As a result, Stalin was unprepared for war when it finally came and the Soviet Union suffered heavy casualties in the early phases of the war that could have been avoided.

Stalin's Postwar German Policy

In the postwar period, Germany again played a central role in Soviet policy. Indeed, more than anything else the Cold War was about the fate and future of Germany. As Pierre Hassner has aptly put it, Germany was "the prize, the pivot, the problem of European politics."[4] To a large degree the breakdown of allied cooperation over Germany paved the way for the onset of the Cold War.

The reasons for the breakdown of cooperation have been extensively treated elsewhere and need not be repeated here. Suffice it to say, however, that Soviet actions, particularly the wholesale dismantling of German industry in its zone of occupation and its failure to make an accounting of its reparations in its zone, played an important role — indeed the critical role — in the collapse of allied cooperation and the decision by the Western allies to halt their deliveries in the spring of 1946. The breakdown of allied cooperation over the issue of reparations set the stage for the progressive erosion of the allied administration of Germany and the effective partition of the country into two separate entities with the introduction of the currency reform in the Western zones in the summer of 1948.

It would be wrong, however, to assume that Stalin consciously sought the division of Germany. Had Stalin foreseen or desired the division of Germany, he hardly would have agreed to the exclusion of Berlin from the Soviet zone or to placing the territory East of the Oder-Neisse under Polish administration, thereby diminishing the Soviet zone. Moreover, he did not immediately embark upon the full-scale Bolshevization of the Soviet zone. For the first two years after the war, references to the "class struggle" were scrupulously avoided and an effort was made to set up an "anti-fascist democratic state."[5] It was only after the Western allies decided to proceed with the currency reform and fusion of their zones in 1948 that the full-scale Sovietization of Moscow's occupation zone began.

Indeed, Stalin does not appear to have had a coherent plan for Germany. Rather, he pursued a policy of "watchful waiting" that would allow him to keep his options open and exploit opportunities as they arose. His policy evolved incrementally, often inconsistently, in response to events themselves. At times he seems to have entertained the possibility of the Communization of all of Germany, whereas at other moments he seems to have been ready to settle for half a loaf.

Stalin never seems to have fully resigned himself to the division of Germany, however. One small piece of evidence is contained in his book, *Economic Problems of Socialism in the USSR*, which was published shortly before his death.[6] In the book he predicted that Germany and Japan would rise again and throw off U.S. tutelage. From the context of Stalin's remarks, Germany is clearly a capitalist country belonging to the Western camp. Nowhere is there mention of East Germany. This suggests that, even in 1952, he expected that Germany would be reunited at some point.

Stalin's controversial notes to the Western allies in the spring of 1952, in which he suggested that the Soviet Union might be willing to accept a neutral, independent, and reunified Germany, should be seen against this background. A detailed discussion of this fascinating chapter in Soviet postwar diplomacy, which has provoked much heated debate between those who see the notes as a "missed opportunity" and those who regard them as a propaganda ploy designed to block West Germany's entry into the European Defense Community (EDC), is beyond the scope of this essay.[7] Both views, however, seem oversimplified. Clearly, Stalin designed his notes to prevent, or at least delay, Bonn's entry into the EDC. Nevertheless, it is also conceivable that Stalin would have been willing to strike a bargain had he found some interest on the part of the Western allies and had he been able to ensure a strong Soviet right to veto developments in a weak, reunified Germany.[8]

Clearly, only a very urgent danger would have induced Stalin to entertain ideas of a reunified Germany. The prospect of a million West German soldiers armed in a strong Western alliance when the Soviet Union had not fully recovered from the ravages of war and when its control in Eastern Europe, particularly in East Germany, was by no means solidified, might have been enough to counsel such a step. As the German historian Waldemar Besson has noted, it has frequently been underestimated "what it must have meant psychologically when seven years after the end of the war German soldiers once again appeared on European soil and this time on the side of the powerful adversary, the United States."[9]

From Stalin's viewpoint, a "Rapallo" policy at this point would have offered a number of advantages. First, it would have prevented the unification of Europe under U.S. leadership. It was not just the strengthening of the western half of Germany that Stalin wished to avoid but the consolidation of Europe as a whole. By 1952, however, it was clear that the two were closely linked and that, in order to prevent Western integration, Stalin had to prevent Germany from becoming the Western linchpin. Second, a neutral Germany could form part of a belt of neutral states that could act as a *cordon Stalinaire* between the Soviet sphere of influence and the West. Third, a Rapallo policy offered the possibility that, once the linchpin of European unity had been removed, the United States might eventually be tempted to withdraw its troops from Europe. The result would be a weak, neutral Germany increasingly open to Soviet pressure and influence, perhaps even to intimidation.

Whatever Stalin's true intentions were will never be known because the allies never pursued this offer. Moreover, Stalin made his proposal too late. Had he made his proposal in 1947, before the Cold War had intensified and Western perceptions of the Soviet threat had solidified, it undoubtedly would have fallen on more fertile soil. By the time of the Soviet diplomatic offensive in the spring of 1952, however, plans for West Germany's rearmament had gained too much momentum to be halted. Too much effort had been invested in the plans to risk the possibility of their collapse while the West engaged in long, weary, and frustrating negotiations to probe ambiguities contained in the Soviet proposals.

Shift to a Two-State Policy

Exactly when the Soviet Union abandoned the idea of reunification as a realistic policy goal is difficult to say. Clearly, however, the June 1953 uprising in East Berlin was a watershed. The revolt significantly increased the Soviet stake in East Germany. Having decided to pay the price of intervention, the Soviet leadership was forced to ride out the storm. Thereafter, the Soviet commitment to the German Democratic Republic (GDR) — and to East German party leader Walter Ulbricht personally — increased, and Soviet interest in reunification declined accordingly.

With the entrance of West Germany into the North Atlantic Treaty Organization (NATO) in May 1955, Soviet support for reunification for all purposes was dead, if not buried. Although lip service continued to be paid to it in Soviet statements for some years to come, from that point on Moscow openly shifted to a two-state policy, and its diplomacy followed a two-track course aimed at stabilizing East Germany and integrating it more tightly into the bloc and securing Western, particularly West German, recognition of the postwar *status quo*.

Indeed, the continuity of Soviet objectives in Europe after 1955 is striking. For the next 15 years, the main goal of the USSR's policy vis-a-vis West Germany remained constant: to obtain Bonn's acceptance of the postwar borders and the permanent division of Germany. Nikita Khrushchev sought to do this through a policy of strategic bluffing designed to exploit advances in Soviet missile and space technology in order to force a settlement of the German Question.[10] This, in essence, was the meaning of the series of crises over Berlin between 1958 and 1962. The allies called Khrushchev's bluff, however, forcing him to back down.

After the Cuban missile crisis in 1962, Khrushchev shifted gears and sought to achieve through courtship what he had failed to obtain through intimidation. Having been rebuffed by the allies, he sought to open direct bilateral contacts with Bonn. Khrushchev's ouster in October 1964 on the eve of his planned visit to West Germany ended one of the most intriguing chapters in Soviet-West German relations. What Khrushchev had in mind will probably never be known, but there is little reason to think that the visit would have led to a major breakthrough. His main goal, then as before, was to obtain recognition of the postwar territorial *status quo*. At that point, neither the allies nor West Germany were willing to entertain this option.

The continuity of objectives extended under Leonid Brezhnev. What changed after Khrushchev's removal in October 1964 were not the goals but the style and methods of Soviet policy and, above all, the *context* in which the new Soviet leadership sought to achieve a relatively constant set of objectives. Whereas Khrushchev had tried — and failed — to obtain Bonn's acceptance of the postwar territorial *status quo* by threats and missile diplomacy, his successors sought to exploit Western European desires for change and the breakdown of rigid Cold War boundaries in the mid-1960s in order to solve the German Question within the wider framework of a campaign for European security.

When the Soviets launched this campaign at the July 1966 Bucharest meeting of the Warsaw Pact, its main aim was largely offensive: to mobilize Western European public opinion against Bonn in order to force it to revise its policy and accept the territorial *status quo*. By the April 1967 Warsaw Pact conference in Karlovy Vary, however, the main goals of Soviet policy, particularly its campaign for European security, had clearly become defensive: to blunt the impact of Bonn's new *Ostpolitik* and halt the erosion of Moscow's own authority in Eastern Europe.

An important symbiotic relationship existed between the developing state of crisis in Eastern Europe in the late 1960s and the evolution of Bonn's *Ostpolitik*. Although West Germany's *Ostpolitik* did not cause the ferment in Eastern Europe, which reached a climax in 1968, the changes in Bonn's policy tended to reduce the fear of West Germany on the part of its Eastern European neighbors — a fear that traditionally had been a major source of cohesion in Eastern Europe — and thus accelerated polycentrist tendencies in the area. The unrest during the 1968 Prague Spring in particular reduced Moscow's room for maneuver and prompted a hardening of Soviet policy towards Bonn. In the face of growing instability in Eastern Europe, the German threat remained one of the few cards that Moscow could play to bolster its crumbling position there. After January 1968, therefore, whatever hopes Moscow may have had of inducing Bonn to change the basic tenets of its policy were largely subordinated to an all-out campaign to discredit the *Ostpolitik* and isolate West Germany.

The August 1968 Soviet invasion of Czechoslovakia marked an important turning point in Soviet policy in Europe and toward West Germany in particular. Paradoxically, although the invasion was a reflection of the weakness of the Soviet position in Eastern Europe and a response to forces that Bonn's *Ostpolitik* had encouraged, it helped to create the very conditions of stability that allowed Moscow gradually to abandon the German bogy image and move toward a rapprochement with Bonn. The invasion not only halted efforts to implement change in Czechoslovakia but also reversed the whole trend toward dissolution of Soviet control that had been gathering momentum during the previous two years.

At the same time, the invasion underscored for Moscow the importance of achieving a settlement with the West that would recognize the legitimacy of Soviet interests in Eastern Europe, thus reducing the prospect of another Prague Spring emerging elsewhere in Eastern Europe. As long as the West did not accept the postwar *status quo*, a threat to Soviet hegemony, however latent, existed. This consideration highlighted the necessity of achieving a settlement with Bonn. It had become increasingly clear that West Germany held the keys to solving the outstanding issues of European politics — the recognition of the Oder-Neisse line and East Germany. Moreover, West German detente initiatives made it more difficult to portray Bonn as the seat of revanchism and militarism, thus reducing the effectiveness of the German "threat" as a means of forging cohesion within the Warsaw Pact.

The invasion also had an important impact on West German policy. Prior to the invasion, Bonn had given priority to Eastern Europe in its *Ostpolitik* and focused only secondarily on the Soviet Union. The invasion of Czechoslovakia, however, made clear that "the road to Prague led through Moscow" — that is, that any opening to Eastern Europe had to have the Soviets' blessing if it was to be successful. Thus, in the aftermath of the invasion of Czechoslovakia, West Germany began to concentrate its main detente efforts on the Soviet Union rather than on Eastern Europe.

Rapprochement and Reconciliation

It is against this background that the shift in Soviet policy toward West Germany in the wake of the invasion of Czechoslovakia should been seen. This shift began to manifest itself much earlier than is generally thought — well before the assumption of power in Bonn by the coalition of Social Democrats and Free Democrats in autumn 1969 — and was influenced by a number of factors.[11] Among the most important were: (1) Charles de Gaulle's fall in early 1969 and the subsequent shift in French policy toward Atlanticism, which removed the main *raison d'être* for centering Soviet detente efforts on Franco-Soviet rapprochement; (2) the emergence of the People's Republic of China (PRC) from its isolation after the Cultural Revolution and the beginning of a thaw in U.S.-PRC relations, which threatened to reduce Moscow's room for maneuver; (3) growing Soviet economic problems, which gave Moscow a new sense of urgency about expanding ties with industrially advanced countries of the West; (4) a desire to improve relations with the United States, particularly to stabilize the arms race; and (5) the election of the Brandt-Scheel "small coalition" in October 1969 and the new government's willingness to sign the Non-Proliferation Treaty and abandon its claim to speak for all Germans (*Alleinvertretungsanspruch*). This important shift in West German policy was signalled by the new Chancellor Willy Brandt in his inaugural address, when he acknowledged the existence of "two German states in one German nation."[12]

The change in Soviet policy toward West Germany was part of a larger Soviet reassessment of policy toward the West as a whole and particularly the United States. Moscow's interest in improving relations with the United States — particularly its desire to proceed with the Strategic Arms Limitation Talks (SALT) — forced it to view its actions elsewhere with an eye to the impact those actions would have on relations with the United States and played a crucial role in the shift in Soviet policy toward West Germany. There was, in effect, an implicit linkage between European detente and the SALT negotiations, and this linkage accentuated the Soviet leadership's desire to seek the resolution of the German Question, the main source of East-West tension.

The rapprochement between Moscow and Bonn in 1969-70 culminated in the signing of an agreement on the Renunciation of Force in August 1970. The Agreement laid the basis for the normalization of relations between West Germany and the USSR. In the treaty, both parties agreed to regard the borders in Europe as inviolable and to settle all disputes by peaceful means.[13] From the Soviet point of view, the treaty's significance lay in the fact that it signaled Bonn's official acceptance of the postwar territorial *status quo*, which Moscow regarded as the *sine qua non* for the stabilization of the situation in Eastern Europe.

The Bonn-Moscow treaty is often portrayed as a victory for the Soviet Union. Yet, this interpretation ignores the important, though less obvious, concessions that the Soviet Union also made. Article III of the treaty contained the most important concession. Originally, Moscow had insisted that the borders were "unchangeable" (*nezyblemyi*). In the end, however, Moscow was forced to accept the stipulation that the borders were simply "inviolable" (*nerushimyi*).[14] This, in effect, left open the possibility of peaceful change, that is, that at some point the borders between the two Germanys could be changed by common consent. Moreover, in contrast to Adenauer's visit to Moscow in 1955, the Soviet Union accepted without comment the receipt of the West German government's Letter of German Unity (*Brief der deutschen Einheit*), which reasserted the right of all Germans to self-determination, thus holding open — at least theoretically — the possibility of German reunification.[15]

In the course of negotiations, Moscow also grudgingly accepted the West German argument that Bonn could not recognize the GDR under international law — as the GDR insisted — because this would erode Four-Power responsibility for Germany as a whole. The acceptance of this argument by the Soviet Union, in effect, decoupled Soviet interests from those of the GDR and made clear that Moscow was not ready to sacrifice its own wider interests in European detente to support the demands of its East German ally. At the same time, it underscored Moscow's desire to maintain allied legal responsibility for

"Germany as a whole" should Germany ever be reunited and to retain control over any process of East-West detente that might make reunification possible some day.

In short, the Bonn-Moscow treaty united in one document two separate but not mutually exclusive concepts: the acceptance of the postwar European borders, which had been a chief goal of Soviet policy in Europe, and renunciation of force, which had been the central feature of Bonn's *Ostpolitik* after 1966. However, although the treaty represented a *modus vivendi* based on the acceptance of the postwar territorial *status quo*, the goals of each side in accepting the *status quo* were fundamentally different. Whereas the Soviet Union desired a sanctification of the territorial *status quo* in Eastern Europe in order to ensure its permanence, West Germany agreed to accept the territorial *status quo* in order to hold open the long-term possibility of changing it. As the Letter of German Unity reaffirmed, Bonn had not given up reunification as a basic goal of its foreign policy. It had simply agreed *not to try to change the current status quo in Europe by force* — something which it had no intention of doing anyway.

By agreeing to accept the borders as inviolable rather than insisting that they be unchangeable, the Soviet leadership may have hoped that it would be able to elicit a much stronger commitment to the permanency of the borders at the Conference on Security and Cooperation in Europe (CSCE), which could then be trumpeted as superseding the bilateral Soviet-West German treaty. If this was the Soviet hope, it remained unfulfilled. West Germany also managed to ensure that the possibility of "peaceful change" of borders was preserved in the CSCE Final Act signed at Helsinki in August 1975.

Disappointment and Discord

The ratification of the Bonn-Moscow treaty established the basis for the normalization of relations and served to remove the German Question from the East-West agenda — at least formally. Moscow's hopes for a significant revitalization of Soviet-West German relations, however, were never fully realized. On the economic side, trade increased significantly, but it never reached the volume that Moscow initially anticipated.[16] Moreover, after a steady increase in the 1970s and early 1980s, it has since declined.

On the political side, too, Moscow's early hopes were not fulfilled. During the 1970s, West Germany occupied pride of place in the Soviet Union's *Westpolitik*; it was Moscow's most important economic and political partner in Western Europe. Toward the late 1970s, however, bilateral relations began to deteriorate. Several factors contributed to this deterioration. One was a change in West German leadership. The first change came in 1974 with the resignation of Willy Brandt as chancellor and his replacement by Helmut Schmidt.

Schmidt, although a Social Democrat, was a confirmed Atlanticist and never shared Brandt's enthusiasm for *Ostpolitik*. Rather, he directed his major energies toward trying to revitalize the Western alliance and advising the Americans on how it should be run. As a consequence, *Ostpolitik* received a somewhat lower priority.

The collapse of the SPD-FDP coalition in Bonn in October 1982 and its replacement by a CDU/CSU-FDP coalition headed by Helmut Kohl reinforced the general stagnation of relations. Kohl came to power determined to avoid the growing friction with the United States that had characterized Schmidt's last years in office and to re-establish a more solid partnership with Washington. His greater willingness to follow the U.S. lead — especially on security issues — as well as his stronger emphasis on the openness of the German Question, contributed to a further cooling of relations.

The lack of a strong leader in the Kremlin also enhanced the deterioration of relations between Bonn and Moscow. After 1978 Brezhnev's health declined precipitously, and he was no longer able to give Soviet policy the strong direction that he had provided in the early 1970s. During much of this period the Soviet leadership was preoccupied with the succession issue. As a result, its policy in Europe was characterized by vacillation and drift.

Andropov's death in February 1984 exacerbated this sense of drift. His successor, Konstantin Chernenko, had little experience in foreign affairs and he largely left foreign policy matters in the hands of Foreign Minister Andrei Gromyko. During the Chernenko period Gromyko virtually monopolized foreign affairs, and Soviet policy was characterized by increasing rigidity and defensiveness toward the West. This was particularly true with regard to relations with Bonn, which were viewed mainly through the larger prism of Moscow's competition with the United States. Moreover, Gromyko remained highly suspicious of the long-term implications of an intensification of the German-German dialogue and tried as much as possible to keep it under tight control.

A third important factor contributing to the erosion of Soviet-West German accord was the INF ("Euromissile") controversy. Bonn was the key to the implementation of the deployment decision. Moscow appears to have calculated that, if Bonn could be persuaded to forego deployment — either through intimidation or enticement — then other countries in the alliance would not be willing to implement the decision either. Hence, Soviet policy during this period focused strongly on West Germany, which was alternatively wooed and warned of the dire consequences following any deployment of U.S. missiles.[17]

At the same time domestic developments in West Germany, particularly the growth of the peace movement and the erosion of the defense consensus after 1979, encouraged Moscow to believe, erroneously, that it could prevent deployment without making major concessions. In so doing, it overestimated the strength of pressure from below and underestimated the ability of the Western alliance to stand firm despite obvious divergences.

The Soviet walkout from the INF talks in November 1983 and Bonn's willingness to proceed with deployment despite Soviet threats underscored the failure of the "Gromyko line."[18] The confrontational policy pursued by the Soviet foreign minister neither prevented deployment nor split the NATO alliance. At the same time it led to growing friction between the USSR and several of its Eastern European allies. Hungary and East Germany in particular — for somewhat different reasons — resisted the Soviet effort to return to a policy of confrontation.[19] Indeed, for a period in 1984 a tacit alliance between Budapest and East Berlin seemed to be developing in an effort to convince Moscow to return to a more cooperative policy.

Perhaps most important, the policy of confrontation created serious strains in Soviet-East German relations. Although the GDR's Erich Honecker on several occasions had warned that German-German relations "could not flourish in the shadow of U.S. missiles," after the collapse of the INF talks he embarked on a course consciously designed to insulate German-German detente from the deterioration of overall East-West relations. In a key speech that set the outlines for East German policy over the ensuing months, he noted at the seventh plenum of the East German Communist Party (SED) in November 1983 that, although the start of deployment had altered the basis of inter-German relations, the prime task now was "to limit the damage" resulting from this development.[20] Rather than deteriorating, as had been predicted, inter-German relations actually improved. This growing rapprochement between Bonn and East Berlin ran counter to the general trend in Soviet policy toward the West and created growing friction between Moscow and East Berlin.

After the collapse of the INF talks, Soviet policy toward West Germany shifted noticeably. The shift did not manifest itself immediately, but by the time of Foreign Minister Hans-Dietrich Genscher's May 1984 visit to Moscow the cooling of Soviet-West German relations was clearly visible. Soon thereafter Moscow initiated a campaign against West German "revanchism" and "neo-Nazism" — charges that had largely disappeared from the Soviet press since the early 1970s.[21] The revival of the revanchism campaign was a clear signal that Soviet policy toward Bonn had shifted and that Bonn was being placed in the docks of the accused for having followed through with deployment.

The campaign, however, was as much aimed at East Berlin as at Bonn. It was designed to signal Moscow's displeasure at Honecker's continued pursuit of closer ties with Bonn, which ran contrary to Moscow's larger interest in freezing East-West relations. Initially, Honecker resisted the mounting Soviet pressure, in part because it was unclear whether the attacks represented the view of the top Soviet leadership or simply that of Gromyko and the Foreign Ministry. By the end of summer 1984, however, Moscow's displeasure with the

German-German detente was unmistakeable, and Honecker felt compelled to postpone a planned visit to Bonn.

The Evolution of Gorbachev's German Policy

Soviet policy toward West Germany — and the German Question — underwent a major shift under Gorbachev. Gorbachev's German policy, however, was not animated by any sort of grand design to resolve the German Question. Rather, it emerged incrementally, largely in reaction to events that Gorbachev unleashed but then proved powerless to control.

Gorbachev did not set out to unify Germany. On the contrary, he initially saw its division as a key element of a new European security order. However, his policy underwent a marked evolution over time. During the first year and a half after Gorbachev assumed power, West Germany continued to be the subject of constant vituperation for its "revanchist" policy.[22] Gorbachev made highly visible visits to Paris and London in 1985 and 1986, but Bonn was consciously excluded from Soviet detente efforts.

By 1986, however, the Soviet attitude showed signs of moderating. The campaign against German "revanchism" initiated in the spring of 1984 gradually began to abate. During Foreign Minister Hans-Dietrich Genscher's visit to Moscow in July 1986, Gorbachev offered to open a "new page" in relations. A number of important bilateral agreements were initiated or signed, including a long-delayed framework agreement on scientific and technological cooperation.

Genscher's visit was followed by other small but important signs that the Soviet attitude toward West Germany was softening: a visible increase in the number of high-level visits, an increase in the number of ethnic Germans allowed to emigrate to West Germany, and a more cooperative attitude regarding Berlin.[23] These changes contributed to an improvement in relations and paved the way for Chancellor Kohl's visit to Moscow in October 1988.

Kohl's visit was a watershed in Soviet-West German relations. The visit essentially ended the quarantine that had been imposed on West Germany in the aftermath of the Soviet walkout from the INF talks. During the visit, six new agreements were signed in areas ranging from environmental protection to nuclear and maritime safety. In addition, more than thirty new contracts with West German firms were signed, including a major deal for the sale of a high-temperature nuclear reactor.

The Kohl visit was the culmination of the shift in Soviet policy that had begun soon after Gorbachev assumed power. In effect, it represented an effort by Moscow to bring its policy toward West Germany into harmony with its policy toward the rest of Western Europe. Given West Germany's key role in Europe and within the Western alliance, any detente policy that excluded Bonn had little chance of success.

This rapprochement, however, did not imply a shift in the Soviet approach to German unification or Berlin. During Kohl's visit, Gorbachev emphasized that Germany's division was the result of specific historical developments. Any attempt to change the situation or to pursue "unrealistic policies," he said, would be "an unpredictable and even dangerous business."[24] Similarly, he warned that efforts to seek improvements in the status of West Berlin contradicted the 1971 Four Power Agreement on Berlin as well as the Helsinki Accords.

Signs of New Thinking

Despite Gorbachev's continued insistence that relations had to be based on postwar "realities," especially the existence of two independent German states, there were signs that Moscow might be beginning to rethink its approach to the German Question as part of its overall policy toward Europe as a whole. One small but important sign of a shift in Soviet thinking on the German Question came during the visit of West German President Richard von Weizsäcker to Moscow in July 1987. In response to von Weizsäcker's insistence on the "unity of the German nation," Gorbachev stressed that there were two Germanys with two different political and economic systems. What would happen in 100 years, he said, "would be left to history to decide."[25] While his response did not substantially depart from the well-established Soviet insistence on the continued existence of two German states, it was less categorical than previous Soviet statements and left open the possibility of change at some time in the (distant) future.

In addition, there were reports that Gorbachev had commissioned four policy experts — Georgi Arbatov, Valentin Falin, Daniil Melnikov and Nikolai Portugalov — to examine alternative ways of dealing with the German Question. Soviet officials also began to drop hints that a withdrawal of foreign troops from the two Germanys might be possible and that such a development could contribute to increased cooperation between the two German states.[26] Other officials suggested that the Berlin Wall might come down. While such statements did not necessarily reflect official Soviet policy, they suggested that some reassessment of Soviet policy might be underway.

The visit by Gorbachev to Bonn in June 1989 provided another indication that this was indeed the case. At West German insistence, the Joint Declaration issued at the end of the visit explicitly noted the "right of all peoples and states" to freely determine their destiny and "the respect for the right of peoples to self-determination."[27] In effect, this implicitly acknowledged that the Germans had the right to self-determination — and unity.

This does not mean, however, that Gorbachev was ready to accept or endorse German unification. On the contrary, he continued to stress the "realities" of the existence of two German states, noting that "time would take care of the rest. "[28] In other words, he was willing to concede that in principle the Germans, like other peoples, had a right to self-determination. However, he continued to see any change in the German Question as a *long-term process* that would come about as a transformation of the overall security situation in Europe. Until this transformation had taken place — which might take decades — two German states would continue to exist.

To be sure, some analysts, such as Vyacheslav Dashichev, Deputy Head of the Institute for the Study of the World Socialist Systems and a consultant to the Foreign Ministry, advocated much more radical change.[29] However, such figures were in the minority and did not represent official thinking. Moreover, even the advocates of more radical change such as Dashichev did not envisage unification in the near future. Rather they called for reforms in the GDR and a gradual rapprochement between the two German states as part of a gradual transformation of the two-bloc system into pan-European structures.

Soviet-East German Divergences

At the same time, Gorbachev adopted a more flexible position toward the German-German dialogue. East Germany was given wider latitude to pursue its own interests as long as these did not conflict with basic Soviet interests. The long postponed Honecker visit to Bonn was allowed to go forward in September 1987. In addition, the GDR initiated a dialogue with the West German Social Democrats on chemical weapons. While this initiative was clearly coordinated with Moscow, it also provided an opportunity for East Germany to pursue its own national interests.

However, Moscow was careful to ensure that the GDR's policy was closely coordinated with its own policy agenda and did not give Honecker entirely free reign. In the spring of 1986, for instance, Gorbachev reportedly intervened to stop initial preparations for a Honecker visit to Bonn that summer, presumably because he felt that the timing was wrong. Soviet pressure also appears to have played a role in Honecker's decision to decline an invitation to attend the opening celebrations of Berlin's 450th anniversary in West Berlin in April 1987.[30]

It was in domestic policy, however, where the greatest divergences occurred. Gorbachev's emphasis on *perestroika* and *glasnost* was regarded with consternation and growing alarm in East Berlin. While Gorbachev did not force the GDR to adopt the Soviet model — on the contrary, he emphasized that each socialist country was free to choose its own path of development — his policy unleashed a strong reform impetus within East German society, especially among intellectuals.

Gorbachev's calls for reform presented particularly acute problems for the GDR because they threatened to undermine the very rationale for its existence.

The GDR, as East German ideologist Otto Reinhold argued, could only exist as an "anti-fascist, socialist alternative to the Federal Republic." A capitalist GDR would have little reason to exist as a separate state. Hence the strategy of the East German leadership, he warned, had to be uncompromisingly aimed at "solidifying the socialist order" in the GDR.[31]

In order to legitimize its rejection of reform, the Honecker regime gradually developed its own ideological rationale. This rationale had two basic elements. First, the GDR economy was doing much better than the economies of the Soviet Union and the rest of Eastern Europe. Hence, there was no need for reform. Second, there was no "universal model of socialism." Each socialist country had to develop socialism according to its own specific national conditions and traditions. Or, as Honecker put it, the GDR would develop socialism "in the colors of the GDR."

Perhaps the most striking indication of the Honecker leadership's effort to legitimize its anti-reform course, however, was its revival of the concept of a "special German road to socialism," first put forward by Anton Ackerman in 1946 and repudiated by the party in the late 1940s under pressure from Stalin. In explaining why the GDR would not emulate Gorbachev's policy, Kurt Hager, the party's chief ideologist and a member of the Politburo at the time, quoted from the Appeal of the German Communist Party (KPD) in June 18, 1945, which stressed that "a policy of imposing the Soviet system on Germany would be false, such a policy does not correspond to the current conditions in Germany."[32] For a generation of Communists educated on the slogan "To learn from the Soviet Union is to learn victory," the resurrection of the Ackerman thesis was a dramatic *volte face* that underscored the lengths to which the SED leadership was prepared to go to resist reform.

Divergences between Moscow and East Berlin were also evident in the area of foreign policy. These manifested themselves in particular in the different approach adopted by each side to the CSCE process. Whereas Moscow pushed for a rapid conclusion of CSCE negotiations, East Germany, along with Romania, initially refused to sign the concluding document because of its objection to certain provisions regarding human rights. East German resistance threatened to derail the CSCE summit, scheduled to be held in Paris in November 1990, and was only overcome after considerable pressure from Moscow.[33]

The most serious differences, however, occurred over Moscow's policy toward the Federal Republic. The Honecker leadership watched Moscow's rapprochement with Bonn with growing anxiety, fearing that Gorbachev might be willing to sacrifice vital East German interests in order to obtain much-needed financial assistance from the FRG. Gorbachev's visit to Bonn in June 1989 particularly disturbed the East German leadership. The communiqué issued at the end of the visit, which referred to the right of all nations to self-determination, was regarded in East Berlin as a departure from Moscow's traditional position on the German Question and as a betrayal of the GDR.

The differences over Moscow's rapprochement with Bonn added to the strain already caused by Honecker's anti-reform course. As a result, after 1988 relations between East Berlin and Moscow deteriorated and genuine communication became increasingly difficult and infrequent. The East German leadership apparently expected that Gorbachev would be overthrown by conservative forces in the USSR surrounding Yegor Ligachev and behind the scenes they actively sought the backing of these forces for their cause.[34] This collusion contributed to a further worsening of relations between the two sides.

The Impact of the Crisis in the GDR

The intensification of the crisis in the GDR in the autumn of 1989, which was touched off by the effort of tens of thousands of GDR citizens to emigrate to the Federal Republic, opened a new phase in Soviet policy toward the German Question.[35] The Soviets had been concerned about the deterioration of the situation in the GDR for some time and feared that Honecker's continued resistance to reform might lead to a popular explosion.[36] However, they did not wish to interfere directly in East German affairs or destabilize the GDR. During Gorbachev's visit to East Berlin on October 6-7, 1989, for the 40th anniversary celebrations of the founding of the GDR, the Soviet leader sought to gently nudge Honecker to introduce more far-reaching reforms. While stressing that policy regarding the GDR was made in East Berlin, not Moscow, he also noted that "life punishes those who come too late."

Privately, moreover, he reportedly warned the East German leadership that if unrest broke out, Soviet troops would remain in their barracks.[37] This dramatically changed the dynamics of the crisis. In the past, the East German leadership felt confident that it could count on Soviet "fraternal assistance" — as in 1953 — in case it faced serious popular unrest. In East Berlin, however, Gorbachev made clear that the rules of the game had changed and that the East German Communist regime could not rely on Soviet help if unrest broke out. This, in effect, pulled the rug out from under Honecker and paved the way for his overthrow — and the acceleration of the crisis.

In sanctioning — or at least not stopping — the opening of the Hungarian borders in September 1989, Gorbachev clearly did not intend to precipitate the collapse of the GDR. Rather, he hoped to encourage the removal of Honecker and the installation of a more reform-oriented leader who would be more flexible but could still be counted on to maintain firm control of the reform process. Wittingly or not, however, Gorbachev's actions did contribute to the collapse of the GDR and the growth of pressure for unification. Once it was clear that the Soviets would not intervene militarily, the demands for reform took on a momentum of their own, sweeping first Honecker, then his successor Egon Krenz, and finally the whole Socialist Unity Party (SED) from power.

The rapidity of the collapse of the GDR caught the Soviet leadership by surprise. While Gorbachev was willing to endorse the general principle of self-determination, he was not initially prepared to accept unification. In his public remarks after the fall of the Wall, he continued to emphasize the "inviolability of borders" and the "reality" of the existence of two German states, which he said had to be respected.[38]   During Foreign Minister Genscher's visit to Moscow in early December, Gorbachev called for "restraint" and said that the GDR was a reliable partner and an important guarantor of peace and stability.[39]

Similarly, in his speech to the European Parliament in Strasbourg on December 19, 1990, Shevardnadze supported the principle of self-determination, but quickly qualified this by saying that self-determination could not infringe upon the territorial and political *status quo*.[40]

In other words, while Gorbachev was willing to concede that Germany had the right to self-determination, he continued to stress the need to take into consideration certain "realities," particularly the existence of the two German states and their territorial status and alliance obligations. He was ready to accept internal change within the GDR as long as the GDR remained a member of the Warsaw Pact and the basic structure of the postwar security order was not destabilized. In short, a "Polish East Germany" was acceptable, but not a fundamental and potentially destabilizing change in postwar borders.

The Problem of NATO Membership

The rapid collapse of the GDR in the following weeks, however, forced Gorbachev to modify his position. During a meeting with East German Prime Minister Hans Modrow at the end of January 1990, Gorbachev agreed in principle to German unification. He warned, however, that it was essential to "act responsibly and not seek a solution in the streets."[41] A few weeks later, during a meeting with Chancellor Kohl, he formally gave the green light for unification.[42]

Gorbachev's agreement in principle to unification introduced a new phase in Soviet policy. Thereafter the main thrust of Soviet policy was aimed at preventing the membership of a united Germany in NATO and slowing down the unification process. During the next several months, the Soviet Union put forward a variety of schemes designed to forestall or prevent the integration of a united Germany in NATO: neutrality, a continuation of Four Power rights for an extended duration after unification, the integration of Germany into both alliances, a pan-European security system based on the CSCE, and finally, a "French" solution in which Germany would be a member of the alliance but not of its military command.[43] None of these proposals were acceptable to West Germany or the other Western powers, however. Moreover, the USSR found itself isolated within its own alliance. The majority of the Eastern European members of the Warsaw Pact, including Poland, favored a united Germany integrated into NATO.

Gorbachev's resistance to accepting the membership of a united Germany in NATO was primarily conditioned by security considerations: German membership in NATO would represent a fundamental shift in the balance of power in Moscow's disfavor. Domestic factors, however, also played an important role in shaping Soviet policy. During the months leading up to the 28th Party Congress in July 1990, Gorbachev faced mounting criticism of his policies on a wide variety of issues. On the domestic front the policy of *perestroika* came under increasing attack. In addition, he was accused of having "lost" Eastern Europe.[44] Concern was also expressed about a "new German danger." At the CPSU plenum in February, Yegor Ligachev, the number two official in the Politburo, pointed to the dangers posed by a powerful Germany, warning that "it would be unforgivably short-sighted and mistaken not to see that a Germany with vast economic and military potential has begun to loom on the horizon."[45]Ligachev's views were echoed by other conservatives who warned of the dangers of "Pan-Germanism."[46] With a tough Congress approaching, Gorbachev could not afford to give his domestic critics more ammunition to use against him. He thus continued to stonewall on the German issue. However, once the Congress was over and the conservative challenge to his leadership had been defeated, he quickly turned to the German issue.

The critical breakthrough came during the discussions between Kohl and Gorbachev in Zheleznovodosk, July 15-16.[47] At the end of the talks, Gorbachev gave his blessing to Germany's full membership in NATO. In return, Kohl agreed to: a) reduce the strength of the German army to 370,000; b) provide financial assistance for the withdrawal of Soviet troops from the GDR; c) renounce the production of nuclear, biological, and chemical weapons; and d) forego the stationing of nuclear weapons or foreign troops on the former GDR's territory as long as Soviet troops were on East German soil.

Gorbachev's sudden about-face at Zheleznovodosk caught the Germans as well as many of Gorbachev's own advisors by surprise. What precipitated such a sudden change in Soviet policy? Several factors appear to have played a role. First, the defeat of Ligachev and the conservative opposition at the 28th Party Congress freed Gorbachev's hand domestically and allowed him to make concessions that he felt unable to make prior to the Congress.

Second, the communiqué at the NATO summit in London (July 5-6, 1990) indicated that NATO was embarking upon a far-reaching transformation, including a shift in nuclear strategy.[48] This was an important signal that the West was also ready to make fundamental changes and strengthened Gorbachev's argument that Germany's unification would contribute to a reduction of the military threat facing the Soviet Union. Indeed, the changes in NATO strategy embodied in the London Declaration may well have been the decisive factor that led Gorbachev to drop his objections to Germany's membership in the alliance.[49]

Third, West Germany's pledge to reduce the size of its army to 370,000 men also played an important role. A significant reduction in the size of the *Bundeswehr* had been one of Moscow's primary objectives in the "two-plus-four" talks.[50] A reduction to 370,000 men represented a cut of nearly 45 percent in the combined size of West German and East German forces. This was an important sign that Bonn was willing to make a concrete contribution to East-West detente.

Fourth, Bonn's agreement to provide a $3 billion credit in June provided a strong incentive to agree to unification. The credit was not tied to any specific projects, and the interest rate on the credit was below commercial rates.[51] In addition, Bonn agreed to provide financial assistance for the withdrawal of Soviet troops, especially the construction of housing for the returning troops. This cushioned the economic costs of troop withdrawal and opened up new perspectives for long-term economic cooperation between the two countries.

Finally, time was not on Moscow's side. With the creation of an economic and currency union between the FRG and GDR on July 1, 1990, unification was rapidly becoming a *fait accompli*. The longer Soviet troops stayed in East Germany, the greater was the chance that they would become the focus of popular resentment and hostility. Moreover, continued delay could have jeopardized the conclusion of a CFE (Conventional Forces in Europe) agreement that was scheduled to be formally signed at the CSCE summit in Paris in November. Without a completed CFE agreement, the summit would have had to be postponed and Moscow would have been blamed for the delay.

The Final Settlement

The agreements at Zheleznovodsk paved the way for the rapid conclusion of the "two-plus-four" talks and the signing of the Final Settlement regulating the external aspects of German unification on September 12, 1990. The agreement returned to Germany full sovereignty and lifted the Four Power rights for Germany and Berlin. At the same time, the Soviet Union agreed to withdraw its troops from the GDR by the end of 1994.[52]

In addition, in September, West Germany and the USSR signed a separate Treaty of Good-Neighborliness, Partnership and Cooperation, designed to expand and update the Renunciation of Force Agreement signed by the two countries in August 1970.[53] Like the 1970 treaty, the new agreement emphasized that the two sides would refrain from using force to resolve their differences. However, it went considerably further than the 1970 treaty and contained a controversial non-aggression pledge (Article 3).[54]

As part of the overall settlement of German unification, Bonn also agreed to provide a 12 billion DM (about $8 billion) package to help underwrite the cost of the housing and withdrawal of the 380,000 Soviet troops stationed in East Germany. This package also included a 3 billion DM interest-free credit to aid the ailing Soviet economy, as noted earlier.

The signing of the "two-plus-four" agreement and the German-Soviet bilateral treaty closed an important period in Soviet-German relations and East-West relations generally. In effect, both documents marked the end of the Cold War in Europe. The division of Germany had been the cornerstone of the division of Europe. As many West German officials had for years emphasized, it was impossible to overcome the division of Europe without overcoming the division of Germany: the two were intimately linked. Thus it was inevitable that the revolutionary changes in Eastern Europe would eventually have an impact on the German Question, and require a reassessment of Soviet and Western policy toward Germany.

As always in history, however, timing is important. The German and U.S. determination to proceed rapidly with unification proved to be both historically "correct" and farsighted. Had the West and the Kohl government not pressed ahead with rapid unification as they did, unification might have been significantly delayed and would have been far more difficult to achieve. In the late fall of 1990, Gorbachev came under strong pressure from conservative forces in the Soviet leadership, especially the military and party *apparat*, to adopt a more conservative policy, both internally and externally. As a result, Soviet policy began to harden visibly shortly after the conclusion of the "two-plus-four" agreement in September.[55]

Had the West not pressed for a rapid settlement of the external aspects of German unification, the "two-plus-four" negotiations could have gotten caught up in the Soviet internal debate, and it would have been much more difficult to bring them to a rapid and successful conclusion. However, by the time the hardening of Soviet policy began to occur, the "two-plus-four" agreement had already been safely concluded. While some conservatives in the Supreme Soviet, led by the "black Colonels" Viktor Alksnis and Nikolai Petrushenko (the "lads in epaulets," as Shevardnadze derisively called them in his resignation speech), tried to block ratification and force a significant revision of the agreements, their effort failed.[56] The two agreements, together with an economic cooperation accord, were approved by the Supreme Soviet by a wide margin on March 4, 1991. In addition, the two remaining agreements on the stationing and withdrawal of Soviet troops were approved in principle and formally ratified several weeks later.

Bonn and Moscow in a New Era

The unification of Germany has significantly changed the dynamics and the nature of Moscow's relations with Bonn. As a result of unification, Bonn's influence and room for maneuver have visibly increased, while Moscow's have declined. As long as Germany was divided, Moscow had an informal *droit de regard* over West German policy and Bonn had to be sensitive to Soviet interests. With German unification, Moscow has lost its ability to manipulate the German Question and has been deprived of one of its prime sources of leverage over German policy.

The disintegration of the USSR as an integral state has further shifted the balance of power in Bonn's favor. Russia will remain a formidable military power, but its economic weakness will make it difficult for Moscow to use its military power to pose a substantial threat to Europe in the near future, even if Yeltsin is overthrown and there is a return to authoritarian rule. For the next decade or so, Russia is likely to turn inward and be preoccupied with its own internal problems. Its main foreign policy efforts will be directed at trying to stabilize relations with the surrounding former republics, especially Ukraine.

Given its geographic position on the edge of the former Soviet empire, however, Germany will maintain a strong interest in stability in the former USSR. Any large-scale unrest in what is now a "Commonwealth of Independent States" (CIS) would have important implications for Germany. Hence Chancellor Kohl took the lead in trying to work out a stabilization and aid package for the former Soviet Union at the G-7 summit in Munich in July 1992. In addition, Germany is currently the largest single source (circa 56 percent) of Western assistance to the CIS, providing more than half of all Western assistance to the former USSR.[57] However, there are distinct limitations to Bonn's ability to underwrite Russia's transformation. The FRG's main priority in the next decade will be the reconstruction of the *Länder* of the former GDR. This task will absorb the lion's share of Bonn's resources, limiting the amount of assistance available to Russia and the other republics of the former USSR. As a consequence, Bonn has increasingly emphasized that assistance must be multilateral and that Germany cannot bear the burden alone.

Moreover, Russia's economic difficulties are likely to limit the enthusiasm of German business to invest heavily in Russia in the near term. Bilateral trade has plummeted in the last few years. In addition, due to its economic difficulties, Russia has had trouble paying its debts to Germany. This has had a further dampening effect on trade and prompted the Kohl government to toughen the criteria for extending export credits to the former USSR in early 1992.[58] As a result, German trade with Russia and the other former Soviet republics has come to a virtual standstill. Indeed, many in the German business community feel that the long-term trade prospects are better with Ukraine than with Russia.

The changed atmosphere was readily evident during Yeltsin's visit to Bonn in November 1991. The visit lacked the drama of previous visits by Gorbachev. Kohl and Yeltsin signed a 14-point document pledging cooperation in a number of areas, including arms control, scientific research, and minority rights. However, the establishment of diplomatic relations was made conditional on the creation of a legally binding structure that would provide provisions for Russia's assumption of the Soviet Union's foreign debt. Moreover, the response of the German business community to Yeltsin's appeal for German investment was reserved.[59]

The question of the German minority in Russia is also likely to have an important impact on bilateral relations in the future. The Kohl government has faced a growing influx of ethnic Germans (*Aussiedler*) from Russia in recent years. In 1990, 147,950 Germans emigrated to Germany from the Soviet Union. This was one-third more than the number in 1989 and triple the number in 1988.[60] Moreover, recent estimates show that another 650,000 could emigrate over the next few years.[61]

The large influx of ethnic Germans from the former USSR has added to Germany's mounting refugee problem, causing severe social tensions.[62] Hence Bonn has pressed the Yeltsin government to grant the two million strong German minority its own autonomous republic in the Volga area in the hope of encouraging the minority to stay home rather than emigrate. In addition, Bonn has allocated nearly 200 million DM ($130 million) for financial assistance in the construction of schools, hospitals, and cultural facilities.

During his visit to Bonn, Yeltsin promised to restore the Volga Republic disbanded by Stalin in 1941. After months of vacillation, in March 1992, he signed a decree establishing national regions for the German minority in Saratov and the Volgograd *oblasts*. In addition, on April 24 a formal agreement was signed between Bonn and Moscow re-establishing the Volga Republic in stages. Under the agreement, the German minority is guaranteed the right to maintain its language, religion, and cultural identity.[63]

The agreement re-establishing the Volga Republic removes an important stumbling block in bilateral relations. It remains to be seen, however, whether the agreement will stem the flow of German emigrants from the former USSR. Many members of the German minority feel that even with the establishment of their own republic, economic prospects are so bleak that they would be better off emigrating. Thus, many may still apply to emigrate unless the overall economic situation in Russia and the other former Soviet republics improves significantly in the near future.

In short, relations between Bonn and Moscow have entered a period of restructuring and transition as both countries grapple with the consequences of the Cold War. In the coming decade Russia will primarily be preoccupied with its internal problems. This will limit its diplomatic engagement and influence on the European scene. At the same time, Germany is likely to devote primary attention to rebuilding the former GDR and European integration. Both tasks, however, could be adversely affected by chaos in Russia and the other former Soviet republics. Thus, whatever Bonn's priorities, German leaders will still need to pay heed to Bismarck's famous dictum — "always keep a line open to Russia."

However, Western fears about the dangers of a new "Rapallo" are unwarranted. Rapallo was the product of a particular set of historical circumstances — an alliance of two international pariahs. Today Germany is not an international outcast; it is an integral member of the Atlantic Alliance and the cornerstone of an expanding European Community that is moving towards greater economic and political unity. Bonn is unlikely to put the benefits of this association at risk for the uncertain gains of an alliance with the "new sick man of Europe."

Notes

This chapter was written under a grant from the Ford Foundation, whose support is gratefully acknowledged.

1. See his *Russia and Germany* (Boston: Little, Brown and Co., 1965), p. 13.

2. Victor Frank, "The Ambivalent Heritage," *Survey*, October 1962, pp. 66-73.

3. On the military cooperation between Russia and Germany, see in particular F. L. Carsten, "The Reichswehr and the Red Army," *Survey*, October 1962, pp. 114-32.

4. Pierre Hassner, "Europe West of the Elbe," in Robert S. Jorden, ed., *Europe and the Superpowers* (London: Allyn and Bacon, 1971), p. 103.

5. For a good discussion of Soviet policy in Germany in the early months after the war, see Henry Kritsch, *German Politics Under Soviet Occupation* (New York: Columbia University Press, 1974). For an informative account by an inside participant, see Wolfgang Leonhard, *Child of the Revolution* (Chicago: Henry Regnery Company, 1967), pp. 359-471.

6. Joseph Stalin, *Economic Problems of Socialism in the USSR* (New York: International Publishers, 1952), pp. 28-29.

7. For a balanced discussion, see Boris Meissner, "Die deutsch-sowjetischen Beziehungen seit dem zweiten Weltkrieg," *Osteuropa*, September 1985, pp. 631-52. For the argument that Stalin's offer represented a "missed opportunity," see Paul Seth, *Zwischen Bonn und Moskau* (Frankfurt: Verlag H. Scheffler, 1956). For a more recent interpretation of this view, see Rolf Steininger, *Die vertane Chance, Die Stalin Note vom 10. März 1952 und die Wiedervereinigung* (Berlin: Verlag J.H.W. Dietz Macht, 1985).

8. This position has recently been argued by Daniil Melnikov, who assisted in the preparation of the Note. See Daniil E. Melnikow, "Illusionen oder verpasste Chance?," *Osteuropa*, September 1990, pp. 593-601. See also his interview, "Stalins gewagtes Spiel," *Der Spiegel*, December 3, 1990. For a recent counterargument, see Gerhard Wettig, "Die Stalin-Note vom 10. März als geschichtswissenschaftliches Problem," *Deutschland Archiv*, February 1992, pp. 157-67.

9. Waldemar Besson, *Die Aussenpolitik der Bundesrepublik* (Munich: R. Piper Verlag, 1970), p. 125.

10. On Khrushchev's use of strategic bluffing, see Arnold L. Horelick and Myron Rush, *Strategic Power and Soviet Foreign Policy* (Chicago: University of Chicago Press, 1966).

11. It is impossible to date the change precisely. However, preparations for it seem to have been undertaken some time between mid-October 1968 and the beginning of 1969. For a detailed discussion, see F. Stephen Larrabee, "The Politics of Reconciliation: Soviet Policy Toward West Germany, 1964-1972" (unpublished Ph.D. dissertation, Columbia University, New York, 1978), pp. 180-218.

12. Brandt insisted, however, that West Germany could not recognize East Germany under international law — one of the major preconditions postulated by the East German leadership for the normalization of relations — because East Germany was "not a foreign country." For the text of Brandt's address, see *Europa Archiv*, No. 21, 1969, pp. D499-506.

13. For the provisions of the treaty, see *Der Vertrag vom 12. August 1970 zwischen der Bundesrepublik Deutschland und der Union Sozialistischer Sowjetrepubliken* [The Treaty of 12 August 1970 Between the Federal Republic of Germany and the Union of Soviet Socialist Republics] (Bonn: Presse- und Informationsamt der Bundesregierung, 1970), pp. 7-9. The Russian text is in *Pravda*, May 16, 1972.

14. Compare the final wording of the treaty (*Pravda*, August 13, 1970) with Gromyko's speech to the Supreme Soviet on July 10, 1969 (*Pravda,* July 11, 1969) where the demand that the borders be considered unchangeable (*nezyblemyi*) is used throughout.

15. The acceptance of the letter without comment contrasted with the public rejection of Adenauer's letter to Bulganin at the time of the establishment of relations between West Germany and the Soviet Union in September 1955, which reaffirmed West Germany's intention to pursue reunification as a fundamental goal of its foreign policy. For the text of the letter on German unity, see *Der Vertrag vom 12. August 1970*, p. 10.

16. A detailed analysis of Soviet-West German economic relations is beyond the scope of this essay. For a comprehensive discussion, see Angela Stent, *From Embargo to Ostpolitik* (Cambridge: Cambridge University Press, 1981).

17. For a detailed discussion of Soviet policy and West German reactions to the missile crisis at this time, see Elizabeth Pond, "Andropov, Kohl and the East-West Issues," *Problems of Communism*, July-August 1983, pp. 35-45.

18. Gromyko (along with Dmitri Ustinov) is largely credited with being the architect of the confrontational policy pursued by Moscow after the collapse of the INF talks in November 1983. As noted below, his removal as Foreign Minister was an important prerequisite for the shift in Soviet policy on INF as well as relations with Bonn.

19. For a good discussion of the East European reaction, see Charles Gati, "The Soviet Empire: Alive But Not Well," *Problems of Communism*, March-April 1985, pp. 73-86, especially pp. 77-81. See also Ronald D. Asmus, "The Dialects of Detente and Discord," *Orbis*, Winter 1985, pp. 753-57.

20. For Honecker's speech, see *Neues Deutschland*, November 26-27, 1983.

21. For background, see Ronald D. Asmus, *East Berlin and Moscow: The Documentation of a Dispute*, Radio Free Europe Research, Background Report 158, August 25, 1984.

22. For details, see Fred Oldenburg, "Das Verhältnis Moskau-Bonn unter Gorbatschow," *Osteuropa*, August-September 1986, pp. 774-86.

23. For details, see F. Stephen Larrabee, "Soviet Policy Toward Germany: New Thinking and Old Realities," *Washington Quarterly*, Fall 1989, pp. 43-44.

24. For Gorbachev's speech, see *Izvestiya*, October 16, 1988.

25. See *Pravda*, July 8, 1987. Gorbachev's remarks are repeated almost verbatim in his book, *Perestroika: New Thinking for our Country and the World* (New York: Harper and Row, 1987), p. 200.

26. For details, see Fred Oldenburg, "Neues Denken in der sowjetischen Deutsch-land-Politik?," *Deutschland Archiv*, November 1987, pp. 1154-60.

27. For the text of the Joint Declaration, see *Bulletin des Presse- und Information-samtes der Bundesregierung* (Bonn), No. 16, 1989, pp. 542-44. There was also another small sign that Moscow was rethinking its position on the German Question. The declaration refers to the FRG as *Federativnaya Respublika Germaniya* rather than *Germanii*. This construction implies that there was only one single Germany (*Germaniya*) with a federal structure rather than two Germanies, with only one having a federal structure. See Hannes Adomeit, "Gorbachev and German Unification: Revision of Thinking, Realignment of Power," *Problems of Communism*, July-August 1990, pp. 5-6.

28. *Pravda*, June 16, 1989. For a detailed discussion of the visit, see Fred Oldenburg, "Vier Tage in Juni — Gorbatschow in Bonn," *Osteuropa*, nr. 11/12, 1989, pp. 981-994. Also Adomeit, "Gorbachev and German Unification," pp. 5-6.

29. Dashichev's influence, however, has been vastly overrated, especially in Germany. Dashichev was somewhat of an intellectual gadfly and his views had little direct impact on Soviet policy. Far more influential were figures like Valentin Falin, Head of the International Department of the CPSU Central Committee, and Yuri Kvitsinski, Soviet Ambassador to Bonn at the time, both of whom took a fairly tough line on unification.

30. See Larrabee, "Soviet Policy Toward Germany: New Thinking and Old Realities," p. 46. On Soviet pressure in April 1986 for Honecker to postpone the visit to Bonn, see also Jens Kaiser, "Zwischen angestrebter Eigenständigkeit und traditioneller Unterordnung," *Deutschland Archiv*, May 1991, p. 489.

31. See his interview with DDR Radio II, August 19, 1989. See also Barbara Donovan, "Reform and the Existence of the GDR," *Radio Free Europe Background Report* (German Democratic Republic), August 25, 1989.

32. See his interview in *Der Stern*, April 8, 1987. Reprinted in *Neues Deutschland*, April 10, 1987.

33. According to a well-informed East German source, the critical breakthrough came as a result of direct intervention by Gorbachev, who sent his personal envoy to East Berlin to lobby Honecker. See Kaiser, "Zwischen angestrebter Eigenständigkeit und traditioneller Unterordnung," pp. 493-94.

34. In the spring of 1988 the GDR was the only socialist country to reprint the infamous Nina Andreeva article from *Sovetskaya Rossiya*, which was widely regarded as an attack on Gorbachev's policies by conservative forces close to Ligachev. On the Honecker leadership's ties to the conservatives in the Soviet leadership, see also Kaiser, "Zwischen angestrebter Eigenständigkeit und traditioneller Unterordnung," p. 490.

35. For a comprehensive discussion of the background and evolution of the crisis, see Elizabeth Pond, "A Wall Destroyed: The Dynamics of Unification in the GDR," *International Security*, vol. 15, no. 2, Fall 1990, pp. 35-66. For an insightful view by an influential West German insider, see Horst Teltschik, *329 Tage* (Berlin: Siedler Verlag, 1991). Teltschik was chief foreign policy advisor to Chancellor Kohl and played an important role in the formulation of the Kohl government's policy toward unification.

36. See the memorandum by Valentin Falin, Head of the International Department of the Central Committee and one of Moscow's top German specialists, in *Die Welt*, September 15, 1989. In the memorandum, a copy of which was obtained by West German Intelligence, Falin expressed concern about growing public dissatisfaction and the possibility of mass demonstrations that could prove difficult to control. He also pointed to the sense of vacillation and drift within the East German leadership, which was unable to handle the growing crisis. However, he expressed doubt that Honecker would retire before the May 1990 Party Congress, if then.

37. See Craig Whitney, "German Upheaval Reviewed," *International Herald Tribune*, December 19, 1989. Also Fred Oldenburg, "Sowjetische Deutschland-Politik nach der Oktober-Revolution in der DDR," *Deutschland Archiv*, January 1990, p. 70.

38. See his speech to the Central Committee Plenum, *Pravda*, December 9, 1989. The same points were reiterated in even stronger terms in a letter from Gorbachev to Kohl on December 18. See Teltschik, *329 Tage*, p. 85.

39. *Pravda*, December 3, 1989. Gorbachev and Shevardnadze took a tough position at the meeting and rejected Kohl's 10-Point plan as a *Diktat*. See also Teltschik, *329 Tage*, p. 68.

40. For Shevardnadze's speech, see *Pravda*, December 20, 1989. See also "Schewardnadze nennt Bedingungen für Wiedervereinigung," *Frankfurter Allgemeine Zeitung*, December 20, 1989. For a detailed discussion of Soviet policy during this phase, see Oldenburg, "Sowjetische Deutschland-Politik nach der Oktober-Revolution in der DDR," pp. 68-76. Also Gerhard Wettig, "Stadien der sowjetischen Deutschland-Politik," *Deutschland Archiv*, January 1990, pp. 1070-78.

41. See Mark Nicholson, "Gorbachev Agrees to Principle of German Unification," *Financial Times*, January 31, 1990. Also "Gorbatschow hat 'prinzipiell' nichts gegen eine Vereinigung der beiden deutschen Staaten," *Frankfurter Allgemeine Zeitung*, January 31, 1990.

42. Craig A. Whitney, "Kohl Says Moscow Agrees Unity Issue is up to the Germans," *New York Times*, February 11, 1991. For a detailed discussion of the historic meeting, see Teltschik, *329 Tage*, pp. 135-44.

43. For a detailed discussion of the various shifts, see Suzanne Crow, "The Changing Soviet View on German Unification," Radio Liberty, *Report on the USSR*, August 3, 1990, pp. 11-14.

44. For a detailed discussion, see F. Stephen Larrabee, *Retreat from Empire: The Gorbachev Revolution in Eastern Europe and its Consequences* (Santa Monica: RAND Corporation, forthcoming). See also Suzanne Crow, "Who Lost Eastern Europe?," Radio Liberty, *Report on the USSR*, April 12, 1991, pp. 1-5.

45. *Pravda*, February 7, 1990.

46. See Alexander Rahr, "Conservative Opposition to German Unification," Radio Liberty, *Report on the USSR*, May 11, 1990.

47. Quentin Peel and David Marsh, "Gorbachev and Kohl Agree on NATO Membership, Troop Cuts," *Financial Times*, July 17, 1990. For a detailed discussion of the talks, see Teltschik, *329 Tage*, pp. 313-42.

48. R. W. Apple, "An Alliance for a New Age: Has NATO Donned a Velvet Glove?," *New York Times*, July 7, 1990. For the text of the London Declaration, see "NATO Transformed: The London Declaration," *Selected Document No. 38*, United States Department of State, Bureau of Public Affairs, July 1990.

49. On the importance of the London Declaration, see Eduard Shevardnadze, *The Future Belongs to Freedom* (New York: Free Press, 1991), p. 141. See also the interview with Valentin Falin, Head of the International Department of the CPSU Central Committee and former Ambassador to West Germany, *Stern*, October 31, 1990. In the interview Falin claims that the London Declaration was "the decisive factor" that persuaded Gorbachev to accept the membership of a united Germany in NATO.

50. See Serge Schmemann, "Shevardnadze Seeks Curb on Forces in New Germany," *New York Times*, June 23, 1990. Originally the Soviets wanted a reduction to 250,000 men but eventually they agreed to settle for 370,000.

51. Ferdinand Protzman, "Bonn to Aid Kremlin Reforms with $3 Billion Bank Credit," *New York Times*, June 23, 1990.

52. For the text of the treaty, see *Bulletin des Presse- und Informationsamtes der Bundesregierung* (Bonn), No. 109, September 14, 1990, pp. 1153-56. For a discussion of the various provisions, see Fred Oldenburg, "Sowjetische Europa-Politik und die Lösung der deutschen Frage," *Osteuropa*, August 1991, pp. 751-73.

53. For the text of the treaty, see *Bulletin des Presse- und Informationsamtes der Bundesregierung* (Bonn), No. 133, November 15, 1990, pp. 1379-82.

54. Although the new treaty specifically stated that it did not infringe on rights and obligations arising from other bilateral and multilateral agreements signed by the two parties (Article 19), the non-aggression clause raised concerns in some Western capitals that it could lead to a weakening of Germany's commitment to Western defense.

55. While this hardening was primarily reflected in the domestic area, it also had an impact on foreign policy. Among its most important signs were the resignation of Shevardnadze, the intensification of the debate over "who lost Eastern Europe," the effort by the General Staff to evade the CFE treaty, stagnation in the START negotiations, the refusal of the Soviet Union to agree to withdraw its troops from Poland, and the crack-down in the Baltics.

56. See Petrushenko's criticisms of the German treaties in *Veteran*, No. 10, March 1991, and his interview in *Sovetskaya Rossiya*, March 2, 1992. See also, "Petrushenko: Abzug dauert 19 Jahre," *Frankfurter Allgemeine Zeitung*, March 4, 1991.

57. See Chancellor Kohl's "Tanner Lecture" at the University of California, Berkeley, *Press Release*, Consulate General of the Federal Republic of Germany, September 13, 1991, p. 11.

58. Ferdinand Protzman, "Germany Curbs Trade Aid for former Soviet States," *New York Times*, July 23, 1991. The curtailment of export credits has had a particularly serious impact on firms in the former GDR, which are highly dependent on the Soviet market, confronting many of them with imminent collapse.

59. Stephen Kinzer, "Yeltsin's Free Market Promises Leave his German Hosts Skeptical," *New York Times*, November 23, 1991; "Russlands Suche nach dem deutschen

Partner," *Neue Zürcher Zeitung*, November 26, 1991; and Ewald König, "Mit leeren Händen zurück nach Moskau," *Die Presse*, November 23, 1991.

60. For a comprehensive discussion of German emigration from the Soviet Union, see Sidney Heitman, "Soviet Emigration 1990" (Cologne: Bericht des Bundesinstituts für ost-wissenschaftliche und internationale Studien, 1991).

61. "650,000 Russlanddeutsche denken an Ausreise," *Frankfurter Allgemeine Zeitung*, January 21, 1992.

62. For a detailed discussion, see F. Stephen Larrabee, "Down and Out in Warsaw and Budapest: Eastern Europe and East-West Migration," *International Security*, Spring 1992, pp. 5–33.

63. "Abkommen über Wiedererrichtung der Wolga-republik," *Frankfurter Allgemeine Zeitung*, April 24, 1992.

10

Poland and Germany: From Foes to Friends?

Arthur R. Rachwald

Since its beginning at the end of the 10th century, the Polish state has been confronted by powerful neighbors on its western and eastern borders, and by the lack of natural barriers to shield the nation from external political and military pressures. The slice of Europe occupied by the Polish nation functions as a wide passageway between two distinct parts of the continent and as a natural gate from the West to the Euro-Asian plains in the East. Poland's survival as an independent state has always depended on the country's ability to repel aggressors and on the competence of its diplomacy to prevent multipower coalitions from plotting to liquidate the Polish state. Consequently, the Poles learned very early in their history to scrutinize every domestic and foreign policy move from the perspective of national security.

The choice between the Eastern and Western patterns of Christianity was the first in a long chain of dilemmas to confront the Polish state. The determination to join Poland with Western Europe through baptism, according to the Roman rite, was a politically inspired safeguard against the Holy Roman Empire which had resolved to advance Christianity by force. In 966 Poland selected Bohemia rather than the medieval Germanic empire as a source of Christianity to highlight Polish independence from the Empire, Poland's Slavic heritage, and the voluntary nature of conversion. All these steps, however, failed to immunize Poland against imperial territorial and political pressures until the battle of Grunwald in 1410, when combined Polish-Lithuanian forces reversed the expansionism of the Teutonic Knights and removed the Germanic threat against Poland for the next three hundred years.

The emergence of an independent Prussian state at the beginning of the 18th century precipitated another two and a half centuries of struggle with Poland's western neighbor. This painful epoch included three partitions of Poland (1772, 1792, 1795) by the combined forces of Prussia, Russia, and Austria, occupation of Polish territories in the 19th century, and the signing of the 1939 Nazi-Soviet pact, conceived to dismember the Polish state and to terminate the Versailles security system in Europe. The 1939 pact also inaugurated World War II, which among countless other victims claimed close to seven million Polish lives and resulted in a major territorial and political reorientation of Poland and Germany. After one thousand years of mutual antagonism and oscillation from east to west, Poles and Germans again were facing each other across the Odra-Nysa (Oder-Neisse) rivers. Thus began the second millennium of Polish-German relations.

The legacy of history plays a very special role in Polish-German relations. It is a natural ethical framework and a point of reference for an understanding of current developments. All Poles, regardless of their political views and religious affiliations, are extraordinarily sensitive about any matter involving Germany. This sensitivity reflects bitterness and indignation about wartime German brutality against the Poles, persistent German territorial claims, and a negative German perception of the Polish people and culture. It is also a consequence of political calculation among many Poles that in the realm of morality Poland has the upper hand over Germany and that moral factors are a very important element of politics today. It is not coincidental, therefore, that various strains of the "German menace" dominate intellectual and political life in Poland. One of best-known bits of common "wisdom" in Poland is that "as long as the world exists a German would never be a brother to a Pole."

Although this troubled Polish-German legacy in general, and the disputed Odra-Nysa border in particular, will be the primary subject of attention in this essay, we shall also have occasion to note some positive aspects of historical Polish-German relations. Poles and Germans have made major contributions to each other's cultural and intellectual life, for example, beginning at least as far back as the 12th century, and continuing through the Hanseatic era, the Renaissance and Baroque, and into the 19th and 20th centuries. Such notable figures as Copernicus, Leibnitz, and Nietzsche served as particularly prominent representatives of a significant degree of Polish-German civilizational interaction.

Poland, the Germans, and the Odra-Nysa Question after 1945

The war left both nations defeated, economically ruined, and politically exposed to foreign influence. While Germany's territorial losses and political divisions resembled those of Poland at the end of the 18th century, Poland was once again under foreign domination with only nominal sovereignty vested in the hands of its pro-Soviet government in Warsaw. This new reality was a product of the military outcome of the war and the consequence of diplomatic negotiations among the three leading members of the anti-Nazi coalition. The future of both nations was determined during the conferences in Teheran and Yalta and sealed in 1945 at Potsdam. While Germany lost its eastern territories and was divided into five occupational zones, Poland lost half of its prewar territories to the Soviet Union and was compensated by acquiring the right to expel its German population and to "administer" the formerly German areas east of the Odra-Nysa rivers. The "final delimitation" of this Great Powers' bequest, however, was to "await the peace settlement" concluding World War II.[1] The ambiguous nature of the Potsdam Protocol triggered another round of Polish-German confrontation, which became an integral element of the Cold War showdown in Europe.

Poland's post-World War II foreign policy was entirely shaped by the experience of German occupation, the territorial shift to the west, and the mandatory character of the alliance with the Soviet Union. Communist authorities in Warsaw formulated two diametrically opposed policies toward Germany. Proclamations of friendship and goodwill toward Communist East Germany contrasted sharply with accusations of neo-Fascism and territorial revisionism aimed at the Federal Republic, allied with the Western powers. Poland adopted a policy of complete integration into the Soviet sphere of influence with the expectation of being rewarded with unequivocal Soviet support for the Odra-Nysa line as a permanent international border with Germany.[2]

The first tangible dividends of this policy emerged in 1950, when the German Democratic Republic's Communist government signed a treaty with Poland recognizing the Odra-Nysa line as the "established and existing frontier . . . [that] constitutes the state frontier between Poland and Germany."[3] This wording became known as the Zgorzelec (Görlitz) formula for recognizing the Polish-German border. It constituted a binding agreement between Poland and one German state, without encroachment on the rights of the other German state to make its own decision, and without breaching the rights of a united Germany and the Big Four to make the "final" determination as directed by the Potsdam Protocol.

This agreement concluded between two Soviet satellites infuriated both the people and the government of the Federal Republic of Germany. An anti-Polish theme became an ingredient in a number of pronouncements delivered by Federal Chancellor Konrad Adenauer, and was skillfully used on the Polish side to build a consensus behind the Communist government in Warsaw around the idea of the "German menace." Adenauer's frequent, politically motivated promises to return expelled Germans to their prewar homes was privately welcomed in Warsaw as the most impressive evidence that the Communist government was driven by patriotism, and that any attempt to alter either the internal or the international orientation of Poland could lead to another partition. For more than two decades after the war, West Germany's official insistence on non-recognition of the Odra-Nysa border had the paradoxical effect of stabilizing both the domestic political and the international status quo in Europe, including Germany's division into separate states.[4]

Eventually West German politicians noticed the intrinsic contradiction between two major goals of the FRG's foreign policy. Bonn's drive to reunify the two German states was hindered by the unrealistic insistence that the united Germany include certain Polish territories. Poland, for its part, focused its entire attention on cementing the political and territorial status quo in Europe, assuming a key role in the Soviet bloc's support for East Germany. Despite deep ethnic animosities between Poles and East Germans, the Polish government in Warsaw enthusiastically promoted East Berlin's cause in the international arena and actively worked toward international isolation of the Federal Republic, which was successfully portrayed as the only state in Europe interested in reversing the effects of the victory over Fascism.

However, interest in the idea of returning to the Odra-Nysa territories declined among West German voters during the 1960s, and with the 1969 electoral defeat of the Christian Democratic party, the Social Democrats were ready to negotiate with Warsaw. The breakthrough came at the end of 1970, when Poland and West Germany signed a treaty recognizing the Odra-Nysa line as an international border. As expected, the 1970 treaty was a result of mutual concessions. Poland failed to obtain either "final" recognition of the Odra-Nysa line or Germany's admission of guilt for the 1939 invasion of Poland and for wartime crimes against Polish citizens. The treaty adopted the Zgorzelec formula, stating that the "existing boundary line . . . shall constitute the western state frontier of the People's Republic of Poland." However, the West Germans augmented this rather *de facto* recognition of the Odra-Nysa border by guaranteeing the "inviolability of the existing frontiers now and in the future" and declaring that both countries had "no territorial claims whatsoever against each other and that they will not assert such claims in the future."[5]

The treaty also served as a warning to the Communist regime in East Germany. Offered the opportunity to settle its own affairs with the Federal Republic, Poland abandoned its multilateral Warsaw Pact approach to East-West relations in Europe and without scruples proceeded to look after its own national interest. East Germany insisted on a united front approach that would require all Soviet bloc states to negotiate simultaneously with West Germany. Under such circumstances West German recognition of the Odra-Nysa border would come concurrently with Bonn's recognition of the East German state. The Polish regime and the general public shared a fundamental distrust and dislike of the East German state, which was perceived as a successor to Prussian expansionism and authoritarianism. By the early 1970s, it was increasingly obvious that Polish relations with East Berlin were motivated by necessity rather than by sympathy or a common ideological outlook. Consistent with its more liberal proclivity, Poland was highly apprehensive about East Germany's predisposition for Communist orthodoxy, dogmatic influence on Moscow, and the brutality of its internal order.

Once the Federal Republic of Germany normalized relations with all its eastern neighbors,[6] including East Germany and the Soviet Union, it was the German Democratic Republic that became an aberration in European politics. Polish support for East Germany continued for another two decades, but the East German regime lost its monopolistic claim to speak for all of Germany within the Soviet bloc. As East German politics appeared to petrify and the country's economic system began to decay, the Communist states of Central and Eastern Europe slowly shifted their attention from East Berlin to Bonn.

The normalization of Polish-West German relations had the effect of further isolating East Germany among its Eastern European allies. Poland, traditionally committed to East Germany's survival, had become the main target of Bonn's *Ostpolitik*. Poland's economic weakness and its relatively liberal form of Communism provided a solid foundation for the peaceful involvement of the Federal Republic in Warsaw's internal and foreign policies. The 1968 Soviet crackdown on the liberalization movement in Czechoslovakia left the entire bloc deeply divided into liberal and orthodox camps, and Poland welcomed this opening to the West as leverage against conservative East Germany and Czechoslovakia, and as a source of economic assistance no longer available from Moscow. Once the Federal Republic abandoned its territorial claims against Poland, both countries discovered that they had shared interests on numerous political and economic issues.

During the 1970s West Germany became Poland's main economic partner in the West and the dominant source of foreign credits necessary to keep the Polish economy alive and Polish society willing to tolerate Communism. Still a political satellite of the Soviet Union, Poland had become an economic ward of the Western powers, especially West Germany.[7] For more than a decade this economic assistance sustained Poland's liberal form of Communism. By the end of the 1980s, however, the Communist system collapsed, having reached the limits of its ability to implement effective political and economic reforms. Politically, close relations between Bonn and Warsaw elevated Poland's international prestige during the negotiations at the Conference on Security and Cooperation in Europe (CSCE) in Helsinki in 1975 by creating the impression that as the second most powerful member of the Communist bloc (after the Soviet Union) Poland had achieved international parity with West Germany.

The emergence of Solidarity in Poland in the course of the 1980s brought the two nations even closer. The best evidence of the West German perspective on the Polish situation surfaced immediately after the imposition of martial law on December 13, 1981. The Federal Republic joined other NATO countries in denouncing the regime of General Jaruzelski for its attempt to enforce a military solution to the crisis and in imposing economic sanctions on Poland. At the same time, however, at the end of February 1982, Chancellor Helmut Schmidt dispatched Social Democratic *Bundestag* member Herbert Wehner to Poland for a "private visit," and subsequently voiced his reservations regarding Poland's growing economic and political isolation. In his view, the West had overreacted to the Polish crisis, and the economic quarantine of Poland could only have a counterproductive effect by deepening that country's domestic turmoil and delaying a return to normalcy.[8]

As far as their respective reactions to developments in Poland were concerned, democratic and prosperous West Germany contrasted sharply with belligerent and dogmatic East Germany. The SED regime in East Berlin explicitly favored a military solution of the Solidarity crisis in Poland.[9] Perhaps more ominously yet, East Germany's leaders now made it clear that deploying their troops in Poland would result in territorial alterations, specifically, the return of the port-city of Szczecin (Stettin) to Germany. Polish and East German naval forces faced off over the dispute involving Poland's navigational rights in the Bay of Szczecin. On January 2, 1985, the GDR's Council of Ministers issued an order extending East Germany's territorial waters from three to twelve nautical miles. This unilateral decision placed the main navigational channel connecting Szczecin with the Baltic Sea within GDR jurisdiction and thus obstructed access to Poland's third-largest port. The result was a series of confrontations between Polish and East German naval forces, enhancing an attitude of intransigence in both countries. Polish anxiety over this showdown was rooted in the fear that the GDR's move was merely the first step in an effort to undermine Poland's sovereignty over its western territories. Unable to reach a direct bilateral settlement, the Polish government secured Moscow's support for a redefinition of the Polish-East German maritime boundary, and subsequently invited Gorbachev to visit Szczecin during his July 1988 trip to Poland, in order to highlight Soviet support for the existing Odra-Nysa frontiers.[10]

East Germany thus presented a direct, immediate danger to Poland and its vital international interests at a time when the Federal Republic was offering unprecedented compassion, financial support, and an understanding of both Solidarity and the military government in Warsaw. Despite its suppression of the labor union, the Jaruzelski regime never resorted to the systematic purges that prevailed in Hungary and Czechoslovakia after the restoration of Communism, and slowly responded to Western pressure to respect human rights in Poland. Even under martial law Poland was more tolerant of opposition than East Germany under its "legitimate" authority, and East Berlin became an oasis of Prussian militarism in Europe. Ironically, the German Democratic Republic, which had long been presented by the Polish regime as a friendly neighbor and buffer against the aggressive West German state, now increasingly seemed to have become itself such a threat to Poland as well as a barrier to closer contact with the democratic and economically affluent West. By the end of the 1980s, East Germany had lost much of its political usefulness for Poland and, most likely, for the other countries of the Soviet bloc, including the disintegrating USSR.

Poland and Germany's Reunification

The spontaneous revolutionary explosion in Central and Eastern Europe in 1989 came to its perhaps most dramatic climax with the fall of the Honecker regime and the crumbling of the Berlin Wall. In the absence of Communism, new political forces came to the fore in GDR politics, the most consequential of which was the East German population's desire for unification with the FRG. East Germany's Communist leaders had failed in their efforts to insulate their subjects hermetically from Eastern and Western political influences. Consequently, the breakdown of East Germany signalled nothing less than the end of the bipolar international order in Europe established after World War II.

These developments had crucial implications for Poland. The Cold War division of Europe in two spheres of influence had numerous disadvantages for Poland, but it also had the benefit of protecting its western border. The Soviet Union was the ultimate patron of the Odra-Nysa line, because it became a fall-back position for Soviet influence in the West and a territorial arrangement designed to weaken Germany and guarantee a pro-Soviet orientation in Poland. The simultaneous liquidation of the East German state and the breakdown of the Soviet Union's international and domestic structure presented Poland with a completely new security dilemma. Poland's reaction to these developments was two-fold.

The first reaction was the result of Poland's inability to derail or delay the process of German unification. The Polish government adopted an "if you can't beat 'em, join 'em" attitude toward events taking place in the West, and decided to take the best possible advantage from the changes taking place in Europe. Consequently, the unification of Germany was presented as a natural side-effect of post-Cold War politics in Europe, and much more desirable than the alternative of Soviet intervention in East Germany to halt reunification. A return to Cold War politics in Europe could threaten the very existence of the Polish state, and could seriously jeopardize the success of Poland's transition to democracy. A peaceful solution to the suddenly resurfaced issue of German unification was in Poland's best interest, as it could claim that the final outcome of the Cold War, including territorial integrity and the democratic political system, was highly advantageous to the Polish nation.

However, Poland's original expectation was that the process of unification would assume the form of a merger between two roughly co-equal partners rather than West Germany's ultimate takeover of the GDR. The Polish government soon discovered that there was nothing to spare in East Germany, and concluded that any attempt to hamper the "two-plus-four" talks could produce only short-term advantages and a considerable long-term political risk for Poland. Any attempt to frustrate unification could fuel nationalistic sentiments in Germany and renew the anti-Polish "Versailles syndrome" among the German public. The Polish government came out in favor of unification, but maintained that this process should be harmonized with the emergence of all-European security structures, and that it should be contingent upon Germany's acceptance of the Odra-Nysa line as the "final" border between Poland and Germany. Unlike Moscow, Poland never favored mandatory neutrality for the united Germany for fear that without powerful international constraints Germany might drift toward nationalism. From the beginning Poland advocated continued German membership in NATO, which would provide the most reliable system of international constraints on any revival of Germany's militaristic legacy.

Moreover, the Poles saw the unification of Germany and Solidarity's success in confronting Communism as two sides of the same coin. The end of Soviet hegemony in Eastern Europe should be equally beneficial to all parties involved, and a democratic Germany was the best possible alternative for Poland. Two other hypothetical scenarios, the unification of Germany on East German terms and, alternatively, perpetuating the division regardless of cost and consequence, were far more dangerous, if not unrealistic. The Poles were fully aware that the countries that had left the Soviet sphere of influence, Austria and Finland, had not turned toward militarism and had never threatened their neighbors. The same applied to NATO, which, once the Federal Republic of Germany dropped its territorial claims against Poland, was seen in Poland as a voluntary alliance of democratic countries able to enforce Germany's obligation never to become a nuclear, chemical, or bacteriological power. Finally, Germany's consent in 1990 to reduce its armed forces to about 370,000, or half the number of combined East and West German forces and only 100,000 more than the East German military, assured Poland that the Western economic giant would not become a military superpower.

Another very important element in Polish calculations involved the future European military balance. Specifically, Poland was apprehensive about the military potential of the Soviet Union. Stricken by economic collapse, the USSR continued to be a dreadful military power. It was in Poland's best interest to renounce any hostility toward Germany and thus remove any cause for the united German state to search for special bonds with Moscow at Poland's expense. Completely new security dimensions began to arise on its eastern border, and the old notion of the "German menace" could not serve any useful purpose. Poland needed close, strong ties with the West to counter nationalistic euphoria and instability in the East.

Poland's second reaction to the changes in Germany and the Soviet Union involved an evolution in Poland's traditional attitude toward Germany, from the perception of an evil Teutonic state resolved to dislodge its Slavic neighbors to a view that West Germany had become a benevolent member of the Western alliance of democratic nations. Polish opinion on the "German character" was the result of a bitter historical experience with the Prussian state, and the "German question" was a real issue for Poland. Old fears inspired by the memory of partitions and two world wars were renewed by the unification of two German states with a combined population of about 80 million and enormous economic potential, as well as by the resurgence of what appeared to be neo-Fascist tendencies among some segments of the German population. Poland was prepared to accept German unity as long as its legitimate security interests, including its western border, received adequate attention and international recognition.

The final stage of Polish-German reconciliation began in November 1989, when the West German parliament declared that Poland's "right to live within secure borders will not be questioned now or in the future by territorial claims from us Germans."[11] This attitude opened the door for Chancellor Helmut Kohl's visit to Poland and created favorable conditions for addressing the moral aspects of mutual relations. Poland demanded an explicit German admission of guilt for atrocities committed during World War II, and Germany sought Poland's acknowledgment that expelling some nine million Germans from the Odra-Nysa territories also violated norms of human behavior. This latter admission was integral to Bonn's campaign to counter ultra-conservative pressures at home. The symbolic act of spiritual reconciliation between the two nations involved the attendance of Chancellor Kohl and Poland's Prime Minister Tadeusz Mazowiecki at a Roman Catholic mass in the Silesian town of Krzyzowa, the site of a 1921 Polish uprising against Germany.

Nevertheless, Kohl was very sensitive to the political influence of irredentist forces in Germany, and consistently refused to issue a clear statement of support for the Odra-Nysa line on behalf of the German government prior to unification. This attitude alarmed Poland and several other European states, including France and the Soviet Union, and prompted Warsaw to demand direct participation in the "two-plus-four" talks on Germany's unification. Kohl played his domestic games fully aware that unification had to be acceptable to the international community. This meant that the united Germany would inherit all international obligations of the FRG and the GDR, including the principles of international behavior agreed upon in the 1975 Helsinki Accords. Europe was not inclined to return to Germany's pre-1937 borders.

Eventually, and largely for symbolic reasons, Poland was invited to join the negotiations, but only during the discussion of Germany's territorial configuration. Both German governments pledged on behalf of the future united Germany to conclude without delay a treaty recognizing the Odra-Nysa line as a permanent *de jure* border between Poland and Germany. In mid-November 1990, a month after Germany's formal unification, representatives of the Polish and German governments agreed in Warsaw on the text of the border treaty, which stated:

> The parties to the treaty declare that the border existing between them is inviolable now and in the future and undertake to respect each other's sovereignty and territorial integrity without restriction.

> The parties to the treaty declare that they have no territorial claims whatsoever against each other and will not assert such claims in the future.[12]

The Germans obtained Poland's confession that this territorial transfer resulted in "the great suffering . . . , particularly the loss of . . . homes suffered by numerous Germans and Poles."[13]

On October 23, 1991, the Polish Senate, the upper house of the Polish legislature, unanimously approved the German-Polish border treaty. Officially, the treaty is seen as a guarantee that the existing borders are final and inviolable, and that in the new Europe international borders should unite rather than divide nations. Unofficially, however, Poland noted certain legal flaws in the status of the Odra-Nysa line. There are at least five international documents dealing specifically with the Polish-German border issue: a) the Potsdam Protocol of 1945, b) the 1950 Zgorzelec agreement between Poland and the German Democratic Republic, c) the 1970 Polish-West German treaty, d) the September 12, 1990, treaty between the four great powers and the two German states (concluding the two-plus-four talks) reaffirming that the borders of a united Germany will be the same as the borders of the two German states, and e) the Polish-German treaty of 1991. All these documents systematically avoid using the phrase "final recognition of the border" as required by the Potsdam Protocol, and instead use the much weaker term "confirmation of the border," leaving some degree of ambiguity over the finality of this settlement.

After the 1970 treaty was signed it was assumed, in Warsaw and Bonn and elsewhere, that this act constituted final recognition of Poland's western border by the Federal Republic, and that the agreement was binding on existing and future German states. Shortly after signing the treaty, however, some West German politicians with revisionist orientations seemed to prevail in Bonn, and the official West German interpretation of the treaty (in part backed by the FRG's Constitutional Court) became that the agreement constituted only a provisional solution to the Polish-German border question, and that a final settlement of the matter required a peace conference attended by a united Germany. In conclusion, all bilateral Polish-German arrangements had no "final" effect as required by the Potsdam Protocol.

At the same time, there has been no formal peace conference with Germany, only the surrogate two-plus-four talks, which for all practical purposes addressed the issues related to the German question but in a legal framework different from that specified at Potsdam. Since Germany is not likely to demand a peace conference, the 1990 Moscow agreement that concluded the two-plus-four negotiations is the "final settlement regarding Germany" and the last international document focused on the border issue. Specifically, in Article 1, the 1990 Moscow treaty stated:

1. The united Germany shall comprise the territory of the Federal Republic of Germany, the German Democratic Republic and the whole of Berlin. Its external borders shall be the borders of the Federal Republic of Germany and the German Democratic Republic and shall be definitive from the date on which the present Treaty comes into force. The confirmation of the definitive nature of the borders of the united Germany is an essential element of the peaceful order in Europe.

2. The united Germany and the Republic of Poland shall confirm the existing border between them in a treaty that is binding under international law.

3. The united Germany has no territorial claims whatsoever against other states and shall not assert any in the future.

4. The Governments of the Federal Republic of Germany and the German Democratic Republic shall ensure that the constitution of the united Germany does not contain any provision incompatible with these principles . . .

5. [The Big Four] take formal note of the corresponding commitments and declarations . . . and declare that their implementation will confirm the definite nature of the united Germany's borders.[14]

In some extreme, politically inspired, legalistic interpretation, the Polish-German border question is still open. Hypothetically, it is still possible that some ultra-nationalistic party in Germany may obtain political power, as the Nazis did in 1933, and declare that Germany had never "recognized" the Odra-Nysa line as the "final" border with Poland as defined by the Potsdam Protocol. The old rhetoric about protecting the German minorities in Silesia and Pomerania could be employed to renew territorial claims against Poland.

This attitude is especially prevalent among members of the Silesians Association and the League of Expelled Germans. These and similar organizations continue to be active in Germany, and despite their relatively small numbers they receive an excessive amount of public attention. In an interview with the Wroclaw daily *Gazeta Robotnicza*, Herbert Hupka, a representative of these groups, explained:

Silesia has always been my native land, and for more than 700 years it was a part of Germany, so I believe that I have now arrived in my native land. This is because, in my opinion, the Polish-German treaties acknowledged the border on the Rivers Odra and Nysa but, nevertheless, they still do not recognize it.[15]

In addition, Hupka pointed out that the border was established illegitimately, the result of pacts made among the wartime Big Three (U.S., USSR, and United Kingdom) but with neither Polish nor German participation. Hupka called the expatriation of ethnic Germans a crime against humanity. The Odra-Nysa line, in his opinion, is an act of "communist and nationalist lawlessness" that should be rectified by "joint management of these territories and joint restoration of Silesia to prosperity."[16]

It is difficult, at least at this point in time, to imagine any further changes in the territorial configuration of Poland. World War II and all the international agreements that resulted created a completely new political, legal, and military situation that cannot be changed without a major war. While in no danger of repeating its experience of 1939, Poland nevertheless is vulnerable to Germany owing to its fragile economic structure and the difficult problem of German minority rights.

German-Polish Cultural Relations and the Question of Ethnic Germans in Poland

The issue of German nationals living in Poland has its roots in the 1944-45 expulsion of the "enemy population" from the Polish territories, including the newly acquired Odra-Nysa land. The question of ethnic Germans living in Poland was never brought to the public's attention in Poland until the 1970s, when both countries agreed to discuss the border issue. For the first time, the Communist authorities in Warsaw admitted that an ethnic German minority was still living in Poland, but they argued that it was strictly an internal matter and not a subject to be included in an international treaty dealing with the border issue. The 1970 treaty made no reference to the status of ethnic Germans in Poland, but the Polish government agreed to publish a unilateral *Information* promising to permit "any persons . . . owing to their indisputable ethnic German origin to leave to East or West Germany," and to give consideration to the petitions of "mixed and separate families as well as . . . Polish nationals who, either because of their changed family situation or because of their earlier decision, express the wish to be reunited with near relatives."[17]

According to the 1970 estimate presented by the West German government, up to one million ethnic Germans still resided in Poland. As a result of the Polish-West German treaty, Warsaw acknowledged that approximately one-fourth of them wished to leave for Germany. Poland accepted an emigration rate of 2,000 to 3,000 persons per month.[18] The Polish authorities were not opposed to the idea of German emigration, but were concerned that many Polish nationals would take advantage of this opportunity to flee the country to Germany and other affluent West European states for economic and political reasons alone. The Polish government feared that a wealthy West Germany would be a magnet for many Poles, especially considering that under West German law any person born in the Odra-Nysa territories could easily be naturalized as a German citizen.

Over the next twenty years the German minority issue escalated, eventually becoming the main source of disagreement between the two nations. Following the establishment of Polish-West German relations, Bonn was confronted with powerful internal pressure to defend and promote the rights of ethnic Germans who were disinclined to leave Poland. In particular, Germany insisted on a Polish commitment to pursue specific and individual solutions, especially concerning cultural identity, double citizenship, and the establishment of a Polish-German commission to guarantee satisfactory conditions for the German minority in Poland. Naturally the issue was highly emotional, because the German public's approval of the territorial changes would come easier from a give-and-take transaction than Germany's unilateral surrender of the Odra-Nysa territories. The West German government, therefore, advanced the notion that Germans living in Poland be granted special privileges and freedoms.

From the early 1970s onward, Bonn attempted to link the border question to the minority issue or economic matters. Yet, Warsaw succeeded in decoupling recognition of the Odra-Nysa border from the issue of Poland's treatment of ethnic Germans or any other problem in the huge inventory of items requiring attention to achieve a complete normalization of bilateral relations. By the beginning of the 1990s, all matters of mutual concern other than the state border were crammed together in one vast agreement entitled "The Treaty on Good-Neighborliness and Friendly Cooperation," which was signed in Warsaw on June 17, 1991, and ratified on January 16, 1992.

Both sides were brought together by a sincere desire to overcome the difficult past and to start a new and better era of bilateral relations. Personnel changes in the Polish government that accompanied the replacement of Prime Minister Mazowiecki by the much younger Jan Krzysztof Bielecki in 1991 contributed to a substantial change in Poland's attitude toward Germany. Instead of dwelling on Germany's history of crimes against the Polish state and nation, and on its economic intimidation of Poland, the new generation of leaders in Poland began to look forward to the unfolding opportunities to strengthen Poland's European policy presented by a new partnership between democratic Germany and Poland.

While the Mazowiecki government, Poland's first non-Communist government since 1945, perceived German unification as a serious threat to the security and territorial integrity of Poland, the younger generation of Polish leaders sees German unification as a way to accelerate the unification of Europe, as a whole recognizing the two unification processes as complementary and in Poland's best interests. Poland decided to cast its future with European political, economic, and even military integration, fully aware that the country cannot become an active member of the European Community over the Germans' heads. On the contrary, Poland's road to Europe leads through Germany, and can succeed only with vigorous German support assured by an open-minded attitude. The parochial outlook that envisioned the Odra-Nysa line as another Berlin Wall against the West would confine Poland to isolationism and lasting economic inferiority. Addressing the Polish parliament on the German-Polish treaty, Prime Minister Bielecki pointed out that the "European character of the treaty is expressed in . . . the fact that the Federal Republic of Germany is pledging to support the strategic aim of our policy, which is precisely to enter the European Community. That is why relations with the Germans have a strategic rather than an opportunistic significance for Poland."[19]

This new perspective on Polish-German relations required a revision of the post-World War II interpretation of mutual relations. According to Communist propaganda, the dominant theme of Polish history was an incessant struggle against military, economic, and cultural German intrusions. From its first years, according to the Communist view, the Polish nation had to combat eastward thrusts, from the Holy Roman Empire, the Teutonic Knights, Prussian militarism, and the Germanization drives of the Second Empire and the Nazi Third Reich. An additional element of this distortion involved a flawed interpretation of the historical role of the German minority in Poland, which was presented as a kind of fifth column constantly conspiring against the Polish state. Finally, Communist propaganda asserted that following the 1945-48 expulsions, there was no German minority left in Poland. Implicit in this misrepresentation was the notion that the presence of up to 1.5 million ethnic Germans in pre-World War II Poland (approximately 4 percent of the total population) constituted the major threat to Polish national security.

This greatly distorted view ran contrary to much of the historical record, selectively using a number of incidents, some indeed very painful and tragic, to generalize about the entire one thousand years of Polish-German relations. Besides military confrontations and territorial disagreements, Polish-German relations have generally been characterized by a high degree of cooperation and considerable German contribution to the development and enrichment of Polish culture, as well as to Poland's technological and scientific progress. Settlers from Germany began to arrive in Poland as early as the end of 12th century. The development of Polish towns and cities was based on German law and fostered by the newcomers from the West, who became rapidly Polonized. Some of the most famous and most patriotic Poles had German parents, including Copernicus, who on behalf of the Polish crown defended Polish cities against the Teutonic knights. The long list of prominent Polonized Germans includes the names of royal scribes, patricians, publishers, scientists, poets, linguists, architects, and several military leaders who fought for the Polish cause against both Germany and Russia.

It is important to add that this cultural bond was never a one-sided phenomenon. The most famous Germanized Poles were Leibnitz and Nietzsche, and over one thousand noble names listed in German heraldry books are derived from the Polish nobility. Today, the names of numerous German political and cultural leaders indicate their Polish roots, and several regions in Germany, notably the Ruhr valley, include high concentrations of Poles who settled in Germany. The simple fact is that western Slavs and Germans lived side-by-side long before the Polish state appeared, and together contributed to the development of civilization rooted in Roman culture and Christianity. Officially, there are today about one million German citizens who claim Polish ethnic origin. Some are organized in 45 Polish parishes within the Federal Republic, and in 270 German towns and cities there are churches celebrating mass in the Polish language. The actual number of Poles living in Germany is unknown, but is estimated to be nearly two million. The 1991 treaty grants the same rights to Polish and German minorities, but the definition of minority covers only those individuals who are citizens or permanent residents, excluding legal and illegal guest workers.[20]

To enlist German support for its European ambitions, Poland had to compromise on such points as the rights of German minorities, German emigration to Poland, and full freedom of movement for people, capital, goods, and services. In this sense, it was a barter trade — minority rights for Germans in exchange for supporting the "Europeanization" of Poland. As expected, those who regard themselves as ethnic Germans have promptly taken advantage of the new treaty. Some 326,000 Polish citizens living in Silesia, Pomerania, and other parts of Poland have signed the declaration claiming membership in the Cultural-Educational Society of the German Minority and demanding the return of churches, the restoration of cemeteries, access to mass media and German language training, as well as bilingual names for cities, streets, and institutions.

Under current law, the ethnicity of a citizen in Poland is his or her private affair and the state has no authority to verify declarations of ethnic origin. Under the criteria applied by German legislation, about 1.5 million Poles are qualified to claim dual citizenship, and whoever declares his or her nationality to be German automatically acquires German citizenship, including a German passport and the right to live in the West. Also, there are persistent rumors in Poland that the *Heimat Bünde* (Home Associations) follow an open door admission policy in recruiting Poles willing to sign a declaration claiming German origin. The recruits are paid 300 to 1,000 D-Mark and their children are provided with supplementary meals and numerous other benefits, creating a *de facto* two-class society in Poland.[21] Poland's program of economic decentralization, which has created semi-autonomous economic regions, greatly facilitates German penetration of selected regions, particularly Silesia, which has been designated for rapid "Europeanization" with the help of German investments.

It is important to note, however, that the members of these German organizations in Poland are not known for questioning the territorial changes, but rather appear to focus on cultural and educational liberties, reconciliation between Poles and Germans, and assisting in regional Polish-German ventures across the Odra and Nysa rivers. "The minority does not want to destabilize the state," declared the chairman of the Gross-Strehlitz Friendship Circle from the Opole region in Silesia, "but would like to actively support economic reforms in Poland." This attitude was confirmed by the October 27, 1991, parliamentary elections in Poland, when seven deputies and one senator representing "Poles of German descent" entered the Polish parliament. Their political program envisions broad involvement in all issues, avoiding provincialism and a narrow focus on minority affairs.[22]

German-Polish Economic Relations

The historical experience indicates that political and territorial disputes have had relatively little effect on economic relations between Poland and Germany. Opening the Polish economy to the West was one of the main achievements of the October 1956 revolt, and by the late 1960s the Federal Republic of Germany had become Poland's largest economic partner and its major creditor in the West, while East Germany was Poland's second-largest economic partner in the Soviet bloc.[23] Poland's economic fortunes and misfortunes can be related to the ups and downs in the country's trade with Western nations. The rapid expansion of the Polish economy in the 1970s was sustained by Western, and above all West German, credits and access to hard currency markets. Western economic sanctions against Poland in the 1980s, following the suppression of Solidarity and the imposition of martial law by the Jaruzelski regime, seriously hurt the Polish economy and contributed to the final breakdown of the Communist system at the end of the decade.

When, in 1990, the Polish government launched a bold program of stabilization and transition to a market economy, its package of economic reforms included complete decentralization and market-oriented foreign trade. Developed in cooperation with the International Monetary Fund, the main pillars of structural change in the Polish economy include intensive privatization, the promotion of foreign trade, and foreign investments in Poland. In order to encourage Western economic involvement in the Polish economy, the government eliminated almost all subsidies and taxes on exports, introduced full internal convertibility of the Polish currency, and allowed full repatriation of hard currency earnings by foreign investors. Now there are no limits on the access to hard currency for purchases of imports and services abroad.

This liberalization of Poland's economic system produced an immediate geographic reorientation of foreign trade toward Germany, which replaced the former Soviet Union as Poland's principal trading partner. Prior to the unification of Germany, about 13 percent of Poland's foreign trade was with the Federal Republic and 7 percent with the former East Germany. Since unification, about 20 percent of Poland's imports and exports involve the Western neighbor. The preliminary data indicates, however, that in 1991 Poland's exports to Germany have declined by approximately 3 percent and imports from Germany by over 8 percent. Explanations for this decline vary, but it could be attributed to the weakness of the Polish accounting system and the collapse of the East German economy. At the same time, Polish trade with Western states increased by about 40 percent, especially with the other members of the European Community.[24] In addition, the united Germany leads Western countries in the amount of humanitarian aid to Poland and in investments in the Polish economy. Following the 1990 Paris Club arrangement, the Federal Republic agreed to a 50 percent reduction of the Polish debt, which at the end of 1990 exceeded $40 billion. About 25 percent of this debt is owed to German banks.

It is apparent that Polish-German economic relations will have the greatest impact on the success of Poland's transition to a market economy in a reasonable period of time. Germany was one of the first Western nations to recognize Poland's economic potential. The latter has the largest gross national product and the most numerous population among all Central European nations, and its commitment to a socially bearable transition to a free market economy continues to be strong. Germany appears to have more confidence than any other Western country in a dynamic growth of the private sector in Poland,[25] and the German people and government are aware that Poland's failure to make a successful transition would have a direct and negative impact on German politics and Germany's economy. In an interdependent world Poland's economic condition is also a German problem.

Conclusion

After a rather difficult past Poland and Germany are trying as best as they can to overcome the painful historical legacy. Without any doubt, internal and international conditions for a permanent Polish-German reconciliation are now better than at any other time in recent history. Motivated by a common heritage and by a mutual interest in European stability and security, Polish-German reconciliation has its own spontaneous dynamic independent of governments and politicians. Friendly relations between Poles and Germans are as essential for peace and security in Europe as cordial links between France and Germany. In political terms, the current and future course of Polish-German relations will have a direct bearing on the architecture of both the entire European continent and that of Germany and Poland more specifically.

But the process of Polish-German reconciliation will take a long time and is likely to suffer many tactical setbacks. Cultural differences between both nations are substantial and will continue to hamper mutual understanding. In addition, Polish mistrust of Germany's long-term strategic objectives on a European continent free of hegemonic superpowers is likely to handicap bilateral relations as well. The Germans, for their part, are disappointed by a chronic and self-inflicted political instability in Poland and angered by the zig-zagging course of Poland's economic reforms. A stable Polish state could make a decisive contribution to the security and prosperity of Europe. However, should Poland's condition as a "sick man of Europe" become irreversible, the country would default on its chance to mature into a full-fledged partner of other European nations, including Germany. Poland has a choice of becoming either an extension of the West and a key international player safeguarding Western Europe and Germany from the uncertainties in the East, or continuing to be a source of aggravation for other nations. Protracted political paralysis in Poland would inhibit Polish-German reconciliation. Eventually, Polish-German relations must rise above the emotions generated by a burdensome past to the level of a give-and-take, business-like partnership. Germany is Poland's most important neighbor, but the character of their bilateral relations will be determined by Poland's ability to fulfill that which is expected of a productive and reliable associate.

Notes

1. Quoted in James T. Shotwell and Max M. Laserson, *Poland and Russia, 1919-1945* (New York: King's Crown Press, 1945), p. 110. For the German perspective on the border question, see Frederick H. Hartman, *Germany Between East and West: The Reunification Problem* (Englewood Cliffs, NJ: Prentice-Hall, Inc., 1965), pp. 15-23. For a more general review of German-Polish relations in English, see Dennis L. Bark and David R. Gress, *A History of West Germany*, Volume I: *From Shadow to Substance, 1945-1963* (Oxford/New York: Basil Blackwell, Ltd., 1989), pp. 47-73.

2. For a discussion of Polish attitudes regarding Germany after 1945, see Helmut Schmidt, *The Balance of Power* (London: William Kimber, 1971), pp. 119-23.

3. Andrzej Lesniewski, ed., *Western Frontiers of Poland* (Warsaw: Polish Institute of International Affairs, 1965), p. 31.

4. On Konrad Adenauer's attitude toward Poland, see Immanuel Birnbaum, "Germany's Eastern Policy, Yesterday and Tomorrow," in Walter Stahl, ed., *The Politics of Postwar Germany* (New York: Frederick A. Praeger, 1963), pp. 454-55.

5. Lawrence L. Whetten, *Germany's Ostpolitik; Relations Between the Federal Republic and the Warsaw Pact Countries* (London: Oxford University Press, 1971), p. 163. The border issue is also discussed in Karl Kaiser, *German Foreign Policy in Transition* (London/Oxford/New York: Oxford University Press, 1968), pp. 34-35. See

also J. K. Sowden, *The German Question, 1945-1973* (New York: St. Martin's Press, 1975), pp. 228-51.

6. On the evolution of the FRG's attitudes towards the countries of East-Central Europe, see Michael Balfour, *West Germany. A Contemporary History* (New York: St. Martin's Press, 1982), pp. 221-24. See also Eugene K. Keefe et al., *Area Handbook for the Federal Republic of Germany* (Washington, DC: U.S. Government Printing Office, 1975), pp. 240-46; Wolfram F. Hanrieder, *Germany, America, Europe. Forty Years of German Foreign Policy* (New Haven/London: Yale University Press, 1989), pp. 198-202, 209-10.

7. Marian Podkowinski, "Olbrzym czy Karzel?," *Perspektywy* (Warsaw), January 31, 1975.

8. Reported in the *Financial Times*, March 10, 1982.

9. See *Der Spiegel*, Nr. 42, October 12, 1992, pp. 95, 97, 99.

10. See *Keesing's Record of World Events*, Vol. 35, No. 5, 1989, p. 36577.

11. Quoted in Horst Teltschik, "Republika Federalna Niemiec a Polska-Trudne Partnerstwo," *Profil* (Hamburg), January 1991, p. 37.

12. *Gazeta Wyborcza*, (Warsaw), November 14, 1990, p. 1.

13. *Gazeta Wyborcza*, November 14, 1990, p. 1. For a useful review of international developments prior to 1989 that made the successful conclusion of the 1991 German-Polish agreement possible, see Bark and Gress, *A History of West Germany*, Volume II: *Democracy and Its Discontents, 1963-1988*, pp. 330, 469-74.

14. *U.S. Department of State Dispatch* (Washington, D.C.: U.S. Government Printing Office), October 8, 1990, p. 165.

15. November 13, 1991, pp. 1-2.

16. *Gazeta Robotnicza*, November 13, 1991, pp. 1-2.

17. *The Treaty Between the Federal Republic of Germany and the People's Republic of Poland* (Bonn: Press and Information Office of the Federal Government, 1971), p. 8.

18. Quoted in *The New York Times*, December 7, 1970, p. A11.

19. *Polska Zbrojna* (Warsaw), January 17-19, 1992, p. 1. See also Krzysztof Skubiszewski, "Traktat o Dobrym Sasiedztwie i Przyjaznej Wspolpracy z Niemcami," *Tygodnik Powszechny* (Cracow), November 24, 1991, p. 1. For Prime Minister Bielecki's statement, see FBIS-EEU-91-203, October 21, 1991, p. 13.

20. Wlodzimierz Kalicki, "Ukryci Niemcy," *Gazeta Wyborcza* (Warsaw), September 21, 1991, pp. 10-14. Also, Wolfgang Krischke, "Germanowie i Slowianie," *Profil*, February 1991, pp. 40-41, and "Spotkania z Polska," *Profil*, March 1991, pp. 38-40.

21. *Przeglad Tygodniowy*, (Warsaw), June 23, 1991, p. 3.

22. Quoted in *Süddeutsche Zeitung*, April 25, 1991. For the status of German deputies see *Frankfurter Allgemeine Zeitung*, November 29, 1991, p. 3.

23. *The New York Times*, October 31, 1974.

24. Based on data provided in Keith Crane, "Polish Foreign Trade in 1990 and the First Half of 1991," *Plan Econ Report*, Volume VII, Numbers 30-31, August 30, 1991, p. 6, Table 3. See also Keith Crane, "Post-Communist Economic Transformation: Hungary vs. Poland," *American Economic Review*, Volume 81, Number 2, May 1991, pp. 318-320.

25. *National Trade Data Base*, November 25, 1991.

11

The Czechs and the Germans: A One-Thousand-Year Relationship

Milan Hauner

The special Czech-German relationship,[1] which spans at least one thousand years, has become yet again extremely topical since the end of the memorable year of 1989. In the last two months of that year, the relationship underwent a profound change that demands a fresh interpretation. The much feared "German Problem" has been recognized as a common European problem concerning all of Germany's neighbors. FRG President Richard von Weizsäcker, visiting Prague on the fateful day of March 15, 1990 (51st anniversary of the German occupation of Czechoslovakia), reiterated that Germany had no territorial claims against any of its neighbors. Aware of the centrality of German history and geography for the peoples of Europe, he declared:

> Our history has never belonged to us alone. Why? Because of our specific European responsibility that reflects our precarious geographic location in the heart of the continent. We Germans have more neighbors than any other country. Our position in the center seriously affected historical events elsewhere. . .[2]

There is a second reason for a new interpretation. As the question of ethnicity and new nationalism is gaining in importance all over Eastern Europe, and even tragically so in the Balkans, it becomes necessary, while assessing Czech-German relations in the post-1990 era, to refer to the critical Czech-Slovak nexus that threatens to split the Czechoslovak state apart. Whatever the future holds for Czechoslovakia, the new Germany is about to give the Germans of the 21st century a new identity. Consequently, Germany's close neighbors will be deeply affected by this process; they, too, will have to adjust their own national identities to the new phenomenon of German unity.

The Breakthrough in 1989

"Germany can be as large as she wants to, as long as she stays democratic." When President Václav Havel uttered these very words in East Berlin on January 2, 1990,[3] in front of the Brandenburg Gate, in the eyes of many Czechs the very symbol of the hated "Prussianism" (*prušáctví*), he destroyed in one swoop several petrified stereotypes that had blocked any reasonable improvement in Czech-German relations ever since the end of World War II.

Does it really matter how big Germany is as long as she appears to be democratic? Was it not the traditional political instinct of the Czechs to support particularism and separatism among the Germans? This centuries-old geopolitical instinct was intuitively shared by the first Czech medieval chroniclers, Kosmas and Dalimil. One can trace its axiomatic impact on the political thinking of Thomas G. Masaryk and Eduard Beneš, the co-founders of the Czechoslovak Republic in 1918. Could the Czechs, as well as other direct neighbors of Germany, forget their perennial geopolitical instincts? How could they disregard the size and power of the new united Germany, solely because its internal institutions appeared democratic for the time being? Moreover, while the greatest "blood transfusion" in history, as German unification is sometimes called, seems to be proceeding without major hiccups, Czechoslovakia is undergoing a reverse trend of ethnic tensions between the Czechs and Slovaks that is ever more clearly leading to political disunity.

Yet, there is a hope that this time the new Germany is an entirely different country. This hope is undoubtedly based on the optimism that democratic institutions, developed in the western half between 1949 and 1989 under the protective shield of NATO, can be successfully transplanted into the five new *Länder* of the former German Democratic Republic. There is much reassuring evidence that this time Germany's direct neighbors need not worry any longer about the resurgence of Prussian militarism, revanchism, expansionism, and so forth. Yet, at the same time, it seems that the wise principle of the European balance of power, established in 1815 (but lost in 1871), and again in 1945, and strongly advocated by statesmen ranging from Disraeli to Kissinger, has been abandoned once again.

Václav Havel, however, a few weeks before his "no-matter-how large" Germany speech, contributed to the Czech-German theme with another even more radical declaration. He issued an unequivocal moral condemnation of the postwar expulsion of three million Czechoslovak citizens of German ethnicity which, as Havel explicitly wrote in his personal letter to President Richard von Weizsäcker, "has always struck me as a deeply immoral act, inflicting heavy damage not only on the Germans, but perhaps even more on the Czechs, both in the moral as well as material sense." As if this were not enough, Havel added in his letter that he wished to ask the Germans "for forgiveness in some form, similar to that which the Germans themselves had already asked several other nations who had suffered from them so terribly during the Nazi era."[4]

Because von Weizsäcker used several passages from Havel's letter in his Christmas address, Havel's private reflections about the necessity of a public apology to the Germans had become public property. The passionate reaction of the Czech public was not only caused by the fact that Havel's words must have injured a great number of patriotic Czechs who had suffered because of the Nazi occupation of Czechoslovakia,[5] but especially because Havel had conscientiously shattered most taboos that since 1945 had clouded Czech-German relations. Furthermore, he explicitly distanced himself from the official thesis of German collective guilt that had dominated Czech political thinking at home as well as in exile for so long.

If it was the "German Question" that had inspired Václav Havel during his first days as statesman to fly instantaneously to Berlin and Munich, the German Question turned out to be, in retrospect, the strongest catalyst for the so-called Velvet Revolution in Czechoslovakia. Without the daily reminder of thousands of East German refugees, streaming to the Lobkowicz Palace in Prague in the late summer of 1989, without the breach of the Berlin Wall on November 9 that symbolized the collapse of the "Iron Curtain" dividing Europe into two camps since 1945, the revolutionary events of November 17 in Prague would hardly have taken place.

The Dissidents and the Czech-German Question

While praising Václav Havel for his brave gestures that helped to redefine fundamentally the Czech-German relationship, one must not forget dissident authors, mostly historians living both at home and in exile, who had prepared the terrain for Havel's courageous deed ever since 1968, the year when the "Prague Spring" had been crushed. The first breakthrough in the discussion of the Nazi occupation of Czechoslovakia and the taboo subject of the expulsion of German Czechs occurred in the spring of 1968 on the pages of the literary journal *Host do domu* [Guest in the House].[6] Further articles on various aspects of the Nazi occupation, including such forbidden topics as collaboration, followed in the historical review *Dějiny a současnost* [Past and Present].[7] The reintroduction of censorship in mid-1969 interrupted the debate for a while, until it was resumed by the underground press at the end of the 1970s.

The debate on the expulsion of the Germans thus entered into its second stage when in 1978 the exile periodical *Svědectví* ["Témoignage"] in Paris published the most direct and sentiment-provoking "Theses on the Eviction of the Czechoslovak Germans," by Jan Mlynárik, a Slovak historian living in Prague and using the pseudonym "Danubius."[8] Mlynárik's aggressive style provoked a whole series of critical comments from Czech authors at home and abroad, summarized in a critical but balanced assessment by a collective of Prague authors using the name "Bohemus."[9] This closed the second round of what one might call the Czech version of the *Vergangenheitsbewältigung* debate.[10]

Historian and journalist Johann Wolfgang Brügel, a prewar German Social Democrat from Czechoslovakia, entered the debate as one of the first "non-Czech" participants. He had a point to make: in spite of the good will of many Czechs to debate this taboo question openly, the second volume of his essential monograph on this subject, *Tschechen und Deutsche 1939-46*, published already in 1974, had not been reviewed four years later by a single Czech historian in exile. Brügel denounced the decision of the Czechoslovak government to expel three million German-speaking citizens as an "abdication of faith in political democracy capable of solving even the most complicated problems."[11] For years Brügel maintained the view that without the expulsion of the Germans after 1945 the Communist takeover in 1948 would not have been possible.

The third stage in this quest for a new formula in the Czech-German relationship opened in the first half of the 1980s in the context of the search for a common denominator among the Western European anti-nuclear pacifists and the Eastern European democratic movement. The Czech and Slovak dissidents came gradually to the conclusion that they should step out from the vicious circle of the German expulsion debate. In the Prague Appeal of March 1985 the Charter 77 signatories, for the first time within the European Peace Movement, demanded recognition of the Germans' right to self-determination as the fundamental prerequisite for the termination of the Cold War in Europe.[12] If Europe were to be united without nuclear weapons and military pacts, the unification of Germany would be the essential prerequisite for such a process. These ideas were clearly spelled out in the fundamental texts of the leading Czech dissidents, such as Václav Havel's "Anatomy of Reticence," or Jiří Dienstbier's "Pax Europeana," which were part of the remarkable Prague Appeal.[13]

What the Average Czech Thinks of the Germans

In 1985, a clandestine inquiry, the first of its kind, was conducted by human rights activists in "normalized" Czechoslovakia. It included a section on the "German Question." About 70 percent of the respondents refused to endorse the official propaganda stereotypes that classified the inhabitants of the Federal Republic of Germany as "bad Germans" and those in the German Democratic Republic as "good Germans." Of the sample, 66 percent rejected the official

Communist view that the Federal Republic was an aggressive power ready to attack Czechoslovakia. Only a mere two to five percent supported the official Communist Party line on the German Question. On the sensitive issue of the postwar expulsion of the Sudeten Germans, around 42 percent disagreed with the brutal methods used. The generation gap was conspicuous: 21.7 percent among the older generation still approved of the expulsion, whereas only 13.6 percent of the middle and 12 percent of the younger generations agreed.[14]

After the "Velvet Revolution" brought Václav Havel to power, a nation-wide poll of 1000 persons was conducted in the spring of 1990, which provided a more representative sample of Czech and Slovak public opinion: 65 percent of the Czechs and Slovaks were in favor of German unification. Only 15 percent perceived unified Germany as a threat. As to the disquieting question of guilt for the brutalities committed by the Czechs during the expulsion of Sudeten Germans, polling data was not available at the time of this writing. In an earlier poll, however, some 2000 fairly representative citizens voted on "the most unpopular measures" taken by President Havel. His apology for the expulsion of the Sudeten Germans together with the amnesty for criminals figured at the top of list.[15]

It is fair to estimate that more than half of the Czechoslovak population welcomed German reunification. Reservations were recorded among the generation of 57 years of age or older (32 percent against), as compared with the optimism of the youngest group (26 percent against). University graduates on the whole supported reunification (60 percent). There was a significant difference between Czech and Slovak polls. In the Slovak Republic, reunification was less popular. Slovak women were less in favor (47 percent) than men (57 percent). To the question, "who are our best friends," 39 percent of Slovaks named Austria, followed by 25 percent in favor of the United States; Germany ranked third with 5.2 percent.[16] The Public Opinion Institute of Prague compared two samples of responses to the question: "Does united Germany threaten the security of Czechoslovakia?" In January 1990, 44 percent answered yes, but only 27 percent did so in May 1991.[17] In a local survey conducted in the city and region of Ústí nad Labem during the summer of 1990, the opening of the borders with both Germanys and Austria was welcomed by 50 percent of the locals. About the same number said they would not mind living with Germans and Austrians, but over two-thirds resolutely rejected the idea of working under German superiors.[18]

The question of returning property to Sudeten Germans has become a hot issue since the autumn of 1990 when it was first discussed in the Federal Assembly. The Czech public was deeply divided on this issue. A pronounced majority of Czech citizens in the middle and older age brackets was resolutely opposed. When a Czech reporter asked a few Czechs at random in the renowned spa resort of Karlovy Vary (Karlsbad) what they thought about returning property to Sudeten Germans, only a few teenagers supported the proposition. Those who were old enough to remember Munich 1938 responded with anger.[19] In a poll conducted at the beginning of December 1990 by the Public Opinion Research Institute, 70 percent of the respondents declared themselves against the return of former Sudeten German property either in the form of restitution or compensation. Only four percent of the 743 respondents over the age of 15 favored return of the property, 11 percent supported financial compensation, while 15 percent was confused. Those living in the former Sudeten German districts were almost without exception against returning property.[20]

A Slovak View

Although there is no shortage of old-style interpretations, with hardly any recognizable change since the Communist era,[21] the German Question can today be seen rather differently from the increasingly popular angle of Slovak nationalism. According to this view, the German settlers in Slovakia, who were also expelled after 1945, are not seen in historical perspective as enemies any longer but rather as allies of the Slovaks against the real enemies of Slovak ethnic survival: the Hungarians. The expulsion of three million Sudeten Germans from Bohemia and Moravia, and of 150,000 Carpathian Germans from Slovakia, is blamed on Prague and Czech authorities. The other startling element in the new Slovak interpretation is the way in which the years 1939-1945, during which the first independent Slovak Republic existed, are interpreted today. Two salient facts are usually glossed over. First, that it was a German puppet state, created by Hitler, and second, that two-thirds of its Jewish citizens (over 60,000) did not survive the war because the Slovak authorities shipped them to extermination camps in German-occupied Poland.

One of the most elaborate views from the contemporary Slovak standpoint is that of the writer Miloš Mistrík, who sums up his interpretation in four points.[22] First, he argues that, in historical perspective, the German presence in Slovakia must be rated rather positively, especially in the cultural and economic spheres, because Slovakia remained sheltered from large-scale German colonization. Only relatively small German settlements were founded in the Spiš district and in several mining towns. Germans and Slovaks together opposed aggressive Magyarization. Very good contacts existed, for instance, between Slovak and German Protestants. It was through the vehicle of German language and culture, argues Mistrík, that Slovak intellectuals developed contacts with Western Europe.

Second, the main culprits responsible for spreading an anti-German mentality among the Slovaks after 1918, Mistrík further implies, were, of course, the Czechs, and after 1945 the Russians. The Czechs, however, carried a larger share of the blame because they had dragged the Slovaks into a new state after

1918 in which the Sudeten Germans were the main element of destabilization. Thus, anti-German propaganda was for the first time introduced in Slovakia by Czech authorities, while the Slovaks had little reason to be anti-German, especially since Hitler was not explicitly threatening Slovakia's national existence. Consequently, the expulsion of the Carpathian Germans from Slovakia was "cruel." Mistrík calls it a "serious mistake," but not a "crime" requiring moral apology. Slovak Germans never represented a threat, not even during World War II. There were too few of them, argues Mistrík. The genocidal threat came from the Magyars, not from the Germans.

Third, regarding the contemporary unification of Germany, Mistrík somewhat clumsily uses the analogy of the alliance between the Slovak Republic and Hitler's Greater German Reich. Such a forced analogy shows a serious handicap in present Slovak political thinking which is incapable of joining the mainstream of an integrating Europe of the 1990s. Mistrík admits Slovak guilt for the expulsion of Slovak Jews, but defends the Slovaks by arguing that they should not suffer disproportionately more criticism than other nations.

Fourth, Mistrík supports President Havel's "strong orientation on Germany," but is aware of the mounting opposition among the Czechs against the sell-out of the national patrimony to the Germans. He thinks that future Slovakia can confidently become a close German ally without fear of losing its national identity. It could even aspire to become Germany's bridgehead (*predpolie*) for further penetration of Central and Eastern Europe and the Balkans:

> German capital, German culture, even German policy played an important role in Slovakia in the past, and there is no reason to avoid it today. The German element (*Nemecký živel*) will, whether we want it or not, advance eastward. From our point of view it would be best to open the door to it. . . . If Slovakia wants to exist in the future, it must play the German card and must do it independently from all sentimental considerations vis-à-vis its closest western, northern, eastern or southern neighbors.[23]

The Three Levels in the Thousand-Year-Old Relationship

The complexity and uniqueness of the Czech-German relationship becomes obvious when the investigation is conducted along its *three levels* of contact. First, the Germans have been the Czechs' most important *external* neighbors with whom they still share their longest border. There is no harm in being reminded of these seemingly trivial geographic realities. Taking as a benchmark the 1938 Czechoslovak-German border, measuring 1200 kilometers, it was twice as long as the German-Polish border and even three times as long as the Franco-German border. After World War II Czechoslovakia became the only country bordering on two German states — and if one included Austria, it had common borders with three "German" states! In contrast to the constantly forward and backward moving Polish-German border, the geographic location of the Bohemian quadrangle turned out to be perhaps the most stable natural border in Central Europe. Since the permanent acquisition of the Cheb region (Egerland) in the 14th century, the German-Czech border (excluding the former hereditary lands of the Bohemian Crown, Lusatia and Silesia), has remained fundamentally unchanged despite numerous wars and violent political changes until the annexation of the Sudeten districts by the Third Reich following the Munich Conference of September 1938.[24]

Second, from time immemorial until 1945 the Germans and Czechs had also been close *internal* neighbors. Czech and German historians used to argue passionately over the question who had first settled permanently in the Bohemian quadrangle after the departure of the Celts, whether the *Urgermanen*, such as the Markomans, or the Slavs.[25] Since the 13th century, however, when German colonization began in earnest, the share of Germans in Bohemia increased from one quarter to one third and remained roughly at that level until their expulsion in 1945. The rapid rise of the Přemysliden dynasty to Central European supremacy, other factors being equal, derived from the successful German colonization connected with the foundation of cities, mining of silver, international trade, and improved agricultural technology.

Western influences were coming to Central Europe through the German filter. This physical closeness between the Czechs and Germans contributed to the emergence of earlier forms of ethnocentric consciousness.[26] The geographic location could not be changed. Nevertheless, the core lands of the Bohemian crown, Bohemia proper with Moravia, maintained their Czech majority throughout the ages, which was furthermore strengthened under the Hussites — the Czech equivalent of the German Reformation in the early 15th century. However, if we include the remaining hereditary lands of the St. Wenceslas Crown into the comprehensive linguistic survey, that is, Upper and Lower Lusatia (acquired by Electoral Saxony in 1635) and rich Silesia (lost to Prussia in 1742), where German colonization had spread much faster, then simple arithmetic will tell us that the majority of the inhabitants of the Czech Kingdom spoke German at least since the 14th century. During the 19th century, when the concept of linguistic nationalism seized the minds of politicians, Czech nationalists never seriously claimed back those Germanized former provinces of the Czech Crown.

Until the emergence of the Czechoslovak Republic in 1918, the Bohemian Germans did not regard themselves as a separate German tribe with a specific cultural or political individuality, which was, for instance, the case of the Bavarians and Saxons across the border. Prior to 1918 the Germans of Bohemia considered themselves to be part of a broader universal German community, along with their Austrian fellow-Germans. This was true until the demise of the Habsburg monarchy, when the last vestiges of supranational identity disappeared. Only thereafter did their cultural identity fall into conflict with the new geopolitical reality. In contrast to the Austrian Italians, the Czech Germans discovered political irredentism only in 1918, while a "cultural irredentism" had been present for at least a century. The latter can be easily documented by a long list of outstanding representatives of German culture born in the Czech lands during the 19th century: Franz Kafka, Rainer Maria Rilke, Adalbert Stifter, Berta von Suttner, Karl Kraus, Max Brod, Franz Werfl, Egon Erwin Kisch, Sigmund Freud, Gustav Mahler, Edmund Husserl, Karl Kautsky, and so on.

For the greatest Czech historian of the 19th century, František Palacký (1798-1876), the German factor remained the dominant one in his principal work, *Geschichte von Böhmen* (1836). He identified the Czech Question with the German Problem. In Palacký's interpretation, Czech history was nothing but a continuous struggle between Slavdom and Germandom, "a contest as well as an emulation, a rejection as well as an acceptance of German customs and laws by the Czechs . . . leading not only to victory or subjection but also to reconciliation . . . Even today history and geography pose the same task to the Czech nation: to serve as a bridge between Germandom and Slavdom, between the West and East in Europe in general."[27] Josef Pekař, perhaps the most original Czech historian of the early 20th century, considered the influence of Western Europe together with the cultural impact of the Germans as the two most important factors in Czech history.[28]

The "Czech Question," as conceived by Palacký, could, of course, be alternatively referred to from the Czech standpoint as the "German Question." The adjectives were interchangeable. At least ten centuries of mutual "contest and emulation" between the two peoples lay behind it, until it was terminated tragically in 1945 by the expulsion of the entire German-speaking population from Czechoslovakia. The year 1945 also marked the final victory and the simultaneous demise of the traditional doctrine of Czech nationalism based on the linguistic and cultural struggle between the two tribes. How could there be, in the dialectical sense (for Palacký was a Hegelian!), any "Czech Question" left after 1945, when the main antagonist of the Czechs, namely the Germans, had disappeared forever from the equation?[29] One dictatorship replaced the other, the German inhabitants of Bohemia and Moravia were forcibly moved across the border, but a thousand years' history with its complex Czech-German relationship could not be erased from memory forever. Even without a substantial German population in their midst (from around 3 million in 1945 there are just under 50,000 Germans still living in Bohemia and Moravia today), the Czechs remain, geographically and historically speaking, among Germany's closest neighbors.

As for the third dimension in the Czech-German relationship, it is difficult to find a neutral and exhaustive formula for it. In the present essay, I shall use the term *Universal Connection*. If it were confined to the sphere of literature and music, nothing would be simpler to define, for one could read one's own

Goethe or listen to one's own Beethoven on the island of Zanzibar, without feeling the need to elucidate the impact of "German universalism." It becomes much more complicated in the precarious environment of East Central Europe [*Ostmitteleuropa*], however. Moreover, the Bohemian State had been connected for a considerable time with the *Regnum Teutonicum* in a much more intimate way than any of Germany's other eastern neighbors. It became the most strategically important element in the chain of the eastern *Zwischeneuropa* ["intermediate Europe"].

Since the arrival of Christianity in the Czech lands in the 9th century, despite the brief aberration with the Byzantine rite, Bohemia became part, both geopolitically and culturally, of the Holy Roman Empire of the German Nation, the heir of the empires created by the Romans and by Charlemagne. It was through this link that Bohemia entered the *Orbis Europaeus Christianus*. The Duke of Bohemia, confirmed since 1212 as the hereditary King, became the most important of the four secular electors in the Empire. His unique position, reinforced by the Golden Bull of 1356 issued by Charles IV, enabled him to intervene in the affairs of the Reich without allowing much interference from the other side. The Bohemian kings of the Luxembourg and Habsburg dynasties received the imperial crown as the natural extension of their status and power and made Prague the Reich's capital for a while. From the legal point of view, the independent position of Bohemia vis-à-vis the Empire was not really comparable with any other German principality: no imperial Diets were ever convened on Bohemian territory, the bishops of Prague and Olomouc (Olmütz) were no *Reichsfürsten*, the Bohemian nobles could not be made into direct vassals of the Emperor, and so forth.[30]

Jan Patočka (1907-1977), the Czech philosopher (and co-founder of the human rights movement Charter 77), addressed the question of "great nations" in his essay "Who are the Czechs?"[31] In contrast to the Germans, who inherited greatness because of the adoption of the "Imperial Idea" (*Reichsidee*), and because of their numbers combined with the central geographical location in the midst of Europe, Patočka believes that the Czechs could have become a "great" nation if they had tried to turn themselves, from the 13th century onward, into the champions of this "Imperial Idea" on the eastern frontier.

After all, the Czech medieval realm had all the perfect prerequisites to become a great nation: a strong dynasty, a fortuitous location behind the natural frontiers of the Bohemian quadrangle, and a perfect national saint, St. Wenceslas, a princely ruler and martyr for the Christian cause in one person. The second prominent Czech saint was St. Adalbert (956-997), who, perhaps even more significantly than St. Wenceslas (murdered in 935), was to epitomize the new Czech mission in the East under the joint banner of the *Reichsidee* and of the *Sacrum Imperium*. Having baptized Hungary's future Stephen the Great (St. István) in 994, he was appointed as first archbishop of Polish Gniezno by his friend and promoter Emperor Otto III, and died a true martyr's death a few years later while trying to convert the heathen Prussians.[32]   The violent conversion of the Prussian and Lithuanian tribes was a joint work of Eastern Europe's Christian rulers and of the implanted Order of the Teutonic Knights.

One and a half century after Adalbert's martyrdom, the "Iron and Golden King" of Bohemia, Přemysl Otakar II, led two crusades against the Prussians. At that time the Mongol invasion through the open steppes of Eurasia had seriously threatened Christian Europe. It was not in remote Palestine, but on Europe's exposed Eastern frontier, as Bishop Bruno of Olmütz urged the Pope in his letter of 1273, that the *paries proximus nobis* of the *Sacrum Imperium* should be defended by the strong hand of the Bohemian King.[33]

The Czech State of the Přemysliden and Luxembourg dynasties, and for the same reasons the Polish and Hungarian monarchies of the time, could have aspired to fulfil the mission of defenders of Christendom on the Empire's most exposed frontier. Instead it was the Habsburg dynasty with its newly acquired domestic base in the "Eastern marches" of the Empire (*Öster-reich*), which emerged as the ultimate arbiter as well as the "Defender of the Faith" in the strategically important Czech-Polish-Hungarian triangle.

It is not possible within the narrow framework of this essay to cover the entire range of contrasting relationships between Bohemia and its German neighbors, implied by the universal *Reichsidee*. The Bohemian vote was still counted at the election of an emperor even after the kingdom lost its sovereignty, and it became therefore vital to the Catholic Habsburgs, the hereditary kings of Bohemia since 1526, to safeguard the Bohemian electorship against the three other secular electors who were Protestant.[34]   The creation of the German Confederation in 1815 followed the old boundaries of the German Empire and thus included, without much afterthought, Bohemia, Moravia, and Silesia. That something called Czech nationalism would emerge in Bohemia within the next generation did not occur to anyone.

Palacký and His Followers

In 1848 the Czech historian Palacký decided to break with the centuries-long attachment of Bohemia to the *Reichsidee*. He hoped that the Habsburg Empire would restructure itself into a federation separate from the existing German Confederation whose future was at the time passionately debated in Frankfurt. Palacký explained his reasons for not accepting the invitation from Frankfurt in his famous letter.[35]   In the first part of the letter Palacký made an eloquent plea on behalf of Czech nationalism, deliberately twisting the historical evidence of the continual political, dynastic, and ecclesiastical association of the Bohemian Kingdom with the German Empire for the sake of the nascent Czech national cause.   Since the major task of the German National Assembly, as Palacký understood it, would be to unify the German nation-state, he could not participate in such a scheme because he did not think of himself as German. While arguing from the standpoint of natural rights of all the Austrian subjects, Palacký deliberately overlooked in his passionate plea the fact that one-third of the Kingdom's population, namely those using German as their mother tongue, might not share his view and prefer to join Greater Germany instead.

The second point in Palacký's letter addressed the federation principle, which he defended against the image of an absolute monarchy, or a republic as personified by the French revolutionary experiment. If the negotiations in Frankfurt succeeded in creating a united Germany, Palacký went on, it would inevitably result in the collapse of Austria as an independent empire. He was against it, because the existence of Austria remained the best guarantee for the small nations of Central and Southeastern Europe. Furthermore, the Russian empire in the East would continue to expand its influence precisely into these parts of Europe. Consequently, the many small nations living in that area, the Slavic, Romanian, Hungarian, Greek, Turkish, and Albanian nations, would not be able to withstand this pressure unless they joined a larger Danubian federation. Palacký felt strongly that Austria, which "by nature and history is destined to be the bulwark and guardian of Europe against Asiatic elements of every kind," should continue to play this role of a protector against Russian expansionism:

> Certainly, if the Austrian state had not existed for some time, we would have to create it in the interest of Europe and humanity itself. . . . When I look behind the Bohemian frontiers, then natural and historical reasons make me turn not to Frankfurt but to Vienna to seek there the center which is fitted and destined to ensure and defend the peace, the liberty, and the right of my nation. Your efforts, gentlemen, seem to me now to be directed . . . toward utterly destroying that center from whose might and strength I expect the salvation not only of the Czech land.[36]

Finally, Palacký's third reason against Czech participation in Frankfurt was his fear that the success of German revolution would inevitably lead to the proclamation of a German republic. Such a form of government, Palacký was convinced, would create a multitude of "teeny" republics (*Republikchen*, as he contemptuously called them), that would present a delightful target for a "universal Russian monarchy." He was equally worried about a universal German monarchy brought about by Prussian militarism — as became true some twenty years later. "There is nothing more dangerous than to have in our neighborhood a united, militaristic German universal monarchy," Palacký argued in 1870. Two years later he declared the Prussians sworn enemies of the Czechs because of their "Germanic furor."[37]

Palacký's decision to reject the Greater German solution also meant an unequivocal breach in the tradition of bilingual Bohemian patriotism and a departure from the precepts of ethnically neutral "Bohemianism," which he clearly formulated in the first edition of his *Geschichte von Böhmen* (1836).

Here, Palacký described himself as a "Bohemian" who had conceived his *History of Bohemia* as a synthesis of three elements: the Slavic that had initially prevailed, the German that since the 10th century had steadily gained in importance, and the specific Bohemian element that was partly a mixture of the other two.[38]

Palacký's philosophy of Czech history is best preserved in his *Idea of the Austrian State* (1865), in which he recognized the geopolitically crucial role the Habsburg monarchy played in history, having defended Europe against the successive waves of Turkish invaders.[39] But what *raison d'être* could the Habsburg monarchy claim in 1848 to justify its continued existence? Palacký believed that the only possible option to safeguard the principle of multi-ethnic co-existence within the increasingly anachronistic political framework would be the transformation of the Habsburg Empire into a federated "Austrian Commonwealth of Nations," consisting of eight territorial units with equal legal rights, representing the major nationalities. For the first time a leading Czech politician was ready to give up the historical rights of the Bohemian Kingdom in exchange for a restructured Habsburg federation. Thus, Palacký conceded, at least in principle, the partition of the historic Czech lands into their German- and Czech-speaking units, with the Czech districts to be augmented by the entire Slovak region from what was then Hungary's "Upper Highlands" (*Feldvidék*). For the first time Czech politics was burdened with two fateful decisions that would in the future complicate the delineation and survival of an independent Czech State.

Meanwhile, Czech society underwent a remarkable transformation. The liberal Austrian Constitution of 1867 not only introduced Austro-Hungarian dualism, but replaced centralism and neo-absolutism by basic democratic rights. During the succeeding years a modern Czech society emerged with most of the necessary attributes in politics, economics, social life, self-governing communes and, above all, with a wide network of schools that raised the level of education by the end of the century to one of the highest in the world. Czech entrepreneurs began to compete successfully with their German counterparts. By 1900, nearly six million Czechs resided in the three provinces of Cisleithania (Bohemia, Moravia, Silesia), the Austrian half of the dual monarchy, as compared with over three million Germans. The Czech lands developed into the prime industrial area in the monarchy and ranked first in all the important categories of industrial progress, such as length of railway lines, production of iron, steel, black and brown coal, machinery equipment and tools, ceramics, glass, paper, textiles, electrical goods, and chemicals. Czech enterpreneurial talent and skill, combined with the resourcefulness of its peasantry, made possible a breakthrough in the food industry (for instance, breweries and sugar refining), which became almost completely Czech-dominated. By the turn of the century, the Czech lands with 36 percent of the Czech and German population employed 53 percent of all industrial workers. In Cisleithania, the Czechs ranked only second to the Germans in the number of self-employed persons and in per capita income. Based on these industries and on agriculture, the newly founded Czech banks, with the *Živnobanka* at the center of the Czech financial web, provided the necessary economic independence from Viennese and German capital. By 1914 the Czech banking network controlled almost 24 percent of all corporate banking stock in Cisleithania. By 1913 the capital investments in Czech banks reached 226 million Austrian Crowns as compared with 138 million in German banks located in the Czech lands.[40]

All these achievements in industry and finance, along with the cultural and educational advancement, stimulated Czech aspirations for larger political autonomy within federated Austria. The Czechs became a modern nation lacking but one essential attribute: their own state.[41] These 60-odd years from the mid-19th century until the break-up of the Habsburg monarchy following the defeat in World War I were the most important formative years for the social, economic, and political development of the Czechs into a modern nation.[42] "What a remarkable transformation our nation underwent between 1848 and 1916!," commented the Czech historian, Josef Pekař, at his funeral oration for the deceased Emperor Francis Joseph.[43] Less than two years later this legacy would be seriously challenged by the break-up of the Habsburg monarchy and the victory of Pekař's political and intellectual opponent, Thomas Garrigue Masaryk (1850-1937), the founder and first president of the new state, the Czechoslovak Republic. However, the negative implications of this remarkable revival of the Czech nation, driven by the vehicle of linguistic nationalism, must not be overlooked. It meant further segregation between the Czech and German communities in Bohemia. All common institutions, schools, and political parties were divided into Czech and German counterparts. When even the Social-Democratic trade unions split, there seemed to be no hope of reconciling the two linguistic groups.

Palacký's letter to Frankfurt and *The Idea of the Austrian State* remained key documents for Czech political aspirations until the outbreak of World War I, despite the serious setback caused by the German-Hungarian compromise of 1867 and all subsequent political disappointments the Czech politicians suffered in Vienna. Meanwhile, the Germans of Bohemia were losing their faith in the future of their separate identity as Austrian Germans and began to drift toward the militant ideology of Pan-germanism. Professor Masaryk, who entered Czech politics in the 1880s, defined the Czech Question primarily on moral grounds as a religious question, as a matter of ethics rather than ethnicity. He passionately believed that the Czech national genius was determined by the Hussite Reformation when it struck Bohemia in the 15th century.[44] Palacký's interpretation of the Czech Question as a continual struggle against Germandom was refuted by Masaryk, who instead emphasized the humanist contents behind the national idea. "The nation is not detached from humanity, it is part of humanity to which we all belong," Masaryk wrote.[45] Political independence should not be the ultimate aim, but merely the means to achieve higher ambitions in the sphere of moral improvement. He argued that the Czech political program must be founded on a strong cultural component that would bring the Czech nation, despite its small population, into the intellectual mainstream of the modern world.

It was only after he went into exile in late 1914 to work against Austria for the independence of Bohemia, that Masaryk was forced by circumstances to modify his humanitarian interpretation of the Czech Question and return to the notion of a narrow Czech-German rivalry revolving around a territorial nationalism in which, ironically for someone who was himself of German background, the language difference became the major characteristic. That he would also accuse the Bohemian Germans of Pan-germanism, and then asked them in turn to live with the Czechs as second-rate citizens in the new state, was inevitable. The Bohemian Germans, because they happened to belong to the defeated ethnic group, were found guilty of war crimes by the victorious Allies and forbidden to apply the right of self-determination just as the Slavs were encouraged to take advantage of it.

The fundamental flaw in Masaryk's vision of postwar Central Europe and the future Czech-German coexistence can be found in his programmatic booklet *The New Europe*,[46] written to challenge the rival German model of *Mitteleuropa* (1915) by Friedrich Naumann. Masaryk recommended that the space emptied by the collapse of four empires be filled by creating a large buffer zone of new anti-German and anti-Bolshevik states sandwiched between the former German and Russian empires (later known as the *cordon sanitaire*).[47]

It was the principle of democracy that defeated the "theocracy" embodied in the German, Austro-Hungarian, and Turkish empires, Masaryk maintained. He proposed a radical reorganization of East Central Europe in the direction that Palacký had detested and contemptuously referred to as "dwarf republics" (*Republikchen*). Masaryk's nation-state apotheosis was, of course, meant for the fortunate nation-states that happened to win the war — not the defeated ones like Germany, Hungary, Bulgaria, and Turkey, who were forced to accept the new Carthaginian peace conditions. Since it was the dreaded *Drang nach Osten*, inspired by Pan-germanism, that was the incarnation of all evils, there was no way the Germans could be readmitted into the world community without paying a heavy penalty, for at least a generation to come. This manichean world was to be sanctified by the new international supervisory body, the League of Nations, but in reality controlled by the victorious Entente powers and their allies, acting like "angels of light" against the vanquished "children of the devil."[48] Was national independence for the small nations in Central Europe, on the ruins of Pan-german supremacy, the ultimate goal of Masaryk's thinking? In *New Europe*, he wishfully suggested the creation of a genuine federation of "free and liberated nations [that] will organize themselves, as they find necessary, into greater units."[49] But how realistic was an East Central

European confederation without Germany, Austria, Hungary, Bulgaria, and so on?

Consider now the precarious position of the Germans living in the new Republic of Czechoslovakia. As former Austrian subjects, they shared the humiliation of the Versailles and St. Germain Peace Treaties with their fellow Germans across the border. Czechoslovakia granted them equal rights as citizens and drafted them into the military to shed blood for a country that many of them regarded as artificial. The "Czechoslovak" language (linguistic nonsense because it was two languages, not one) was declared the state language. Although the Germans were the second largest ethnic group in the country with over 3 million citizens (22.5 percent overall, while in Bohemia and Moravia their combined share was 30 percent), they had to relinquish their rights of secundogeniture to the Slovaks. Other important minorities were the Hungarians (5 percent) and Ruthenes (4 percent). The Jewish minority in Czechoslovakia was numerically weak and divided into several social and ethnic groups, with the German-speaking segment culturally most prominent. The bulk of Czechoslovakia's minorities could not identify with the new state and strove, like the Slovaks, for greater autonomy or followed, like the Germans, the clarion call of irredentism from across the border. The Czechs now replaced the Germans as the ruling ethnic group. Because the Czechs numbered just over 6.5 million, about 50 percent of the entire population, the Slovaks (15.6 percent), who had never belonged to the Bohemian state, were eagerly co-opted in order to give Prague a comfortable "Czechoslovak" majority.

Solving the German Problem in the new republic was clearly a question of survival. In his first public address after his return from exile in 1918, Masaryk the President-Liberator described the Bohemian Germans as second-rate citizens, who originally came to the country as "immigrants and colonists."[50] This harsh treatment sounded astonishing from someone who was of German origin himself.[51] Although Masaryk tried immediately to rectify the negative impact of his comments by delivering a speech in German the following day at the German Theater in Prague, reassuring his German fellow-citizens that they would enjoy equal rights with the Czechs, the damage was already done. In his 1920 New Year's address, Masaryk called the Czech-German Question the single most important issue for Czechoslovakia.[52] He tried hard to convince the leading Czech Germans to enter the government, but did not succeed until 1926. After the German Christian and Agrarian Parties joined the Prague government, the German Social Democrats entered the coalition in 1929. Thus, shortly before the world depression hit Central Europe and propelled Hitler's party to the fore, most of the Sudeten Germans in Czechoslovakia abandoned their earlier hostile attitude toward the new state. Only about one-quarter of the German voters continued to support the German National Party (DNP) and the German National Socialist Workers' Party (DNSAP).[53] When the sister Nazi party under Hitler (NSDAP) came to power in Germany in 1933, the Prague government decided to ban the two extremist German parties. This did not prevent Konrad Henlein from forming a new party, the *Sudetendeutsche Heimatfront*, which in 1935 changed its name to *Sudetendeutsche Partei*, and became the main vehicle for German irredentism in Czechoslovakia with the full moral and financial support of Nazi Germany. Consequently, attitudes on both sides of the German-Czech political schism hardened, resulting in a cultural "apartheid" between these two peoples who had worked and lived together, but now preferred to ignore each other.

If the prominent ideologues of Czech nationalism such as Palacký and Masaryk ended up by interpreting the Czech-German relationship as a permanent struggle, was there no voice of reason that could prevent the inevitable clash? Such a voice did sound briefly. In 1928 the solitary Czech author Emanuel Rádl published *The Struggle between Czechs and Germans*.[54] Rádl refused to participate in the degeneration of the Czech-German relationship into what he aptly called "tribal warfare." A philosopher-moralist like President Masaryk, but with roots in the natural sciences rather than in sociology, Rádl was the ultimate intellectual Don Quixote in Czech politics. Was there no other way, Rádl asked in exasperation, than the path of tribal war that would end in the mutual destruction of two peoples? He criticized the official state doctrine that fused the Czechs and Slovaks into one artificial "Czechoslovak" state-nation (*Staatsnation*) and excluded Germans and Hungarians. Why, Rádl kept asking, could there not be a "Czechoslovak" nation with three state languages following the Swiss model?[55]

Alas, Rádl's premonitions proved right. Five years after the publication of his book, an Austrian political adventurer named Adolf Hitler assumed power in Germany. Within a few years, the Nazi movement irresistibly attracted the Germans outside the Reich, especially those in Austria and Czechoslovakia. If the Czechs wanted to keep the Germans inside their new state against their will, they would have to fight a war that Hitler keenly wanted, but the other European powers did not. Under the Munich *Diktat* of September 1938, the Czechs were compelled to surrender the Sudeten German areas along the centuries-old border to Hitler's Germany. Six months later rump-Czechoslovakia was invaded by Hitler and annexed as "Protectorate of Bohemia and Moravia" to the "Greater German Empire," which was to last a thousand years. The phantom of the *Reichsidee* in its worst metamorphosis became a reality. It was degraded *ad nauseam* through the propaganda machinery of Joseph Goebbels and his press organ *Das Reich*. The wartime atmosphere exacerbated the antagonism between the Czechs and Germans to the point of pathological hatred, especially after the assassination of Reinhard Heydrich in Prague and the subsequent destruction of the Czech village Lidice in June 1942 by the Nazis. Had Hitler won the war, plans existed to deport half of the Czech population eastward to Siberia and to Germanize the rest.[56]

In 1945 the Czechs retaliated with the expulsion of the entire German population from Czechoslovakia. This was first urged by the Czech underground from as early as 1939, and after 1942 it was supported by the exile government of President Beneš, and gradually won the backing of all political parties including the Communists — with the exception, obviously, of the German Social Democrats. With the approval of the Allied Powers, these plans were put into effect when the war ended. The consequences of the state doctrine based on linguistic nationalism were most terrible. The two protagonists, the Germans and the Czechs, concluded respectively that they must get rid of each other, shredding the fine texture of at least seven centuries of coexistence in Bohemia. Almost three million Sudeten Germans were expelled under harsh conditions, and only about 200,000 were allowed to stay behind, mostly miners and experts needed to keep the economy going. German statistics claim that about 225,000 Sudeten Germans died during the forced transfer.[57] Approximately the same number of Czech victims (including Jews) also died during the entire Nazi occupation.

Recalling Palacký's dictum of Czech history as a continual struggle, this was its final act and consummation. What new meaning could Czech history have after this tragedy, if the main antagonist of the Czech nation ceased to exist? Although Masaryk was adored during his lifetime as the founder of the Czechoslovak Republic, its President-Liberator, and as the king-philosopher, today his model nation-state is often seen skeptically as a failure.[58]

All political parties in Czechoslovakia accepted the inevitability of German expulsion. Given the division between two worlds in the middle of Europe, exemplified by the partition of Germany and Austria (the latter until 1955), Czechoslovakia became after 1949 the only country in Europe bordering on three — if we include Austria — successor states of Hitler's short-lived Greater (Third) German Reich. The partition of Germany was welcomed by all Czech political parties without exception, since they all believed that it was the necessary prerequisite for their country's security. While the German Democratic Republic turned overnight into the "first workers' and peasants' state in German history," the Federal Republic of Germany was regarded in official Communist propaganda as no better than Nazi Germany. Diplomatic relations between Prague and East Berlin opened in June 1950 with a joint declaration stating that there were no border or population problems between the two equal partners. The so-called Hallstein Doctrine, put into effect by the West German government in 1955, prevented Prague from opening diplomatic relations with Bonn during the 1950s and 1960s, although the opposition West German Social Democratic Party pressed for negotiations throughout the entire period. The Prague government was also the absolutely last one among the Warsaw Pact countries to react to the new West German *Ostpolitik*. Diplomatic relations between Bonn and Prague finally opened in December 1973. During the "Prague Spring," conditions were almost ripe for such an act, had it not been thwarted by the Soviet-led Warsaw Pact invasion of August 21, 1968, in which GDR troops participated as well.[59]

The Future of the Czech-German Relationship

One of the leading Sudeten German authors, Rudolf Hilf, has called the brutal dissolution of the historic Czech-German community in Bohemia "the example of total failure in the coexistence of two peoples."[60] One of the possible ways of rebuilding the Czech-German relationship and giving Václav Havel's message of reconciliation a chance is to try to disconnect the notion of the German state as a great power from that of the German nation as an ethnic and cultural entity. Whether this is more than a mere intellectual exercise remains to be seen, but it should be attempted, as Lev Kopelev does so eloquently in the case of German-Russian relations.[61]

When President Havel transmitted his good wishes to the united democratic Germany in early October 1990, the amicable atmosphere was marred by the intervention of the Sudeten German Association (*Landsmannschaft*), which requested to be directly involved in bilateral discussions between the German and Czechoslovak governments on the issue of restitution of pre-1945 Sudeten German property.[62] Obviously, the apology repeatedly offered by Václav Havel was not satisfactory. Moreover, the new Czechoslovak legislation concerning re-privatization and restitution of private property as far as back as 1948 must have encouraged the Sudeten German organizations to press their claims.

The traditional position of the Prague government on the Munich Agreement did not help very much in clarifying the issue. Since 1945 the Czech official mind had been confronted with a dilemma, between its desire to punish the culprits on the one hand, and the legal consequences of Munich on the other hand. In order to carry out with exemplary severity the collective punishment of the Sudeten Germans for their betrayal of Czechoslovak statehood to Hitler in 1938, the Czechoslovak authorities confiscated their property and expelled them from the country. Presidential Decree No. 33 of August 2, 1945 declared every German (with the rare exception of a few hardened anti-Nazis) and Hungarian, including even the yet unborn descendants, to be *persona non grata*, deprived of any rights of Czechoslovak citizenship and protection under international law. Therefore, whenever the question of restitution of former property to ex-Czechoslovak citizens of German ethnicity was raised, the Prague authorities reacted with indignation, applying the collective guilt principle that traitors could not enjoy the rights of Czechoslovak citizens. This property and the Sudeten German districts incorporated in the Third Reich after September 29, 1938 with the consent of three European powers (Great Britain, France, and Italy), and the subsequent legal approval (under duress) by the Czechoslovak authorities, could no longer be regarded as valid after the collapse of Hitler's Germany in 1945.[63] President Beneš's device to overcome the obvious legal discrepancies was the so-called "Continuity Theory," that is, the notion that the Czechoslovak Republic, founded in 1918, never ceased to exist in its entirety regardless of the changes brought about by German conquest and occupation (and similarily by the Soviet annexation of the easternmost region of pre-Munich Czechoslovakia, the Trans-Carpathian Ukraine, one might add). Hence Prague's insistence that the Munich Agreement should be declared null and void.

This was also the legal position of the Czechoslovak Communist leadership in dealing with the two German states after 1949. It was not a problem in the relationship between East Berlin and Prague. With regard to Bonn the situation was obviously more complicated because of the strong political influence exerted in West Germany during the 1950s by the *Landsmannschaften*. Gradually, however, their influence began to dwindle, and successive West German governments were able to repudiate the Munich Agreement in 1966, 1968, and again in the last of the "Eastern Treaties" that the Brandt government signed with its eastern neighbor in December 1973 as part of the new *Ostpolitik*. Although the other three parties to the Munich Agreement repudiated their signatures, this matter of citizenship and property would remain until a final peace treaty with Germany could be formally concluded.[64] However, such a treaty will probably never be signed.

The Czechoslovak Federal Government has so far refused any Sudeten German claims for restitution of specific property, stating that the four Allied Powers settled the question at the Potsdam and Paris Peace Conferences in 1945. It has also refused to negotiate about compensation directly with any of the Sudeten German associations, considering them private organizations. Taken at face value, the Czech and Sudeten German claims regarding damages due to forced deportation and war destruction probably amount to roughly similar astronomic figures (360 billion versus 300 billion prewar Czechoslovak crowns), which, for all intents and purposes, cancel out each other.[65] It is obvious that this sensitive matter is far from being resolved, but it does not need to become a major bone of contention in Czechoslovakia's future relations with the united Germany. During his visit to Prague in November 1990, German Foreign Minister Hans-Dietrich Genscher expressed hope that the future bilateral treaty between the two countries, which is to update the "Normalization Treaty" of 1973, would take into account the radically changed political situation and settle most of the outstanding issues, including the property claims of the Sudeten Germans.[66] In April 1991, however, during his follow-up visit to Prague, Genscher deliberately omitted the alleged claims of the Sudeten German *Landsmannschaft* from his statement. Both sides agreed that the final text of the new bilateral Czechoslovak-German treaty must not touch property questions predating February 1948.[67] Predictably the Sudeten Germans reacted with anger. Their spokesmen did not wish to be excluded from the negotiations.[68]

Prague is actually much more concerned about the estimated loss of 1.8 billion DM in broken trade contracts with the former German Democratic Republic. The joint communiqué stressed the necessity of building stable institutions of a future united Europe, which should also include the former Soviet Union. Since February 21, 1991, when Czechoslovakia became the 25th member of the Council of Europe in Strasbourg, the emphasis on joining the "chosen twelve" of the European Community has been one of the principal aims of Czechoslovak foreign policy. Within this strategy Prague considers Germany's sponsorship as the most important asset. Recently, German private investors cemented this sponsorship with the biggest single deal concluded so far in Eastern Europe: at the beginning of 1991, the largest German car manufacturer, Volkswagen, announced that it would invest $6.45 billion over several years in its Czech counterpart, the Škoda car plant. This was followed by the announcement by Daimler-Benz that it was taking over the two Czechoslovak truck makers, LIAZ and AVIA. German investment in Czechoslovakia had become so extensive by the end of 1991 (around 80 percent of foreign dollar investment), that the Czech Premier Petr Pithart asked distrustfully at a press conference: "What is German capital? Does it have the same geopolitical context as in the 1930s?"[69]

Finally, on October 7, 1991, the long-awaited treaty of "good neighborliness and friendly cooperation," for the duration of ten years, was signed in Prague by Genscher and Dienstbier, and in the presence of President von Weizsäcker himself. With regard to the future, the treaty underlines the aspiration of the Czech and Slovak Federation to join the European Community. With regard to the past, the treaty is a not altogether happy compromise between Prague and Bonn. While both parties agreed to drop the demands for compensation for destroyed or confiscated wartime property, Bonn succeeded in prevailing upon Prague to allow German citizens to settle in Czechoslovakia in the future, "gradually as the process of European integration will make its progress." The difficulty over the wording of references to Czechoslovakia's legal status between 1938 and 1945 was apparently overcome through the statement in the preamble which "recognized the fact that the Czechoslovak State never ceased to exist since 1918 . . ."[70] As anticipated, the Slovak government, without actually preventing the signing of the treaty, was infuriated by the preamble's reference to the Czech theory of "legal continuity" because such a statement is in open conflict with the Fascist Slovak Republic of 1939-1945, which has now become cherished by Slovak nationalists as the first Slovak State in history.[71]

It was the "German Problem" and the perversion of the *Reichsidee* in 1938-39 that led to the multiple break-up of pre-Munich Czechoslovakia and that became the major catalyst for the split between the Czechs and Slovaks. Fifty years later one is inclined to attribute to Germany a more positive geopolitical function in Eastern Europe. A great deal of political responsibility and maturity, however, will be demanded from Prague and Bratislava. Bonn has so far done more than others. It is an irony of history, but it seems as if the next chapter in Czech-German relations will be shaped in Bratislava rather than in Bonn or Prague — and there is very little we can do about it.

A hundred years ago some Czech intellectuals, like Hubert Gordon Schauer,[72] feared German expansionism, both political and cultural, and were therefore alarmed by the prospects of forced Germanization. Eduard Beneš certainly feared German expansionism, which compelled him into exile during both world wars. Václav Havel does not seem to be much bothered by such anxieties:

> To me, my Czechness is a given fact . . . If I lived during the national revival in the nineteenth century, my Czechness might still have been a matter of personal choice, and I might have tormented myself with the question of whether it was worth the effort. The problem whether we should develop the nation or simply give up on it is not something that I have to solve. These matters have already been decided by others.[73]

With Berlin, the old *Reichshauptstadt*, now restored as the capital of reunited Germany, the center of gravity of German political activities will move eastward in a few years to supervise the unique work of economic reconstruction in the former GDR and beyond. "The geographical situation cannot be changed," Egon Bahr, a leading foreign policy expert for Germany's opposition Social Democratic Party, aptly remarked recently. "Germany's role is as an interpreter of interests and problems in countries east of Germany. Our economic role is quite remarkable and this carries a certain responsibility in this region . . ."[74] The end of the Cold War may also unfasten the oldest political concept on the European continent. In the search for their new identity, the Germans of the 21st century will become more assertive and may give the *Reichsidee* a new meaning, which the Czechs will observe with mixed feelings and apprehension.

Notes

1. In this article I deal almost exclusively with the Czech-German, not "Czechoslovak"-German, relationship. Although it is correct to use the adjective "Czechoslovak" for inter-state activities following the foundation of the Czechoslovak Republic in 1918, it cannot be done so for the last 1000 years during which the Czechs and Slovaks developed largely in separate historical and cultural entities. Although a number of compact German settlements had existed in Slovakia from the Middle Ages until 1945 (for example the Spiš region, and several mining and trading towns founded by German colonists), it was the Magyar-Slovak relationship that formed a certain analogy to the German-Czech one.

2. The speeches of Václav Havel and Richard von Weizsäcker in the Prague daily, *Svobodné Slovo*, March 16, 1991. Even in the age of highly sophisticated public opinion polls, the "German Question" remains difficult to quantify. "Geography and history were

responsible," German historian Michael Stürmer argued before Germany's unification. "The German Question never belonged to the Germans alone . . ." See Michael Stürmer, "Kein Eigentum der Deutschen: die deutsche Frage," in Werner Weidenfeld, ed., *Die Identität der Deutschen* (Munich: Carl Hauser, 1983), p. 99.

3. Reported, among others, in *The New York Times*, January 3, 1990.

4. Václav Havel's letter to Richard von Weizsäcker, November 5, 1989. Text obtained at the Czechoslovak Documentary Center, Scheinfeld. Cited with permission of the Director, Dr. Vilém Prečan. President von Weizsäcker quoted a portion of the above passage in his Christmas address (see *Süddeutsche Zeitung*, December 23-26, 1990).

5. *Svobodné Slovo*, January 5, 1990. See also Craig R. Whitney, "Glee for Communists: Havel suffers a Miscue," *The New York Times*, January 6, 1990.

6. *Host do domu* (Brno), 5 (1968).

7. See the articles by B. Černý, M. Hauner, T. Pasák and J. Tesař in *Dějiny a Současnost* (Prague), nos. 5, 6 (1968) and 1, 3, 5, 8 (1969).

8. *Svědectví* ([Témoignage], Paris), 57 (1978), pp. 105-22.

9. *Bohemus*, "Slovo k odsunu" ["A Word About the Transfer"], *Právo Lidu* (Zürich), nos. 1-3, 1980. See also Ernst Nittner, "Die Ausweisung der Sudetendeutschen vor vierzig Jahren als tschechisches Problem," *Bohemia*, No. 26 (Munich, 1985), pp. 9-21. Most of these texts, including correspondence, are now available in a separate volume, *Češi-Němci-odsun (Czechs-Germans-Transfer): A Discussion between Independent Historians*, edited by B. Černý et al. (Prague: Academia, 1990).

10. The term *Vergangenheitsbewältigung* usually refers to the postwar German attempt to "come to terms with the past," specifically the legacy of the Third Reich.

11. J. W. Brügel in *Svědectví*, 57 (1978), pp. 103-04.

12. See Milan Hauner, "Anti-militarism and the Independent Peace Movement in Czechoslovakia," in Vladimir Tismaneanu, ed., *In Search of Civil Society: Independent Peace Movements in the Soviet Bloc* (London: Routledge, 1990), pp. 88-117.

13. For the English version of Václav Havel's essay, see *Cross Currents*, vol. 5, 1986. Jiří Dienstbier, "Pax Europeana," *Listy*, vol. XIV, no. 6 (Rome, December 1984), pp. 15-20. Expanded into *Snění o Evropě* [Dreaming about Europe], samizdat typescript 1986, reprinted by the publishing house Lidové Noviny, Prague, 1990.

14. See *Svědectví*, 78 (1986), pp. 258-334, here pp. 300-03. It took almost a full year to carry out this highly unusual independent public opinion survey, consisting of 85 questions among 342 Czechoslovak citizens, selected mostly from among the urbanized and best educated individuals. Forty-three percent had university education whereas the national average is a mere 6 percent. The questionnaires were sent under difficult circumstances to France where they were evaluated with the aid of computers by CRITS (Centre de Recherche Interdisciplinaire des Transformations Sociales), under Dr. Zdeněk Strmiska, who until the Soviet invasion of 1968 was the director of the Institute of Sociology in Prague.

15. Personal communication to the author on November 5, 1990 by Dr. Illner of the Institute of Sociology in Prague.

16. Letter to the author by Dr. Jan Hartl, November 12, 1990; data samples from the Institute of Sociology in Prague.

17. According to *Respekt* (Prague), July 22-28, 1991, pp. 7-8.

18. Conversation with Professor F. Zich from the Socio-Economic Institute, Ustí nad Labem, in *Rudé Právo*, December 10, 1990.

19. *Mladý svět* [Young World] (Prague), November 26, 1990, p. 3.

20. *FBIS: Eastern Europe*, January 8, 1991, p. 18.

21. See, for example, Dušan Kováč, *Německo a německá menšina na Slovensku (1871-1945)* (Bratislava: SAV, 1991).

22. Miloš Mistrík, "Nemecká karta," in *Literárny týždenník* (Bratislava), October 12, 1990.

23. Mistrík, "Nemecká karta."

24. An earlier precedent occurred at the end of 1918, following the acceptance of the armistice by Austria-Hungary, when four majority German-speaking regions carved themselves out of Bohemia and Moravia (*Deutschböhmen, Sudetenland, Böhmerwaldgau* and *Deutschsüdmähren*), in the hope that they could merge with Germany and Austria. Nothing came of it since the Allies would neither tolerate self-determination on the part of any defeated nation, nor approve of German-Austrian unification through the Bohemian bond.

25. See, for instance, the polemics between the Czech historian Josef Pekař and the Moravian archivist Bertold Bretholz, concerning the latter's *Geschichte Böhmens und Mährens* (Reichenberg: Sollors Nachfolger, 1921-24). The first historical record of the settlements of Germanic "Marcomanni" and "Quadi" in Bohemia and Moravia was of course *Germania* by Tacitus, written at the end of the first century AD.

26. F. Graus, "Bildung eines Nationalbewußtseins im mittelalterlichen Böhmen," *Historica* (Prague: Academia, 1966), vol. XIII, pp. 22-24; F. Šmahel, *Idea národa v husitských Čechách* (České Budějovice: Růže, 1971), pp. 184-85; F. Šmahel, "The Idea of the 'Nation' in Hussite Bohemia," *Historica* (Prague: Academia, 1969), vol. XVI, pp. 143-247, and vol. XVII, pp. 93-197.

27. F. Palacký, *Dějiny národu českého w Čechách i w Morawě*, vol. I (Prague: Kalve & Tempsky, 1848), pp. 12-13.

28. J. Pekař, *Smysl českých dějin* (Prague: Památník Národního Osvobození, 1928). See also Milan Hauner, "Josef Pekař: Interpreter of Czech History," *Czechoslovak and Central European Journal*, vol. 10, no. 1 (Summer 1991), pp. 13-35.

29. See Milan Hauner, "Values and Evaluation in Czech Historiography," *Promeny* [Metamorphosis], (Montreal), vol. 14/2 (1977), pp. 72-80, and "Recasting Czech History," *Survey*, Summer 1979, pp. 214-25.

30. Ferdinand Seibt, "Zwischen Ost und West: Versuch einer Ortsbestimmung," in Ferdinand Seibt, ed., *Die böhmischen Länder zwischen Ost und West. Festschrift für Karl Bosl* (Munich: Oldenbourg Verlag, 1983), pp. 10-12.

31. J. Patočka, "Co jsou Češi?" [Who Are the Czechs?], *150,000 Slov*, vol. 4, no. 12 (Paris, 1985), pp. 1-32.

32. H. G. Voigt, *Adalbert von Prag* (Berlin: W. Faber, 1898); R. Holinka, *Svatý Vojtěch* (Brno: Brněnské tiskárny, 1947); R. Nový, "Svatý Vojtěch — První Evropan" [St.Adalbert — the first European], in *Dějiny a současnost* (Prague), 4 (1991), pp. 10-15.

33. Josef Šusta, *Poslední Přemyslovci a jejich dědictví* (Prague: Česká akademie císaře Františka Josefa pro vědy, slovesnost a umění, 1917), p. 286.

34. Hajo Holborn, *A History of Modern Germany, 1648-1840*, vol. 2 (New York: A. Knopf, 1964), p. 8.

35. Palacký's famous letter to Frankfurt of April 11, 1848. For the English translation, see Hans Kohn, *Pan-Slavism* (New York: Vintage Books, 1953), pp. 75-80.

36. Kohn, *Pan-Slavism*, pp. 75-80.

37. See Ivan Pfaff, "Tschechoslowakei," in Walther Hofer, ed., *Europa und die Einheit Deutschlands* (Cologne: Verlag Wissenschaft und Politik, 1970), pp. 206-08.

38. See Franz Palacký, *Geschichte von Böhmen* (Prague: Kronberger & Weber, 1836), vol. 1, pp. vi and ix.

39. František Palacký's *Idea státu rakouského* consisted of a series of eight articles published in the daily *Národ* during April and May of 1865. A German translation appeared the following year as *Österreichs Staatsidee*. See also the excellent analysis by Jan Křen, "Palackýs Mitteleuropavorstellungen, 1848-1849," in V. Prečan, ed., *Acta Creationis: Independent Historiography in Czechoslovakia, 1969-1980* (Hannover: Prečan's own copyright, 1980), pp. 119-146.

40. Compiled from: *Die Habsburgermonarchie 1848-1918*, vol. 1, *Die wirtschaftliche Entwicklung* (Vienna: Verlag der österreichischen Akademie der Wissenschaften, 1973); Otto Urban, *Kapitalismus a česká společnost* (Prague: Svoboda, 1978), pp. 53-186; Bruce M. Garver, *The Young Czech Party 1874-1901 and the Emergence of a Multi-Party System* (New Haven: Yale University Press, 1978), pp. 15-28.

41. See Jiří Kořalka, "Národ bez státu," in F. Graus, ed., *Naše živá i mrtvá minulost* (Prague: Svoboda, 1968), pp. 136-57.

42. See Otto Urban, *Česká společnost 1848-1918* (Prague: Svoboda, 1982).

43. According to Willy Lorenz, *Monolog über Böhmen* (Vienna: Herold, 1964), pp. 63-70.

44. T. G. Masaryk, *Česká otázka* (Prague: Čin, 1895), p. 176; T. G. Masaryk, *Palackého idea národa českého* (Prague: Čin, 1926). See also Otto Urban, "Masarykovo pojetí české otázky," *Československý časopis historický* (Prague), vol. 4 (1969), pp. 527-52.

45. T. G. Masaryk, "Humanita a národnost," *Naše doba* (Prague), no. 3 (1897).

46. T. G. Masaryk, *Nová Evropa: Stanovisko slovanské* (Prague: G. Dubský, 1920). See also George J. Kovtun, "Masaryk's *New Europe*: the History and the Purpose of the Book," *Czechoslovak and Central European Journal*, Vol. 8, nos. 1 and 2 (Summer/Winter 1989), pp. 81-89.

47. Masaryk was not alone in proposing such a scheme. The remarkable British geographer Sir Halford Mackinder, in order to improve the stability of Eastern Europe, also proposed the creation of a "tier of independent States between Germany and Russia." See Mackinder, *Democratic Ideals and Reality* (London: Constable, 1919), p. 205.

48. This was the description of John Maynard Keynes, who resigned his position as economic advisor to the British government and left the Paris Peace Conference in disgust in June 1919. See his *Economic Consequences of the Peace*, [1919] (New York: Penguin, 1988), p. 267.

49. T. G. Masaryk, *The New Europe: the Slav Standpoint* (Lewisburg: Bucknell University Press, 1972), p. 77.

50. Josef Dubský, "Masaryk a Němci" [Masaryk's Concept of Germandom in His Struggle for the Creation of an Independent State and His Relationship to the Germans after 1918], in *T.G. Masaryk a naše současnost*, vol. 2 (Prague: samizdat, 1980), pp. 217-18.

51. See Lorenz, *Monolog über Böhmen*, pp. 112-20.

52. Dubský, "Masaryk a Němci," p. 220.

53. The DNSAP traced its origins to the German Workers' Party founded in 1904 in Trautenau, in northern Bohemia, and must thus be regarded as the oldest "Nazi" party. See J. W. Brügel, *Tschechen und Deutsche: 1918-1938* (Munich: Nymphenburg Verlag, 1974), pp. 64-65; Ronald M. Smelser, *The Sudeten Problem 1933-1938* (Middletown: Wesleyan University Press, 1975).

54. E. Rádl, *Válka Čechů s Němci* (Prague: Čin, 1928), p. 13. For the German edition, see *Der Kampf zwischen den Tschechen und Deutschen* (Reichenberg: Verlag Gebrüder Stiepel, 1928).

55. Rádl, *Válka*, pp. 13, 89, 213.

56. Helmut Heiber, "Der Generalplan Ost," *Vierteljahreshefte für Zeitgeschichte*, vol. 6 (1958), p. 318.

57. See Bundesministerium für Vertriebene, *Die Vertreibung der deutschen Bevölkerung aus der Tschechoslowakei* (Bonn, 1957); J. W. Brügel, *Tschechen und Deutsche, 1939-1945* (Munich: Nymphenburger Verlag, 1974).

58. See F. Gregory Campbell, "Empty Pedestals?," *Slavic Review*, Vol. 44, No. 1 (Spring 1985), and the rejoinders by Gale Stokes and Roman Szporluk, pp. 1-29. For the contemporary Czech criticism emphasizing Masaryk's failure to contribute to the solution of the German Question, see Rudolf Kučera, *Kapitoly z dějin střední Evropy* (Munich: Tschechischer Nationalausschuß in Deutschland, 1989), p. 123.

59. Compiled from A. Müller & B. Utitz, *Deutschland und die Tschechoslowakei* (Freudenstadt: Eurobuch Verlag, 1972); Libor Rouček, *Die Tschechoslowakei und die Bundesrepublik Deutschland 1949-1989* (Vienna: Tuduv, 1990).

60. Rudolf Hilf, *Deutsche und Tschechen. Bedeutung und Wandlungen einer Nachbarschaft im Mitteleuropa* (Opladen: Leske Verlag, 1973), pp. 7-8.

61. Lew Kopelew, "Fremdenbilder in Geschichte und Gegenwart," in Mechthild Keller, ed., *Russen und Russland aus deutscher Sicht, 9.-17. Jahrhundert* (Munich: W. Fink, 1985), pp. 11-34, here p. 24; Lew Kopelew, *Worte werden Brücken* (Munich: n.p., 1989), pp. 118-119. See also Peter M. Pflüger, ed., *Freund- und Feindbilder: Begegnung mit dem Osten* (Olten/Freiburg: n.p., 1986), pp. 45-69; Stefan Plaggenborg, "Russen und Deutsche — Bemerkungen zu einem alten neuen Thema," *Osteuropa*, No. 10 (1990), pp. 975-90.

62. *Hospodářské noviny* (Prague), September 11, 1990 and September 16, 1990.

63. See Brügel, *Tschechen und Deutsche 1939-1945*, pp. 252-58; Roucek, *Die Tschechoslowakei und die Bundesrepublik Deutschland 1949-1989*, pp. 179-81; Hermann Raschhofer and Otto Kimminich, *Die Sudetenfrage: Ihre völkerrechtliche Entwicklung vom Ersten Weltkrieg bis zur Gegenwart* (Munich: Olzog Verlag, 1988).

64. On the international legal aspects of the Munich Agreement of 1938, see Sir John Wheeler-Bennett and Anthony Nicholls, *The Semblance of Peace: The Political Settlement After the Second World War* (New York: St. Martin's Press, 1972), pp. 611-13.

65. See the statements of Dr. Richard Král, the legal expert of the Czechoslovak Foreign Ministry, in *Práce* (Prague), November 30, 1990, and *Lidové Noviny* (Prague), December 11, 1990.

66. German Press Agency (DPA), communiqué of November 2, 1990.

67. *Lidová demokracie* (Prague), April 12, 1991.

68. *Sudetendeutsche Zeitung* (Munich), March 1, 1991. It would not be surprising if the German government followed in this situation the recent precedent set by the country's highest court, which ruled on April 23, 1991 that former legal owners of agricultural and industrial properties confiscated by Soviet authorities during the period 1945-1949 in the former GDR territory are entitled to compensation, but not to the return of the property. See F. Protzman in *The New York Times*, April 21, 1991.

69. Stephen Engelberg in *The New York Times*, January 23, 1992.

70. Cited from the faxed text of the Treaty made available to me through Herr Fritjof von Nordenskjoeld, Minister at the Embassy of the Federal Republic of Germany in Washington, whom I wish to thank for his kind assistance.

71. Ariane Genillard, *The Financial Times*, October 8, 1991.

72. In December 1886 a young Czech journalist, Hubert Gordon Schauer, challenged the Czech-German dilemma in an upfront manner. Playing the devil's advocate, he asked the existentialist question of whether a small nation like the Czechs should waste all their energy on the preservation of their language, instead of merging with the stronger German culture. Schauer's "Our Two Questions" were published in the literary magazine *Čas*, edited by T. G. Masaryk in Prague.

73. See Václav Havel, *Disturbing the Peace: A Conversation with Karel Hvížďala* (New York: Alfred Knopf, 1990), pp. 178-79.

74. According to Marc Fischer in *The Washington Post*, September 18, 1991, p. A27.

12

Hungary and Germany:
Two Actors in Search of a New Play

Ivan Volgyes

The relationship between Germany and Hungary, or the Hungarian version of the "German Question," has never existed in a vacuum of dispassionate academic discourse. As in many other European countries, the German Question has always been fraught with emotion. At various times, it has been used politically, as in the promotion of Hungarian nationalism during the Rakoczi rebellion of 1703-1711, or in the propagation of anti-Habsburg, anti-monarchist (and hence anti-German) nationalist sentiments in the 19th century. In the first half of the 20th century, Hungary's relationship with Germany dominated three significant policy debates. In the military-strategic area, it was crucial in the controversy over whether to seek or oppose an alliance with the Third Reich. Economically, the German Question overshadowed the choice between protectionism and increased commerce with Germany. And in Hungary's cultural and intellectual domain, a pivotal issue concerned whether to embrace or reject a closer intellectual alignment with German *Kultur* and *Philosophie*.[1]

This essay is an attempt to reflect on Hungary's "German Question," in order to discover what is particular and unique in Hungary's relations with Germany and the Germans. It is my contention that these relations are the result of the delicate interplay between objective mutual interests, on the one hand, and the perception of such interests among the elites and the people, on the other hand.

For the new Europe that is emerging today, after the collapse of Communism in Eastern Europe, the very expression "German Question" evokes painful memories on all sides. It is essential for this new Europe, however, that time-worn clichés are discarded, and that the terms "national" or "nationality question" be given a new meaning and generate new practices. This is crucial, because the return of a new tribalism in the Balkans and in many parts of what used to be the Soviet realm amply illustrates that the traditional invocation of a "nationality question" brings up old grievances, old concerns, and old sources of vengeance for the wrongs committed.[2] In reference to Germany and the "Germans," it raises the ugly specter of anti-Semitism as much as the highly positive evaluation of German *Kultur*. In short, while for professional historians the "German Question" may be an interesting academic query, for the vast majority of Hungarians the problem discussed here is not just a matter of dispassionate analysis. Rather, it is a cathartic exercise in national and individual self-justification. For even if Europe shares certain historical traditions based on the experiences of Western Christianity, the Renaissance, the Reformation, and the Enlightenment, and even if Germany and Hungary have both been part of these developments in European civilization, the tension and the stress between Germany and Hungary have at various times in their common history reached extremely high levels.

The purpose of this essay, therefore, is to put the "German Question," the relation between Germany and Hungary, and between Germans and Magyars, in a broader context. We shall examine the historical antecedents, analyze the ideological and policy orientations of recent years, discuss the divergent implications resulting from the rise and demise of East Germany, and summarize the developments resulting from the great transformation of 1989-1991.

History Revisited:
An Uncomfortable Journey through Time

The "German Question" is, of course, a somewhat misleading term, since the term "German," historically, has been used as a reference to many a different identity. In our analysis, where practicable, we will refer to "Germans" as those who possess a German mother-tongue, including those of Austrian or Swiss-German heritage, whose fate intertwined them with that of the people of Hungary, and identify as "German" those areas (with the exception of Switzerland) where German is (or perhaps was) the predominant mother-tongue. Thus, the lands of the Habsburg Empire in Central Europe or Saxony, the many small *Fürstentümer* or the Prussian realm, are all treated as part of the "German Question" just as much as the people, whether they hailed from Swabian, Bavarian or Saxon background.

It must also be noted from the very outset that throughout the existence of Hungary, Germans have been an inextricable part of the history of the Hungarian people.[3] Along with the Bohemian, Polish, French, and Italian royal houses, German nobles — ranging from the pre-Habsburgs to the Wittlesbachs — have served as rulers over the Magyars. Throughout its history, and until very recently, parts of Transylvania and most of Hungary's cities were populated by hard-working, industrious "Germans."[4] The beginnings of commerce and urban modernization could not have been accomplished without the participation of the Germans in Hungary. The development of education and the professions, as well as culture and science, in medieval and post-medieval Hungary could not have taken place without the contributions of the Germans.

The role of "Germany" or of the "German states" is more difficult to delineate, since Hungarians historically referred to Germans as those living in a part of the Habsburg realm. It is this identification of the Habsburgs with things "German" that compelled Sandor Petofi, Hungary's best known and most ardently nationalistic poet of the 19th century, to title his poem "What Does that German Really Want?" when, in reality, he was referring to Franz Josef's Habsburg Monarchy, rather than to "the Germans" in a generic sense of the word. And one should be reminded that although the Habsburgs, indeed, came to liberate Buda from the Turks in 1686, they stayed on as oppressors of Hungary's national aspirations until Hungary's *Ausgleich* with Austria in 1867. Thus, German aspirations were historically regarded negatively by Hungarian nationalists, since it was the "Germans," after all, who suppressed the great struggles for Hungary's independence in 1703-1711 and 1848-1849. While the usage of the concept of "Germany" began to change in 1870-1871 with the rise of a unified German state, the negative connotations attached to "Germany" among Hungarian nationalists remained a fact until recently.

German aspirations of becoming an imperial power at the beginning of the 20th century caused little resentment in Hungary. On the one hand, Magyar nationalists viewed the united Germany as limiting the very viability of the Habsburg realm. On the other hand, they viewed the emerging strength of the new German state as a positive force in stopping Russian expansionism.

World War I and its aftermath altered these evaluations, however. Austria-Hungary as a co-equal realm disappeared and Hungary became an independent state, sharing the fate of being the real loser of the great conflagration with Germany.[5] In light of the awkward and brutal postwar attempt of Bela Kun and his compatriots to establish a Communist system in Hungary,[6] the eradication of the "Commune" at the hands of the Entente, and the degradation suffered by a country that retained only one-third of its former territory and a quarter of its people, the choice of "joining" the Entente or "opting" for closer relations with that other pariah, Germany, was not a genuine "choice" for Hungary's decision-makers.[7]

The choice facing Hungary was not a genuine one for the following reasons. First, a real pro-Entente orientation was doomed from the beginning by the infamous Vyx note — the *démarche* by the Entente practically ordering Hungary to accept the Allies' *Diktat* regarding the territorial division of Hungary — and the subsequent policy directives of the Allies to dismember Hungary.[8]   The allies of the Entente in Eastern Europe — Romania, Czecho-Slovakia, and Serbia-Croatia — all received preferential treatment from the Allied leaders at Paris.   Moreover, precisely because of these policy preferences, Hungary could not possibly have been allowed by its neighbors to become a trusted member of an interwar alliance system aimed, in part, precisely against Hungary and the Hungarian population.   Second, while Hungary's traditional markets — Germany and Austria — continued to provide opportunities for commercial integration, neither France and England, nor the United States and Hungary's newly created neighboring states, were eager to deal with the new Hungarian government in a preferential manner.   Third, a possible pro-Entente orientation was also doomed by the emergence of the clearly anti-democratic Horthy regime.   While it is also clear that — with the exception of Czecho-Slovakia — there was little democracy in the surrounding states, the methods of rule employed by the Horthy regime guaranteed that Hungary would not march in the forefront of the nations toward democracy.

In short, *even if* Hungary had possessed a genuinely democratic government after 1919, it still would have been treated in pretty much the same manner by France or England and its allies as it actually was.   Consequently, the efforts of the Anglo- or Francophiles, such men as Istvan Bethlen or Pal Teleki during the 1930s, to transform Hungary into a pro-Entente stronghold, were doomed by history, *realpolitik*, and nationalism in the surrounding states.[9]   My thesis bears repeating again: Hungary had little or no option other than to draw ever closer to Germany, because — aside from Mussolini in Italy — only Germany appeared to be interested after 1933 in redressing the injustices it (and, thus, indirectly, Hungary) had suffered in the Paris Peace Treaties.   It was not, as some have argued, due to the common "Fascist," "racist," or "dictatorial" orientations of the Hitler and Horthy regimes that an alliance between Hungary and Germany became inevitable, but the fact that realistically Horthy's Hungary had nowhere else to turn![10]   All other roads were blocked, either by the sorry record of the failed attempt at Bolshevization in 1919, or by the policies of the sworn enemies of Hungary — the building blocks of Entente policy.

The question of whether there *really* was an alternative for the country has, of course, been a matter of historical debate both in Hungary and elsewhere. Due to a limitation of space, and thus without any attempt at completeness, let me merely outline the various schools of thought on this thorny issue.   The interpretation by both the Liberal and the Socialist/Communist schools of historiography has been the most consistent in this regard.   They have held that Hungary should have consistently courted France, England, and especially its future ally, the USSR,[11] and that it should have consistently rejected the Right, the Fascists, and eventually the Nazis both outside Hungary and the policy options propagated by their cohorts inside the country.   This is a tempting generalization in light of the horrors brought on by the Right.   Yet, it ignores two facts. First, Hungary attempted to play along with Germany only for purposes of regaining the "losses of Trianon," while rejecting becoming a third party to the "Pact of Steel." Second, Hungary made continuous efforts to avoid direct conflicts with England and the latter's allies until very late in the development of events during World War II. In fact, Hungary's relationship with Soviet Russia became normalized only after the Molotov-Ribbentrop Pact, and the school of thought that accuses Hungary for being a willing ally of Fascism tends to forget both the lack of options offered by the Western alliance system, as well as the impact of the intricate relations between Hitler's Germany and Stalin's Russia.

The Right attacks Hungarian foreign policy and its cautious activities precisely from the opposite perspective. Especially influential during the 1930s within Hungary's own Fascist circles and after the ravages of war within the right-wing emigré community, this school of thought regards Hungary's timidity *vis-a-vis* the "holy battle" against Communism as a historical weakness and a lost opportunity to prove Hungary's innate national values. In fact, the reassertion of the "holy cause" has been most noticeable following the re-establishment of Hungarian democracy in 1989. The sorry speeches of General Kalman Keri, Jeno Fonay, and especially Istvan Csurka, and the subsequent re-emergence of anti-Bolshevism as a "holy national cause" that justified Hungary's beastly behavior toward its own Jews in the circles around such periodicals as the *Szent Korona* and *Hunnia* in 1991-1992, are representative of such views.[12]

The centrist view, which is closest to my own, is, as noted above, that Hungary's choices were rather circumscribed by history, limited by geopolitical considerations, and constrained by the sorry record of statesmanship of the politicians both in Hungary and in Europe as a whole. Clearly, Hungary should have sided with the Allies and even with Soviet Russia against Hitler's Fascism. But the Allies would not admit Hungary onto their side, they were far away and uninterested, while Soviet Russia made its peace with Hitler quite happily. Clearly, Hungary should not have entered the war, but remained neutral, or after 1944 if it had to enter the war at all, it should have opposed Hitler's legions, like Romania and Bulgaria did later on. Horthy was a bungler, however, and his ineptness as much as the presence of Hungary's own Fascists doomed these efforts. It was a tragedy, but not one so much of commission as of omission of acts that would have been desirous in retrospect. At any rate, we all know that history is not a visit of condolences and that nations act in ways that are never totally consistent with their own interest, especially from a historical perspective.

Let me touch briefly on one of the most painful issues relating to the relationship between Germany and Hungary, namely the role of the German minorities in post-Trianon Hungary. It is an issue that affected and influenced the relationship between these two states more profoundly than is the case for most other states of the region, although in its severity it did not approach the dislocations that occurred in Poland and the Czech lands. Nevertheless, the fate of the German minority in Hungary became of enormous importance in the immediate postwar years.

As noted earlier, "Germans" have been present in Hungary throughout the centuries. As peasants, artisans, and merchants, and as the members of the fledgling bourgeoisie, they were a part of the realm. Following the demise of Latin, their language in its myriad variations was a common tongue spoken by the people of Austria-Hungary. After the demise of the Monarchy, the number of Germans in Hungary dwindled, and Hungary became a virtually homogenous state in ethnic terms. According to the census of 1920, the German minority in post-Trianon Hungary comprised only 6.9 percent of the country's population.[13] While Weimar Germany began to build a democracy in the 1920s, Budapest started to implement discriminatory measures against the local German population — most of whom were identified as "Donau-Schwaben," though, in reality, they hailed from many different parts of the German realm.[14] Although these measures were highly restrictive, the vast majority of the Germans shrugged them off and remained loyal citizens of Hungary. Until the mid-1930s little noticeable friction existed among Magyars and Germans living in Hungary. The German communities continued to cling together, and newspapers and magazines were published in German. In fact, the German language daily, the *Pester Lloyd*, was one of the best papers in Budapest.

The advent of Hitler and the spreading of the great-German and pan-German message, as well as the rise of German expansionism, began to change this pattern of coexistence. The Hitler regime considered the Germans in Hungary to be *Volksdeutsche*, and the Horthy regime also adopted this term. In an effort to draw Horthy ever closer to his own camp of supporters, Hitler began to utilize the *Volksdeutsch* population as a Fifth Column, an open and willingly mobilizable interest group working on behalf of the German Reich.[15] Although not the entire *Volksdeutsch* population supported Hitler uniformly, a good percentage of the ethnic Germans did back Fascist German aims and policies in Eastern Europe.

We noted above that the Horthy regime had no real alternative to joining Germany — if it desired to recapture at least some of the territories where Hungarians lived in the surrounding successor states. Its options were further limited because, until very late in the game, the Allies refused to accept Hungary as a part of the alliance system of the West.[16] While realizing that in the Europe of the late 1930s only Germany could muster the political, military, and industrial force that mattered, Horthy nonetheless tried a sort of balancing act of semi-independence. Prime Ministers Miklos Kallai or Pal Teleki continued to flirt with the Allies, exploring opportunities at least to stay neutral in a potential conflict between Germany and the Allies, and hoping for a match, even if their efforts, in historical retrospect, were doomed to failure in the ever more polarized European world.[17]

We should also admit, however, that there was a great deal of similarity of values between a large portion of the German and Hungarian Fascist political elites, and between the racist policies of Hitler and the conservative Horthy. That Hitler was vociferous in his desire to exterminate the Jews, and that the salon anti-Semite Horthy simply did nothing to save most of Hungary's rural Jews from extermination — at least until the summer of 1944 — is a distinction that is academic at this stage of our ethical evaluation. But the fact remains that Hitler's policies concerning the extermination of the Jews in the German sphere of influence were accepted by Horthy as a norm. When Horthy was no longer willing to carry out Hitler's "requests," when in a final, desperate attempt, he tried clumsily to extricate Hungary from the already lost war, the Hungarian Fascist Arrow-Cross leader Ferenc Szalasi could be put in Horthy's place by German bayonets overnight. Szalasi, in turn, willingly carried out Hitler's demands to the very end.[18]

The net result of Hitler's *Endlösung* in Hungary, and Horthy's inaction in saving the Jews, was the extermination of nearly 500,000 Jews (out of a prewar total of 750,000), deported to the gas-chambers from Hungary between 1942 and the summer of 1944. Szalasi's brief reign between October 1944 and January 1945 ended the lives of another 125,000 Jews trapped in Budapest.[19] The Germans and Hungary's Magyar Arrow-Cross Fascists were together responsible for the extermination of Hungarian Jewry in the Holocaust to an extent replicated only in Poland. Germans and Magyars alike have had to live with the legacy of these horrors.

Enter Ideology

As noted at the outset, the "German Question" found an ideological expression in Hungary long before 1945.[20] However, after World War II it took on a new and different hue. The horrors of the war, the destruction and cruelties caused by Fascism, and the revulsion at the murder of millions of innocents by the Nazis, brought forth an outburst of anti-German feelings everywhere in Europe. In Hungary these feelings were amplified, however, by other considerations as well. First, there was a strong emphasis placed on the role of the *Volksdeutsch* minority during the war. Second, there were feelings of guilt as a result of Hungary's loyalty as Hitler's last ally, the brutal acts and deeds of Hungarian Fascists, and Magyar support for Szalasi and native Fascism. And third, the ascendance of Communism under Soviet tutelage added a further dimension to the intensely anti-German feelings in Hungary.

It was relatively easy to deal with the wartime role of the *Volksdeutsch* minority: the forcible expulsion of approximately one-third of the German minority, 278,000 people of German origin (as well as the expulsion of some 73,000 Slovaks), expiated the national consciousness.[21] This "forcible repatriation," along with the expulsion of Magyars from Slovakia, and Germans from Czechoslovakia and Poland — already decided in Potsdam by the Allied leaders in August 1945 and in Paris in February 1946 — remains one of the sorriest episodes of the history of the region.

The two other aspects of the problem, however, became immediately intertwined. Former Fascists and members of the Arrow-Cross party swelled the ranks of the tiny postwar Communist party in Hungary. Eager to please their new masters, they sought legal and political protection from the deeds of their Fascist past.[22] By joining the Communist party, they also sought to escape the wrath of those returning from concentration camps, and of those assorted Communists coming home from Moscow who tried to seek punishable culprits for the crimes of the previous regime.

It should be noted, however, that the common policy orientation toward the "German Question" was already manipulated from Moscow. The primary goal of this policy became clear in a relatively short time: never again to allow Germany to become a threat to Soviet power. One of the primary tools of this policy in the region was the eradication of positive orientations toward Germany from Eastern Europe. "German," in short, had to become synonymous with "Fascist" or "Nazi." To be a German was to be considered *ipso facto* a Hitlerite, an enemy of humanity, of decency, of culture, and, consequently, an opponent of "progress," and of the "inevitable dawn" of Communism.[23] In short, the preferred method of dealing with the "German Question" was to be the eradication of the positive attributes of German culture, commerce, influence, and presence, in the name of *both* "humanity" and Communism throughout Eastern Europe. As one observes the textbooks and the literature produced between 1950 and 1965, the uniformity of negativism becomes glaring.[24]

The implications of treating the "German Question" in such a negative manner remained essentially the same throughout the first two decades of postwar Communist rule. The emergence of the Federal Republic as a democratic state, the successes of the *Wirtschaftswunder*, and the increasing role played by the Federal Republic in Europe — both as a member of the European Community and as a member of NATO — only re-enforced the negative treatment of the German problem. West Germany was always identified as an inheritor of the Fascist past, as the home of former Nazis. Further, the Hungarian Communists never missed a chance to equate German policy with presumed aspirations for "imperialist revanchism." By the mid-1960s, however, some subtle changes in these formulations in Hungary became noticeable. Slowly the centrally projected, heavy-handed "image" of Germany as a Fascist state began to be slightly altered.

There were, of course, good reasons — in both the domestic and foreign policy realms — for the change in the negative treatment of Germany. In the domestic realm, the coming to power of the Social Democratic Party in West

Germany, the subsequent lifting of the Hallstein Doctrine, the subsequent adoption and implementation of *Ostpolitik*, and the gradual welfarization and democratization of German domestic affairs, should be noted. Faced with these developments in West Germany, Hungarian ideologists found it increasingly hard to refer to Germany as a land of rampant capitalism, as a state interested in "recapturing" the East by force, or as a country that was still governed by Fascists. In the face of an emergent reality that included Rudi Dutschke and the Baader-Meinhoff gang just as much as it had included the triumphs of Germany's labor unions, to continue to hold on to an image of the "Fascist, totalitarian Germany" would have been implausible and ludicrous.

Moreover, the Social Democrats' *Ostpolitik* began to turn German interests in an eastern direction. Hungary proved to be a good partner for Bonn: Budapest welcomed increasing — though still largely symbolic — trade contacts with the Federal Republic, and, most notably, it quietly opened its borders to greater West German tourism. This was especially important for West Germany. Since East Germans could not travel readily to the West, Hungary's Lake Balaton (the *Plattensee*) provided a readily available and relatively cheap location for long separated German families to spend their vacations together.

In the foreign policy area the image of Germany also changed, as the USSR continued to play with the idea of splitting up NATO by enticing Western Europe away from its close links with the U.S. and into a less strictly transatlantic posture vis-a-vis the Warsaw Pact. Though it failed to reach that goal — in spite of having received unwitting support for these goals from the adoption of such Western European rhetorical devices as "Europe for the Europeans" or a "Europe from the Atlantic to the Urals" — the USSR continued to hope for the neutralization of West Germany. The 1975 Helsinki Accords could be seen as major triumph for the USSR: though it failed to neutralize the Federal Republic, the USSR received a guarantee from all parties concerning the "final borders" of divided Europe.

As far as Hungarian-German relations were concerned, however, following the adoption of the Helsinki Accords, the Federal Republic could no longer be depicted as desiring to alter by force the territorial boundaries established in the postwar years. Furthermore, as the need of the Eastern European states for trade with the West and the infusion of Western technology and funds into their economies grew, culminating in a heavy reliance on importing these goods especially from the Federal Republic, the projected image of an aggressive "Fascist" and "revanchist" West Germany slowly began to fade.

East Germany: The "Good" Germans as Comrades?

At this stage it is important to note a major confounding factor in the Hungarian treatment of the "German question:" the rise of the German

Democratic Republic. It must be admitted that in the totally negative conception of the German Question by the Communists in the postwar decades, the Russians already tried a "gentle shading" when they referred to the German Communists — from Luxemburg and Thälmann to Ulbricht, Pieck and company — as the "good Germans." The rise of the GDR as a state, after 1949, also began to mitigate the negative treatment of the German Question, at least insofar as the depiction of Communist Germany was concerned. Thus, from 1950-51 onward, the Hungarian media took great pains to separate "good East Germans" — allegedly all cultured, humane, and Communists — from the "bad West Germans" who were all supposed to be Fascists and capitalists, or at best duped and exploited by American imperialism. Using such tools as the deliberate indictment of the expelled *Volksdeutsche* as having had a Fascist past and now seeking vengeance through their influence in the political life of West Germany, the regime tried to use fear to depict the Federal Republic negatively, on the one hand, while further identifying "progressive East Germany" with policies the Hungarian Communists themselves advocated, on the other hand.

Moreover, the progress of East Germany in the industrial arena also provided the regime with new ammunition. The successes of the GDR in the rebuilding of its economy, with advances in most productive areas, were often compared with West Germany's "soaring unemployment," its riots, and "the exploitation of the masses." It was a convenient tool that worked until the tourist trade opened up in both directions and real comparisons could be made. Paradoxically, therefore, it was the very existence and progress of East Germany that forced the re-emergence and opened up the reinterpretation of the "German Question" once again in Hungary.

From the mid-1960s on, however, the very comparisons were disastrous for East Germany. For every Trabant in the East there was a Volkswagen, for every Wartburg belching fumes, a new *Straßenkreuzer* could be seen cruising on Hungary's main thoroughfares. The little pup-tents of the East German tourists provided glaring examples of poverty when contrasted with the huge campers of the "other" Germans. The comparisons were even more glaring in the industrial sphere: technology in the West qualitatively overshadowed the technology from East Germany, even if the GDR, in fact, *was* ahead of Hungary in most industrial areas. In culture, too, the restrictive East German interpretations became staid mockeries of *Kultur* when compared with the new culture of West Germany. Only in allegedly "amateur" sports could the GDR excel over its Western counterpart. In spite of all the propaganda aimed at them, the people of Hungary understood the vast differences between West and East Germany.

Perhaps, it is an irony of Hungarian history that it turned out to be the German Question that would sound the death-knell of Communism. This is not the place to delineate the collapse of the system we used to call Communist, suffice it to say, however, that its approaching demise was nearly invisible for a long time. The extent of the internal rot of the system was not obvious even to practiced observers. That the people were fleeing the system was obvious, but the extent of the East Germans' desire to escape from the system or otherwise discard it, went unobserved by most social scientists or political analysts for a long time.

Therefore, the 1989 mass exodus from East Germany caught most observers by surprise. The sight of East German citizens climbing desperately into West German embassy enclaves in Prague, Warsaw or Budapest was witnessed by camera-crews — both alerted and ever-ready for news — and broadcast live into the living rooms of most TV owners across the globe. In Hungary the number of refugees grew practically from hour to hour. Camps had to be set up by the Hungarian authorities to house the refugees. In a twist of history, even those camps at Budapest's Csilleberc, the 1944 "home" for the Jews scheduled to be shuttled off to Auschwitz by Eichmann's *Einsatzkommandos*, had to be readied for the literally thousands of East German refugees.

The government of Prime Minister Miklos Nemeth deliberated. On September 10, 1989, word came that a group of East Germans was setting off on foot toward Austria. General Jozsef Horvath, the head of the III/III Department of the Ministry of Interior — the Department normally charged with internal surveillance — was on duty that day. Based on Hungary's obligations resulting from its membership in the Warsaw Pact, General Horvath had standing orders to shoot. Yet, like many others around him, he had already realized that it was futile to stop the exodus by force. "In the end," he said, "I commanded the head of the District Border Guard unit not to fire at them. The ball-game was over."[25]

The government, notified of Horvath's decision, came to the same conclusion. At a stormy session, with Prime Minister Nemeth, Foreign Minister Gyula Horn, and Education Minister Ferenc Glatz leading the pack, the government decided to let the East Germans go to Austria and then on to West Germany. Nemeth and Horn ordered a plane to stand by and in near total secrecy they subsequently flew to Bonn to see Chancellor Helmut Kohl. There, Prime Minister Nemeth told the Chancellor that he intended to let the East Germans have free passage to Austria. Alluding to Hungary's obligations to the Warsaw Pact, the Chancellor inquired whether Nemeth realized what the Hungarian government was doing. Nemeth barely waited for the translation before giving his affirmative reply.

Now it was only a matter of agreeing on the price. "What do you want from us to do this?" Kohl inquired. "Nothing," said Nemeth, "It is our human duty." Kohl's eyes filled with tears. "We will never forget what you have done," he said and offered his hand to both men. The Iron Curtain ceased to exist, and with it Communism was bound to disappear just about overnight.

Did everyone realize this at the time? Did they know that this single event would lead to the collapse of the Wall and the speedy and inevitable reunion of

the two Germanys? Did they know that that was the end of the Communist
system, of the Warsaw Pact, of the Soviet realm? Every one of the participants
probably had a different interpretation of the events that were to take place
within the next few months, but everyone also realized that as of that moment
German-Hungarian relations, and the "German Question," would be placed on
a new basis.

The nagging question remains whether there were economic and financial
promises made to Hungary at the time when Nemeth and Horn made their
decisions. Certainly, if promises were made that would differentiate Hungary
in any way from the other former Bloc countries, they appear not to have been
kept. Hungary received, to be sure, some German investment, but German
investment has been far more extensive in Czechoslovakia than in Hungary.
Though there exists today a Basic Treaty between the two states that underlines
a special relationship — signed by Chancellor Kohl and Prime Minister Antall
on February 6, 1992 — there are no visible signs of either Hungary's demands
for or German promises of favors for allowing the East Germans to leave
unhampered for the West during those historical few days.

Reflections on German-Hungarian Relations
since the Fall of Communism

A great deal has happened since the fall of Communism in Hungary, which
is also reflected in the political, economic, and cultural relations between unified
Germany and democratic Hungary. While these changes cannot be directly
linked to Hungary's earlier deeds, the development of a new "special"
relationship must be noted.

Politically, the center-right government of Prime Minister Jozsef Antall
draws much of its inspiration and some of its policy orientation from Germany's
current government. At least until mid-1992, there were oft-reported frequent
telephone-calls between the Prime Minister and Chancellor Kohl that were
symbolic of the type of relations between the two countries as well. The
conclusion of the German-Hungarian Basic Treaty in February 1992 brought
Hungary still closer to Germany politically, economically, and culturally.[26] In
spite of some haphazard and inadequate steps by the United States to establish
close links to Hungary, the Magyar state appears to be solidly situated in the
new Germany's sphere of interest.

The close relationship is reflected in a myriad contacts between the two
countries. These extend from activities undertaken by all of the German
political *Stiftungen* (foundations) in promoting democratic institution and culture
building, through the already well-established system of exchanges in every
conceivable field of governmental operations, to the teaching of German as a

replacement for Russian, or to the political and institutional ties that are now woven ever stronger between the two states.

Economically, in spite of the fact that the largest foreign investments in Hungary are undertaken by non-German firms, Germans are making enormous inroads. Concentrating mostly on investment in small to mid-size firms, Germans are quietly corralling the market, orienting Hungary's trade toward Germany. In short, Germany is establishing for itself a dominant position in Hungary's economy.

Culturally, the relationship between these two states has never been better. The German minority's rights in Hungary have been fully restored, and the community is vibrant and strong once again. A new project is aimed at republishing the *Pester Lloyd* in German, and German is very rapidly becoming a respected language of culture and commerce once again. Unlike Western European capitals, where German businessmen — until very recently! — have been virtually indistinguishable from other European businessmen in their unified use of English as a common language, German in Hungary is now accorded the right of being at least on a par with English as the language of commerce. Hungary — along with Austria — once again appears ready to become a part of the German-dominated cultural sphere within this decade.

In short, Germany has resumed a pivotal role in Hungary. What it failed to achieve militarily in 1944-1945, it is managing to accomplish peacefully: a dominant influence in Hungary's political and economic life. However, the Germany of the 1990s does not stand alone, but is a respected member of the European and the global community. It shares with the members of the European Community common values concerning the rights and duties of people. And in this respect, that is, in regard to the tolerance and freedom it provides for its citizens, and in regard to the institutions, policies, and operations of democracy, Germany can and does provide a shining example of a working democracy for Hungary. It can only be hoped that Hungary will try to emulate the best examples set by this new Germany, and that Germany, in turn, will stick to the democratic course forged by its leaders and its people after World War II.

Notes

This chapter is, in part, based on an earlier study entitled "Hungary and the German Question," in Günther Wagenlehner, ed., *Die Deutsche Frage und die internationale Sicherheit* (Koblenz: Bernard und Gräfe, 1988), pp. 242-47. The author would like to express his appreciation to Professor Joseph Held for his insightful comments on this chapter.

1. Zoltan Horvath, *Magyar szazadfordulo: A masodik reformnemzedek tortenete* (Budapest: Kossuth, 1961), pp. 65, 72, 80-92.

2. For a cogent summary of the ancient wrongs, see Gyula Szekfu, *Harom Nemzedek . . . es ami utana kovetkezik* (Budapest: Cserepfalvi, 1920 and 1934), 2 vols., especially vol. 1, pp. 379-401.

3. German settlers were invited to Hungary by Hungary's kings as early as the 13th century. Gyula Kristof, "Erdely XI-XIII. szazadi tortenetehez," in Istvan Racz, ed., *Tanulmanyok Erdely torteneterol* (Debrecen: n.p., 1988), pp. 60-65.

4. Lately, this contention has been disputed. For recent figures on the city populations of Transylvania, see Laszlo Makkai and Ferenc Mucsi, eds., *Erdely tortenete* (Budapest: Akademia, 1986), 3 vols., vol. 1, pp. 287-301.

5. Adam Magda, *Magyarorszag es a kisantant a harmicas evekben* (Budapest: n.p., 1978).

6. Ivan Volgyes, ed., *Hungary in Revolution, 1918-1919* (Lincoln, NE: University of Nebraska Press, 1971).

7. For a thoughtful argument on the options available to Hungary after World War I, see the late Gyorgy Ranki's especially cogent analysis of the economic and political consequences of great power policies in the Danube Valley in *Golyavari estek* (Budapest: Kozgazdasagi es Jogi Konyvkiado, 1984), pp. 140-74.

8. For the most cogent explanation of the Vyx note, see Gabor Vermes, "The October Revolution in Hungary: From Karolyi to Kun," in Volgyes, ed., *Hungary in Revolution*, pp 56-58.

9. Interestingly, given the political line adopted by the Hungarian decision-makers after 1956, Hungarian historians explored this issue far more early, and more objectively, than elsewhere in the region. For the earliest post-1956 effort, see Ivan T. Berend and Gyorgy Ranki, *Magyarorszag a fasiszta Nemetorszag elettereben* (Budapest: Kozgazdasagi es Jogi Konyvkiado, 1960).

10. The lack of choice, of course, is not reflected in the thinking of a large number of historians and writers in contemporary Hungary. Basing their ideals on an essay by the Hungarian poet Endre Ady, they wistfully assign Hungary the role of a "Ferry-state," ferrying back — either voluntarily or forcibly — between two shores. The contention of this essay is that freedom to attach oneself to *either* of the opposing "shores" or partners was never really open to Hungary before World War II.

11. The Communist school of historiography maintains that Hungary's interest in seeking territorial revisions was also shared by the USSR, for the Soviets — especially in the 1920s and 1930s — were vociferous in rejecting the dictates of Trianon as well. See Laszlo Zsigmond, *Magyarorszag es a masodik vilaghaboru* (Budapest: Kossuth, 1961), pp. 16-17.

12. See *Tallozo*, February 6, 1992, pp. 4-7; cf. *Magyar Forum* (Budapest), August 20, 1992.

13. "Magyar Statisztikai Szemle," Nos. 1-3 (1944), p. 14.

14. Ingomar Senz, *Die nationale Bewegung der ungarländische Deutschen vor dem ersten Weltkrieg* (Munich: n.p., 1977) and G. C. Paikert, *The Danube Swabians* (The Hague: Martinus Nijhoff, 1967).

15. For the most detailed study of the *Volksdeutsch* problem, see Thomas Spira, *The German-Hungarian-Swabian Triangle, 1936-1939: The Road to Discord* (New York: East European Monographs, 1990). See also Lorant Tilkovszky, *Ez volt a Volksbund* (Budapest: Kossuth, 1978).

16. This point is made forcefully in C. A. Macartney, *October 15: Hungary between the World Wars* (Cambridge: Cambridge University Press, 1961).

17. Teleki, before he committed suicide as a desperate response to Hungary's attack on Yugoslavia, succinctly summed up the necessity — and impossibility — of balancing between German power and Hungarian national interests. On Teleki's policy, see *Magyarorszag a masodik vilaghaboruban* (Budapest: Kossuth, 1987).

18. On Szalasi and the Arrow Cross movement, see Miklos Lacko, *Nyilasok, Nemzetiszocialistak* (Budapest: Kossuth, 1969); Nicholas Nagy-Talavera, *The Green Shirts and Others: A History of Fascism in Hungary and Rumania* (Stanford, CA: Hoover Institution, 1970). Two fine essays on Hungarian Fascism are Gyorgy Ranki, "The Problem of Fascism in Hungary," and George Barany, "The Dragon's Teeth: The Roots of Hungarian Fascism," in Peter Sugar, ed., *Native Fascism* (Santa Barbara, CA: ABC-CLIO, 1971), pp. 65-72 and 73-82.

19. For the best study of the fate of Hungarian Jewry, see Randolph A. Braham, *The Politics of Genocide* (New York: Columbia University Press, 1981) and his *The Destruction of Hungarian Jewry* (New York: World Federation of Hungarian Jews, 1963).

20. Laszlo Kovago, *Nemzetisegek a mai Magyarorszagon* (Budapest: Kossuth, 1981), p. 5.

21. Kovago, *Nemzetisegek*, p. 19, and *Az 1960 evi nepszamlalas* (Budapest: Statisztikai Kiado, 1964), v. XIII, p. 27. For the most thorough analysis of the problem, see Stephen B. Kertesz, *Between Russia and the West: Hungary and the Illusion of Peacemaking, 1945-1947* (South Bend: Notre Dame University Press, 1984), especially pp. 4-8.

22. Although there are no figures that indicate the exact number of such "transfers," recent notes found in the former party archives indicate that at least 35,000 Communist party members in 1946 had "no references," a term reserved for those who had most probably been admitted to the party with a tainted past (XIV/1946/doc. 3-5). The task of ferreting out this information is all the more difficult because many former Fascists were not members of the Arrow Cross Party. The extent of the cross-over, however, may also be indicated by the similarity of voting patterns in the working-class districts of Budapest, Csepel, and Zuglo. Known, for instance, as "red Csepel" after 1945, in the early 1940s it was called "green Csepel." See Gyorgy Ranki, *A masodik vilaghaboru* (Budapest: Gondolat, 1973), and his *1944: marcius 19* (Budapest: Kossuth, 1978). For an extensive English-language discussion, see Charles Gati, *Hungary and the Soviet Bloc* (Durham, NC: Duke University Press, 1986), especially chapter 1.

23. We should reiterate that the failure of these attempts could not be confirmed by any scientific surveys until very recently. Starting in 1987, however, Hungarian sociologists and political analysts, notably Laszlo Keri, Istvan Schlett, and Istvan Stumpf, began to question the success of the entire process of political socialization, and concluded that those values projected by the regime were considerably less internalized by the population than officials assumed.

24. See, for example, *Vilagtortenelem* (Budapest: Tankonyvkiado, 1963), a world history textbook for graduating seniors in Hungary's gymnasia, especially pp. 135-52.

25. Personal interview. This section as a whole is based on interviews with most of the participants, including Ferenc Glatz and Gyula Horn, as well as the relevant members of the Foreign Ministry apparat. Gyula Horn, in his *Colopok* (Budapest: n.p., 1991),

offers a different version, while former Prime Minister Nemeth counters with still another story in his numerous interviews given on the subject.

26. For the text and negotiation of the Basic Treaty, see *Nepszabadsag* (Budapest), February 10, 1992, pp. 1, 4-5.

13

Romania and Germany: An On-Again, Off-Again Relationship

Robert R. King

Romania is one of Germany's more distant neighbors. It is separated by a greater physical and cultural distance than many of them, and the two countries have been spared direct territorial disputes with each other. At times, however, their relations have been marked by dramatic forms of cooperation or estrangement with political consequences that have had much more than a bilateral impact. At other times, their involvement with each other has drifted into one of relative unimportance. Some observers would see these mercurial swings as more Latin than Teutonic in style. Such a characterization no doubt would appeal to many Romanians, who like to view themselves as constituting an island of Latin culture in the midst of a vast sea of Slavs and Hungarians.

The see-saw nature of the relationship predates the Cold War period, and it took a particularly acute form during the years of Nazi rule in Germany. The Third Reich developed friendly relations with Romania in order to exploit the latter's economy for Germany's military mobilization and war effort. It manipulated Romanian interests, and ultimately betrayed Romania's territorial integrity. Romania, in turn, followed its own more limited options in power politics. Initially its dependence upon Germany increased, but as the war moved toward a defeat for the Axis Powers, Romania made a timely turn against the Third Reich by joining in the Allied effort to expel the *Wehrmacht* from Eastern Europe.

In the period since 1945, there have been similar undulations in the relationship between Romania and West Germany. There were no outstanding territorial issues between the two countries, but they became junior members of opposite blocs in the Cold War confrontation. As a result of its ideological and geopolitical priorities, the development of normal bilateral ties between Bucharest and Bonn was delayed and enormously complicated. In the late 1960s, however, there was a sudden and sensational improvement in their relations which marked the first breakaway from West Germany's Hallstein Doctrine. This shift in turn had significant ramifications for West Germany's relations with the Soviet Union and all other members of the Warsaw Pact. Indeed, it is possible in retrospect to detect here the beginning of a new era in East-West relations as a whole. Ironically, relations between Bonn and Bucharest soon cooled once more, as detente expanded to the rest of Central and Eastern Europe, while Romania's Communist regime became increasingly rigid and repressive during the 1970s and 1980s.

The substantial ethnic German population in Romania adds another distinctive dimension to the relationship between the two countries. The Transylvania Saxons and the Danube Swabians were a legacy of imperial policies of earlier centuries, but during the 1930s and 1940s they provided members for a fifth column in Romania, manipulated for the benefit of the Third Reich. Though their numbers were substantially reduced after the war, their presence has continued to be an important issue between Romania and Germany.

The Legacy of Romanian-German Relations during World War II

To understand the dynamics of Romanian-German interaction since 1945, it is important to appreciate their previous history. During the 19th and early 20th centuries relations between Germany and Romania were generally good. Ties were cultivated by Romania as a counterbalance to expanding Russian and Austrian influence in the Balkans, and in 1866 when no Romanian noble could win support as prince of the united provinces of Wallachia and Moldavia, Prince Charles of the German House of Hohenzollern-Sigmaringen became the Romanian sovereign. In the first third of the 20th century, economic ties between the two developed positively.

Following the establishment of the Nazi regime in 1933, Germany became increasingly involved in Balkan politics for both strategic and economic reasons. Strategically, Germany was anxious to protect its southern flank, particularly vis-a-vis what it perceived as an adversary and potentially expansionist Soviet Union. Romania was the principal front-line state in this area, sharing a long border with the USSR, as well as possessing the territory of Bessarabia, which was claimed by the Soviets. Economically, Germany was particularly interested in Romanian oil, since the Ploeşti oil field was the largest reserve reasonably near Germany. Romania was a source of agricultural products and other natural resources, as well as a market for German manufactured goods.[1]

Nazi Germany entered into trade agreements with Romania to buy surplus agricultural products at fixed prices with the purchases handled through controlled accounts that required off-setting purchases of German products. These agreements led to substantial Romanian sales to Germany and resulted in improvement in the Romanian economy, but they also tied Romania to Germany. By 1938, 37 percent of Romania's imports were from Germany (which by that time also included Austria) and 27 percent of its exports went to Germany.[2]

Nazi policy toward Romania before and during World War II included support for local Fascist groups. The organizational expression of the Fascist movement in Romania, the Iron Guard and the Legion of the Archangel Michael, embraced the key elements of Fascism as it emerged elsewhere – anti-Semitism, extreme nationalism, racial glorification, and dictatorial government. Fascism in Romania, however, was more socially radical than elsewhere because of the weakness of the traditional leftist political parties (Communists and Socialists).[3] Although Hitler supported the Romanian Fascists on ideological grounds, his principal concern was that Romanian government policy support Nazi aims, and he was willing to overlook the suppression of the Iron Guard by King Carol II when it was necessary for his broader purposes. At other times, however, Hitler championed the Iron Guard in order to put pressure on the Romanian government.

Despite the effort to cast Germany as a protector of Romanian interests, Hitler had no reluctance secretly to negotiate away Romanian territory when he considered it to be in his own interest. Once Hitler had determined to continue his territorial aims in Central Europe, even if it meant war with Britain and France, he entered into the Non-Aggression Treaty of August 23, 1939, with Stalin. Under the terms of that agreement, Germany and the Soviet Union carved up spheres for themselves in Central and Eastern Europe. In a secret protocol to the non-aggression pact, the boundaries of the two countries' spheres of influence were delineated. The Soviets called attention to their interest in Bessarabia, and Germany declared "its complete disinterestedness in these areas."[4] On June 26, 1940, the Soviet Union massed troops on the Romanian border, Moscow demanded that Romania immediately cede Bessarabia, and the German government counseled Bucharest to yield to the Soviet ultimatum and refused to support armed Romanian resistance to the demand.[5]

The Germans were even more directly and overtly involved in the decision to take the northern part of Transylvania from Romania and grant it to Hungary. Under terms of the Second Vienna Award of August 30, 1940, Italian Foreign Minister Count Galeazzo Ciano and German Foreign Minister Joachim von Ribbentrop reviewed the rival claims of Romania and Hungary to the contested territory and then gave the northern part to Hungary, while allowing Romania to retain only the southern part.[6]

This territorial dismemberment was a devastating blow to Romania. On September 6, 1940, King Carol abdicated and fled the country, the government in office collapsed, and a new government dominated by the Fascist Iron Guard took power. The new Prime Minister, General Ion Antonescu, however, soon suppressed the Fascist revolutionaries and, with German approval and support, established his military dictatorship over Romania. This suited the German interest in stability, which was necessary to exploit Romania's economy for the benefit of the German war machine.[7]

After 1940, the overriding interest of the Romanian people and their government was to regain the lost territories of Transylvania and Bessarabia. Under existing conditions, support for Nazi Germany was the best way to accomplish that. During the war both Romania and Hungary competed for Hitler's favor in order to gain all of Transylvania. When Germany attacked the Soviet Union in June 1941, Romanian troops enthusiastically joined German troops in moving across the border to retake Bessarabia. Romania annexed Bessarabia directly and also took over the administration of a much larger occupied Soviet territory between Bessarabia and the Soviet Black Sea port of Odessa. Although Romania had limited interest in this new territory, it was given to Bucharest by Germany in part as compensation for the loss of northern Transylvania.[8]

Though some leaders of the traditional (or "historical") political parties, particularly those with a more liberal ideology, opposed the close links with Germany, the dictatorship of Antonescu and the general perception of German invincibility discouraged efforts to alter Romania's foreign policy orientation. That perception began to change as German troops, with the support of the Romanian army, suffered defeat after defeat in the USSR and began to retreat in the face of the advancing Red Army. By August 1944, conditions were ready for change. It was clear that the future boundaries of Romania would be determined by the Soviet Union and the Western allied powers. On August 23, 1944, the leaders of the historical parties and a small group of Communist operatives, with the support of King Michael, engineered a coup d'etat against Antonescu. A new national unity government was established, and Romania switched sides in the war. Romanian officials recognized that there was no possibility of retaining Bessarabia, so they focused their efforts on regaining northern Transylvania from Hungary. Relations with Germany were severed, and Romanian troops joined the Soviet Army in driving German and Hungarian troops from Transylvania and then in moving against their positions in Hungary.

The Legacy of the Ethnic German Population in Romania

A pre-war legacy that has had an important impact on Romanian-German relations since 1945 is the large ethnic German population living in Romania.

The Romanian census of 1930 reported a German-speaking population of 745,421 — 4.1 percent of the population.[9] The ethnic German population in Romania was the fourth largest living outside Germany at the time — exceeded only by minorities in Czechoslovakia, the Soviet Union, and Poland. The ancestors of some of these ethnic Germans moved into what became Romania as early as the 11th and 12th centuries, when the Hungarian kings encouraged Saxons to settle in Transylvania to strengthen their hold in that region. The largest and latest mass migration came in the 18th century, when large numbers of Swabians settled in the Danube River Valley at the invitation of the Austrian emperor, who sought to strengthen his borders against the Ottoman Empire.

As a result of the upheaval of World War II, however, the number of ethnic Germans in Romania was substantially reduced. Some voluntarily left Romanian territory to settle in areas annexed to Germany during the war. In 1941, after the USSR seized Bessarabia and Bulgaria was ceded Southern Dobruja, large numbers of Bessarabian and Dobrujan Germans were resettled in newly acquired territories of the Third Reich in what had been Poland. After Romania's switch of alliances in 1944, others were forced to leave because of their links with Nazi Germany. Ethnic Germans had been permitted by the Romanian government to enlist in German military units without this affecting their status as Romanian citizens, and many had taken advantage of the opportunity. After Romania switched sides in August 1944, however, ethnic Germans who served in the Nazi military lost their Romanian citizenship. Many of them and their families fled to Germany as the *Wehrmacht* retreated. They were joined by other ethnic Germans, including some who had been heavily involved in pro-German activities in Romania.[10]

Under the Antonescu government, ethnic Germans enjoyed a privileged status. After the August 1944 coup d'etat, however, the new government reversed this policy and took punitive action against this ethnic minority. The citizenship of everyone who had held a prominent position in German ethnic organizations or who had worked with pro-Nazi groups was revoked. In January 1945 the Soviet occupation army in Romania mobilized able-bodied ethnic Germans and transported them to the Soviet Union to rebuild war-devastated areas. Two months later, the Communist-dominated Romanian government seized property owned by ethnic Germans who had ties to Nazi organizations. During the next four years it implemented further punitive and confiscatory legislation against this minority that was regarded as having been disloyal. In 1949, however, most of the legislation directed specifically against ethnic Germans was repealed, and their civil rights were restored.[11]

The wartime upheaval and these post-war punitive actions against ethnic Germans reduced the German population by more than half. At the time of the 1930 Romanian census, the German population was 745,421. The 1948 census, however, showed only 382,400 claiming German nationality and only 343,913 with German as their mother tongue. Germans went from 4.1 percent of the population in 1930 to less than 2 percent 18 years later.[12]

Although the German population was substantially reduced, it was still a significant portion of the Romanian population. After the massive expulsion of ethnic Germans from Czechoslovakia, Poland, Yugoslavia, and Hungary during the immediate post-war period, Romania had the second largest German minority after the Soviet Union. Furthermore, the Germans in Romania were generally well educated and made up a significant portion of the industrial labor force in Transylvania.

The Long Road to the Establishment of Diplomatic Relations

For nearly two decades after the end of World War II, Romania's relations with West Germany were limited. Immediately after the war, Romania endured the convulsion of a Communist seizure of power and the restructuring of its political, economic and social system. At the same time, West Germany's principal focus was domestic reconstruction. Furthermore, Romanian-West German relations were clearly subordinate to the larger East-West confrontation between Western Europe and the United States on the one hand and the Soviet Union and its client states in Eastern Europe[13] on the other hand. Until the late 1950s or the early 1960s, Romanian foreign policy was subservient to the Soviet Union, and Bucharest's relations with Bonn were subordinate to Moscow's broader concerns. West Germany had much more important concerns with the Soviet Union and East Germany, and clearly relations with these countries took precedence over relations with Romania. At this time, West Germany's Hallstein Doctrine permitted no diplomatic relations and only limited political, economic and cultural ties with any state (other than the USSR) that maintained diplomatic relations with East Germany. As a Soviet client state, Romania had full diplomatic ties and extensive links with East Germany.

By the early 1960s, however, conditions were changing. Romania began to move away from Soviet control for a number of interrelated reasons. First, Romania resented and resisted the economic pressure by the Soviet Union, East Germany, and Czechoslovakia for greater economic integration under the Council for Mutual Economic Assistance (CMEA) and continued its own Stalinist program of autarchic economic development focused on rapid industrialization. Second, Romania began to realign its foreign trade toward Western Europe, and West Germany in particular, because of the availability of superior Western technology and better credit terms. Romania's substantial crude oil resources permitted it greater flexibility in trade with the West than other Eastern European countries enjoyed at that time. Third, by the late 1950s, the Soviet Union's reconsolidation of its hegemony in Eastern Europe, which followed the Hungarian Revolution and Polish upheaval of 1956, began to give way to greater domestic and international flexibility for the Eastern European countries. Fourth, the inter-party differences between the Soviet Union and China began to emerge, and this provided greater maneuvering room for Eastern European Communist regimes that wished to exploit these differences.[14]

In West Germany, as well, conditions were favorable for movement. The Adenauer government began to pursue a more activist role in Eastern Europe. Initially, in order to avoid the complications of the Hallstein Doctrine's *Alleinvertretungsanspruch* (by which the FRG claimed to be the sole legitimate representative of the German nation as a whole), Foreign Minister Gerhard Schröder sought to establish trade missions in Eastern Europe and extend higher levels of government-guaranteed credits for the purchase of West German industrial products. Since there were no unresolved territorial questions from World War II between Romania and West Germany, as there were with Poland and Czechoslovakia, it was considerably easier to reach agreement on trade issues with Romania. Trade negotiations with Poland were the first to be initiated, but Romania was the first of the Eastern European countries to actually sign an agreement establishing a joint trade mission. The Romanian agreement was signed on October 17, 1962. Other agreements followed: with Poland five months later, with Hungary 13 months later, and with Bulgaria 17 months later.[15]

The establishment of trade missions was followed by an intensification of economic contacts, which expanded into other spheres. A series of key visits took place in 1966. In February an important Romanian trade delegation visited Bonn, which paved the way for a visit three months later by the Romanian Foreign Trade Minister Gheorghe Cioara. In September West German Economics Minister Kurt Schmücker was in Bucharest, and during the visit he extended an invitation to Romanian Foreign Minister Corneliu Manescu to visit Bonn. In Bonn on January 31, 1967, Manescu and West German Foreign Minister Willy Brandt signed the agreement establishing full diplomatic relations.[16] This dramatic action was a watershed event for both Romania and West Germany. For Romania it was the boldest act of defiance of the Soviet Union thus far, and for West Germany it marked the abandonment of a key principle of its foreign policy – the Hallstein Doctrine. This act was a critical step in the rapprochement between the Soviet Bloc and West Germany which ultimately led to full normalization of relations between Bonn and Eastern Europe.

The Romanians were more anxious for full diplomatic ties than the West Germans. For Bucharest, this was another important step in expanding its foreign policy autonomy from the Soviet Union, and one that the Romanians hoped would bring concrete benefits in terms of trade and credits. While Romania remained within the Soviet orbit as a member of the Warsaw Pact and CMEA, Romanian leaders frequently made a point of emphasizing their differences with the Soviet Union. They pressed against the limits of Soviet tolerance and occasionally provoked an angry Soviet reaction, but they managed to avoid Soviet military intervention while continuing their foreign policy autonomy.

As noted, Romania's principal reason for seeking full diplomatic relations with West Germany was to underscore further its autonomy within the Soviet bloc. Ironically, however, this desire proved to be a major stumbling block for West Germany, which was now preparing to abandon the Hallstein Doctrine and establish full relations with all the countries of Eastern Europe. Bonn therefore offered to negotiate the exchange of ambassadors with Czechoslovakia and Hungary at the same time as with Romania. In the end, both Prague and Budapest caved in to pressure from East Berlin and Moscow. Territorial questions would in any case have constituted an additional obstacle for Czechoslovakia, as for Poland. Romania thus remained the only one of West Germany's Eastern European prospects that was eager to move ahead, but Bonn now had to consider the possible trade-off of affronting the Soviet Union and obstructing possible later diplomatic progress with Moscow's more pliant Eastern European allies. The Federal Republic finally took the step, as a demonstrative move toward a new *Ostpolitik*, after the establishment of a new government in Bonn. Chancellor Kurt Georg Kiesinger (CDU) headed the Grand Coalition of Christian Democrats and Social Democrats, but the new foreign policy came to be identified with Willy Brandt (SPD), the foreign minister.

East German Reaction to Romania's
Diplomatic Relations with West Germany

The principal difference between Romania and its Warsaw Pact allies on relations with West Germany was over strategy for resolving outstanding issues with Bonn. Romania took the position that problems should be solved on a bilateral basis. The validity of the Munich Agreement, the Oder-Neisse border, and recognition of East Germany should be resolved between West Germany and Czechoslovakia, Poland, and East Germany, respectively. Settling these issues should not be a precondition for Bucharest to improve its relations with Bonn.

This approach became clear in Romania's and West Germany's contradictory treatment of the Hallstein Doctrine, which was of vital importance to East Germany. Bonn left no doubt that diplomatic relations with Bucharest did not represent any change in its attitude toward East Germany. Two days after the agreement with Romania was signed, Chancellor Kiesinger made a statement to the *Bundestag* reaffirming that "the Federal Government alone has the right and obligation to speak for the entire German people."[17] The Romanian news agency, however, issued an official response to the Kiesinger statement, affirming the Romanian view that one of the fundamental realities of post-war

Europe was "the existence of two German states" and "acknowledgement of this reality is one of the prerequisites for the development of co-operation among European countries."[18] In other words, Romania disagreed with Bonn, but it would not make West Germany's recognition of East Germany a precondition for its own establishment of diplomatic relations with Bonn.

The East Germans were furious with Bucharest because recognition by West Germany was a vital question for East Berlin. SED party leader Walter Ulbricht claimed authority on this issue over all other Warsaw Pact countries except the Soviet Union. Ulbricht was quoted as telling Polish party chief Wladislaw Gomulka, "Regarding relations with West Germany, we have the ultimate competence. Not every socialist country can go its own way."[19] In a speech in East Berlin just two weeks after the signing of the Romanian-West German agreement on diplomatic relations, Ulbricht charged that West Germany's *Ostpolitik* was intended to "isolate the DDR, then play off the socialist states against each other."[20]

When it became obvious that Bonn and Bucharest were moving toward formal establishment of diplomatic relations, East Berlin went on the attack. A week before the agreement was signed, *Neues Deutschland* (January 25, 1967) issued a declaration denouncing West Germany's "aggressive and expansionist policy." After the agreement was signed, East German media viciously attacked "the Romanian Foreign Minister" who "was not willing to reject the presumptuous [West German] claim to sole representation," hence, "the preconditions for diplomatic relations did not exist."[21] As polemics between East Berlin and Bucharest escalated,[22] relations between the two fraternal countries were so strained that Romania refused to send a representative to East Berlin for a conference of Warsaw Pace foreign ministers to discuss the issue of relations with West Germany. When the conference was shifted to Warsaw to ensure Romanian participation, Romania sent its *deputy* foreign minister while all other states sent their foreign ministers.

Although Romania's establishment of diplomatic relations with West Germany was the most important single reason for a precipitous decline in relations with East Germany, it was only one of several irritants in Soviet-Romanian relations. Initially the Soviet Union was cautious but not critical of Romania's move, and Bulgaria was permitted to continue negotiations with Bonn on diplomatic relations for two months after the Romanian-West German agreement was signed. Ulbricht's cassandra-like warnings, however, soon persuaded the Soviet Union that the Romanian action represented a serious threat to the stability and cohesion of the Warsaw Pact. By April 1967, East Berlin had won full Soviet backing for a strong line against any further approaches from Bonn.

Relations between Romania and East Germany continued to be severely strained as a result of the decision to proceed with diplomatic relations with West Germany.[23] After relations between East and West Germany were normalized in 1971, relations between East Berlin and Bucharest again became civil, but they remained formal and not cordial.

The Subsequent Development of Relations
between Bucharest and Bonn

For Romania, the agreement with West Germany was a major triumph in its policy of establishing foreign policy autonomy from the Soviet Union. Despite strong Soviet, East German, and Polish disapproval of the Romanian-West German exchange of ambassadors, relations between the two countries progressed rapidly. In August 1967 Willy Brandt paid an official visit to Romania, and had extensive discussions with all Romanian leaders. This was his first official trip to any Eastern European country. During that visit an accord on technical and economic co-operation was signed, and agreement was reached to begin negotiations on a cultural exchange accord.[24]

One issue of concern to the West Germans that continued to be a problem even after the establishment of diplomatic relations was the migration of ethnic Germans in Romania to Germany. In December 1967, West Germany's Minister for Refugees and Expellees Kai-Uwe von Hassel declared that the number of Germans granted permission to leave Romania was unsatisfactory. The number had fallen from 2,700 in 1965 to 609 in 1966, and only 314 were permitted to leave Romania during the first ten months of 1967.[25] The Romanian ambassador in Bonn responded that Romania had too great an investment in the education and training of its Germans to permit free emigration. In part this was accurate – the Germans were a well-educated segment of the Romanian work force. At the same time, however, this argument was part of the Romanian propaganda effort to extort economic compensation from Germany for permitting these Germans to leave. Further-more, the Romanian Communist regime was reluctant to permit the emigration of any segment of its population for fear that it could trigger a large-scale exodus of other groups of the population.

West Germany did extend credits and provide other incentives to encourage Romanian authorities to permit migration. They were somewhat successful, and during the early 1970s the numbers permitted to emigrate increased. In 1974 some 8,000 Germans were given exit visas. After the signature of the Helsinki Accords in 1975, there was hope that Romania might permit a greater flow of people. Those hopes, however, proved illusory. During the years following the Helsinki Accords, it became even more difficult for ethnic Germans to receive permission to leave the country. In 1975 the number was about 5,000 and in 1976 it dropped below 4,000.[26] Romanian President Nicolae Ceauşescu feared the impact upon ethnic Romanians as well as Hungarians if Germans were permitted to leave. The human rights provisions of the Helsinki Accords, which

Romania strongly and consistently opposed, were considered by Ceauşescu to be part of a plot to undermine the stability of his regime. From the early 1970s through 1989, Romania was the Warsaw Pact state with the most stringent travel restrictions on its own citizens. Ceauşescu took a particularly hard line, arguing that migration under the guise of family reunification, in fact, perpetuates family disunity. He contended that since ethnic Germans in Romania enjoy "full rights and liberties," there was no reason for their leaving.[27]

The Romanian decision to establish full diplomatic relations with West Germany vindicated Romania's policy of seeking closer economic ties with the West and lessening its dependence upon the Soviet Union. Trade expanded rapidly after diplomatic relations were established. From 1958 to 1960, Romanian-West German trade averaged $57 million annually, with an average yearly Romanian surplus of $7 million. This increased gradually to $215 million in 1966, when Romania had a deficit of $65 million. When diplomatic relations were established, Bonn, primarily for political reasons, extended a generous trade credit to Romania. In 1967, Romanian imports from West Germany jumped by 73 percent while exports grew by only 29 percent. Bilateral trade was $347 million, with a Romanian deficit of $153 million. West Germany took second place (behind the Soviet Union) as Romania's most important trade partner.

For the next few years, Romanian-West German trade moved toward balance, and in 1971 Romania had a positive surplus of $21 million with total trade of $409 million. West Germany continued to extend significant credits during the 1970s, with Romania running a total trade deficit with West Germany from 1967 through 1981 of nearly $1.8 billion.[28]

Relations with the Two Germanys in Ceauşescu's Later Years

The uniqueness and drama of Romania's establishment of diplomatic relations with West Germany in 1967 were largely due to the fact that it occurred contrary to the wishes of the Soviet Union, East Germany, and Poland. Yet it served Romanian interests because it gave Bucharest another public opportunity to highlight its foreign policy autonomy in an area of vital Soviet and Eastern European interest, and it led to concrete benefits in the area of trade. For West Germany, as well, the decision with Romania was a milestone. It gave West Germany and its new Foreign Minister, Willy Brandt, a quick and striking success that strengthened support for *Ostpolitik*. At the same time, however, it galvanized East German and Soviet attitudes on the issue of relations with Bonn. Ultimately, it was one of the important factors that led to the resolution of outstanding problems on the divided continent. After the establishment of the SPD-FDP coalition with Willy Brandt as West German Chancellor in the fall of 1969, the Soviet Union and the Eastern European countries exhibited a greater willingness to work toward the settlement of outstanding problems with Bonn. Within a relatively short time span, West Germany had resolved thorny bilateral problems with Poland and Czechoslovakia, and relations between East and West Germany were normalized. The 1975 Helsinki Conference on Security and Cooperation in Europe represented the culmination of that effort toward detente.

The success of West Germany's *Ostpolitik* and the progress of the Helsinki process led to a decline in the importance of relations with Romania for West Germany. When Bucharest was the only Eastern European capital (with the exception of the special case of Moscow) with a West German ambassador, it was important as a symbol of Bonn's interest and intentions toward the East. After relations were established with other Eastern European states, however, Romania was no longer unique. West Germany had many broader and more important political and economic interests with the Soviet Union, East Germany, Poland, and Czechoslovakia. Clearly the relationship was much more important for Bucharest than it was for Bonn, particularly with regard to trade and economic cooperation. The volume of trade with West Germany was an important segment of Romania's economic exchanges and a significant source of heavy equipment and Western technology. Moreover, Bonn showed consideration for Bucharest despite the lessened importance to the West Germans of this first full diplomatic link to an Eastern European country (other than the Soviet Union).

Although independence from the Soviet Union was a critical element that permitted the establishment of diplomatic relations between Romania and West Germany in 1967, the limits of Romania's foreign policy autonomy soon became evident and the significance of the policy became less important to the West. The Soviet-led invasion of Czechoslovakia in 1968 and Moscow's response to other crises in Eastern Europe emphasized the limits of Soviet toleration for Romanian independence, and Nicolae Ceauşescu was acutely aware of those constraints. It also became increasingly evident to the West Germans and the NATO allies that there was no alternative to direct cooperation with the Soviet Union in key areas such as arms control and regional issues. The Helsinki process and the Western policy of detente were the consequence of this rethinking of Western policy. In the context of improving relations with Moscow, it could have been counterproductive to such broader and more important foreign policy goals to encourage an unruly Soviet client state like Romania.[29]

The Helsinki process focused greater international attention on domestic liberalization and basic human rights — freedom of speech, press, religion, protection of the rights of ethnic minorities, and intellectual dissent. With this emphasis, Romania's repressive internal policies caused growing problems in its relations with Bonn and other Western allies. Ceauşescu's treatment of the minorities intensified the problems with West Germany. Bonn's interest in a more liberal Romanian migration policy clashed with Ceauşescu's fear that permission for ethnic Germans to leave would open the floodgates for all.

As a result of these growing tensions with West Germany and the member countries of the European Community, there were unpleasant exchanges between Bonn and Bucharest, restriction of trade benefits by the European Community, the withdrawal of credits, suspension of discussions on a trade agreement with the European Community, and other sanctions against Romania. During the last few years of the Ceauşescu regime, Romania's flagrant violations of human rights became the dominant element in its relations with the Western countries. Its intransigence in the face of strong Western protests resulted in the further deterioration of relations with Bonn.

During Ceauşescu's final year in power, relations reached a low point. West Germany was one of the nations of the European Community that sent its diplomats to meet with Romanian dissidents in order to provide them with a measure of protection and to make its displeasure with Romanian human rights policies known. Bonn formally protested to Bucharest about a number of cases of individual human rights abuses. The West German ambassador to Bucharest was recalled in April 1989, and the following month a strong protest was issued following an "unbelievable" incident in which the wife of a West German diplomat was attacked in broad daylight by Romanian *Securitate* forces while she was walking near her home.[30] A series of unpleasant diplomatic messages were exchanged between Bonn and Bucharest that same year over an invitation to visit Germany extended to former Romanian Foreign Minister Corneliu Manescu, who was out of favor with President Ceauşescu.

Economic relations with West Germany underwent a major transformation during the 1980s as a result of a massive centrally-directed effort to eliminate Romania's foreign debt. Although by the 1980s most Eastern European states had moved away from Stalinist economic autarchy, Ceauşescu continued to pursue self-sufficiency. Romania incurred substantial foreign debt in the late 1960s and 1970s to encourage domestic economic growth, and a significant portion of that debt was owed to West Germany. This became a serious irritant to the Romanian dictator. In particular, Ceauşescu resented the fact that international lending institutions and foreign bankers criticized his economic policies and demanded changes.

In the early 1980s, Romania reduced imports to the absolute minimum, while it sought to push its own exports, such as agricultural products, to the limit. As a result, virtually all high-quality meat and produce went out of the country. Romanian consumers were left with bruised, spoiled fruits and vegetables and chicken feet or pork bones. In order to cut hard currency imports of increasingly costly petroleum products, the government rationed gasoline and imposed strict controls on energy consumption. Even the press of the Soviet bloc found the consequences to be dismal. In mid-1989, on the eve of a visit to Romania by Soviet party leader Mikhail Gorbachev, the Soviet Communist party daily

Pravda reported: "For several years Romanians have not been receiving enough food and manufactured goods. Lines, infamous shortages, ration cards, and the strict conservation of fuel and energy, sometimes contrary to the interests of the people – this is the reality of Romania today."[31]

Between 1981 and the end of 1988, Romania reduced its foreign debt from some $10 billion to about $2.5 billion. As a result of this massive repayment effort from the early 1980s until the collapse of the Ceauşescu regime at the end of 1989, Romania ran a consistent trade surplus with West Germany that totalled some $2.7 billion.[32] The policy of seeking foreign credits to encourage economic development, which Ceauşescu had supported since his designation as party leader in 1965, was completely reversed. At a plenary session of the Romanian Communist Party Central Committee in April 1989, Ceauşescu announced that Romania had completely repaid its foreign debts, and three days later the Romanian parliament adopted legislation barring the country from ever again accepting foreign loans.[33]

As Romania's relations with West Germany and the Western countries went into decline from the late 1970s through the 1980s, relations with East Germany improved. This was particularly true after Mikhail Gorbachev came to power in the Soviet Union in 1985. As Romania's paranoia about economic and political reforms in Hungary and Poland increased, it sought improved ties with those Communist states in Eastern Europe that opposed reform. Noticeably warmer relations developed between Ceauşescu and East German party leader Erich Honecker as both maintained their adamant opposition to Soviet-encouraged reform. In fact, one of the last foreign visits made by Romanian President Ceauşescu in October 1989 was to attend the celebrations in East Berlin that marked the 40th anniversary of the German Democratic Republic. That occasion, however, also marked the end of the GDR, as popular opposition surged to the surface during the anniversary celebrations, and shortly thereafter overwhelmed the East German Communist regime.

Romanian Relations with Germany after Ceauşescu

In December 1989 Ceauşescu, too, was overthrown in a bloody uprising against his repressive regime. With the exception of maverick Albania, Romania was the last Eastern European country to be swept up in the democratic transformation. The violent overthrow of the old regime in Romania was in marked contrast to the generally peaceful transformations that took place elsewhere in the old Soviet bloc. This was a reflection of the repressive, Stalinist system that Ceauşescu had maintained in Romania during the quarter century he remained in power. Although there are serious questions about the democratic credentials and aspirations of the National Salvation Front government that was swept to power in Romania after Ceauşescu's summary execution by a military firing squad on Christmas Day 1989, there is no question that the lot of the Romanian people has improved.

West Germany was one of the countries to provide immediate assistance to the Romanian people after the revolution, and it was one of the most generous contributors. Three weeks after Ceaușescu's overthrow, West German Foreign Minister Hans-Dietrich Genscher was in Bucharest to show support for the new government and to assess the need for humanitarian and economic assistance to the beleaguered Romanian people. This generosity was reflected in the trade figures. During 1990, West German exports to Romania jumped to record levels, reaching a value of $1.113 billion.[34] At the same time, Romanian exports to Germany fell off sharply, reflecting the economic disorganization and political upheaval. Although Germany was initially supportive of the new government in Bucharest, it joined the Western chorus of criticism of the government-inspired violence of the Romanian miners against democratic protesters in Bucharest during the summer of 1990 and the other all-to-frequent anti-democratic actions of Romanian officials.

The collapse of the Ceaușescu regime brought a significant change in the migration of ethnic Germans from Romania to Germany. During his visit to Bucharest in January 1990, just after the establishment of the new government, Foreign Minister Genscher said that he expected 60 to 80 percent of Romania's ethnic Germans to migrate to Germany.[35] The German government moved quickly to establish consulates in the cities of Timișoara, Brașov, and Sibiu to handle matters involving the German minority, including the distribution of visas for permanent residence in Germany. There followed a flood of applications. By mid-1990, from five hundred to a thousand Germans were arriving daily at the Nürnberg center for processing emigrants from Romania. Between January 1 and August 12, 1990, West German authorities reported that 86,623 emigrants had arrived in Germany from Romania.[36] In October 1991, less than two years after Ceaușescu's overthrow, it was estimated that the German population in Romania numbered only 74,000 – a drastic decline from the 200,000 to 220,000 still in Romania in December 1989.[37]

As freedom of movement permitted ethnic Germans to leave Romania, however, other groups also sought to leave Romania and this created new problems. For example, large numbers of Romanian Gypsies attempted to enter Germany illegally. In May of 1990, seven hundred Romanian refugees, mostly Gypsies, were crowded into an army barracks outside East Berlin, while another two thousand sought refuge in and around the railroad station in Dresden. Thousands more were reported in other locations.

The instability and serious domestic political, economic and social problems have forced the Romanian government to focus predominantly upon internal issues. Until fundamental domestic problems are resolved, Bucharest is unlikely to give international relations a high priority. Romania's principal foreign policy concern has been to improve its image in order to overcome its diplomatic isolation, an isolation that endures despite the overthrow of the Ceauşescu regime. Germany, as one of the leading powers in the European Community, has played an important role in EC policy toward Romania. Romania, in turn, has gone out of its way to maintain cordial relations with Bonn. The unification of Germany in October 1990 posed few, if any, problems for Bucharest, and the Romanian government welcomed the event as marking the end of the Cold War era.

For Romania, the key element in relations with Germany is likely to continue to be trade and economic cooperation. The Romanian economy is still in difficult straits, and only serious reform and restructuring will make it possible to progress. Germany is still of special importance in this endeavor, but increasingly it will be the European Community that sets the agenda for economic issues.

Traditional diplomatic and economic ties with Germany are likely to continue to be a greater priority for Romania than for Germany. German credits and technology will continue to be important, as in the past. Furthermore, with the disintegration of the Soviet Union, which was the largest single trading partner of Romania until 1989, Germany is likely to become even more important as a market for Romanian food, industrial and energy products. Germans, however, might see Romania as less important economically than in the past. The economic integration of the former East German *Länder* will absorb considerable German effort and resources. German enterprises are also facing new competition at home and new opportunities elsewhere in the European Community, as the Common Market integrates further. Even among the countries of Central and Eastern Europe, Romania is now among the least important to Germany. Poland, Czechoslovakia, and Hungary are closer to Germany physically and culturally, more economically developed, and more important politically than Romania. Hence they are likely to rank higher in Germany's hierarchy of foreign interests.

The undulating, on-again/off-again nature of Romanian-German relations clearly appears to be in an "off" phase at present. That does not mean, however, that it will always remain so. At critical times over the past century Romanian-German relations were highly significant — not only to the two countries involved, but in a much broader international context. Romania is one of German's smaller neighbors and it lies a good distance from Germany's borders. At the same time, however, Romania is now the largest Balkan state. With the disintegration of both the Soviet Union and Yugoslavia, Romania will assume a much more prominent role in that traditionally unstable region, particularly if its political system stabilizes and its economy recovers. Germany has historically had a strong geopolitical interest in the Balkans. The newly united Germany's obvious interest in containing the recent instability in Yugoslavia, including Bonn's leadership within the European Community on extending diplomatic recognition to Croatia and Slovenia, reflects an enduring interest in that region. Germany and Romania may well emerge from the present bilateral lull to a revival of their traditionally intense and significant relationship.

Notes

1. On German policy toward the Balkans and Romania during the Nazi period, see Hugh Seton-Watson *Eastern Europe Between the Wars, 1918-1941* (New York: Harper and Row, 1967), *passim*; and Marilynn Giroux Hitchens, *Germany, Russia, and the Balkans: Prelude to the Nazi-Soviet Non-Aggression Pact* (Boulder, Colorado: East European Monographs distributed by Columbia University Press in New York, 1983). Two accounts of this period by Romanian diplomats who participated in them are also of importance in understanding that period: Grigore Gafencu, *Prelude to the Russian Campaign: From the Moscow Pact (August 21st 1939) to the opening of hostilities in Russia (June 22nd 1941)*, translated by E. Fletcher-Allen (London: F. Muller, 1945) and Alexandre Cretzianu, *The Lost Opportunity* (London: Jonathan Cape, 1957).

2. Figures cited in Henry L. Roberts, *Rumania: Political Problems of an Agrarian State* (New Haven: Yale University Press, 1951), p. 214. For additional details on the economic aspects of Romanian-German relations during this period, see Roberts, *Rumania*, pp. 214-22; William S. Grenzebach, Jr., *Germany's Informal Empire in East-Central Europe: German Economic Policy Toward Yugoslavia and Rumania, 1933-1939* (Stuttgart: Franz Steiner Verlag Wiesbaden GMBH, 1988); H.W. Arndt, *The Economic Lessons of the Nineteen-Thirties* (Oxford: Oxford University Press, 1944), pp. 174-206; and Antonin Basch, *The Danube Basin and the German Economic Sphere* (New York: Columbia University Press, 1943), *passim*.

3. See Robert R. King, *History of the Romanian Communist Party* (Stanford, CA: Hoover Institution Press, 1980), pp. 26-27. On Romanian Fascism, see the following works by Eugen Weber: "The Men of the Archangel," *Journal of Contemporary History*, Vol. 1, No. 1 (1966), pp. 105-22; "Romania," in Hans Rogger and Eugen Weber, eds., *The European Right* (Berkeley and Los Angeles: University of California Press, 1966), pp. 501-74; and *Varieties of Fascism* (Princeton, N.J.: Princeton University Press, 1964). Others who have given good insight into Romanian Fascism include Nicholas M. Nagy-Talavera, *The Green Shirts and Others: A History of Fascism in Hungary and Rumania* (Stanford, CA: Hoover Institution Press, 1970); Emanual Turczynski, "The Background of Romanian Fascism," and Stephen Fischer-Galați, "Fascism in Romania," in Peter F. Sugar, ed., *Native Fascism in the Successor States, 1918-1945* (Santa Barbara, CA: ABC-Clio, 1971), pp. 99-121. Roberts also provides helpful insights into Romanian Fascism, *Rumania*, pp. 223-33.

4. Raymond J. Sontag and James S. Beddie, eds., *Nazi Soviet Relations 1939-1941: Documents from the Archives of the German Foreign Office* (Washington, D.C.: Department of State, 1948), p. 78.

5. Bessarabia, which makes up the bulk of the former Soviet Socialist Republic of Moldavia and of the current Republic of Moldova, is the territory that lies between the Prut and Dniester rivers. Turkish until 1812, when the area was added to the Russian Empire, it became part of Romania in 1918 when Russia was too preoccupied with its

own revolution to prevent the loss. The Soviet Union never accepted that forfeiture of territory. For background on Bessarabia, see Robert R. King, *Minorities Under Communism: Nationalities as a Source of Tension Among Balkan Communist States* (Cambridge, MA: Harvard University Press, 1973), pp. 31-35 and 91-108; *Facts and Comments Concerning Bessarabia, 1812-1940* (London: G. Allen and Unwin, 1941); and Charles Upson Clark, *Bessarabia: Russia and Roumania on the Black Sea* (New York: Dodd, Mead and Co., 1927).

6. The western third of Romania, known as Transylvania, was a part of the Austro-Hungarian Empire until 1918 when it was annexed to Romania. Historically it was a part of Hungary, and it was the first area to be settled when the wandering Hungarian tribes arrived in Europe in the 9th century. That territory still has a substantial ethnic Hungarian minority population of as many as 2 million. For background on Transylvania, see King, *Minorities Under Communism*, pp. 35-44, 76-90 and 146-69.

7. On the relations between Nazi Germany and Romania during the period 1933-1945, see Andreas Hillgruber, *Hitler, König Carol und Marschall Antonescu* (Wiesbaden: Steiner, 1965).

8. On Romanian administration of the province of Transnistria, see Alexander Dallin, *Odessa, 1941-1944: A Case Study of Soviet Territory under Foreign Rule* (Santa Monica, CA: Rand Corporation, 1957).

9. *Anuarul Statistic al Romîniei 1939* (Bucharest, 1939). These 1930 figures were for the territory of Romania as it was at that time, including Bessarabia and Northern Bukovina, which were ceded to the Soviet Union in 1940 and confirmed by peace treaty in 1947, and southern Dobruja, which was ceded to Bulgaria in 1940 and confirmed after the war.

10. On the policies of the Nazi government toward the ethnic Germans in Romania, see Wolfgang Meige, *Das Dritte Reich und die Deutsche Volksgruppe in Rumänien 1933-38: Ein Beitrag zur nationalsozialistischen Volkstumspolitik* (Frankfurt/M: Herbert Lang, 1972) and Johann Böhm, *Das Nationalsozialistische Deutschland und die Deutsche Volksgruppe in Rumänien 1936-1944: Das Verhältnis der Deutschen Volksgruppe zum Dritten Reich und zum rumänischen Staat sowie der interne Widerstreit zwischen den politischen Gruppen* (Frankfurt/M: Peter Lang, 1985).

11. The most thorough discussion of the numbers of Germans who were relocated, fled, or were expelled during the period between 1940 and 1949 is Joseph B. Schechtman, *European Population Transfers, 1939-1945* (New York: Russell & Russell, 1946), pp. 174-213 and 225-37; and Joseph B. Schechtman, *Postwar Population Transfers in Europe, 1945-1955* (Philadelphia: University of Pennsylvania Press, 1962), pp. 263-71. George C. Paikert, *The Danube Swabians: German Populations in Hungary, Rumania and Yugoslavia and Hitler's Impact on their Patterns* (The Hague: Martinus Nijhoff, 1967), pp. 243-60. On the regulations adopted by the Romanian government against its German citizens, see Werner Conze et al., eds., *Dokumentation der Vertreibung der Deutschen aus Ost-mitteleuropa* (Berlin: Bundesministerium für Vertriebene, Flüchtlinge und Kriegesgeschädigte, 1957-1961), volume on Romania.

12. *Anuarul Statistic al Romîniei 1939* (Bucharest, 1939) and *Recensămîntul Populaţiei din 21 Februarie 1956. Structura Demografică a Populaţiei* (Bucharest, n.d.).

13. "Eastern Europe" is a term that has been criticized as having a negative connotation, and some have argued that "Central" or "East-Central Europe" is a better phrase. While that description may be somewhat more accurate geographically and more

relevant in describing current aspirations of the countries involved, it is a much less precise term than "Eastern Europe," which was used consistently in the past to refer to the group of six countries that formerly were Soviet client states and members of the Warsaw Pact — Poland, East Germany, Czechoslovakia, Hungary, Romania, and Bulgaria. When "Eastern Europe" is used in the chapter, it refers specifically to this group of six countries at the time prior to the revolutionary changes that took place at the end of 1989.

14. Romania's autonomous foreign policy during the period 1960-1989 has been the subject of a number of descriptive and analytical works. The following deal with this period in considerable detail: R. L. Braham, "Rumania Onto the Separate Path," *Problems of Communism*, 13:2 (May-June 1964), pp. 14-24; J. F. Brown, "Rumania Steps Out of Line," *Survey*, No. 49 (October 1963), pp. 19-34; R. V. Burks, "The Rumanian National Deviation: An Accounting," in Kurt London, ed., *Eastern Europe in Transition* (Baltimore: The Johns Hopkins Press, 1966); Robert Farlow, "Romanian Foreign Policy: A Case of Partial Alignment," *Problems of Communism*, 20:6 (November-December 1971), pp. 54-63; Stephen Fischer-Galaţi, *The New Rumania: From People's Democracy to Socialist Republic* (Cambridge, MA: The MIT Press, 1967); David Floyd, *Rumania: Russia's Dissident Ally* (New York: Praeger, 1965); Graeme J. Gill, "Rumania's Background to Autonomy," *Problems of Communism* 15:1 (January-February 1966), pp. 16-28; and Kenneth Jowitt, *Revolutionary Breakthroughs and National Development: The Case of Romania, 1944-1965* (Berkeley and Los Angeles: University of California Press, 1971), pp. 198-272. For my own analysis of Romania's autonomous foreign policy, see *History of the Romanian Communist Party*, pp. 135-49; "Autonomy and Detente: The Problems of Rumanian Foreign Policy," *Survey*, No. 91-92 (Spring-Summer 1974), pp. 105-20; and "Romania's Struggle for an Autonomous Foreign Policy," *The World Today*, 35:8 (July 1979), pp. 340-48.

15. For information on the agreement, see Auswärtiges Amt der Bundesrepublik Deutschland, *Die Auswärtige Politik der Bundesrepublik Deutschland* (Cologne: Verlag Wissenschaft und Politik, 1972), p. 504.

16. On the agreement to establish diplomatic relations, see *Die Auswärtige Politik der Bundesrepublik Deutschland*, p. 588-89.

17. *Frankfurter Allgemeine Zeitung*, February 2, 1967.

18. Agerpres [Romanian press agency], February 1, 1967.

19. Quoted by Erwin Weit, "Ostbloc Intern," *Der Spiegel*, August 17, 1970.

20. Reported by ADN, February 15, 1967; see also *Neues Deutschland*, February 16, 1967.

21. *Neues Deutschland,* January 25, 1967; ADN February 1, 1967 and *Neues Deutschland*, February 2, 1967. See the front page editorial in *Neues Deutschland*, February 3, 1967.

22. See, for example, the Romanian reply to the *Neues Deutschland* editorial in *Scînteia*, February 4, 1967. The Romanian party daily observed: "The foreign policy of a socialist state is laid down by the party and government of the country in question, and they need render account only to their people . . . The attempt of the newspaper [*Neues Deutschland*] to set itself up as the foreign policy advisor to another state, its interference in the internal affairs of another country, does not serve the interests . . . of friendship and cooperation between socialist countries."

23. East Germany publicly attacked Romania for deviating from Warsaw Pact policy on East-West relations (*Neues Deutschland*, May 11, 1967) and for maintaining diplomatic relations with Israel following the June 1967 Middle East War (see *Neues Deutschland*, June 12, 1967). The harshest criticism, however, was for Romanian relations with West Germany, and the visit of Willy Brandt to Romania in August 1967 brought forth a new round of vituperation (see *Neues Deutschland*, August 6 and August 10, 1967; *Berliner Zeitung*, August 10, 1967).

24. Final communiqué on Brandt's visit, Agerpres, August 6, 1967. The cultural exchange agreement continued to be a problem in Romanian-West German relations. Efforts to negotiate such an agreement earlier had floundered on the question of Berlin (see *Handelsblatt*, May 20, 1965; *Welt am Sonntag*, August 16, 1965; and *Die Welt*, November 24, 1965). Although negotiations were begun after the Brandt visit, a number of documents, but not the cultural exchange agreement, were signed in May 1969.

25. dpa, December 12, 1967.

26. dpa, October 15, 1976 and January 19, 1977.

27. See Ceauşescu's strong statement against German migration in his speech to the Congress on Political Education and Socialist Culture, *Scînteia*, June 3, 1976. See also his interview in *Frankfurter Rundschau*, July 27, 1976, and his comments to the newly-arrived West German ambassador to Romania, Radio Bucharest, October 7, 1976.

28. Trade figures are from *Direction of Trade Yearbook* (Washington, D.C.: International Monetary Fund and International Bank for Reconstruction and Development), issues for 1958-1962, 1963-1967, 1968-1972, 1970-1976, and 1980.

29. For a discussion of the impact of detente upon Romania's quest for an autonomous foreign policy, see King, "Autonomy and Detente: The Problems of Rumanian Foreign Policy."

30. dpa, May 10, 1989.

31. *Pravda* [Moscow], July 7, 1989.

32. Trade figures from *Direction of Trade Statistics* (Washington, D.C.: International Monetary Fund and International Bank for Reconstruction and Development), Yearbook 1987 and Yearbook 1991.

33. Agerpres, April 14, 1989; *Scînteia*, April 15, 1989 and April 19, 1989.

34. Trade figures from *Direction of Trade Statistics* (Washington, D.C.: International Monetary Fund and International Bank for Reconstruction and Development), Yearbook 1991.

35. Rompres [Romanian press agency], January 15, 1990.

36. *România Liberă*, May 31, 1990; dpa, August 18, 1990. The report on emigrants from Romania did not specify how many were ethnic Germans and how many were of other ethnicity. Since only ethnic Germans were receiving official permission to enter Germany, however, it is clear that most, if not all, were German.

37. Arpres [Romanian press agency], October 24, 1991. See also Michael Shafir and Dan Ionescu, "Romania: The Minorities in 1991: Mutual Distrust, Social Problems, and Disillusion," *REF/RL Research Institute: Report on Eastern Europe*, 2:50 (December 13, 1991), p. 27.

PART FOUR

Neighbors to the South

14

Yugoslavia and the Two Germanys

Sabrina Petra Ramet

Germany — and in the years 1949-89/90, the two Germanys — has always loomed large in Yugoslav foreign policy. The Federal Republic of Germany (FRG) was long one of Yugoslavia's top three trading partners, and for a while, was its most important trading partner, in terms of the overall value of commodities exchanged. German tourism was more important to the Yugoslav economy than tourism from any other country. And remittances from Yugoslav *Gastarbeiter* (literally, "guest workers") resident in West Germany provided an important source of revenue for Yugoslavia throughout the 1970s and 1980s.

The following pages trace the course of Yugoslav-German relations from 1948 to the present, highlighting the distinct relationships pursued by Belgrade with both Bonn and East Berlin, and the attendant complications associated both with that triangular relationship and with Yugoslavia's nonaligned course. The chapter ends with a discussion of the current Yugoslav civil war and Germany's response to it. German-Yugoslav relations in the interwar period and during World War II are touched on later in the chapter, in the context of contemporary recollections of that period. For the purposes of this chapter, the story begins at the close of World War II.

The Early Years

Comparing the documents issued as a result of Yugoslav-West German talks with those issuing from Yugoslav-East German talks, it would seem, at first sight — at least where the late 1970s and the early 1980s are concerned — that the latter were "warmer." With the East Germans, the Yugoslavs could agree on Marxism-Leninism, on the threats to world peace, even on the need to keep West Germany from acquiring nuclear arms.[1] In talks with the West Germans, by contrast, the Yugoslavs agreed on the importance of trade and cooperation.[2] The wording seemed to suggest greater bonding among Communist comrades. The reality, of course, was more complex.

The early post-war years of the Yugoslav-German triangular relationship (i.e., Yugoslavia, the Federal Republic of Germany, and the German Democratic Republic) were very much affected by the expulsion of Yugoslavia from the Cominform in June 1948 and the subsequent Cominform blockade. The East German Communists obediently picked up Moscow's tune in the dispute, and continued to bombard Belgrade with hostile rhetoric until 1955.[3]

As a result, Yugoslavia was frozen out of the socialist camp at a time when it badly needed to continue with post-war economic reconstruction. The Yugoslavs looked West for assistance, and became the first Communist government to recognize the Bonn government — 16 years before Romania did so. In 1951, Stane Pavlić, Yugoslavia's representative in Bonn, was raised to the rank of ambassador. The German Consulate General in Belgrade was elevated to embassy status later, on February 24, 1952. The first economic agreement between Yugoslavia and West Germany was signed already in 1951, which granted the Belgrade regime 180 million DM in credit, later raised in 1953. The two countries signed a trade agreement in June 1952, followed by four additional agreements in the years 1952-57. By 1957, West Germany accounted for 13.2 percent of Yugoslav exports and 11.4 percent of Yugoslav imports.[4]

The most difficult issue affecting the Yugoslav-West German relationship in these early years (up to 1957) was that of German indemnification for suffering and damage caused in World War II. As part of the Potsdam Declaration of 1945 and subsequent documents, individual countries that had suffered war losses were referred either to the Federal Republic or to the German Democratic Republic (GDR) for reparations. Yugoslavia was one of 18 countries instructed to refer claims to the Bonn government. Yet when the Yugoslav government presented its bill of 2 billion DM to Bonn in 1955, the latter offered, instead, total reparations of 300 million DM — 60 million in the form of an immediate cash payment, and 240 million in interest-free credits, with a 99-year term.[5] In return for this indemnification for Yugoslav losses, the Germans sought the repatriation of German soldiers held in Yugoslav POW camps. As early as January 1946, the Yugoslavs had released some 1,500 German prisoners from the POW camp at Brčko, releasing another 2,100 two weeks later.[6] The repatriation of German POWs in Yugoslavia continued during 1948 and 1949. The total number of Germans held in Yugoslav POW camps had been 53,130.[7] At the same time, the Yugoslav government allowed its ethnic Germans to leave the country. Most of them took refuge in the American zone of occupied Germany.[8]

By 1955, however, Yugoslav President Josip Broz Tito was patching up his relationship with the Soviets, and appeared eager to be readmitted into the socialist camp. Hence, he offered a partial (and quite adequate) endorsement of the Soviet invasion of Hungary in November 1956, and, on September 10, 1957, officially recognized the Oder-Neisse line as the legitimate German-Polish border. The West Germans, who did not recognize the legitimacy of that border at the time, wondered what else Tito was planning, and asked the Yugoslav ambassador accredited to Bonn if the Yugoslav president intended to recognize East Germany. The ambassador answered, not in the foreseeable future. Yet, exactly a month later, on October 10, 1957, the Tito regime recognized the GDR. Bonn immediately broke off diplomatic ties, citing the Hallstein Doctrine. Named after Walter Hallstein, one of Adenauer's principal foreign policy aides, the Hallstein Doctrine, first set forth in 1955, declared that the West German government would deny diplomatic recognition to any government that maintained diplomatic ties with East Germany. Bonn exempted the Soviet Union, when it became possible, in 1955, for Bonn and Moscow to exchange ambassadors. But Yugoslavia's extension of diplomatic recognition to East Germany two years later was not granted a similar exemption and was treated by Bonn as an infraction of the doctrine.[9]

Yugoslav Relations with West Germany, 1957-68

With the rupture in diplomatic ties, relations between Yugoslavia and the FRG seriously deteriorated. Consular relations were maintained, and official contacts were conducted through intermediaries — Sweden and France. But these arrangements were not fully adequate, and the discussion of major issues in the relationship became extremely difficult.[10] All the same, economic and cultural cooperation not only continued, but grew. No new trade agreements were signed, but the validity of earlier agreements was confirmed and extended on a year-to-year basis, through notes exchanged via the countries serving as intermediaries. At that time, the bulk (65 percent) of Yugoslav exports to West Germany consisted of foodstuffs and other agricultural products, and raw materials. More than half (53 percent) of Yugoslav imports from the FRG at that time consisted of finished products (chiefly industrial machines and means of transportation).[11] Immediately after the rupture in diplomatic relations, Bonn withdrew the "Hermes" guarantees for business deals with Yugoslavia (state guarantees for credits). These were largely restored in October 1959, but with clear limits set on that occasion.

Two issues dominated the Belgrade-Bonn agenda in the late 1950s and early 1960s: indemnification, and Croatian exiles in Germany. Where the former was concerned, Belgrade insisted on further payments, while Bonn refused to undertake any action as long as there were no diplomatic ties. Belgrade interpreted this as diplomatic blackmail, since Bonn's condition for re-recognition was the former's termination of ties with East Berlin. Since Bonn had, by the early 1960s, satisfied the other 17 countries with war damage claims, the Yugoslav government took particular offense at this impasse. Belgrade drew attention, moreover, to the fact that Yugoslavia had been one of the first countries to release German prisoners of war, allowing them to return home.

The second issue was perhaps even more tangled. The Yugoslavs insisted that Bonn undertake effective action to suppress certain Croatian emigré organizations, which the Yugoslav government claimed were involved in anti-Yugoslav terrorism.[12] Belgrade cited various terrorist actions, which it blamed on Croatian emigrés living in West Germany. On November 24, 1962, an attack on the Yugoslav Trade Mission in Bad Godesberg — blamed on Croatian *Ustasha* — resulted in one death.

Little could be done as long as Konrad Adenauer remained West German chancellor. But in 1963, Adenauer retired and was succeeded in office by Ludwig Erhard, a man widely touted for his "pragmatic," nononsense approach. Soon after Erhard's accession, Bonn sent three notes to the Yugoslav government, replying to various Yugoslav demands and signalling Erhard's desire to end the deadlock.

By 1964, relations were on the mend. A new economic agreement was signed, which provided for more liberal regulation of Yugoslav exports to West Germany. The agreement also postponed the Yugoslav debt, increased the credit-level set by the "Hermes" guarantee, and granted new prospects in the field of transport. Of special importance in the 1964 agreement was the establishment of a mixed inter-governmental committee to foster economic cooperation without recourse to intermediaries.[13] But a pall was soon cast over this limited rapprochement, by two events.

The first was the announcement by the Bonn government in January 1965 that it might suspend further prosecution of Nazi war criminals. The Yugoslav Federal Assembly immediately issued a note condemning the proposal.[14]

The second was Tito's visit to the GDR in June 1965. During this visit, Tito explicitly echoed the East German position that, in any discussion of German reunification, ". . . it is impossible to speak about any solution of the German problem without taking into account that there are two sovereign German states with different social systems."[15] The Bonn government declared that this visit betrayed Yugoslav disinterest in friendship with West Germany, and backed away from its earlier suggestion that relations might be "normalized." It was to be a year before Vice Chancellor Erich Mende would signal renewed West German interest in a restoration of diplomatic ties.[16]

This overture must be seen in the context of Bonn's larger *Ostpolitik*. Bonn had already signed major trade agreements with Poland (1963), Romania (1964), Hungary (1964), and Bulgaria (1964). In March 1966, Chancellor Erhard sent a note to the East European capitals that figured very much as an olive branch. By July 4, 1967, Bonn had established an embassy in Romania (waiving the Hallstein Doctrine). The new West German chancellor, Kurt-Georg Kiesinger, continued the concept of restoring ties with Yugoslavia. In 1967, the FRG banned Croatian emigré political organizations — thus satisfying a major Yugoslav desideratum. In February 1968, diplomatic ties were finally restored, and in October of that same year, an agreement was signed regarding the employment of Yugoslav *Gastarbeiter* in West Germany.

After a rather shaky start in the 1950s, Yugoslav-West German trade grew more steadily in the 1960s. From a total value of 252.5 million DM in 1950, the volume of their bilateral trade grew to the level of 1,981.6 million DM by 1968. As of 1967, Yugoslavia accounted for only 1 percent of total West German foreign trade, while West Germany accounted for some 12.8 percent of total Yugoslav foreign trade that same year.[17]

Yugoslav Relations with East Germany, 1957-71

The establishment of diplomatic ties between Yugoslavia and the GDR in 1957 did not usher in a period of friendly and harmonious mutual appreciation. Quite on the contrary, new polemics and frictions were ignited just six months later, when the SED (the East German ruling party) obediently followed Moscow's course and condemned the Yugoslav Seventh Party Congress of April 1958 as "revisionist." As a result, neither side took any move to consolidate the new ties by elevating the provisional diplomatic representatives to the rank of ambassadors. This proved possible only much later — in September 1966, when SED party chief Walter Ulbricht visited Yugoslavia.

As in the relationship with the FRG, economics proved easier than politics. Indeed, between 1958 and 1963, bilateral trade increased by 175 percent, and in early 1963, Yugoslavia and the GDR signed a trade agreement valued at 100 million (East) German marks. This was followed by the signing of a long-term trade agreement in December 1965 and by the establishment of a standing Commission for German-Yugoslav Scientific-Technical Cooperation in 1966. The commission had held six sessions by June 1969. At the same time, Walter Ulbricht's support for Yugoslavia's application for association with COMECON played a key role in COMECON's agreement, in 1965, to grant Yugoslavia this special status.[18] On the political side of the ledger, neither side would accommodate the other. Thus, for example, while Tito worked to promote the two-Germanys concept (favored by East Berlin) among members of the Nonaligned Movement, he declined to make resumption of diplomatic ties with Bonn contingent upon a full repudiation of the Hallstein Doctrine (as the GDR wanted).

For that matter, East German attacks on Yugoslavia's system, in the context of polemics over the Seventh Party Congress, were sharp, and assured that there would be lingering bitterness on the Yugoslav side. The East Germans had declared at that time (1958) that the Yugoslavs were giving up Marxism, that "so-called self-management" was restoring "capitalism," and that the Yugoslavs had abandoned the principle of revolutionary class struggle.

Visits to East Berlin by Assembly President Edvard Kardelj (May 1964) and Republic President Tito (June 1965) helped to nurture the relationship. On the latter occasion, the Yugoslavs seemed to be bending over backwards to accommodate the GDR. Not only did Tito expressly endorse the GDR's two-Germanys concept (a move he knew would ruffle feathers in Bonn); he also joined Walter Ulbricht in signing a joint communiqué expressing opposition to any FRG acquisition of nuclear arms.[19] In so doing, Tito abandoned his much-vaunted posture of "balance" between East and West. Or would the Yugoslavs have ever dreamt of using a joint communiqué with the FRG as a vehicle for making a comparable statement regarding the GDR?

But Yugoslavia's relationship with the GDR under Ulbricht was always hostage to its relationship with the USSR. Hence, when Moscow sent tanks rolling into Czechoslovakia in August 1968, to remove a liberal government with which Belgrade had become very friendly, Belgrade condemned the Soviet invasion, and the East German regime, which had committed a contingent to participate in the Soviet invasion, joined other bloc states in condemning Yugoslavia. The old arguments of 1958 were revived, with East Berlin now throwing in criticism, in the wake of Yugoslavia's Ninth Party Congress (March 1969), of Yugoslavia's deconstruction of the party and its allegedly "petit-bourgeois" and "anarcho-syndicalist" orientations.[20] These renewed attacks seriously undermined Tito's relationship with Ulbricht. After that, there was to be no rapprochement until Ulbricht was removed from office in January 1971.

Yugoslavia between East and West

As the foregoing discussion makes clear, Yugoslavia did not enjoy full diplomatic ties with either West or East Germany from October 1957 to September 1966. Yugoslavia had had exclusive diplomatic relations with Bonn from 1951/52 to 1957, and would now have exclusive diplomatic relations with East Berlin from 1966 to 1968. On January 31, 1968, immediately following six days of bilateral talks on neutral ground (Paris), Yugoslavia and West Germany resumed ties. From that moment until the collapse of the GDR some 20 years later, Yugoslavia maintained diplomatic missions in both German states.

After Erich Honecker's accession to power in East Berlin in January 1971, Yugoslavia's ties with the GDR became markedly friendlier. Already in

February 1971, the two states signed a major trade agreement.[21]   This was followed, in May 1973, by an official visit of Yugoslav Prime Minister Džemal Bijedić to the GDR.[22]   Tito visited the GDR in November 1974, and Honecker reciprocated in January 1977 with a visit to Yugoslavia.   Yugoslav-GDR trade doubled in the years 1971-75, and by 1974, the GDR was Yugoslavia's tenth most important trading partner.   Yugoslavia was, at that time, eighth in importance among the GDR's major trading partners.   As of 1988, the GDR ranked tenth among markets for Yugoslav exports and tenth among sources for Yugoslav imports.[23]   Yugoslav-GDR relations in the Honecker era (1971-89) were by and large cordial, and free of the acerbic, dogmatic polemicizing that had characterized the Ulbricht era.   Cooperation between the two states included contacts between officials at all levels (including the municipal), between enterprises, and between social institutions, and extended to cooperation in the fields of social security, medicine, and transport.   The cordial relationship survived Tito's death in May 1980, and in 1985, East Berlin hosted a high-ranking Yugoslav military delegation headed by Fleet Admiral Branko Mamula, Yugoslav Minister of Defense.[24]   In November of that year, the two countries signed what was perhaps their last major bilateral economic accord, coordinating trade for the five-year plan period, 1986-90.   The agreement called for East Germany to import aluminum, copper, zinc, and wood pulp from Yugoslavia, and to sell the Yugoslavs potash, organic and inorganic chemical products, pharmaceuticals, and photographic materials.[25]

Where relations with the FRG are concerned, the fallout from the Soviet invasion of Czechoslovakia coincided with the resumption of diplomatic ties and reinforced tendencies toward rapprochement.   After the 1968 invasion, Yugoslavia ceased to fantasize about a special *political* relationship with the socialist bloc, and renewed its emphasis on its nonaligned status.   Ties with Romania, Albania, and China — all socialist critics of the USSR — were strengthened and developed, and ties with Western states were given greater weight.

Hence, while the Bonn regime ultimately refused to satisfy Belgrade's demands for indemnification, Bonn's extension of 1 billion DM in credits, between 1973 and 1974, helped to place the Yugoslav-West German relationship on sound footing.[26]   West Germany continued to be generous with credits, in fact, and already by 1971, 11 percent of Yugoslavia's foreign debt was owed to West Germany.[27]

West Germany rapidly became Yugoslavia's most important economic partner — this for four reasons.   First, there were the aforementioned credits, which placed West Germany third among Yugoslavia's creditors (behind the United States and Italy).   Second, the presence of more than half a million Yugoslav *Gastarbeiter* in the FRG was an important element in the Yugoslav economic strategy of the 1970s.   The exodus of Yugoslav workers peaked in 1973, when there were some 1.1 million Yugoslavs working abroad (constituting

12 percent of the Yugoslav labor force). Nearly half of them were working in West Germany. The remittances from Yugoslavs working abroad in 1972 alone came to $800 million, accounting for 18 percent of total foreign currency earnings and 25 percent of convertible foreign currency earnings.[28]

Third, tourism was becoming big business for Yugoslavia in the 1970s, and the tourist trade would continue to provide a major source of foreign currency revenue to the end of the 1980s. The major centers for touristic development were along Croatia's Adriatic coast (especially Dubrovnik, Makarska, and Opatija) and in Slovenia. The German contribution was not merely important; it was critical. Already in 1978, 68 percent of Yugoslavia's foreign tourist trade came from six countries: in descending order of importance, West Germany, Austria, Italy, France, Britain, and the Netherlands. Of that total, 32 percent came from West Germany alone.[29] By 1981, these six countries accounted for 71 percent of tourist traffic in Yugoslavia, with West Germans accounting for 34 percent. The trend continued in this direction, and the 1983 figures were even more dramatic: 41.6 percent from West Germany, 10.7 percent from Austria, 9.1 percent from Italy, 7.8 percent from Britain, 6.8 percent from Czechoslovakia (a new entrant in Yugoslav tourism), 4.4 percent from the Netherlands, and 2.9 percent from France. These seven countries accounted, thus, for 83.3 percent of Yugoslav tourism.[30]

And fourth, in the sphere of foreign trade, West Germany figured among Yugoslavia's leading partners throughout the 1970s and 1980s. By 1981, the FRG ranked second in total commodity exchange between Yugoslavia and foreign countries. It was Yugoslavia's no. 1 source of imports, and placed third among markets for Yugoslav exports.[31]

At first, despite the restoration of diplomatic relations, Bonn declined to grant Yugoslavia most-favored-nation status, and listed it rather on the so-called "B list." All the same, Yugoslavia and the Federal Republic signed more than 200 contracts on inter-enterprise technical and industrial cooperation between 1968 and early 1971 alone.

Meanwhile, Yugoslavia had been granted preferential status in trade with the European Community (EC), and was broadening its ties with West European countries generally.[32] More specifically, Yugoslav-West German relations were elevated through contacts at the highest levels: Yugoslav Foreign Minister Mirko Tepavac visited Bonn in July 1969, and Willy Brandt, the incoming West German chancellor and the first Social Democrat to head a government in Bonn, visited Belgrade in April 1973. Significant bilateral agreements were signed in the economic, cultural, insurance, and legal spheres, and the visa requirement for travelers between the two countries was abolished.

The West German government also showed goodwill by addressing Yugoslavia's two major concerns: anti-Yugoslav terrorism and war reparations. In the first case, the ban on Croatian political organizations has already been mentioned. In the second instance, Bonn offered a compromise: if Belgrade would set aside its tally of the dead, and its demand for per capita compensation, Bonn would agree on a package of very favorable investment credits. Belgrade accepted the compromise, and this source of discord could now be set aside.

Subsequent contacts — for example in the course of Tito's visit to the FRG in 1974 and Chancellor Helmut Schmidt's visit to Yugoslavia in 1977 — seemed to augur well for the relationship. The arrest by Yugoslav authorities of four German-based terrorists, led by a certain Stjepan Bilandžić, created some tensions between Belgrade and Bonn in summer 1978.[33] But the Yugoslav government later released the terrorists and the two governments were able to ride out the crisis.

The improvement in Yugoslav-West German relations, which had begun while Willy Brandt had been foreign minister and had continued under his and Helmut Schmidt's chancellorships, did not come to an end when the Social Democrats were turned out of office in Bonn. On the contrary, under Helmut Kohl's conservative coalition, the relationship continued to grow and develop, involving, *inter alia*, interparliamentary exchanges, ties between trade unions, and special ties of cooperation between different federal units in the respective states.

West Germany gave its blessing to the political status-quo in the Balkans. Specifically, West German Chancellor Helmut Kohl used the occasion of his summer 1985 visit to Belgrade to underline the FRG's "great interest in maintaining the internal and external stability of Yugoslavia. Yugoslavia's stability," he said, "is an important factor of . . . the political balance in Europe."[34]

Despite a slight decline in total trade volume between the two countries during 1986-87, West Germany remained Yugoslavia's second most important trading partner. As of 1989, West Germany bought 12.4 percent of Yugoslavia's exports (third, behind the USSR and Italy), and accounted for 17.6 percent of Yugoslav imports (marginally behind the USSR). By contrast, Yugoslavia made only a small dent in the massive West German economy, accounting for only 1.1 percent of West German exports and 1.2 percent of West German imports in 1989.[35]

Germany's Interest in the Yugoslav Civil War

The reunification of Germany in 1990 seemed to promise to make Germany all the more important in Yugoslavia's foreign economic ties. This inevitably proved hostage to three factors.

First, the rapid incorporation of the territory of the GDR into the FRG within the space of less than a year, and thus without any structural preparation of any consequence, gutted the economy of eastern Germany, by exposing its fragile enterprises too quickly to the tough competition of West German producers. The resultant economic disintegration in eastern Germany became a problem for all of Germany, and had some effect on its willingness to offer credits and economic benefits to other countries. The nature of German import and export needs may also change with reunification, and German authorities may hope to boost the economy in the eastern part of the country by negotiating business deals on its behalf.

Second, Yugoslavia itself reached a political impasse in 1989, and throughout 1990 and the early months of 1991, Yugoslavia's constituent republics searched for a new formula to preserve some form of union. Slovenia and Croatia threatened to secede from the federation by June 26, 1991, unless the governments of Serbia and Montenegro agreed to negotiate the reconstruction of the political system in the form of a loose confederation. Bosnia and Macedonia — the remaining two republics in the Yugoslav federation — found themselves forced to choose sides, and, although they preferred the preservation of a loose federation to either the confederalism favored by Slovenia and Croatia or the tight centralized rule advocated by Serbia and Montenegro, they ultimately endorsed the confederal proposal. Bosnia and Macedonia therefore threatened to follow Slovenia and Croatia out of the federation, if no agreement could be reached. Yet for all that, there were few signs of any meeting of minds, and progress toward a negotiated solution appeared torturously difficult.[36] Yugoslavia's constituent republics had enjoyed considerable freedom of action in their foreign trade relations for many years. But whether these developments would culminate in peaceful confederalization or in civil war, Yugoslavia's ties with foreign countries, including Germany, would inevitably be affected.

And third, the processes of general European integration have the potential to change the context and framework within which bilateral relationships in Europe are developed. Yugoslavia, for its own part, had recently placed great emphasis on improving and strengthening its ties with the OECD, the European Free Trade Association (EFTA), and above all, the EC.[37]

The Yugoslav civil war broke out because the republics could not agree on anything except that the existing constitutional system was completely unacceptable. All the other issues and controversies are secondary though in many cases quite real, but were stoked by political leaders in the two chief squabbling republics (in the first place, Serbia, but, according to some observers, also though to a lesser extent Croatia). Even the claims made by the Serbian minority in Croatia (11.6 percent of the Croatian population in 1981) must been seen as derivative from the more fundamental breakdown of the system.

The outbreak of civil war in Yugoslavia was *not* a surprise. The country had been sliding toward civil war for at least a decade, if not, in some ways, since the suppression of the Croatian liberals in December 1971.[38] Yet, when it broke out, there was little consensus in the West as to whether it even mattered. The Soviets, the French, the Indians, the Portuguese, the Danes, and for a while the Dutch and the Americans, all issued statements to the effect that the Yugoslav civil war was an internal matter for Yugoslavs and that foreign powers should not get involved: the implication was that the Yugoslav civil war lacked serious consequences for foreign states. Germany and Austria were among the few countries to express some views to the contrary already at an early juncture. These two states had built up extensive trade ties with Yugoslavia and had developed a certain sympathy for Yugoslavia as such. In addition, and more to the point, many Germans and Austrians had made regular summer visits to Croatia's Dalmatian coast as well as to parts of Slovenia (especially Bled) over the years — as mentioned earlier — and in the process of doing so, had made friends among the Croatian and Slovenian populations. For these Germans and Austrians, the Yugoslav civil war was not just an abstraction, but a catastrophe affecting their friends. In addition, most of the 600-700,000 Yugoslav *Gastarbeiter* in Germany were Croats, and some of these became very active in pressing for German recognition of Croatian independence. These consider-ations were among the factors that encouraged the two German-speaking states to begin talking of unilateral recognition of the breakaway republics of Slovenia and Croatia soon after the outbreak of civil war.

As early as July 1, 1991, German Foreign Minister Hans-Dietrich Genscher threatened to cut off all German aid to the Yugoslav government (which totaled about $550 million in 1990) if Belgrade continued to use force to prevent Slovenia and Croatia from exercising their right of self-determination.[39] Subsequently, Genscher also threatened to extend unilateral diplomatic recognition to the two secessionist republics. But while Genscher only talked of this eventuality, Karl-Heinz Hornhues, deputy chairperson of the CDU/CSU, criticized Genscher's hesitations and demanded the immediate recognition of both Slovenia and Croatia.[40]

Reports surfaced alleging that Germany and Austria were arming the Slovenes and Croats,[41] that German trainers had been dispatched to Slovenia and had instructed members of the Slovenian Territorial Defense in the use of anti-tank and anti-aircraft weaponry,[42] even that German mercenaries had fought on Slovenia's side during the brief engagement between the Yugoslav National Army and the Slovenian forces in late June and early July, and that members of German and Austrian special forces were operating in Slovenia.[43] Many of these allegations originated in the Serbian press, and all of them were denied by German and Austrian foreign ministry spokespersons.

In some Serbian reports, the charges had a garish quality. These included charges that a Vatican archbishop had acted as an intermediary between the Republic of Croatia and a private German arms exporter,[44] claims that German generals were meeting in Sofia to discuss military options against Serbia,[45] and allegations that some 40 members and instructors from *Bundeswehr* Special Forces had trained the elite 27th Brigade of the Slovenian Territorial Defense, modeling it after the Brandenburger Regiment of Hitler's *Wehrmacht*.[46]

At least in part because of such propaganda, the civil war has deepened the traditional enmity Serbs have felt for Germans since World War II. Even without the present civil war, Serbs have always remembered the German dismemberment of Yugoslavia in 1941 and German support for Fascist Croatia during the war, but tended to forget the fact that the wartime Serbian Chetnik "resistance" headed by Draža Mihailović also collaborated with the Axis,[47] and that even Tito entered at one time into discussions with the Nazis about possible collaboration.[48]

The Nazi war crimes have made it difficult, if not impossible, for even a democratic Germany to play an independent role in foreign affairs. Perhaps feeling that Germany might have regained some of its former self-confidence in the wake of reunification, Serbia in essence played on German war guilt to try to prevent Germany from undertaking any decisive action to help embattled Croatia. In the summer months of 1991, the Serbian press compared Kohl to Hitler,[49] asserted that "national socialism" was being revived in Germany,[50] justified their own anti-German sentiments by claiming that Germany had drafted plans for a "Fourth Reich," intending ". . . to put the entire Europe, including Yugoslavia, under its command,"[51] and, more specifically, avowed that Germany hoped to "gain access to the Mediterranean" through Slovenia and Croatia,[52] implying — one can only suppose — that the Serbian media believed that united Yugoslavia had systematically obstructed the transport of German goods through Adriatic ports.

One must concede that in interwar Europe, Yugoslavia had slipped steadily into a position of economic dependence on Germany and Italy, because only these two states were ultimately willing to buy substantial amounts of Yugoslav exports and to sell Yugoslavia goods it needed at competitive prices. Indeed, Nazi Germany routinely paid 30 percent above world prices for its imports, which made it an attractive buyer for exports. Similarly, German investment in Yugoslavia, as a proportion of total foreign investment in that country, rose sharply toward the end of the 1930s.[53] But affirming that Kohl's Germany has ambitions in the Balkans that are in any way similar to those to Adolf Hitler, as the Serbian press now routinely asserts,[54] is another matter, and would require that relevant supportive evidence be adduced. So far no such evidence has been adduced, whether in the Serbian press or anywhere else.

But Germany has had to tread carefully because, as excessive as the Serbian caricature of German foreign policy may be, it nonetheless has resonance on a continent that has not yet forgotten (or forgiven) that it was Germany that, more than 50 years ago, took Europe down the path to war. Hence Kohl's care to emphasize publicly and repeatedly that any deployment of German troops in the Balkans is precluded for both constitutional and historical reasons.[55] Hence also Germany's care in obtaining general European Community agreement on the principle of recognition of Slovenia and Croatia before proceeding with the establishment of diplomatic ties with these two new states.

All in all, Germany acted with particular care and caution here, despite the fact that the welfare of Croats has been dear to German hearts. Hence, when the Serbs of eastern Slavonia (located in eastern Croatia) set up a political body to function as an interim representative organ for Slavonia's secessionist Serbs, Foreign Minister Genscher proposed that the Conference on Security and Cooperation in Europe (CSCE) could provide a framework for negotiating the issue of the partition of Croatia. The National Council of the Autonomous Region of Slavonia, Baranja, and Western Srem, however, did not appreciate the suggestion and issued a statement to the effect that "in such a [proposal] the Serbian people have unmistakably identified the atmosphere of Munich's beer cellars of fifty years ago and their contribution to the history of human insanity and the most horrendous genocide in human history."[56] The Serbian daily, *Politika*, tried to cast doubt on Germany's motives and feigned wonder "whether a country which was the aggressor in two world wars and responsible for vast destruction in Yugoslavia can now competently judge the Yugoslav crisis," and accused Germany of seeking anew to achieve "supremacy in Europe."[57]

German diplomats held a series of meetings with Slovenian and Croatian leaders in the months following the two republics' declarations of independence. Genscher met with Slovenian President Milan Kučan and Slovenian Foreign Minister Dimitrij Rupel in Villach, Austria, in early July 1991.[58] Kohl received Croatian President Franjo Tudjman in Bonn in mid-July.[59] And Kohl made use of the Austrian resort village of St. Gilgen-am-Wolfgangsee to meet with Slovenian Prime Minister Lojze Peterle in mid-August.[60] Meanwhile, Genscher declared, on September 4, 1991 — in a threat that Germany seemed ill-poised to back up — "We will not be able to stand by and watch any longer."[61]

In late July, Chancellor Kohl met with French President François Mitterrand at the resort town of Bad Wiessee. After a day of discussions, they issued a statement to the effect that it was "too early" to extend diplomatic recognition to Slovenia and Croatia.[62] In spite of this statement, Bonn was clearly becoming distressed as one cease-fire after another collapsed and the war continued. The European Community and the UN had shown no capacity to bring the war to a close even by late November 1991, five months after it had begun. By then, Serbian irregulars, backed by the Serbian-dominated Yugoslav National Army, controlled more than 35 percent of Croatian territory; Vukovar, once a bustling east Slavonian town of 50,000 inhabitants, lay in ruins, abandoned by its population; and Osijek, the capital of Slavonia, was under siege and seemed destined for the same ultimate fate as Vukovar. Germany did not believe that economic sanctions alone could induce Serbia to call off its offensive against Croatia,[63] and had recommended that the CSCE set up a peacekeeping force to enforce a cease-fire in Yugoslavia.[64] But if EC economic sanctions did not seem to bend Serbia's will, by the same virtue, Serbia repeatedly rejected peace proposals tendered by the European Community.[65] Yet, even as the fourteenth ceasefire crumbled in the last days of November, no one in the West was so bold as to suggest the dispatch of armed force into the country, except by agreement of all combatants. Croatia repeatedly indicated its willingness to see a peacekeeping force in place. Serbia repeatedly rejected such a force as "foreign interference." Meanwhile, the war continued and casualties mounted.

At the height of hostilities, the Organization of Former Yugoslav POWs presented a demand, out of the blue, for some 10 million DM in additional war reparations (that is, for World War II) from Germany.[66] Since Germany and Yugoslavia had settled the question of war reparations more than 25 years earlier, this new demand had no hope of success, least of all in view of the fact that the Organization was based in Belgrade.

Chancellor Kohl received Bosnian President Alija Izetbegović for an official visit in November 1991. In early December, Slovenian President Milan Kučan came to Bonn. Within Germany, pressure continued to build, both from the ranks and the leaderships of various parties, for recognition of the two northern republics. The opposition Social Democratic Party criticized Kohl for moving too slowly in this regard. The CSU, the CDU's sister party in Bavaria, loudly endorsed the Slovenian and Croatian right of self-determination. Within Foreign Minister Genscher's Free Democratic Party, support for Slovenia and Croatia was "overwhelming," as it was in Kohl's CDU.

Kohl had promised to recognize Slovenia and Croatia "by Christmas." As Christmas neared, he took measures to prepare for this eventual step. In early December, for example, Germany closed its borders to Serbian trucking and closed its airports to the Serbian airline, JAT. The German government also laid the groundwork for diplomatic relations with Slovenia by establishing a general consulate in Ljubljana, the Slovenian capital. Germany had already had a general consulate in Zagreb, capital of Croatia, for many years.[67]

Germany also increased the pressure on its European allies to agree to a coordinated recognition of the two breakaway republics. Finding little sense of urgency among Germany's EC partners, Foreign Minister Genscher announced in mid-November that if the other EC members did not come around, Germany would act unilaterally. Chancellor Kohl immediately endorsed Genscher's statement and added that Bonn's recognition of Slovenia and Croatia would occur "by Christmas." Lord Carrington, the head of the EC mediation effort, argued that any "premature" recognition by Germany would undermine the peace conference underway. The U.S., together with UN Secretary-General Boutros Boutros-Ghali, bore down on Germany to try to compel it to abandon its pledge to proceed with recognition. But Germany was adamant, and first Austria, then Italy, and finally the other EC partners came around.

Finally, on December 17, Bonn got what it wanted, in the form of an EC agreement to recognize the two republics by January 15, 1992, contingent on a provision of assurances by both republics on the rule of law, democracy, and human rights, and an acceptance of the inviolability of all borders and European arbitration of the war by means of the Hague Peace Conference.[68] The agreement also required the two republics to guarantee the rights of ethnic minorities. On December 23, Bonn decided that further delay was unnecessary and declared its recognition of the two republics, thus keeping Kohl's "by Christmas" promise. In the meantime, the German government had already entered into talks with Croatian government officials on future economic and humanitarian assistance. Bonn assured the Croats of its "determination to support Croatia in the reconstruction of the country and in setting it on the path to democracy and a market economy."[69] At the same time, Germany suspended the "German-Yugoslav" trade agreement, under which trade with Serbia and Montenegro had remained technically open.

The U.S. criticized the German initiative, even though the other members of the EC followed the German lead, and expressed concern that the extension of recognition could prolong and aggravate the conflict. But within ten days of the German move, the Serbs seemed to show a sudden flexibility in negotiations, and the fifteenth cease-fire, unlike any of the preceding cease-fires, kindled unusual optimism in Western diplomatic circles. Cyrus Vance, the UN special envoy who had been trying for months to bring the Croats and Serbs to an agreement, conceded, "We, I think, have made some real progress. I have seen steps taken that have not been taken before — the acceptance of our proposed plan in its entirety by both sides. The situation is radically changed."[70] Radically changed, he could have added, as a direct result of the German initiative and the agreement by the European Community, which the U.S. had criticized. On January 1, 1992, the warring Serbian and Croatian republics agreed to the deployment of a 10,000-strong UN peacekeeping force in Croatia, specifically in three zones: East Slavonia, West Slavonia, and the so-called Krajina.[71]

The War in Bosnia

By January 1992, the Serbian militias had accomplished most of their strategic goals in Croatia. It was only now that they agreed to the emplacement of UN "peacekeeping" forces along the edge of their new conquests. As early as September 1991, however, behind closed doors, Radovan Karadžić, president of Bosnia's Serbian Democratic Party, and Serbian President Slobodan Milošević prepared plans for the expansion of the war into Bosnia.[72] When the Bosnian government called for a referendum on independence, on February 29-March 1, 1992, local Serbs did not even bother to vote. Even with the Serbian boycott, some 63.4 percent of the total eligible voting population of Bosnia took part, and of this number, 99.7 percent of valid ballots endorsed Bosnian independence.[73] Karadžić's party responded with a call for the attachment of all regions of Bosnia inhabited by Serbs to the new Serb-Montenegrin federation. Subsequent EC-sponsored negotiations foundered, and in late March, the JNA began bombarding Bosanski Brod, a town with mixed Muslim, Serbian, and Croatian population. Shortly thereafter, Serbian militias put Sarajevo under siege and began daily shelling of civilian targets. By June 1992, Serbian militias controlled more than 70 percent of the territory of Bosnia-Herzegovina.

The UN, CSCE, EC, and governing council of the General Agreement on Tariffs and Trade (GATT) imposed various sanctions on Serbia between May and June.[74] But Serbia was clearly undeterred, and it gradually became clear to many in the West that only international military intervention against Serbia could bring an end to the conflict. Support for a military option gathered strength in Germany in particular, where, in June 1992, Klaus Kinkel, Genscher's successor as Foreign Minister, demanded the creation of an international military force for use against Serbia. But Kinkel, like other German spokespersons, specifically ruled out the use of German troops, for well-known "historical reasons."[75]

On July 14, the UN Security Council met to discuss an Austrian proposal (backed by Germany) to take steps toward the creation of an international military force under UN auspices. The U.S., Britain, and France rejected the plan.[76] But about the same time, Chancellor Kohl created a sensation by agreeing to allow the German destroyer *Bayern* to join an allied sea and air patrol monitoring UN sanctions against Serbia and Montenegro. The opposition SPD expressed outrage that Kohl had taken the decision without consulting the *Bundestag*. The SPD also threatened to challenge the move in the German Constitutional Court, on the grounds that the Basic Law did not permit the deployment of German forces "outside NATO."[77]

This, in turn, opened a broad debate within Germany about just what *is* provided in the constitution, and as to whether the long-standing policy should be changed. General Klaus Naumann, the first Inspector-General of the German *Bundeswehr* since unification, commented: "Everyone seems to have the idea that the constitution forbids the use of German troops outside [the NATO] area. It is not true."[78] Meanwhile, opinion surveys conducted in July found that 69 percent of Germans felt that German participation in a broader UN peacekeeping force should be allowed (with 24 percent opposed), while 41 percent thought that Germany should feel free to dispatch its troops abroad unilaterally (with 54 percent opposed).[79]

Although it had been sparked by developments in the Balkans, the debate in Germany quickly assumed dimensions far transcending the Balkan stage. And while Foreign Minister Kinkel and Justice Minister Sabine Leutheusser-Schnarrenberger urged that German forces be authorized to participate in the UN peacekeeping mission in Croatia and Bosnia, Kohl explicitly ruled out any combat role for German forces in the region of former Yugoslavia.[80]

Of the "big four" in Europe, Germany is by far the most directly affected by the war in the Balkans, if only because it has absorbed some 220,000 refugees from Croatia and Bosnia (as of early August 1992).[81] Britain and France, by contrast, have accepted fewer than 2,000 Croatian/Bosnian refugees each, while Italy has taken in only some 7,000. In this context, it is not surprising to see Klaus Kinkel call for the establishment of an International War Crimes Tribunal to judge Serbia's guilt and to weigh evidence of genocide. Nor is it surprising that Kinkel's initiative provoked a sharp rebuke from Belgrade.[82]

Thus far, the recent German-Serbian relationship appears relatively "simple." But in late August, German customs authorities uncovered a smuggling operation through which certain German arms manufacturers had been selling weapons to Serbia, in contravention both of the UN embargo on trade with Serbia and of German law.[83] Similar operations supplying Croatia have also been uncovered.[84]

Conclusion

This chapter has discussed the relations between a country long split in two but eventually reunited and a country long united but eventually falling apart. The resultant multiplicity of interests, perspectives, personalities, and strategy options exceeds the norm for the "usual" sort of bilateral relations.

Yet for all that, there have been some constants. Certainly, throughout the entire period of their interaction, Yugoslavs have always viewed Germans with deep ambivalence. On the one hand, they have viewed the Germans with a sense of expectation: Germans bring higher technology, investments, trade opportunities, markets. On the other hand, Yugoslavs (or at least the Serbs) have always feared the Germans, whether the Hohenzollerns or the Nazis or the Germans of the postwar republic.

Again, whether one talks of the interwar period or the postwar era, Germany has been vastly important for the Yugoslav economy, regardless of changes in political and economic systems on both sides.

And finally, whether in the 1930s or today, the Germans have been saddled with war guilt. In the 1920s and 1930s, the Germans labored under the weight of ascribed guilt for World War I, and it was only at the risk of international opposition that Germany even remilitarized its own Rhineland region (in 1937). In the 1990s, Germany (not just Nazism) is still held to blame for the sufferings of World War II, and would have to risk international rebuke if it attempted to undertake any unilateral action to assist its friend, Croatia. Serbia seems to worry, however, that just as Germany was willing to take the risk in 1937, it may be willing to take the risk in intervening more decisively in the civil war.

Notes

1. See, for example, SED Politburo member Paul Verner's expressions of enthusiasm for "the heroic struggle of the Yugoslavs in World War Two" (against the Germans themselves) and for the two states' alleged shared understanding of socialism and Marxism-Leninism, in his speech of May 29, 1974, reprinted in *Dokumente zur Aussenpolitik der Deutschen Demokratischen Republik 1974* (Berlin: Staatsverlag der Deutschen Demokratischen Republik, 1978), pp. 257-62.

2. There were many such talks and agreements, and the more important of them were dutifully reported in Belgrade's *Review of International Affairs*.

3. Heinz Timmermann, "Jugoslawien und die 'Eurokommunisten'," in Hans-Adolf Jacobsen et al., eds., *Drei Jahrzehnte Aussenpolitik der DDR* (Munich: R. Oldenbourg Verlag, 1979), p. 539.

4. P. Jovanić, "Economic Relations with Federal Germany," in *Review of International Affairs*, no. 291 (May 20, 1962), p. 11.

5. Thomas Brey, "Bonn und Belgrad," in *Osteuropa*, Vol. 29, No. 8 (August 1979), p. 635.

6. K. W. Böhme, *Die deutschen Kriegsgefangenen in Jugoslawien 1941-1949*, Vol. 1, Part 1 (Munich: Verlag Ernst und Werner Gieseking, Bielefeld, 1962), p. 277.

7. Böhme, *Die deutschen Kriegsgefangenen*, p. 278.

8. Böhme, *Die deutschen Kriegsgefangenen*, p. 280.

9. Henry Ashby Turner, Jr., *The Two Germanies since 1945* (New Haven, Conn.: Yale University Press, 1987), pp. 87-88.

10. T. Ranić, "Belgrade-Bonn Relations," in *Review of International Affairs*, no. 314 (May 5, 1963), p. 13.

11. Ranić, "Belgrade-Bonn Relations."

12. For details of alleged activity, see Milo Bošković, *Antijugoslovenska fašisticka emigracija* (Belgrade and Novi Sad: Sloboda and Dnevnik, 1980).

13. Branko Skrinjar, "Yugoslav-West German Arrangements," in *Review of International Affairs*, no. 344-5 (August 5-20, 1964), p. 6.

14. Even within Germany, the issue was controversial, however. Under German criminal law, the statute of limitations for murder was 20 years. When applied to Nazi crimes in World War II, this signified that Nazis not brought to justice by May 8, 1965, would thereafter be immune from prosecution. The West German parliament at first postponed the issue by declaring, arbitrarily, that the statute of limitations would begin on January 1, 1950, even for crimes committed before May 1945 — which meant that Nazis could be prosecuted until January 1970. Inevitably, the issue was revived with a vengeance in the early months of 1969. Most of the German public was opposed to any further extension of the limitation; but the Bonn government was sensitive to foreign public opinion, and ultimately decided, on June 26, 1969, to abolish all limits for the prosecution of acts of genocide. See Dennis L. Bark and David R. Gress, *A History of West Germany, Vol. 2: Democracy and its Discontents 1963-1968* (Oxford: Basil Blackwell, 1989), pp. 34, 144-45; and Albrecht Götz, *Bilanz der Verfolgung von NS-Straftaten* (Cologne: Bundesanzeiger Verlag, 1986), pp. 143-44.

15. "Tito on the German Question," in *Review of International Affairs*, no. 365 (June 20, 1965), p. 25.

16. Irena Hendrichs, "Westdeutsche Ostpolitik: Die Beziehungen zu Bulgarien, der CSSR, Polen, Rumänien, Ungarn und Jugoslawien," in Hans-Peter Schwarz, ed., *Handbuch der deutschen Aussenpolitik* (Munich: Piper Verlag, 1975), p. 296.

17. *Savezna Republika Nemačka kao privredni partner SFR Jugoslavije* (Cologne and Zagreb: Bundesstelle für Aussenhandelsinformation, 1969), pp. 36-37.

18. Peter Christian Ludz, *Die DDR zwischen Ost und West* (Munich: Verlag C. H. Beck, 1977), p. 125; and *Dokumente zur Aussenpolitik der Deutschen Demokratischen Republik 1969*, Vol. 17, Part 1 (Berlin: Staatsverlag der Deutschen Demokratischen Republik, 1971), pp. 145-46.

19. "Joint Communique on Tito-Ulbricht Talks," in *Review of International Affairs*, no. 365 (June 20, 1965), p. 26.

20. Timmermann, "Jugoslawien und die 'Eurokommunisten'," p. 545.

21. The official communiqué is reprinted in *Dokumente zur Aussenpolitik der Deutschen Demokratischen Republik 1971*, Vol. 19, Part 1 (Berlin: Staatsverlag der Deutschen Demokratischen Republik, 1974), pp. 345-46.

22. *Dokumente zur Aussenpolitik der Deutschen Demokratischen Republik 1973*, Vol. 21, Part 1 (Berlin: Staatsverlag der Deutschen Democratischen Republik, 1976), pp. 209-14.

23. *Statistički godišnjak Jugoslavije 1989*, Vol. 36 (Belgrade: Savezni Zavod za Statistiku, 1989), p. 330.

24. *Dokumente zur Aussenpolitik der Deutschen Demokratischen Republik 1985*, Vol. 33, Part 1 (Berlin: Staatsverlag der DDR, 1988), p. 167.

25. *Dokumente zur Aussenpolitik der Deutschen Demokratischen Republik 1985*, p. 175.

26. Hendrichs, "Westdeutsche Ostpolitik", p. 303.

27. Vinod Dubey et al., *Yugoslavia: Development with Decentralization*, Report of a mission sent to Yugoslavia by the World Bank (Baltimore: Johns Hopkins University Press, 1975), p. 292.

28. Dubey et al., *Yugoslavia*, p. 288.

29. John B. Allcock, "Yugoslavia's Tourist Trade: Pot of Gold or Pig in a Poke?," in *Annals of Tourism Research*, Vol. 13 (1986), No. 4, p. 583.

30. Boris Vukonić, "Foreign Tourist Expenditures in Yugoslavia," in *Annals of Tourism Research*, Vol. 13 (1986), No. 1, pp. 62-63.

31. Nikola Čičanović, "The Socialist Federal Republic of Yugoslavia and the Federal German Republic," in *Review of International Affairs*, no. 742 (March 5, 1981), p. 4.

32. Gordana Kovačević, "Spoljnotrgovinska saradnja Jugoslavije sa EEZ," in *Medjunarodni problemi*, Vol. 39 (1987), nos. 2-3, pp. 176-77. See also: Ljubiša S. Adamović, ed., *Jugoslavija i Evropska Ekonomska Zajednica* (Belgrade: Institut za medjunarodnu politiku i privredu, 1988); and Boris Šnuderl, "Saradnja Jugoslavije s Organizacijom za ekonomsku saradnju i razvoj (OECD)," in *Medjunarodni problemi*, Vol. 25 (1973), no. 4.

33. Brey, "Bonn und Belgrad," p. 643.

34. Quoted in Jansjörg Eiff, "German-Jugoslav Relations," in *Review of International Affairs*, no. 916 (June 5, 1988), p. 4.

35. *Direction of Trade Statistics, Yearbook 1990* (Washington DC: International Monetary Fund, 1990), pp. 186-88, 417-18.

36. For details, see Sabrina P. Ramet, "The Breakup of Yugoslavia," in *Global Affairs*, Vol. 6, No. 2 (Spring 1991). For a detailing of Yugoslavia's long path to decentralization, confederalization, and eventual civil war, see Sabrina P. Ramet, *Nationalism and Federalism in Yugoslavia, 1962-1991*, 2nd ed. (Bloomington, Ind.: Indiana University Press, 1992).

37. See the special issue of *NIN* devoted to "Europe 1992": *NIN* (Belgrade), no. 2021 (September 24, 1989).

38. For an early warning about the risk of eventual civil war, see my article, "Yugoslavia and the Threat of Internal and External Discontents," in *Orbis*, Vol. 28, No. 1 (Spring 1984), especially pp. 114, 118.

39. *The New York Times*, July 2, 1991, p. A6.

40. *Süddeutsche Zeitung*, July 6/7, 1991, p. 7.

41. For example, Tanjug (July 8, 1991), in FBIS, *Daily Report* (Eastern Europe), July 9, 1991, pp. 41-42; and *NIN* (August 2, 1991), as reported in DPA (Hamburg), August 2, 1991, translated in FBIS, *Daily Report* (Eastern Europe), August 5, 1991, p. 39.

42. Tanjug (July 17, 1991), in FBIS, *Daily Report* (Eastern Europe), July 18, 1991, p. 38.

43. Both allegations in Tanjug (July 7, 1991), in FBIS, *Daily Report* (Eastern Europe), July 8, 1991, p. 39.

44. RTV Belgrade (July 31, 1991), translated in FBIS, *Daily Report* (Eastern Europe), August 1, 1991, p. 31.

45. *Politika* (Belgrade), as summarized in Tanjug (July 3, 1991), in FBIS, *Daily Report* (Eastern Europe), July 8, 1991, p. 39.

46. Tanjug (July 7, 1991), in FBIS, *Daily Report* (Eastern Europe), July 8, 1991, p. 40.

47. Jovan Marjanović, *Draža Mihailović izmedju Britanaca i Nemaca* (Zagreb and Belgrade: Globus/Narodna knjiga/Prosveta, 1979), especially pp. 133-45, 183-213, 233-63, 283-301; Marko Galić, *Politika u emigraciji: Demokratska alternativa* (Zagreb: Globus, 1990), pp. 159-63; and Walter R. Roberts, *Tito, Mihailović and the Allies, 1941-1945* (New Brunswick, N.J.: Rutgers University Press, 1973), pp. 101-06, 111, 118.

48. This is recounted in Milovan Djilas, *Wartime* (New York: Harcourt, Brace, Jovanovich, 1977).

49. Cited in *Corriere della sera* (Milan), September 9, 1991, p. 1.

50. *Politika ekspres* (Belgrade), as summarized in DPA (Hamburg), July 4, 1991, translated in FBIS, *Daily Report* (Eastern Europe), July 8, 1991, p. 59.

51. *Borba* (Belgrade), as summarized in Tanjug (July 25, 1991), in FBIS, *Daily Report* (Eastern Europe), July 26, 1991, p. 29.

52. Tanjug (July 7, 1991), in FBIS, *Daily Report* (Eastern Europe), July 8, 1991, p. 39.

53. Frank C. Littlefield, *Germany and Yugoslavia, 1933-1941* (Boulder, Colo.: East European Monographs, 1988), especially chapters 2 and 4; and John R. Lampe and Marvin R. Jackson, *Balkan Economic History, 1550-1950* (Bloomington, Ind.: Indiana University Press, 1982), pp. 503-19.

54. For a recent example, see *Politika*, May 14, 1992, p. 4.

55. *Neue Zürcher Zeitung*, November 29, 1991, p. 1.

56. Quoted in Tanjug (August 5, 1991), translated in FBIS, *Daily Report* (Eastern Europe), August 6, 1991, p. 40.

57. As summarized in Tanjug (September 8, 1991), in FBIS, *Daily Report* (Eastern Europe), September 9, 1991, p. 38.

58. Radio Slovenia (Ljubljana), July 2, 1991, translated in FBIS, *Daily Report* (Eastern Europe), July 3, 1991, p. 57.

59. ADN (Berlin), July 20, 1991, translated in FBIS, *Daily Report* (Eastern Europe), July 22, 1991, p. 43.

60. *Süddeutsche Zeitung*, August 17/18, 1991, p. 2.

61. Quoted in *Los Angeles Times*, September 5, 1991, p. A16.

62. *Neue Zürcher Zeitung*, July 25, 1991, p. 1.

63. *Financial Times*, August 7, 1991, p. 2.

64. *International Herald Tribune* (Paris), September 5, 1991, p. 1.

65. See, for example, *Süddeutsche Zeitung*, October 26/27, 1991, p. 1.

66. *Süddeutsche Zeitung*, September 7/8, 1991, p. 2.

67. *Süddeutsche Zeitung*, November 30/December 1, 1991, p. 2; *Neue Zürcher Zeitung*, December 6, 1991, p. 2.

68. *Financial Times*, December 18, 1991, p. 3.

69. Quoted in the *Financial Times*, December 20, 1991, p. 2.

70. Quoted in *The New York Times*, January 2, 1992, p. A3.

71. *Neue Zürcher Zeitung*, January 4, 1992, p. 2.

72. *Vreme* (Belgrade), September 30, 1991, p. 5.

73. Commission on Security and Cooperation in Europe, *The Referendum on Independence in Bosnia-Hercegovina, February 29-March 1, 1992* (Washington, DC: Commission on CSCE, 1992), p. 23.

74. For details, see Sabrina Petra Ramet, "War in the Balkans," *Foreign Affairs*, Vol. 71, No. 4 (Autumn 1992).

75. *Neue Zürcher Zeitung*, June 19, 1992, p. 2. Regarding other German politicians who supported this option, see *Süddeutsche Zeitung*, May 30/31, 1992, p. 4; also *Neue Zürcher Zeitung*, June 4, 1992, p. 2.

76. *Neue Zürcher Zeitung*, July 16, 1992, p. 1.

77. *International Herald Tribune*, July 15, 1992, p. 1; *The New York Times*, July 16, 1992, p. A4; *Financial Times*, July 22, 1992, p. 2.

78. Quoted in the *Financial Times*, July 13, 1992, p. 24.

79. *Süddeutsche Zeitung*, July 11/12, 1992, p. 10.

80. *Süddeutsche Zeitung*, August 14/16, 1992, p. 6; and *Neue Zürcher Zeitung*, August 26, 1992, p. 2. For a lengthy discussion of the debate in Germany, see *Welt am Sonntag* (Bonn), July 12, 1992, pp. 1, 3.

81. *Süddeutsche Zeitung*, August 8/9, 1992, p. 7.

82. *Süddeutsche Zeitung*, August 22/23, 1992, p. 2.

83. *Neue Zürcher Zeitung*, August 25, 1992, p. 2.

84. *Frankfurter Allgemeine Zeitung*, August 29, 1992, p. 2.

15

Austria and Germany:
A Not-So-Foreign Relationship

Max E. Riedlsperger

Introduction

The "German Problem" that has again been thrust to the center of the world's attention is a manifestation of the extraordinary strength that the country has exerted since its unification as a nation-state. Throughout most of prior German history, however, the "Problem" was one of German weakness stemming from political fragmentation and depredation by stronger neighbors. The solution was national unification and the movement towards this realization provoked the question of whether and how German-speaking Austrians should be included. Thus, unlike the other neighbors of Germany that had a strong sense of their own national identity, Austrians have been perplexed by the question of whether or not they were in fact German, making the "Austrian Question" a component part of the "German Problem" since it was first identified in the 18th century. For most "non-Austrian Germans" Prussia's conquest of Germany by 1871 solved the historic problem of weakness and by the turn of the 20th century the Second Reich matured into an economically and militarily powerful and self-assured nation. The "Austrian Question" became irrelevant for the Reich; however, for the nationally conscious among the over ten million ethnic Germans in the Habsburg Empire, the question became whether they should be loyal to their perceived German nation or to their homeland. This dilemma was exacerbated after 1918 when the almost monolithically German rump state of Austria was denied *Anschluß* to the

Weimar Republic; it was resolved only when Hitler ended the "Austrian Question" by absorbing his homeland into the Third Reich in 1938.

In 1945, a second Austrian republic was created, but no new "Austrian Question" resulted. Given the burden of the Nazi experience, the founders of the new state expediently disassociated Austria from the German past and set about inculcating the idea that it constituted a unique nation. In the post-war era, history has been the handmaiden for both neighbors in their respective efforts to deflect tradition and forge a new public consciousness. In the 1960s, historians in the Federal Republic took up this burden and set about to conquer their country's uncomfortable past, while their colleagues in Austria accepted the national construct of 1945 and worked to write its history as separate and distinct from the German experience. Public opinion gradually followed and under the beneficent influence of political stability and growing economic prosperity normal neighborly relations became possible for the first time since political nationalism had confused matters.

From 1945 until 1990, the "German Problem" was again one of division and was subsumed in the overarching problems of the Cold War. The end of the Cold War and the 1990 rush to reunification reveals that Germany, whether divided or united, is problematic for at least some of Germany's neighbors. As a consequence of over a millennium of intertwined history, Austria has been a part of the "German Problem" since it emerged. In order to assess the question of its present and future position vis-a-vis a united Germany it is first necessary to trace the lengthy evolution of this "not-so-foreign" relationship.

The "German Problem" and the "Austrian Question"

The incorporation of the territory of modern Austria into what for a thousand years was considered to be Germany began already in the 8th century with its conquest by the Franks and establishment as the *Ostmark* against the threat of the Avars and Slavs. When Pope Leo III invested the Frankish King Charlemagne with the title of Holy Roman Emperor on Christmas Day, 800, he also implied the unity of a medieval German nation that included the eastern Marches. By the end of the next century the *Ostmark* was commonly known as *Ostarrîchi*, the oldest form of the modern German *Österreich*, meaning "region in the east,"[1] and by the 13th century was among the strongest of the German principalities. Indeed, by the end of the 15th century the Austrian Archduke Maximilian, who was at the same time the German King and Holy Roman Emperor, had come to view his Habsburg domains as an independent state in the modern sense,[2] within the loose confederation that made up the Holy Roman Empire of the German Nation. Vienna had become the preeminent southern German trade metropolis and one of the main centers of culture and learning for all of German-speaking Europe.

In the 16th and 17th centuries, Habsburg emperors attempted to use the power of their dynastic holdings to transform the illusion of German unity into political reality. Although they failed, Austria remained the most important German state, but became something much more as the consequence of its incorporation of Bohemia, Hungary and later much of the Balkans in the wake of the ebbing of Ottoman power. With this expansion of Austria from a southern German state into an eastern and southeastern empire, the "Greater-Austrian" idea of a pluralistic, supranational empire replaced that of the pre-national, but nevertheless German, Austrian state. Germanized elites from the newly incorporated areas moved into important positions in the bureaucracy, the Church, and the economy, and although Vienna did not cease to be one of the most important German cities, it did take on a cosmopolitan character that set it apart. Nowhere was this more evident than in the cultural sphere. By the turn of the 19th century a German high culture had begun to emerge and Vienna was one its most important centers. German-Austrians like Haydn, whose hymn has been used and abused as the German national anthem, and Mozart, as well as "non-Austrian Germans" like Gluck and Beethoven flocked to the Austrian capital which was graced by many of the finest architectural examples of the German Baroque and Rococo. The German National Theater, founded by Joseph II in 1776, became the leading stage in German-speaking Europe, but with the difference that in addition to important works of the general German Enlightenment, dramas in German by Austrian authors on Magyar and Slavic historical themes were also produced.

In this era before political nationalism, there was no question that Austria was a part of Germany, albeit understood only in a cultural sense. The only German problem was that of weakness, which promoted civil war and invasion by Germany's neighbors. It was finally the French Revolution and Napoleonic domination that stimulated in Germans a nascent sense of political nationalism. Indeed the Austrian General, Archduke Karl, appealed to nationalism to mobilize the defense ". . . to restore to Germany the independence and the national honor due it."[3] His goal was clearly the realization of a community of German states built on illusory memories of bygone unity in the old Holy Roman Empire of the German Nation and on nascent feelings of modern nationalism aroused by foreign oppression. Once the victory over Napoleon had been won, however, the dominant German powers, Austria and Prussia, put self-interest above any putative national interest by creating a German Confederation with only enough unity to provide the image of sufficient power to fill the vacuum that in the past had invited almost constant invasion by Germany's neighbors. This historic problem of German weakness was resolved, but the future "German Problem" of a strong nation in Central Europe did not yet exist. Nor with Austria as leader of the German Confederation was there yet a "Question" about its role in Germany.

It was only as the idea developed that a people of similar language, culture and ethnicity (*Kulturnation*) should, to as great a degree possible, be incorporated in their own political nation (*Staatsnation*)[4] that Austria's place within Germany became subject to question. In 1848, when revolutionaries attempted to solve the historic problem of German weakness by uniting the nation along political lines, the "Austrian Question" emerged. There was no argument that Austria, or at least German-Austria, was part of the greater German ethnic and cultural community; rather, the dilemma was how to include it. Finally, historians Johann Gustav Droysen, and Friedrich Christoph Dahlmann, whose later historical writings made the subsequent *kleindeutsch* state appear to be an inevitable Prussian synthesis of historic German contradictions, formulated, with others, the "Question to Austria" that asked whether Austria could accept a constitution that forbad the association of any part of the German Reich with non-German lands except by way of a personal union.[5] Austria emphatically rejected the proposition and in the coming years attempted to ensure that no other prince accept the German crown either. But Austrian obstructionism could not forever block the unification, and from 1864-1871 the force of Prussian arms solved the "German problem" and answered the "Austrian Question," at least from the perspective of the new, Second Reich. Although this new Germany incorporated only part of the nation as historically identified, by the 20th century most Reich-Germans had accepted their state as *the* German nation and Austria-Hungary became a neighbor to be dealt with through normal international diplomatic and trade agreements.

After initial disagreements over trade practices had been resolved, Germany began a vigorous program of trade and investment in Austria-Hungary, which in turn became a partner in joint ventures such as railroad construction in the Balkans and the Middle East and oil exploration in Rumania. It was a special relationship, albeit with Austria as junior partner, not because of any pan-German affinity, but rather due to the economic, diplomatic and ultimately military advantages it offered the Reich.

One area in which Austria was not subordinate was culture, and the extent and intensity of the relationship between the two countries reveals just how artificial national boundaries can be. Late national unification meant that German-speaking Central Europe had many cultural centers, a fact that was not changed by the establishment of Berlin as the political capital of the Second Reich. German literature has always transcended political boundaries, both before and after 1871. Outside the "Austrian nation" school[6] there seems to be little argument that Franz Kafka and Rainer Maria Rilke from Prague, the Moravian-Jewish Stefan Zweig, the Viennese Hugo von Hoffmannsthal and Arthur Schnitzler, and the Salzburger Georg Trakl, all born in the old Austro-Hungarian Empire, are central to the German literature of the late 19th and early 20th centuries. Efforts to suggest that these authors are part of "Austrian literature" rather than writers of German literature, writing perhaps about Austrian themes and with Austrian sensitivities, imply a provincialism that did not exist. Likewise, in the dramatic arts, the *Burgtheater*, ensconced in its grandiose new home on the Vienna *Ringstrasse* after 1888, remained an important German stage, although in an age of literary modernism rather too conservative to be considered any longer the most significant. In the more cosmopolitan musical and visual arts where, with the exception of song, language is less significant, attempts to distinguish the Austrian from the German is even less meaningful. Vienna dominated German music in the 19th century, and its *fin-de-Siècle* Succession art and architecture can also be seen in Berlin and Munich. The artists who kept Vienna at least a capital of the German cultural world were Alpine Germans, Germanized Slavs, Hungarians, Rumanians, and Jews; all, however, used German as their mother tongue. They enriched the cultural life of the German Reich just as the artistic production of the Reich contributed to the vibrancy of Austria. Politically, however, by the last third of the 19th century, the Austrian Empire was obsolete. It was a construct of many nationalities assembled in a pre-nationalist age and never developed a modern GreaterAustrian identity to thwart the centrifugal aspirations of its myriad peoples. As a result, when the predominantly non-German lands that for centuries had defined the Empire seceded in 1918, the provisional government of "German-Austria" declared itself a constituent part of Germany.[7] In early 1919, the Austrian and German Foreign Ministers signed a protocol that would have provided for unification, but the victorious Allies wrote a ban on *Anschluß* into their peace treaties with both countries. Forced to be independent, Austria was even required to remove the prefix "German" from its name.

Anschluß was a matter of only peripheral concern for Weimar Germany, but in Austria it dominated political debate, the media and the pages of the publications of political, religious and sporting organizations to such a degree that it must be seen as pervasive.[8] Plebiscites for *Anschluß* to Catholic south Germany won majorities of 90 percent and 78 percent respectively in Tyrol and Salzburg in 1921, and a similar result in Styria in 1922 was avoided only when the Federal Government banned the vote and renounced *Anschluß* for twenty years as the price for desperately needed international loans. For a time, inflation and political tumult in Germany dampened *Anschluß* sentiment in Austria, but with the economic upturn after 1924 in the Weimar Republic, it resumed and gathered strength throughout the remainder of the decade. Unlike Weimar Germany, Austria never recovered from the loss of its industrial and agricultural heartlands, and Social Democratic workers as well as broad segments of the educated middle-classes supported *Anschluß* as the only way out of the crisis. In 1931, economic distress caused Germany to take a half-step in this direction as well, when the Brüning government attempted to negotiate a customs union with Austria as a vehicle for economic expansion into southeastern Europe. Under pressure from France and its client states, both countries renounced the project, which in turn led to the radicalization of the *Anschluß* movement to the benefit of the Nazis in Austria.

In 1933, fearful that the National Socialist revolution developing in Germany would engulf his own country, Chancellor Dollfuß created an authoritarian, Catholic-corporatist dictatorship with the aid of the fascistic, Catholic-conservative, para-military *Heimwehr* and encouragement of Mussolini. He renounced *Anschluß* as an option and began to formulate the idea of an Austria distinct from Germany. But this authoritarian and sometimes brutal regime inspired no Austrian nationalism among the majority of citizens.

Thousands of Greater-German nationalists were arrested and tens upon tens of thousands more went into the illegal Austrian Nazi party or fled to the ranks of the Austrian Legion in Bavaria from where they hoped to be able to bring about the *Anschluß* by force. During this time the German government had no fixed policy on *Anschluß* and did nothing to promote it. Without Reich-German support, the Austrian Nazi leadership turned to negotiations with Dollfuß in hopes of gaining entry into the government as a means of achieving union through legal means. When that failed, they increased the terror and ultimately mounted the unsuccessful *Putsch* attempt that ended with the murder of Dollfuß on July 25, 1934. No evidence of direct German involvement in the *Putsch* has ever come to light,[9] and its only overt actions against Austria were a 1,000 Mark exit fee placed on Germans traveling to Austria and an embargo on Austrian goods, both of which had a devastating impact on the depression-crippled Austrian economy.

Kurt Schuschnigg, who assumed the Chancellorship after the *Putsch*, unlike Dolfuß, was committed to the principle that Austrians were German, indeed, after 1933, "the better Germans," making him by nature an appeaser in the struggle for Austria. In an effort to undercut the now almost totally Nazi-dominated *Anschluß* movement and to combat a fifty percent drop in exports since 1930, Schuschnigg negotiated the Agreement of July 11, 1936 with Germany. On the surface, it appeared to be a victory for Schuschnigg. Germany recognized Austria as a sovereign state and promised not to interfere in its internal affairs, even where Austrian National Socialism was concerned. In return, Schuschnigg promised policies determined by the fact that Austria was a German state and signed a secret, "Gentlemen's Agreement" that may be seen as a first step in the *Gleichschaltung*, or "co-ordination," of the institutions of Austria with the Third Reich. As the price for a normalization of press, cultural and economic relations and the tourist trade, Schuschnigg agreed to include two "emphatic German-Nationals" in his government and allowed German newspapers to disseminate Nazi propaganda in Austria, while any criticism of Nazism by the Austrian press was proscribed.

In February 1937, Germany forced a currency union and the incorporation of Austrian industry, and on February 12, 1938, Hitler intimidated Schuschnigg into accepting all but the formal elimination of Austrian independence. The

Austrian Nazi Seyß-Inquart was imposed on Schuschnigg as Minister of Interior, and another Nazi was placed in charge of German-Austrian economic relations. Others, many of whom had been dismissed for participating in the *Putsch* of 1934, were placed in important posts in government, the army, the economy and in cultural institutions. By early March, pro-Nazi demonstrations had built a frenzy of public support for *Anschluß*, sweeping along the non-Nazi but pro-*Anschluß* middle-class and peasantry. Even Karl Renner, a prominent Socialist and first Chancellor of the republic, gave public support to the *Anschluß*, while his party colleagues took a perverse pleasure in the prospect of the fall of the "clerical-fascist" regime that had persecuted them so vigorously since 1933.

Confronted by the prospect of an imminent Nazi revolution from within, Schuschnigg seized upon the idea of a plebiscite, which in turn triggered the German military occupation of Austria on March 11. The overwhelming enthusiasm with which Austrians went "home into the Reich" created the impression of a massive popular revolution that neutralized any possibility of resistance. Their jubilation was, however, not approbation for what Nazi Germany was and would become, but rather for what they saw as national unification and the economic salvation they expected would result.

However, *Anschluß* turned out not to be the long-desired completion of German national unification, but rather Hitler's first conquest on his road toward European hegemony. Unlike the Second Reich, which after 1871 left its constituent parts substantial elements of their former identity, the Third Reich designated Austria as the "*Ostmark*," returning it to the status it had held as a military outpost against the East eleven hundred years before. Austrians who had thought they were joining their brothers and sisters in a united German nation, were instead treated as step-children or worse. Government and the bureaucracy suffered political and racist purges and Reich-Germans replaced those who were sent to concentration camps or executed. The gold reserve and other currency assets worth 17 times those of the Reich itself were confiscated. Austrian workers did not receive wage and social benefits comparable to those in the *Altreich*, and even most of the largely pro-*Anschluß* middle classes suffered from integration into the larger German economy. Discrimination and persecution of the Catholic Church also alienated the religious. Most of these negative consequences were not widely known at the time, however, due to a combination of terror and totalitarian control over the media.

Yet, at the same time, widespread enthusiasm for the long-delayed completion of German unification, the real economic gains that came from the redistribution of "aryanized" property, and the success of propaganda that created the illusion of a social revolution that submerged traditional class differences in the totality of the united *Volk*, brought Austrians into the NSDAP in even larger numbers than in Germany proper. Fully one-quarter of all adult Austrian males became "party comrades" and many believed in the "German

Dream" until it turned into a nightmare. But at this same moment, when the historic ambiguity of national identity was solved for most Austrians, the seeds of a new national identity were sown. When the German nationalism that had been rooted in the liberalism of the 19th century became synonymous with the Nazism that had swallowed it, the politically suppressed and imprisoned elites of the old Socialist and Catholic-conservative political camps began to formulate the concept of a new, "non-German" Austria.

In 1945, a revolution occurred in the relationship between Austria and the Germans. Given the strength of the German-national tradition and a different course of events after the *Anschluß*, it is conceivable that Austria could have emerged from the war as one more state of the divided German nation, just as were the FRG and GDR. In 1945, however, it was expedient for Austria, under the influence of the Allied Occupation, to break with the concept of a common national community. Already before the *Anschluß*, a handful of ideologues in the monarchist wing of the Christian-Social Party and also in the Communist Party had begun separately, out of a common hatred and fear of Nazi-dominated German nationalism, to promote the idea of a distinct Austrian nation. During the Nazi "Occupation" and war, more politically conscious Austrians came to embrace the dream of an independent Austrian nation, built on a "social partnership" that would end the civil war mentality that in the First Republic had made *Anschluß* appear the only salvation. Austrian Communist émigrés in the Soviet Union also impressed this vision of an independent Austria on Stalin. Accordingly, at the Moscow Conference in October 1943, Soviet Foreign Minister Molotov rejected wording for a final declaration by Britain and the United States that, tacitly, would have accepted the legitimacy of the *Anschluß*. Instead, the final text implied support for future independence by describing the *Anschluß* not as a "union" of the "Austrian people" with Germany as in the Anglo-American draft, but as an "annexation" making Austria ". . . the first free country to fall victim to Hitlerite aggression."[10]

This Moscow Declaration became one of the first "myths of creation" for the new Austrian nation that was fabricated after 1945 and fit into the post-war policies of both East and West as the realities of the Cold War precluded other alternatives for restructuring Central Europe. In reality, however, as new research by Keyserlingk proves, the Moscow Declaration was simply a propaganda ploy intended to stimulate an Austrian revolt against Hitler and created no legal precedent for independence.[11] Indeed, Keyserlingk cites a 1944 State Department planning report complaining that "[t]he Moscow Declaration poses the Austrian question without specifying a clear-cut solution," and proves that at least the United States was still considering the possibility of a confederation of the old Habsburg succession states or even another *Anschluß* with Germany.[12]

In 1945, however, it suited Allied purposes to lend legal substance to their off-handed Moscow Declaration. As a result, under the supervision of the

Allied Occupation, Austria, unlike Germany, was permitted to elect a government that then proceeded with the business of inculcating a sense of nation where none had existed before. *Österreichische Monatshefte*, the ideological organ of the Christian-conservative ÖVP (Austrian People's Party), as well as Fritz Fischer, the most prominent ideologue of the Austrian Communist Party, began to define Austrians as different from Germans by virtue of their history, their distinct ethnic character, and even their humanity. German was equated with Prussian and then in turn with pan-Germanism and National Socialism.[13] This effort to distance Austria from all things German was nowhere more ludicrously evidenced than in the insistence of Minister of Education Felix Hurdes that composition and grammar in the schools be called classes in the "Language of Instruction" [*Unterrichtssprache*] so as to avoid calling them German classes [*Deutschunterricht*].

Certainly few Austrians still longed to be part of any German state, but by no means were most yet willing to surrender the traditional concept of a nation defined by a common language and culture. But to argue against the Austrian nation was to risk charges of neo-Nazism, and over the course of forty-five years, the collective influence of government, education, and the media has proven irresistible.

In contrast to 1964, when only 47 percent of Austrians polled thought that Austria was a nation and another 23 percent agreed that it was slowly beginning to become one, by 1987 these percentages had increased to 75 and 16, respectively, with only 6 percent identifying themselves as belonging to the German nation and another 3 percent as German-Austrians.[14]

Austrian Relations with the Federal Republic of Germany

If a broad consensus has now developed among Austrians for joining the European Community, which thereby means a partnership with Germany, such a step would have seemed impossible in 1945. At that time, as a means of defining an identity for the infant Austrian state, "Austrian nationalists" evoked a hatred of all things German, and Allied restrictions on economic, cultural, and even personal contacts initially drew a curtain between Austria and Germany almost as impermeable as that to the east. To be sure, Austrians met with Germans at the international meetings of their sister political parties and in the international councils formed to implement the Marshall Plan, but there was no official, bilateral contact.[15] By 1949, Allied restrictions were relaxing, but Austrians were reluctant to give even the appearance of closer relations with the newly formed Federal Republic out of anxiety about awakening the *Anschluß* paranoia of Germany's other neighbors. It was only in 1950-51, within the framework of GATT negotiations in England, that the first official meetings between representatives of the Austrian and Federal German governments took place.

In 1953, the first step in the direction of normalized relations came with the visit in Bonn of Austrian Minister of Foreign Affairs Karl Gruber and his assistant State Secretary Bruno Kreisky, where they established the framework for future negotiations on the whole range of Austrian-German relations with Chancellor Adenauer and members of his government. Deferring to the Four-Power control that gave the Soviet Union a veto over Austrian foreign relations, the two countries agreed to establish offices in each other's capital that would be staffed with diplomats. The first issue to try the tentative new relationship arose in October 1954, when the Administrative Court of the Federal Republic ruled that German citizenship acquired by Austrians as a consequence of the *Anschluß* was legal and that those who had remained in Germany after the war retained their rights as citizens. The Soviet Union, which had been protesting West German integration into NATO, claimed that the court's decision was evidence of a "malicious" new effort to subordinate Austria and used it as an excuse to question the wisdom of concluding a State Treaty with Austria, which was being negotiated at that time. Anxious that the treaty not be jeopardized, all three Austrian parties nervously overreacted, charging the Federal Republic with plans for a new *Anschluß*. Embarrassed, Bonn responded that it considered the *Anschluß* annulled and before the end of the year passed a law on the citizenship matter declaring the *Anschluß* Law of 1938 without substance.

As it turned out, these events, combined with Khrushchev's ascendancy in the Soviet Union, may have removed the final barriers to the negotiation of the Austrian State Treaty. In a major speech before the Supreme Soviet on February 8, 1955, Foreign Minister Molotov argued that the remilitarization of West Germany increased the danger of a new *Anschluß* that could only be stopped by the conclusion of a State Treaty with Austria.

In return, it was expected that Austria would obligate itself not to join in any military alliance directed against any state that had fought in the war against Nazi Germany. Within a little more than three months the State Treaty was finalized, and before the end of the year, the Austrian parliament had passed its law of "permanent neutrality." In November 1955, ambassadors were exchanged between Austria and the FRG. Visits by officials at all levels increased in frequency and cordiality, creating by 1957 what West German Chancellor Adenauer called a "basis for the friendship that has developed between the two countries."[16] Over the next four years, potentially serious problems over residual "German assets" in Austria, compensation for the Austrian victims of National Socialism, and ethnic German refugees from the east who had settled in Austria, were taken up by a "Mixed Commission" designed to negotiate all questions still open between the two countries. In the 1961 Kreuznach Treaty it was agreed to settle these claims for a sum of 321 million D-Mark, paving the way for a new era in German-Austrian relations that was symbolized by the state visit of Federal German President Heinrich Lübke to Austria in March of 1962. After 1961 the relationship between Austria and West Germany grew increasingly intimate. No sector provides statistical evidence more demonstrative of this fact than foreign trade. In 1952, exports to and imports from the Federal Republic comprised only 20.1 percent and 21.6 percent of Austria's total foreign trade, respectively. By 1988, despite Austria's decision at the end of the 1950s to join the European Free Trade Association rather than follow the Federal Republic into the developing Common Market, this share had climbed to 34.5 percent and 43.6 percent, respectively.[17]

In 1989, Austria decided to apply for admission to the EC, and the Ministry of Foreign Affairs emphasized the importance of German support in this bid. As Austrians have grown more accustomed to their new national identity, the need to distance themselves from Germany has declined. Geographic propinquity, linguistic, historic and cultural ties created an intimacy that is described in recent reports by the Austrian Ministry for Foreign Affairs as dynamic and positive.

Nevertheless, disagreements inevitably occur between neighbors, particularly when they are of such disparate power and size. One such problem arose out of the Austrian environmental movement, ultimately leading to a successful referendum in 1979 against the use of nuclear power. High amounts of fallout from the Chernobyl disaster in 1986 and fear about similar plants in neighboring Yugoslavia and Czechoslovakia only added to the concern. Bilateral negotiations with the Federal Republic on a wide range of nuclear issues began in 1984, but ground to a halt in 1987, largely due to Austrian opposition to German plans for the construction of an atomic waste recycling plant at Wackersdorf in eastern Bavaria, not far from the border. The abandonment of these plans in February of 1989[18] led to the resumption of negotiations. A much more serious problem has been the growing Austrian concern over the ten-fold increase in north-south truck traffic through Austria between 1978 and 1988, which has posed serious problems for noise and air pollution, highway maintenance, and customs control. The completion of the economic integration of the EC promises a further doubling of traffic by the year 2000, and the opening of Eastern Europe adds a totally new dimension to the transit problem. Although commercial truck traffic can flow to Italy entirely through EC countries, Austria remains the route of choice for most shippers, either because of the shorter distance or because of tonnage limits that are much closer to EC norms than those of neighboring Switzerland. At the end of 1989, Austria banned night driving for loud trucks over 7.5 tons on transit highways,[19] and disagreements over the weight and volume of truck traffic escalated during the first half of 1990. The situation reached a crisis point in August when a bridge collapse closed the Brenner *Autobahn*, forcing large numbers of trucks onto surface arteries. When the states of Salzburg and Tyrol closed their roads to transit traffic in protest, Italy blockaded Austrian commercial traffic to the south and Bavaria threatened to suspend an agreement that treated inner-Austrian transit across a corner of Germany as domestic. Politicians in the 1990 parliamentary campaign went to great lengths to assure voters that they had not sold out the ecology of the transit region for membership in the European Community, while "Asphalt Cowboys" talked about digging the trenches for a "war of the roads."[20] An EC summit meeting finally produced a truce by the end of August and negotiations over the next year produced an agreement incorporating Transportation Minister Streicher's proposal using so-called "Eco-points" to reduce nitrogen and other emissions by 60 percent by the year 2003 and effectively freezing the number of truck transits at 1.38 million per year.[21] Despite this, the legacy of threats by German negotiators to hold Austrian acceptance into the European Community hostage to its acceptance of EC transit norms continues to strain a German-Austrian relationship that on most other matters has been quite harmonious.

In intellectual and cultural matters there is a paradox in the relationship between Austria and the Federal Republic. Because it was too much a part of Germany from 1938 to 1945, Austria's academics have made vigorous efforts to write their country out of German political and cultural history. German history was not taught as a discrete subject in the schools, and the proposition that the Austrian experience was a part of German history prompts accusations of cultural imperialism if posed by a German, or suspicions of questionable loyalty, if not neo-Nazism, if suggested by an Austrian. The "Austrian Question" has been treated as an aberration, and the post-1945 "German Question" has been largely ignored.

Then, suddenly, after forty years of indoctrination had successfully implanted the perception of Austria as a nation, separate and distinct from Germany, Austrians were suddenly reminded of their German past by the international uproar caused in 1986 by their election of Kurt Waldheim to the Federal Presidency. Investigative reporters in Austria as well as in the foreign press revealed the details of his military service that Waldheim had suppressed in his autobiography, and implications that he had been involved in committing war atrocities were raised. Not only was Austria's role in the German war effort exhumed, but the American Jewish Congress went so far as to charge that "by electing a man with a Nazi past, the majority of Austrians had 'knowingly and deliberately associated themselves with that past.'"[22] Even some Germans gloated that Austrians, who had largely escaped their Nazi past, were now forced to come to grips with their complicity.[23] What was ignored in the press hysteria, which commonly saw in Waldheim's election confirmation of Austria as an unreconstructed remnant of the Third Reich, were the real reasons for his victory. Sympathy for Waldheim's connection to Nazi Germany and its war effort, as implied in some U.S.[24] and British media coverage,[25] was not what won him the presidency. Rather, distinctly Austrian political considerations were the primary factors. Space limitations do not here permit a full discussion of the Waldheim election victory, but a few observations will illustrate the tendentious nature of its coverage by the media.

First of all, Waldheim was nominated by the conservative ÖVP because, as former Secretary-General of the U.N., it thought it could elect Austria's only internationally known politician. In a backlash against the Socialist Party's exploitation of the information about Waldheim's war record and what they regarded as unsubstantiated and hypocritical attacks by countries, including Germany, that had cleared Waldheim for election as SecretaryGeneral, Austrians closed ranks against what they considered to be foreign interference in the internal affairs of their country. This can readily be seen in the campaign slogan: "We Austrians will vote for whomever *we* want." In explaining why Green, Socialist, and indifferent voters voted for the ÖVP candidate, one analyst put it: ". . . they didn't vote for Waldheim because they wanted him, but rather because the Americans, Jews and other foreigners didn't."[26] Waldheim remained an embarrassment, particularly in 1988, the year given over to contemplation about the *Anschluß* and its consequences. Nevertheless, he became a symbolic figure, who, even if in a negative manner, contributed to a continuing rise in Austrian national consciousness. Between 1987, when the Waldheim Affair put Austria on the front pages of the world's newspapers, and 1990, the numbers of Austrians answering the standard poll questions testing Austrians' identity with their nation and implicitly their lack of identification with Germany rose to an almost unanimous 94 percent.[27] Neither the fall of the Iron Curtain on the borders to its old territories in the east, nor the unification of Germany dampened this trend.

If, by 1990, Austria as a distinct political nation had definitively emerged, its relationship to the German cultural community was more equivocal. To be sure, pre-1938 literature, music, art and architecture were portrayed as outgrowths of the Habsburg tradition and post-1945 works as distinctly Austrian. Nevertheless, after the initial post-war restrictions on contact with Germans had relaxed, Austria resumed its place in the German cultural and intellectual world. Herbert von Karajan could easily move from the Vienna Philharmonic to the Berlin Philharmonic and back to the Salzburg Festivals, and Federal German citizens have dominated as directors of the *Burgtheater* since 1968.

While there is no question that Austria is politically independent and while it follows that its literature is therefore Austrian, the reality of artistic survival means that the works of Austrian writers must find their public in the wider, German-speaking world. Their successes and prizes won in the Federal Republic are matters of great pride in official publications of the Austrian government. The works of Peter Handke and Thomas Bernhard, which have forced Austrians to confront the uncomfortable past when Austria was part of Nazi Germany, have won the most international attention and parallel those of German writers who had done the same for the Federal Republic. To argue, therefore, that Austrian literature is independent unto itself and not a branch of

German literature, albeit with elements that are distinct and unique, is to superimpose political borders on areas of human activity that transcend state boundaries. Nor are the technicalities of citizenship a bar to other trans-national activities. German academics hold a significant number of professorial posts in Austrian institutions of higher education, and the majority owners of the daily newspapers read by the overwhelming majority of Austrians are Germans. At the personal level, Germans are valued as the single most important source of tourist income as well as for the overall importance of the Federal Republic to the Austrian economy, but they are also somewhat resented for many of the same reasons that large, wealthy, and powerful countries are always resented by their smaller neighbors. Nevertheless, in a poll in 1987, 64 percent of respondents identified the Federal Republic of Germany as the country with which Austria was the most intimately related and ranked "Germany" as the first in a list of "nations" towards which the respondents were the most sympathetic.[28]

Austria's Relations with the German Democratic Republic

In stark contrast to the harmonious relationship that developed after 1949 between Austrians and Germans in the West, since Bohemia was lost to the new state of Czechoslovakia in 1918, Austria became first geographically separated and after World War II politically isolated from its old Saxon and Thuringian neighbors in the East. Although a trade agreement was reached with the German Democratic Republic in 1953, Austria followed the example of Switzerland and Sweden and did not recognize the GDR until after the Basic Treaty of December 21, 1972 was signed between the two German states. A ten-year treaty on economic, technical and industrial cooperation was agreed to the following year, but trade between the two countries never became significant for Austria. Even fifteen years later, the GDR did not appear in the list of Austria's top ten trading partners. Official visits between the two countries did not begin to take place until after the signing of the Final Act of the Conference on Security and Cooperation in Europe (CSCE) in 1975, although it should be noted that in 1977, Austrian Chancellor Kreisky was the first Western head of state to make an official visit to East Berlin.

The pace of official visits increased considerably throughout the decade of the 1980s, but the increasingly cordial relations did not mask the fact that Austria has been tied to the southern part of what was the Federal Republic of Germany for over a millennium, while its relationship with Protestant and Prussian-dominated eastern Germany has always been problematic. Nevertheless, with the new openings to the East precipitated by the events of 1989, Austrian politicians across the political spectrum from the Social Democratic Party to the Freedom Party have begun to comment about historic Austrian ties to Saxony and the possibility of a Lower Austrian-Bohemian-Saxon economic axis.

Austria and the "New Germany," 1990 and Beyond

Despite over a millennium of closely intertwined destiny, Austrians were markedly subdued in their enthusiasm as German unification rushed to completion in 1990. They opened their arms and their pocketbooks in the late summer and fall of 1989 to the East Germans fleeing over the Hungarian border and aided them on their way to their new homes in the Federal Republic, but after the initial euphoria at the collapse of the Berlin Wall and the end of the Cold War, public opinion began to show reservations. Although proponents of the concept of the Austrian nation worry about latent German nationalism and discount expressions to the contrary as political expediency,[29] a poll in early 1990 found that only 58 percent regarded unification as "rather positive," while 31 percent expressed negative feelings.[30] Certainly German reunification would have revitalized a movement for the inclusion of Austria if *Anschluß* still held any appeal. The total absence of any such movement indicates that by 1990 Austria had evolved a strong sense of independence and for most Austrians a separate national identity.[31] In a public opinion poll conducted late in the year of German unification on the attitudes of Austrians towards neighboring states and the recent changes affecting them, only 12 percent in the sample favored incorporation into the new, united Germany. Even among FPÖ (Austrian Freedom Party) voters, whose party still asserts the membership of Austria in the German ethnic and cultural community, only 18 percent stated a desire for *Anschluß*.[32]

To reassure Germany's other neighbors, Chancellor Vranitzky stated unequivocally that Austria was no longer a part of the "German question."[33] As if to underscore this view, official Austria reacted to the dramatic changes affecting its closest and most important neighbor with classic understatement: "The Federal Government, in alert consciousness of our history, welcomes . . . the unification of the two . . . divided German States, and looks forward to good neighborly cooperation in all questions of mutual interest as well as within an all-European framework."[34] This lack of open enthusiasm may also be attributed to more than concern about reawakening the fear of a new *Anschluß*. Like West Germans, Austrians also were anxious about the disruptive impact of rapid unification on their economy. The fear that former markets for Austrian goods in the Federal Republic and the EC might be taken over by East German production was real, as was the concern that the enormous cost of rebuilding the German east might adversely affect the D-Mark and thereby weaken the closely related Austrian Schilling. However, within less than a year, this anxiety was replaced with optimism that Austria was at the beginning of an unprecedented economic upsurge. Austria's 1990 economic growth rate of 4.6 percent was second in the world only to that of Japan, with a full one percent of that increase attributable to German unification. Despite the onset of a world-wide recession, year-end estimates for growth in 1991 were still 3.3 percent, again second only to Japan in the entire world.[35]

Furthermore, the Eastern European revolution of 1989 has influenced more international relationships than just the one between Austria and Germany. In the first half of 1990, the term "*Pentagonale*" suddenly emerged, referring to five countries that wholly or partially made up the old Austrian Empire: Austria, Italy, Yugoslavia, Czechoslovakia, and Hungary. It appears that Italy is promoting this idea as a possible counterbalance to what it sees as a German-dominated Common Market, although for the other four such a regional alignment is definitely of lesser importance than entrance into the European Community. While the civil war in Yugoslavia diverted attention from this discussion, certainly the newly independent and former Habsburg territories of Croatia and Slovenia can be expected to resume efforts for integration into this Central European alignment.

Despite the prospects for an economically reunified Danubian basin, the center of gravity of Austria's foreign policy is its bid for entry into the European Community, the acknowledged key to which has been the support of the Federal Republic of Germany. German unification, however, has prompted muttered fears in some European quarters about "too many Germans" in the EC and may be jeopardizing Austria's chances for early admission. This perception was intensified in the summer of 1991, with Germany supporting Austria's sympathetic response to the attempts by neighboring Slovenia and Croatia to establish their independence. Sharp criticism by France, with increasing references to a German-speaking Axis, and Brussels' continued deferral of the issue of Austrian membership have only increased Austrian defensiveness on the "German Question."

A related problem that has been the subject of intense and sometimes emotional debate within Austria, among EC members, as well as with the Soviet Union, is Austria's policy of "permanent neutrality." Adopted voluntarily in 1955 in return for the Soviet Union's agreement to negotiate the State Treaty, neutrality has become one of main ideals by which the Austrian nation has established its identity, separate and distinct from the Germans. Since Austria first applied for admission to the EC on July 17, 1989, expressions of concern about neutrality were heard, but it was the end of Communism in Eastern Europe, German unification, and the crisis in the Persian Gulf that made it an explosive issue in 1990.

As a domestic political issue, neutrality is as emotionally wrapped up in the complex relationship between Austrians and Germans as is the concept of the Austrian nation. This was illustrated by the uproar that followed a speech given by Jörg Haider, Chairman of the German-nationalist FPÖ, in Munich on the day of the ratification of the treaty of German unification. In this speech he called neutrality a "home-made stumbling block" on the path toward towards EC membership and implied the need to renegotiate the State Treaty because it more severely restricted the sovereignty of Austria than did the treaty signed that day limit the sovereignty of Germany. His political opponents back in Austria immediately charged him with jeopardizing the State Treaty and Austria's neutrality and with appealing to the old Nazis (*Ewiggestriger*) and "propagating *Anschluß*."[36] Several months later, Günter Winkler, one of Austria's most prominent experts on international law, made much the same case as Haider,[37] albeit without the latter's demagogic instinct for place and time. Haider's statement was, however, nothing more than a particularly pointed formulation of his party's position which since its founding has regarded the neutrality law as an evil that had been necessary to win the State Treaty, but one that unfortunately isolated Austria from the remainder of the Western European community. European integration was one of the FPÖ's earliest and most consistent goals. Thus, when EC members initially expressed reservations about the compatibility of Austrian neutrality with the political implications of membership, the FPÖ was ready to reopen the debate on its importance.

For the ÖVP, neutrality is more problematic. The ÖVP led the way to its initial adoption, and its former chairman and current Minister of Foreign Affairs, Alois Mock, continues to contend that neutrality has a function in the post-Cold War world in that it can strengthen the position of Vienna as the third home of the United Nations and can increase the Austrian role as a mediator beyond the traditional East-West conflict. At the same time, the ÖVP, with its strong ties to the business community, cannot afford to jeopardize what is seen as Austria's vital economic integration into Western Europe and has indicated its willingness to reinterpret neutrality in the light of recent events.

In contrast, Austrian Socialists had always opposed entrance into the European Common Market and saw neutrality as a bulwark against both the Communist East and the capitalist West. Recently, however, Franz Vranitzky, Chancellor and Chairman of the newly renamed Social-Democratic Party, and the pragmatists who support him, have won the party over to a pro-EC course that accepts the need for the reinterpretation of neutrality in the light of recent history. Only in late summer, 1991, did the left-wing of the party reluctantly accept this new direction, while remaining vehement in its defense of the *status quo* on neutrality and the State Treaty.[38]

Before the explosion of the Persian Gulf crisis and the election campaign, public opinion on neutrality and EC membership seemed clear. Polls early in 1990 showed a clear majority with optimistic expectations regarding the impact of entry into the EC on matters such as prices, wages, unemployment and competitiveness, with only 32 percent finding advantage in neutrality. Once the Gulf crisis broke, however, a poll showed 86 percent wanting to take a strictly neutral stance in case of war in the Gulf, while another poll found 29 percent in favor of giving up or modifying the still standing policy of "permanent neutrality." As the Gulf War was coming to an end, 64 percent expressed a willingness to accept exclusion from the EC if it meant surrendering neutrality and 80 percent identified neutrality as an important component of Austrian identity, while another polling organization criticized these results as being in "crass contradiction" to its own "carefully and responsibly conducted survey." Exactly how "permanent neutrality" will be interpreted is still very much in flux, and the volatility of public opinion on the matter can be attributed to the recent and dramatic transformation of the political environment that had shaped the development of Austrian national identity since the founding of the Republic.[39]

All nations are built on myths, and neutrality along with the State Treaty are two of the most important that distinguish the still infant Austrian nation from Germany. Membership in a United Europe, despite all the anticipated economic advantages, promises to blur national boundaries and thereby threatens to make the Austrian nation irrelevant before it even becomes fully established. The concept of the Austrian nation was developed as a means of escaping the German legacy, and absorption into Europe brings a threat to the still fragile identity of Austrians who do not want to be seen as Germans, even if German Europeans.

In contrast, official Germany on the eve of the full integration of the EC at the end of 1992, is embracing the universalism urged by Goethe at the dawn of the age of nationalism, and Thomas Mann's admonition to become European Germans has been made its credo. In the West, nationalism is fading and historic regions and even nationalities that were divided as the outcome of wars and treaties long past seem destined to be reunited under the general umbrella of the United States of Europe. In the East, however, nationalism has reemerged as a force of destabilization and poses new questions for the already complicated task of European unification. Austria, for forty-five years at the seam of East and West, is anxious about individual problems such as the wave of asylum-seekers unleashed by the revolutions of 1989-1990, but is generally optimistic about the future. The elimination of customs barriers that will come with admission to the EC is expected to bring an economic boom and the blurring of all borders will accomplish a kind of national unification for the small percentage of Austrians who still identify with national communities beyond the borders of their homeland. When Austria is admitted to the European Community, it will, in its "not-so-foreign" relationship with Germany, play a significant role in the economic revitalization of Eastern Europe and in the process perhaps realize former German-Austrian dreams of a *Mitteleuropa*, albeit under the democratic, free market umbrella of a United Europe.

Notes

1. Hugo Hantsch, *Die Geschichte Österreichs bis 1648*, vol. 1, 2nd. ed. (Graz-Vienna: Styria Steirische Verlagsanstalt, 1947), pp. 36-37.

2. Georg Wagner, "Zum 20. Jahrestag des Staatsvertrages," in Georg Wagner, ed., *Von der Staatsidee zum Nationalbewußtsein* (Vienna: Gesellschaft Pro Austria, 1982), p. 112, quoting Maximilian I from the year 1495.

3. "To the German Nation," photographic reproduction in Herbert Zippe, ed., *Bildband zur Geschichte Österreichs* (Innsbruck, Frankfurt am Main: Penguin Verlag Innsbruck, Umschau Verlag Frankfurt, 1967), p. 138. The author is responsible for this and all subsequent translations from the original German.

4. Friedrich Meinecke, *Cosmopolitanism and the National State*, translated by Robert B. Kimber (Princeton: Princeton University Press, 1970).

5. Adam Wandruszka, "Grossdeutsche und kleindeutsche Ideologie 1840-1871," in Robert A Kann and Friedrich Prinz, eds., *Deutschland und Österreich: ein bilaterales Geschichtsbuch* (Vienna and Munich: Jugend und Volk Verlaggesellschaft, 1980), pp. 120-121.

6. For example Kurt Jungwirth, "Austrian Literature is Austrian," *Austria Today*, 1 (1984), pp. 45-46.

7. Most of the following factual detail is drawn from Andreas Hillgruber, "Das Anschlussproblem 1918-1945 — aus deutscher Sicht," and Gerhard Botz, "Das Anschlussproblem (1918-1945) — aus österreichischer Sicht," in Kann and Prinz, eds., *Deutschland und Österreich*, pp. 160-98; and Helmut Andics, *Der Staat den keiner wollte* (Vienna: Verlag Fritz Molden, 1962).

8. A recent study by Oliver R. Rathkolb, "The Austrian Foreign Service and the Anschluss in 1938," *German Studies Review*, vol. VIII, nr. 1 (February 1990), pp. 55-83, shows the extent to which this sentiment was pervasive in the Foreign Ministry and how it contributed to the ease with which *Anschluß* was accomplished in 1938.

9. Gerhard Jagschitz, *Der Putsch: Die Nationalsozialisten 1934 in Österreich* (Graz, Vienna and Cologne: Verlag Styria, 1976), and Hilgruber, "Das Anschlussproblem 1918-1945 — aus deutscher Sicht," p. 168.

10. Gerald Stourzh, *Kleine Geschichte des Österreichischen Staatsvertrages mit Dokumententeil* (Graz, Vienna and Cologne: Styria Verlag, 1975), pp. 14-15.

11. Robert H. Keyserlingk, "Austria Abandoned: Anglo-American Propaganda and Planning for Austria, 1938-1945," in F. Parkinson, ed., *Conquering the Past: Austrian Nazism Yesterday & Today* (Detroit: Wayne State University Press, 1989), pp. 225-40.

12. Keyserlingk, "Austria Abandoned," p. 236.

13. Fritz Fellner, "The Problem of the Austrian Nation after 1945," *The Journal of Modern History*, vol. 60, nr. 2 (June 1988), p. 269.

14. Gerald Stourzh, ed., *Österreichbewußtsein, 1987* (Vienna: Dr. Fessel & Co., Institut für Meinungsforschung, 1987), pp. 6, 10.

15. Much of the following section is based on Alfred Ableitinger, "Österreichisch-Deutsche Nachkriegsbeziehungen seit 1945," in Kann and Prinz, eds., *Deutschland und Österreich*, pp. 199-219.

16. Quoted by Ableitinger from *Europa-Archiv*, 10/2, 1955, 84438 f.

17. *Jahrbuch der österreichischen Außenpolitik: Außenpolitischer Bericht, 1989* (Vienna: Manzsche Verlag und Universitätsbuchhandlung, 1989), p. 176.

18. *Jahrbuch der österreichischen Außenpolitik, 1989*, p. 265.

19. *Jahrbuch der österreichischen Außenpolitik, 1989*, p. 259.

20. "Kein Friede im Herrgottswinkel," *Kurier*, in *Österreich Bericht*, September 4, 1990, p. 4.

21. Helmut Weixler, "Man muß uns glauben!," *Profil*, November 11, 1991, pp. 50-51.

22. Quoted by Richard Basset, *Waldheim and Austria* (New York: Penguin, 1988), p. 155.

23. Klaus Harprecht, *Am Ende der Gemütlichkeit: Ein österreichisches Tagebuch* (Munich: Deutscher Taschenbuch Verlag, 1989).

24. "Papers Show Waldheim was SS Butcher," *New York Post*, March 26, 1986.

25. Richard Basset's articles for *The Times* of London encapsulated in his book *Waldheim and Austria*.

26. Ernst Gehmacher, Franz Birk, Günther Ogris, "Die Waldheim-Wahl: eine erste Analyse," *Journal für Sozialforschung*, 3/4 (1987), p. 327.

27. Gerald Stourzh, *Vom Reich zur Republik: Studien zum Österreichbewußtsein im 20. Jahrhundert* (Vienna:Wiener Journal Zeitschriftenverlag, 1990), p. 102.

28. Stourzh, ed., *Österreichbewußtsein, 1987*, p. 33.

29. Gerhard Botz, "The Breathtaking union: After the 'German Question,' — the 'Austrian Question'?" *Austria Today*, 2 (1990), pp. 7-11.

30. Inge Santner, "Deutsche Einheit und Österreichs Bangigkeit," *Kleine Zeitung*, March 21, 1991, in *Österreich Bericht*, March 24, 1991, p. 4.

31. Gerald Stourzh, "Österreichbewusstsein im Ausgang der Achtzigerjahre — eine Einführung," pp. i-xvii in *Österreichbewusstsein, 1987*.

32. "Österreicher lehnen jedweden 'Anschluß' ab," *Die Presse*, reprinted in *Österreich Bericht*, November 13, 1990, p. 2.

33. Santner, "Deutsche Einheit und Österreichs Bangigkeit," p. 4.

34. Statement by the Austrian Federal Government to Parliament quoted in *Austrian Foreign Policy Yearbook, 1990* (Vienna: Austrian Ministry for Foreign Affairs), 1991, p. 21. Personal interview with Herbert Schambeck, Vice President, Bundesrat der Republik Österreich.

35. "Österreich profitiert am meisten: Starke Wachstumsimpulse durch deutsche Einigung," *Wiener Zeitung*, in *Österreich Bericht*, December 22, 1990, p. 1.

36. Barbara Hoheneder, "Hausgemachter Stolperstein: FP-Chef Haider stellt Österreichs Staatsvertrag und Neutralität in Frage," *AZ*, reprinted in *Österreich Bericht*, September 14, 1990, p. 2.

37. "'Der Staatsvertrag ist zur Gänze obsolet.' Der prominente Staatsrechtler Günter Winkler fordert: Das bevormundete Österreich gehört in die Souveränität entlassen," *Die Presse*, November 26, 1990, reprinted in *Österreich Bericht*, November 30, 1990, p. 4.

38. Andy Kaltenbrunner, "Das Gute im Bösen," *Profil*, September 2, 1991, pp. 30-31. "Verheerende Orientierung," interview with Josef Cap by Hubertus Czernin, George Hoffmann-Ostenhof and Herbert Lackner in *Profil*, January 13, 1992, p. 21.

39. Data from polls by the Gallup Institute, IMAS and SWS are taken from reprints in *Österreich Bericht* from May 1990 through May 1991. A summary of public opinion research appeared in "Opinion Polls in Austria: Yes to EC membership. Yes to neutrality," *Austria Today*, 3 (1990), p. 25.

16

Switzerland and Germany: An Ambivalent Relationship

Mark Stucki

In the seven centuries of Switzerland's political history, the relationship with the Germans has always been important. The Swiss have tended to view their northern neighbors with a cautious ambivalence rather than outright affection or hostility. At the present time, public opinion in Switzerland continues to show a considerable reserve, yet the Swiss are very much aware that there are benefits as well as risks to be derived from Germany's proximity. Moreover, while the Swiss like to complain that they are often overlooked, taken for granted or not fully accepted as equal partners by the Germans, this perceived condition of neglect is not without a positive side. On the whole, Switzerland has experienced less direct interference from Germany in recent history than most of the other neighboring countries.

Over the centuries, to be sure, there has been enough friction in the relationship to justify the Swiss habit of prudence in dealing with the Germans. But there have also been times in modern Germany's problematic history, when its progressive reformers have looked southward to Switzerland and seen something worthy of emulation. The most recent such turn came in the early postwar years, before the Federal Republic of Germany had itself become prosperous and stable, when there was a marked revival of German respect or even admiration for the economic and democratic accomplishments of the small Alpine republic.

Germany's reunification in 1990, after some four decades of division, has renewed the salience of Switzerland's relations with the giant to the north.

Coming just as Switzerland was preparing to celebrate its own 700th anniversary, in 1991, the political transformation of Germany and Europe at the end of the Cold War has intensified a Swiss self-examination that is, in effect, an identity crisis. It is widely recognized in Switzerland that, after decades of partial self-isolation, the country can no longer avoid coming to terms intellectually and politically with a fast changing and increasingly interdependent continent.

It is not yet clear how Switzerland will answer this challenge to its traditional and preferred role as a neutral bystander in the heart of Europe. However, it seems certain that relations with Germany will not only remain the most important external concern for Switzerland but will become even more important than hitherto. At the same time, closer relations with Germany and the rest of Europe do not mean that Switzerland will easily abandon its centuries-old determination to be free of external domination or interference.

Switzerland cannot even pretend to be a nation-state like so many of its neighbors. It is internally divided along several cleavage lines in addition to the more common European ones, based on socio-economic stratification, urban-rural contrasts or regional differences, such as those between mountain and plain areas. Switzerland is exceptional primarily because of its highly concentrated cultural diversity, shaped by the coexistence of four languages and two major religions within a relatively small territory. If the cleavage lines had coincided, the country would probably be ungovernable, even as a loosely knit confederation. They are cross-cutting, however, and normally result in a politics of shifting coalitions rather than coherent and stable linguistic or cultural blocs.

Close to one-half of the country's population is Catholic, and most of the other half is oriented toward a predominantly Calvinist form of Protestantism. A little more than 70 percent or about four million of the Swiss people speak German as their first language, but there are several distinct dialects. Another 20 percent or more than one million Swiss are francophone, about one-quarter of a million are Italian-speaking, and a few thousand speak Romansch, another derivative of Latin.[1] All four tongues enjoy recognition as official languages of Switzerland. The strong federative structure of the country gives the 26 *cantons* considerable autonomy and makes them the primary centers of political life on cultural and many other matters. This structural decentralization of government in turn serves as an important additional check against any tendency for the German-speaking majority to act as a unified and dominant bloc. In recent years, there appears to have been a growing apprehension among members of the linguistic minorities over possible German-language domination in some areas of the corporate economy or the public service. But compared to some other multilingual societies, Switzerland has remarkably little friction among its language groups.[2]

Switzerland's Emancipation from Its German-Speaking Neighbors

Despite some chronological uncertainties and the mythical adornments in the saga of the brave freedom fighter, Wilhelm Tell, the birthdate of the Helvetic or Swiss Confederation is usually set in 1291.[3] In that year, the three *cantons* in the center of present-day Switzerland — Uri, Schwyz, and Unterwalden — formed an Eternal League, a perpetual alliance for the settlement of disagreements among themselves and for "mutual aid against attack and injustice."[4] They created their defensive league out of fear of encroachments by the Habsburg rulers on what the Swiss considered to be their ancient privileges and freedoms within the Holy Roman Empire. Even as they asserted their independence from intermediate rule by the Habsburgs, the Swiss proclaimed their continuing loyalty to the higher imperial authority. In reality, however, they could run most of their own affairs, because the Holy Roman Empire was a loose-knit confederation that exercised little effective control over its many different principalities, kingdoms, and independent towns. This political weakness was a crucial factor in the Swiss ability to gain full independence during a process of separation that stretched over the following two centuries.

During the first century of the Swiss Confederation, the three *cantons* fought off several attempts by the Habsburgs to reimpose their rule. They first defeated the Habsburgs at Morgarten (1315). Here and later, the Swiss gained a reputation as ferocious fighters by using unconventional tactics and refusing to take prisoners. Some seven decades later the league, now expanded by five more *cantons* which added an important urban component (Lucerne, Zürich, Zug, Glarus, and Bern), triumphed again at Sempach (1386) and Nafels (1388). In 1438, however, the Habsburgs gained the throne to the Holy Roman Empire and thereafter renewed their threat to the semi-independent Swiss Confederation by trying to strengthen the imperial bonds. An important turning point came in 1495, when the Imperial *Reichstag* in Worms, under Habsburg influence, moved to provide for an imperial court and tax.[5] Such encroachments triggered the Swabian or Swiss War of 1499, in which the Confederation won a string of bloody battles. Already the same year, the Swiss forced a settlement, the Peace of Basel, which provided for their practical independence from the Holy Roman Empire, a little more than two centuries after the first step in the break-away.

Switzerland continued to expand piecemeal by a combination of persuasion and conquest. By 1513, five more *cantons* had entered the loose Confederation (Fribourg, Solothurn, Basel, Schaffhausen, and Appenzell), raising their number to 13. Only after a major defeat by technically superior French forces in Lombardy, at the battle of Marignano in 1515, did the Swiss finally abandon military exploits abroad and settle on a foreign policy of neutrality. From this year until the French Revolution, the Confederation managed to stay out of foreign conflict. It took considerable effort and some time for the Swiss to learn how to contain internal conflicts of interest and religion in their own increasingly heterogeneous Confederation. On some occasions, their differences spilled over into civil strife, but a spirit of accommodation prevailed in the end. It appears that the long struggle for independence and incremental expansion on the periphery had laid the foundation for a sense of shared political destiny. In later centuries, when the spirit of nationalism swept over much of Europe, this political commonality would overarch the cultural and linguistic diversity of the Swiss Confederation and keep it together as a country that perhaps could be called a politically defined *Staatsnation*.

The Swiss reformers Zwingli and Calvin had been in the theological vanguard of the break-up of Christendom during the 16th century. As elsewhere, the religious split had political repercussions, and it came to conflicts between Swiss Catholics and Protestants on several occasions in the first half of the 17th century. It is therefore remarkable that the Confederation managed to keep itself out of the Thirty Years' War, which *could* have had a devastating impact on the fledgling country. In 1648, the Westphalia peace settlement of Europe's religious conflict nevertheless had an important result for Switzerland. It finally established *de jure* recognition of the country's independence and thus severed the last formal ties of the Swiss *cantons* to the Empire and the emperor.

During the next 150 years, Switzerland's relationship with its politically fragmented German neighbors was defined by the growth of peaceful trade links. Swiss farmers, who specialized in dairy products (mainly cheese) and cattle-breeding, were able to export a significant part of their product to southern Germany in return for grain. Textiles and watches became other important Swiss export articles. As international trade grew, the economy of neighboring German states also came to depend on the passes in Switzerland as increasingly important trade lines with the south of Europe.[6]

Switzerland also laid the foundation for its renowned multicultural profile in this period. It stood at the confluence of three European high cultures, but in these formative years Swiss elites were primarily influenced by France. That was also true for their counterparts in much of the rest of Europe, but French influence on Switzerland appears to have been unusually strong.[7] It left traces that have lasted to this day, and the legacy has served to counterbalance the later cultural primacy of Germany.

The political foundation of modern Switzerland can be traced back to the French Revolution and the Napoleonic wars, as is true for much of the rest of Europe. When French armies invaded the country in 1798, many Swiss welcomed them as liberators from the social and political oppression of the oligarchic patrician families in several of the *cantons*. The old regime collapsed and political reforms carried out under French tutelage turned the loose Confederation into a more unified country, with central authorities and a liberal constitution.

Another threat to Swiss independence came fifteen years later, ironically when the state asserted the policy of neutrality that has been a hallmark of its modern identity. At this point, in 1813, the Swiss refused an offer to join the coalition then forming against Napoleon. The move caused both surprise and consternation among the allies, especially in the German states of the military coalition, whose romantic image of the Swiss fight for liberty had recently been nurtured by Friedrich Schiller's popular play of 1802, *Wilhelm Tell*. Their newspapers now berated the Swiss for cowardice and treachery, denouncing them as slackers and weaklings. It is symptomatic that at this time some of the leading German reformers, including Stein, Humboldt, and Hardenberg, seriously considered a forced integration of Switzerland into a future German nation.[8] Any Swiss hopes to remain outside the fray were dashed. In December 1813, the allies abandoned their self-imposed restraint and marched troops into Switzerland in order to attack Napoleon's exposed flank, but they promised to restore Swiss independence and neutrality as soon as the French were defeated.

The Congress of Vienna (1815) made amends by issuing a formal guarantee of perpetual Swiss neutrality. It also confirmed the admission of nine more *cantons* in a final territorial expansion of the Confederation. Although the Congress restored the old regime of patrician rule, it could not eradicate the new and progressive political ideas that from now on clashed with more conservative sentiments in Switzerland as in other parts of Europe.

In the following decades, relations with many of the German states became even more important. Trade increased as Switzerland embarked on a relatively early industrialization. There was a cultural and intellectual reorientation after the defeat of the French, as German-speaking Swiss turned increasingly toward the dynamic northern neighbors for inspiration.[9] A new and entirely different link was forged, when the Congress system's political suppression of the growing liberal movement brought a first wave of German political refugees and emigrants into Switzerland. This situation led to severe tensions with several German states. Prussia even sought to intervene on behalf of the German Confederation in 1824, but such a move was thwarted by Britain. Thus Switzerland became a refuge for the German Liberals, who in turn had a stimulating effect on the intellectual and political life of their hosts.

Soon Switzerland had a revived and expanded progressive reform movement of its own, which proclaimed as one of its goals a modern and more unified country with central authorities. After a brief civil war in 1847, the victorious Liberals in the following year set up a stronger federal constitution for Switzerland, which included the principle of universal male suffrage. Unlike the German Confederation, where Liberal hopes for constitutional reform and national unification had been dashed in 1848, resulting in another wave of political emigration, Switzerland emerged from the revolution as Europe's first democracy. To be sure, the Swiss would eventually move from the vanguard toward the rear, because their democracy remained a male domain for well over a century.[10]

In the aftermath of the 1848 revolution, a dangerous conflict erupted with Prussia over the Swiss *canton* of Neuchâtel. Although it was legally a member of the Swiss Confederation, Neuchâtel personally belonged to the King of Prussia. Beset by his own revolutionary threat at home, he had not intervened when Neuchâtel proclaimed itself a republic in 1848. Eight years later, however, when royalists were thwarted in an attempted counterrevolution in Neuchâtel, the Prussian king demanded that the imprisoned leaders be released. When the Swiss government refused, Prussia prepared for a military attack, and Switzerland mobilized its army in turn. In the end, the intervention of the other Great Powers defused the conflict, and a conference in Paris settled the issue in 1857 by establishing that Neuchâtel was an integral part of Switzerland in return for a Swiss release of the royalist prisoners. The settlement had symbolic importance for the Swiss. It gave a boost to their growing sense of political identity and self-confidence as a progressive country. Their idealized interpretation of the conflict was captured neatly in a summary comment by the famous Swiss historian, Edgar Bonjour: "The new law-writing radicalism of Switzerland pitted itself against the law-preserving conservatism of Prussia."[11]

The Swiss view of Germany also became less benign after Prussia's victory in the war with Austria (1866). Many correctly recognized that this might be a step toward German unity under Prussian dominance. Swiss apprehensions were linked to considerations of both ideology and power politics, since earlier sympathy for a united Germany had sprung from an identification with the German liberal-democratic efforts for political reform from below. Now, as Bismarck led a conservative effort to unite Germany from above "by blood and iron," Swiss support for the German cause eroded as it became increasingly clear that a major shift in the European balance of power was imminent.

In its first 600 years, Switzerland had managed to free itself from the Holy Roman Empire and had successfully warded off attempts by some of its fragmented German neighbors to interfere in its affairs. These common efforts had forged a sense of shared political identity and purpose among the Swiss, despite their cultural heterogeneity. The relationship with the neighboring Germans had not been defined by such struggles alone. Over time, mutually beneficial economic and cultural ties to the German states had developed, and German liberalism had even helped spawn a Swiss counterpart that gave shape to the new political system after 1847. But the unification of Germany under Prussian leadership in 1871 changed the relationship fundamentally.

New Challenges to Swiss Sovereignty: Political Independence versus Economic Dependence

During the Franco-Prussian War of 1870, the Swiss army had been mobilized to safeguard the vulnerable northwestern frontier. When the nearby conflict was over, however, the presence of a united Germany posed a more lasting problem for the Swiss. As a multicultural country, with a major German-speaking component, Switzerland had special reasons to worry about the growth of nationalism in Europe and, especially, in Germany. For the most part, Swiss public opinion appears to have turned against Germany, or more precisely against Prussia. It was especially working class leaders who expressed fear of German-Prussian dominance in Europe, with its potential threat to absorb smaller countries with ethnic German populations. There was no straightforward crisis between Switzerland and Germany, but it was possible to register a severe cooling in public relations between them. Bismarck's *Kulturkampf* found little understanding in the large Catholic minority of Switzerland, and his anti-socialist laws drove yet another wave of political emigrés into the country from Germany. Like their liberal predecessors, the socialist refugees were often articulate advocates of progressive reforms and incisive critics of an illiberal government and society in their German homeland. They found a ready hearing among many Swiss, who had special reasons for being uneasy about the increasingly powerful and dynamic neighbor.

The somewhat strained political relations, however, were counterbalanced by a strengthening of economic ties between the two countries. German and Italian unification had stimulated trade throughout the western part of Europe, and this in turn made the transit routes through Switzerland even more important than earlier. The Swiss railroad network grew in significance after the opening of the transalpine Gotthard tunnel in 1880, funded in considerable part with German investments.

Switzerland continued to industrialize and, apart from short interludes of recession, experienced remarkable economic growth coupled with an increasing dependence on international trade in the period before World War I. In the Swiss machine industry, the share of exports grew between 1887 and 1913 from 7 percent to 15 percent. It rose to a similar percentage in the food-processing sector and reached 45 percent in the textile sector. Germany replaced Britain as the single most important trading partner in these years. Between 1891 and 1894, it absorbed silk exports worth 57 million Swiss Franks (SFr), about 22 million SFr worth of watches, and 17 million SFr worth of cotton textiles. Meanwhile, Switzerland imported from Germany over 42 million SFr worth of iron, over 34 million SFr worth of wool, and over 24 million SFr worth of coal. Another important economic factor was Switzerland's new position as a major financial center in Europe. At the turn of the century, Switzerland had become the world's biggest international per capita investor.[12]

Switzerland's relations with the wider world changed as a result of these and other osmotic processes with the neighboring countries and especially with Germany. In the 19th century, Switzerland had an overabundant labor supply and, as a result, had experienced a major emigration to North America. By the turn of the century, however, the process reversed itself as Switzerland began to attract workers from the surrounding countries. In 1914, 700,000 foreigners were living in Switzerland, representing 17 percent of the whole population. The single biggest group was of German origin.[13] Most stayed in the German-speaking part of Switzerland, where they made considerable economic contributions that were eventually followed by a major social and cultural impact as well.

While popular ambivalence toward the big neighbor prevailed, the turn of the century and the reign of Kaiser Wilhelm II brought closer political and military ties at the elite level. Indeed, the officer corps in Switzerland embarked upon cooperation with its German counterpart in a manner and degree that aroused suspicions among both the Entente Powers and some parts of the Swiss population itself.[14]

When World War I broke out in 1914, Switzerland reaffirmed its neutrality once again. However, it turned out to be a somewhat biased neutrality, especially during the first years of the war. There were several instances in which Swiss intelligence was illegally transmitted to the Germans, and the Swiss commander-in-chief even contemplated entering the war on the side of Germany. The German-speaking newspapers, except for some Socialist ones, showed support for the German side, despite the invasion of neutral Belgium. A somewhat similar tendency to take sides, but in this case with the Entente, could be detected in the francophone press of Switzerland. As a result, the war created a temporary political divide between many French- and German-speaking Swiss. The prolonged European conflict also caused economic problems for the landlocked country, which was dependent on the import of its raw materials, but it proved possible to continue trade with both belligerent sides. During the first war years, at least, the German economic connection appeared to be more important.

Switzerland survived World War I without completely compromising its independence, but the special relationship with Germany had created tensions within the country and badly discredited the Swiss claim to neutrality. After the war, Switzerland established good relations with the defeated northern neighbor. The official emphasis tended to be mostly on the restoration of trade relations, but the Swiss public did not hide its sympathy for the Weimar Republic whose commitment to democracy helped allay the lingering fear of German hegemony.

The situation changed drastically after the Nazi rise to power in early 1933. Hitler's ideology, with its emphasis on "blood" and "race," implicitly threatened the existence of a country like Switzerland, which relied on the harmonious coexistence of different peoples and cultures. From a Nazi perspective, the German-speaking Swiss belonged to the *Volk* as much as did the Austrians, and their homeland was regarded as an integral part of a future Greater Germany.

Relations between the two countries deteriorated further as a result of a number of developments and events. These included the undercover operations by the German *Gestapo* inside Switzerland, the emergence of a Nazi movement among German nationals living in Switzerland, Berlin's support for the small but aggressive Swiss Nazi organizations coupled with its pressure against anti-Nazi voices in the Swiss press, and the assassination in Davos in February 1936 of the Swiss Nazi leader Wilhelm Gustloff.[15] The Swiss government sought to appease Germany by making concessions, always with a view to maintaining as much independence as possible, as when it imposed new restrictions on the critical press. The most tragic concession, whose full consequences were not foreseen, took the form of a severe limitation on the immigration of Jewish refugees.[16]

In domestic politics, a familiar phenomenon could be observed. Greater external pressure resulted in greater internal solidarity, so that by 1939 the Swiss largely regarded Nazi Germany as a virulent danger. Nevertheless, the small country decided that its military and economic vulnerability made it necessary to follow a path of limited cooperation with the aggressive next-door giant. In retrospect, it would be difficult not to conclude that this cooperation went further than necessary — and most surely so on the refugee issue.[17]

As in 1914, Switzerland declared its neutrality at the outbreak of World War II, on August 30, 1939. Germany's formal response was positive, and included an incongruous insistence on absolute compliance with the rules of neutrality.[18] The Federal Council decided to mobilize the Swiss army. In contrast to World War I, Switzerland this time was united in its perception of Germany as the main threat, and the general public and military shared a broad commitment to defend the country. Among political and economic elites, however, there seemed to be wavering by some individuals. They had been impressed by Germany's swift victory against France in 1940, by its apparent economic achievements before that, and by its "crusade" against Communism thereafter. There was considerable doubt about the capability of Switzerland to safeguard its complete independence in what appeared to be a "new" Europe. This explains the policy of accomodation as well as the presence of scattered collaborationist tendencies among Swiss elites. In retrospect, a fair observer must conclude that the policy of moderation toward Nazi Germany resulted mainly from the perceived need to appease a powerful and aggressive neighbor. This is not to deny that there were individuals who went beyond necessity in their willingness to cooperate. Switzerland, like some other European countries, has not really come to terms with this part of its past. Thinking men and women will continue to be troubled by the question about how Hitler could and should have been resisted more firmly.

Throughout the war, anxiety about a German attack persisted. Such fears could feed on casual aggressive remarks by German leaders or in German criticism of the free and sometimes still outspoken Swiss press. There was also evidence of German military plans and moves that indicated a preparation for attacks on Switzerland. Actual military engagement occurred in the course of the campaign against France. In May and early June 1940, German planes repeatedly violated Switzerland's airspace, and the Swiss air force shot down several *Luftwaffe* fighters. These and later incidents led to diplomatic tensions with Germany, which sometimes reacted with threats of force, backed by some attacks on Swiss fighter patrols. Yet the decisive actions of the Swiss army and air force served as a clear signal of the Swiss determination to resist and may well have had a crucial deterrent effect.[19] The will to fight back was perhaps best embodied in the famous "redoubt strategy."[20]

Switzerland nevertheless was pulled into the German orbit by economic considerations. At the outset of the war, the Swiss conducted long and difficult trade negotiations with both sides, and the Allies finally agreed to a minimal Swiss-German trade that Switzerland regarded as indispensable. After the fall of France, the Swiss were completely surrounded by Fascist powers. At that point, as one historian remarks, "*de facto*, Switzerland was integrated into the German economic system, *de jure* it could keep itself out of the blockade."[21]

Swiss exports became heavily skewed toward Germany. In 1941-42, about 60 percent of the weapons industry, 50 percent of the optical industry, and about 40 percent of the machine industry worked for Germany. Switzerland had become even more important for the Third Reich in financial matters. It was the only country in the world where Germany could trade its gold for freely convertible currencies. This procedure was especially problematic because a significant part of German gold had been acquired illegally and included gold from victims of the concentration camps. In retrospect, it can be argued that economic cooperation with Germany may have done more to keep Switzerland free from a military attack than all of the country's preparations to defend itself. But the moral question lingers: To what degree can the interest in national self-preservation justify the maintenance of an extensive and mutually beneficial trading relationship with a regime like that of the Third Reich?[22]

The victory of the Allies was welcomed throughout Switzerland. Any possible sympathy for Germany had vanished during the war, and the Swiss were repulsed by the record of Nazi brutalities that now became more fully revealed. Throughout the conflict, Switzerland had continued to follow a policy of accommodation and limited resistance in dealing with a Third Reich that for a short time straddled most of Europe. Cut off from the rest of the world, the Swiss had been prepared to resist military aggression, but their strategy for self-preservation had included intensive economic dealings with the Third Reich that raised understandable suspicion and some ill will in the Allied nations. If anything, the experience boosted Switzerland's tendency toward political inwardness and detachment from the outside world.

1945 to 1990: The Priority of Economics

After World War II, Switzerland was among the first countries to lend a hand to devastated Germany. The Swiss gave humanitarian aid in the form of *Schweizerspende*, offered advice on rebuilding the country, and gave political support to the new and democratic institutions set up in the Western zones of occupation. But for the most part Switzerland remained in its inward-looking mood. The traumatic experience of isolation during World War II seemed to reinforce a political tradition of concentrating on domestic matters or those as close to home as possible. Switzerland remained committed to neutrality, and it did not join the United Nations, the European Community, or any of the international defense pacts. At the same time, however, there was never a question of where the country belonged in terms of the East-West division of Europe: Switzerland perceived itself as a member of the Western world, politically, economically, and — despite its official neutrality — even in terms of defense policy.

The capitulation of Germany on May 8, 1945 had interrupted whatever remained of the flow of capital and goods with Switzerland. Thereafter the Swiss government faced the difficult task of liquidating the German-Swiss Clearing, that is, the sum not yet paid for the exports and imports between the two countries during the war. It had given cash advances in the sum of about one billion SFr to stimulate bilateral trade, and there was no chance after the war to liquidate this Clearing through German imports. Moreover, there was no central German monetary institution to deal with after the *Reichsbank* had ceased to exist. In this situation, the Swiss government froze all German assets in Switzerland. Later on, as trade with West Germany increased, there came an opportunity to try collecting on the old war-time debts, but economic rationality made such a course of action seem inadvisable. Switzerland had an interest in opposing protectionism against its own exports, and that made it seem unwise to offend the Germans with old claims that arose out of the liquidation of the Third Reich.[23]

After the war, Swiss officials had been able to conclude agreements with the different occupation zones in Germany as a first step toward normalization of bilateral trade. At first, it was mostly a one-way flow, with German goods sold to Switzerland rather than the other way around. As a result, the Swiss had a strong interest in promoting fair terms of trade with occupied Germany, based on the idea that imports from there should be balanced by Swiss exports. There was rapid progress in this matter. Already by 1949, the western and eastern parts of Germany together had become the third most important purchaser of Swiss products. In the same year, Switzerland concluded a major agreement on trade and payment with the new Federal Republic of Germany. It brought a massive liberalization in their bilateral economic exchanges, with restrictions on imports and exports mostly banned, and resulted in a rapid increase in the volume of trade between the two countries.[24]

After the creation of separate West and East German states in 1949, it was quite natural for Swiss relations to be much closer with the western Federal Republic of Germany than with the Communist-ruled German Democratic Republic. West Germany was not only an immediate neighbor, it also shared with Switzerland a basic commitment to liberal democracy and a market economy.

From 1950 onwards, there was a dramatic increase in Swiss involvement in international trade. The country's balance of trade for 1950 shows exports worth 5.6 billion SFr. Thirty-five years later, in 1985, they reached 117.7 billion SFr.[25] In 1965, 33 percent of the Swiss production of industrial goods was exported, and this share had grown to 46 percent by 1985. A similar pattern shows up in the record of imports into Switzerland. In 1965, the share of imported goods on the Swiss market stood at 31 percent, while twenty years later the share had risen to 40 percent. The conclusion is obvious: Switzerland's economy and its wealth were and still are unusually dependent on a free flow of imports and exports.

The same is true for the small country's financial relations. Despite its tiny population and small domestic market, Switzerland continues to be one of the most important financial powers on earth. It is the world's fifth biggest foreign investor, the foreign credits of its banks are the third largest in the world, and Zürich is the world's third largest foreign currency exchange.[26] This remarkable achievement is not the result of "nature," but is based on a closely woven web of international relations and interdependencies.

In this vast economic and financial network, the Swiss relationship with the Federal Republic of Germany occupies a crucial position. In the early 1950s, West Germany won back the rank long held by Germany as Switzerland's most important trade partner, in both exports and imports. It has kept that primacy until today. Indeed, when compared with former times, the relationship has become even more important. In 1978, the value of Switzerland's imports from West Germany was about 12.2 billion SFr, while exports to West Germany amounted to about 7.5 billion SFr. These amounts represented 29 percent of Swiss imports and 18 percent of Swiss exports, respectively. In 1986, the import-export figures had reached just over 24 billion SFr and 14 billion SFr respectively, almost a doubling in eight years. The West German share of Swiss imports had gone up to 33 percent, while its share of Swiss exports had risen to 21 percent.

The impressive growth of Switzerland's postwar economic relations with Germany and with other countries in Western Europe was made possible by a multitude of bilateral and multilateral agreements. When it came to economics, at least, the Swiss did not pursue isolation from the rest of the world. In 1948, the country joined the OEEC (later: OECD), and in 1958 it signed the General

Agreement on Tariffs and Trade (GATT). Both organizations, to which the Federal Republic of Germany also belongs, have the goals of furthering world trade. In 1960, Switzerland was one of the founding members of the European Free Trade Association (EFTA), a tariff union of seven non-EC countries. In 1972, an important free-trade treaty was concluded with the European Community (EC). This treaty gives Switzerland free access to the German market (except for agrarian products). Because of Germany's membership in the EC (and Switzerland's non-membership), many official contacts are now via EC offices in Brussels. For that reason, bilateral agreements have become less frequent, and trade relations have to be seen more and more in a wider European context.

Aside from international trade, tourism is a very important branch of the Swiss economy. The country's mountain resorts are world-famous, but they are not inexpensive and it has become more difficult to attract budgetminded foreign guests. Germans are among those foreigners who still can afford holidays in Switzerland, and they spend a considerable amount of money there. In 1986, the Swiss tourist industry counted almost two million arrivals of German tourists in Switzerland and almost six and one-half million overnight stays by Germans.[27] While many Germans visit as tourists, however, there appears to have been a decline in some other direct contacts between Swiss and Germans.

At the beginning of the century, many Germans lived and worked in Switzerland. There are still many German residents in the country, but their relative importance in comparison to other foreigners has diminished. In 1960, there were 93,406 Germans with permanent residence in Switzerland, representing about 16 percent of the foreign population. By 1980, their numbers had declined to 87,913 and their share had plummeted to 9.3 percent.[28] The causes for this development seem obvious enough. Germany is today a country almost as rich as Switzerland, and there is no pressing economic reason for Germans to emigrate anymore. Germans who live in Switzerland today are neither economic nor political refugees, as often in the past. They are there overwhelmingly for personal reasons or because they represent German firms. Indeed, the small but very effective Swiss economy has become very dependent on the much larger and very rich German economy.[29] The postwar days in which the Swiss could look upon Germans as poor and needy neighbors have passed into history. Today, the Swiss look upon the German economy with considerable respect and at times even some envy.

Swiss neutrality mandates that military relations with other countries must remain very limited. However, some relations with the Federal Republic of Germany evolved over the years. From the beginning of the Cold War, Switzerland anticipated a military threat only from the Warsaw Pact. From the Swiss perspective, a strong NATO with an armed West Germany as core member represented an essential element of the small and neutral country's own security. In that sense, German troops were no longer regarded as a threat but as a potential source of protection for Switzerland.[30] The Swiss army itself relies almost completely on imported equipment from NATO countries, and in recent years the Federal Republic of Germany became an important source of military imports for Switzerland.[31]

Cultural relations between the two countries are very important, as any visit to a Swiss bookshop makes abundantly clear. The overwhelming number of books in German-speaking Switzerland comes from the Federal Republic of Germany, with a very small additional share of Swiss origin. A similar preponderance of French imports can be found in the francophone parts of the country. German magazines, television, songs, musical performers, and actors all form an important part of the Swiss cultural diet. It is important to add that the most acclaimed contemporary Swiss authors, like Friedrich Dürrenmatt and Max Frisch, always looked upon themselves not primarily as Swiss, but as German-speaking writers.[32] Indeed, it could be argued that some of their best work wrestles with some of the moral problems generated by the politics of 20th century Germany. In a wider sense as well, the cultural world of urban Swiss-Germans is similar to that of their German counterparts in the Federal Republic. There may well be smaller differences derived from the experience of having grown up in Zürich as compared to Cologne than from having lived in the large Swiss city as compared to a small village in the Alps. As for mass culture, the German parts of Switzerland have almost ceased to have their own sense of identity (if we assume they ever had one).

Academic links to science and higher education in Germany have also become more important for Switzerland. To be sure, this development is part of the global trend toward an internationalization of scholarship, but for the Swiss it is probably true that the German influence has grown more than any other. The shared language makes the German choice quite natural when Swiss-Germans want to study abroad, when Swiss universities hire new professors, or when Swiss schools adopt foreign schoolbooks. This is not necessarily an undesirable development, but it can become a problem when German-speaking Swiss students know more about their neighbors to the north than about francophone Swiss people.

Political relations between Switzerland and the Federal Republic of Germany have been astonishingly uneventful during the past thirty years. Of course, the two countries have had close relations at the political level, but they were so smooth and unproblematic that they demanded relatively little attention. The economic relationship clearly has been far more salient. The old saying that Swiss foreign policy is really economic policy applies nowhere so much as in the country's relations with the Federal Republic of Germany. There have been no territorial disputes between the two countries, and their interests have in most cases been congruent. From a Swiss point of view, it makes little sense to risk disagreements with the Federal Republic on minor issues. The only major tension with West Germany (and the EC) in recent years stemmed from

Switzerland's restrictive road policy for trucks on transit through the country.[33] Even here, Switzerland has tried to appease the Federal Republic.

In contrast to the close relationship with West Germany, relations with East Germany were never very close or important. Switzerland tended to follow the West German lead in dealing with the Soviet bloc countries, and this was especially true for the German Democratic Republic. The Swiss widely regarded Communist Germany as a Soviet satellite, and ignorance of or hostility toward East Germany was quite common. This stemmed in part from the presence of a relatively strong anti-Communism in Switzerland, where the Communist Party has never been very popular.[34] But many Swiss also tended to ascribe to East Germany the militarist or authoritarian traits they associated with Prussia or Nazi Germany. For the Swiss, who like to see themselves as among the most democratic and free people in the world, the militant and repressive East German regime held no attraction. For a long time, there were practically no contacts with the Communistruled state in Germany.

Switzerland followed the Western powers in not extending official recognition to East Germany until after Willy Brandt's *Ostpolitik* had led to the *Deutschlandvertrag* or Basic Treaty between the two German states in 1972. After diplomatic relations were established, there was a modest improvement in other areas. Swiss trade with East Germany rose from the insignificant volume of $38 million in 1970 to $313 million in 1987. The balance of trade was always in favor of Switzerland, with an export surplus in 1987 of $159 million. But even these numbers never meant very much to the Swiss economy, and they are completely overshadowed by the trade figures with West Germany for those years. The percentage of trade with the GDR never rose to a level higher than 0.3 percent of total Swiss foreign trade.[35] Moreover, Swiss public opinion continued to perceive the German Democratic Republic as a strange and unattractive country.

German Unification: Switzerland Discovers a New World

The unification of Germany caught Switzerland by surprise. As in other neighboring countries, the event aroused mixed feelings. No major Swiss voice spoke against the merger of East and West Germany, but there were also few if any expressions of unadulterated joy. In an earlier book about German unification, published in 1970, the Swiss historian Hans Rentsch had formulated a view that still seemed characteristic for his countrypeople: ". . . Switzerland has a deeply rooted fear about the word 'unity' on German lips."[36]

Twenty years later, that word had become reality, and the Swiss fear of a united Germany had not completely dissipated. Soberly considered, Swiss relations with Germany are very good today, be they economic, political or personal, but beneath the surface there is still an unease, especially at the level of public opinion. Popularly expressed reflections, such as the common pronouncement heard in taverns that "60 million Germans are enough," constitute the simplest and least controlled formulations of a widespread concern. From the perspective of the small and culturally diverse Alpine republic, a united Germany easily appears as too big, too powerful, too self-confident, and sometimes surely too close for complete comfort.

A Swiss poll taken in early 1990 showed the presence of widespread reservations, but little outright fear, about German unification. The question, whether a united Germany represented a threat to Switzerland, yielded answers showing that almost four-fifth (79.2 percent) of the Swiss did not expect a threat, only 15 percent did, while 5.8 percent did not know or had no opinion. The picture changed, however, when the question was formulated more concretely and personally. Asked if they personally favored German unification, almost two-fifths answered "no" (37.9 percent), while barely more than one-half answered "yes" (52.5 percent). This result becomes even more interesting, when one compares the answers of German-speaking Swiss with those of their francophone counterparts. It was the former who indicated the greatest opposition to German unification (43.9 percent said "no"), whereas their French-speaking compatriots were more supportive (only 20 percent of them said "no")![37] It hardly needs adding that those who did not favor unification seem to have been expressing an understandable preference for a smaller neighbor. They clearly were not being supportive of the dictatorship in East Germany.

Negative feelings toward Germany immediately before unification were quite common among the Swiss. In a ranking of sympathies toward the country's four neighbors, Germans ranked last with 10.1 percent, while the French were first with 30.8 percent. Asked about typical qualities of Germans, the one with the highest percentage in the German-speaking parts of Switzerland was "bragging" (74 percent), while only 46 percent agreed that Germans are "nice."[38]

In a commentary in the influential Swiss magazine, *L'Hebdo*, publicist Frank A. Meyer expressed with some eloquence the fear that a multicultural Switzerland could be endangered by a united Germany. If the already dominant German-speaking part of Switzerland would become even stronger through German unification, if everything German would dominate Europe, centrifugal tendencies in Switzerland would intensify, he wrote. Such a catastrophe could be avoided if Switzerland were to join the European Community and help ensure that "Europe does not become German, but that Germany instead becomes European."[39] This widely used phrase, coined by Thomas Mann in another context decades earlier, had become a central theme in Hans-Dietrich Genscher's reassurances to Germany's neighbors, and it had clearly found appreciative ears also in Switzerland.

Public statements by Swiss politicians fit into this picture of prudent reactions to German unification. The president of the Swiss parliament for 1991 was thinking aloud, when he said that "many people are asking themselves if more Germany is indeed better Germany." The president of the powerful Free Democrats had "reservations" about German unification, while his Social Democratic counterpart temporarily broke free of restraint and referred to a "nightmare."[40]

However, it would be a mistake to exaggerate the depth or scale of Swiss fears about German unification. Indeed, with the exception of Austria, Switzerland may have been the European neighbor with the fewest reservations about the developments in Germany. One reason could be the fact that the Swiss have not been drawn into recent wars with Germany. Another would surely be the beneficial if dependent economic relationship with Germany, united or not. When they really think about the issue, most Swiss would probably put the economic benefits first. The title of a commentary on German unification, which appeared in the influential magazine, *Politik und Wirtschaft*, introduces a sober Swiss assessment of the bottom line of economic benefits that is probably more widely shared than the polls suggest: "Freuen wir uns an Deutschland" or "Let's be happy about Germany."[41]

Switzerland's relations with today's Germany are too important to be defined in terms of historically derived prejudices against the giant neighbor. Much of the old distrust will perhaps vanish with generational shifts, growing personal contacts, and even closer bilateral links.[42] It would be unrealistic to expect public opinion polls in Switzerland to reflect a newly discovered love for Germany, but a growth in mutual respect and acceptance would be desirable. An absolute precondition for such a development among the Swiss would be a continuation of democratic tolerance in Germany. The recent series of right-wing spasms among German voters, in such neighboring states as Baden-Württemberg and Bavaria as well as the new eastern *Länder* and Schleswig-Holstein, could rekindle old fears in Switzerland.

The Swiss business community is understandably far more optimistic about German unification. Switzerland can only thrive from a continued and growing access to German markets. An enlarged Germany appears to Swiss business as an even larger market for goods, services, or investments. Because there is a shared language along with many common cultural traits, the Swiss see possibilities for setting up subsidiaries in the eastern part of Germany, itself a gateway to much of Central and Eastern Europe. At the same time, they cannot afford to forget that the Germans are also their strongest competitors in business and industry.[43] It is clear that Switzerland must adapt flexibly to the new economic situation in Germany and Europe, but also that it stands to gain much by doing so.

German unification and the transformation of Europe in the wake of Communism's collapse have triggered another even more basic question: Has

Switzerland outlived itself? For centuries, the coherence of Switzerland was rooted in seeing itself as being better (or sometimes just better off) than the neighboring countries — be this in terms of local autonomy and international neutrality or, later, constitutional government and democracy as well as economic well-being. In recent years, the outside world has changed rapidly, while Switzerland seems to have remained much the same. Europe is now no less democratic than Switzerland, and the economic performance of a country like Germany is astonishing.

Switzerland differs from most of its European neighbors in that it never developed a distinctive Swiss ethnoculture to complement its well-established territorial and political identity. Given the small country's cultural diversity, that might have been an impossible task. It was never seriously tried. Instead, the strategic and political interests sufficed to keep the Swiss *cantons* together and give them an overarching confederal identity before and after the emergence of nationalism in modern Europe. The Helvetic Confederation had been formed and maintained by the Alpine *cantons* for the purpose of guarding their considerable freedoms and, later, wealth against foreign intruders. For a long time these common interests could continue to serve as a substitute for the national identity that came to define many other European countries. A distinctive Swiss constitutional identity or *Verfassungspatriotismus* could be said to have emerged after 1847. But with today's ideological, political, and economic transformation of the continent, Switzerland's often negatively defined identity of standing apart and aloof seems to have become increasingly obsolete.

At the beginning of its eighth century of political existence, then, Switzerland faces an existential dilemma. By sticking to its traditional course, the country would be in danger of becoming a kind of historical museum that would attract antiquarian interest among tourists but radiate little vitality as a community. However, the attempt to become integrated into the larger, uniting Europe could also have unintended and unwanted consequences in addition to the expected and desired economic benefits. For Switzerland, membership in the EC could raise more than the problem faced by all other small countries as well, namely that of falling under the economic and political domination of the far larger Community partners. EC membership could also weaken the common political bond between Switzerland's different cultures, if they were to lean even more than now towards their much larger external counterparts in France, Italy and, especially, Germany. Thus Switzerland could eventually disappear, with the larger German-speaking part absorbed more fully than now into a German *Kulturnation*.

Such considerations played a role in the small country's orgy of self-examination, as it celebrated its 700th anniversary. In 1992, the die seemed to be cast in favor of "joining the world," or at least Europe. In a referendum in May of that year, a majority of Swiss voters supported membership for their country in the International Monetary Fund and the World Bank. A week later, the Swiss government decided to explore membership in the European Community.[44]

However, in a referendum in early December, the Swiss voted "no" on a plan to have their country join the EC-EFTA "European Economic Area." Analysts suggested that the narrow "no" vote in the referendum (50.3 percent versus 49.7 percent) also implied trouble for Switzerland's EC membership application. Alan Riding of *The New York Times* reported that "[t]he vote also exposed a potentially dangerous split in a multicultural country that has long favored consensus over confrontation: All but one of the German-speaking cantons opposed closer ties with Europe, while all six French-speaking cantons strongly backed the plan. Sentiment in the smaller Italian-speaking areas was generally opposed to union."[45]

For some people in the Alpine republic, the present time offers a special opportunity for reviving what they would call the "Swiss idea." They take pride in remembering that over the centuries Switzerland emerged as one of the most progressive countries in Europe. Even when ideal and reality often matched poorly, the Swiss idea could serve as a "normative model" of a federal and democratic form of government that presented unusual opportunities for civic involvement in community affairs and demonstrated the possibility of a pluralist coexistence of different cultures.[46]

In our century, Swiss attention to this ideal seems to have faded or been overshadowed by concern for the bottom line of economic benefits. However, if a united Europe were truly — not just rhetorically — to become one of regions, the Swiss could possibly seek allies in other countries who care about guarding or, more often, reviving such a tradition of devolutionary, pluralist, and republican ideas against the technocratic and centralist tendencies that many see as a crucial problem of the European Community. In such democratic company, Switzerland could once more be something of a political pioneer and become a part of the needed "liberal heart" of the continent. As an experienced multicultural society, moreover, it could perhaps even serve as something of a prototype for the more nationally defined countries of the continent. In order to achieve such a role, Switzerland would have to overcome its outdated tendency toward petty-bourgeois smugness as well as its distrust of what lies outside its borders. The Swiss would have to revive some of their former self-confidence in a civic culture that could serve as their most important political contribution to Europe.[47]

In seeking to overcome political isolation, the Swiss might discover that they work well with their neighbors to the north, who today appear to share their commmitment to federalism, regional diversity, and liberal democracy. Despite some inevitable differences of interest that may increase as a result of its recent growth, the Federal Republic of Germany would appear to be a very congenial partner for a small country committed to the "Swiss idea" — far more congenial than any other German state in over a century.

Notes

1. The percentages have been fairly constant since 1848, but see also T. W. Netter, "Swiss Language Gap Widens," *The New York Times*, August 19, 1985, p. 6.
2. See Jürg Steiner, "Switzerland," in Gerald A. Dorfman and Peter J. Duignan, eds., *Politics in Western Europe*, second edition (Stanford: Hoover Institution Press, 1991), pp. 298 and 312-13.   See also Arend Lijphart, *Democracies: Patterns of Majoritarian and Consensus Government in Twenty-One Countries* (New Haven: Yale University Press, 1984), pp. 23-33.
3. Denis de Rougemont, a Swiss cosmopolitan, suggested that even if Wilhelm Tell did not exist, the myth would be important for an understanding of the Swiss people who created and maintained it.   See his book, *La Suisse ou l'histoire d'un peuple heureux* (Paris: Hachette, 1965) and, for a witty and insightful commentary on this and other aspects of Swiss identity, Willy Goetschel's essay, "Switzerland, for Example: 700 Years Old and Still Going Strong . . . ," *Telos*, Nr. 88, Summer 1991, p. 163.   As Goetschel points out, although the Tell myth began more than 500 years ago, it did not become "institutionalized" until the 18th century.
4. See the text of the *Bundesbrief* establishing the Helvetic Confederation in Hans Tsani, *Das Neue Profil der Schweiz* (Zürich: Werd, 1990), p. 41.
5. See Herbert Grundmann, ed., *Handbuch der Deutschen Geschichte*, vol. 2 (Stuttgart: Klett, 1954), p. 12.
6. See Ulrich Im Hof et al., *Geschichte der Schweiz, und der Schweizer*, 3 volumes (Basel: Helbling und Lichtenhahn, 1982/1983), vol. 2, p. 106ff.
7. For example, the Swiss-German idiom of today still uses many words that have a French origin, and Swiss cultural life shows a considerable French influence even outside the francophone areas.
8. See Edgar Bonjour, *Geschichte der schweizerischen Neutralität*, 9 volumes (Basel: Helbling und Lichtenhahn, 1965-1976), vol. 1, p. 172f.
9. Many Swiss students went to German universities for their higher education, helping to establish close links with Germany at the elite level.
10. By the time Switzerland, as the last country in Europe, extended the franchise to women in 1972, it had long since lost the image of a vanguard of political reform.
11. Bonjour, *Geschichte der schweizerischen Neutralität*, vol. 1, p. 357.
12. For the statistics in this paragraph, see Im Hof et al., *Geschichte der Schweiz, und der Schweizer*, vol. 3, pp. 79-82. Swiss investments abroad averaged between $550 and $750 per capita.
13. Im Hof et al., *Geschichte der Schweiz, und der Schweizer*, vol. 3, p. 91f.
14. See Joseph Hardegger, Markus Bolliger, et al., eds., *Das Werden der modernen Schweiz*, vol. 2 (Luzern: ilz, 1989), pp. 10-11.
15. See Werner Rings, *Schweiz im Krieg* (Zürich: Ex Libris, 1974), p. 63.
16. See Rings, *Schweiz im Krieg*, p. 324f.
17. See Rings, *Schweiz im Krieg*, p. 315ff.
18. See Bonjour, *Geschichte der schweizerischen Neutralität*, vol. 4, p. 24.
19. See Bonjour, *Geschichte der schweizerischen Neutralität*, vol. 4, p. 85ff. According to Wilhelm Mark, there were 6,501 intrusions into Switzerland's neutral airspace during the war, and its armed forces downed 16 aircraft. See Mark, "Die

Sicherheitspolitik der Schweiz," in Dieter S. Lutz and Annemarie Grosse-Jütte, eds., *Neutralität — eine Alternative?* (Baden-Baden: Nomos Verlagsgesellschaft, 1982), p. 63.

20. The Swiss army had been massed in the natural fortress of the Alps. This strategy left the industrialized parts of the country vulnerable but ensured that there could be a continued resistance out of the mountains against any invader.

21. Im Hof et al., *Geschichte der Schweiz, und der Schweizer*, vol. 3, p. 171.

22. On German-Swiss economic relations during World War II, see Jakob Tanner, *Bundeshaushalt, Währung und Kriegswirtschaft* (Zürich: Limmat, 1986), p. 285ff.

23. On these matters, see Albert Kiessling, *Deutsch-Schweizerische Handelsbeziehungen* (Brackenheim: Kohl, 1953), p. 22ff.

24. On the development of Swiss-German trade in the late 1940s, see Kiessling, *Deutsch-Schweizerische Handelsbeziehungen*, chapter 2.

25. See *Die Schweizer Wirtschaft 1946-1986: Daten, Fakten, Analysen* (Zürich: SBG, 1987), p. 65.

26. Rudolf Strahm, *Wirtschaftsbuch Schweiz* (Zürich: Ex Libris, 1987), p. 219f.

27. *Statistisches Jahrbuch der Schweiz* (Basel: Birkenhauser, 1988), p. 192.

28. *Statistisches Jahrbuch der Schweiz* (1988), p. 24.

29. In 1989, the economic performance of each country is reflected in the following figures. Population in millions: FRG 61.7, GDR 16.7, Switzerland 6.6. GNP in billion SFr: FRG 1933, GDR 250, Switzerland 226. GNP per capita in SFr: FRG 31,320, GDR 14,976, Switzerland 34,128.

30. When mobilized, however, the Swiss army was bigger in numbers than its German counterparts. At the end of 1989, the numbers were as follows: FRG 495,000 (without reserves), GDR 120,000, and Switzerland 625,000.

31. In the last years, Switzerland procured 350 Leopard II main battle tanks from the Federal Republic, one of the country's biggest defense contracts in recent years.

32. See Willy Graber, Arno Mulot, et al., eds., *Geschichte der deutschen Literatur* (Munich: Bayerischer Schulbuch Verlag, 1983), p. 330.

33. The Swiss have imposed size restrictions on trucks that transit through Switzerland. This is an important issue, because there are not many alternatives to the Swiss roads for getting through the Alps.

34. For a description of Swiss anti-Communism, see Jürg Frischknecht et al., *Die unheimlichen Patrioten* (Zürich: Limmat, 1987), p. 56ff.

35. See Konrad Adenauer Stiftung, *Die Westpolitik der DDR. Beziehungen der DDR zu ausgewählten westlichen Industriestaaten in den 70er und 80er Jahren* (Melle: Ernst Knoth, 1989), p. 336f.

36. Hans Ulrich Rentsch, "Neutraler Kleinstaat am Rande des Reichs," in Walther Hofer, ed., *Europa und die Einheit Deutschlands. Eine Bilanz nach 100 Jahren* (Cologne: Verlag Wissenschaft und Politik, 1970), p. 62.

37. See "Link poll," *Politik und Wirtschaft* (Glattbrugg), February 14, 1990, p. 18f.

38. "Link poll," p. 18f.

39. See Frank A. Meyer, "La fin de la Suisse?," *L'Hebdo* (Lausanne), February 15, 1990, p. 16.

40. See Kurt Zimmermann, "Wir und die Deutschen," *Politik und Wirtschaft*, February 14, 1990, p. 18f.

41. Peter Hartmeier, "Freuen wir uns an Deutschland!," *Politik und Wirtschaft*, February 14, 1990, p. 24f.

42. It is not surprising that there also is a marked generational difference among the Swiss in their attitudes toward integration with the European Community, with younger people being more supportive of such a move. See the poll results from April 1992, as reported in *The New York Times*, May 17, 1992, p. 6.

43. See Bernard Rappaz, "Un géant à notre porte," *L'Hebdo*, February 22, 1990, p. 14.

44. See *The Economist*, May 9, 1992, p. 58. See also "Switzerland and Europe," *The Economist*, November 28, 1992, pp. 51, 52, 54.

45. December 7, 1992, p. A4.

46. See the conclusion to Goetschel's essay, "Switzerland, for Example," pp. 164-66. In much of his commentary, he stresses the gap between the normative ideal of the Swiss model of democratic federalism and the practical failure to realize its promise. But he returns to an appreciation of the model's contemporary relevance for a Europe in which the "super-state" would appear to be obsolete yet not improbable.

47. Recently, the Swiss theologian Hans Küng, who has lived abroad for three decades, ruminated along these lines on the subject of Switzerland's role in today's world of politics. See his book, which has become a best-seller in Switzerland, *Die Schweiz ohne Orientierung? Europäische Perspektiven* (Zürich: Benziger Verlag, 1992). His thoughts bear some similarity to the reflections of Denis de Rougemont (see note 4) in the early postwar period. See Konrad Mrusek's review, "Ohne Orientierung?," *Frankfurter Allgemeine Zeitung*, August 1, 1992, p. 6.

17

Italy and Germany: Historical Memory and the Impact of 1989-90

Gian Enrico Rusconi

Introduction

For the Italians of today a German Question apparently does not exist — either politically or culturally. Italo-German relations are formally excellent, as is convenient for two countries with a common political interest in strengthening the European Community and a common economic interest in maintaining their close economic relationship. Germany, in fact, is Italy's most important commercial partner.

Recently, bilateral relations between the two countries have been further strengthened by an intergovernmental accord (the "Joint Declaration of Rome" of May 1988) intended to promote systematic contacts between German and Italian politicians, scholars and experts in various disciplines. On the basis of this agreement regular meetings are now held at a very high governmental level indeed (the so-called *"Foro di Dialogo Italo-Tedesco"*[1]).

This important effort at reciprocal understanding and debate, however, has not prevented crucial political-economic questions from provoking frictions between the two countries — over the timing and form of European monetary union, for example. And, beyond the actual issue concerned, these frictions are unconsciously aggravated by latent and reciprocal suspicions, a phenomenon that is the outward symptom of an enduring historical memory that is still partially unresolved. Germans and Italians thus sometimes display a deep-seated mistrust for each other that has its origins in unfortunate or even tragic historical experiences.

The intensity of this problem of unreconciled historical memory became evident in the years 1986-88 with the enormous stir caused in Italian public opinion by the so-called *Historikerstreit* ("historians' dispute").[2] The effect of this debate was to heighten the simultaneous, although unrelated, controversy then raging in Italy over the "revision" of the great historicopolitical paradigms of Fascism and anti-Fascism.

Despite the deep social, political, and cultural transformations that have taken place in Germany and Italy over the last forty years, the historical complex created by Fascism and Nazism and their consequences represents a sort of trauma in collective memory that is only slowly being reworked and critically overcome.

From this point of view, there is no doubt that German reunification, and the form it took, dramatically accelerated this process. But the relationship between the two countries' cultures has yet to find a satisfactory point of equilibrium.

Although, today, German reunification is universally regarded as a "normal" event, it was certainly not viewed as such until 1989. Only a few months were needed to cancel out arguments that in then current political culture (in all its variants) had for decades not only legitimated the partition of Germany but also regarded the existence of two German states as politically expedient.

We may take as an example Giulio Andreotti, the best-known and most eminent of Italian Christian Democrat politicians. In the mid-1980s he created a sensation in Germany and Europe by publicly warning against a possible revival of "pan-Germanism." His declaration was prompted by the rumors (which proved to be unfounded and indeed ridiculously unrealistic) of direct cooperation and convergence between the two German states. These were the years in which Erich Honecker was being received in Bonn by Helmut Kohl with all the honors due to a head of state, including a flag-raising ceremony and the playing of the GDR national anthem. For Paris and London, Andreotti's alarmism over the danger of pan-Germanism was not exaggerated. In Italy, however, it reflected and reaffirmed a postulate of "anti-Fascist" political culture — particularly among the Italian Left, whose support Andreotti (a man of the moderate center) then needed for his domestic political purposes.

A certain suspicion of the influence of Germany's past on her present, a suspicion that derived from the anti-Fascist (and anti-German) Resistance, was (and still is) part of common Italian political culture. Thus, beyond declarations of principle in favor of German unity (which in any case was thought to be unachievable in practice), the division of Germany was seen not only as an implicit "just punishment" for Nazi war crimes but as a guarantee against the rebirth of German nationalism, and therefore as favoring balance and detente in Europe. This historico-political view could coexist with the positive image of West Germany's efficiency and modernism.

So far, we are dealing with the "image of Germany" as held by current political culture and taken up by political commentators and the mass media. But matters are very similar if we examine the behavior of some Italian scholars and "specialists" on Germany. The situation here is a curious one. German culture — from literature to philosophy — obviously enjoys enormous prestige in Italian universities and academic culture. But this is mostly a historical interest that is only with difficulty connected with the political present. Not a few scholars give the impression of regarding the cultural, social, and political reality of postwar Germany as a "posthumous" event. Contemporary Germany is studied in a highly selective manner according to whether the past is judged positively or negatively. This is due in part to a certain imbalance between scientific and academic interest in Germany. It is in fact mainly historians and students of German literature who cultivate an interest in Germany, while Italian political scientists and sociologists are not particularly oriented towards study of German society.

In addition, historians and Germanists mostly belong to the political Left, which has been extremely distrustful and critical of developments in the Federal Republic since the war.[3] By contrast, their attitudes toward the GDR have been rather positive: it was not by chance that precisely in Italy a school of Germanists specializing in the literature of the GDR emerged. And it was these scholars and historians critical of the FRG who voiced most of the reservations regarding German reunification.

In the wake of the extraordinary events of 1989-90, the attitudes of Italian politicans were, at least in the beginning, highly ambivalent towards the extremely rapid progress of German reunification. They would have preferred a slower kind of transition, comprising what the rhetoric of those months termed the effective "Europeanization" of the whole process.[4]

Andreotti rapidly adapted to the new course of events. During the latter months of 1990, when it was Italy's turn to hold the presidency of the European Community, the Italian government made the maximum effort to ease the formalities of German unification.

Andreotti's change of attitude was not only dictated by considerations of *Realpolitik* within a changed international setting. It also arose from political calculations of a domestic nature. German reunification was closely connected not only with the downfall of the Communist regime of the GDR but also with the definitive loss by "real socialism" of its historical, political, and cultural legitimation. It was the final blow to the *Partito Comunista Italiano*, which had been in crisis for some time. The leaders of the PCI decided to expunge the word "Communist" from the party's name, and accordingly changed it to *Partito della Sinistra Democratica* (Party of the Democratic Left).

All this had inevitable repercussions for the historical culture disseminated by the PCI, with its rather negative image of Germany. The crisis of the PCI

meant that proclaiming the values of historical anti-Fascism no longer necessarily entailed suspicion of the "new great Germany."

Self-Deception over the GDR?

The incredulity with which the Communist Left greeted the collapse of the
GDR reflected its difficulties in evolving politically and ideologically, and in
redefining its conception of Socialism and Communism.

Italian Communists never really liked the government of the GDR.
However, they believed that the East German system was "functional" and
"efficient," even if its standards were different from those of Western
"capitalist" systems. They considered it to be more "reformable" than those of
Poland or Hungary — perhaps more reformable than the Soviet system itself.
They never suspected that the GDR's efficiency was a fiction built by manipulat-
ing statistics and by concealing the country's technological backwardness and
managerial incompetence. They were unaware of the size of the police
apparatus and the huge network of informers in the country (the "Stasi"). They
dismissed as propaganda any suggestion that the SED regime only managed to
stay on its feet because it was propped up by the Red Army. They were wrong,
of course.

In their convictions regarding the GDR, the Italian Communists were no
more stupid or uninformed than the many German Social Democrats who
thought (until 1989) exactly the same. The GDR's positive image was boosted
by dozens of "scientific" sociological and economic articles written and
published in the West (often as empirical studies based on research in the field)
that described the East German system as "functional" and even as "legitimated"
by the population.

What can we say today about all this — now that we are aware of the
effectively precarious state of the GDR's system — or about its almost
unanimous repudiation by the East German population? Were the experts, the
Italian Communists, and the German Social Democrats acting in bad faith? I do
not believe so. Were they gullible, if not entirely innocent? Perhaps. The only
certainty is that it was a colossal act of "scientific" and "ideological" self-
deception, probably dictated by a misguided ideological benevolence towards the
subjects being studied.

Even after the fall of the Berlin Wall and the institution of the first,
presumably "reformist" government in East Berlin (the Modrow Government),
many on the Italian left hoped for a "third way" between bureaucratic socialism
and capitalism, in keeping with the social and political models they also envisaged for Italy. There was a call for the preservation of real or alleged specific
"social/socialist" features of the GDR in the cultural and social areas, which
would be annihilated by *Anschluß* with the FRG.

This is not the place for a critique to show how unrealistic these worries were. In the GDR of 1989-90 any point of view associated with the idea of "socialism" had no chance of achieving consensus. Moreover, the "November Revolution" had hardly any of the features of a political upheaval with the deliberate aim of establishing a new, autonomous political order. It was a popular revolt for the fundamental rights of liberty that was not followed by any real politico-institutional planning. When the people in the streets demanded immediate reunification with the FRG (a demand that at first was excluded by everyone), no political force was able to stop it. "Unconditional" reunification was the only political demand that emerged clearly from the GDR elections of March 1990.

Neo-Nationalism?

Apart from the bewilderment of the Left, the Italian mass media, even though they looked benevolently on German reunification, had for months disseminated an image of a Germany become "great and powerful once again." Between the lines, however, one read the question of whether a new, dangerous German nationalism had not been born. Nonetheless, in spite of the rather demagogic abuse of the expressions "Fourth Reich" or "GDR *Anschluß*," all observers had to acknowledge the baselessness of fears of neo-nationalism in a united Germany or more particularly in its eastern regions.

It would in fact be a mistake to interpret the irresistible demand for reunification voiced in the GDR as signalling the resurgence of a national feeling that had survived decades of "socialist/internationalist" manipulation. The uprising by the people of the GDR cannot be interpreted as a national/ nationalist protest. This would be to underestimate the economic, practical, and indeed idealistic reasons for the revolt. Its aim was to achieve "the freedoms of the West," or better the "affluence" associated with those freedoms, not to build "the German nation" as such.

There is another point that needs clarifying. One must distinguish between old-style nationalism and the reaffirmation of "national identities" now in progress in many European countries. In the German case, this might simply be a matter of recovering language and patterns of thought banished from public discourse in recent decades. Naturally one cannot assert that this revival of national identities is not partly regressive in character. But it is a problem that concerns not just the Germans, but the British and the French as well. The Italians, however, seem more immune than others to national/nationalist enthusiasms.

But there is another aspect to German behavior — in this case West German — that Italian commentators associate (rightly or wrongly) with a disguised form of "nationalism": Germany's pride in its industrial and economic performance,

DM-Nationalismus. This apparently has scant ideological content, and restricts itself to proclaiming the liberal values of the market and capitalist efficiency. However, behind the enthusiasm for "the social market economy" and for standards of economic performance expressed in general terms, may lurk an intolerance for any criticism or objection to the capitalist model in West Germany. A model now ready to extend itself, monolithic and inflexible, as far as the Oder and to impose itself as the European model *tout court*.

This sometimes generates a polemical attitude towards other, less efficient systems and countries. And Italy is often the direct or indirect target of censure. Much of this criticism is justified: for example, the admonitions by the Bundesbank, worried by the problems involved in the creation of a common European currency and therefore by Italy's management of its national debt. But what irritates the recipients of this criticism, such as the Italian politicians in the government, is its tone, which provokes the counter-accusation against the Germans that they are pursuing their own narrow national/nationalist interests with indirectly hegemonic intent.

All these factors have created the expectation within Italian public opinion that a united Germany will assume a new leading role. A role that will induce the country to loosen its traditional ties with its Western partners to go in search of new privileged relationships in Eastern Europe and the (former) Soviet Union. Hence the worries over a possible resurgence of the German "special way" or *Sonderweg*. But this expectation has been proved to be unfounded by the increasingly dramatic situation in the five new *Länder* (the ex-GDR).

There has been no lack of those (in Germany even more than in Italy) who draw a parallel between the difficulties of East Germany and the "*Mezzogiorno* question" in Italy — that is, the endemically unresolved problem of Italy's South.

I believe this comparison to be inaccurate, and for a number of reasons. In Italy, the problem of the *Mezzogiorno* is one of a depressed, mainly agricultural region that has failed to achieve economic growth. Apart from their deep historical roots, the difficulties of southern Italy have been aggravated by a series of misguided investment policies that then became unexpectedly bound up with organized crime. East Germany, by contrast, has a relatively well-developed, even though technologically backward, economic system that collapsed because its politico-institutional support was removed. The productive paralysis and unemployment induced by this collapse cannot be compared with the endemic backwardness and unemployment of the Italian South. In addition, the two areas have very different kinds of work culture: in East Germany an "industrial" culture had grown up, while in the Italian *Mezzogiorno* a substantially "pre-industrial" culture still persists, aggravated by a mentality of welfare dependency or even parasitism.

Normality and "Normalization" of the Past

Has Germany therefore become a "normal" nation for the Italians, one like any other? Most recent public opinion surveys seem to show that this is the prevalent attitude: only a minority of Italians still express open reservations over the "incorrigibility" of the Germans.

Nevertheless, the "normality" of Germany continues to possess a "special" character of its own, one that differentiates it from other countries. Is this diversity due to Germany's extraordinary industrial and economic capability? Is it due to its geopolitical location in the heart of Europe? Or is it still the shadow of its past?

Even if these three factors blend together in the mixture of admiration and fear, attraction and wariness that characterizes the Italian attitude to the Germans' new-found normality, there is no doubt that it is the third of them (historical memory) that explains the latent Italian diffidence towards Germany most.

This became apparent — even before reunification — in the sensation caused in Italy by the *Historikerstreit* mentioned above. Indeed, we may say with hindsight that the controversy it aroused prepared the ground for arguments that once again centered on the hopes and fears of reunification. These discussions were the culmination of a series of debates — which in Italy were conducted outside a narrow circle of intellectuals — on the issue of the revival of notions of "fatherland/nation" and the issue of "German identity."

I shall not go into the many different Italian reactions to the "historians' dispute." As is well known, the controversy was sparked by Ernst Nolte's thesis of a "causal nexus" between Bolshevik/Stalinist crimes and those committed by the Nazis. This is not the place for an examination of Nolte's exact intentions, or of the plausibility of his claims. They were interpreted in Italy (at least at first) as a scandalous attempt to trivialize Nazi crimes by denying the historically "unique" character of the Holocaust. Nolte and the other "revisionists" were charged with trying to offload the Nazis' guilt onto their Bolshevik predecessors in an attempt to "normalize" Germany's past.

The exponents of the culture of the Left and of the Resistance in Italy have had no hesitation in recognizing the enormity of the crimes of Stalinism and the other forms of twentieth-century genocide, but they reject any "causal nexus" between these and the extermination of the Jews. The Holocaust is still "unique."

The argument over the "guilt" of the Germans is more complex. The political culture that has descended from the Resistance rejects the idea of the "collective guilt" of the German people. The blameless Germans of today therefore need have no "guilt obsession," but they are expected to keep alive the memory of the crimes committed in the name of the German nation. No "normalization" of the German past is possible because Auschwitz will always remain a cardinal point of reference for German historical identity. One may therefore say that the culture of the Resistance found expression in the positions that Jürgen Habermas took up in the *Historikerstreit*.

It is difficult to specify the effects of this debate on Italian public opinion at large. There is no doubt that the close scrutiny made of Stalinist crimes within the context of the generalized terror of the age of totalitarianism has had a major impact. There is equally no doubt that the historical equivalence of Hitler and Stalin has been definitively confirmed. But demonstrating this parity has led not so much to a "cutting down to size" of Nazi crimes as to a distinct distancing from the Communist regime that made Stalinism possible. This has led to the definitive demise of the historical myth of the Soviet Union so central to "progressive" postwar ideology.

The debate on Nazi crimes inevitably raised the question of the similar behavior of Italian Fascism. There is a long historical tradition of examination of the analogies and differences between the Italian (Fascist) and German (National Socialist) totalitarian regimes.[5] Recently, the tendency has been to emphasize differences over similarities. The Fascist regime, in fact, lacked the extreme features of totalitarianism because of its institutional context, such as the continuation of the monarchy, guarantees for the relative autonomy of the army and the top levels of the state bureaucracy, and the decisive influence of the Church, especially in its social and cultural control over the majority of the population. With regard to the specific issue that interests us here — the crimes committed by the Fascist regime — these factors were responsible for a tardy and relatively tolerant anti-Semitic policy and fairly minor episodes of indiscriminate violence against ethnic groups. This is not to imply that these crimes (massacres committed during the colonial conquests in Africa or during the war in the Balkans) cannot be compared with those of the Nazis. But, not by coincidence, the most serious episodes coincided with the phase of Italian cooperation with the Germans during the last years of the war.

This brings us, therefore, to the historical experience that has had the greatest impact on the collective memories of the Italians and the Germans: wartime collaboration (1941-43), and then its dramatic cessation during the Italian "civil war" (1943-45). An understanding of this period requires a brief historical *excursus*.[6]

The Historical Roots of Italo-German Collective Imagery

We may begin our political-cultural analysis with Italy's and Germany's common political experience as latecomer nation-states in the second half of the 19th century. Each country achieved its respective national "*Risorgimento*" by out-maneuvering the two great continental European powers, France and Austria, and by playing them off against each other — in different ways but in the same period (1848-1870). It is significant that the last acts of Italian unification were accomplished either with the direct help of Prussia (when it acquired Venice from the Austrians in 1866) or in coincidence with Prussia's war against France (the taking of Rome in 1870). The *"Risorgimento"* of both countries was led by a monarchical-military power (Prussia and Piedmont) that managed to combine its own dynastic and expansionist interests with popular national feelings.

Once unified, each country had to deal with grave internal problems that were both socio-economic and politico-institutional in character. The Germany of the Bismarck years saw an illiberal hardening process (*Kulturkampf*, anti-socialist laws) as the country attempted to deal with the deep social contradictions deriving from its accelerated industrial development. United Italy faced problems made even more serious by its lack of an industrial structure comparable to Germany's. The premises for its economic and administrative backwardness, especially dramatic in Southern Italy, were already in place. And the gap between the relatively developed North of the country and the South with its social pathologies (banditry) rapidly widened.

It was the requirements of the international balance of power, not domestic political considerations, that led to the Triple Alliance (1882-1914) between Germany, Austria and Italy. This was an alliance formed to counteract France, and then also Russia, as the situation in the Balkans steadily worsened. Nonetheless, one cannot deny that influential sections of the Italian ruling class looked with admiration to the semi-authoritarian regime of Germany under Kaiser Wilhelm, which they saw as the politico-institutional model to follow in correcting the "liberal" Italian regime. They believed the Italian regime to be incapable of resolving the serious problems that blocked industrial take-off at home, and unable to conduct "power politics" abroad that were coherent with Italy's geopolitical position. These were the years of Italy's costly and bloody colonial conquests (Eritrea, Somalia, and Libya). But ever present in nation-al/nationalist public opinion was the problem of reclaiming the "unredeemed" (*irredenti*) regions (Trento and Trentino, Trieste, and Dalmatian and Julian Venetia) for the motherland. In this context, alliance with the Austro-Hungarian Empire, the historic enemy of unified Italy, appeared "unnatural." And there seemed to be little difference between Germany and Austria, insofar as Germany was supporting Austria in its endeavour to keep its multinational empire intact and, indeed, to extend and strengthen it in the Balkans (where Italy was also intent on increasing its power).

It must be said that in Italy this vision of small-scale imperial expansionism, and *irredentismo* itself, only expressed the views of the most turbulent sections of the bourgeoisie and the intellectuals. It was fairly weak among the Catholic and Socialist masses of the population. In effect, Italy's decision in May 1915 to enter World War I on the side of France and England — thereby reversing its alliances — was brought about by pressure from small political and social groups that had managed to impose themselves on parliament, and especially on the more reluctant population. The slogan of the Italian Socialists, *Ne' aderire ne' sabotare* (Neither agree nor sabotage) was typical of the impasse in which the political groups against the war found themselves.

The Great War, therefore, achieved the same effect of "national integration" in Italy as it did in other nations involved in the hostilities. The nationalist catch-phrase current in the war against Austria, *compimento del Risorgimento* (Fulfillment of the Risorgimento), strengthened by the ideology of "the struggle against German militarism," seemed to give valid legitimation to a conflict that was otherwise disproportionately costly in terms of casualties and moral damage.[7]

For our purposes here, there are two points that warrant examination. Neither combatants nor the civil population made any distinction between "Austrian" and "German." Indeed, the enemy was once again indiscriminately referred to as "the German," as in popular usage during the *Risorgimento*. On the Austro-German side, the legend grew of the "Italian treason": Italy's switching of its allies in 1915 and its entry into the war on the side of France and Great Britain — which was perfectly legitimate in terms of the treaties it had signed as well as being politically expedient — was regarded as treachery. And Italy's behavior was demagogically presented as such to the German soldiers and the many "peoples" (Croatian, Czech, Slovenian) fighting under the flag of the Habsburg Empire. The legend of Italy's treason would continue to undermine politico-military relations between Italy and Germany in the decades that followed World War I. And it was revived again in 1943-45 when Italian duplicity was confirmed — in the eyes of the Germans — when the first post-Fascist government broke Italy's alliance with Nazi Germany (September 1943) and the Resistance began.

After World War I, the resentment felt by Weimar Germany and Italy over the Paris peace treaty brought the two governments together in what came to be called the "revisionism" of Versailles. Italy's main preoccupation, however, was its extremely serious domestic social, political, and institutional situation — to which protest against the "mutilated victory" at Versailles was only a contributory factor. The crisis was defused in October 1922 when the king appointed Benito Mussolini, leader of the "revolutionary" Fascist movement, to head the government. As a movement, Fascism managed to combine extra- and anti-institutional action, to the point of blatantly breaking the law as it waged its violent campaign against left-wing and Catholic groups and organizations under the pretext of institutional legality. It counted on the strong support of broad sections of the bourgeoisie, the capitalists, and the great landowners who wished to crush the Communists and Socialists, and on the complicity of the monarchy and much of the army. The first Fascist government was born as a "strong" government of coalition and "national" concentration. Only gradually did it turn into the personal dictatorship of the *Duce* Mussolini and the monolithic Fascist

Party that absorbed the other "national" forces, a process that could only be said to be complete in 1925.

The Fascist experiment was followed with great interest in Germany, especially by the nationalist and conservative Right, for whom Fascism seemed an original and effective way of dealing with the threat of Communism. Mussolini's greatest admirer in Germany was Adolf Hitler, who in 1923 had gained notoriety with his failed *Putsch* against the government in Munich.

In the 1920s and 1930s, Fascist Italy, despite its anti-democratic domestic policy, was unreservedly welcomed into the community of European nations. Its claims to being a "Mediterranean power" were taken seriously, and its international image was anything but disreputable. In the second half of the 1930s — this was also an effect of the great economic slump — a considerable number of European countries had authoritarian political structures that were fairly similar to Italian Fascism. For friends and enemies alike this was the "alternative model," as much to traditional Liberalism as to Communism.

Germany became National Socialist with the appointment of Hitler as Chancellor on January 30, 1933, and although he adhered to his native roots and traditions, in particular racism (which was alien to Fascism), the Führer never hid his admiration for Mussolini's regime. The Italian Fascists for their part, and Mussolini in particular, regarded Hitlerism with a mixture of suspicion and self-conceit. Apart from idiosyncratic attitudes towards Germany as such (Italian nationalism always cultivated a negative image of the "German"), there were two issues in particular that divided Italy and Germany: the question of the South Tyrol and the Austrian question in general.

At the end of World War I, Italy moved its northernmost border to the Brenner Pass, thus incorporating into the country a vast mountainous region of German language and tradition (the South Tyrol, now named Alto Adige). Under Fascism a program for the forced Italianization of the region began, with large-scale immigration by Italians (mostly from the South) and a campaign to eradicate the local Germanic culture. This provoked stubborn passive resistance and hostility among the population of the Alto Adige, which looked to Vienna and Berlin for help. But neither Austria nor Weimar Germany was able to change the situation. Hitler himself had already written in *Mein Kampf* that he would ignore the South Tyrol question, so that he could count on Italy as an ally in his larger project for expansion towards the East. In fact, he never laid claim to the South Tyrol, despite the protests of the pan-Germanists.

More complex was the question of Austria which, relegated by the peace treaty of 1919 to the status of a German-speaking outpost, certainly wanted to "join up with" the German Reich. However, the victors in the war were firmly opposed to any such plan: Italy too wanted Austria to remain autonomous and separate from Germany, and therefore became the guarantor, militarily as well, of the *status quo* beyond the Brenner.

Hitler took exactly the opposite view. His program for the "revision of Versailles" included *Anschluß* with Austria (which was his country of birth). But in 1934, when Germany was apparently seeking to exploit to its advantage a crisis in the Austrian regime, Mussolini sent his troops to the Italo-Austrian border, thus making his opposition to any German interference in Austrian affairs unequivocally clear. The situation changed in the years that followed, however. In 1935, Fascist Italy decided to extend its colonial empire by conquering Ethiopia. In the ensuing conflict, condemned by the League of Nations, the only European power to voice its approval of the Italian action was Germany. This brought renewed rapprochement between the two countries, which was soon strengthened even further by their joint intervention in the Spanish Civil War (from 1936 onwards) on the side of the anti-republican generals led by Franco.

Thus, when in March/April 1938 an opportunity arose for Hitler to achieve his *Anschluß* of Germany with Austria, Mussolini gave his consent provided that the Brenner border was left untouched. This marked the beginning of the most tormented and fateful period of the Italo-German alliance. Mussolini wanted both to dampen and to exploit the aggressive German politico-diplomatic activism that, piece by piece, was dismantling the Versailles order while the Western powers watched impotently. Despite the ideological affinities between the two regimes, Mussolini was preoccupied by German hegemony in Europe; hence his mediation in the Munich Agreement of September 1938. However, when a year later — after the shock announcement of the pact with Stalin — Germany attacked Poland in direct defiance of the Western powers, Mussolini announced the "nonbelligerence" of Italy. The Duce's attitude was influenced not only by the unpreparedness of the Italian army, but also by his bewilderment over Hitler's gamble. However, when the *Wehrmacht* achieved its lightning victory in the French campaign in June 1940, he scrambled into the war on Germany's side. Mussolini's intention was to reap the fruits of victory and to maneuver himself into a position where he could deal with the Germans on an equal footing.

With this in mind, the following year Italy attacked Greece (launching its campaign from Albania, which was already under its control) and thus inaugurated its "parallel war" alongside Germany's. This war initiative, which in fact ended in military disaster (as did the war in the desert against the British), was not simply dictated by opportunism, but also by a desire to have pre-established points of strength with which to counteract German hegemony in Europe. The outcome was exactly the reverse, however. Because of their lack of military preparedness, the Italians had to call on the Germans for help in Greece as in Libya, and this made them increasingly dependent on the *Wehrmacht*. After the German attack on the Soviet Union in June 1941, Mussolini sent an army to Russia. However, in the winter of 1942, the Italians were caught on the Don river by the Soviet offensive at Stalingrad and forced into disastrous retreat. The retreat from Russia has become embedded in Italian popular memory as a crucial event in the country's history: together with the Resistance, it is the most frequent subject of memoirs written about the war years. Indeed, a close link was established in popular tradition between that tragic military campaign and the beginnings of anti-Fascist consciousness among the Italian people.

During this period of wartime collaboration, the Italians' negative image of the German grew sharper, an image that, despite a quantity of evidence to the contrary, solidified into that of the cruel, haughty, and racist ally. Inevitably, German writings about the same period portrayed the Italian, in turn, as cowardly, treacherous, and opportunist.

These reciprocal images were already in place, so to speak, when the momentous political decisions of 1943 were made: the dismissal of Mussolini from the government on July 25 and the virtual dismantling of the entire Fascist apparatus in Italy, as well as the formation of a government that signed the armistice with the Allies on September 8 on terms so irresponsible and ill-considered that it practically delivered the Italian army (scattered throughout Europe) into the hands of the Germans.

For their part, the Germans saw the decisions of the Italian government as yet another "act of treason" and treated their Italian prisoners accordingly (mass executions, deportations to Germany). Only a small minority of Italian soldiers managed to evade capture by hiding in the mountains, where they established the first nucleus of the armed Resistance. While the German army in Italy trans-formed itself from ally into occupying force in the central-northern regions of the country, those Fascists who survived established a puppet republic, the *Repubblica sociale italiana*, in the North.

This marked the beginning of the civil war between Nazi-Fascists and democratic and Communist forces. In fact, the Resistance was conducted on three fronts: there was the national war against the Germans, a democratic war for the restoration of the rights of political freedom, and a social or class war oriented towards Communist values. In this complex interweaving of motives, certainly least problematic was the national struggle against the Germans, which, among other things, could draw upon deep-rooted anti-German feelings that dated back to the *Risorgimento* and World War I. It was a simplification, although one understandable in view of the ferocity with which the war was fought in Italy between 1943 and 1945.

The climate soon became more tense as the horrific news of the Nazi death camps spread and the Italian survivors began to return home. Inevitably, therefore, this emotion-charged atmosphere nourished feelings that were to be indiscriminately hostile towards the Germans for many years after World War II.

I have dwelt on these seemingly distant events because they are today still the most profound source of the collective imageries and reciprocal stereotypes of Germans and Italians. Or better, all subsequent experiences or knowledge, positive or negative, have had to reckon with this basic datum, which so often brutally and unexpectedly crops up in everyday conversation.

Toward the Building of Europe

The more recent history of relations between Italy and Germany, with their governing classes working side-by-side to build a political Europe, has been marked by two significant social phenomena. In the 1950s and 1960s large numbers of Italian workers (mainly from the South) migrated to the Federal Republic. These were the *Gastarbeiter*, who made such a major contribution to the German "economic miracle" in return for the good wage benefits they received. Not a few of them stayed on in their host country to settle down. Of course, emigration is always an "unfair exchange" between giver and taker. And on the subject of prejudices and stereotypes it is unclear to what extent the *Gastarbeiter* were responsible for, and to what extent they were subjected to, their updated versions: Germans as efficient but arrogant and latently racist, Italians as good workers but unpredictable and unreliable. Or, perhaps, they helped to overcome these stereotypes.

Similar questions arise over the phenomenon of mass tourism, which for years has brought millions of Germans of every social class to Italy. Even if certain forms of organized mass tourism create spatio-temporal enclaves with impoverished human and social relations, instead of opportunities for contact, one can argue that this rubbing of shoulders among hundreds of thousands of people cannot help but adjust their stereotypes of each other.

In strictly political terms, relations between Italy and Germany since the 1950s have been straightforward and increasingly mediated by their common reference to European institutions. In many respects, Europeanism is the only choice possible for the two countries — which for the decisive decade after the war were led by men of the political stature of Adenauer and De Gasperi, when there seemed to be no alternative to a Western and Europeanist stance after the tragedies of Fascism and Nazism. The discrediting of nationalism, and of "nationalist" values — in the strict, myopic sense of the term — induced Italy and Germany to behave much less equivocally in their pursuit of supranational objectives than the countries that had emerged victorious from the war (France and Britain). In fact, both Italy and Germany had the highly viable "neutralist" alternative of non-alignment between West and East. The reasons for this were different in each country. In Germany the Westernism and Europeanism of Adenauer seemed to harm the country's chances of reunification (especially after the creation of the FRG and GDR as separate states). This was the opinion of the Social Democrats, who wished to conjugate the prospect of national reunification with neutralism. In Italy, it was the powerful Left (dominated by the Communists) that campaigned for the loosening of economic and military ties with the West and with capitalist and imperialist Europe.

In fact, with the passing of the years and in the face of the evident advantages of European integration, the opposition of the Left in the two countries has dwindled. The Italian and German governments have become two of the most convinced proponents of the need to accelerate and strengthen the building of the European Community, and they have worked together in the Community to overcome the doubts of the other member states. Thus, in the early 1980s, thanks mainly to the efforts of the two foreign ministers, Colombo and Genscher, the process was set in motion that led in 1983 to the Declaration on European Union. And the Treaty passed in 1984 by the European Parliament, inspired by the Italian Altiero Spinelli, had the unreserved support of the Federal Republic.

In the meantime the economic interdependence of the two countries has grown ever closer. Germany absorbs more than 18 percent of Italy's exports (compared with 16 percent by France and 9.6 percent by the U.S.), while more than 19 percent of Italy's overall imports are from Germany (compared with 14.5 percent from France and 5.3 percent from the U.S.). Italy, for its part, is the fifth largest exporter to Germany (with 8.7 percent) and is the third largest importer of German products (with 9.6 percent, after 11.6 percent by the Netherlands and 11 percent by France). This dense flow of trade involves almost all production sectors, and follows a pattern that renders the two countries interdependent, if not complementary.[8]

Recently, however, a number of analysts and scholars in Italy have voiced their disquiet over the increasing asymmetry between the two economies.[9] This is not so much a fear of implicit Italian dependence on uncontrolled German "economic hegemony" (a fear also felt by other European countries) as a preoccupation over the growing structural weakness of the Italian economy, a weakness that is aggravated by the size of the national debt, high rates of inflation, and inadequate fiscal policy. In Italian and German public opinion these phenomena are directly linked to other pathological features of the Italian political and social system, such as the instability of governments and government coalitions, and political delegitimation induced by the apparently unstoppable growth of organized crime, especially in the South.[10]

The result has been the widespread impression that Italy is undergoing an economic and political decline of major proportions, a view that has been succinctly expressed by the debate on "*Italia partner di serie B*" (Italy a second-rate partner) in the European Community. By comparison, Germany is not only the European super-partner, but also the country pushing most (in a disguised and indirect manner) for Italy to be discriminated against in the Community. At least this is the belief of a number of Italian observers and opinion-makers, and it accounts for the ill-feeling and friction between the political and economic leaders of the two countries that I mentioned at the beginning of this essay. In reaction to this situation, there has been a resurgence of the polemical thesis that Germany is seeking its own "special way" or *Sonderweg* — a road distinct from, if not antagonistic to, that followed by the other European nations. It goes without saying that the accusation or suspicion of a German *Sonderweg* is charged with contentious allusions to Germany's history (Wilhelm's Empire, the final period of the Weimar Republic, the Third Reich) and to the immense suffering that Germany's past decisions brought to itself and to Europe.

I do not believe that it would be right or appropriate to exhume this old historical notion for polemical purposes. Above all, historically speaking, there can be no German *Sonderweg* in isolation from the international context in which it has somehow been created and shaped. The "special German way" has always been an unsatisfactory solution for more general European and global problems that could have been solved in a less traumatic manner. The restless empire of Wilhelm, which unleashed the war of 1914-18, corresponded to a balance of European and world power that had already run its course a decade before. To the turmoil of Weimar (of which the campaign to revise Versailles was a symptom before it triggered the tragedy of Hitler) corresponded the inability of Europe in the 1920s and 1930s to build genuine European cooperation.

Likewise, when today we ask ourselves with some trepidation as to the likelihood of a new "special German way," we should not just look at Germany's political class, at its desire for economic and financial leadership combined with a reluctance to assume international political responsibilities. Nor should we consider only the nationalist-neutralist stance of certain sections of the German population mixed with the fervent Europeanism of others. We must also examine the national/nationalist revivals now in progress in France and Britain (but absent in Italy). Above all, we should bear in mind the difficulties that stand in the way of a political Europe. Far from being a solid "supranational community," Europe is still only a fragile web of national checks and balances, where — recast and refined — such traditional notions of the nation-state as "balance of power" and "geopolitical zones" hold sway. For a long time to come, Europe will continue to live by a system of balance and counterweight among (diminished) national sovereignties. Not only will Germany be no exception to this rule, it will continue to fulfill the "special" role assigned to it by economic power and geopolitical position.

It is within these objective and subjective coordinates that any reemergence of the German *Sonderweg* should be measured; coordinates that meet on Germany's "position at the center." Although the concepts of "center" and "balance" both belong to the same old European geopolitical paradigm, their meanings have changed as world history has moved onward. United Germany does not and cannot aspire to the "centrality" it enjoyed under Bismarck or during the 1930s, for the simple reason that the European center has been downgraded, so to speak, with respect to the past. What used to be *welt-*

geschichtlich, that is, an area of immediate historicoglobal significance, is today only a "region," albeit the most important one in the world. Germany, however powerful, does not have the autonomy or the economic-financial and above all military independence of the past. It amicably but unequally shares these requisites of sovereignty with its European partners. This new "communitarian" pattern, or better this novel "interdependence," is irreversible, and it constitutes the robust framework within which the new political and cultural relations between Germany and Italy are taking shape.[11]

Notes

1. See the *Atti* (Proceedings) of the first *Foro di Dialogo Italo-Tedesco* of 1989: Maurizio Ferrera and Elfriede Regelsberger, eds., *Italia e Germania protagoniste dell'integrazione europea* (Bologna: Il Mulino, 1990). These official meetings concentrate mainly on major economic questions. More properly cultural initiatives are carried forward by other institutions, notably "Villa Vigoni" and the Goethe Institut centres distributed throughout Italy.

2. The main texts in the debate have been published in Italy: see Gian Enrico Rusconi, ed., *Germania: un passato che non passa* (Turin: Einaudi, 1987), which came out independently and prior to the German collection *Historikerstreit* (Munich/Zurich: Piper, 1987). On the first Italian and international reactions see Dan Diner, ed., *Ist der Nationalsozialismus Geschichte?* (Frankfurt a. M.: Fischer, 1987), and the Italian debate in the journal *Passato e presente*, vol. 16, January-April, 1988.

3. The historian Enzo Collotti's important *Storia delle due Germanie* (Turin: Einaudi, 1968) for many years conditioned much of contemporary Italian historiography on the two Germanies and led to a great deal of very critical analysis of federal Germany from commentators on the political Left. See, for example, *Modello Germania. Strutture e problemi della realta tedesco-occidentale* (Bologna: Zanichelli, 1978). A milder position has recently been expressed in Antonio Missiroli, *La questione tedesca* (Florence: Ponte alle Grazie, 1981).

4. On this problem see Gian Enrico Rusconi, *Capire la Germania. Un diario ragionato sulla questione tedesca* (Bologna: Il Mulino, 1990). This book analyses German events in 1989/90 also from the point of view of their first interpretation in Italy and Europe.

5. See Wolfgang Schieder, ed., *Faschismus als soziale Bewegung. Deutschland und Italien im Vergleich* (Hamburg: Hoffmann und Campe, 1976); Karl Dietrich Bracher and Leo Valiani, eds., *Fascismo e nazionalsocialismo* (Bologna: Il Mulino, 1986). The scholar who has made perhaps the greatest contribution to historical debate on this subject is Renzo De Felice, whose monumental biography of Mussolini has now reached its fourth volume (*Mussolini, l'alleato*, Turin: Einaudi, 1990), devoted to Italian-German relations. The German historian who has gone most deeply into the historical period is Jens Petersen: *Hitler e Mussolini la difficile alleanza* (Bari: Laterza, 1975) and "Italia e Germania: due immagini incrociate" in Francesca Ferratini Tosi, Gaetano Grassi, and Massimo Legnani, eds., *L'Italia nella seconda guerra mondiale e nella resistenza* (Bologna: Il Mulino, 1988).

6. Systematic analysis of the relationships and the convergences between the two countries is relatively limited. An exception is the series of research studies promoted by the *Istituto trentino di cultura* (of Trento, Italy) in collaboration with Italian and German historians and published by Il Mulino of Bologna between 1977 and 1987. Among the various titles, of interest to us here are the following: Ettore Passerin D'Entreves and Konrad Repgen, eds., *Il cattolicesimo politico e sociale in Italia e Germania dal 1870 al 1914*; Leo Valiani and Adam Wandruszka, eds., *Il movimento operaio e socialista in Italia e Germania dal 1870 al 1920*; Rudolf Lill and Nicola Matteucci, eds., *Il liberalismo in Italia e in Germania dalla rivoluzione del 1848 alla prima guerra mondiale*; Peter Hertner and Giorgio Mori, eds., *La transizione dall'economia di guerra all'economia di pace in Italia e in Germania dopo la prima guerra mondiale*; Rudolf Lill and Franco Valsecchi, eds., *Il nazionalismo in Italia e in Germania fino alla prima guerra mondiale*; Umberto Corsini and Konrad Repgen, eds., *Konrad Adenauer e Alcide De Gasperi: due esperienze di rifondazione della democrazia*; Karl Dietrich Bracher and Leo Valiani, eds., *Fascismo e nazionalsocialismo*; Gustavo Gozzi and Pierangelo Schiera, eds., *Crisi istituzionale e teoria dello Stato in Germania dopo la prima guerra mondiale*. On the topic of Fascism and the war, apart from the literature cited in note 5, see Hans Woller, ed., *Italien und die Grossmächte 1943/49* (Munich: Oldenbourg, 1988), and Rudolf Lill, ed., *Deutschland-Italien 1943-45* (Tübingen: Niemeyer, 1990).

7. See Claus Gatterer, *Erbfeindschaft Italien-Österreich* (Vienna: Europa Verlag, 1972).

8. Data taken from "Introduction" to Ferrera and Regelsberger, eds., *Italia e Germania protagoniste dell'integrazione europea*, p. 14.

9. See Valerio Valli, ed., *L'economia tedesca. La Germania federale verso l'egemonia economica in Europa* (Milan: Etas, 1981); Onoris Clauser, Peter Mooslechner, and Giovanni Pegoretti, eds., *Finanz, Industrie und Währung in Italien und im deutschsprachlichen Raum* (Berlin: Duncker und Humblot, 1990). For a worried diagnosis of the Italian situation, see Romano Prodi, *Multinazionale Germania* (Il Mulino, 1/1991).

10. Among German works that give a pessimistic analysis of the Italian sociopolitical situation, see Theodor Wieser and Frederik Spotts, *Der Fall Italien. Dauerkrise einer schwierigen Demokratie* (Frankfurt a. M.: Wörner, 1983).

11. It was in this spirit that the second "*Foro Italo-Tedesco*" was held in Venice in November 1991.

PART FIVE

A Transatlantic Neighbor

18

The United States and the German Question: Building a New European Order

*Alice Ackermann and
Catherine McArdle Kelleher*

Introduction

"Here we made the choices and took the stands that shaped today's world,"[1] Secretary of State James Baker said in his landmark speech at the Berlin Press Club on December 12, 1989. Reacting to the spectacular revolutions witnessed in Central and Eastern Europe only recently, Mr. Baker's introductory remarks presented more than a sentimental statement of an American foreign policy-maker to the revolutionary events in Europe. Nor were they merely intended to introduce an American declaration on the principles of a new Europe and a "new Atlanticism." Rather, Mr. Baker above all alluded to the influential role the United States played in the creation of the postwar European order.

As in 1989, four decades ago, the construction of a new European order had been an equally pressing task for American leaders. As in 1989, Berlin was not only the visible symbol for the dramatic changes that were to manifest themselves over the next four decades — the Cold War, the East-West conflict, detente, and gradually, the transformation of Eastern Europe and the Soviet Union. More so, then as now, the divided city stood for the new role the United States vowed to play: a role that would inaugurate a revolutionary change in American foreign policy, and a role that would not only yield impressive global power but also demand unexpected and, most often, burdensome obligations and commitments. America's involvement in the construction of a new postwar order in Europe meant nothing less than assuming responsibility for the solution of the German Question. This would ultimately require active American engagement in European affairs, spanning almost half a century — an unprecedented "first" in the history of U.S.-European relations. From its very beginnings, this new relationship entailed a strenuous process of bargaining and tough choices, many of which the early "creators" never fully anticipated.

But what exactly is the German Question from the American perspective? What is its origin? How has it evolved over time? Why is the German Question, as seen through American eyes, inevitably embedded in the "European Problem?" Why did the United States after the revolutions of 1989 face revisiting some of the policy choices it made nearly 40 years ago? Many of the answers can be found by exploring the critical years of 1946 to 1948. But the genesis of America's German Question as the essential component of the "European Problem" is anchored far deeper in U.S. history than the immediate postwar period. For those who crafted and implemented the postwar order, the vision of a new Europe devoid of the instabilities of previous centuries largely emanated from the belief of learning the lessons provided by the Great War, the failures of European reconstruction by victorious, yet divided allies, and the upheavals of the interwar era. Therefore, to American policy-makers, the major motivation for solving Europe's German Question rested in the conviction that a repetition of history must be avoided. Critical conclusions were thus drawn in that European and German reconstruction must not only be facilitated but that constructive and active American participation was crucial in this process. The major foreign policy transformation that resulted from these deliberations forever toppled a U.S. foreign policy fundamental: a deliberate avoidance of European entanglements.

In the ensuing decades, the German Question, at least from the American perspective, became redefined as policy concerns over European reconstruction were surpassed by other issues. These were growing increasingly complex given that Germany and Europe became more prosperous and politically independent. Moreover, as the peaceful revolutions in Central and Eastern Europe took their course and the unification of Germany became an irreversible reality, to many American observers the German Question had reached its final demise. Yet, to manage the revolutionary transformations in Europe in a constructive manner, America's present foreign policy formulation toward Germany and Europe again demands a participatory commitment that in so many ways should be reminiscent of the immediate post-World War II era.

This essay explores America's German Question as encompassing two intertwined dimensions. First, in its broader context, America's German Question displays two prominent underlying themes, namely: 1) that the German Question mostly concerns a revolutionary development in the history of American foreign policy, the restructuring of a new foreign policy course that would eventually even surpass the visions of its mentors; and 2) that the German Question was largely fuelled by a determination to prevent the fallacies of the past, to compensate for what was commonly perceived as an unsuccessful, or perhaps unfinished, American endeavor toward changing European power structures after World War I. Second, in its more narrow focus, notably the post-1945 context, America's German Question is not only about the division of Germany but also about the management of a "special relationship," repeatedly challenged by West German economic and socio-cultural changes. In its final stage, America's German Question is about the German revolution of 1989, the unification process that followed it, and Washington's readjustment to a fully sovereign Germany and a transforming Europe.

In essence, this essay will view America's German Question as intricately linked to, and thus inseparable from, "the European Problem." The analysis refrains from providing a condensed account of those events that traditionally are associated with the post-1945 German Question — the division of Germany and the many ill-fated attempts toward reunification. Rather, the objective is to re-examine the broader themes and patterns that comprise the German Question from the American perspective. We define the German Question mostly in the framework of a U.S. endeavor to establish a postwar European order in which a democratic and economically prosperous Germany was to be firmly embedded. The ingredients for this new order came largely from the positive and negative lessons that American statesmen had drawn from history, especially their experiences in the aftermath of World War I. The cornerstone of this new European order in 1945 was not merely confined to preventing a resurgence of German power. It was equally concerned with promoting European reconstruction and integration, which was to serve as a damper on the nationalist politics prevalent in pre-1945 Europe.

This essay will first probe the historical infancy of America's Germany Question as it emerged prior to and in the aftermath of World War I. It will then explore the crucial decisions reached by American foreign policy-makers in 1946-47 that spelled out the provisions for a constructive engagement in the creation of a European postwar order. Furthermore, the essay will focus on the economic and socio-cultural dimensions of America's German Question. The concluding section will analyze the decisiveness of American action toward facilitating the resolution of the "second" German Question after the peaceful revolutions of 1989, and it will comment on German-American relations in the post-unification era.

Setting the Stage:
The Making of the German Question

Much has been written about the genesis of Europe's German Question or German Problem, two concepts that are not only used interchangeably but also denote historical longevity. European and German scholars generally trace the origin of the German Question/Problem to the Peace of Westphalia in 1648, thus referring in essence to the futile search of Germany to find its place in the European state system.[2] To most Europeans, the German Question/Problem has always been Germany's search for belonging, of "looking westwards or wandering between East and West,"[3] the inherent dilemmas posed by the country's central position.[4] Others view the German Question solely in a post-1945 context, exploring the historical phases that instigated Germany's division and the subsequent attempts at reunification.[5] From the American perspective, the German Question differs from the European conception, mostly in historical context, but also in semantic reference and policy approach. To the United States, the German Question is embedded in the complex process of postwar European reconstruction. At its basis lay the transformation and rehabilitation of a devastated Germany, mainly through the institutionalization of stable democracy and economic prosperity. Underlying it all was the wish to "do it right" this time, to restore Europe with all available resources — to avoid a repeat of history's painful lessons.

To understand the genesis of America's German Question as rooted in the historical experiences that the country has had, one must first recapture the specifics that characterize the U.S.-German relationship from the beginning of the 20th century. It is from there that America's German Question took its course. Far from harmonious, U.S.-German relations at the turn of the 20th century were determined by competitive behavior resulting from the simultaneous evolution of both countries as global powers. Although Germany certainly was "most anxious to preserve the tradition of German-American friendship,"[6] and the United States equally "did not go out of its way to pick a quarrel with the Wilhelmian Reich,"[7] conflictive tensions between the two states were more than occasional occurrences. Naval rivalries were the cause of most of these imbroglios, as both nations expanded their maritime forces. In turn, it enhanced the perception that this newly-acquired naval mobility would foster German territorial ambitions overseas, particularly in traditional U.S. spheres of interest, such as the Far East or Latin America. By and large, however, U.S. irritation with Germany was limited to economic disputes that focused on trade tariffs, quotas, and competition for global markets rather than overt military confrontation.[8]

The German Problem became more precarious with the outbreak of World War I. Although the War initially produced a U.S. proclamation of neutrality delivered in ten different statements beginning August 4, 1914 — four of which were solely directed at Germany[9] — President Wilson was eventually compelled to abandon the neutral U.S. stance because of relentless German submarine warfare. Conducted systematically and voraciously, it flagrantly violated American neutral rights and staged indiscriminate attacks on unarmed American merchant and passenger vessels. On February 3, 1917, diplomatic relations with Germany were severed, followed by a U.S. declaration of war on April 6, 1917. In his address to Congress four days prior to the war declaration, Wilson also articulated another U.S. objective: to make the world safe for democracy.[10] This implied above all the destruction of the autocratic regime in Germany. Thus, the introduction of liberal democracy as a means toward the resolution of the German Question was a Wilsonian concept. Nearly thirty years later, other American statesmen, such as George Kennan, Dean Acheson, and George Marshall, would resume this idea, intent on completing the task in which previous American administrations presumably had failed.

Having envisioned a more "liberal peace" for Germany, Wilson pursued two conflicting U.S. foreign policy objectives at the Paris peace conference. On the one hand, he sought to establish a stable and responsible Germany,[11] a goal enhanced by Washington's fear of a possible Bolshevik revolution in Germany.[12] To this end, the Wilson government initiated a massive humanitarian assistance program, especially food aid. It aimed at providing a remedy against Socialist-inspired revolutions in Germany and Eastern Europe and carried a strong anti-Communist message.[13] On the other hand, there was a hesitancy regarding U.S. involvement in Europe.[14] Domestic opposition pushed most of the political discourse toward limited engagement. The U.S. Senate did not only vehemently reject American participation in the League of Nations but also opposed any U.S. responsibilities in Germany, including a minimal troop presence, a U.S. zone of occupation, and participation in several postwar settlement commissions. On March 19, 1919, the Versailles Treaty failed Senate ratification, seriously hampering U.S. moderating efforts vis-a-vis the French government, which had embarked on an aggressive policy toward Germany.

As a result of these harsh realities of European power politics, Wilson's moral vision of a lasting and stable European peace was an idealist vision at best. Europe remained a breeding ground for mutually incompatible security and national interests, German revisionism, and national hatred. What also remained in Europe was a Germany that throughout the 1920s would be inflicted with serious political and economic instabilities and societal disorientation as well as psychological insecurities.

While the "men of the creation" would later consider the Wilsonian idea of establishing a liberal democracy in Germany as a crucial element in the process of acting on the lessons of history learned, another U.S. post-World War I initiative, that is, assisting in the reconstruction of Europe, including Germany, also influenced policy-makers in the 1940s. Guided by pragmatic and idealist considerations, European reconstruction was not only seen as crucial to the national interest of the United States.   It also reflected American liberal economic thinking that equated economic prosperity with the promotion of democracy and peace.   The newly elected Republican administration in 1920/21 therefore adopted a concerted approach to advance its objective of building a lasting global peace.   It strongly advocated the integration of Germany "into the western community of liberal-democratic and capitalist states, so as to prevent a spill-over of social revolution."[15]   This meant above all economic reconstruction and the rebuilding of Germany's monetary and banking system through loans, credits, and investment.   Although the introduction of a legitimate democratic political system was also thought to enhance the prospects for a peaceful Germany, most of America's efforts were placed on reinstituting economic prosperity, mainly with the assistance of its bankers and financiers.

By mid-1922, U.S. support for Europe and Germany acquired an imminent urgency.   It was in this year that Germany was confronted with a near political, economic, and societal collapse.   Other European nations were also suffering from the economic and social burdens that the war had unleashed on their respective societies.   So dramatic was the economic and social chaos that fear of a Bolshevik-style revolution was widespread, not only in Germany but on the entire European continent.   In a letter to the Secretary of State in October 1922, the U.S. Ambassador to Germany, A. B. Houghton, outlined the vulnerability of a devastated Europe, in particular Germany, Great Britain, France, and Italy, to a Bolshevik take-over.   Based on rhetoric that resembled the later arguments for containment, Ambassador Houghton appealed for American assistance that would supersede the mere rescheduling or abrogation of debt payments.   He warned in particular that Germany might turn for relief to the East if the allies would not modify their punitive policies.[16]

Acting on such dire warnings, the United States signed a trade treaty with Germany in December 1923.   It extended most-favored-nation status to the Weimar Republic.   Furthermore, in 1924, U.S. influence was also crucial in negotiating the Dawes Plan — a major revision with respect to the problematic war reparations question and a crucial instrument in U.S. efforts for the stabilization of Europe's war-torn economies.[17]   The Dawes Plan signified "the full-fledged entry of the United States as an economic — though by careful design not as a political or military — force into the affairs of Europe."[18]   Although President Calvin Coolidge explicitly referred to U.S. actions as a "policy of permanent peace with independence,"[19] the Dawes Plan, from the U.S. perspective, was "the first decisive step in the economic and political revival of Germany."[20]   Its political significance rested on the premise that the collapse of Germany would constitute a security threat to all of Europe.[21]

Thus, U.S. policy toward Germany in the interwar years did not at all reflect the staunch image of isolationism or non-entanglement so commonly held in the literature.[22]   It is therefore more appropriate to refer to U.S. foreign policy as exhibiting an attitude of separateness that did not necessarily equate with aloofness to European concerns. In fact, U.S. foreign policy in the 1920s displayed already most of the basic principles and themes that came to underlie the country's policies vis-a-vis Europe and Germany in the 1940s: the economic reconstruction of Europe and Germany as a prerequisite to peace and security; the institutionalization of liberal democracy in Germany; and the integration of Germany into Western European security, economic, and political institutions. In the aftermath of World War II, these principles would again constitute the essential American blueprint for solving Europe's German Question. The detrimental consequence that non-participation in the League of Nations had for the stability of the European system would later be another vital lesson drawn from past policy failures. So would the need for collective security, also a Wilsonian concept, incorporated first in the legal provisions of the League of Nations, and reinstituted in post-World War II international and regional security arrangements.

The Crucial Years, 1946-48:
Avoiding a Repetition of History

Two related and difficult questions guided American thinking on a new post-World War II order. How should this new order be constructed to afford a permanent solution to Europe's German Question, and how could this new order function as a crucial bulwark against the ideological persuasiveness of Soviet Communism? In many ways the answers rested with already existing and previously tested policy directives that originated from America's political experiences after World War I. Then, as in 1945, the re-establishment of the international economic and political order required the recovery of Europe. To restore Europe meant invariably to include Germany. To prevent the re-emergence of another German threat to European security in the future, meant to create a Germany that would be both democratic and economically stable. To prevent the spread of Communism, all possible efforts toward European and German reconstruction had to be made. Underlying all this was the determination that history should not be repeated; that one had therefore best draw on lessons provided by the successes and failures of past U.S. foreign policy experiences; and that the United States should assume "guardianship" over the German Question.

To a large extent, such determination was influenced by the collective experiences of the men who would shape American foreign policy after the war. They were the experiences of a George Kennan, whose intimate knowledge of Soviet behavior became the subject of a secret and lengthy embassy telegram that he sent to the State Department on February 22, 1946, as chargé d'affaires at the U.S. Embassy in Moscow. Most instrumental in the debate over Soviet postwar objectives, it formed the basis of what would later be known as containment.[23] But there were also the experiences of men like Dean Acheson, later Secretary of State, who would describe his decisive role in the formulation and implementation of the Truman Doctrine and the Marshall Plan as having been "present at the creation."[24] He and others, such as John J. McCloy, Averell Harriman, and Robert Lovett, had acquired formidable knowledge as bankers and lawyers during the 1920s when European recovery had been on the U.S. agenda. Theirs was the conviction that economic stability for Europe and Germany was the best guarantee against the expanding forces of Communism.[25] There was also the belief of policy-makers such as Secretary of State James Byrnes who drew from history the lesson that America's mentality of separateness, its unwillingness to participate in Europe's security arrangements and to oversee German disarmament had been a mistake; that therefore not repeating that mistake translated into continuing "our interest in the affairs of Europe and of the world."[26] Even President Truman relied on history for advice, believing that "most of the problems a President has to face have their roots in the past."[27]

But unlike the aftermath of World War I, this time there was growing awareness that any blueprint to solve the German Question and, thus, the "European Problem" would inevitably require a redefinition of the American role in the international arena. The multiplicity and complexity of objectives was clear even prior to the emergence of a national consensus on the nature of the postwar order: to safeguard against a future German threat, to engage actively in the containment of Soviet ideological and political power, and to redesign power configurations in such a way as to provide the United States with a leading global role. The immensity of the task ahead can never be really sufficiently captured in words. Europe's political, economic, and social structure had been destroyed; millions of soldiers and civilians had lost their lives; many were maimed, starving, dislocated, and demoralized; cities had gone up in flames; industrial and agricultural production had come to a halt. On the international level, the balance of power had shifted not only in Europe but in Asia as well. What emerged out of the discussions on the nature of the postwar setting was the unshakable perception that America's interests were to be global. At a minimum, this would require an international balance of power.[28] As far as Europe was concerned, the United States had decided to act on previous policy lessons; to alleviate Europe's German Question would therefore also be in the U.S. interest. The perception that Europe was to be the prize and the price in the emerging struggle with the Soviet Union largely assisted in the process of U.S. foreign policy restructuring. So was the perception that Europe and the United States had something in common, that is, that Europe was largely like "us."[29] It was this sentiment that gradually tilted the balance in favor of a prominent American role in orchestrating the transformation of the German problem.

How was the German Question to be solved permanently? How was democracy to be expanded and the ideological power of Marxism-Leninism to be curtailed? How were U.S. political and economic interests best secured in the long term? The policy of containment offered one solution to these problems. Its rudimentary principles were first outlined by George Kennan, who originally proposed a short-term postwar assistance plan that subsequent administrations expanded in scope and nature. As a theoretical construct, containment was strictly a political and psychological strategy, devoid of any military connotation. As a policy instrument it envisaged the reconstruction of Europe, including Germany, primarily through economic means. Fearing that a political vacuum created in Germany could leave the devastated country susceptible to Soviet influences, the rehabilitation of Germany was considered to be a central task in the establishment of European security and stability.[30] As a U.S. policy approach to Europe and Germany, it was endorsed in a study by the State Department's Policy Planning Staff on May 23, 1947, then under Kennan's directorship. The study, commissioned by Secretary of State George Marshall after his return from the Council of Foreign Ministers Conference in April 1947, specifically stated that not Communism was the "root" of the problem, but the war-shattered political, economic, and social order in Europe and the psychological problems associated with this condition. Instead of combating Communism militarily, a measure not deemed necessary since the Soviet Union was not perceived to be a military threat, emphasis should be placed on providing assistance in the form of a European recovery program. Its centrality rested on an unprecedented amount of U.S. financial assistance that would only be allocated under provisions of an explicit and joint European request.[31]

On June 5, 1947, Secretary of State Marshall, in a commencement speech given at Harvard University, outlined the basic conceptual tenets of America's European recovery policy. It was followed by a State Department draft legislation on the European recovery program submitted to the Senate Foreign Relations Committee on December 19, 1947.[32] Subsequent hearings on the European Recovery Bill (S.2202) took place from January 8 to February 5, 1948. Supporters of the bill rallied around the common theme that the United States had a special interest in the economic recovery of Europe and Germany; that it was "a major step in the development and promotion of a peaceful and prosperous world;"[33] and that "without the restoration of their [Europe's] social and political strength necessarily associated with economic recuperation, the prospects for the American people, and for free people everywhere to find peace with justice and well-being and security for themselves and their children will be gravely prejudiced."[34] The bill — passed despite considerable Congressional opposition — was signed by President Truman on April 3, 1948, appropriating $13.2 billion to the European Recovery Program, which came to be known as the Marshall Plan.[35] The price for European security was without doubt a heavy one. But, as has been suggested, "the Marshall Plan was simply the down-payment for a future of common benefits and continuing American growth."[36] While the most extensive assistance program in U.S. history was being implemented in Europe, signs of a "second" German Question had already appeared on the horizon.

The Evolution of the "Second" German Question

The second dimension of America's German Question is largely associated with the post-1945 events that ushered in the territorial and political division of Germany and the onset of the Cold War. Although the wartime coalition had hammered out a joint authority and responsibility during the Potsdam Conference in July and August 1945, dividing the war-torn country and Berlin into four zones, the United States and the Soviet Union soon thereafter drifted apart on issues of reparations, administration of the zones, the nature of Germany's political order, and disputes over the occupied country's eastern frontier. The reparations question in particular invoked the ghosts of the past, reminding President Truman and the U.S. government of not committing a similar mistake as during allied negotiations after World War I. Between 1945 and 1947, the rivalry between the Soviet Union and the United States grew more tense, gradually transforming Germany from a defeated enemy into a contested prize, one which would allow each competitor to increase dramatically its potential power position. The failures of the Council of Foreign Ministers meetings, first in Paris in June 1946 and again in Moscow and London in 1947, signalled the ultimate breakdown of the coalition's attempt to reach consensus on a quadripartite arrangement for Germany.

By 1947, the Western allies introduced elements of a separate West German state, fusing the American and British zones. This act marked the beginning of Germany's division, which largely came to be viewed as the best solution for the German Question. It was soon followed by massive economic assistance under the Marshall Plan, preliminary discussions with respect to the Brussels Defense Treaty, and the 1948-49 Berlin Crisis as the Soviet response to a separate Western currency reform. By early 1948, the long-lasting period in U.S-Soviet relations commonly referred to as the Cold War had begun.

What followed the creation of the Federal Republic in 1949 were several Soviet attempts toward the reunification and neutralization of Germany. The United States, meanwhile, was actively promoting the politico-economic and military integration of West Germany into the Western "camp." From a broader perspective, such integration would thwart popular German attraction toward Soviet "concessions" with respect to a reunified and neutralized Germany. Moreover, U.S. policy-makers, who had no interest in a prolonged and massive occupation force in Germany, perceived Western European integration to be a most suitable solution to the European security problem, and thus, the German problem. Lastly, integration would also ease Western European concerns over the prospect of a rearmed Germany. While in some U.S. circles the possibility of German rearmament had already been contemplated as early as 1948,[37] the outbreak of the Korean War in 1950 was the principal event that would ultimately lead to the termination of occupation, the re-establishment of a West German military, and West German membership in NATO in 1955.

Despite the emergence of two separate German states in 1949, during the 1950s diplomatic endeavors toward settling the division of Germany played themselves out between the four powers and the Federal Republic. Most of the political correspondence spelling out the preliminary conditions for a united Germany — a peace treaty and all-German elections — was exchanged prior to 1955 as the Soviets attempted to prevent the Federal Republic's entrance into NATO. But even after the Federal Republic had regained its sovereignty, all interested parties continued to pursue the question of reunification, although more as a rhetorical device than a real policy option. Since the Western powers and the Soviet Union had mutually exclusive objectives, very little common ground could be found to facilitate the reunification of the two Germanys. Soviet overtures insisted on a Germany that was neutral, whereas the Western allies were asking for a united Germany that would be entrenched in the West. To show Western solidarity and collective resolve, the United States supported reunification. Yet underneath lurked its incompatibility with Soviet containment and U.S. policy toward the integration of the Federal Republic into Western Europe's institutions.[38]

A crisis precipitated by Nikita Khrushchev in November 1958 over allied access to Berlin marked the beginning of a series of events that were to freeze the German Question in time. The building of the Berlin Wall on August 13, 1961 was merely the coup de grâce after an exhaustive process that had sought to remedy the German Question. A week later, President Kennedy, in a speech to the United Nations General Assembly, solemnly warned that peace in Germany and in Europe was in danger and that the crisis constituted a threat "against the vital interests and the deep commitments of the Western Powers."[39] However, as the subsequent negotiations on Berlin between 1961 and 1962 indicated, the United States was not willing to risk a military confrontation over Berlin.

At the same time, cleavages between the Adenauer government and the Kennedy administration over issues of nuclear control sharing and arms control began to disrupt U.S.-German relations. Bestowed with a pragmatic vision for the present, President Kennedy broke with "the polite words and ritualistic pledges of the past"[40] to turn Washington's attention to more pressing issues: to reduce the risk of war over Berlin and to improve superpower relations so as to ameliorate conditions in Europe. To this end, Washington sought bilateral talks with the Soviet Union, which would soon after constitute the major context for detente.   Acceptance of the division of Germany as a political reality abruptly ended America's engaged commitment to German reunification. Washington's sacrifice of the German Question, that is, its reversal on a promise of the past, was deemed to be justified.   President Kennedy's "Ich bin ein Berliner" speech in 1963 could do little to bridge the growing U.S.-West German rift.   As superpower detente progressed, the Federal Republic also pursued its own detente, *Ostpolitik*, which, through a series of treaties with the East, gave not only status-quo recognition to a divided Europe but also a permanency to an unresolved German Question.

The Impact of Economic and Socio-Cultural Winds of Change

While in the immediate postwar years German-American relations focused primarily on political-military affairs, by the 1960s the first signs of economic and socio-cultural changes in the Federal Republic were giving America's German Question another dimension.   Although the most profound impact of these changes was not felt until the 1970s and 1980s, its roots can be traced to the 1960s.   It was a decade that not only witnessed the manifestation of successful economic recovery, portrayed best in the West German economic miracle, or *Wirtschaftswunder*, but also the revolt of the young against traditional norms and structures of authority.   The rift between the two allies became first most contentious in the economic sphere as the Federal Republic gradually emerged as a major competitor to the United States in global markets. Soon, it also permeated the socio-cultural domain.   By the time Ronald Reagan assumed the presidency, the mixture of chronic economic disagreements and volatile anti-Americanism imposed serious strains on the management of the bilateral relationship.

In economic matters, several bones of contention surfaced.   There were serious imbroglios over monetary and trade policies that were particularly prevalent in the 1970s and 1980s.   But more significant than the economic rivalries between the two countries were the disputes that broke out over contending perceptions and practices with regard to East-West trade, the major focus of the following discussion.   The conduct of East-West economic affairs was a particularly controversial issue, since it involved not only a clash over diverging national economic policies but also over different perceptions of national security.   While it was the U.S. foreign policy objective to limit Eastern bloc access to Western technology, to reduce Western dependence on energy resources from the East, to restrict the availability of export-credits, and to impose sanctions when deemed necessary for leverage with the Soviet Union, the Federal Republic primarily utilized economic policies for the pursuit of political objectives.   Not only was West Germany's *Osthandel*, that is, its trade with the East, a fundamental component in Brandt's *Ostpolitik*, the Federal

Republic also became the biggest trading partner of the Soviet Union and Eastern Europe. East-West trade, then, was crucial to Bonn's foreign policy as an instrument for building peace in the region.[41] Thus, Bonn had many reasons not to yield willingly to Washington's call for restrictions on economic activities with the East. This was especially so because the Federal Republic viewed normalization with the East as a continuous process that required more often the provision of carrots than the wielding of sticks.

Among the earliest cases of alliance disagreement was the pipe embargo of 1962-1963 that a U.S.-sponsored NATO resolution imposed on the export of large-diameter steel pipes to the Soviet Union. It was triggered largely over an American political objective to prevent the establishment of a Soviet oil-exporting industry.[42] Despite German compliance with the embargo, the measure had serious repercussions for the German and American governments but also for West German domestic politics. Other incidents of U.S. imposed trade restrictions followed, including President Carter's sanctions on drilling equipment for oil and gas in 1978 and his partial grain embargo in 1980 in retaliation for the Soviet invasion of Afghanistan. By far the most severe conflict between the United States and the Federal Republic broke out over the Urengoi Pipeline sanctions of 1981-1982. It clearly exposed the different perceptions that Washington and Bonn held regarding the implementation of sanctions and embargoes. As a result, there was not only non-compliance with U.S. policies, but the impact of such enforced sanctions was so immense that it threatened to damage the cohesion of the Western Alliance.[43]

Fundamental to an understanding of such conflicts over economic policy vis-a-vis the East were above all the differing perceptions of security that the two countries held. For the United States, the limits set on East-West trade or its use as a tool of leverage were among the fundamentals of its national security policy, whereas for the Federal Republic the expansion of economic relations with the East was a policy aimed at assuring security by political and economic means.

Yet another disturbing phenomenon appeared on the horizon in the 1960s, again reaching its zenith in the early 1980s, coinciding with the confrontational course pursued by the Reagan administration. It was in the 1960s that the first signs of anti-Americanism appeared, expressed primarily by students and intellectuals with leftist inclinations. Anger over Germany's Nazi past and the widely perceived "oppressiveness" of authoritarian structures, but also U.S. intervention in Vietnam and other Third World countries, fuelled the unrest. In the 1970s, a broader spectrum of concerned citizen groups surfaced that challenged the Bonn government on nuclear and other environmental and social issues. By the early 1980s, these grass-roots movements gained unprecedented momentum in response to the planned deployment of new nuclear missiles and in opposition to deterrence for moral reasons. As Washington grew more hostile toward the Soviet Union, the fear intensified that the deterioration of

East-West relations could provoke an outbreak of armed conflict in Europe. Public pressure on Bonn to continue with its arms control and detente policies thus were substantial. Given the Reagan administration's policies on East-West relations, a strong anti-American rhetoric accompanied many of the public protests. Although complex socio-cultural processes were responsible for the manifestation of changing German sentiments toward the United States, Washington's policy community most often only gave attention to the profound anti-Americanism displayed in the public protests.

Even to this day, there are conflicting perspectives on the causes of societal unrest in the Federal Republic, especially among West German youths, and the anti-American sentiments that accompanied such outbursts. Those who ground their analysis primarily in cultural explanations speak of anti-Americanism as positively linked to the search for national identity. The essence of such an argument is that postwar West German society filled its national identity void by building an alternative collective identity that was largely modelled on American culture. By the early 1980s, this "surrogate" identity was collapsing and, along with a generational change, gave way to popular discontent that the newly emerging social movements successfully captured.[44]

Most American policy-makers also regarded generational change as the primary cause for the shift in German attitudes toward the United States. President Reagan expressed this view when he spoke of a German generation that had not been present at the creation and thus was not able to appreciate the Western Alliance for its role in the maintenance of peace.[45] Arthur Burns, the U.S. Ambassador to the Federal Republic during the early 1980s, adopted a similar standpoint, arguing that the emergence of a new generation with less knowledge of the constructive U.S. postwar role accounted for the waning interest in strong U.S.-German ties. But he also recognized the significance of diverging perceptions of security issues for the rift between the two countries.[46] To make matters worse, Washington's reaction to such negative public sentiments further encouraged a re-emergence of West German neutralist aspirations and severance of links with the West.[47] The situation became particularly exacerbated as the security consensus among West German foreign policy elites broke down over the deployment of intermediate-range nuclear forces (INF) in the early 1980s.[48] Even as late as 1989, U.S. suspicions regarding the upsurge of anti-Americanism in the Federal Republic remained a powerful psychological barrier in the relationship between the two countries.

From a sociological point of view, the emergence of new social movements, the political protest over nuclear weapons, and anti-American sentiments are seen more as the expression of change in social and cultural norms than as a search for national identity or a shift to neutralism. Described as a long-term process in the transformation of the political culture of all advanced industrialized nations, the societal protests of the 1980s are taken as evidence of a change in social consciousness, the emergence of participatory politics, postmaterial value changes, and even a cultural shift.[49]   However, all these explanations never alleviated the basic misperceptions that existed on both sides: for the United States, the manifestation of socio-cultural disturbances mostly were an indication of German nationalism and neutralist tendencies triggered by a new generation, while for the Federal Republic, they were increasing evidence of the divergences in political-security matters that rendered bilateral relations more divisive throughout the 1980s.

The German Question Revisited:
The German Revolution of 1989

When President Bush in his speech on May 31, 1989 in Mainz pleaded to "bring glasnost to East Berlin,"[50] little did he know that this would soon be a reality, leading to arduous but fast-paced negotiations on German unity. Bush's speech did not merely reaffirm long-standing U.S. support for German unification. When it finally resurfaced as a viable issue, America's decisive leadership was also crucial in formulating and implementing the appropriate framework in which negotiations could proceed in a cooperative manner. Within the context of its bilateral relationship with the Federal Republic, the "reopening" of the German Question meant revisiting the reunification promises of the past. Within the Allied power framework — a remnant of the early postwar days — it meant the recognition and the accommodation of psychological as much as political needs, and the promise of continued "guardianship" over European security given the prospects of a united, and thus substantially enlarged Germany.

Despite balancing acts that were at times conflicting, the United States moved surprisingly swift on formulating its policy on German unification, deciding perhaps as early as June or July 1989 that it was in America's best interest to support German unity decisively rather than join the forces opposing it. One motivating factor was that the Bush administration was eager to preserve its role in a new Europe, willing to submit to a "change in form but not in fundamentals"[51] as President Bush suggested in his Thanksgiving Day Address. Moreover, it also was intended to maintain its newly defined "partnership in leadership" with the Federal Republic that it had launched during President Bush's visit there in 1989. Unlike most Europeans, Washington's sentiments, then, as in the later course of negotiations, were that the United States was the least worried about unification.[52] The events associated with the reopening of the German Question during the summer of 1989 are numerous and need not be recaptured in their entirety. What is pivotal, though, is an exploration of how the United States further facilitated the unification process, careful not to antagonize its three Allied partners nor preclude German participation as an equal member in the conduct of the negotiations that followed.

What appeared first to be a West German problem, as the country struggled between September and November 1989 to manage the logistics of the mass exodus of discontented citizens from the German Democratic Republic, soon became the concern of the Western allies and the Soviet Union as the Berlin Wall crumbled on November 9, 1989 and the prospects of German unity once more brought the "European Problem" to the fore. In reaction to the large mass migration to the Federal Republic, Chancellor Kohl on November 28, 1989, had presented a ten-point plan that suggested a gradual and carefully monitored creation of a federation between the two Germanys. Without proposing any special time-table, Bonn envisioned a process leading from economic assistance to establishing confederated structures, ultimately resulting in a federation. Having already pledged support for a unified Europe in May 1989 and having expressed that, from the U.S. perspective, German unification seemed inevitable,[53] Washington, although caught by surprise, was hardly stunned by Mr. Kohl's unilateral November initiative. It responded positively to the Chancellor's speech, but it approached the subject of German unity with unmistakable diplomatic caution, largely because of the sensitivities of the other three Allied powers. Therefore, Washington first disguised its open support for Bonn's policies, stressing that unity was "a goal that we and [West Germany] have long shared" but also signalling to the Soviet Union, France, and Great Britain that questions with respect to European security deserved primary attention.[54]

To alleviate anxieties over German unity, Secretary of State Baker in his speech on the "new Atlanticism" at the Berlin Press Club on December 12, 1989, reiterated the four U.S. conditions on which German unification was to be based: German self-determination, a German commitment to NATO and the European Community, a peaceful and gradual transition toward unification, and resolving border issues according to the provisions of the 1975 Helsinki Final Act. In addition, Mr. Baker affirmed "a recognition of a need for an active U.S. role in Europe."[55] Despite such reassurances, two critical issues hampered negotiations. But here again the United States acted decisively and in support of the West German position. One disputed problem was how the new and united Germany was to be incorporated into NATO. In this case, Washington lent a sympathetic ear to West German Foreign Minister Hans-Dietrich Genscher, whose suggestion of a united Germany in NATO without stationing NATO troops on former East German territory found Mr. Baker's endorsement.[56] In the subsequent talks with a hesitant Soviet Union concerning the latter's consent to a united Germany's membership of NATO, the Bush administration largely allowed the Federal Republic to negotiate bilaterally the conditions for such acceptance.[57] Imperative in the entire process also was Washington's offer of a nine-point plan that it had worked out with Bonn at an earlier stage. The plan made substantial concessions to Moscow, promising not only a reform of NATO strategy, but also a commitment to a Germany free of nuclear, chemical, and biological production capabilities, a renunciation of German border claims toward the East, substantial economic and technological assistance to the Soviet Union, and, most important of all, the institutionalization of the 35-nation Conference on Security and Cooperation in Europe (CSCE) with a leading role for the Soviet Union.[58]

Another problem, solved because of decisive U.S. action and maneuvering and cajoling behind the scene, was the issue of how negotiations on German unity were to proceed. To accommodate the Federal Republic within a more cooperative framework instead of the simple Four Power context demanded by France, Great Britain, and the Soviet Union, and also to avoid the sensitive matter of a peace conference with all former war parties, Washington hammered out the "two-plus-four" concept. It allowed both Germanys to assume responsibility over the internal dimensions of their unification and interact as participatory members with the four other parties. Mr. Baker's shuttle diplomacy to Paris, London, and Moscow, as well as his continued successful lobbying during the Ottawa Open Skies Conference in February 1990 (creating the impression that the five foreign ministers[59] were only engaged in meetings with each other), at last produced the desired result of a two-plus-four arrangement.[60] The final outcome, the "Treaty on the Final Settlement with Respect to Germany" was signed on September 12, 1989 in Moscow by the four former Allied powers and the two Germanys. It allowed for German membership in NATO and bestowed full sovereignty on a united Germany. With the internal unification completed on October 3, 1990 and all-German elections on December 2, 1990, a chapter in European and U.S. postwar history had come to a successful close. The beginnings of a new Europe were ushered in in late November 1990, when the 35 CSCE nations signed the Charter of Paris, thereby establishing the structures and institutions for a united Europe. This act was to some extent reminiscent of the earlier visions of U.S. and European statesmen who had believed all along that a united Europe would most likely hold the solution to the German problem.

Conclusion: Adjusting to a New Germany
in the Post-Unification Era

Although none of the post-unification scenarios predicting a Germany more aloof and disengaged from the United States so far have become a reality, German-American relations in the aftermath of the dismantling of the Berlin Wall have not been tension-free, nor will they be so in the future. Most of the recent policy disagreements, such as over the Gulf War or the conflict in Yugoslavia, however, are not so much the result of a more assertive Germany, as is often suggested in Washington's policy circles. Rather, they are partially rooted in Bonn's inability to meet U.S. expectations regarding the country's new international responsibilities, expectations that German leaders often perceive as unrealistic, contradictory in nature, and even incompatible with Germany's foreign policy approach. In addition, German-American discord also results from differing notions of power, security, and peace, and with it, diverging foreign policy styles that exacerbate conflictive perceptions over Germany's international role.

It is thus crucial for U.S. policy-makers to understand how Germany perceives itself. Not only have Bonn's foreign policy leaders, in particular Foreign Minister Genscher, molded the image of Germany as a major actor engaged in bringing about the resolution of the East-West conflict through peaceful means. They have, moreover, significantly shaped the construction of a new post-1989 European order, emphasizing peaceful outcomes to conflict, a shift toward cooperative security, the use of a spectrum of non-military methods before force is invoked, multilateral approaches to peacemaking and peacekeeping, reconciliation among ethnically, culturally, and linguistically diversified peoples, economic interdependence, and pan-European integration.[61]

Perhaps the most telling example exposing Washington's and Bonn's diverging expectations and perceptions came in the aftermath of the Iraqi invasion of Kuwait in August 1990. While Bonn repeatedly pressed for a peaceful resolution of the conflict using a plethora of bilateral and multilateral channels, voices in Washington asked accusingly why a united Germany did not assume greater international responsibilities that befitted its political and economic prowess. To Bonn, having been the subject of rekindled anxieties over its future resurgence as a European military power only a few months ago, U.S. demands for a more active role in the war effort seemed at best contradictory. In an interview in the German weekly newspaper, *Die Zeit*, German President Richard von Weizsäcker poignantly uncovered this apparent contradiction and the confusion it had elicited in Germany when he noted:

> The one contradiction is that in 1990 everyone perceived Germany to be a new European power marching ahead of others — now everyone thinks that the Germans are running behind everyone, applying brakes or being hesitant objectors.
> Another contradiction is indeed that in the entire postwar era all our neighbors and all our alliance partners always proceeded from the assumption that because of our historical burden no new German military potential could ever again arise. In the year 1990 there were many fears about what a Germany, strengthened in power by unification, would one day do with it militarily — and now, at the beginning of the year 1991, Germans are faced with the accusation that they do not want to participate in war.[62]

Not only did the Gulf War raise eyebrows in the United States over German inaction, although Secretary of State Baker underlined during Genscher's visit in March 1991 that "we are extraordinarily pleased with the economic and financial support we've received from the Federal Republic of Germany,"[63] but

Germany's active diplomatic engagement in the Yugoslav conflict drew a similar reaction. As early as July 1991 a consensus among all German parties had emerged calling for the right of self-determination for Slovenia and Croatia, whereas the United States, along with France and Britain, urged the preservation of the territorial integrity of Yugoslavia.[64] Fearing that armed conflict in Yugoslavia could sabotage endeavors toward the creation of a European peace order and arguing that only a recognition of the two republics could force Serbia to negotiate a peace, Germany lobbied hard in the EC forum to gain collective diplomatic recognition for the break-away republics. It came about on December 15, 1991, amid protests by the United States and the United Nations that such recognition would at best excacerbate but not end the war.[65] Yet by April 1992, the United States had also moved closer to the German position on Yugoslavia, with Genscher and Baker discussing measures to stop further violence against the civilian populations by the Yugoslav army.[66]

Thus, while disagreements over international and European policies will continue to characterize German-American relations, German leaders have also adopted Bush's theme of "partners in leadership." During his first visit in Washington after unification, Chancellor Kohl reacted positively to U.S. policy-makers who emphasized that the partnership with a united Germany would continue to play a key role in U.S. foreign policy. Kohl furthermore commented on the essentiality of a security community between the United States and Europe. But he also proposed an expansion of the Atlantic relationship through economic means and particularly through cultural exchange,[67] even suggesting the creation of a German-American Academy of Sciences.[68]

Moreover, in September of the same year Kohl made one more step in the direction of extending cultural relations with the United States. On September 12, 1991 he opened a new institute on German and European studies at the University of California at Berkeley, an initiative he had sponsored, duplicating a similar endeavor that had led to the establishment of academic centers at Harvard and Georgetown Universities in 1988. Even with regard to European security, several joint U.S.-German initiatives have been crucial, such as establishing a NATO link to Central and Eastern Europe and to the Commonwealth of Independent States (CIS) via the North Atlantic Cooperation Council, or coordinating international economic assistance to the East. Perhaps Washington even finds itself adopting some of Germany's political discourse. In April 1992 Secretary of State Baker impressed on an American audience at the Council of Foreign Relations in Chicago that U.S. financial support for democratization and economic reform in the CIS should be seen as investments in security. This was similar to Chancellor Kohl's statement made during his March visit in the United States, when he spoke of such assistance as an investment in peace.

The German-American partnership, then, will remain part of a political community that was built more than 40 years ago, as part of an American endeavor to construct a new European order.   Although much of this task has now been assumed by Germany and its European neighbors and a plethora of multilateral institutions such as the EC, NATO, and CSCE, the United States, despite its changing status in Europe, will continue to be a vital transatlantic partner.

Notes

The authors would like to thank Michael McKinley for his valuable research assistance.

1. Secretary of State Baker, "A New Europe, A New Atlanticism: Architecture for a New Era," Speech given at the Berlin Press Club, December 12, 1989, *Current Policy*, no. 1233 (1989), p. 1.
2. See, for instance, Renata Fritsch-Bournazel, *Das Land in der Mitte: Die Deutschen im europäischen Kräftefeld* (Munich: Iudicium Verlag, 1986) and "The Changing Nature of the German Question," in F. Stephen Larrabee, ed., *The Two German States and European Security* (New York: St. Martin's & Institute for East-West Security Studies, 1989); Gert Krell, "The German Question and the European Peace Order, 1648 to 1990" (Frankfurt: Peace Research Institute Frankfurt, September 1990).
3. Fritsch-Bournazel, "The Changing Nature of the German Question," p. 49.
4. Anne-Marie LeGloannec, "France's German Problem," in Larrabee, ed., *The Two German States and European Security*, pp. 242-68.
5. There is little consensus on whether or not the term used should be the "German Question" or the "German Problem."   The literature on the subject reveals that both concepts are often employed interchangeably.   Some scholars make the usage of either term contingent on the historical context examined.   Others adopt a framework that refers to the specific geopolitical and legal parameters of the phenomenon.   J. K. Sowden asserts that there are two dominant views on the German Question/Problem that determine the appropriate linguistic usage.   Accordingly, "the historical approach sees it principally in the constitutional, territorial and geo-political context over centuries. The post-1945 viewpoint considers it to be intrinsically the present-day set of questions relating to division and reunification, stressing not only the national factor, but also its significance in European — and even in world-politics" (*The German Question 1945-1973: Continuity in Change*, New York, St. Martin's Press, 1975, p. 17).   Representative of the first approach, the German Problem, is Gerhart Ritter's *Das deutsche Problem: Grundfragen deutschen Staatslebens gestern und heute* (Munich: Oldenbourg Verlag, 1962); the second approach, the German Question, is found in Walther Hubatsch's *Die deutsche Frage*, 2nd ed. (Würzburg: Plötz, 1964).
6. Manfred Jonas, *The United States and Germany: A Diplomatic History* (Ithaca and London: Cornell University Press, 1984), p. 34.
7. Jonas, *The United States and Germany*, p. 34.
8. On U.S.-German relations in historical perspective, see for example, Jonas, *The United States and Germany*; Hans W. Gatzke, "The United States and Germany on the Eve of World War I," in Imanuel Geiss and Bernd Jürgen Wendt, eds., *Deutschland in*

der Weltpolitik des 19. und 20. Jahrhunderts (Düsseldorf: Bertelsmann, 1973), pp. 271-86; Manfred Jonas, "The Major Powers and the United States, 1898-1910: The Case of Germany," in Jules Davids, ed., *Perspectives in American Diplomacy* (New York: Arno Press, 1976), pp. 30-77.

9. Department of State, "Proclamation of Neutrality — The President's Appeal to the People of the United States," *Papers Relating to the Foreign Relations of the United States, 1914*, supplement (Washington, DC: GPO, 1928), pp. 547-51.

10. Department of State, "Address of the President of the United States Delivered at a Joint Session of the Two Houses of Congress, April 2, 1917," *Papers Relating to the Foreign Relations of the United States, 1917*, vol. 1, supplement 2 (Washington, DC: GPO, 1932), p. 201.

11. Jonas, *The United States and Germany*, p. 147.

12. See Klaus Schwabe, "America's Contribution to the Stabilization of the Early Weimar Republic," in Hans L. Trefousse, ed., *Germany and America: Essays on Problems of International Relations and Immigration* (New York: Brooklyn College Press, 1980), pp. 21-28.

13. Werner Link, *Die amerikanische Stabilisierungspolitik in Deutschland 1921-1932* (Düsseldorf: Droste Verlag, 1970), pp. 79-80.

14. Jonas, *The United States and Germany*, p. 147.

15. Link, *Die amerikanische Stabilisierungspolitik*, p. 78.

16. Department of State, "The Ambassador in Germany (Houghton) to the Secretary of State, October 23, 1922," *Papers Relating to the Foreign Relations of the United States, 1922*, vol. 2 (Washington: GPO, 1933), p. 173.

17. On the influential role of American economic reconstruction in Germany after 1920 see the extensive account by Link, *Die amerikanische Stabilisierungspolitik*; see also Herbert Feis, *The Diplomacy of the Dollar, 1919-1932* (Baltimore: Johns Hopkins Press, 1950); Manfred Jonas, "Mutualism in the Relations Between the United States and the Early Weimar Republic," in Trefousse, ed., *Germany and America*, pp. 41-53; Werner Link, "Die Beziehungen zwischen der Weimarer Republik und den USA," in Manfred Knapp et al., eds., *USA und Deutschland 1918-1975* (Munich: C.H. Beck, 1978); Schwabe, "America's Contribution to the Stabilization of the Early Weimar Republic," pp. 21-28, and his "The United States and the Weimar Republic: The Special Relationship that Failed," in Frank Trommler and Joseph McVeigh, eds., *America and the Germans: An Assessment of a Three-Hundred Year History*, vol. 2: *The Relationship in the Twentieth Century* (Philadelphia: University of Pennsylvania Press, 1985). For an analysis of the different schools of interpretation, see the chapters by Hans-Jürgen Schröder, "Twentieth-Century German-American Relations: Historiography and Research Perspectives," and Arnold A. Offner, "Research on American-German Relations: A Critical View," in Trefousse, ed., *America and the Germans*, pp. 147-67 and 168-82, respectively.

18. Jonas, *The United States and Germany*, p. 181.

19. Department of State, "Message of the President of the United States to Congress, December 3, 1924," *Papers Relating to the Foreign Relations of the United States, 1924*, vol. 1 (Washington, DC: GPO, 1939), p. xx.

20. Department of State, "Message of the President" (see note 19).

21. Department of State, "Message of the President" (see note 19).

22. For an account on the "myth" of U.S. isolationism, see, for example, Werner Link who takes a critical view of isolationism as a driving component of American foreign policy during the era of the Weimar Republic; see his *Die amerikanische Stabilisierungspolitik*, and "Die Außenpolitik der USA 1919-1933, Quellen und neue amerikanische Literatur," *Neue Politische Literatur* vol. 7, no. 3 (1967). See also Schröder, "Twentieth-Century German-American Relations."

23. See "Moscow Embassy Telegram #511: 'The Long Telegram'," in Thomas H. Etzold and John Lewis Gaddis, eds., *Containment: Documents on American Policy and Strategy, 1945-1950* (New York: Columbia University Press, 1978), pp. 50-63.

24. Dean Acheson, *Present at the Creation: My Years in the State Department* (New York: W.W. Norton, 1969).

25. For an excellent account of these statesmen, see Walter Isaacson and Evan Thomas, *The Wise Men: Six Friends and the World They Made* (New York: Simon & Schuster, 1986); also Thomas Alan Schwartz, *America's Germany: John J. McCloy and the Federal Republic of Germany* (Cambridge: Harvard University Press, 1991); Acheson alludes to these fears of Communism, even on U.S. territory, in *Present at the Creation*, pp. 358-59.

26. Department of State, Historical Office, "Address by Secretary of State Byrnes on United States Policy Regarding Germany, Stuttgart, September 6, 1946," *Documents on Germany 1944-1970*, Prepared for the Senate, Committee on Foreign Relations, 92nd Congress, 1st session (Washington, DC: GPO, 1971), pp. 59-67.

27. Harry Truman, *Memoirs, Vol II: Years of Trial and Hope* (New York: Signet Book, 1956), p. 13.

28. Catherine McArdle Kelleher, "Containment in Europe: The Critical Context," in Terry L. Deibel and John Lewis Gaddis, eds., *Containment: Concept and Policy*, vol. 2 (Washington, DC: National Defense University Press, 1986), pp. 381-400.

29. For an elaboration on American images of Europe, see Catherine McArdle Kelleher, "America Looks at Europe," in Lawrence Freedman, ed., *The Troubled Alliance: Atlantic Relations in the 1980s* (London: Heinemann Educational Books, 1983), pp. 44-66, and also her "U.S. Foreign Policy and Europe, 1990-2000," *Brookings Review* (Fall 1990), pp. 4-10.

30. See George F. Kennan, "The Origins of Containment" and Kelleher, "Containment in Europe," in Deibel and Gaddis, eds., *Containment: Concept and Policy*, pp. 23-31 and 381-400, respectively.

31. "PPS 1, May 23, 1947: Policy with Respect to American Aid in Western Europe," in Etzold and Gaddis, eds., *Containment: Documents on American Policy and Strategy*, pp. 102-106.

32. U.S. Congress, Senate Committee on Foreign Relations, *Outline of European Recovery Program*, Draft Legislation and Background Information, Submitted by the Department of State, 80th Congress, 1st session (Washington, DC: GPO, 1948).

33. U.S. Congress, Senate Committee on Foreign Relations, *European Recovery Program*, Report of the Committee on Foreign Relations on S. 2202, February 26, 1948, 80th Congress, 2nd session (Washington, DC: GPO, 1948), p. 1.

34. U.S. Congress, Senate Committee on Foreign Relations, "Statement of Hon. George C. Marshall, Secretary of State," *United States Assistance to European Economic Recovery*, 80th Congress, 2nd session, January 8, 1948, Part 1 (Washington, DC: GPO, 1948), p. 1.

35.Alexander DeConde, *A History of American Foreign Policy, Vol. II: Global Power*, 3rd ed. (New York: Charles Scribner's, 1978), pp. 225-26.

36. Kelleher, "U.S. Foreign Policy and Europe," p. 6.

37. Kelleher, "U.S. Foreign Policy and Europe," p. 6.

38. Wolfram Hanrieder, *Germany, America, Europe: Forty Years of German Foreign Policy* (New Haven: Yale University Press, 1989), p. 142; Frank Ninkovich, *Germany and the United States: The Transformation of the German Question Since 1945* (Boston: Twayne Publishers, 1988).

39. Department of State, Historical Office, "Address by President Kennedy to the United Nations General Assembly, September 25, 1961," in *Documents on Germany* (see note 26), pp. 585-86.

40. Catherine McArdle Kelleher, *Germany and the Politics of Nuclear Weapons* (New York: Columbia University Press, 1975), p. 192.

41. Hélène Seppan refers to West German economic policy objectives vis-a-vis the Soviet Union as a phenomenon of "buying peace" in "The Divided West: Contrasting German and US Attitudes to Soviet Trade," *Political Quarterly*, vol. 61, no. 1 (January-March 1990), pp. 51-65.

42. See, for instance, Angela Stent, *From Embargo to Ostpolitik* (Cambridge: Cambridge University Press, 1981).

43. For a discussion on the differing perspectives, see, for example, Philip Hanson, *Western Economic Statecraft in East-West Relations* (London: Routledge & Kegan Paul, 1988); Hanns-Dieter Jacobsen, "East-West Trade and Export Controls: The West German Perspective," in Gary K. Bertsch, ed., *Controlling East-West Trade and Technology Transfer* (Durham: Duke University Press, 1988); Angela E. Stent, *Economic Relations with the Soviet Union: American and West German Perspectives* (Boulder: Westview Press, 1985).

44. See, for example, Andrei S. Markovits, "Anti-Americanism and the Struggle for a West German Identity," in Peter H. Merkl, ed., *The Federal Republic of Germany at Forty* (New York: New York University Press, 1989), pp. 35-54; David R. Gress, "Die deutsch-amerikanischen Beziehungen von 1945 bis 1987," *Aus Politik und Zeitgeschichte* B3/88 (January 15, 1988), pp. 16-27; Fritz Stern, "Conclusion: German-American Relations and 'The Return of the Repressed'," in James A. Cooney, Gordon A. Craig, Hans-Peter Schwarz, and Fritz Stern, eds., *The Federal Republic of Germany and the United States: Changing Political, Social and Economic Relations* (Boulder: Westview Press, 1984), pp. 234-53; Stephen F. Szabo, "West Germany: Generations and Changing Security Perspectives," in Stephen Szabo, ed., *The Successor Generation: International Perspectives of Postwar Europeans* (London: Butterworths, 1983), 43-75. For a discussion on cultural change and national identity, see also Dirk Verheyen, *The German Question: A Cultural, Historical, and Geopolitical Exploration* (Boulder: Westview Press, 1991).

45. Statement made at the National Press Club, Washington, DC, November 18, 1981.

46. Arthur F. Burns, *The United States and Germany: A Vital Partnership* (New York: Council on Foreign Relations, 1986).

47. Hans-Peter Schwarz, "The West Germans, Western Democracy, and Western Ties in the Light of Public Opinion Research," in Cooney, Craig, Schwarz, and Stern, eds., *The Federal Republic of Germany and the United States*, pp. 56-97.

48. Discussed at length in Thomas Risse-Kappen, *Die Krise der Sicherheitspolitik: Neuorientierung und Entscheidungsprozesse im politischen System der Bundesrepublik Deutschland 1977-1984* (Munich: Kaiser, 1988).

49. Representatives of such perspectives are Russell J. Dalton and Manfred Kuechler, *Challenging the Political Order: New Social and Political Movements in Western Democracies* (New York: Oxford University Press, 1990); John K. Gibbins, *Contemporary Political Culture: Politics in the Postmodern Age* (London: SAGE, 1989); Ronald Inglehart, *Culture Shift in Advanced Industrial Society* (Princeton: Princeton University Press, 1990).

50. President George Bush, "Four Proposals to Overcome Europe's Division, Mainz, FRG, May 31, 1989," in Adam Daniel Rotfeld and Walther Stützle, eds., *Germany and Europe in Transition* (Oxford: Oxford University Press, 1991), p. 94.

51. "Text of President Bush's Address," *Washington Post*, November 23, 1989, p. A24.

52. This statement was made by Deputy Secretary of State Lawrence Eagleburger in an interview on November 25, 1989; in "U.S. Aide Sees Unification," *New York Times*, November 26, 1989, p. A21.

53. "U.S. Aide Sees Unification."

54. Marc Fisher, "Kohl Proposes Broad Program for Reunification of Germany," *Washington Post*, November 29, 1989, pp. A1 & A33.

55. Secretary of State Baker, "A New Europe," p. 2.

56. See "Baker begrüßt Genschers Vorschlag," *Süddeutsche Zeitung*, February 7, 1990, p. 2; Al Kamen, "Baker Said to Back Bonn Unification Plan," *Washington Post*, February 7, 1990, p. A19.

57. R. W. Apple, "As Bush Hails Decision, Many see Bonn Gaining," *New York Times*, June 17, 1990, p. A1.

58. Thomas L. Friedman, "U.S. Will Press the Soviets to Accept Plan on Germany," *New York Times*, June 5, 1990, p. A17.

59. The Ottowa Open Skies conference was attended by all NATO and Warsaw Pact foreign ministers. Five foreign ministers met informally to discuss the idea of "two-plus-four" negotiations on German unification: Hurd (UK), Genscher (FRG), Dumas (France), Shevardnadze (USSR), and Baker (US). After these five ministers had reached basic agreement, the East German foreign minister (Meckel) joined the others to pose for the photographers. Only after these photos were taken was a statement on the "two-plus-four" talks released.

60. For a detailed analysis of the non-public diplomacy involved in the two-plus-four concept, see Thomas L. Friedman with Michael R. Gordon, "Steps to German Unity: Bonn as a Power," *New York Times*, February 16, 1990, pp. A1 & A9. For a more in-depth analysis of the events leading to unification, see Elizabeth Pond, *After the Wall* (New York: Priority Press, 1990), and Catherine McArdle Kelleher, "The New Germany: An Overview," in Paul Stares, ed., *The New Germany and the New Europe* (Washington, DC: Brookings Institution, forthcoming 1992).

61. On this point, see Alice Ackermann, *Building Peace with Adversaries: The Case of Postwar Germany* (Ph.D. dissertation, University of Maryland, College Park, 1992); Lily Gardner Feldman, "The Architecture of a European Peace Order: Concepts, Actors, and Institutions," in J. J. Lee and Walter Korter, eds., *Europe in Transition: Political, Economic, and Security Prospects for the 1990s* (Austin: University of Texas, 1991), pp.

229-56; Hanns W. Maull, "Germany and Japan: The New Civilian Powers," *Foreign Affairs* vol. 69, no. 5 (Winter 1990-91), pp. 91-106; Catherine McArdle Kelleher, "The New Germany: Unification One Year On," *Brookings Review*, vol. 10, no. 1 (Winter 1992), pp. 18-25.

62. Gunter Hoffmann, Robert Leicht, and Theo Sommer, "Der Golfkrieg weist nicht in die Zukunft," Ein Zeit-Gespräch mit Bundespräsident Richard von Weizsäcker, *Die Zeit* (Hamburg), February 8, 1991.

63. "US Pleased with German Support of Coalition, Transcript of Baker-Genscher Remarks," *U.S. Policy Information and Texts*, March 4, 1991.

64. "Bonn stärkt die Slowenen und Kroaten," *Die Welt*, July 5, 1991, p. 8.

65. See William Drozdiak, "EC to Recognize Independence of Croatia, Slovenia Next Month," *Washington Post*, December 17, 1991, p. A15; Steve Vogel, "Germany Recognizing New States," *Washington Post*, December 20, 1991, p. A39; William Drozdiak, "Old Fears Stirred as Germany Asserts New Aggressive Role," *Washington Post*, December 23, 1991, p. A14.

66. Laura Silber, "Clashes Rage in Bosnian Capital Despite Warnings to Serbia," *Washington Post*, April 22, 1992, p. A23.

67. See Helmut Kohl, "Aufgaben deutscher Politik in den neunziger Jahren, Rede in Washington am 20. Mai 1991," *Bulletin* (Bonn), May 22, 1991, Deutscher Bundestag, Pressedokumentation, File #050-40; Helmut Kohl, "Deutsch-amerikanischer Beitrag zu Stabilität und Sicherheit, Erklärung vor der Presse, 21. Mai 1991," *Bulletin* (Bonn), May 28, 1991, Deutscher Bundestag, Pressedokumentation, File #050-60; "Enge Partnerschaft zwischen Kohl und Bush," *Neue Zürcher Zeitung*, May 22, 1991.

68. "Bundeskanzler Dr. Helmut Kohl zur Situation in der Sowjetunion sowie zu den deutsch-amerikanischen Beziehungen," Interview given at Deutschland-Funk on May 22, 1991, *Fernseh- und Hörfunkspiegel*, May 22, 1991, Deutscher Bundestag, Pressedokumentation, File #050-40.

About the Book

For Germany's neighbors, perhaps more acutely than for observers elsewhere, the 1990 reunification of divided Germany has raised old memories and new concerns in public and scholarly discourse. The shape and influence of these issues are the subject of this unique, ambitious book.

Organized into country-specific chapters, the book offers original, expert analyses of Germany's relations with seventeen European neighbors as well as with the United States. The contributors explore the essential concerns these nations have faced in their bilateral relations with Germany—past, present, and future.

In their introduction, the editors trace both commonality and diversity in various national conceptions of the "German Question" and the ways in which these perceptions in turn generate shared as well as divergent national policy agendas vis-à-vis united Germany.

About the Editors
and Contributors

Alice Ackermann is a citizen of Germany and received her doctorate from the University of Maryland, College Park. A recipient of dissertation fellowships from the Institute for the Study of World Politics and the United States Institute of Peace, she is currently an assistant professor of political science at Washington State University in Pullman.

Jens Drews, a native of Schleswig in Germany, is a Ph.D. student in political science at Pennsylvania State University, University Park, completing a dissertation on East Germany's failed strategies of legitimacy-building and the revolution of 1989.

John Fitzmaurice has worked for the European Commission in Brussels since 1973. He is a part-time lecturer at the Free University of Brussels, where he teaches European politics. He is the author of *Politics in Belgium: Crisis and Compromise in a Plural Society* (1983), in addition to articles on Belgian affairs.

Trond Gilberg is a native of Norway and an independent consultant on comparative political systems, specializing in Western and Eastern European and Soviet affairs. His publications include *The Soviet Communist Party and Scandinavian Communism: The Norwegian Case* (1973), *Modernization in Romania since World War II* (1975), *Coalition Strategies of Marxist Parties* (1989), and *Nationalism and Communism in Romania* (1990), in addition to many scholarly articles and chapters in edited books on European affairs.

Anthony Glees is director of European Studies and senior lecturer in the Department of Government at Brunel University in the United Kingdom. He is the author of *Exile Politics During the Second World War: The German Social Democrats in Britain* (1982) and *The Secrets of the Service: British Intelligence* *and Communist Subversion, 1939-51* (1987), in addition to numerous other articles on contemporary German history and politics as well as aspects of Anglo-German relations. In 1989-90 he served as advisor to the War Crimes Inquiry set up by the British government's Home Office and in 1992 directed the *Daily Mail* team's publication of excerpts from the Goebbels Diaries.

Milan Hauner is a visiting professor of history at the Center of German and European Studies at Georgetown University in Washington, DC. Born in Germany during World War II, he is a native of Czechoslovakia and was educated at Charles University in Prague and at Cambridge University, UK. Dr. Hauner has lived in the U.S. since 1980, and is the author of *India in Axis Strategy: Germany, Japan, and Indian Nationalists in the Second World War* (1981), *Hitler: A Chronology of His Life and Time* (1983), *What is Asia to Us? Russia's Asian Heartland Yesterday and Today* (1990), *The Soviet War in Afghanistan: Patterns of Russian Imperialism* (1991), and a variety of articles on Czechoslovak affairs.

Catherine McArdle Kelleher is a senior fellow in the Foreign Policy Studies Program at the Brookings Institution in Washington, DC. She is currently on leave from her posts as director of the Center for International Security Studies (CISSM) and professor in the School of Public Affairs, both at the University of Maryland, College Park. Among her many publications in the fields of national security, arms control, and German and European affairs are *Germany and the Politics of Nuclear Weapons* (1975) and *Evolving European Defense Policies* (co-edited with Gale A. Mattox; 1987).

Robert R. King served as assistant director of research at Radio Free Europe in Munich, Germany, and on the staff of the U.S. National Security Council during the Carter Administration. He is currently chief of staff to a member of the U.S. Congress. He has published *Minorities under Communism: Nationalities as a Source of Tension among Balkan Communist States* (1973) and *A History of the Romanian Communist Party* (1980), as well as articles and chapters in many scholarly journals and books.

Steven S. Koblik is president of Reed College in Portland, Oregon. He has served as dean of the faculty at Scripps College in California and has taught in the departments of history and international relations at the Claremont Graduate School in California. Educated in the U.S. and Sweden, he is the author of *The Stones Cry Out: Sweden's Response to Persecution of the Jews, 1933-1945* (1988) and *Sweden: The Neutral Victor* (1973).

F. Stephen Larrabee is a senior staff member in the International Policy Department at RAND in Santa Monica, California. From 1983 until 1989, he served as vice president and director of the Institute for East-West Security Studies (IEWSS) in New York. Before joining IEWSS, Dr. Larrabee was co-director of the Soviet and East European Research Program at the Johns Hopkins University School of Advanced International Studies (SAIS) in Washington, DC. From 1978 until 1981, he served on the U.S. National Security Council staff as a specialist on Soviet-East European affairs and East-West political-military relations. He has written widely on Soviet-East European and German affairs. His publications include *The Two German States and European Security* (editor; 1989) and *Conventional Arms Control and East-West Security* (co-edited with Robert Blackwill; 1989). He is currently completing *Retreat from Empire: The Gorbachev Revolution in Eastern Europe and Its Consequences*.

Anne-Marie LeGloannec is a research fellow at the Centre d'Etudes et de Rélations Internationales of the Fondation Nationale des Sciences Politiques in Paris. A visiting fellow at the Woodrow Wilson Center in Washington, DC, in 1985, and at the Institute for East-West Security Studies in New York in 1986, she is the author of *Un mur à Berlin* (1985) and *La Nation orphéline. Les Allemagnes en Europe* (1989/1990).

Arthur R. Rachwald is professor of political science at the U.S. Naval Academy in Annapolis, Maryland. Born in Poland and educated at the University of Marie Curie-Sklodowska (Poland) and the University of California at Santa Barbara, he is a specialist in Soviet and East European Politics and Soviet National Security Affairs. He is the author of *Poland between the Superpowers: Security vs. Economic Recovery* (1983) and *The Search for Poland* (1989), as well as the surveys of Polish affairs in the Hoover Institution's *Yearbook on International Communist Affairs* (1984 through 1990) and a variety of articles on Polish/East European affairs.

Sabrina Petra Ramet is associate professor of International Studies at the University of Washington in Seattle. She is the author of *Cross and Commissar: The Politics of Religion in Eastern Europe and the USSR* (1987), *The Soviet-Syrian Relationship since 1955: A Troubled Alliance* (1990), *Social Currents in Eastern Europe: The Sources and Meaning of the Great Transformation* (1991), *Balkan Babel: Politics, Culture, and Religion in Yugoslavia* (1992), *Nationalism and Federalism in Yugoslavia, 1962-1991* (2nd. edition, 1992), in addition to eight edited works as well as numerous scholarly articles.

Max E. Riedlsperger is professor of history at California Polytechnic State University in San Luis Obispo. He is the author of *The Lingering Shadow of Nazism: The Austrian Independent Party Movement since 1945* (1978), as well as a variety of articles on Austrian politics and history.

Gian Enrico Rusconi is professor of political science at the University of Turin in Italy. Among his publications on German affairs are *La crisi di Weimar* (1977), *Rischio 1914: come si decide una guerra* (1987), and *Capire la Germania* (1990).

Alpo Rusi is a member of the Finnish foreign service. Having served in the Finnish foreign ministry as director of planning and research and as director of the Bureau on Nordic and Other Western States, and as counsellor in Finland's U.N. Mission, he is currently minister, Deputy Chief of Mission, at the Finnish Embassy in Bonn. He also holds an adjunct professorship at Tampere University in Finland. His many publications include *Press Censorship during the Continuation War, 1941-44* (1982), *Public Opinion and Foreign Policy* (1985), and *After the Cold War: Europe's New Political Architecture* (1991), in addition to articles and chapters on Finnish and European affairs.

Christian Søe is professor of political science at California State University, Long Beach. Born in Denmark, he received his doctoral degree at the Free University of Berlin. He has written extensively on the FDP, German political liberalism, and party coalition politics. He is the editor of the anthology *Comparative Politics*, now in its 11th edition, and is director of the Pacific Workshop on German Affairs.

Mark Stucki holds a Licence in Political Science and Current History from the University of Bern, Switzerland. After a year in the U.S. on a research scholarship at the University of North Carolina in Chapel Hill, he is currently an editor at a Bern radio station.

Dirk Verheyen is assistant professor of political science at Loyola Marymount University in Los Angeles, California. Born in the Netherlands, he completed his graduate studies at the University of California at Berkeley. He is the author of *The German Question: A Cultural, Historical, and Geopolitical Exploration* (1991).

Ivan Volgyes was born in Budapest, Hungary and emigrated to the United States in 1957, after the Hungarian Revolution. His many publications include *Social Deviance in Eastern Europe* (1978), *Hungary: A Nation of Contradictions* (1982), *The Reliability of the East European Armies: The Southern Tier* (1983), and *Politics in Eastern Europe* (1989). Dr. Volgyes is professor of political science at the University of Nebraska in Lincoln and visiting distinguished professor of political science at Rutgers University-Camden.